8979

55 *Victorian Prose Writers Before 1867,* edited by William B. Thesing (1987)

56 *German Fiction Writers, 1914-1945,* edited by James Hardin (1987)

57 *Victorian Prose Writers After 1867,* edited by William B. Thesing (1987)

58 *Jacobean and Caroline Dramatists,* edited by Fredson Bowers (1987)

59 *American Literary Critics and Scholars, 1800-1850,* edited by John W. Rathbun and Monica M. Grecu (1987)

60 *Canadian Writers Since 1960,* Second Series, edited by W. H. New (1987)

61 *American Writers for Children Since 1960: Poets, Illustrators, and Nonfiction Authors,* edited by Glenn E. Estes (1987)

62 *Elizabethan Dramatists,* edited by Fredson Bowers (1987)

63 *Modern American Critics, 1920-1955,* edited by Gregory S. Jay (1988)

64 *American Literary Critics and Scholars, 1850-1880,* edited by John W. Rathbun and Monica M. Grecu (1988)

65 *French Novelists, 1900-1930,* edited by Catharine Savage Brosman (1988)

66 *German Fiction Writers, 1885-1913,* 2 parts, edited by James Hardin (1988)

67 *Modern American Critics Since 1955,* edited by Gregory S. Jay (1988)

68 *Canadian Writers, 1920-1959,* First Series, edited by W. H. New (1988)

69 *Contemporary German Fiction Writers,* First Series, edited by Wolfgang D. Elfe and James Hardin (1988)

70 *British Mystery Writers, 1860-1919,* edited by Bernard Benstock and Thomas F. Staley (1988)

71 *American Literary Critics and Scholars, 1880-1900,* edited by John W. Rathbun and Monica M. Grecu (1988)

72 *French Novelists, 1930-1960,* edited by Catharine Savage Brosman (1988)

73 *American Magazine Journalists, 1741-1850,* edited by Sam G. Riley (1988)

74 *American Short-Story Writers Before 1880,* edited by Bobby Ellen Kimbel, with the assistance of William E. Grant (1988)

75 *Contemporary German Fiction Writers,* Second Series, edited by Wolfgang D. Elfe and James Hardin (1988)

76 *Afro-American Writers, 1940-1955,* edited by Trudier Harris (1988)

77 *British Mystery Writers, 1920-1939,* edited by Bernard Benstock and Thomas F. Staley (1988)

78 *American Short-Story Writers, 1880-1910,* edited by Bobby Ellen Kimbel, with the assistance of William E. Grant (1988)

79 *American Magazine Journalists, 1850-1900,* edited by Sam G. Riley (1988)

80 *Restoration and Eighteenth-Century Dramatists,* First Series, edited by Paula R. Backscheider (1989)

81 *Austrian Fiction Writers, 1875-1913,* edited by James Hardin and Donald G. Daviau (1989)

82 *Chicano Writers,* First Series, edited by Francisco A. Lomelí and Carl R. Shirley (1989)

83 *French Novelists Since 1960,* edited by Catharine Savage Brosman (1989)

84 *Restoration and Eighteenth-Century Dramatists,* Second Series, edited by Paula R. Backscheider (1989)

85 *Austrian Fiction Writers After 1914,* edited by James Hardin and Donald G. Daviau (1989)

86 *American Short-Story Writers, 1910-1945,* First Series, edited by Bobby Ellen Kimbel (1989)

87 *British Mystery and Thriller Writers Since 1940,* First Series, edited by Bernard Benstock and Thomas F. Staley (1989)

88 *Canadian Writers, 1920-1959,* Second Series, edited by W. H. New (1989)

89 *Restoration and Eighteenth-Century Dramatists,* Third Series, edited by Paula R. Backscheider (1989)

90 *German Writers in the Age of Goethe, 1789-1832,* edited by James Hardin and Christoph E. Schweitzer (1989)

91 *American Magazine Journalists, 1900-1960,* First Series, edited by Sam G. Riley (1990)

92 *Canadian Writers, 1890-1920,* edited by W. H. New (1990)

93 *British Romantic Poets, 1789-1832,* First Series, edited by John R. Greenfield (1990)

94 *German Writers in the Age of Goethe: Sturm und Drang to Classicism,* edited by James Hardin and Christoph E. Schweitzer (1990)

95 *Eighteenth-Century British Poets,* First Series, edited by John Sitter (1990)

96 *British Romantic Poets, 1789-1832,* Second Series, edited by John R. Greenfield (1990)

97 *German Writers from the Enlightenment to Sturm und Drang, 1720-1764,* edited by James Hardin and Christoph E. Schweitzer (1990)

98 *Modern British Essayists,* First Series, edited by Robert Beum (1990)

99 *Canadian Writers Before 1890,* edited by W. H. New (1990)

100 *Modern British Essayists,* Second Series, edited by Robert Beum (1990)

101 *British Prose Writers, 1660-1800,* First Series, edited by Donald T. Siebert (1991)

102 *American Short-Story Writers, 1910-1945,* Second Series, edited by Bobby Ellen Kimbel (1991)

103 *American Literary Biographers,* First Series, edited by Steven Serafin (1991)

104 *British Prose Writers, 1660-1800,* Second Series, edited by Donald T. Siebert (1991)

105 *American Poets Since World War II,* Second Series, edited by R. S. Gwynn (1991)

106 *British Literary Publishing Houses, 1820-1880,* edited by Patricia J. Anderson and Jonathan Rose (1991)

107 *British Romantic Prose Writers, 1789-1832,* First Series, edited by John R. Greenfield (1991)

108 *Twentieth-Century Spanish Poets,* First Series, edited by Michael L. Perna (1991)

109 *Eighteenth-Century British Poets,* Second Series, edited by John Sitter (1991)

110 *British Romantic Prose Writers, 1789-1832,* Second Series, edited by John R. Greenfield (1991)

111 *American Literary Biographers,* Second Series, edited by Steven Serafin (1991)

112 *British Literary Publishing Houses, 1881-1965,* edited by Jonathan Rose and Patricia J. Anderson (1991)

113 *Modern Latin-American Fiction Writers,* First Series, edited by William Luis (1992)

114 *Twentieth-Century Italian Poets,* First Series, edited by Giovanna Wedel De Stasio, Glauco Cambon, and Antonio Illiano (1992)

115 *Medieval Philosophers,* edited by Jeremiah Hackett (1992)

(Continued on back endsheets)

Sixteenth-Century British Nondramatic Writers

First Series

Dictionary of Literary Biography® • Volume One Hundred Thirty-Two

Sixteenth-Century British Nondramatic Writers

First Series

Edited by
David A. Richardson
Cleveland State University

A Bruccoli Clark Layman Book
Gale Research Inc.
Detroit, Washington, D.C., London

The trademark ITP is used under license.
10 9 8 7 6 5 4 3 2 1

For Sharon

"Strowe me the ground with Daffadowndillies."

Contents

Plan of the Series

. . . Almost the most prodigious asset of a country, and perhaps its most precious possession, is its native literary product — when that product is fine and noble and enduring.

Mark Twain*

The advisory board, the editors, and the publisher of the *Dictionary of Literary Biography* are joined in endorsing Mark Twain's declaration. The literature of a nation provides an inexhaustible resource of permanent worth. We intend to make literature and its creators better understood and more accessible to students and the reading public, while satisfying the standards of teachers and scholars.

To meet these requirements, *literary biography* has been construed in terms of the author's achievement. The most important thing about a writer is his writing. Accordingly, the entries in *DLB* are career biographies, tracing the development of the author's canon and the evolution of his reputation.

The purpose of *DLB* is not only to provide reliable information in a convenient format but also to place the figures in the larger perspective of literary history and to offer appraisals of their accomplishments by qualified scholars.

The publication plan for *DLB* resulted from two years of preparation. The project was proposed to Bruccoli Clark by Frederick C. Ruffner, president of the Gale Research Company, in November 1975. After specimen entries were prepared and typeset, an advisory board was formed to refine the entry format and develop the series rationale. In meetings held during 1976, the publisher, series editors, and advisory board approved the scheme for a comprehensive biographical dictionary of persons who contributed to North American literature. Editorial work on the first volume began in January 1977, and it was published in 1978. In order to make *DLB* more than a reference tool and to compile volumes that individually have claim to status as literary history, it was decided to organize volumes by topic, period, or genre. Each of these freestanding volumes provides a biographical-bibliographical guide and overview for a particular area of literature. We are convinced that this organization — as opposed to a single alphabet method — constitutes a valuable innovation in the presentation of reference material. The volume plan necessarily requires many decisions for the placement and treatment of authors who might properly be included in two or three volumes. In some instances a major figure will be included in separate volumes, but with different entries emphasizing the aspect of his career appropriate to each volume. Ernest Hemingway, for example, is represented in *American Writers in Paris, 1920–1939* by an entry focusing on his expatriate apprenticeship; he is also in *American Novelists, 1910–1945* with an entry surveying his entire career. Each volume includes a cumulative index of the subject authors and articles. Comprehensive indexes to the entire series are planned.

With volume ten in 1982 it was decided to enlarge the scope of *DLB*. By the end of 1986 twenty-one volumes treating British literature had been published, and volumes for Commonwealth and Modern European literature were in progress. The series has been further augmented by the *DLB Yearbooks* (since 1981) which update published entries and add new entries to keep the *DLB* current with contemporary activity. There have also been *DLB Documentary Series* volumes which provide biographical and critical source materials for figures whose work is judged to have particular interest for students. One of these companion volumes is entirely devoted to Tennessee Williams.

We define literature as the *intellectual commerce of a nation:* not merely as belles lettres but as that ample and complex process by which ideas are generated, shaped, and transmitted. *DLB* entries are not limited to "creative writers" but extend to other figures who in their time and in their way influenced the mind of a people. Thus the series encompasses historians, journalists, publishers, and screenwriters. By this means readers of *DLB* may be aided to perceive literature not as cult scripture in the keeping of intellectual high priests but firmly po-

From an unpublished section of Mark Twain's autobiography, copyright by the Mark Twain Company

sitioned at the center of a nation's life.

DLB includes the major writers appropriate to each volume and those standing in the ranks immediately behind them. Scholarly and critical counsel has been sought in deciding which minor figures to include and how full their entries should be. Wherever possible, useful references are made to figures who do not warrant separate entries.

Each *DLB* volume has a volume editor responsible for planning the volume, selecting the figures for inclusion, and assigning the entries. Volume editors are also responsible for preparing, where appropriate, appendices surveying the major periodicals and literary and intellectual movements for their volumes, as well as lists of further readings. Work on the series as a whole is coordinated at the Bruccoli Clark Layman editorial center in Columbia, South Carolina, where the editorial staff is responsible for accuracy of the published volumes.

One feature that distinguishes *DLB* is the illustration policy – its concern with the iconography of literature. Just as an author is influenced by his surroundings, so is the reader's understanding of the author enhanced by a knowledge of his environment. Therefore *DLB* volumes include not only drawings, paintings, and photographs of authors, often depicting them at various stages in their careers, but also illustrations of their families and places where they lived. Title pages are regularly reproduced in facsimile along with dust jackets for modern authors. The dust jackets are a special feature of *DLB* because they often document better than anything else the way in which an author's work was perceived in its own time. Specimens of the writers' manuscripts are included when feasible.

Samuel Johnson rightly decreed that "The chief glory of every people arises from its authors." The purpose of the *Dictionary of Literary Biography* is to compile literary history in the surest way available to us – by accurate and comprehensive treatment of the lives and work of those who contributed to it.

The *DLB* Advisory Board

Introduction

The early modern period from 1485 to 1603 is commonly referred to as "the Renaissance" in England and as "the age of the Tudors," for it can be conveniently divided into the reigns of Henry VII, Henry VIII, Edward VI, Mary I, and Elizabeth I in deference to an unbroken string of idiosyncratic Tudor monarchs. But just as there is no Grand Unified Theory (GUT) in modern physics, there is no single theory, history, concept, or tag for sixteenth-century British nondramatic literature — none at least that inspires widespread and lasting conviction. In matters of literary history every defining term and each generation of scholarship have been succeeded by new information, interpretations, and labels.

Twentieth-century scholarship is first characterized by historical, philological, and bibliographical work, with the New Criticism especially dominant after World War II. The latter half of this century — and especially the final third — has seen an explosion of scholarship influenced by Freudian and other psychologies, Marxist theories of history and economics, feminist and gender issues, and deconstruction and a vast array of other French theory. Each has had or is having its day, as the New Historicism, for instance, is succeeded by "New New Historicism," and historical studies of the British literary empire are reassessed in light of postcolonial anthropological or ethnographic criticism. Two important background studies for sixteenth-century scholarship were made by Jacob Burckhardt (1860) and E. M. W. Tillyard (1944). Some of the most influential works of the twentieth century include studies by Douglas Bush (1939), Hallett Smith (1952), C. S. Lewis (1954), Mikhail Bakhtin (1968), Michel Foucault (1979), and Stephen Greenblatt (1980). The present state of sixteenth-century literary history is nothing less than effervescent. (For a list of titles, please see the Checklist of Further Readings.)

For a quick overview of the scholarly status quo, see Leah S. Marcus's essay "Renaissance/Early Modern Studies" (1992). An evolving history of sixteenth-century literature is implicit — often aggressively explicit — in "Recent Studies in the English Renaissance" (annually in *Studies in English Literature,* winter issue), and readers will quickly spot trends from articles in respected journals such as *English Literary Renaissance* and from book reviews in *Renaissance Quarterly* and *Sixteenth Century Journal.* Although now two decades old, *The New Cambridge Bibliography of English Literature* (volume 1, 1974) is an invaluable guide to primary and secondary materials, including literary history. Michael J. Marcuse's "Literature of the Renaissance and Earlier Seventeenth Century" (1990) is another important bibliography.

This introduction does not pronounce on what is past or passing, nor does it predict what is to come in the understanding of sixteenth-century literary history. Instead, it draws attention to some of the recurrent points made in the entries in this volume: literary innovations, widely used forms, and some observations about the historical origins and careers of authors. From these points one sees, for example, how the sixteenth century is not only an era of literary renascence but also of revolution, how its nondramatic "literature" spills vigorously over into Reformation history and politics, and how a tradition of courtly belles lettres coexists with the bumptious birth of a new world of professional writing. These emphases will inevitably change with the discovery of new documents, reinterpretations of standard texts, and the rise and fall of theoretical schools in the universities. For the last decade of the twentieth century, however, the entries in this volume show the following as some important traits of sixteenth-century British nondramatic literature.

Innovation. Although conveniently labeled "Renaissance authors," the writers discussed in this volume are far more than literary discoverers and revivers, or adapters and imitators, of classical texts. Their works are often strikingly new, even revolutionary. Collectively, their literary biographies document innovation on a scale certainly unprecedented and perhaps unequaled in the entire history of English writing.

In the matter of lyric genres, for instance, it is common knowledge that early in the century Sir Thomas Wyatt is the author of the first English sonnets, published in Richard Tottel's collection *Songs and Sonnets* (1557, familiarly known as "Tottel's Miscellany"). Less well known is that the commendatory versified prose of William Baldwin in Christopher Langton's *Treatise of Physic* (1547) is the first English sonnet to be printed. Also at mid century, Barnabe Googe's *Eclogues* (1563) is the first volume of English personal poetry published in the modern era by a gentleman during his lifetime – a major challenge to traditional notions of decorum. Later, Thomas Watson's *Hekatompathia* (1582) is the first published sonnet sequence in English with the dominant theme of love. And, at the end of the century, the 181 love poems of Barnabe Barnes make up the longest collection of such verse in English to date (1593); they include the only triple sestina in English, which ends his sequence with a rape.

In different literary veins, Alexander Barclay is the first to write pastoral verse in English (probably circa 1509–1514), along with Googe, whose eclogues follow some half-century later. In addition to his sonnets, Wyatt is also the author of the first true satires in English, some exposing the court, others treating the theme of female mutability and fickleness with downright anti-Petrarchan misogyny. Baldwin's *Wonderful News* (1552?) is the first Italianate and neoclassical satire to become popular in England in the seventeenth century; his *Beware the Cat* (1570) has been called the first original English prose-fiction novel – a collection of interlaced stories satirizing Catholicism in particular and superstition generally.

Separate genres are also created and sometimes synthesized into new forms during this period. Stephen Hawes, for instance, is the earliest author in England to try "to combine allegory with the romance form, to create a literary hybrid that seeks to adapt old forms to new purposes." In 1586 William Webbe is responsible for the first extensive critical treatise specifically on English poetry, a "not-unpleasant hotchpotch" of criticism that saw print a decade before Sir Philip Sidney's contemporaneous *Defense of Poesy* (1595).

New translations are important in the literary history of sixteenth-century England, especially in the context of the humanists' revival of classical Greek and Latin and the Reformers' work with Scripture (often related enterprises). Even here innovation is endemic. Bishop Gavin Douglas, for instance, who rendered Virgil's Latin *Aeneid* into his native Scots early in the century, may be considered the "first great Renaissance translator" in Great Britain and his *Eneados* (1553), the "first translation of a great classical work into any form of English"; Douglas is also the first Scots author to distinguish his literary language from that of England (in the prologue to his translation of Virgil). Among the

Reformers, William Tyndale is distinctive for his many "firsts" in making the Bible available in modern English: the first translation of the entire New Testament from Greek into English, the first English translation of any text written in Hebrew (his Old Testament Pentateuch), and the first modern English printed edition of part of the New Testament. Sir John Cheke's translation of Saint John Chrysostom is reputedly the first book to be set in Greek type in England and a chief force in moving scholars away from a preoccupation with Latin toward concern with Greek authors. Baldwin is not the first to translate the *Song of Songs* (1549), but his publication eight years before "Tottel's Miscellany" rivals that more famous work in its diversity of verse forms and meters for its sacred poetry.

In the sister field of history, sixteenth-century authors are equally enterprising. Polydore Vergil, for instance (the "father of English history" on whom Edward Hall and John Stow built their works), published his *Anglica Historia* (1533), "arguably the first humanist history to be written in and about England." With Robert Ridley he coedited Gildas's sixth-century *De excidio, et conquestu Britanniae*, the first critical edition of any English medieval source. (Vergil was interested in "firsts" in his own right, having compiled lists of inventors ["first begetters"] of a wide variety of things in his *De inventoribus rerum* of 1499.) Hall is the first to enunciate many of the principal themes of Shakespearean drama and of Elizabethan and early-Stuart prose historiography, and Stow published the first scholarly history of an English town in his *Survey of London* (1603).

The history and philosophy of politics also elicited many volumes of prose and several important firsts in the sixteenth century. Reginald Pole is recognized today as the first well-known anti-Machiavellian. John Ponet, the first Protestant advocate of limited monarchy, influenced John Milton, John Adams, and U.S. political theory. Edmund Grindal is responsible for creating a "groundbreaking conception of the church's autonomy from civil power" and set himself against Elizabeth I in the antithetical rhetoric of his letter opposing her policies. By contrast, Richard Hooker wrote his *Laws of Ecclesiastical Polity* (1593) at the queen's behest; it is the first major treatise in English on political theory, especially on the "nature and kinds of law" and the role of consensus in a constitutional monarchy.

Innovative writing is also associated with formal education and informal learning throughout the century. A notable nonliterary text is Cuthbert

Tunstall's treatise on arithmetic (1522), the first in England and acclaimed throughout Europe. At mid century Thomas Wilson published both the first logic textbook and the first comprehensive rhetoric written in English (1551, 1553). The 1547–1550 travel journal of Thomas Hoby is the prototype for a young Englishman on the grand tour; it reflects a mind striving for self-knowledge and understanding and (although not published until 1902) is part of the foundation of English autobiography.

In passing, it is worth noting that William Cornish introduced dramatic performances by the Children of the Chapel in 1517. He is one of the most important and influential devisers of court entertainments in the early sixteenth century, and his composition "Pleasure it is" is included in the first songbook printed in England (1530).

Forms. In addition to their innovations, British authors from 1485 to 1603 write in a great variety of literary forms in both verse and prose. Three recur frequently in this volume: autobiography and biography, dialogue, and satire.

Autobiography and biography. Among the Scots authors, Douglas early in the century creates striking correspondences to his real-life personality in self-portraits of himself as dreamer and as poet in his *Palice of Honor* (circa 1535); and Sir David Lindsay uses chivalric romance as a guise for biography. In England there seems to be an autobiographical element in Hawes's *Comfort of Lovers* (1515). The works of Henry VIII are more problematic, but some of his songs are autobiographical because they are singable *only* by Henry and suggest that "our usual distinctions between fact and fiction do not apply" to the king. It is hard to distinguish Wyatt's authorial voice from his persona in his paraphrases of the Seven Penitential Psalms – but, as autobiographical mouthpieces, his secular lyrics seem to transcribe his life as a courtier. (The lyrics of Thomas, Lord Vaux, by contrast, are not useful for autobiographical purposes, for they are abstract, reaching "for the normative rather than the individualistic.") Also in the secular realm, Hoby kept "one of the most important mid-sixteenth century autobiographical travel journals in English." And, despite poor skills in almost every other genre, Thomas Churchyard was best at structuring autobiographical materials, as in his fast-paced "Story Translated out of French" (1580).

Autobiography and biography flourished also as part of the Reformation, from the noblest authors to the most humble. A favorite autobiographical subject for Pole, for instance, was his having been asked by Henry VIII to help win support for the king's divorce from Anne Boleyn; after he broke with Henry, he wrote flattering autobiographical images of himself in contrast to royal portraits that Henry considered demeaning. The final letters of Lady Jane Grey to her father and sister are notable as personal yet public autobiographical statements. John Knox reveals much about his public and private life in his *History of the Reformation* (1587). To answer anti-Reformation opposition in his own parish, John Bale wrote his quasi-autobiographical *Expostulation* (1552?), and later his highly readable *Vocation of Bale* (1553) while he was bishop of Ossory in Ireland.

The most widely known of all Reformation biographers is John Foxe. His *Acts and Monuments* (called the "Book of Martyrs," 1563) is designed as polemical martyrology; its purpose is to laud Protestant loyalty under persecution, to reject the miracles of traditional hagiography as lying "fables," and to supplant medieval saints' legends, such as Jacobus de Voragine's *Golden Legend*. Foxe also edited the complete works of the martyred Reformers Tyndale, John Frith, and Barnes (1573) and added his own biographies to their publications. Despite his spirited Protestantism, vestiges of the medieval and Catholic traditions survive in these and similar works: in the "Book of Martyrs," his life of Tyndale, for instance, is itself an "idyllic, hagiographic picture."

Other Reformers co-opting biography in their cause include Bale, who edited and commented on the autobiographical *Examinations of Anne Askew* (1546–1547) as a Protestant saint's life much as he did in his earlier chronicle about Sir John Oldcastle. William Latymer's encomiastic eyewitness biography of Anne Boleyn seems intended to rehabilitate her as a Protestant heroine and champion of the Reformation. From another perspective John Colet is presented in less-than-flattering epistolary portraits in Desiderius Erasmus's correspondence with him and other humanists. And, overtly for the Roman Catholic cause, Pole directed the creation of the "saintly" Thomas More; much of his other writing is also biographical, almost entirely in Latin.

Dialogue. The sixteenth century is often associated with the efflorescence of drama and especially the works of William Shakespeare at the end of the century. But take away Shakespeare and the stage, and an astonishing array of dialogue remains in the nondramatic works of the age.

As the historical context might suggest, much dialogue is an instrument of the Protestant Reformation. Tyndale, for example, uses the form in his pamphlet debates with More. Foxe fully transcribes the public debate between Grey and Mary Stuart's confessor, Dr. John Feckenham. Much of the career of Knox can be understood as a running dialogue of vituperation with religious opponents. The dialogue structure in many of Grindal's works shows his "polemical bent," not only in Protestant-Catholic debate but also in his own conflicts with Elizabeth I over temporal versus scriptural authority. In his 1549 translation of Bernardino Ochino's Latin dialogue between warring forces in Christian history, Ponet creates a "biting and amusing satirical dialogue," and his *Short Catechism* (1553) is notable for its dialogue form modeled explicitly on Socrates and Apollinaris. Baldwin, in his fictional *Beware the Cat,* uses dialogue to satirize Catholicism and superstition. Other examples include Thomas Starkey's vernacular *Dialogue between Pole and Lupset* (which preceded More's English dialogues but remained in manuscript and unknown until the nineteenth century). The form is a favorite of Pole, who used it in composing his *De summo pontifico* (1569) when he might rather have been campaigning as a candidate for pope. Other Reformation figures, however, are fundamentally opposed to the form, as seems apparent in John Whitgift's rigorous enforcement of rules, conformity to oaths, suppression of debate, and other control of the intellectual and spiritual exchange that is implicit in dialogue.

The form is equally prevalent on the secular scene. Wyatt writes epistolary satire as dialogues of cynical advice on how to succeed at the English court. At the Scottish court, Lindsay counsels through dialogue about civil as well as spiritual governance in Scotland; and George Buchanan uses the form to debate the peoples' rights versus the divine rights of kings. In the first English pastorals, Barclay heightens the dramatic argument by changing his prose source to verse dialogue. Dialogue appealed to William Barker, who translates Giovanni Battista Gelli's ten dialogues and paraphrases Lodovico Domenichi's *Nobility of Women.* Beyond traditional literary circles, dialogue is the choice of Thomas Smith in his economic analysis of mid-Tudor inflation caused by a debased coinage, as it is for Wilson in his *Discourse upon Usury* (1572).

Satire. This reprobative genre finds its butt most often in the court and the church. Although Henry VIII did not himself write satire, courtiers used it directly and indirectly to criticize the corruption of his later court, even transforming erotic verse into a form of protest literature. Among these courtiers Wyatt was admired during the seventeenth century and much of the eighteenth as a satirist rather than as a love poet. His epistolary satires are adapted from the Italian, while his satiric epigrams are as biting as Martial's and go beyond the conventional satire of his anticourt sources. Barclay castigates categories of folly in his *Ship of Fools* (1509) and contrasts pastoral delights with the miseries of court life in the anticourt satire of Eclogues 1–3.

Nor is the Scottish court immune from the barbs of satire. William Dunbar mocks the court fool Sir Thomas Norny in a parody of Geoffrey Chaucer's *Sir Thopas* (in *The Canterbury Tales,* composed 1386–1394), writes a mock-encomium of a black woman at the Scottish court, and caricatures courtly ideals in his "eavesdropping poems" – all this in addition to his mock-serious macaronics that parody wills, the Paternoster, the Office of the Dead, and the city of Stirling ("lead us not into the temptation of Stirling, but deliver us from its evil"). In addition to dramatic modes in his *Satire of the Three Estates* (1602), Lindsay includes a broad range from farce to irony in his nondramatic work, with admonitions to the king and to religious and civil leaders. The didactic and admonitory elements of his *Dream* (1554?) reappear in his "wildly satiric" *Complaint* (1554?), which attacks political and religious corruption in Scotland. His further satires deride commoners who ape court behavior and courtiers' manner of dress (his satire of women's dress becomes an invective against women), and he uses forthright satiric dialogue in "Kitty's Confession" (1568) to condemn church corruption.

Among the Reformers, Tyndale writes caustic satire against More (who seems surprisingly petty and vicious in the "no-holds-barred style typical of early sixteenth-century religious controversy"). Buchanan satirizes corruption in the Franciscan order in a dream vision based on Dunbar, as well as in sarcastic palinodes, hostile catalogues of hypocrisy, and epigrams. Ponet is notable for his skill with "biting and amusing satirical dialogue" in dramatic exchanges between warring forces in Christian history. The last pamphlet of Knox contains violent satire of the popes, and his *History of the Reformation* is literary art for its "superbly dramatic narrative" as well as its "powers of sarcastic invective and ironic description," full of "pointed jabs and epithets."

At virtually the same time at the end of the century, the controversial *Marprelate Tracts* deserve special mention. They are among the finest examples of prose satire in the Elizabethan era: informal, sarcastic, and full of puns, banter, and racy insinuations, they often descend to personal attacks in matters traditionally respected as dignified and sober. The tracts include scandalous stories and spicy gossip about the personal lives of particular bishops (the result of a "decision to forego deference"), parody the defenses of the establishment, and defend satire as a means to "bring the truth to light."

Among other works William Lily's *Antibossicon* (1521) contains virulent satire in his epigrams and short poems. Churchyard wrote three autobiographical court satires, but they are undistinguished and indistinguishable. Googe's *Ship of Safeguard* (1569) is a satiric allegory of the voyage of life, with similarities to Edmund Spenser's approach to the Bower of Bliss in *The Faerie Queene* (1590).

Origins. This volume includes biography as well as the literary matters sketched above. One of the most interesting life facts to emerge in the following entries is that while some of the authors enjoyed aristocratic or otherwise comfortable origins, more of them came from relatively humble or straitened backgrounds. Among the fortunate few, Douglas, for instance, was the well-educated younger son of the fifth earl of Angus and ended up ensconced in the church. Wyatt was the son of "a powerful and wealthy Privy Councillor." The father of Colet was from the merchant class but enjoyed political success (including election as lord mayor of London); Colet's mother was from the nobility. Googe's father held extensive property in Nottinghamshire, Lincolnshire, and around London. Cheke was the son of an official at Cambridge; Hall, of a successful grocer; and Whitgift, of a middle-class merchant and ship owner. The most conspicuously elevated, of course, were Henry VIII and Lady Jane Grey.

More typical of Tudor authors, however, Sir Nicholas Bacon was the son of a sheep reeve before rising to lord chancellor, keeper of the Great Seal. Thomas Smith, coming from similar origins, was insulted by Sir Nicholas Throckmorton's charge that he was but recently "a beggarly scholar" and throughout his social climb resented being snubbed by his superiors as an upstart. Historian Stow began as apprentice to a tailor. Grindal was the son of a poor tenant farmer but later distinguished himself academically to become vice-master of Pembroke Hall, Cambridge, later bishop of London, and finally Elizabeth I's archbishop of York and archbishop of Canterbury.

Careers. It is important at the end of the twentieth century to realize that few authors in the sixteenth century were professional writers in the current understanding of the term. For example, on the secular scene, Churchyard scraped together a living as a soldier and as a not-very-good minor writer in almost every marketable genre. Among Reformation figures, Tyndale devoted his life to a much more successful career as translator of Scripture and author of instructions in reformed theology; he is understandably the single most influential prose stylist in the English language.

But, in contrast to such full-time "professional" writers, most sixteenth-century authors scribbled outside or in the interstices of another career, sacred or secular. Douglas, a litigious and politically dynamic churchman, wrote most of his poetry during his early years. During much of his life Barclay was a teaching Benedictine monk at Ely, yet he was among the first English writers honored with publication of a nearly complete edition of his own works during his lifetime (he is also the only native writer of the early Tudor period whose works went immediately and regularly into print, as he capitalized on the new technology of the movable-type press in cooperation with the printer Richard Pynson).

Henry VIII's break from Rome, the Protestant Reformation of the church, and Nonconformist dissent from the established Church of England are three events of the sixteenth century that have enormous literary importance, for they created an urgent demand for writers. One reads Thomas Cranmer, for example, as the second most influential prose stylist in the history of English letters (although he would likely have identified himself in other terms — as a researcher of divorce materials for Henry VIII, liturgist for the reformed church, and archbishop of Canterbury). After his conversion from Rome, Bale ("Bilious Bale") served the Protestant Reformation through virtually uninterrupted activity as publisher, editor, cleric, antiquarian, dramatist, and historian. Colet wrote in the context of his ecclesiastical life and in the cause of Saint Paul's School, which he founded. The interdependent religious and authorial careers of Grindal are not unlike those of his predecessor Ponet. Details about other authors remain uncertain from the pseudonymous *Marprelate Tracts,* which attacked the established church at the end of the century; the very nature of their enterprise made such writing occasional and surreptitious. As spokesmen for Elizabeth I's church, Whitgift and Hooker turned their pens to her service, with Hooker devoted almost wholly in the end to his apodictic *Laws of Ecclesiastical Polity.* Knox's prolific writing career rubs elbows, sometimes violently, with his experiences as tutor, armed bodyguard, galley slave, preacher, and minister to Marian exiles on the Continent and later to his Edinburgh congregation.

(For other writers whose work has bearing on the Reformation, see the entries on William Alabaster, Baldwin, Cheke, Foxe, Googe, Grey, Hall, Henry VIII, Latymer, Lindsay, Pole, Thomas Sternhold and John Hopkins, Tunstall, Vaux, Vergil, Wilson, and Wyatt.)

Outside of the church and its concerns, many well-known authors were best known as courtiers. In Scotland, Lindsay was the nation's highest-ranking herald as Lyon King of Arms and led his adult life at the court of James V. In England, Wyatt enjoyed various posts from patronage and informed his poetry with the dark, bitter side of court life. Sir Thomas Sackville was a courtier and statesman as well as a patron of literature and learning in his own right.

Others wrote incidentally or for other ends while occupying themselves in different ways. Cornish wrote music and lyrics while teaching, singing, directing the Children of the Chapel, and creating many of the magnificent entertainments at the courts of Henry VII and Henry VIII. Lily was educator and master of Colet's new school at Saint Paul's in London. Webbe tutored the children of his patron. Wilson led a multifaceted career as humanist, tutor, political activist, lawyer, member of Parliament, statesman, and translator. In addition to being a courtier, Thomas Smith served as ambassador to France and vice-chancellor of Cambridge University, where he lectured brilliantly in law. Pole is notable for his triple achievements in religion, literature, and politics – and so on. The list can be extended to most of the figures presented in this volume, for nondramatic writing in the sixteenth century was more often an instrument or an avocation rather than a career in itself.

Other. This introduction has focused on four large descriptive categories that are conspicuous in the entries in this volume: literary innovations and forms, authorial origins and careers. Other important topics are treated throughout the sixteenth century and are listed here for convenience in following up particular interests:

Education and teaching: Baldwin, Bale, Barclay, Barker, Buchanan, Cheke, Cranmer, Douglas, Dunbar, Googe, Grey, Hall, Hawes, Henry VIII, Knox, Latymer, Lily, Lindsay, Pole, Ponet, Sternhold and Hopkins, Tunstall, Tyndale, Vaux, and Wilson.

History: Hall, Knox, Pole, Smith, Stow, and Vergil.
Humanism and the classics: Baldwin, Barker, Buchanan, Cheke, Colet, Cranmer, Douglas, Grey, Hawes, Henry VIII, Hoby, Hooker, Lily, Pole, Ponet, Sackville, Smith, Starkey, Tunstall, Tyndale, Vergil, Watson, Webbe ("Tudor humanism in a nutshell"), and Wyatt.
Medievalism and native traditions: Baldwin, Bale, Churchyard, Douglas, Foxe, Googe, Hawes, Henry VIII, Lindsay, Sackville, Stow, and Wyatt.
Neo-Latin literature: Alabaster, Buchanan, Colet, Henry VIII, Lily, Pole, Vergil, Watson, and Wilson.
Patronage, networking: Bacon, Baldwin, Bale, Barclay, Barker, Buchanan, Churchyard, Colet, Cranmer, Douglas, Dunbar, Foxe, Googe, Grindal, Hall, Hawes, Henry VIII, Hooker, Knox, Latymer, Lily, Lindsay, Pole, Ponet, Sackville, Starkey, Sternhold and Hopkins, Stow, Tunstall, Tyndale, Vergil, Whitgift, Wilson, and Wyatt.
Politics: Buchanan, Grindal, Henry VIII, Hooker, Knox, Latymer, *Marprelate Tracts,* Pole, Ponet, Starkey, Tunstall, Tyndale, Whitgift, and Wyatt.
Style: Alabaster, Bale, Colet, Cranmer, Douglas, Dunbar, Grindal, Hawes, Hooker, Knox, *Marprelate Tracts,* Starkey, Tyndale, Vaux, and Vergil.
Women: Barker, Dunbar, Grey, Hawes, Knox, Lily, Lindsay, and Wyatt.

Note: Titles in the front matter of entries are reproduced as given in the *Short Title Catalogue,* second edition. Titles and quotations in the articles themselves are modernized for spelling and punctuation to make them more readily accessible to modern readers.

– *David A. Richardson*

ACKNOWLEDGMENTS

This book was produced by Bruccoli Clark Layman, Inc. Karen L. Rood is senior editor for the *Dictionary of Literary Biography* series. David Marshall James was the in-house editor.

Photography editors are Edward Scott and Timothy C. Lundy. Layout and graphics supervisor is Penney L. Haughton. Copyediting supervisor is Bill Adams. Typesetting supervisor is Kathleen M. Flanagan. Samuel Bruce is editorial associate. Systems manager is George F. Dodge. The production staff includes Rowena Betts, Steve Borsanyi, Barbara Brannon, Patricia Coate, Rebecca Crawford, Margaret McGinty Cureton, Denise Edwards, Sarah A. Estes, Joyce Fowler, Robert Fowler, Jolyon M. Helterman, Tanya D. Locklair, Ellen McCracken, Kathy Lawler Merlette, John Morrison Myrick, Pamela D. Norton, Thomas J. Pickett, Patricia Salisbury, Maxine K. Smalls, Deborah P. Stokes, Jennifer Carroll Jenkins Turley, and Wilma Weant.

Walter W. Ross and Brenda Gross did library research. They were assisted by the following librarians at the Thomas Cooper Library of the University of South Carolina: Linda Holderfield and the interlibrary-loan staff; reference librarians Gwen Baxter, Daniel Boice, Faye Chadwell, Cathy Eckman, Gary Geer, Qun "Gerry" Jiao, Jean Rhyne, Carol Tobin, Carolyn Tyler, Virginia Weathers, Elizabeth Whiznant, and Connie Widney; circulation-department head Thomas Marcil; and acquisitions-searching supervisor David Haggard.

Sixteenth-Century British Nondramatic Writers

First Series

Dictionary of Literary Biography

William Alabaster
(27 January 1568 – 28 April 1640)

Michael O'Connell
University of California, Santa Barbara

BOOKS: *Apparatus in Revelationem Jesu Christi* (Antwerp: A. Coninex, 1607);
De Bestia Apocalyptica (Delft, 1621);
Roxana tragædia (London: William Jones, 1632);
Ecce sponsus venit (London: William Jones, 1633);
Spiraculum tubarum sive fons spiritualium expositionum ex æquivocis Pentaglotti significationibus (London: William Jones, 1633).

Editions and Collections: *The Sonnets of William Alabaster,* edited by G. M. Storey and Helen Gardner (London: Oxford University Press, 1959);
"Alabaster's Conversion," transcribed, with an appendix of other documents relating to Alabaster, by John Fabian (Rome: English College, 1978);
Roxana tragaedia, in *Antigone / Thomas Watson. Roxana / William Alabaster. Adrastus Parentans sive vindicata / Peter Mease,* prepared, with an introduction, by John C. Coldewey and Brian Copenhaver (Hildesheim & New York: G. Olms, 1987).

TRANSLATION: *The "Elisæis" of William Alabaster,* translated and edited by Michael O'Connell, *Studies in Philology,* Texts and Studies, 76 (Winter 1979).

William Alabaster, a poet in Latin and English, wrote an interesting and too little known collection of devotional sonnets late in the reign of Queen Elizabeth I. The sonnets, which belong to a late-Renaissance tradition of meditative verse, frequently forecast seventeenth-century religious poetry in style and manner. At his best he can bring to mind certain of George Herbert's poems, and even

William Alabaster (frontispiece to his Ecce sponsus venit, *1633)*

the less successful of Alabaster's sonnets share the taste for witty paradox that characterizes the period. Edmund Spenser praised Alabaster's fragmentary Neo-Latin epic on the career of Elizabeth, *Elisaeis,* and urged the queen to extend her patronage to its

3

young author. Though of little more than historical interest, the single completed book of the poem does vindicate Spenser's praise of Alabaster's learning. Alabaster also wrote, or adapted, a lurid academic Latin tragedy, *Roxana* (1632), that enjoyed a contemporary reputation. Finally, his life and career illustrate something of the religious and political volatility of the late Elizabethan period. After a promising academic career at Cambridge and patronage by Robert Devereux, second Earl of Essex, Alabaster suddenly converted to Roman Catholicism in 1597, courted the legal persecution this involved, then fled to the Continent for a time before returning with messages to the earl apparently encouraging a Catholic alliance. He endured four years of imprisonment and banishment to the Continent, studied again at the English College in Rome, then after difficulty with the Roman Inquisition returned to England in 1610 and eventually resumed his interrupted career as a clergyman in the Church of England.

Alabaster was born 27 January 1568 at Hadleigh in Suffolk, the eldest of six surviving children, three boys and three girls. He recorded in an interrogatory signed thirty-one years later at the English College that his paternal family was of ancient Norman extraction. His father, Roger, was born in reduced circumstances and had been an unsuccessful merchant in the Spanish trade. He was living on a slender, though adequate, income at the time of William's birth. William's mother, Bridget, was of the distinguished, prosperous Winthrop family and was an aunt of John Winthrop, the first governor of Massachusetts. Having attended Westminster School, Alabaster went as a Queen's Scholar to Trinity College, Cambridge, in 1584, where his uncle by marriage, John Still, was master. He proceeded B.A. in 1588, was elected a fellow in 1589, and became M.A. in 1591. He appears to have continued at Cambridge until his conversion to Catholicism. His early verse in Latin, including *Elisaeis* and *Roxana,* was composed during this time.

What survives of the *Elisaeis* is the first of what was projected as a twelve-book epic in Latin hexameter verse on the career of Queen Elizabeth. Then in his early twenties, Alabaster very likely intended to attract notice and patronage at court through the project; he reports that he presented the first book to the queen himself. Spenser's warm commendation of the poem in *Colin Clouts Come Home Againe* provides the only means of dating it. Since Spenser's poem records his sojourn in England from the fall of 1589 to the spring of 1591, and since the opening lines of the *Elisaeis* refer to the Spanish Armada, the poem must have been written between the fall of 1588 and early 1591. Spenser's puff, whatever it might have been worth, came too late; *Colin Clout* was not published until 1595. Alabaster, in his account of his conversion, implies that he had written a second book by this time, which he was about to present to the queen. But after converting he would have had no further motive to continue work on the virulently anti-Catholic poem and must have destroyed what he had written of the second book.

The surviving first book treats Elizabeth's tribulations early in Mary I's reign, her estrangement from Mary, her transportation from her sickbed at Ashridge to London, and her imprisonment in the Tower of London during the spring of 1554. Elizabeth is portrayed as an innocent victim who must endure what is thrust upon her by powerful evil forces. Only some 120 of the book's 753 lines are taken up with undoubted historical events. Most of the book traces figures of allegorized evil in their encircling of the future queen: Satan appears to Papacy, personified as the Whore of Babylon, to stimulate her to sow Catholicism and dissension in England; Papacy in turn appears in sleep to Stephen Gardiner, bishop of Winchester and Mary's lord chancellor, to bring Elizabeth into Mary's disfavor. Gardiner then accuses Elizabeth of complicity in Sir Thomas Wyatt's rebellion against Mary. Alabaster's historical source is the *Actes and Monuments* (1563) of John Foxe (a work he refers to satirically in sonnet 5). But his poetic inspiration is clearly Virgil, to whom he alludes frequently. Alabaster's malevolent Juno is Satan; his Carthage, Catholic Rome; his Allecto, the Papacy; and so on. But the style of the poem is far from Virgil's measured gravity and appears to owe more to such silver-age poets as Lucan and Statius. While the poem has some interesting descriptive successes, the main failing of the *Elisaeis* is a slow-moving and often-interrupted narrative. Alabaster's real preoccupation was style. Terse epigrams punctuate his florid descriptions and similes, and these alternate with elaborately rhetorical speeches. When, for example, Papacy appears in sleep to Stephen Gardiner, she berates him for his apparent unconcern over the losses Catholicism has suffered:

An tenues curae Papiae, quae vertere possunt
Imperium? tenues, quae formidabile regnum
Restituant Christi? tenues, quae momine rerum
Deturbare tuos possunt Ventane triumphos.
Atque utinam tantum possint, iam fervere vidi
Undique seditione urbes, ipsosque ministros
Concilia horrenda et turmas glomerare rebelles.

Engraved title page for Alabaster's 1632 tragedy. The panel at bottom, center, depicts an English theater with the unusual detail of patrons seated behind the stage.

(Insignificant, then, are these anxieties of the Papacy, which can overthrow our empire? Can they be insignificant, which may restore the powerful kingdom of Christ? Insignificant, which can by the momentum of events overturn all your triumphs, Winchester? Oh, that these things were only possibilities! Already I have seen cities everywhere seething with sedition and the ministers and bands of rebels gathering in frightening councils.)

As Gardiner, disturbed by the visitation, walks distracted through his garden, Alabaster applies a curious simile to his motion:

> Buxeus ut rapida volitat vertigine turbo
> Quem torvae sub regnum hiemis glaciemque furentem
> Marmoreis pueri subigunt discurrere claustris,
> Ille autem crebra lunatae grandine plagae
> Ebrius: et pastu satiatus, dormit oberrans.

Lactea turba stupet puerûm, ridetque natantes
Dum cernit glomerare orbes: et scribere marmor:
Areolas pede lymphato sic Gardiner errat.

(As a boxwood top flies about in rapid circles, which during the rule of grim winter and its icy rage some boys have wound up to run from the marble-white cage of their fingers; but fed to the full and drunk with the hail of curved blows, it sleeps as it weaves about; the milk-white troop of boys gapes over it and laughs as they see it form wavering circles and inscribe the icy marble.)

Alabaster's Latinity, often elliptical or asymmetrical in its syntax, appears to represent stylistic experimentation. In Latin as well as in English, he was a forerunner of what has been variously called mannerist, baroque, or metaphysical style. The poem had some circulation in manuscript and was still being read in Cambridge in the 1620s. The young John Milton appears to have read it and been influenced by it in his own miniature epic on the Gunpowder Plot, *In Quintum Novembris* (composed 1626), and Phineas Fletcher may well have found inspiration in it for his *Locustae* (1627) and its English amplification, *The Apollyonists* (1627).

Alabaster's tragedy *Roxana* was written shortly after the *Elisaeis* and performed at Trinity College, Cambridge, around 1592. When a revised version was published in 1632, in response to an unauthorized edition, he said that some forty years earlier, "more or less," he had composed it in two weeks for a single night's performance. Adapted from Luigi Groto's *Dalida* (Venice, 1567), the play participates in a fashion for Italian drama – and equally in contemporary fondness for Senecan horror. It begins with the ghost of King Moleo returning from the dead to curse his native Bactria and vowing vengeance for his death at the hands of his nephew, the present king, Oromasdes. When Moleo, appointed regent for Oromasdes, refused to relinquish the kingdom to his impatient nephew, the latter fled to India, married the princess Atossa, then returned to kill his uncle and reclaim his kingdom. But Oromasdes fell in love with Moleo's daughter, Roxana (Dalida in the Italian play), whom Moleo had hidden from him in a remote region but whom he discovered and seduced while hunting. At the time of the action of the play, Oromasdes has a son and a daughter by Roxana, whose love for Oromasdes also represents betrayal of Moleo. Their relationship has been concealed from all but his councillor, Bessus.

The ghost of Moleo, desiring vengeance over all his kin and supported by allegorized Death and Suspicion, presides over – and prompts – the action of the play. Events are precipitated by Bessus's falling in love with the queen and his revelation to her of Oromasdes' secret. Driven by a personified figure of Jealousy, Atossa promises Bessus satisfaction of his passion if he will deliver up Roxana and her children. When he does so, Atossa imprisons them and forces Roxana to kill the children and herself. She then fulfills her vow to Bessus. Still ignorant of the fate of Roxana and his children, Oromasdes learns of the adultery of Atossa and Bessus and has the latter killed. Pursuing her vengeance, Atossa invites Oromasdes to a Thyestean banquet at which Roxana and his children are served up with poisoned wine. Oromasdes, still unaware of what he has eaten, presents Atossa with the head of Bessus. She counters with the heads of Roxana and his children, then to his demand for their bodies reveals

they have already been served to him. But Oromasdes has also given Atossa poisoned wine. To the satisfaction of Moleo, a double murder thus concludes a clean sweep of the principals of the tragedy.

Thomas Fuller reports in his *Worthies of England* (1622) that this last scene, so feelingly acted in its single performance, caused a gentlewoman to fall distracted and never fully to recover her senses. Whatever its contemporary effect and reputation, the play shares much with the *Elisaeis* in its allegorized figures of evil and above all in the highly rhetorical character of its speeches. In his *Life of Milton* (1779), Samuel Johnson cited *Roxana* as being perhaps the finest Latin verse produced in England before Milton's elegies.

In the account of his conversion that Alabaster wrote at the English College in 1598, presumably at the behest of its rector, Robert Parsons, and addressed to an unnamed former schoolfellow at Westminster, he makes clear that in 1597 he was on the verge of a distinguished career in the Church of England. In addition to presenting the first book of the *Elisaeis* to the queen, he had preached at court. He had for some time been chaplain to the earl of Essex and the previous year had gone with him on the famous and successful raid on Cadiz. He was, moreover, engaged to be married and in the spring of 1597 was in attendance at court to obtain the prebend on which he would settle. (The previous fall he had obtained the living of Landulfe in Cornwall, worth four hundred crowns, from Essex.)

But during the Michaelmas term of 1596 he had been appointed to catechize in Trinity and had consequently begun a course of reading that had included Catholic as well as Reformed writers. He reports that he found himself sometimes defending the Catholic position against John Calvin and that he intended to study matters further when the question of his preferment was settled. Moreover, he began to feel a more than Protestant warmth toward the Passion of Christ and to experience religious visions in his sleep. Just before leaving Cambridge for London, he says he gave a Good Friday sermon that surprised his hearers in the fervency of its devotion. While in London he visited an old acquaintance, Dr. Gabriel Goodman, dean of Westminster, who had a Jesuit, Thomas Wright, under house arrest. Alabaster engaged in theological discussion with Wright, then borrowed from him William Rainolds's defense of the Rheims translation of the New Testament (1583). He says that he took the book back to his lodgings and read in it for fifteen minutes after supper, then was astounded to find himself suddenly changed. He felt entirely persuaded "of all and every point of Catholic religion together . . . and feeling this in myself upon the sudden with such inward light of evidence as I could not contradict and with such force of affection as I could not resist, I leapt from the place where I sat, and said to myself, now I am a Catholic, and fell down on my knees and thanked God most heartily, humbly, and affecteously for so rare a benefit."

Alabaster communicated this event only to Wright and to the schoolfellow whom he would later address in the account of his conversion, then the next morning took his leave of Essex and immediately returned to Cambridge. Clearly his whole course of life was now utterly overthrown. His first business when he arrived in Cambridge was to write and break off his engagement, which understandably caused much consternation in the families on both sides. His next was to lay out some twenty-two pounds on works by Catholic authors and to begin a concentrated course of reading. This, combined with the ascetic practices he suddenly undertook, caused his friends to fear for his sanity. Though he says he longed for the imprisonment and suffering that discovery of his conversion would entail, he prayed to be spared six months in which to study and fit himself for the trials he knew lay ahead. During this time he abstained from attending Protestant services, made known his conversion to certain individuals, and apparently traveled to Suffolk, where he seems to have converted his parents and a sister as well. The earl of Essex was abroad during this time, and Alabaster rashly addressed him in writing, sending to London a manuscript of his "Seven Motives" for his conversion. (It is not known whether the work was later printed; it was, however, well enough known to be answered in print by his Trinity colleague John Racster in 1598 and by Roger Fenton in 1599.)

Not surprisingly, a copy of this came to the eyes of the authorities, and orders were sent to Cambridge for his arrest – at just the time, Alabaster notes, when the six-month truce he had prayed for was due to expire. Accordingly, on 21 September 1597 the vice-chancellor of the university sent a beadle to Dr. Thomas Neville, the master of Trinity, to hold Alabaster in house arrest if he refused to attend Protestant services. Neville, who was well disposed to Alabaster, dealt mildly with him and attempted to dissuade him from his present course. But Alabaster held his ground and was taken by the beadle to the vice-chancellor, where he received similarly mild treatment. But still refusing to yield, he was kept under close arrest in the university beadle's house for about six weeks until the government could make a further determination. During this time, Alabaster says, some of his friends came at night to the street window of his chamber and confessed leanings similar to his own. He encouraged them and gave them devotional sonnets that he had written. He was also spoiling for theological combat, which came in part in visitations by Dr. John Overall, the chief university reader in divinity, and by the Greek and Hebrew readers. He also thought of posting points for public disputation on the gates of the colleges, but his friends were not willing to take the risk. He says he was on the point of slipping out of his room at night to accomplish this himself when the order came for his removal to London.

Accompanied by a pursuivant, Alabaster arrived in London on 1 November and was taken to the newly appointed bishop of London, Dr. Richard Bancroft. The mild treatment continued as Bancroft attempted by persuasion and dispute to bring Alabaster back to Protestantism. In a second interview the bishop was joined by Neville, then a few days later by Still, now bishop of Bath and Wells. With Still came Dr. Edward Grant, Alabaster's old schoolmaster at Westminster, and Overall. As a talented and learned young man, Alabaster was evidently considered a serious loss to the church and the university, and every attempt was made to persuade his return by argument and by appeal to the bonds of affection, but to no avail. Alabaster's account of the meetings indicates the degree of absolute certainty and youthful arrogance they were up against.

A bigger gun was trained on the target in the person of Lancelot Andrewes, then master of Pembroke Hall, Cambridge, but Alabaster was if anything even more contemptuous of Andrewes. More conferences with Bancroft and Stills followed, but Alabaster remained unmoved. Throughout he maintained a hope in the earl of Essex. Eventually he was secretly able to obtain ink and paper and to write to Essex, asking that he be allowed books and the opportunity of public disputation against the bishops. Alabaster says that Essex was well disposed to the request and made it known at court, even to the queen, who he reports was angry that her bishops should fear dispute. Unlikely though both responses would appear, he was allowed paper and ink, but not books, whereupon he set down some "seven or eight score of reasons," listing general Protestant positions against the Catholics, then answering them in brief form, hoping thereby to provoke a public disputation. Not surprisingly, he failed in this. On 21 February 1598 he was brought before the bishop of London, Thomas Sackville of the Privy Council, Edward Coke (the queen's attorney), Andrewes, and various members of the clergy and was deprived of Anglican orders. More private conferences followed with old connections among the clergy, including Still and Goodman. During this time he continued to be kept under house arrest by the pursuivant.

But when three months elapsed and he continued to be frustrated of a public confrontation, Alabaster simply walked away from his place of confinement and was hidden in London by a Jesuit, John Gerard. He believed that the authorities at least half intended his escape as a means of being rid of him, since no attempt was made to keep him locked up or under guard. In any case a search was mounted and a watch maintained at all the ports for some six or seven weeks. Meanwhile, Gerard had given him a copy of Saint Ignatius's *Spiritual Exercises,* and Alabaster reportedly voiced his intention of joining the Jesuits. He stayed in London throughout the summer of 1598, writing two polemical books of "observations," as he termed them, on Protestantism. In September, about a year after his arrest in Cambridge, he managed to escape from England to France, with three hundred florins from Gerard for expenses, and went by way of the Catholic seminary at Douai through Germany to Italy. He arrived at Rome in mid November and immediately went to stay at the English College.

The composition of most of Alabaster's sonnets must have occurred in the period between his conversion in the spring of 1597 and his escape to the Continent some eighteen months later; many were likely written during the six-month "truce" and his confinement in Cambridge. He says that shortly after his conversion he devised "what sonnets and love devices I would make to Christ." During that summer before his arrest, he walked in the fields around Cambridge, "where I could not be seen nor heard of others and here pass the time in conference between almighty God and my soul, sometimes with internal meditation uniting my will to God, sometimes forming and contriving the same meditations into verses of love and affection, as it were hiding of the fire under ashes, with the reading whereof I might afterwards kindle my devotion at new time again." He composed the verses and sonnets, he adds, not only for himself but to stir others to a like devotion, and he gave them to sympathetic friends at Cambridge. One manuscript compiled by an Elizabethan recusant contains thirteen of the son-

nets and lists the date 1597 at their head; since the poems were passed in manuscript among recusants, it seems likely that these may have come to the compiler shortly after their composition. Alabaster likely continued writing sonnets during his confinement in London and his summer in hiding. But it is possible that some may predate his conversion; the more fervent devotion to Christ's Passion that he says came over him in fall 1596 may have stimulated the beginning of this activity and perhaps the early poems in the collection.

Save one (and that anonymously), none of Alabaster's sonnets was printed during his lifetime, but they continued to circulate in manuscript. Three of the six manuscripts of his poems represent collections, one containing as many as sixty-four of the seventy-seven that can be certainly ascribed to him. Few of the sonnets seem designed to stand by themselves, but rather they fall into identifiable groups. Since the sonnets that the major manuscripts share occur in the same order in each, it seems clear that Alabaster intended them to be read in such groupings as series of meditations. Modern editors give these groupings such titles as "The Portrait of Christ's Death," "Penitence," "Resurrection," "New Jerusalem," and "The Incarnation"; one grouping is entitled "Upon the Ensigns of Christ's Crucifying" in the manuscript. In addition, one sequence of seven poems is called "Personal Poems" by the editors and contains sonnets concerned with Alabaster's conversion and spiritual progress; poem 49 reads as if it might have been written to his fiancée after the engagement was broken off.

Nearly all of Alabaster's sonnets show a fine clarity both of language and of argument. Because they are all meditations on religious themes and must therefore portray a sense of personal engagement with their subjects, they generally avoid the preciosity and overly learned allusiveness of his Latin poetry. The conceits that structure the arguments of the poems are frequently clever without appearing to strain after cleverness; some of them — man's soul as a microcosm of the world (number 15, "My soul a world is by contraction"), tears of penitence as purifying seas or fertile rain, the Incarnation as God's love suit to man, the crucified Christ as a cluster of grapes pressed into wine — would also serve John Donne, George Herbert, and their followers in the tradition of meditative verse. Other conceits (as in number 64, "Jesu, the handle of the world's ball, / By which the finger of omnipotence / Took hold of us") express a kind of wit proper to Alabaster. One of the most effective, number 43, develops a conceit in which the beatific vision is likened to the discipline of reading and unfolding the text of the Scripture:

> Thrice happy souls and spirits unbodied,
> Who in the school of heaven do always see
> The three-leaved bible of one Trinity,
> In whose unfolded page are to be read
> The incomprehended secrets of the Godhead,
> Who only read by love that mystery,
> And what you read is love's infinity,
> Who learn by love, and love is what is learned.
> O happy school whose master is the book,
> Which book is only text, which text unwrit
> Doth read itself, and they that on it look
> Do read by being read, nor do they flit
> From word to word: for all is but one letter,
> Which still is learnt, but never learnt the better.

The conceit depends on the Protestant discipline of reading and interpreting the Bible, but this Book of the Trinity reads its readers and is self-interpreted. All difficulty of interpretation collapses for those "who learn by love" the Book that is love. By imagining the mystical union of "book" and reader, the poem projects the elision of textuality and interpretation.

In poem 75, Alabaster, like Donne, puns on his own name; he imagines himself sending his Lord an alabaster box as a New Year's gift, which he hopes may be filled with the treasure of spiritual graces. Though Catholic in inspiration, the poems arguably express a blending of Counter-Reformation traditions of affective meditation with a stamp of Protestant inwardness. Some of the sequences, such as those on Christ's Passion and on the "Ensigns" of the Crucifixion, make use of specifically Catholic techniques of visualizing scenes and objects. The first poem of this sequence, number 24, on the sponge that conveyed the vinegar to Jesus' mouth, unfolds a witty, Herbert-like argument that expresses the paradox implied in the desire to achieve a psychic engagement with the Passion and the contrary demand of passive acceptance of its grace:

> O sweet and bitter monuments of pain,
> Bitter to Christ who all the pain endured,
> How shall I full express such loss, such gain?
> My tongue shall be my pen, mine eyes shall rain
> Tears for my ink, the place where I was cured
> Shall be my book, where, having all abjured,
> And calling heavens to record in that plain,
> Thus plainly will I write: no sin like mine.
> When I have done, do thou, Jesu divine,
> Take up the tart sponge of thy Passion,
> And blot it forth; then be thy spirit the quill,
> Thy blood the ink, and with compassion
> Write thus upon my soul: thy Jesu still.

Others, such as the sonnets engaging his personal experience and penitence, seem to depend on a Calvinist desire to scrutinize the self, even though their doctrine has been directed away from the specific need to discover signs of election. Only a few of the sonnets seem to express specifically Catholic doctrine. One celebrates the Virgin through the witty development of her as "graceful morning of eternal day"; a small handful (numbers 5, 9, and 76) engage in polemics with Protestantism. Still, Alabaster is clearly aware of a difference of style in the devotion of contemporary Catholics and Protestants, and he plays on this implicitly in some of the sonnets. Number 71, for example, contrasts a dry-eyed viewing of the Passion of Christ with a tearful devotion that enables the viewer to feed upon the blood that comes from Christ's side.

Because the sonnets were not printed and their circulation appears to have been limited to a small handful of manuscripts, it is difficult to gauge their influence. While readers will be reminded of Donne, Herbert, and Richard Crashaw at times, it is perhaps more likely that those poets drew upon the same poetic and meditative traditions than that they read Alabaster's sonnets. Before the late eighteenth century there is only a single reference, by Edward Leigh in 1656, to Alabaster as an English poet.

Alabaster's sojourn at the English College in Rome lasted only four months. He was much impressed by the level of religious devotion and charity in Counter-Reformation Rome, by the multitude of religious congregations, and by the monuments of early Christianity. He says at the conclusion of the account of his conversion that he intended only a short stay for study, after which he intended to return to England and martyrdom at Tyburn. College records indicate that he received minor orders between 6 March and 10 April 1599, which suggests that at that point he intended to become a priest. In May, the record concludes, he left because of ill health. But this reason may have been a cover for a mission from Parsons. From Rome, Alabaster went to Barcelona, then to La Rochelle, where he was taken and handed over to the English authorities. On 8 August he was committed to the Tower.

Immediately he attempted to impart information to the government, perhaps about efforts by the "French party" among English Catholic exiles to contact the king of Scotland regarding the succession. In any case he finally did give information in July 1600, but regarding the "Spanish party," which included Parsons and those with whom Alabaster dealt in Spain. Alabaster had been charged by them, he said, to deliver messages to Essex persuading him to favor the title of the infanta of Spain in return for the loyalty of English Catholics and the promise of important position in the new government. A truce with Hugh O'Neill, second Earl of Tyrone, was urged upon Essex, under which Tyrone would rule Ireland as a papal subject until Essex was established in control of the English Crown, then the pope would order Tyrone's submission to England. Alabaster's motives in revealing this are not at all clear. By this time Essex was in disgrace in England after the collapse of the Irish campaign the previous summer. Alabaster had been in ill health after nearly a year in the Tower, and he may have grown disillusioned over the intrigues of his coreligionists in Rome and Spain. He nevertheless remained firm in his Catholic convictions. He was held in the Tower until 7 July 1601, when he was transferred to Framlingham Castle in his native county; he was kept prisoner there another two years. He was released and pardoned in September 1603 after the accession of James I.

Shortly after his release Alabaster again entered into religious polemics, and by June 1604 he was incarcerated in the King's Bench prison in London. Here he remained until late 1605 or early 1606, when – upon learning he was to be banished – he wrote to Robert Cecil offering his services as a spy on emigrant English Catholics. It is not known whether his offer was accepted, but by July 1606 he was a guest at the Catholic seminary at Douai. He appears to have stayed at Douai and at Brussels for the next two years, writing the *Apparatus in Revelationem Jesu Christi,* a work of mystical theology that he published in Antwerp in 1607, against the advice of Parsons, and that would shortly land him in trouble with the Holy Office in Rome. Late in January 1609 Alabaster was back at the English College in Rome. By September he appears to have come into serious conflict with Parsons, for the latter wrote that although Alabaster was sound in the Catholic faith, he was unwilling to conform to the discipline of the College and would be better off at an Italian university or monastery. Shortly after this Alabaster appears to have rebelled against his Jesuit patron and denounced him to the Inquisition. Alabaster's denunciation backfired, however, and he was himself called before the Inquisition and imprisoned. In January 1610 the *Apparatus in Revelationem* was declared heretical; he was released from prison but ordered to stay in Rome.

Alabaster left the city, however, bitterly insulting both the Inquisition and the Jesuits and declaring his intention to return to the Protestant church. By midsummer 1610 he was in Marseilles making wild charges that Parsons had been involved in the Gunpowder Plot and that Cardinal Robert Bellarmine had advised the assassination of James I. A month later he was in Amsterdam, where he was soon suspected of an attempt on the life of Prince Maurice of Nassau and imprisoned. The authorities were clearly dubious about the sincerity of his return to Protestantism, though he protested his desire to write against the Jesuits. He was turned over to English authority and returned under guard to London, where he was confined in the house of his old adversary at Cambridge, Overall, now dean of Saint Paul's. It is possible that the government wished to use Alabaster to harass English Catholics, in particular to exploit his hatred of the Jesuit William Baldwin, whom he suspected of denouncing him to the Inquisition. But by February 1611, still in confinement at the deanery of Saint Paul's, Alabaster declared his intention to live and die a Catholic.

Nothing is known of Alabaster in the next three years. By early 1614 he appears not only to have returned to Protestantism but to have accomplished this so persuasively that he was high in royal favor. By March of that year Donne wrote to Henry Goodyer that Alabaster had obtained from the king the dean of Saint Paul's "best living, worth above 300 pounds." In May he formally abjured his allegiance to the Catholic church before a synod at Westminster and was absolved of his seventeen-year infidelity to the Church of England. The following month he was restored to Anglican orders and at the king's command made doctor of divinity at Cambridge. In late June he took possession of his benefice at Therfield, Hertfordshire, where he resided after late June and where his mother died the following November. It has been suggested that Alabaster again converted to Catholicism late that same year, but this appears to rest on a mistaken identification. Since he was reported in January 1615 to have preached before the king at Whitehall, and since he was listed as chaplain to the king in his admission to Gray's Inn on 2 August 1618, another reconversion seems unlikely. In London on 22 August 1618 he married Katherine Fludd, widow of Thomas Fludd, and thereby became stepfather to the alchemist and physician Robert Fludd. Not surprisingly, Alabaster continued to be suspected of Catholic opinions, and no less

SPIRACULUM
'BARUM
*iue.
*Fons spiritualium expositionum
ex æquivocis Pentaglotti
significationibus
Authore Guilielmo Alabastro
Anglo.
Londini
Ex officina Guil: Jones.
Extant in cœmeterio
D. Pauli ad insigne
Papæ.

Per ambages exercitus omnes emicuit.

Engraved title page for Alabaster's last book, which examines biblical prophecy

than Oliver Cromwell, in his first parliamentary speech, mentioned what he called the "flat popery" of a sermon preached by Alabaster in 1617.

In esoteric interpretation of apocalyptic biblical prophecy, Alabaster's difficult and rather arrogant personality found an outlet more conducive to a settled life than active theological controversy. He continued his interest in such interpretation of the Book of Revelation – begun in the *Apparatus in Revelationem* – with another commentary, *De Bestia Apocalyptica* (1621). He followed with *Ecce sponsus venit* (1633), a Latin treatise that includes "an exposition of the signs given by Christ for knowing the state of the double Church of Catholics and Protestants and the time of the coming of Christ" (chapter 47). His final work, *Spiraculum tubarum sive fons spiritualium expositionum ex aequivocis Pentaglotti significationibus* (1633), includes a lexicon of Hebrew words traced through Chaldean, Aramaic, Talmudic Hebrew and Aramaic, and Arabic to aid in the mystical and numerical interpretation of prophecy. This is the Alabaster whom Robert Herrick commended as one

In whom the spirit of the gods does dwell,
Firing thy soul, by which thou dost foretell
When this or that vast dynasty must fall
Down to a fillet more imperial;
When this or that horn shall be broke, and when
Others shall spring up in their place again;
When times and seasons and all years must lie
Drowned in the sea of wild eternity.
(*Hesperides* 763: "To Dr. Alabaster")

In addition, Alabaster continued to write Latin epigrams in elegiac verse, and these survive in manuscripts. His final work was an abridgment of a Hebrew lexicon, *Schindleri lexicon pentaglotton, in epitomen redactum a G.A.* (1635). He died in London on 28

April 1640 and was buried at Saint Dunstan's-in-the-West.

Alabaster's poetic activity in English represents one brief and intense moment in a life much taken up with the religious struggles that embroiled England in the reigns of Elizabeth I and James I. It is significant that the psychic turmoil precipitated by his conversion should immediately impel him toward vernacular poetry and specifically to the sonnet. This form clearly represented for him and his contemporaries a means of controlled expression through which the self could portray, both for itself and others, serious thought and emotion with a kind of dramatic intensity. If the generation of Edmund Spenser and Philip Sidney had used the sonnet to portray the intensity of love, it now represented as well a vehicle for intense religious expression. It is not known whether Alabaster ever returned to the sonnet during the next forty-odd years of his life. His earlier poetry in Latin was composed in an academic context that encouraged the display of learning and rhetorical mastery. Only the English sonnets appear to come of a desire to explore and express a self experiencing the upheaval – including the apprehension of torture and death – that conversion meant at the end of the sixteenth century. Beyond the poetry Alabaster appears to have been someone whose talent, learning, and volatile intelligence fascinated, rather than charmed, his contemporaries. Though he was only one of the earl of Essex's many protégés, and this for a comparatively short time, it may be that in his case patron and client were mutually well chosen.

Alabaster's contemporary literary reputation, as reflected in printed references to him, was exclusively as a Latin poet. In fact, only one reference from the mid seventeenth century places him among poets who wrote in English. His modern discovery came in 1903 when Bertram Dobell published six of his sonnets from the Bodleian manuscript in the *Athenaeum*. Louise Imogen Guiney published five sonnets in her anthology of recusant poetry in 1939. But a full sense of Alabaster's accomplishment as an English poet had to wait until the publication of G. M. Storey and Helen Gardner's edition of his poems in 1959. By this point, however, the early vogue of the metaphysical poets had passed, and commentary on his poetry has most frequently occurred in the context of his better-known successors Donne, Herbert, and Crashaw. Alabaster's poetry continues to be too little known and anthologized.

References:

John C. Coldewey, "William Alabaster's *Roxana:* Some Textual Considerations," in *Acta Conventus Neo-Latini Bononiensis,* edited by R. J. Schoeck (Binghamton, N.Y.: Medieval & Renaissance Texts and Studies, 1985), pp. 413–419;

Louise Imogen Guiney, "William Alabaster," in *English Recusant Poets* (New York: Sheed & Ward, 1939), pp. 335–346;

Michael O'Connell, "Introduction," in *The "Elisæis" of William Alabaster,* translated and edited by O'Connell, *Studies in Philology,* Texts and Studies, 76 (Winter 1979): 1–12;

G. M. Storey and Helen Gardner, "General Introduction," in *The Sonnets of William Alabaster,* edited by Storey and Gardner (London: Oxford University Press, 1959), pp. xi–xliii.

Papers:

Seventy-seven of Alabaster's sonnets survive in six manuscripts; three contain collections of the poems: Bodleian Library MS. Eng. Poet.e.57 (forty-three sonnets identified as Alabaster's); Saint John's College, Cambridge, T.9.30 (sixty-four sonnets); and Oscott College Ms. E.3.11 (contemporary recusant manuscript of thirteen sonnets). In addition, Bodleian Library Ms.Rawl.D.293 contains a collection of eighteen Latin poems, including an epitaph on Spenser. Guiney lists other manuscripts containing individual Latin poems and smaller groupings of them.

Sir Nicholas Bacon

(circa 1510 – 1579)

James A. Riddell
California State University, Dominguez Hills

EDITIONS AND COLLECTIONS: *The Recreations of His Age,* edited by Charles Daniel (Oxford: Daniel Press, 1919) – includes Bacon's poems, with a few expurgations;

Sir Nicholas Bacon's Great House Sententiae, edited by Elizabeth McCutcheon, *English Literary Renaissance* supplements, no. 3 (1977);

"The Poems of Sir Nicholas Bacon, Continued," edited by Steven W. May, *American Notes and Queries,* new series 5 (April–July 1992): 103–106 – includes the matter expurgated by Daniel.

Sir Nicholas Bacon, lord keeper of the great seal during the first twenty years of Elizabeth I's reign, was widely admired in his own age, not only for his political wisdom but also for his eloquence in expressing that wisdom. The latter, or rather the reputation for it, is largely responsible for his place in literary history. There have been few commentators on Bacon's rhetorical skill since the sixteenth century – probably because a collection of his speeches and orations has never been published. Some of his speeches in Parliament have been reproduced by parliamentary historians, from Sir Simonds D'Ewes in the seventeenth century to John Neale in the present, but never with any attempt to group them together. His poems have fared somewhat better: a limited (and expurgated) edition of them was published in 1919, and versions of the expurgated poems were published in 1992. Although several manuscript copies survive, apparently Bacon's poems were not widely circulated in his own day; thus, in contrast to his contemporary reputation as an orator, such reputation he has as a poet is entirely a modern one.

Bacon was born about 1510, the son of a sheep reeve of the monastery of Bury Saint Edmunds in Suffolk. Nicholas was one of at least five children (three sons and two daughters) born to Robert and Isabel Cage Bacon. One can infer from Robert's position that although he was a man of no more than modest wealth, he could both read and write. He was also able to arrange for Nicholas to attend Corpus Christi College, Cambridge, which he entered at the age of thirteen in 1523 and from which he graduated bachelor of arts four years later. Where Nicholas was educated before he went to Cambridge is unknown, but it very likely was at the abbey school of Bury Saint Edmunds. How he was occupied during the five years after he left Cambridge is also unknown; it has been suggested that he traveled abroad, which remains plausible, but unsupported, conjecture.

He was admitted to the study of law in Gray's Inn in 1532 and seems to have advanced in his profession at a rapid rate. Beginning in the late 1530s he served in the Court of Augmentations, helping to distribute the property confiscated from the churches after King Henry VIII's break with Rome; Bacon maintained this position for about ten years. In 1540 he married Jane Fernely, the daughter of William Fernely, a man of some property and significant connections. She died twelve years later, having borne three sons and three daughters. Within a few months Bacon was again married, this time to Anne Cooke, daughter of Sir Anthony Cooke. She was reputed to be one of the best-educated women in England. They had two sons – one very able and one who became extraordinary – Anthony and Francis.

The only poem by Nicholas Bacon that can be dated with certainty was written about his wife Anne, and it seems likely that at least one other was written with her in mind. The title of the latter, "An Ode of Horace turned at the desire of my Lady his Lordship's wife," sits much more with what is known of Anne's education and interests than with Jane's. The other is titled "Made at Wimbleton in his Lordship's great sickness in the last year of Queen Mary." It is a charming address to his wife, thanking her for her attention to him during his illness in 1557 and 1558. In the poem, which is rather unusually personal for its day, Bacon suggests that a good many, if not all, of the poems in his collec-

Sir Nicholas Bacon (National Portrait Gallery, London)

tion had been written by a time in his life that he then fancied to be advanced, for he had already produced "fruits of [his] mind" that were both "young and old." The "fruits" that were his poems he in effect dedicates to Anne:

> For you I could not find
> A more deep thing than fruits of mind.
>
> A mind I have such as it is
> And fruits thereof both young and old,
> Not precious much nor all amiss,
> But as they be, lo, here them hold:
> I wish them better a hundreth fold:
> The recreations of both mine ages,
> Go and serve her as humble pages.

Other poems in *The Recreations of His Age* (1919) deal with topics that seem to have interested Bacon for most of his life. This matter is discussed at some length by Elizabeth McCutcheon in the introduction to her edition of the sententiae that Bacon had painted on the walls of the long gallery of his house at Gorhambury, near Saint Albans. His ideas – like his life itself – were remarkably coherent. He took seriously the moral implications of the Renaissance notion of the "mean estate," which is not to say that he failed to advance himself in the world. Indisputably he did, but the genuineness of his belief in such an ideal of existence is not therefore subject to doubt.

For one thing, no man writes poems for his own entertainment that are products of hypocrisy, poems such as those titled "Against Ambition," "Against Covetousness," and, most to the point, "In Commendation of the Mean Estate." The first two lines of the last poem are "The surest state and best degree / Is to possess mediocrity," and the last six lines are:

Busts of Bacon and his wife, Lady Anne, circa 1568. They were the parents of Anthony and Francis Bacon (Gorhambury Collection).

Wherefore by right I may conclude
Of the three estates two are eschewed,
As two extremes by reason's lore,
And the mean state is set before,
Who brings and breeds these jewels three:
Safety, Quiet, and Liberty.

These notions are succinctly put in Bacon's personal motto, *Mediocria Firma* ("moderate things endure" or "steadfastly moderate"), and they recur frequently in his speeches and orations. Indeed, Bacon's reputation among his contemporaries is based on his eloquent expression of sensible opinions. An early comment was made by the French epic poet Guillaume de Salluste, Seigneur Du Bartas, who in 1584 called Bacon, along with Sir Thomas More and Sir Philip Sidney, one of the three "pillars" of the English tongue. Eight years later Thomas Nashe noted Du Bartas's observation with approval. George Puttenham was scarcely less extravagant than Du Bartas in his praise of Bacon's eloquence. In the *Art of English Poesy* (1589), he declared that from Bacon's "lips I have seen to proceed more grave and natural eloquence than from all the orators of Oxford or Cambridge," and continued, "I have come to the Lord Keeper Sir Nicholas Bacon and found him sitting in his gallery alone with the works of Quintilian before him; indeed

he was a most eloquent man, and of rare learning and wisdom, as ever I knew England to breed."

Bacon's reputation for eloquence persisted into the seventeenth century, partly as the residue of earlier notice (for instance, in the many editions of Du Bartas that were printed in the first part of that century). In his *Annals* of 1615 William Camden noted Bacon's death among the events of 1579, mentioning as well the great man's great bulk and his eloquence. Two additional comments on Bacon's eloquence from the early seventeenth century are by Henry Peacham, in the sixth chapter of *The Complete Gentleman* (1622), and by Camden's pupil Ben Jonson. If the former's comment seems merely to echo Puttenham's, the latter's has the ring of authority and independent thought that one would expect in a statement from Jonson. In a passage in his *Discoveries* (1640) devoted to eloquence, Jonson makes the compelling remark that "Sir Nicholas Bacon was singular, and almost alone, in the beginning of Queen Elizabeth's times."

Several dozen Bacon speeches survive; they range from long, elaborate rhetorical exercises to rather short (one- or two-page) responses to questions that had been put to him. A brief survey of the structure of one formal speech can give a sense of the sort of approach that Bacon took in his more fully developed presentations. This speech, made before the Privy Council in late 1559, early in Bacon's tenure as lord keeper, reflected the lingering doubts of some of the councillors about the wisdom of sending an expedition into Scotland to help the Scots drive out the French, whose presence in the land was a matter of increasing concern. Bacon's chief adversary in the debate was his wife's brother-in-law William Cecil, at the time Elizabeth's chief secretary of state; Bacon later abandoned his initial position and took up Cecil's. The structure of the speech, however, is the issue here, and Puttenham's comment on finding Bacon alone reading Quintilian proves very much to the point. In the *Institutio Oratoria,* Quintilian points out the virtues and defects of *partitio,* which he explains "may be defined as the enumeration in order of our own *propositions,* those of our adversary or both." He then elaborates: "Our first *partition* will be between admitted and disputed facts. Admitted facts will then be divided into those acknowledged by our opponent and those acknowledged by ourselves. Disputed facts will be divided into those which we and those which our opponents allege."

Bacon's proposition in the speech is posed as a question: should the English aid the Scots openly or clandestinely? The two major divisions are then partitioned into two subdivisions, each supported by points. First, open aid is discussed and partitioned into the "admitted fact" (subsequently to be ignored) that open aid will provoke war with France. Second, the "disputed fact" that England cannot maintain war with France is addressed point by point under the heads of (1) England's weakness and (2) France's strength. Bacon contends that England cannot maintain war with France because of her lack of money, men, and friends (foreign princes), along with other respects. Each of these first three parallel reasons is supported in turn by an argument.

So far as money is concerned, the queen has too little, the nobility have too little, the gentlemen and commons have too little, and the clergy have none. So far as men are concerned, soldiers have had their numbers decimated by pestilence and by wars, there are not enough yeomen and husbandmen to tap their store for new soldiers, and foreign soldiers cannot be paid – even if they could be, there would be the danger of foreign troops on English soil. So far as friends are concerned, the queen has none who are obliged to her, she cannot afford mercenary friends, and, in any case, during the reigns of Henry VIII, Henry VII, Edward VI, Edward III, and so forth, friends have

not proven terribly useful. "Other respects" is likewise divided into a series of points. Then, having detailed the English weakness, Bacon depicts the French strength, partitioning it into the same categories as the English weakness: money, men, friends, and other respects.

After showing the French strength he turns to the second major division of his proposition: that the Scots should be aided secretly. This portion is also partitioned into two subdivisions, each one supported by points. The first subdivision, that the English will (relatively, at least) gain strength, is dependent upon the second, that the French will be enfeebled by protracted wars with the Scots. The second subdivision, therefore, is the one that is developed. Bacon contends that the French cannot begin war with England for at least a year and a half because they would not be able to maintain a war on two fronts and they could not conquer Scotland short of that time, which is supported by examples of historical precedent and the "fact" that men will fight harder to protect their own lands than to conquer others'. Bacon's general conclusion, which thereupon follows, is a recapitulation of the entire argument.

In addition to their structural sophistication, Bacon's speeches are characteristically salted with pithy observations, both in Latin and in English, often in the manner of the sententiae that adorned the long gallery of his house at Gorhambury. "Bis dat qui cito dat" (he gives twice who gives at once), he several times exhorted the houses of Parliament when he was attempting to raise money; or, when he was interested in that which motivates a man: "Such as have done well may hear thereafter, and such as [have] done otherwise may feel thereafter." Indeed, such observations became associated with his name, some with more justice than others. An example of each may be found in two comments dealing with Queen Elizabeth and with Bacon's considerable bulk.

On one occasion, when the queen visited him at his house, she is supposed to have said, "My Lord, what a little house you have gotten," to which Bacon replied, "Madam, my house is well, but it is you who made me too great for my house." On (perhaps) another occasion she is supposed to have said, "My Lord Bacon's soul lodgeth well." The first is reported by Bacon's son Francis in his *Apopthegms* (1624); the second is said to have appeared for the first time in Robert Naunton's *Fragmenta Regalia,* first printed almost forty years after Elizabeth's death and more than sixty after Bacon's, but which in fact seems to

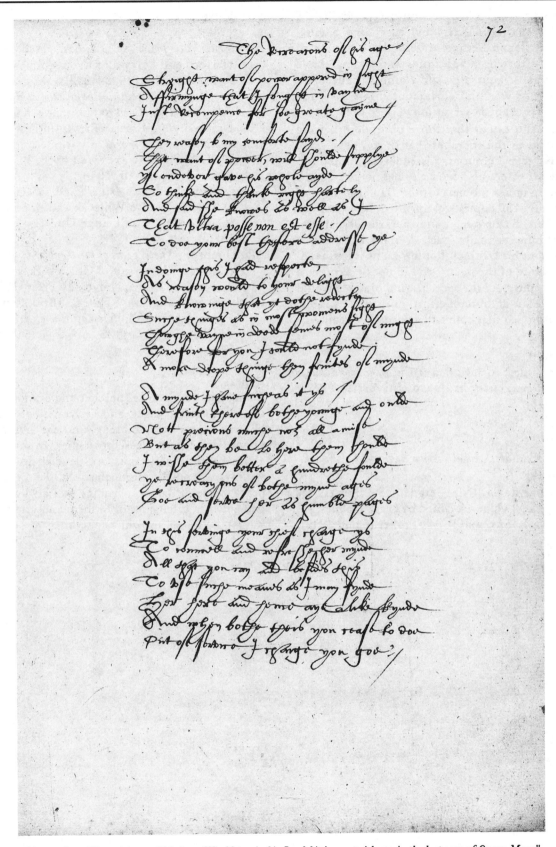

Manuscript of Bacon's poem "Made at Wimbleton in his Lordship's great sickness in the last year of Queen Mary"
(Henry E. Huntington Library and Art Gallery, HM 1340 fol. 72r)

date from even later in the century in David Lloyd's *State Worthies* (1665). In any case, like Samuel Johnson, Bacon became one of those figures in history with whom anecdotes and sayings have become associated, almost certainly because, like Johnson, he was himself famous in his own day for his trenchant observations.

To the extent that those observations were embedded in the speeches that Bacon gave, they have, in recent centuries, passed largely unnoticed. To a lesser extent his poetry also has not been much noticed in modern times, for the Daniel edition, of which only 130 copies were printed, is not easy to find. Thus, Bacon's reputation as a rhetorician and poet is today virtually spectral. Many know something about his writings, but few know it firsthand. A reprinting of the poetry would not be a difficult task; an edition of the speeches and orations would require a fair amount of effort. Both are desirable, and it is hoped that both will someday be realized.

Biography:

Robert Tittler, *Nicholas Bacon: The Making of a Tudor Statesman* (Athens: Ohio University Press, 1976).

References:

William Camden, *Annales rerum Anglicarum* (London, 1615);

Guillaume de Salluste, Seigneur Du Bartas, *The Works,* 3 volumes, edited by U. T. Holmes, Jr., J. C. Lyons, and R. W. Linker (Chapel Hill: University of North Carolina Press, 1935–1940);

Ben Jonson, *Ben Jonson,* 11 volumes, edited by C. H. Herford and Percy and Evelyn Simpson (Oxford: Clarendon, 1925–1952);

Steven W. May, *The Elizabethan Courtier Poets: The Poems and Their Contexts* (Columbia & London: University of Missouri Press, 1991);

Thomas Nashe, *The Works,* 5 volumes, edited by R. B. McKerrow, revised by F. P. Wilson (Oxford: Blackwell, 1958);

George Puttenham, *The Arte of English Poesie,* edited by Gladys Doidge Willcock and Alice Walker (Cambridge: Cambridge University Press, 1936);

Alan Simpson, *The Wealth of the Gentry, 1540–1660* (Chicago: University of Chicago Press / Cambridge: Cambridge University Press, 1961);

Gladys Scott Thomson, "Three Suffolk Figures," *Proceedings of the Suffolk Institute of Archaeology and Natural History,* 25, no. 2 (1951): 149–163.

Papers:

Manuscripts of Bacon's speeches and orations are in the Huntington, Folger, and University of Chicago libraries, the British Library, and the libraries of Oxford and Cambridge Universities. In some cases entire bound manuscripts are devoted to Bacon's writings; in others, particularly at the British Library, some of Bacon's writings (not always identified either in catalogues or in the manuscripts themselves) are bound up with the writings of others.

William Baldwin

(circa 1515 – 1563)

Nancy A. Gutierrez
Arizona State University

BOOKS: *A treatise of morall phylosophie, contaynyng the sayinges of the wyse. Gathered and Englyshed by W. Baldwyn* (London: Printed by Edward Whitchurch, 1547);

The canticles or balades of Salomon, phraselyke declared in Englysh metres (London: Printed by W. Baldwin, servant with Edward Whitchurch, 1549);

Westerne Wyll, vpon the debate betwyxte Churchyarde and Camell [attributed to Baldwin] (London: Printed by William Powell, [1552?]); reprinted in *The contention bettwyxte Churchyeard and Camell, vpon Dauid Dycers dreame* (London: Printed by O. Rogers for M. Loblee, 1560);

The funeralles of King Edward the sixt. Wherein are declared the causes of his death (London: Printed by Thomas Marshe, 1560);

A marvelous hystory intitulede, Beware the Cat (London: Edward Allde, 1584) – two editions were printed in 1570, one by John Arnold and another by William Griffith; a careful transcription of the now-lost Arnold edition, which has primary textual authority according to William A. Ringler, Jr., and Michael Flachmann, was made in 1847.

Editions: *The Mirror for Magistrates,* edited by Lily Bess Campbell (Cambridge: Cambridge University Press, 1938; New York: Barnes & Noble, 1960);

Beware the Cat, and The Funerals of King Edward the Sixth, edited by William P. Holden (New London: Connecticut College, 1963);

"A Critical Edition of *The Canticles or Balades of Salomon Phraselyke Declared in English Metres,*" edited by Frances Camilla Cavanaugh, Ph.D. dissertation, Saint Louis University, 1964;

"William Baldwin's *A Treatise of Moral Philosophy* (1564): A Variorum Edition with Introduction," edited by Paul M. Gaudet, Ph.D. dissertation, Princeton University, 1972;

Beware the Cat: The First English Novel, edited by Ringler and Flachmann (San Marino, Cal.: Huntington Library, 1988).

OTHER: Christopher Langton, *A very brefe treatise, ordrely declaring the principal partes of phisick,* with a commendatory sonnet by Baldwin (London: Printed by Edward Whitchurch, 1547);

A Myrrovre for Magistrates, edited by Baldwin and including fourteen tragedies written by him (London: Printed by Thomas Marshe, [1559]; another edition, [1563]) – revised edition of *A memorial of suche princes, as since the tyme of king Richard the seconde, haue been vnfortunate in the realme of England* (London: Printed by John Wayland, [1554?]), of which survives only a fragment of the title page plus two duplicate leaves of the text beginning with Owen Glendower.

TRANSLATION: Publius Esquillus, *Wonderfull newes of the death of Paule the .iii.* (London: Printed by T. Gualtier, [1552?]).

During the middle years of the sixteenth century, William Baldwin was a recognized author, editor, and translator whose published works show both a linguistic and narrative complexity and a sophisticated acumen about the political power of writing. As editor of *A Mirror for Magistrates* (1559), as compiler of a popular philosophical compendium, as translator of the biblical Song of Songs and of Italian satire, and as writer of original works of poetry and prose, Baldwin demonstrates the range of his interests and the scope of his literary experimentation. Equally important, these works chart his appropriation of Erasmian humanism in the service of the Protestant Reformation. Consequently, his writings must be examined as contributions both to the artistic and to the political and social culture of the English Renaissance.

In spite of Baldwin's reputation during his own time as a learned moralist (John Bale called him an English Cato in his *Scriptorum Illustrium maioris Britanniae . . . Catalogus,* 1557–1559), he has left few clues about his family background and personal life. Anthony à Wood notes that William Bal-

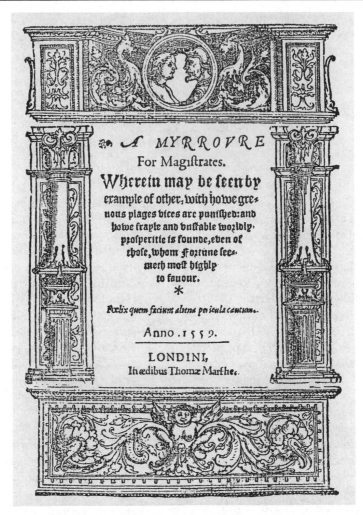

Title page for William Baldwin's edition of twenty historical tragedies, including fourteen of his own, compiled to warn rulers not to repeat the errors of their predecessors. This work was used as a source by many Elizabethan writers, among them William Shakespeare and Edmund Spenser.

dwin "seems to have been a Western man born," and he is called a Welshman in the 1587 edition of *A Mirror for Magistrates,* but the place and date of his birth remain a mystery. There is a record of two William Baldwins from Shropshire, one of whom served as a cupbearer to Queen Mary I and another who is reported to have died in 1544. A Baldwin family moved from Wales to Shropshire (near Diddlebury) and to Staffordshire, which is mentioned in *Beware the Cat* (1570). However, whether William Baldwin the author is a member of any of these families cannot be documented. Most scholars take Wood's assertion as true that Baldwin supplicated the regents of Oxford University for a degree in January 1533, but this cannot be verified. Prior to 1547, when his name is first associated with the printer Edward Whitchurch, he may have been a schoolmaster, as Wood suggests, or he may have served in the military, perhaps in Ireland, as did his

later collaborators in *A Mirror for Magistrates* – George Ferrers, Thomas Chaloner, and Thomas Churchyard. Until 1547, however, the details of Baldwin's life are only conjecture.

However he spent his young adulthood, his path led to the printing house of Whitchurch, where in 1547 his commendatory sonnet to Christopher Langton's *A Very Brief Treatise, Orderly Declaring the Principal Parts of Physic* was printed (verso of title page):

William Baldwin
Who so desireth health got, to preserve:
And lost, to procure: ought chiefly to know
Such natural things, as thereto may serve:
Great knowledge whereof, this book will him show.
Which small though it seem containeth as much
Of art to be known of them that are wise,
As big mighty books agastful to touch
As well for the weight, as for the heavy price.

Read it therefore all ye that love your health,
Learn here in an hour, elsewhere in a year
Scarce read, the which Langton willing our wealth
Hath englished brief, as it doth appear.
To whom the free giver of your so great gain,
Yield thanks and praises, a payment for his pain.
Consule valetudine.

The sonnet is versified prose rather than poetry, advertisement rather than art, in its recommendation of the book as more informative, less expensive, and less weighty than other such manuals. Nevertheless, the poem has the distinction of being the first English sonnet to be published: it is written in Shakespearean form of decasyllabic lines with a four- (rather than a five-) stress line.

In the next twelve years Baldwin either authored, translated, or compiled six major works: a collection of ethical sayings from the classics, an English translation of the biblical Song of Songs, a satire on the pope, the first extended work of English prose fiction, a politically motivated elegy on the death of Edward VI, and an anthology of narrative *de casibus* lives (stories of how people of high rank or position, through either bad fortune or their own error or vice, fall from high to low estate). A poem of social criticism is also attributed to him. The prolificity and diversity of these publications have caused recent scholars to describe Baldwin as "the literary voice of the reign of Edward VI" and "the preeminent imaginative author of the English Reformation." William Herbert (in augmenting Joseph Ames's *Typographical Antiquities,* published 1785–1790) was the first to point out, however, that Baldwin's literary career was developed to further the cause of the Reformation. The production of his works, especially in light of the censorship difficulties he experienced, illuminates the relationship between literature and politics in the tension-filled years of the mid sixteenth century.

In 1547, in addition to his commendatory sonnet for Langton, Baldwin published one of the two works for which he was perhaps best known during his lifetime and for several generations afterward, *A Treatise of Moral Philosophy,* a work that "served to introduce ancient learning to a reading public with an avid commitment to self-education," according to John N. King. Revised seven times between 1547 and 1564, the *Treatise* was reprinted twenty-four times by 1651. With the dedication to Edward Beauchamps, the son of Edward Seymour, Protector Somerset, Baldwin at once demonstrates the political nature of his text and marks it as a vehicle for the education of youth. According to Paul M. Gaudet, editor of a 1972 variorum edition of the

Treatise, the components of the first edition include the following:

> A dedicatory epistle, a prologue and four books: "Of lives and answers," which includes four introductory chapters on the origins and nature of moral philosophy, plus a table of contents for the first book and a general description of the other three, and several biographical accounts; "Of precepts and counsels"; "Of proverbs and adages"; and "Of parables and semblables"; [a] table of contents for the entire work, arranged according to book and chapter . . . placed at the end.

Gaudet counts 1,235 translations of classical sayings and the lives of twenty-four philosophers. He argues that the didactic objective of the work is served by the structure, in that the work "systematically progresses from the simplest and most overt form of teaching, precepts, to the most complex and allusive, parables." Further, the *Treatise* begins with biography and history, so as to provide a narrative in which to place the ethical formulations. Baldwin marries classical literature to Scripture in this work, and this activity — along with the book's appeal to a popular audience evident in its use of the vernacular, its explicit address to youth, its belief (implicit in its structure) in the rational perfectibility of man, and its many references to Erasmus — reveals that *A Treatise of Moral Philosophy* is a work written in the tradition of Erasmian humanism.

The printing history of the *Treatise* not only shows Baldwin's inability to maintain control of his work, but it also demonstrates the fragility of the humanist program. Baldwin republished this work in 1550, circa 1552, and 1555. In 1554 Thomas Palfreyman published an unauthorized edition from the print shop of Richard Tottel, making no mention of Baldwin as author and severely altering the content and structure. These revisions eliminate the progressive nature of the book's structuring, thus stunting its capacity as a tool for a reader's intellectual growth; the work becomes merely a repository of sayings for a reader to consult instead of a challenging system of learning that actively engages the reader for the purposes of self-reformation.

In spite of Baldwin's complaints in his 1555 edition, probably published in response to Palfreyman's pirated edition, Palfreyman published yet another edition in 1557, commenting in his preface that anyone who criticizes his efforts does so "contrary to the virtue of their good gift and calling (through the devil's flighty invasion and forgetfulness of the charity of God)." In the 1564 edition, apparently according to a compromise

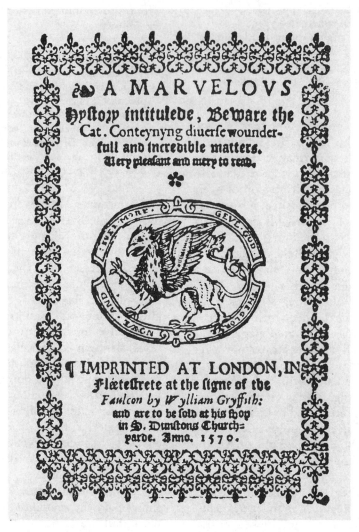

Title page for Baldwin's only work of prose fiction, sometimes called the first English novel

worked out by the two printers, Baldwin incorporated Palfreyman's changes within his humanist agenda, thus restoring the work's integrity as a process-oriented guide to individual perfection. The *Treatise* maintained this form into the seventeenth century.

In 1549 Baldwin published *The Canticles or Ballads of Solomon,* his metrical translation of the Song of Songs, dedicated to the young King Edward. The arrangement of the book signals his didactic intent: a chapter of the Great Bible preceding each chapter as preface, followed by the original text divided into sections, Baldwin's own paraphrase, the "argument" of the passage, and its versified translation. A companion piece to Baldwin's *Treatise,* Solomon's wise sayings are the divine counterpoint to the pagan philosophy Baldwin made available in the earlier book. In publishing his translation of the Song of Songs, he enters the reformist debate concerning the biblical canonicity of the work, obviously asserting that it is. He harmonizes its apparent profanity with divine truth by seeing its form as an epithalamium, a stance taken by most reformers, including John Calvin. Baldwin also suggests that the allegory makes reference to Reformation strife, although his commentary is rather abstract and not polemical.

Appearing eight years before *Tottel's Miscellany,* the work most often cited as the first published example of the "new poetry," *The Canticles* rivals this later secular poetic collection in its diversity of verse forms and meters, as it includes heroic couplets, trimeter lines, fourteeners, poulter's measure, hexameters, ballads, anapestics, and iambics. In his dedication to Edward, Baldwin makes explicit his desire to replace secular poetry with divine:

> For here shall your majesty hear Christ and his church singing the one in praise of the other: and that such sweet and musical ballads, as I doubt not but will delight any Christian-hearted ear. Would God that such songs might once drive out of office the bawdy ballads of lecherous love that commonly are indited and sung of idle courtiers in princes' and noble men's houses.

In the colophon Baldwin identifies himself as a servant of Whitchurch, with whom he may have collaborated as a publisher. Whitchurch's publications included the Great Bible of 1539, as well as the *Primer* in 1545. Further, with Richard Grafton, he had been given the privilege for all service books authorized by church authorities. This close association of Whitchurch's shop with the aims of Edwardian reform, as promoted by Archbishop Thomas Cranmer and Protector Somerset, suggests that Baldwin's work may have had official sanction.

The remaining five works attributed to Baldwin also reinforce the Erasmian humanist program, albeit from a more explicitly secular point of view. In circa 1552 a pamphlet entitled *Western Will, upon the Debate betwixt Churchyard and Camell* was printed by William Powell. Attributed to Baldwin by the *Short Title Catalogue*, this verse is part of the flyting between Thomas Churchyard and Thomas Camell, which generated a dozen or so ballads and longer poems during the early years of the 1550s. (This flyting was initiated by Camell, who accused Churchyard of deliberately challenging the social order with his poem "Davy Dicar's Dream," a dream vision by a Piers Plowman type of a utopian world free from social ills.) The larger portion of Baldwin's poem, thirty-five six-line stanzas written in fourteeners in an *ababcc* rhyme scheme, is a frame for the twenty-eight-line "Davy Dicar's Dream," written in poulter's measure. In this frame three sailors from Maldon visit Saint Paul's, looking for a "thing uncouth" to take back home to their friends, and find a printer who tells them "Davy Dicar's Dream" in the course of telling them about the flyting between Dicar and Camell. This frame is likewise framed by the narrator, who had heard the entire exchange and written it down. Not only interesting as a document of social criticism, the poem also draws attention to the difference between personal experience and that experience transformed into discourse, either by oneself or by another. The poem looks ahead to Baldwin's later fictional works

in its play with narrative point of view, its dialogic structure, and its epistemological thematics.

Also circa 1552 *Wonderful News of the Death of Paul the Third,* by Publius Esquillus, was printed by T. Gualtier. This is a translation from *Epistola de morte,* attributed to Matthias Flacius and to P. P. Vergerio. The title page indicates that the translator is "W. B., Londoner." These initials, along with Baldwin's motto, "Love and Live," allude specifically to Baldwin. This is the earliest example of the kind of Italianate and neoclassical satire that would become popular in England during the 1600s. In the form of a letter, the work ostensibly follows the soul of the late pope to hell, where his crimes — sodomy, incest, licentiousness, poisoning, and the like — are recorded on pillars of adamant. Baldwin labels the work a "tragedy," pointing to the structure and didactic intent of the *de casibus* tradition. Although the anti-Catholic satire certainly must have appealed to him, the literary form of the piece would have been equally attractive.

Baldwin's next work, although written during Christmas 1552, was apparently not published until after Elizabeth's accession. *Beware the Cat,* the first original piece of English prose fiction, has also been called the first English novel. It is an interlaced series of stories satirizing superstition in general and Catholicism in particular. In the "Argument," Baldwin frames his story by setting it during Christmastime 1552, when he was assisting George Ferrers, the master of revels, with the Christmas celebrations. Baldwin himself is the narrator, although he puts on a naive persona. Baldwin — here sharing a room with Ferrers; an "astronomer," Master Willot; and the "divine," Master Streamer — and his companions one evening get into an argument over whether animals can reason. Streamer silences the other men by telling them he knows, through personal experience, that animals can talk and reason.

In "The First Part of Master Streamer's Oration," he retells stories concerning animal speech and reason that had been told to him when he had been staying at the home of a friend (the printer John Day): these stories become increasingly distant in time and removed from narrative authority. In the second part of his oration, he recounts his efforts to concoct a potion that would make the language of cats intelligible to him; in the third part he retells the adventures of Mouselyer, the cat whose story he overheard after he had taken the potion. Whereas the first two parts attack superstitious practices in general, Mouselyer's tale focuses specifically on Catholic practices, and on the Mass in particular, placing this work directly in the tradition of the pamphlet war against the Mass waged several years earlier by Protector Somerset. The "cat" becomes a symbol of the Protestant conscience.

The structure of the fiction is that of a dialogue: "The Argument" is the vestibule that introduces the subject matter, sets the place for the dispute, and presents the proposition that animals can reason; "Streamer's oration" is the contention, the proof of the proposition. Joined with this structure is the classical rhetorical form of the declamation or paradoxical oration, a speech by a foolish speaker, arguing a ridiculous and fantastic point of view. The text is supported with marginal glosses, a convention of learned writings, which through indirection and satiric comment call into question Streamer's assertions. This process-oriented approach to reading is congruent with such famous humanist works as Sir Thomas More's *Utopia* (1516) and Erasmus's *Encomium Moriae* (1509), as well as with Baldwin's own structuring of his *Treatise* and *Canticles:* the humanist author demands an active reader of his works in order to have the reader progress in the humanist agenda. Within this frame of declamation cum dialogue are contained other such genres as the beast fable, dream vision, Skeltonic rhyme, medical treatise, proverb, and history.

As the argument to *Beware the Cat* suggests, Baldwin was involved with court entertainments during the first half of the 1550s. The Revels Accounts mention "a play of the State of Ireland set out by William Baldwin" for the Christmas season, 1552, which apparently was delayed until May Day, 1553, because of the king's ill health. Baldwin may have been part of the Christmas revels in 1551–1552 as well as in 1552–1553, since "we know that an Irish story was being prepared at the time, as Irish properties were required," according to Eveline I. Feasey. In a 1555 letter to Thomas Cawarden, master of the revels, Baldwin describes "a comedy concerning the way to life" (usually wrongly entitled "love and live," Baldwin's motto, which appears at the top of the letter), a morality play with sixty-three characters whose names all begin with the letter *L* and which lasted three hours.

Just as the anti-Catholic *Beware the Cat* could not be published until Elizabeth's accession, so Baldwin could not publish his next literary endeavor until after Mary's reign. A continuation of John Lydgate's *Fall of Princes* (1431–1438), *A Mirror for Magistrates* was licensed to John Wayland (a Catholic scrivener who took over the reformer Whitchurch's printing shop when the Catholic Queen Mary assumed the throne in 1553) but was suppressed in 1555. Thomas Marshe eventually printed its first edition in 1559. In this work Baldwin again creates a frame for the various stories: a series of ghosts from English history appear to him and tell their stories of woe. So popular became this rhetorical frame and Baldwin's position as transcriber of such stories that many later poets allude to Baldwin as they begin their own like poems, such as George Whetstone in his remembrance on Sir Nicholas Bacon (1579) and John Woodward in his tragedy of Mary, Queen of Scots (circa 1601).

Various writers contributed to the *Mirror*, including Churchyard, Ferrers, Thomas Phaer, Thomas Chaloner, Thomas Sackville (whose "Induction" is frequently cited as the best piece in the work), Francis Seager, John Dolman, Raphael Holinshed, a "Master Cavyl," and Baldwin himself. As the title *Mirror for Magistrates* makes explicit, these stories are directed to public officials, and in all cases the *de casibus* motif asserts that the story is a "mirror" that these officials should avoid. A popular book that went through seven more editions by 1610 – with various other authors and printers "borrowing" Baldwin's conception and title – the printing history of *A Mirror for Magistrates* demonstrates yet again Baldwin's difficulty in controlling the shape and the dissemination of his work.

The Funerals of King Edward the Sixth is Baldwin's verse elegy on the death of the young king. It is the last of his works and was printed in 1560 by Marshe. A poem of 380 lines in iambic-pentameter couplets, with an insertion of a twelve-line poem in fourteener couplets, it blames the immoral practices of England's people, especially its government and church leaders, for Edward's death and portrays Mary's accession as a punishment for immoral and seditious behavior. The piece shows an interesting confluence of traditions: the opening is Chaucerian in its astrological setting and personification of the elements; the story of Lot is the paradigm for the plot itself; the visit to the "underworld" for Crasy cold (the virulent disease that ultimately kills Edward) recalls classical literature. *The Funerals* is followed by "An exhortation" to the people of England to reform their behavior, a poem of twelve eight-line stanzas in iambic-pentameter couplets, and by "An Epitaph" on the death of Edward VI, in four rhyme-royal stanzas. This political reading of Edward's death explains the delay in the work's publication. Under the title *A Royal Elegy* the poem with its accompanying apparatus was published in 1610 by J. Windet for H. Holland and wrongly attributed to John Cheke.

Title page for Baldwin's verse elegy on the death of Edward VI

Baldwin's ability to survive during the reign of the Catholic Mary, indeed his apparent court preferment and his continued association with Wayland, who received the exclusive patent to print Roman Catholic primers, demonstrates his probable silence concerning his own religious leanings. The history of the publications of his writings, however, charts the precarious and uncertain course of a reformist writer.

In the last years of his life, Baldwin apparently left the print shop to become a minister. While Wood posits this without providing any authority, an accumulation of evidence seems to demonstrate that the assertion is true and points to Baldwin's death date as 1563. First, in the preface to the 1563 edition of *A Mirror for Magistrates,* Baldwin speaks of being "called to another trade of life," and he is spoken of as a minister in the preface to Churchyard's tragedy of Wolsey in the 1587 edition of the *Mirror.* Second, in 1559 a William Baldwin was ordained deacon by Archbishop Grindal, in a group of men who all were rather older than usual; the author may be the William Baldwin who became vicar of Tortington Sussex (probably in 1559 or 1560) and rector of Saint Michael le Quern in Cheapside in 1561. Third, the hypothesis that he died in 1563 may be confirmed with evidence from the churchwarden's accounts for 1562–1563 that indicates the parson previous to Baptist Willoughby, who was appointed rector on 20 December 1563, died before 1 November 1563. Finally, John Stow's *Historical Memoranda* supports Baldwin's death in 1563:

> Anno 1563, in September, the old bishops and diverse doctors were removed out of the Tower into the new bishops' houses, there to remain prisoners under their custody (the plague then being in the city was thought to be the cause), but their deliverance (or rather change of prison) did so much offend the people that the preachers at Paul's Cross and on other places both of the city and country preached (as it was thought of many wise men) very seditiously, as Baldwin at Paul's Cross wishing a gallows set up in Smithfield and the old bishops other papists to be hanged thereon. Him self died of the plague the next week after.

The coherence of this variety of documentation, along with the fact that no personal revisions of Baldwin's works appear after 1563, seems to disprove the thesis that he "lived well into the 1580s, if not beyond," according to Arthur Freeman. Relevant evidence, mostly poetic allusions to Baldwin as a sympathetic transcriber of tragedies, confuses his fictional persona with the historical person. Thus, Baldwin's last years are as shadowy as his beginnings.

While the chronology of Baldwin's writings might suggest that he moved from religious to more-secular interests (from translating the Song of Songs to editing *A Mirror for Magistrates*), the common thread is certainly his interest in the use of learning as an aid to both religious and social self-reformation. Seen from this perspective his writings thus constitute a significant body of work in the history of the English Reformation, especially in the marked role played by the Erasmian heritage. While *A Mirror for Magistrates* has received a fair amount of scholarly attention, both because of its political content and its role as source for the Elizabethan history play, Baldwin's other works continue to suffer undeserved neglect. The complexity of his narrative writings, both his original works and his translations, particularly demand analysis in light of William A. Ringler, Jr.'s rewriting of the literary history of the novel. Consequently, both historical and aesthetic considerations prompt a reconsideration of Baldwin's contribution to his culture in his career and writings.

References:

Truman W. Camp, "William Baldwin and His *Treatise of Moral Philosophy*," Ph.D. dissertation, Yale University, 1935;

Eveline I. Feasey, "William Baldwin," *Modern Language Review,* 20 (1925): 407–418;

Arthur Freeman, "William Baldwin: The Last Years," *Notes & Queries,* new series 8 (August 1961): 300–301;

Paul M. Gaudet, "William Baldwin and the 'Silence' of His Last Years," *Notes & Queries,* new series 25 (October 1978): 417–420;

Stephen Gresham, "William Baldwin: Literary Voice of the Reign of Edward VI," *Huntington Library Quarterly,* 44, no. 2 (1981): 101–116;

Nancy A. Gutierrez, "*Beware the Cat:* Mimesis in a Skin of Oratory," *Style,* 23, no. 1 (1989): 49–68;

David Scott Kastan, "The Death of William Baldwin," *Notes & Queries,* new series 28 (December 1981): 516–517;

John N. King, *English Reformation Literature: The Tudor Origins of the Protestant Tradition* (Princeton: Princeton University Press, 1982);

William A. Ringler, Jr., "*Beware the Cat* and the Beginnings of English Fiction," *Novel,* 12 (1979): 113–126;

Wilbraham F. Trench, "William Baldwin," *Modern Quarterly of Language & Literature,* 2 (1898–1899): 259–267;

Anthony à Wood, "William Baldwin," in volume 1 of his *Athenae Oxonienses* (London: Printed for F. C. & J. Rivington, 1813), pp. 341–343.

John Bale
(21 November 1495 – 1563)

John N. King
Ohio State University

BOOKS: *Yet a course at the romyshe foxe,* as James Harrison (Zurich [i.e., Antwerp]: Printed by Antonius Goinus as Oliver Jacobson, 1543);

A christen exhortacion vnto customable swearers, anonymous (Antwerp: Printed by Catherine van Ruremund, 1543?);

A brefe chronycle concernynge the examinacyon and death of the martyr syr J. Oldecastell (Antwerp: Printed by Antonius Goinus, 1544);

The Epistle exhortatorye of an Englyshe Christiane, as Henry Stalbridge (Antwerp: Printed by Catherine van Ruremund, 1544?);

A mysterye of inyquyte contayned within the heretycall genealogye of P. Pantolabus (Geneva [i.e., Antwerp]: Printed by Antonius Goinus as Michael Wood, 1545);

The image of both churches, after the reuelacion of saynt Johan the euangelyst, parts 1–2 (Antwerp: Printed by Stephen Mierdman, 1545?); enlarged edition, with part 3 added (Antwerp: Printed by Stephen Mierdman for Richard Jugge, 1548?);

The actes of Englysh votaryes, comprehendynge their vnchast practyses and examples by all ages (Wesel [i.e., Antwerp]: Printed by Stephen Mierdman, 1546);

A tragedye or enterlude manyfestyng the chefe promyses of God vnto man (Wesel: Printed by Derick van der Straten, 1547?);

A brefe comedy or interlude of Johan Baptystes preachynge (lost edition published in Wesel: Printed by Derick van der Straten, 1547?);

A brefe comedy or enterlude concernynge the temptacyon of our lorde (Weselin the County of Cleves: Printed by Derick van der Straten, 1547?);

Illustrium maioris Britanniae scriptorum . . . summarium (Ipswich: Printed by John Overton, 1548; Wesel: Printed by Derick van der Straten [Theodoricus Plateanus], 1549); revised and enlarged as *Scriptorum Illustrium Majoris Britanniae . . . Catalogus,* 2 volumes (Basel: Printed by Joannes Oporinus, 1557, 1559);

John Bale (engraving from the 1557 edition of his Catalogus*)*

A comedy concernynge thre lawes, of nature Moses, & Christ (Wesel: Printed by Derick van der Straten, 1548?);

An answere to a papystycall exhortacyon, pretendynge to auoyde false doctryne, anonymous (Antwerp: Printed by Stephen Mierdman, circa 1548);

A dialoge or communycacyon to be had at a table betwene two chyldren (London: Printed by Stephen Mierdman for Richard Foster, 1549);

The apology of Johan Bale agaynste a ranke papyst, that neyther their vowes nor their priesthode are of the gospell (London: Printed by Stephen Mierdman for John Day, 1550?);

27

An expostulation or complaynte agaynste the blasphemyes of a franticke papyst of Hamshyre (London: Printed by Stephen Mierdman for John Day, 1552?);

The vocacyon of Johan Bale to the bishoprick of Ossorie in Irelande (Rome [i.e., Wesel?]: Printed by Joost Lambrecht? for Hugh Singleton, 1553);

Acta Romanorum Pontificum (Basel: Printed by Joannes Oporinus, 1558); translated, with additions, by John Studley as *The pageant of popes, contayninge the lyues of all the bishops of Rome* (London: Printed by Thomas Marsh, 1574);

A declaration of Edmonde Bonners articles (London: Printed by John Tisdale for Francis Coldock, 1561).

Editions and Collections: *Comedy of John [the] Baptist's Preaching,* in *The Harleian Miscellany,* volume 1 (London: Thomas Osborne, 1744), pp. 97–110;

King John, edited by John Payne Collier (London: Camden Society, 1838);

Select Works, edited by H. Christmas (Cambridge: Parker Society, 1849) – includes *Brief Chronicle concerning Sir John Oldcastle, Image of Both Churches,* and *Examinations of Anne Askew;*

Index Britanniae Scriptorum, edited by Reginald L. Poole and Mary Bateson, Anecdota Oxoniensa, Medieval and Modern Series, part 9 (Oxford: Clarendon, 1902); reprinted with a new introduction by Caroline Brett and James P. Carley (Cambridge: D. S. Brewer, 1990) – from Bodleian Library MS Selden supra 64, in Bale's handwriting, circa 1548–1557;

King John, edited by Barry B. Adams (San Marino, Cal.: Huntington Library, 1969);

Scriptorum Illustrium Majoris Britanniae . . . Catalogus, edited in facsimile (Farnsworth, U.K.: Gregg International, 1971);

The Complete Plays, 2 volumes, edited by Peter Happé (Cambridge: D. S. Brewer, 1985–1986) – includes *Comedy concerning the Temptation of Our Lord, Comedy concerning Three Laws, Comedy of John [the] Baptist's Preaching, King John,* and *Tragedy Manifesting the Chief Promises of God;*

The Vocation of John Bale to the Bishopric of Ossory in Ireland, edited by Happé and John N. King, Renaissance English Text Society, volume 14 [1989] (Binghamton, N.Y.: Medieval & Renaissance Texts & Studies, 1990).

OTHER: Anne Askew, *The first examinacyon of Anne Askewe* and *The lattre examinacyon of Anne Askewe,* each with a commentary by Bale (Mar-

burg in Hesse [i.e., Wesel]: Printed by Derick van der Straten, 1546–1547);

Walter Map?, *Rhythmi Vetustissimi de Corrupto Ecclesiae Statu,* edited by Bale (Antwerp: Printed by Derick van der Straten, 1546);

Marguerite de Navarre, *A godly medytacyon of the christen sowle,* translated by Princess Elizabeth (later Queen Elizabeth I), edited by Bale (Wesel: Printed by Derick van der Straten, 1548);

John Lambert, *A treatyse made by Johan Lambert vnto Kynge Henry the .viij. concernynge hys opynyon in the sacrament of the aultre,* edited by Bale (Wesel: Printed by Derick van der Straten, 1548?);

John Leland, *The laboryouse journey & serche . . . for Englandes antiquitees,* revised and enlarged by Bale (London: Printed by Stephen Mierdman for Bale, to be sold by Richard Foster, 1549).

TRANSLATIONS: Johann Bugenhagen, *A compendious letter which Jhon Pomerane of Wittenberge sent to the faythfull congregation in Englande,* possibly translated by Bale (Southwark: Printed by James Nicholson, 1536);

Justus Jonas, *The true hystorie of the christen departynge of Martyne Luther,* translated by Bale (Wesel: Printed by Derick van der Straten, 1546);

Baptista Mantuanus Spagnuoli, *A lamentable complaynte of Baptista Mantuanus,* translated by Bale (London: Printed by Stephen Mierdman? for John Day, 1551?);

Stephen Gardiner, *De vera obediencia,* possibly translated and edited by Bale (Rouen [i.e., London?]: Printed by John Day as Michael Wood, 1553).

John Bale was an extraordinarily forceful and prolific Protestant propagandist during the early stages of the Reformation in England. His emergence as a Protestant polemicist represented a complete turnabout from his earlier life as a cleric because his education and religious outlook were quite orthodox until well into his maturity. In the course of a career as a cleric, antiquarian, dramatist, historian, and publisher, he mastered a diverse array of genres including the Protestant mystery play, allegorical history play, prose tract, beast fable, Protestant saint's life, biblical commentary, polemical history, bibliography, dialogue, and autobiography. His editions and translations include goliardic verse, devotional meditation, and a variety of propagandistic forms. Although his writings had a great impact upon mid-Tudor and Elizabethan Protestant authors including Robert Crowley,

John Foxe, Edmund Spenser, and the editors of the Geneva Bible (1560), his reputation has suffered from the late-Elizabethan reaction against the conventions and style of the native literary tradition. Because of a general shift toward Continental and neoclassic style and technique after 1580, Bale has been remembered chiefly for his antiquarian research and as the master of an invective style that often lapsed into virulent innuendo inspired by allegations that the clerical vow of celibacy encouraged sexual immorality. Thus Thomas Fuller attached the unforgettable epithet of "Biliosus Balaeus" (Bilious Bale) to him in *The History of the Worthies of England* (1662). In actual fact, scurrilous language of the kind that Bale favored was a conventional feature of Reformation polemics by Martin Luther, Thomas More, and many other authors. It represents a distinctive feature of Bale's energetic literary and dramatic imagination.

Bale was born in humble circumstances to Henry and Margaret Bale near Dunwich in Suffolk on 21 November 1495. After studying from the age of twelve in the house of the Carmelite friars in Norwich, he went up to Cambridge University in his late teens. His early attitudes were apparently untouched, however, by the intellectual ferment of the university, where Hugh Latimer, Thomas Cranmer, Miles Coverdale, and others gathered at the White Horse Tavern during the 1520s to discuss new Lutheran ideas. After a period of study abroad, Bale was awarded the B.D. and eventually the D.D. degrees. He served as prior of Carmelite houses at Maldon and Ipswich in East Anglia during the early 1530s, at a time when Henry VIII approached the rupture of relations between England and the Church of Rome. At some point during the early 1530s, Bale fell under the influence of Thomas, first Baron Wentworth, an East Anglian peer who patronized religious reformers; he credited his departure from the Church of Rome to Wentworth.

Friar Bale underwent a religious conversion prior to his departure from the Carmelite order in 1536. At that time he took a wife, Dorothy, and served as a secular priest in Thorndon in Suffolk. When he was imprisoned in 1537 for preaching heresy, he won release due to the influence of John Leland, the king's antiquarian, to whom he dedicated *Anglorum Heliades,* a historical and bibliographical account of the Carmelite order in England. That work shows how Bale had not yet completed his transition from Catholic to Protestant theology. Encouraged by Leland, Thomas Cromwell intervened on Bale's behalf because of his talent for writing

satiric drama. As Henry VIII's chief minister and vicegerent for religious affairs, Cromwell was then overseeing the dissolution of the monasteries. Bale appears to have been an active member of a dramatic troupe patronized by Cromwell.

Bale's literary career passed through four distinct phases in response to shifts in official political and religious policy. After an initial period of activity under Cromwell's patronage, he fled to the Continent when Henry VIII and Parliament neutralized the process of religious reform; Cromwell fell from favor and was executed in 1540. After returning to England under the genuinely Protestant government of Edward VI, Bale fled into a second exile when a period of Catholic reaction ensued under Mary I. Shortly before the end of his life, he returned to England when Elizabeth I restored most of the Edwardian ecclesiastical reforms. Despite these political and religious shifts, his writings were published at a steady rate by presses in England and on the Continent. In many cases he or his publishers resorted to impudent pseudonyms in order to satirize their enemies with impunity. For example, *The Vocation of John Bale to the Bishopric of Ossory in Ireland* (1553) attacks the papacy with the false claim that it was "Imprinted in Rome before the Castle of Sant' Angelo at the sign of St. Peter in December, Anno Domini 1553."

Although Bale's *Scriptorum Illustrium Majoris Britanniae . . . Catalogus* (1557, 1559) lists twenty-four of his own plays, only five examples have survived. Bale wrote *King John,* which appears to have been his first drama, at some point between Henry VIII's assumption of royal supremacy over the church in 1532 and the performance of the dramatic interlude at the house of Cranmer, archbishop of Canterbury, during Christmastide 1538–1539. Cromwell may have patronized this production. Bale mingles historical and semihistorical figures with allegorical type characters in order to praise Henry VIII as an ideal prince who has supplanted the pope as leader of the church and to encourage the king to embark upon a program of further religious reform of the kind that Cromwell and Cranmer favored.

As the hero of the play, King John (1199–1216) provides a prototype for monarchal reform by unsuccessfully attempting to rescue England, personified as a widow, from papal "tyranny." John's efforts to lead Nobility, Clergy, and Civil Order in this effort are blocked by the Vice characters in appropriate clerical disguise: Usurped Power (as Pope Innocent III), Private Wealth (as Cardinal Pandulphus), Dissimulation (as both the legate

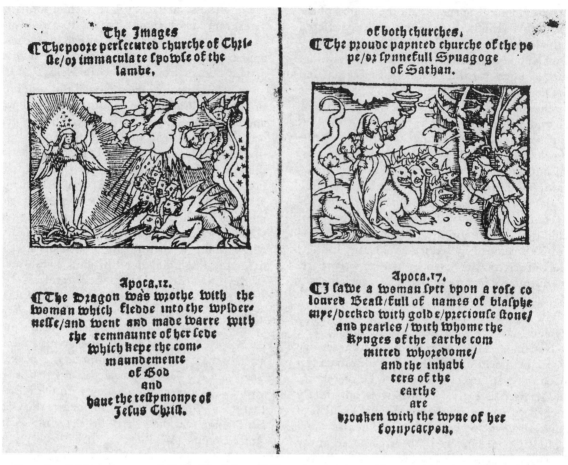

Pages from Bale's commentary on the Book of Revelation, with illustrations depicting the Woman Clothed with the Sun (left) and the Whore of Babylon

Raymundus and the monk Simon of Swinset), and Sedition (as Steven Langton or the Monk). Satiric use of religious costume of this kind is one of Bale's favorite dramatic devices. The play's central scene dramatizes the deposition where the king surrenders his crown to the cardinal. At the death of King John, the play moves into Bale's own age with the advent of Veritas (Truth) and Imperial Majesty, whose role as "true defender" of "the authority of God's holy word" and "the Christian faith" flatters Henry VIII at the same time that it urges him to complete the process of religious reform.

Bale composed his four other extant plays in 1538, presumably under the patronage of Cromwell. They all adapt themes, conventions, and devices of the late medieval mystery and morality plays to Protestant purposes. Bale breaks dramatic illusion for the sake of polemical effect by assigning didactic prefaces and epilogues to himself in the guise of "Baleus Prolocutor." *The Chief Promises of God, John [the] Baptist's Preaching,* and *The Temptation of Jesus Christ* (all 1547?) are tightly interrelated as a

Protestant variation of a cycle of scriptural mystery plays of the kind that Bale probably saw during his youth. *The Chief Promises of God* moves from Adam's tragic fall to a concluding prophecy of the advent of Christ as the Messiah, with its "comic" expectation of the regeneration and salvation of Christ's "elected spouse," the faithful congregation. Instead of achieving fully dramatic action, each of the play's seven acts consists of dialogue between Pater Coelestis (the Heavenly Father), on the one hand, and the succession of patriarchs and prophets who received God's covenantal promises on the other: Adam, Noah, Abraham, Moses, David, Isaiah, and John the Baptist.

The ensuing plays dramatize the transition from Old Law to New Law. *John [the] Baptist's Preaching* dramatizes evangelical reform, with emphasis on the priesthood of all believers, through John's conversion and baptism of lay people including an armed Roman soldier who initially resembles the Plautine miles gloriosus. *The Temptation of Jesus Christ* dramatizes the text of Matthew 4:4–11 by presenting Christ as the paradigm of patient obedience, who will act only when God appoints. The anachronistic presentation of Satan identifies him as a Roman cleric linked with the pope as a type of Antichrist.

A Comedy Concerning Three Laws (1548?) dramatizes the successive downfalls of the personified Virtues: Natural Law, Mosaic Law, and Christian Law. Bale again relies upon allegorical costuming to satirize the victorious Vices as manifestations of Roman Catholic "error." Thus he presents Sodomy as a monk, Covetousness as a bishop, Avarice as a canon lawyer, False Doctrine as a "popish" doctor, and Hypocrisy as a Franciscan friar. The costume of an old witch identifies Idolatry with the Whore of Babylon, a type for papal Rome, just as Sodomy's residence at Rome associates him with the pope as Antichrist. Infidelity possesses the traditional comic attributes of the medieval Vice character, notably the use of blasphemy and vulgar comic diction, which are evident in Infidelity's speech at the beginning of act 3:

Ha, ha, ha, ha, ha, ha, ha, ha, ha.
A pastime, quoth he! I know not the time nor when
I did laugh so much since I was an honest man.
Believe me and ye will, I never saw such sport.
I would ye had been there that ye might have made the fort.

Modeled on Revelation, the last two acts of the *Three Laws* lead up to a climax in which Divine Vengeance banishes Infidelity and restores the three Laws in anticipation of the apocalyptic wedding of the Bridegroom and the Spouse at the descent of the New Jerusalem.

Bale fled with his wife and son, John, into exile on the Continent upon the execution of Cromwell in 1540, at a time when Henry VIII's government began to place tighter restraints upon Protestant publication. During the next eight years Bale composed religious tracts and edited writings that attacked the Church of Rome for ceremonialism, sacerdotalism, veneration of the Virgin Mary and saints, and the doctrine of transubstantiation. These texts include editions of *Apocalypsis Goliae*, a goliardic poem attributed to Walter Map, as *Rhythmi Vetustissimi de Corrupto Ecclesiae Statu* (1546); Justus Jonas's eyewitness account of the death of Martin Luther; and Princess Elizabeth's translation of *A Godly Meditation of the Christian Soul* (1548), a devotional text by Marguerite de Navarre. Many of these works were printed in Antwerp before Bale moved on to Wesel in the county of Cleves in response to the Hapsburg imposition of tighter restrictions upon Protestant publication. Printed in the English language, Bale's books were smuggled into England for surreptitious sale. Bale employed the pseudonyms of James Harrison and Henry Stalbridge because of the danger posed by English and imperial authorities.

The most important publication of Bale's first exile is *The Image of Both Churches* (1545?), the first commentary upon the whole of Revelation that was printed in the English language. It interprets Christian history as a conflict between the "true" church, whose teachings are based upon the Gospel record of commandments by Jesus, and the "false" church, whose headship by the pope results from alleged subversion by Antichrist. Turgid language typical of Bale's propagandistic style may be noted in his interpretation of the golden cup carried by the Whore of Babylon (Rev. 17:4):

This cup is the false religion that she daily ministereth, besides the chalice whom her merchants most damnably abuse; and it contained all doctrine of devils, all beastly errors and lies, all deceitful power, all glittering works of hypocrites, all crafty wisdom of the flesh, and subtle practices of man's wit, besides philosophy, logic, rhetoric, and sophistry; yea, all prodigious kinds of idolatry, fornication, sodomitry, and wickedness. Outwardly it seemeth gold, pretending the glory of God, the holy name of Christ, the sacred scriptures of the Bible, perpetual virginity of life; and all are but counterfeit colors and shadows of hypocrisy in the outward letter and name.

According to Bale, a proper understanding of Revelation should enable believers to trace the historical trajectory of the conflict between the two churches through the seven ages prophesied by the blowing of seven trumpets, the opening of the seven seals, and the pouring of the seven vials. These ages range from an initial period of apostolic purity through the sixth age, which encompasses the persecution of the faithful from the time of John Wycliffe onward. The final age will lead to the end of the world. Despite Bale's insistence that Revelation is deeply implicated in ecclesiastical history, he acknowledges the poetic character of the awe-inspiring visions that are expressed through "pleasant figures and elegant tropes."

Bale's interpretation of Revelation furnishes a historical paradigm that underlies most if not all of his other works. *The Acts of English Votaries* (1546) affords a tendentious history of ecclesiastical "falsity" focused upon allegations that sexual license and perversity were rampant in the monastic houses of England. *Yet a Course at the Romish Fox* (1543) adapts the beast fable to the purpose of attacking Stephen Gar-

The first examinacyon of Anne Askewe, latelye mar
tyred in Smythfelde, by the Romysh popes vpholders, with
the Elucydacyon of
Johan Bale.

BIB
LIA

Psalme 116.
The veryte of the lorde endureth for euer.

Anne Askewe stode fast by thys veryte of
God to the ende.

Fauoure is disceytfull/and bewtye is a vay
ne thynge. But a woman that feareth the
lorde/is worthye to be praysed. She openeth her mouthe to wysdome/and in her lan
guage is the lawe of grace. Prouerb. xxxj.

Title page for Bale's edition of a narrative about a Protestant woman who was tortured for her beliefs

diner, bishop of Winchester and lord chancellor of England, and other prelates who persecuted the Protestants in England.

Bale edited *The Examinations of Anne Askew* (1546–1547), a personal narrative by a Protestant gentlewoman of Lincolnshire concerning her judicial interrogation for heresy and condemnation to die along with several companions at the very end of Henry VIII's reign. The commentary that Bale added treats this text as a Protestant saint's life and attacks Gardiner and Edmund Bonner, bishop of London, for persecuting Askew for her heretical disbelief in transubstantiation and the Roman-rite mass and for ordering her torture by the full rigor of the rack. Askew's own words provide the core of this work and testify with an understated eloquence that may be noted in the beginning of her account of an interrogation by Bishop Bonner: "And as I came before him, he said he was very sorry of my trouble, and desired to know my opinion in such matters as were laid against me." Bale alters the tenor of Askew's plain language, however, by adding a highly tendentious interpretation of the kind that fills his editorial commentary:

> The diligent [may] perceive the greediness of this Babylon bishop, or bloodthirsty wolf, concerning his prey.... He that will know the crafty hawking of bishops, to bring in their prey, let him learn it here. Judas, I think, had never the tenth part of their cunning workmanship. Mark it here, and in that which followeth.

Like Bale's earlier effort at reshaping the medieval genre of martyrology, *A Brief Chronicle Concerning ... Sir John Oldcastle* (1544), his edition of *The Examinations of Anne Askew* identifies the suffering martyr as a "true" saint under attack by agents of Antichrist.

Although *Illustrium Majoris Britanniae Scriptorum ... Summarium* (1548; hereafter cited as *Summarium*) was printed in Wesel soon after Henry VIII's death and the succession to the throne of Edward VI – a minor king whose government was committed to a thoroughgoing program of Protestant reform – the origins of this work are deeply rooted in Bale's continuation of John Leland's antiquarian project of enumerating and preserving manuscripts that were dispersed following the breakup of abbey libraries at the time of the dissolution of the monasteries. (Bale's involvement in this effort may be noted in his expanded 1549 edition of Leland's *Laborious Journey and Search for England's Antiquities*.) *Summarium* employs the apocalyptic periodization of history familiar from *The Image of Both Churches* as the chronological framework for cataloguing the writings of British authors. In so doing, Bale asserts the existence of an unbroken literary tradition that connects Anglo-Saxon authors to their Middle English successors and the authors of Bale's own age. The major British authors are members of an apostolic tradition that contradicts the "false" papal claim to ecclesiastical primacy: Bede, Wycliffe, Geoffrey Chaucer, William Tyndale, and Bale himself. An appendix to Bale's edition of Leland's *Laborious Journey* outlines a plan for a second volume of *Summarium*. His continuing interest in this bibliographic project may be noted in the manuscript list of authors, titles, incipits, and locations of books that Bale started about the time his *Summarium* appeared and continued for the next decade. It has been published in modern times under the title *Index Britanniae Scriptorum*.

As Bale prepared to return home from his initial exile, he incorporated into *Summarium* a dedication and last-minute revisions that praise Edward VI for permitting the return of Protestant activists who went into exile under Henry VIII. Although these additions and the title-page woodcut portraying the author presenting a copy of this work to the boy/king style the text as a request for patronage, his search for royal support was a failure. The returned exile did, however, receive patronage from the duchess of Richmond (sister of the poet Henry Howard, Earl of Surrey), in whose household he resided at the same time as

John Foxe, with whom he forged a long-standing friendship. Bale then received appointment in 1551 as rector of the Church of Saint Mary at Bishopstoke, Hampshire, a benefice in the gift of John Ponet, bishop of Winchester.

During the Edwardian phase of his career, Bale continued to write pamphlets and tracts that cast himself in the role of a militant opponent of religious "error." They include *The Apology of John Bale against a Rank Papist* (1550?) and his quasi-autobiographical *Expostulation or Complaint against the Blasphemies of a Frantic Papist of Hampshire* (1552?). The latter work records Bale's efforts to impose recently instituted Protestant religious reforms against strenuous local opposition in his parish of Bishopstoke. He provides colorful accounts of his effort to track down the recusants who concealed forbidden religious images "in hope of a change" in regime and who opposed Bale's production of his own polemical play, *A Comedy Concerning Three Laws*. In the latter case an old believer rather wittily convinced an actor in Bale's play to insert a new speech insulting to the author:

> In the heat whereof, he most shamefully reviled a servant of [Bale's] house calling him heretic and knave, because he had begun to study a part in such a comedy as mightily rebuked the abominations and foul filthy occupyings of the Bishop of Rome. Moreover he required him in his own stout name to do a lewd message, which was to call the compiler of that comedy both heretic and knave, concluding that it was a book of most pernicious heresy. Therein is largely declared how the faithless Antichrist of Rome with his clergy hath been a blasphemer, darkener, confounder, and poisoner of all wholesome laws. And that with idolatrical sodomitry he hath defiled nature, by ambitious avarice he hath made God's commandments of none effect, and with hypocritical doctrine perverted Christ's most holy gospel.

Bale rose to his highest clerical position in 1552, when Edward VI appointed him to serve as bishop of Ossory, a diocese in southern Ireland that was a hotbed of support for the Church of Rome. *The Vocation of John Bale to the Bishopric of Ossory in Ireland* (1553) records his experience from the time of appointment until his flight into a second Continental exile upon the accession of Mary I one year later. This autobiographical account documents continual conflict between an uncompromising missionary bishop and the Irish clergy, upon whom he vented fury for the breaking of religious vows, and the people whom he attempted to convert. This highly readable and exciting work recounts the poisoning of his superior, Archbishop Good-

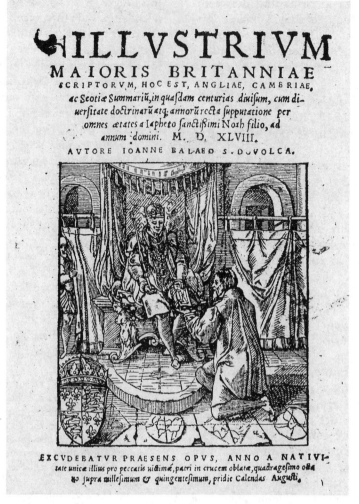

Title page for Bale's description of British writings from the Anglo-Saxon period to his own. The engraving shows Bale presenting this book to Edward VI.

acre; the murder of Bale's own servants for obeying his orders to mow hay on a Catholic feast day; his flight from priests who attempted to kill him; his captivity by a sea rover and ensuing sea voyage; and his eventual arrival at a safe haven on the Continent. In an apparent paradox Bale once again organized a production of his own plays, complete with musical accompaniment and song, to attack religious ceremonialism that he regarded as excessively theatrical. The author expresses delight over the power of his plays to stir up discord within the local populace:

> The young men in the forenoon played a tragedy of God's promises in the old law at the market cross, with organ playings and songs very aptly. In the afternoon again they played a comedy of Saint John [the] Baptist's preaching of Christ's baptizing and of his temptation in the wilderness, to the small contentation of the priests and other papists there.

During his second exile Bale dedicated most of his labors to completion of his massive bibliographical project. He worked on the revised and expanded version of *Summarium* during residence with Foxe in the household of the famous Basel printer Joannes Oporinus and later at Klarakloster, a dissolved convent. Oporinus published this two-volume work as *Scriptorum Illustrium Majoris Britanniae . . . Catalogus* (1557–1559). Historical summaries interspersed throughout the volume supply the apocalyptic context within which Bale sets the careers of British authors. He republished the material concerning the papacy in a separate volume, *Acta Romanorum Pontificum* (1558). Although Mary I died and Elizabeth I came to the throne while Bale's *Catalogus* was in press, he adapted a special issue of that text, preserved at the British Library in London, in order to praise the new queen as the chief hope for the return of England to "true" Protestant religion. When he returned from exile, he received appointment as a prebendary at Canterbury Cathedral from Matthew Parker, archbishop of Canterbury. Although Bale wrote nothing new after *Catalogus*, he revised the ending of *King John* by providing an epilogue in praise of Queen Elizabeth and published his 1554 attack against the Marian bishop of London who was renowned for the persecution of Protestants: *A Declaration of Edmund Bonner's Articles* (1561).

Because so many of Bale's colleagues had been burned as heretics or died in exile, he was arguably the chief radical of the first reformist generation to live on into the reign of Elizabeth I. He died in 1563 at the age of sixty-seven or sixty-eight. Bale's career is notable for the virtuosity with which he mastered a great variety of polemical forms, for his satiric flair, and for the intensity of the invective that he hurled against his enemies. Because a new sense of polite literary taste came into fashion during the last decades of the sixteenth century, when figures such as Sir Philip Sidney and George Puttenham were its important arbiters, Bale's willingness to direct scatological and sexual innuendo at his enemies tended to alienate many English readers. Within a few years of John Studley's adaptation and translation of *Acta Romanorum Pontificum* as *The Pageant of Popes* (1574), Bale's many works went out of print. Nevertheless, apocalyptic ideas that he developed in *The Image of Both Churches* exerted an enduring influence upon such works as the Geneva Bible, Foxe's *Acts and Monuments* (the "Book of Martyrs"), book 1 of Spenser's *Faerie Queene* (1590), and Thomas Dekker's *Whore of Babylon* (1607). Bale has been otherwise influential in later centuries because of his antiquarian research and bibliographic compilations.

Bibliographies:

Honor C. McCusker, "Books and Manuscripts Formerly in the Possession of John Bale," *Library,* fourth series 16 (September 1936): 144–165;

W. T. Davies, "A Bibliography of John Bale," *Oxford Bibliographical Society, Proceedings and Papers,* 5 (1940): 203–279;

Peter Happé, "Recent Studies in John Bale," *English Literary Renaissance,* 17 (Winter 1987): 103–113.

References:

Thora Blatt, *The Plays of John Bale: A Study of Ideas, Technique and Style* (Copenhagen: G. E. C. Gad, 1968);

Leslie P. Fairfield, *John Bale: Mythmaker for the English Reformation* (West Lafayette, Ind.: Purdue University Press, 1976);

Fairfield, "*The Vocacyon of John Bale* and Early English Autobiography," *Renaissance Quarterly,* 24 (Autumn 1971): 327–340;

Peter Happé, "Properties and Costumes in the Plays of John Bale," *Medieval English Theatre,* 2, no. 2 (1980): 55–65;

Jesse W. Harris, *John Bale: A Study in the Minor Literature of the Reformation,* Illinois Studies in Language and Literature, 25, no. 4 (Urbana: University of Illinois Press, 1940);

John N. King, *English Reformation Literature: The Tudor Origins of the Protestant Tradition* (Princeton: Princeton University Press, 1982);

Honor C. McCusker, *John Bale: Dramatist and Antiquary* (Bryn Mawr, Pa., 1942);

Rainer Pineas, "John Bale's Non-Dramatic Works of Religious Controversy," *Studies in English Literature,* 2 (1962): 218–233;

Pineas, "Some Polemical Techniques in the Non-Dramatic Works of John Bale," *Bibliothèque d'Humanisme et Renaissance,* 24 (1962): 583–588;

Greg Walker, *Plays of Persuasion: Drama and Politics at the Court of Henry VIII* (Cambridge: Cambridge University Press, 1991), pp. 169–221.

Papers:

Important holdings of Bale's papers are at the British Library, Bodleian Library, Henry E. Huntington Library, and Cambridge University Library.

Alexander Barclay

(circa 1475 – June 1552)

David R. Carlson
University of Ottawa

BOOKS: *The gardyners passetaunce touchyng the outrage of fraunce,* anonymous (London: Printed by R. Pynson, 1512?);

The fyfte eglog of Alexandre Barclay of the cytezen and Uplondyshman (London: Printed by W. de Worde, 1518?);

The boke of Codrus and Mynalcas. The fourthe eglog of A. Barcley (London: Printed by R. Pynson, 1521?);

Here begynneth the introductory to wryte, and to pronounce Frenche (London: Printed by Robert Copeland, 1521);

Here begynneth the Egloges of Alexander Barclay prest wherof the fyrst thre conteyneth the myseryes of courters & courtes (Southwark: Printed by P. Treveris, 1530?).

Editions and Collections: *The Ship of Fooles . . . with diuers other workes,* edited by John Cawood (London: Printed by John Cawood, 1570);

The Ship of Fools, 2 volumes, edited by T. H. Jamieson (Edinburgh: W. Patterson, 1874; New York: AMS, 1966);

The Mirrour of Good Manners by Alexander Barclay, Spenser Society, 38 (Manchester, 1885; New York: Burt Franklin, 1967);

The Eclogues of Alexander Barclay, edited by Beatrice White, Early English Text Society, Original Series 175 (London: Early English Text Society, 1928);

The Life of St. George, edited by William Nelson, Early English Text Society, Original Series 230 (London: Early English Text Society, 1955);

The Gardyners Passetaunce, edited by Franklin B. Williams, Jr., and Howard M. Nixon (London: Roxburghe Club, 1985).

TRANSLATIONS: Sebastian Brant, *This present boke named the shyp of folys of the worlde was tr. out of Laten, Frenche, and Doche in the college of saynt mary Otery by A. Barclay* (London: Printed by R. Pynson, 1509);

Giovanni Battista Spagnolo, *Here begynnyth the lyfe of the gloryous martyr saynt George, tr. by a. barclay* (London: Printed by R. Pynson, 1515?);

Domenico Mancini, *Here begynneth a ryght frutefull treatyse, intituled the myrrour of good maners, conteynyng the .iiii. vertues. Tr. A. Bercley* (London: Printed by R. Pynson, at the instance of Rychard yerle of kent, 1518?);

Sallust, *Here begynneth the famous cronycle of the warre, which the romayns had agaynst Iugurth. Tr. syr A. Barclay* (London: Printed by R. Pynson, 1520?).

In a brief literary career occupying only fifteen years or so early in the sixteenth century, Alexander Barclay contributed importantly to bringing contemporary Continental literary culture home to England and, in cooperation with his printer/publisher Richard Pynson, to popularizing it. Best known as the first to write pastorals in English, modeling his work on that of Italian humanists, Barclay also introduced the German Sebastian Brant's *Ship of Fools* into England in 1509 and wrote allegories in the manner of Burgundian court literature. Almost all of his writings are translations, if only nominally. In handling the sources he chose – not only Brant, but also his Italian contemporaries Enea Silvio Piccolomini, Giovanni Battista Spagnolo of Mantua, and Domenico Mancini, and the ancient historian Sallust – he inevitably added much of his own, fitting the work to his peculiar circumstance. These literary labors appear to have been undertaken in order to attract patronage, and Barclay may have had some success, especially with Thomas Howard, second Duke of Norfolk. He succeeded best, however, by the printing press: he was the only native writer of the early Tudor period whose works went immediately and regularly into the wide and comparatively popular circulation that print afforded.

Barclay was born around 1475, within a year or so of the advent of printing in England. The

The preface of Alexander Barclay preest/ vnto the
right hye and mighty prince: Thomas
Duke of Northfolke.

Reuerēdiffimo in Chrifto patri ac
dño: dño Ioanni Veyfy exoniēn e-
pifcopo Alexander Barclay prefby
ter debita cum obferuantía. S.

EMINI me fuperiori-
bus annis cū adhuc facel-
li regii preful effes:paftor
vigilantiffime:tuis fuafi-
onibus incitatū :vt Crifpi
Saluftij hyftoriā (quā Iu-
gurthynū bellū dictitant) e romana lin
gua:

Ight mighty/
hye/and magnifi-
cent prince: myne
hūble feruyce/due
vnto pour grace.
And the behement
affection which I
haue vnto pour honour and ppetuall
fame/impelleth me often tymes to de-
vpfe/ and to reuolue in mynde: what
feruyce / or pleafure my fymplenesse
might

*Woodcut of Alexander Barclay (kneeling), from his circa 1520 translation of Sallust's
Jugurthine War. Printer Richard Pynson used this illustration in three of
Barclay's books.*

exact date is not known, and the place of his birth has been a subject of disagreement since the Elizabethan period. Most likely he was born in Scotland; but even if so, he lived in England from an early age, possibly at Croydon or Lincoln, and his literary career was entirely English. By his own testimony he was thoroughly educated (in a prefatory verse to *The Ship of Fools,* he claims to have been "a scholar long, and that in diverse schools"). But here again records are nonexistent and the evidence is scant. Probably, he took a degree or more at one of the English universities; and his knowledge of affairs at certain Continental centers of education, Paris especially, suggests that he may also have studied abroad. The will associated with his name –

proved in June 1552 – calls him "Alexander Barclay, Doctor of Divinity"; that he styles himself "Sir" in his own writings implies that he was at least a *magister artium.*

Within a period of five weeks in March and April 1508, Barclay was ordained successively subdeacon, deacon, and priest by Hugh Oldham, bishop of Exeter, apparently so that he could take a job in the collegiate church of Ottery Saint Mary in the Exeter diocese. The position of *capellanus* that he took up involved teaching, training, and supervising the choirboys and former choirboys in residence, and it necessitated ordination to the priesthood. The warden of Ottery Saint Mary in the period 1490–1511 was Thomas Cornish, to whom Barclay dedicated his translation of *The Ship of Fools;* Cornish was also titular bishop of Tine and suffragan bishop in the diocese of Bath and Wells from 1485 until his death in 1513, and he had been provost of Oriel College, Oxford, from 1493 to 1507, at a time when Barclay may have been studying at Oxford. The colophon to the edition of *The Ship of Fools* printed in 1509 confirms Barclay's association with the college, stating that the translation had been made "in the College of Saint Mary Ottery in the county of Devonshire" in 1508 by Barclay, "priest, and at that time chaplain in the said college." The implication is that, by the time of the book's publication in 1509, Barclay was no longer college chaplain, and there is other evidence to indicate that, at some point before 1514, he left Ottery Saint Mary.

Even though the dates and length of his tenure there are not known precisely, the period is important because it saw the completion of Barclay's first – and probably most important – literary labor: his *Ship of Fools.* It is a translation of Brant's *Narrenschiff,* first printed in 1494 on the Continent, and in dedicating his version to Cornish, Barclay claimed that it was his "first work to be published." He also claimed that his translation was made "out of Latin, French, and Dutch." The evidence suggests, however, that he relied chiefly on the Latin translation of Jakob Locher, the *Stultifera navis,* first printed in 1497 and reprinted with Barclay's translation in 1509, and on a French version, *La Nef des folz du monde,* by the little-known Pierre Rivière, also first printed in 1497.

The work takes the form of a series of chapters – 113 in Barclay's version – each of which is devoted to anatomizing and castigating a particular group of fools taking up space on board the "ship of fools": evil counselors, the greedy and the prodigal, the obsessively modish, old fools, negligent fathers, tale bearers, gluttons and drunkards, ecclesiastical pluralists, the jealous, the willfully ignorant, the indiscreet, "young fools that take old women to their wives, for their riches," dancing fools, gamblers, lofty extortionists, those who show contempt for the poor, usurers, flatterers, and so on. The list is all but endless, for reasons set forth: "All men are fools that cannot themselves guide; / Thus all the world may I well comprehend."

It is a necessarily spacious book, with a certain amount of repetition; but it seems designed to be taken in small doses, one chapter at a time, over a long period. Each chapter is equipped with a propaedeutic woodcut, and each woodcut does a more or less good job of making the chapter's point by itself. Under the woodcut appears a summary stanza, and this is followed by the dilatory chapter itself. In Barclay's version each chapter ends with an original Barclaian envoy, usually addressed to the group of fools in question, exhorting them to mend their ways.

The pattern is varied only by a series of chapters interspersed among the others – but especially concentrated toward the end of the book – that deviate from anatomizing types of folly. These include a sermon addressed by a personified Wisdom to wise men and fools alike (she advises fleeing folly); an allegory of the paths to Heaven and to Hell (the one narrow and beset with difficulties, the other wide and busy); an exhortation to worldly princes to relieve Rome of the threat of the "cursed Turks"; a description of the wise man; a debate between "Virtue" and "Voluptuosity" set in the context of an allegorical choice at a crossroad (Virtue wins); and a concluding "Ballad of the Translator in Honor of the Blessed Virgin Mary, Mother of God," the refrain of which is "Direct our life in this tempestuous sea." Also distinctive about Barclay's version are its frequent references to contemporary, local conditions, including veiled attacks against his putative detractors, as well as extensive encomiums of Henry VII and Henry VIII.

The book's publication represented the first fruits of a collaboration between Barclay and Pynson that was to continue for some years. Pynson, who died in 1530, was a Norman printer who had come to England in about 1490, and for more than thirty years he was a dominant force in English printing. He and Wynkyn de Worde, who inherited William Caxton's business, shared between them about 70 percent of the domestic trade in printed books during the first three decades of the sixteenth century. A growing body of evidence indicates that these early English printers could collaborate with the living writers whom they published; evidently, Barclay was one with whom Pynson was willing to work closely. In *The Ship of Fools,* for example, Barclay mentions Pynson repeatedly (at one point claiming that Pynson was urging him to keep the book short), and he subscribed his preface to it "from Pynson's shop, London." After publication of *The Ship of Fools,* Pynson would appear always to have been the first to print Barclay's work, doing so soon after its completion. Even at the end of his literary career in 1519, Barclay was doing simple editorial work for Pynson on a reissue of the inevitably reissued *Vocabula* of the pervasive grammarian John Stanbridge.

A distinctive feature of the books that Barclay and Pynson produced together is their bilingual format. In *The Ship of Fools,* Locher's Latin precedes Barclay's translation; the other Barclaian books printed by Pynson juxtapose Barclay's English and his Latin source in columns on the same page. Setting up the columns in type and keeping the parallels true would have cost Pynson editorial and compositorial labor; but the format enabled him to offer his customers two books in one, and it may also have helped to keep Barclay happy. Barclay's most detailed discussion of the purposes of the bilingual format occurs in the preface to his translation of Sallust (circa 1520). There he claims that the Latin is for "such as shall disdain to read my translation in English," who are "learned and understand Latin." He also claims that the Latin "shall appear more clear and plain in many places by help of this my translation" and that the translation is after all intended for the "many noble gentlemen who understand not the Latin tongue perfectly": "for by the same, they shall have some help toward the understanding of Latin, which at this time is almost contemned of gentlemen." In his preface to *The Life of Saint George* (circa 1515), Barclay makes further claim that the presence of the Latin proves his *fides* (fidelity) as a translator; but it also serves to highlight his originality: the parallel columns make it especially easy to locate sections where Barclay adds to his source.

Among Barclay's additions to his source in *The Ship of Fools* is "A Brief Addition of the Singularity of Some New Fools" near the end of the book. At the end of this "Addition" occurs a passage that allusively denigrates Barclay's better-known contemporary John Skelton by remarking on Skelton's recently republished *Phillip Sparrow:* "My will is good," Barclay begins,

Men to induce unto virtue and goodness.
I write no jest ne tale of Robin Hood,
Nor sow no sparkles ne seed of viciousness.
Wise men love virtue, wild people wantoness;
It longeth [belongs] not to my science nor cunning
For Phillip the Sparrow the *dirige* to sing.

Much has been made of the quarrel between Barclay and Skelton putatively attested by this remark, even though there is little other clear evidence for it (John Bale attributes the work *Contra Skeltonum* to Barclay; but the work, if ever it existed, is now lost). Certainly their careers ran parallel in many ways, and they would have known, or known of, one another: both began as pedagogues, Barclay at Ottery Saint Mary, Skelton in the royal household; both were priests but were occupied extensively with writing; both wrote didactic works and transla-

tions of ancient historians, Barclay of Sallust and Skelton of Diodorus Siculus; both wrote pro-English propaganda for the wars against France and Scotland in 1512 and 1513, among other points of similarity between their writings; and both enjoyed (or sought) the patronage of the Howard family. They competed to fill the same niche in England's literary economy. Skelton started earlier and was more successful, in part perhaps because of his willingness to entertain. Barclay – a more ostentatiously righteous writer – may well have felt some ill will toward Skelton, as toward the literary system of writing and patronage in general, which never did as well by him as he felt it should. There is little, however, to hint that the professional rivalry between Barclay and Skelton was compounded with personal animosity.

At some point between his completion of *The Ship of Fools* in 1508 and the publication of the first group of his *Eclogues* around 1514, Barclay joined the community of Benedictine monks (familiarly known as "Black monks") associated with Ely Cathedral. This change of residence and of life may have been precipitated by the vacation of the wardenship of the College at Ottery by his early patron Cornish in 1511, or by Cornish's death in 1513; in any event the community Barclay joined had had a history of association with important figures in English ecclesiastical culture. Ely's bishops during Barclay's years there were James Stanley (from 1506 to 1515), a son of Thomas Stanley, first Earl of Derby, and Nicholas West (from 1515 to 1533), the last pre-Reformation bishop. John Morton – in whose household the young Thomas More was fostered – had been bishop of Ely (1479–1486) before being elected archbishop of Canterbury and lord chancellor of England in the first years of the reign of Henry VII; Morton was also a chancellor of Oxford and Cambridge. He was succeeded at Ely by John Alcock, who was bishop from 1486 to 1500 and in that capacity baptized Henry VII's firstborn son, Arthur, in 1486. Barclay lauds the learning and piety of both Morton and Alcock in his writing of this period.

With the exception of *The Ship of Fools,* all of Barclay's writings date from this period he spent as a Black monk at Ely, around 1510 to 1520. The earliest of these are two – *The Gardener's Passetaunce* (1512?) and *The Tower of Virtue and Honor* (1514?) – occasioned by the diplomatic and military events of 1512 and 1513. In early 1512 Pope Julius II excommunicated the French king Louis XII and laid an interdict over his kingdom in response to French attacks on the papal states in Italy; secretly, he also

FOLIVM

Away with this pryde / this statelynes let be
Rede of the Prophetis clothynge oz vesture
And of Adam firste of your ancestrye
Of John the Prophete/theyr clothynge was obscure
Vyle and homly/but nowe what creature
Wyll then ensue/sothly fewe by theyr wyll
Therfoze suche folys my nauy shall fulfyll

De Antiquis fatuis.
Ad patulū q̄uis languēs declino sepulchrum:
Triuerit & metam iam mea vita datam.
Non tamen antiquos fatuorum desero mores.
Stultitięꝗ vias inueteratus amo.

Danielis. xii.	INueterata meę dementia crassa senectę:
Ouidius i fas.	Non solitos linquit mores:vitam ve priorem:
Prouer.xxii.	Sum puer:& centum transacti temporis annos
	Connumerare queo:nec enim sapiētior vsq̄
Esaye.lxvi.	Esse velim:pueris stultorum signa ministro.
	Sulticięꝗ meę regimen pręscribo malignum
	Turpia viuēdi/mihitestamenta reliquo:
	Exemplarꝗ mali sum/duxꝗ & pessimus auctor.
C.ex studis.	Quod puer edidici:facto monstratur inerti:
&.c.cū iniuuē	Stultus ego semper:tamen hac laudarier arte
ture. de p̄sum	Percupio:insanam & sceleris protendere famam:
pti.	Et vitium monstrare meum:moresꝗ pudendos
Laudatur pec	Audeo:de celebri tanq̄ certetur honore.
cator i deside=	Nunc refero per me deceptas vndiꝗ gentes:
ꝛiis suis p̄s.	Me duce nunc iacto tot semina sparsa malorum:
xviij.	Immemor hunc prauum vitę conuertere cursum.
xvii.di.nec li=	Quin doleo:ꝗ non consueto tramite semper
cuit.	Ire queo:& stultas penitus consūmere vestes.
	Sed qa non valeo cursum complere vetustum:
	Hęc nato discenda meo:teneroꝗ nepoti
	Proponam:fingamꝗ vias ad crimina largas.
Decōse. dis.v	Hic alacer/fatui patris/vestigia temtet:
c.vl.in glo.	Et discet prodire gradu genitoris iniquo:
	Gaudet & ipse parens:natus ꝗ crimine maior:
	Progressum sceleris superat/numerūꝗ malorū:
	Spemꝗ gerit pulchram de nato:quom sua gestat
	Signa:quibus vitę malesanos triuerit annos.

Pages from Barclay's 1509 translation of Sebastian Brant's Ship of Fools, *showing its complex typography and layout*

XXII

Moribus in prauis verfabitur illius ætas.   Iuuenalis.
Stulticięꝗ vias nunꝗ poftponet inertes:
Ergo reget pictꝗ ftultorum carbafa nauis
Proh pudor:effœta o quid nūc cupis effe fenecta⸗   Tulliusde feñ
Semper & in tenebris pręfentia vota morari⸗
Inueteratus enim fatuus bene viuere nefcit: Prouer.xxvi.
Nefcit & ex animo fœdos depellere mores.   puer.xviij.

      ❡Of olde folys that is to fay the longer they lyue
         the moze they ar gyuen to foly.

❡Howe beit I ftoup/and faft declyne
Dayly to my graue/and fepulture
And though my lyfe faft vo enclyne
To pay the trybute of nature
yet ftyll remayne I and endure
In my olde fynnes/and them nat hate
Nought yonge/wozs olde/fuche is my ftate

robin þ toule

Inueterata fa
tuitas.

Inueterate di
erum malorū
nunc venerūt
peccata tua ꝗ
opabaris pri⸗
us. A feniori⸗
bus egreffa ē
iniquitas. Pu
er centum an⸗
norum morie
tur . & pecca⸗
tor centū an⸗
norū maledi⸗
ctus erit. Stul
tia eft que me
non finit effe
fenem.

ƱHe madnes of my youthe rotyd in my age
    And the blynde foly of my iniquite
Wyll me nat fuffer to leue myne olde vfage
                d.ii.

promised to recognize Henry VIII's claims to the French throne if Henry could win it by force of arms. The French campaigns in Italy persisted; and, with Henry VIII allied with his father-in-law, Ferdinand of Aragon, the emperor Maximilian, and the pope in a Holy League against the French, France's only remaining ally was Scotland. In support of his dynastic ambitions, Henry VIII led a military expedition to France at the end of June 1513, while Louis XII was laying siege to Milan; in late August, Henry's forces captured Thérouanne, and in late September, Tournai. Meanwhile, the Scots attempted to invade England. They were resoundingly beaten, however, at Flodden Field on 9 September 1513 by English forces under Thomas Howard, later second duke of Norfolk, and evidently Barclay's chief aristocratic patron. These events occasioned an unusual and extensive outpouring of literary propaganda, including Barclay's contributions. Among the better known of those who wrote were Skelton, Bernard André, Erasmus, More, and Andrea Ammonio: an all-but-comprehensive list of poets who were or who wanted to be patronized by the early Tudor court.

The Gardener's Passetaunce ("The Gardener's Pastime" or "Recreation") was first printed by Pynson, without date, but probably in 1512, in the form of a small, twelve-page pamphlet. It is a brief verse allegory of a gardener choosing the sweet-smelling red rose (Henry VIII) over the foul-smelling lily (Louis XII), making the case for English belligerence and lamenting French depredations against papal interests. The work's attribution to Barclay – only by means of a reference in Andrew Maunsell's 1595 *Catalogue of English Printed Books* to "his [Barclay's] figure of our mother holy Church, oppressed by the French King" – is not altogether certain. Like other popular English verse propaganda of the period – for the production of which Pynson, as royal printer, was chiefly responsible – the piece appears to have been written and printed hurriedly, and it appeared anonymously.

The Tower of Virtue and Honor memorializes Edward Howard, who was killed in a naval battle against the French off Brest in 1513. His father, Thomas, the victor of Flodden Field, is praised in Barclay's poem as duke of Norfolk – an honor done him, for his victory at Flodden, late in 1513 and not publicly known until February 1514. *The Tower of Virtue and Honor* is the first in the series of writings that Barclay addressed or dedicated to him. There is no sure evidence that Norfolk ever rewarded Barclay for his literary labors, though it is probable that

he did: hereafter Barclay often claimed to write "at the commandment of" Howard.

The Tower of Virtue and Honor is also an allegory. Barclay describes a rich tower set high on a crag and approached only by an arduous road. Its porter is Labor; inside, Virtue governs; and enthroned in the tower's hall sits Honor. Resident in the tower are the heroes of the 1513 English campaigns against the French, including Henry VIII ("Most high enhanced, as ought a conqueror"), Thomas Howard ("Named of Norfolk the flower of chivalry"), and his son, the young Edward, raised up into the tower by his "own acts and noble chivalry": "a flower of knighthood" and "the flower of his lineage." The poem's epideictic purpose is to praise the living no less than the dead. The allegorical form chosen to convey the encomiums derives if not immediately from Jean Lemaire de Belges's *Temple d'honneur et de vertu* (1503), which has been alleged as the source, then certainly from the tradition of peculiarly chivalric and classicizing allegory associated with the Burgundian ducal courts of the fifteenth century. Barclay's poem, for example, mentions Seneca, Cicero, and Cato the Elder as authorities on "cruel Fortune"; and among the examples of virtuous "chivalry" it uses are Pompey, Julius Caesar, Alexander the Great, Policrates, and Cyrus the Great.

No doubt *The Tower of Virtue and Honor* was circulated separately at the time in manuscript form, but it survives now only as incorporated in the next body of work to which Barclay turned, his *Eclogues*. There are five of them, some so closely interrelated as to form virtual chapters of a single work, others just as clearly separate, discrete pieces in their own right. The five were not published together until 1570. They appear to have been written and revised over a period of some years, around 1509 to 1514, and the dates of their completion and final publication are not exactly known. They were popular, it seems, and were often reprinted, but no edition of any of them earlier than about 1518 survives. All of the earliest surviving editions (many of them in fragmentary form) from this period 1518 to 1530 are evidently derivative rather than authorized. This absence of good textual sources clouds the issue of the relations among the eclogues and Barclay's conception of them, as a single work or a group of works.

The first three eclogues now form a unit. There is some evidence to suggest that the first of them may have been written and published by itself initially. If so, its ending was later altered to lead into the second eclogue, the ending of which leads into the third: as the texts survive, these three eclogues are parts of a single, continuous work. It is a discussion of the courtier's life translated from, or based on, the *De miseriis curialium* of Piccolomini (written before his election as Pope Pius II in 1458), which is a Latin prose epistle addressing a friend, detailing and generalizing from Piccolomini's experiences in the imperial court during the 1440s. The work is a declaration, "all whole," of "the courtly misery" and "the court's wretchedness." As Barclay puts it, "the court is the baiting place of hell," but the success of the anticourt argument that Barclay's version makes is a result in part of the vividly detailed descriptions of contemporary court life that he offers, often amplifying or supplementing his source:

> If the dish be pleasant, either flesh or fish,
> Ten hands at once swarm in the dish.
> And if it be flesh, ten knives shalt thou see
> Mangling the flesh and in the platter flee:
> To put there thy hands is peril without fail,
> Without a gauntlet or else a glove of mail.
> Among all these knives thou one of both must have,
> Or else it is hard thy fingers whole to save.
> Oft in such dishes in court is it seen,
> Some leave their fingers, each knife is so keen.
> On a finger gnaweth some hasty glutton,
> Supposing it is a piece of beef or mutton.

Like other anticourt writings of the early sixteenth century (the "Dialogue of Counsel" at the beginning of More's *Utopia* [1516] being another example), Barclay's anticourt eclogues 1–3 were written, paradoxically, in an effort to attract courtly patronage, by someone who wanted to succeed at court; among other indications of Barclay's ambitions are the encomiums of Henry VII and Henry VIII that he inserted.

Barclay's chief original contribution, however, was generic: his decision to make pastoral verse of Piccolomini's plain prose letter. By casting the material in the form of a dialogue between two shepherds, Cornix and Coridon – the one a former courtier, now grown old; the other a youth eager to leave country life behind for the court – Barclay dramatizes the argument: Coridon has a decision to make, and Cornix seeks to sway him. Also, the pastoral setting enables Barclay to delineate the miseries of court life the more sharply: unlike his source, always present in Barclay's work is a contrast between the good pastoral life the shepherds enjoy and the miserable court life one of them mistakenly desires. If this group of three eclogues is the most successful of Barclay's pastoral efforts, it is in some

measure because here the pastoral conceit has particular aptness to the argument being conducted.

Barclay's fourth eclogue was published separately, and apparently later, under the title *The Book of Codrus and Minalcas* (these being the names of the rustic interlocutors); but the title page of the earliest surviving edition, printed by Pynson, makes a point of the fact that it is also "The Fourth Eclogue of A. Barclay." The success of the first three, it would seem, with printers and their publics, prompted Barclay to extend the series. Like the first three, this one too was a translation of an Italian humanist source, in this case the fifth eclogue of Mantuan – Battista Spagnolo of Mantua – who had also been a source for Barclay's eclogues 1–3. Mantuan was the best-known Latin poet of the Renaissance; his most famous poems were his pastorals, all of which Barclay knew and used. As the basis for his own fourth *Eclogue* Barclay chose one treating a topic of particular concern to him as a patronage seeker: "the behavior of rich men against poets." Again, the poem is a dialogue, this time between Codrus, a rich shepherd, "lusty, gay, and stout," and Minalcas, a poor one, who "yet could ... pipe and finger well a drone." Codrus has been an admirer of Minalcas's poetry; but even after Minalcas details poets' needs for patronal sustenance, the unreliability of the rich, and their ignorant taste for "merry fits" on ribald and vulgar topics, Codrus avoids meeting his responsibilities. Codrus had promised to reward him for a song, but in the end he begs off, pleading the hardness of his circumstances at the moment and so objectifying the meanness of the rich.

The most interesting feature of Barclay's eclogue is something original to it: within the neoclassical, humanist framework that he borrowed from Mantuan, Barclay inserted examples of other kinds of verse making. As proof for Minalcas of his poetic skills, Codrus performs two pieces: one is the Burgundian-style allegory separately circulated in 1513, *The Tower of Virtue and Honor;* the other is a ballad "Of Sapience," hortatory and proverbial, like Sir Francis Brian's "Proverbs of Solomon" and Thomas Wyatt's third satire responding to it, or such earlier poems as the so-called "Moral Ballad" of Chaucer's friend Henry Scogan and the Chaucerian ballad "Truth." The complex construction Barclay built here – out of pieces taken from several origins, in his own and others' work – demonstrates the unusually wide range of the poetic skills that he commanded, and as such should have been particularly apt to overcome the patronal reluctance – "the

Page from Barclay's circa 1515 translation of Giovanni Battista Spagnolo's Life
of Saint George, with a woodcut of Saint George slaying the dragon

behavior of rich men against poets" – that is the poem's ostensive topic.

Barclay's fifth (and last) eclogue was likewise published separately, under the title *The Fifth Eclogue of Alexander Barclay, of the Citizen and Uplandishman* (1518?). Like the fourth, this is a translation of an eclogue by Mantuan (his sixth); here too the title tells the topic. It is a debate about the relative merits of urban and rural life, conducted in part by means of biblical exempla, between two shepherds: Amintas, an admirer of city life, recently returned from London to the country because the city had broken him with impoverishment; and Faustus, poor but content, who had visited the city only for market and had learned thereby "the mad enormity, / Envy, fraud, malice, and such iniquity" of urban life. Country life comes out looking preferable. Much of the discussion is given over to other topics, however: the effects of Fortune and how best to live with them (stoically); and folly again, its extent ("The men of the earth be fools each

one") and its varieties, particularly as practiced among the urban, the wealthy, and the courtly.

With the completion of this series of eclogues, Barclay's important literary work was behind him. During the final five years or so of his literary career (circa 1515–circa 1520), he published three further translations, each from an Italian source, none particularly noteworthy, and a brief didactic piece. It seems likely that he enjoyed the most patronage he ever did during this phase of his career – each of these late works claims to have been written "at the commandment of " some noble patron – but the choices of sources to translate seem predictable, and the work itself contains little that is new.

In the middle of the sixteenth century, Bale imputed to Barclay lives of the saints Etheldreda (who established the monastic foundation at Ely in the seventh century) and Catherine and Margaret (both subjects of lives by Mantuan), but the only saint's life by Barclay that survives is of Saint

George. He finished it at Ely in August 1515, and it was printed by Pynson, probably shortly thereafter. As with the fourth and fifth eclogues, here too Barclay was translating Mantuan. In addition to the appealing humanist source – and, here again, the Latin was printed beside Barclay's English – Barclay's *Life of Saint George* had the added attraction of patriotic appeal. The woodcuts with which Pynson decorated the first half of the book emphasize the story's romancelike qualities: it involves chivalric prowess, after all, with a damsel in distress, and the relief of a city from a dragon's depredations. The second half, narrating George's martyrdom, is less immediately appealing and was left unillustrated. In part by means of a series of digressions that he added to his source, Barclay made of the whole an exhortation to pious fortitude ("constance in hard extremity") addressed explicitly to an English audience. The work's dedication to Thomas Howard – at whose "commandment" Barclay again claims to be working – is especially appropriate: as earl marshal of England, Howard was an officer of the Order of the Garter, whose patron saint was George, and so Howard was "George's worthy knight" in a special sense.

Also "at the commandment of" Howard, Barclay undertook to translate the ancient Roman historian Sallust's *Jugurthine War:* an account of late Republican Rome's wars against the Numidian usurper and tyrant Jugurtha. In the letter published with it, Barclay draws a parallel between Howard, who at Flodden Field had repelled "the invader and violent enemy of the commonweal of England," and "mighty Marius," the Roman general awarded a triumph for finally vanquishing Jugurtha, but the work ought to have been of broader appeal. The story stands as "a warning and admonition unto princes and governors," Barclay says, "thereby to rule and order themselves and a commonweal"; it teaches that the "tyranny of injurious and odious exactors and oppressors" must sometimes be put down "by violence, armor, and battle, by ministration of good and righteous princes, defenders and maintainers of the commonweal." These feats of the ancients – "the deeds most famous of all times, since creation of the world" – Barclay meant to be useful to contemporary "gentlemen, which covet to attain to clear fame and honor, by glorious deeds of chivalry."

Barclay's other late translation – *The Mirror of Good Manners* (circa 1518), from the Latin verse *De quattuor virtutibus* (1484) of Mancini – may likewise have been a commission, though not from Howard. Barclay's preface says that he had translated it "at

the desire of Sir Giles Alington, Knight," about whom little is known, and the colophon to the printed text states that Pynson published it "at the instance and request of the right noble Richard [Grey], Earl of Kent." An Italian humanist in the employ of Angelo Cato, archbishop of Vienne, Mancini had spent some part of 1483 in England and had written an important account of the usurpation of Richard III. His *De quattuor virtutibus* was first published in Paris in December 1484, not long after he left England. It is a work of moral exhortation, meant to encourage espousal of the four cardinal virtues: prudence, justice, fortitude (something Barclay calls "magnanimity or strength of mind"), and temperance. Barclay's translation begins with a prefatory section arguing that, although these four are "natural" virtues, requiring no more than an application of reason to justify them, their origin is ultimately in God. A section is devoted to each of the four, defining and exemplifying. The final section, on temperance, is disproportionately long – as long as the other three combined. Most of it is given over to discussion of forms of intemperance to be avoided, and hence it recalls *The Ship of Fools* and its anatomy of folly.

The Introductory to Write and to Pronounce French (1521) is a compendious guide to the language, comprising a series of lists: pronouns, verb forms, and vocabulary, the last arranged by parts of speech (nouns, adjectives, and so on) and by subject (numbers, days, months, varieties of fish, and so on). It does not appear to be a work of thoroughgoing pedagogy or reference; its nature is perhaps best suggested by the fact that the last page and a half of the thirty-two-page booklet is taken up with a piece on "The Manner of Dancing Base-Dances after the Use of France," translated from French by the man who printed the thing, Robert Copeland. Evidently, it was a vade mecum for the neighborly and for curial and mercantile tourists. Barclay was moved to compose it ("at the commandment of the right high, excellent, and mighty prince, Thomas, Duke of Norfolk"), he claims in his preface, because lately "it hath pleased almighty God to reconcile the peace between the two realms of England and France and to confederate them in love and amity." The book was printed in March 1521, within months of the amicable and magnificent meetings of May and June 1520 between Henry VIII and Francis I, known as the Field of the Cloth of Gold.

The last reference to literary activity on Barclay's part comes in the form of a 1520 letter to Cardinal Wolsey, who was occupied at the time with planning the Field of the Cloth of Gold meetings. On 10 April an agent of his already in France, charged with arranging entertainments for the occasion, wrote asking that "Master Barclay, the black monk and poet," be sent "to devise histories and convenient reasons to flourish the buildings and banquet house withal." The implication of the letter is that Barclay by this time had come to enjoy considerable esteem as a writer in courtly and aristocratic circles. But there is no record of his having gone to France, and no record of any contributions he may have made to the Field of the Cloth of Gold revels; nor is he known to have done any literary work at all at any date after about 1520. The only work of his that postdates the Field of the Cloth of Gold is *The Introductory to Write and to Pronounce French.*

Barclay's literary career ends here, for no apparent reason. There are various records of the later doings of one or more persons by the name of Alexander Barclay, but the records do not sit easily side by side, and links between these doings and those of the poet Barclay before about 1520 are obscure at best. In 1528 an English Alexander Barclay fetches up in Germany, in a group of formerly observant Franciscans, as a Lutheran agitator and pro-reform extremist. In April 1529 a Friar Alexander Barclay was reported to Wolsey in England for criticizing the cardinal as a tyrant. In late 1538, two to four years after the suppression of the Franciscan orders in England, a Friar Alexander Barclay, publicly wearing the habit of a Franciscan, was reported preaching and agitating against reform at several sites in southwest England. This staunchly Catholic Barclay may also have acted as chaplain to Princess Mary some years later, around 1550.

In 1546 an Alexander Barclay was preferred to two vicarages, one in Essex and another in Somersetshire, as someone between the extremes, at least reconciled to the course of reform in England; this parish priest also acted as master of the Wells Cathedral School (only two miles from his Somerset parish) in 1547. This final Barclay died in June 1552, leaving bequests to the poor of his parishes in Essex and Somersetshire, and was buried at Croydon. Bale puts the death of the poet in 1552 and his burial at Croydon; these remarks suggest that the 1552 will is the poet's and hence that, after the dissolution of the monasteries in England in the mid 1530s, the poet had spent at least the last six years of his life as a parish priest. He would have been nearing eighty by 1552. That the poet left the Benedictine order for the Franciscans, or that he was an activist of the Reformation – for or against, or by turns for and against – cannot be asserted

Title page for John Cawood's 1570 edition of Barclay's best-known translation, including sections by Barclay not found in the first edition

with any confidence. These late records probably refer to the doings of more than one Alexander Barclay, possibly none of whom need have been the poet. The poet's work was finished around 1520 in any case.

Barclay was one of the first English writers to be honored with the publication of an edition of his complete (or nearly complete) works. Chaucer's appeared early in the sixteenth century; an omnibus of Skelton's work, edited by John Stow, was printed in 1554; and in 1570 the printer John Cawood published a large volume containing Barclay's *Ship of Fools, The Mirror of Good Manners,* and the five *Eclogues.* Edmund Spenser and Michael Drayton knew the *Eclogues,* and Spenser may have known Barclay's version of the life of Saint George; however, Barclay's reputation has been in eclipse since the late sixteenth century. By the measure of critical and scholarly interest, he appears to be the least of the three vernacular poets – Skelton, Stephen Hawes, and Barclay – attached in some fashion, at some time, to the early Tudor court, seeking to prosper by writing in the peculiar circumstances that prevailed in England in the decades following the introduction of printing.

References:
John M. Berdan, "Alexander Barclay, Poet and Preacher," *Modern Language Review,* 8 (July 1913): 289–300;

Sukanta Chaudhuri, "Barclay's Eclogues: Satire and the Suffering Rustic," in *Renaissance Pastoral and Its English Developments* (Oxford: Clarendon, 1989), pp. 116–125;

L. S. Colchester, "Alexander Barclay," *Modern Language Review,* 37 (April 1942): 198;

Edelgard DuBruck, "Barclay's Veritable Source: *A Ship of Fools* by Pierre Rivière," *Michigan Academician,* 4 (Summer 1971): 67–75;

Alistair Fox, "*Beatus ille:* The *Eclogues* of Alexander Barclay," in *Politics and Literature in the Reigns of Henry VII and Henry VIII* (Oxford: Blackwell, 1989), pp. 37–55;

R. J. Lyall, "Alexander Barclay and the Edwardian Reformation 1548–1552," *Review of English Studies,* new series 20 (November 1969): 455–461;

Lyall, "Tradition and Innovation in Alexander Barclay's 'Towre of Vertue and Honoure,' " *Review of English Studies,* new series 23 (February 1972): 1–18;

Wilfred P. Mustard, "Notes on the Egloges of Alexander Barclay," *Modern Language Notes,* 24 (January 1909): 8–10;

William Nelson, "New Light on Alexander Barclay," *Review of English Studies,* 19 (January 1943): 59–61;

Nicholas Orme, "Alexander Barclay, Tudor Educationalist," in his *Education and Society in Medieval and Renaissance England* (London: Hambledon, 1989), pp. 259–270;

Aurelius Pompen, *The English Versions of the Ship of Fools* (London & New York: Longmans, Green, 1925; New York: Octagon, 1967);

John Richie Schultz, "Alexander Barclay and the Later Eclogue Writers," *Modern Language Notes,* 35 (January 1920): 52–54;

Schultz, "The Life of Alexander Barclay," *Journal of English and Germanic Philology,* 18 (1919): 360–368;

Schultz, "The Method of Barclay's Eclogues," *Journal of English and Germanic Philology,* 32 (1933): 549–571.

William Barker

(circa 1520 – after 1576)

Kenneth R. Bartlett
Victoria College, University of Toronto

BOOK: *Epitaphia et inscriptiones lvgvbres. A Gulielmo Berchero, cum in Italia, animi causa, peregrinaretur, collecta* (London: Printed by John Cawood, 1566) – there is a phantom 1554 edition but no copy survives.

Edition: *A Dyssputac[i]on off the Nobylyte of Wymen betwene Dyvers Ladis and Gentleme[n] off Ytalye at a Place Called Petriolo, One of the Bayns of Siena, the Noble Cyttye of Toscane,* edited by R. Warwick Bond (London: Roxborough Club, 1904–1905).

TRANSLATIONS: Xenophon, *The Bookes of Xenophon Contayning the discipline, schole, and education of Cyrvs (the noble kyng of Persie.) Translated out of Greeke into Englyshe, by M. Wylliam Barkar* (London: Printed by Reynold Wolfe, 1553?);

Giovanni Battista Gelli, *The Fearfull Fansies of the Florentine Couper: Written in Toscane, by John Baptista Gelli, one of the free Studie of Florence, and for recreation translated into English by W. Barker. Pensoso d'altrui* (London: Printed by Henry Bynneman, 1568; reprinted, 1599).

William Barker is unfortunately remembered largely as the faithless servant who betrayed his master, Thomas Howard, fourth Duke of Norfolk, following the exposure of the Ridolfi Plot. It is only appropriate, then, that his reputation be rehabilitated because of his significance as one of the earliest Tudor translators of Italian literature, an important collector of classical inscriptions, and a proponent of humanist education, including the celebration of learned women.

Barker was born about 1520, probably in Norfolk, into a humble family, but he received a good education at St. John's College, Cambridge, through the assistance of the fiercely Protestant queen Anne Boleyn. He was granted his M.A. in 1540 and may have remained at Cambridge as a fellow or received some other educational appointment, perhaps as tutor to a young nobleman. There

is no doubt, though, that Barker was a Roman Catholic and remained one, despite his acceptance of rewards from Queen Anne.

It was probably the more radical direction of the Reformation under King Edward VI (1547–1553) that drove Barker to the Continent and to Italy, but the date of his departure is difficult to determine. He was perhaps in England in October 1551 because he dedicated his translation of the first books of Xenophon's *Cyropaideia* to Sir William Herbert as earl of Pembroke, a dignity not granted him until 11 October of that year. However, there is evidence that Barker had been in Italy during the autumn of 1549, since he was one of the party that accompanied Thomas Hoby, whom he met in Siena, to Rome and Naples that winter. The most likely solutions to this mystery are either that Barker returned to England at some time after October 1551 but quickly set out once more for the peninsula or that Reynold Wolfe, the printer of the book, changed the dedication to correspond to the new earl's title. Both are equally plausible.

The dedication of the *Cyropaideia* to Pembroke asserts that the translation was made to assist in education, and Herbert is especially praised for his care in educating his sons. Whether the translation is directly from the Greek or from a Latin edition or from the Italian versions of Poggio Bracciolini (1521) or, more likely, that of Lodovico Domenichi (1548) is impossible to determine for certain; but it must be remembered that Barker very likely knew Domenichi and translated his Italian *La Nobilità delle donne* (1549). Since Barker has been definitely located in Tuscany in 1549, it is most likely that the work was at least in part a translation from the Italian, although it is probable that he knew the Greek original. Also, the fact that he relied on Domenichi's version for his 1567 completion of his translation of the Xenophon text is very suggestive. This continuation of his work is dedicated to another nobleman, Philip Howard, Earl of Surrey, son of his patron, the duke of Norfolk.

Barker must have returned to England soon after the accession of Mary because one of the fruits of his Italian journey, his *Epitaphia et inscriptiones lugubres,* was first printed in London by John Cawood in 1554. This collection of Latin epitaphs reflects the interest in such inscriptions by humanists. Barker's traveling companion, contemporary, and fellow Cantabrigian Hoby also recorded many funerary inscriptions in his journal, and Italian humanist travelers – Giovanni Pontano, for example – reflected the fashion in Italy. One interesting observation concerning Barker's published epitaphs is that not all of them are ancient; some modern Roman inscriptions appear, and many from Naples are from royal tombs. Like Hoby, therefore, Barker mixed his humanist obsession with the classical world with a manifest concern for the modern.

Although Barker did not write a diary or journal as such, he does reveal a significant amount of information about his travels and activities in Italy in the prefaces to his translations and other works. From his *Epitaphia* his itinerary can be followed precisely as he traveled from city to city collecting funerary inscriptions. He visited Rome, Naples, Padua, Venice, Bologna, Florence, Certaldo, Siena, Alba Longa, Nola, Chiusi, Aversa, Nocera, and Capua. Nevertheless, besides the inscriptions themselves and the route they define, Barker leaves no further evidence of his experiences in the *Epitaphia*.

However, in his translation of Giovanni Battista Gelli's dialogues, Barker admits to having spent some time in Florence in informal literary studies, a subject obviously of interest to this educated and literate gentleman. How long he spent there is not known, but it is probable that he made the acquaintance of Domenichi, whose *La Nobilità delle donne* he was to paraphrase in English probably during his residence in Siena. Domenichi's book had been printed in Venice in 1549, so Barker might well have been working from the printed version; but the fact that he later made use of Domenichi's translation of Xenophon's *Cyropaideia* (when he completed the last books of his own translation, which had been begun and printed before his trip to the Continent) indicates a knowledge of Domenichi's work and career that would most likely have come from personal association. Also, given Barker's literary connections in Florence, it is probable that he would have met a figure such as Domenichi, who was Duke Cosimo de' Medici's librarian and a significant, if perhaps overrated, member of Florentine intellectual society.

The preface to his English paraphrase of Domenichi gives the greatest detail of Barker's life

Title page for Barker's collection of Latin epitaphs, gathered during his travels in Italy

in Siena, where he says he settled after his travels. The character of that life is what might be expected of a gentleman living abroad in order to learn the Italian language, acquire some knowledge of the literature, and polish his manners. His companions were aristocratic ladies and gentlemen, and their hospitality in their villas clearly made his experience in Tuscany very pleasant – indeed, a memory powerfully invoked during his praise of Siena, its surrounding countryside and medicinal baths, the quality of the Italian spoken there, and graciousness of the people.

Barker's *A Disputation of the Nobility of Women* is known to have been written while he was in Siena, probably near the end of 1552 or the very beginning of 1553, because he describes the children of Henry VIII in the positions they occupied while Edward VI was still on the throne; and writing abroad he is also free to praise the Catholic princess Mary:

The two sisters of the most noble prince King Edward the Sixth, of which the elder is the lady Mary's grace . . . so excellent and passing in all kind of learning and language as few have been the like, and therefore I can do no more but pray for her grace's long preservation.

Therefore, although the manuscript text was dedicated and delivered to Queen Elizabeth in 1559, it was certainly composed in Italy during Barker's residence in Siena, at a time when he might well have known Domenichi through the kinds of aristocratic and courtly society who would have had access to the ducal library in Florence, even if Siena at this time had not yet fallen to Cosimo's siege.

In itself the preface to *The Nobility of Women* constitutes an instructive vignette of English travel in Italy in the middle of the sixteenth century; and the civilized, literary character of this preface contrasts sharply with the image of Barker as a kind of Machiavel, trained in conspiracy, cowardice, treason, and faithlessness. Certainly the preface owes much to the frame of the *Decameron* (1349–1351); that Barker knew Giovanni Boccaccio's work is evident from his record of the Italian's inscription at Certaldo. And, of course, there are memories of Baldassare Castiglione's *Cortegiano* (1528) in the characterizations and the situations of the dialogue. Nevertheless, in his desire to describe the life he led there, even if embellished by literary allusion and use of an established topos, Barker emphasizes the aristocratic, courtly atmosphere, the *cortese* he associates particularly with Siena. His hosts and friends come not from a world of power and politics or even the church but from noble Tuscan families taking the waters and sharing the *villeggiatura* of the Borghese family, who had not yet risen to great wealth and power in Rome through the papacy.

Domenichi's setting is moved from a court wedding in Milan to Petriolo; the characters are altered, and the dialogue advanced to 1553 from 1546, the year of Domenichi's original. Moreover, an interesting – and for the history of the English perception of Italy important – addition is Barker's introduction of himself as a character in the dialogues. He produces a disarming and sensitive verisimilitude by recounting in some detail his own travels through Italy, describing its cities and their attractions and charms until he reaches Siena. The Siena he describes moreover is a nostalgic and fleeting moment in history caught between the Spanish occupation that ended in August 1552 and Duke Cosimo's siege of January 1554. This short moment of recaptured freedom created the world in which the dialogue takes place and consequently reminds the reader powerfully of Castiglione's *Cortegiano,* soon to be translated by Hoby, in which the golden age of Italian courtesy and culture lost to the indignities of war and failure can be recaptured only in literature and memory.

At the end of Barker's paraphrase is a catalogue of Englishwomen celebrated for their learning, undoubtedly appended to indicate that England, too, has produced learned women. The names are interesting and confirm the date of composition as 1554. Celebrated are the two Tudor princesses, the daughters of Sir Thomas More and Sir Anthony Cooke, the sisters of the duke of Norfolk, the daughters of Edward Seymour, Duke of Somerset, and Henry Fitzalan, twelfth Earl of Arundel, and even those of Henry Grey, Duke of Suffolk, although Lady Jane Grey is wisely not mentioned by name or title.

It is not known when Barker undertook his other major translation from the Italian, his complete version of ten dialogues of Gelli's *I Caprici del Bottaio* (1549), although it is again probable that the idea was at least conceived in Florence, where Barker had known of Gelli. Barker informs the reader in the preface to this work, translated as *The Fearful Fancies of the Florentine Cooper* (1568):

> For had not I had once a man that used often to talk with himself, and a fellow whose name was Just, as it might well be I had no more remembered the talk of father Just of Florence, which I read when I was there, and thought no more of. But, as John Baptista Gelli, for so is the tailor called, and for his wisdom chief of the vulgar university of Florence, when I was there did publish these communications of Just the cooper.

The nature of this collection of dialogues reflects again Barker's access to and interest in the intellectual world of contemporary Florence in particular and Italy in general. Recording discussions between Just and his soul, the original is reminiscent of Italian literary internal dialogues, which begin with Petrarch's *Secretum;* however, Gelli's have a pungent Florentine quality, illustrating the textures of sophisticated Florentine wit with its anticlericalism, appreciation of the local idiom, and comments on the morality and habits of the time, written by one of the most talented of the *poligrafici* (authors skilled in many subjects). The English is equally racy and was sufficiently popular to result in two printings, first in 1568 and again in 1599.

Once he had returned permanently to England, Barker's career changed fundamentally. Penniless and possessed only of an excellent education and a taste for the polished company of aristocratic circles, his only possible occupation was service in a noble household. Barker wrote that "hard fortune drove me to serve." Some time before the death of Mary, he entered the household of the young duke of Norfolk as his secretary. In this capacity he was returned through the duke's patronage to the Parliaments of 1558 and 1559 for Yarmouth, as "servant to my lord of Norfolk's grace." He sat for Bramber in 1563 and Yarmouth again in 1571.

Because of the Catholic sympathies of the Howards, descriptions of the confessional allegiances of the Norfolk household were categorized by the queen's government some time before 1567: Barker, not surprisingly, is listed as a Roman Catholic. Moreover, besides sitting in Parliament as the duke's man, he was also clearly becoming increasingly involved in his lord's affairs. By 1568 he was trustee of some of the vast Howard estates; and in 1569 he was arrested soon after his master for complicity in the Catholic plots and rising of that year.

However, it was his deep involvement in the Ridolfi conspiracy that made most use of Barker's particular gifts, especially his knowledge of Florence and Italian, and that resulted in his subsequent vilification by posterity. In 1571 Barker brought Roberto di Ridolfi to Howard House and indeed conversed with him in Italian about the plot. As a result he was sent with Norfolk to the Tower in September 1571 and interrogated for months as an active member of the conspiracy. The conclusion of these interrogations, during which Barker showed great fear of the rack, was that he betrayed Norfolk completely and provided the evidence that took his master to the block.

After his testimony Barker was branded by the duke as an "Italianified Englishman" (Norfolk's other accuser, the bishop of Ross, was described as "a shameless Scot"), implying that his word should not have been accepted and that he had been corrupted while abroad in Italy and had in fact been the real instigator of the conspiracy. Norfolk blamed Barker for condemning him for his own treason. This, of course, is the image of Barker that has been recorded: the faithless Judas who betrayed the noble patron who had so graciously advanced and befriended him. Indeed, it is possible that it was Barker to whom William Harrison was referring in the powerfully anti-Italian diatribe in his "Description of England" printed in *Holinshed's Chronicles* (1577). Barker was seen, then, as a classic model of the *inglese italianato* (Italianate Englishman), hence *un diavolo incarnato* (a devil incarnate).

There is no doubt that Barker, faced with torture, turned against his former patron and protector to save his own life; and there is no doubt that Barker was deeply involved in the Ridolfi plot himself, even using his mastery of Italian to treat with the Florentine conspirator in his own language

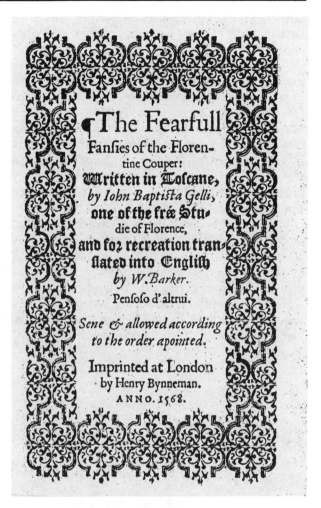

Title page for Barker's translation of ten dialogues by Giovanni Battista Gelli

(William Murdin records Barker's own confession). However, did this cowardice and treason have anything to do with Barker's experience in Italy, or was it merely an opportunity for English Protestant enthusiasts to attack the Roman church, which was deeply involved in the plot against the queen and the established religion, and which had in 1570 declared Elizabeth deposed, thus inciting good Catholics everywhere to rise up against her?

The epithet of "Italianified Englishman" directed against Barker by the condemned Norfolk in his last letter to the queen appears not to have had any substance beyond the general distaste for the former secretary's damning testimony against his master. The epithet is, then, a slur, a slight much like Roger Ascham's almost contemporary indictment of the Italianate Englishman in his *Schoolmaster* (1570) and Archbishop Matthew Parker's caricature of Reginald Pole in *De antiquitate Britannicae ecclesiae*

(1572). To be Italianate, consequently, was to be wicked and treacherous behind a mask of civility and sincerity.

Despite his condemnation of the duke, Barker himself was sentenced to death after his trial. However, he spent only two years in the Tower before receiving a pardon in May 1574. Moreover, his goods and property were returned to him two months later, probably as reward for turning Crown's evidence. The last record of Barker is a suit in the Court of Requests regarding property matters in February 1576. It is probable that he died soon afterward.

It should be noted that other works attributed to Barker – including those translations listed by Thompson Cooper in his brief biography of Barker in the *Dictionary of National Biography* – are most probably by others. There is no significant modern scholarship specifically on Barker, except for a 1957 article by George B. Parks. This neglect is curious, given his notoriety as an "Italianified Englishman"

and the role he played in bridging the English and Italian literary communities. Useful work especially needs to be done on Barker's principles of translation, which so successfully turned the contemporary Italian prose of Gelli and Domenichi into lucid and flexible English.

References:

Peter Hasler, ed., *The House of Commons, 1558–1603,* volume 1 (London: Her Majesty's Stationery Office, 1981), pp. 396–397;

William Murdin, *A Collection of State Papers Relating to Affairs in the Reign of Queen Elizabeth,* volume 2 (London: William Bowyer, 1759), pp. 87–129;

George B. Parks, "William Barker, Tudor Translator," *Papers of the Bibliographical Society of America,* 51 (1957): 126–140;

John Venn and John Archibald Venn, *Alumni Cantabrigienses,* volume 1 (Cambridge: Cambridge University Press, 1922), p. 88.

Barnabe Barnes

(circa March 1571 – December 1609)

George Klawitter
Viterbo College

BOOKS: *Parthenophil and Parthenophe. Sonnettes, madrigals, elegies and odes* (London: John Wolfe, 1593);

A diuine centurie of spirituall sonnets (London: Printed by John Windet, 1595);

Foure bookes of offices: enabling privat persons for the service of all good princes (London: Printed by Adam Islip, 1606);

The Divils Charter: a Tragædie Conteining the Life and Death of Pope Alexander the sixt (London: Printed by G. E. for John Wright, 1607);

The Battle of Hexham (London, 1607?).

Editions and Collections: *Poems,* edited by Alexander B. Grosart (Manchester: C. E. Simms, 1875);

Ten Poems from "Parthenophil and Parthenophe," edited by Madeleine Hope Dodds (Plymouth: Priory Press, 1929);

The Devil's Charter, facsimile edition (New York: AMS, 1970);

Parthenophil and Parthenophe, edited by Victor A. Doyno (Carbondale: Southern Illinois University Press, 1971);

Four Bookes of Offices, facsimile edition (Norwood, N.J.: W. J. Johnson, 1975).

Barnabe Barnes is one of the most important minor sonneteers to write during the reign of Elizabeth I. A member of the leisured rich, he moved easily in literary circles and managed to make friends and enemies among the most luminous courtiers and writers of his day. Although much of his biography is shrouded by the usual blankness typical of Renaissance authors, scholars have been able to piece together enough of his life to appreciate him as a fascinating, if brash, figure in Shakespeare's England. Most of his works have evaded oblivion, but the first edition of his most famous first collection of poems exists in only a single copy. Had that not survived, readers would be tantalized today by various satirical references to his secular poetry without means to substantiate the contemporary criticism.

Far below the status of Edmund Spenser and Sir Philip Sidney, Barnes holds his own poetic niche comfortably with the best of Thomas Watson, Fulke Greville, and William Habington.

Barnes was born circa March 1571, the fourth son of six children, to Richard Barnes, suffragan bishop of Nottingham and chancellor of York Minster. Although the date of his birth is not recorded, Barnabe was baptized 6 March 1571. His father eventually was advanced to Durham in 1577, and his mother died when Barnabe was ten. In 1582 his father married a Frenchwoman named Jane Jerrard from whom the poet may have picked up his knowledge of French. He matriculated at Brasenose College, Oxford, when he was fifteen, but took no degree, possibly because his father died in August 1587. In 1591 he joined the earl of Essex's Normandy expedition, a venture on which he saw little action but which gave him ample matter to boast about and earn a reputation as a braggart. Both Thomas Nashe and Thomas Campion faulted him for exaggeration and attention grabbing. Nashe recounts that Gabriel Harvey had so puffed him up with a sense of flamboyance that Barnes obtained an odd pair of trousers with a huge codpiece, walked around town, entered court, and was generally ridiculed.

In 1593 Barnes published the work on which his literary notoriety would rest both in his day and thereafter. *Parthenophil and Parthenophe* has shocked enough readers to be dubbed "pornographic" by Hallett Smith in *Elizabethan Poetry* (1952), although most of its sonnets, madrigals, odes, elegies, and sestinas are conventional enough. The title of the book is an obvious allusion to Sidney's *Astrophil and Stella* sequence (1591), and many references throughout Barnes's book demonstrate his regard for Sidney's work. The name *Parthenophil* means *virgin-lover,* but the boy in the sequence becomes more a seducer than a lover. The name *Parthenophe* comes from the Greek word for *virgin* also, and the girl introduces herself in sonnet 6, "I am virgin." There is probably no historical basis for the two characters: Barnes never married, and if he was enamored of any particular lady, he never recorded her name, nor did his contemporaries speculate on her identity. *Parthenophil and Parthenophe* contains 181 love poems, making it the longest collection of such verse in English to that date. The first part contains 104 sonnets, 26 madrigals, and a sestina. Part 2 is devoted to 21 elegies, a canzone, and a translation of Moschus. Part 3 has 20 odes, 4 sestinas, 2 canzones, and a sonnet.

The story line in the sequence is simple but compelling. Parthenophil, seduced by Laya and jilted within the first five sonnets, turns his attention to Parthenophe, who gives him little encouragement. In poem after poem the narrator complains of his unrequited love, and various signs of the zodiac fuel his store of images. Gods and goddesses romp plentifully among the lines, and Barnes gives every indication that his use of them is as much whimsical as serious. In the infamous sonnet 63 he invokes Jove's disguises used on Europa and Danaë, wishes he were Parthenophe's gloves so that he might kiss her hands, and ends by imagining himself sweet wine that might "run through her veins, and pass by pleasure's part." Nashe made particular fun of this last image in *Have with You to Saffron-Walden* (1596) when he surmised that Barnes "was very ill advised, for so the next time his Mistress made water, he was in danger to be cast out of her favor." The final shock of the sequence comes in the last poem, the only triple sestina in English. Parthenophil, giving up conventional methods to win his lady, conjures Parthenophe to ride by him naked on the back of a goat, and he rapes her. Whether the act is real or a figment of Parthenophil's jaded imagination, it has never deterred readers from agreeing that it is a most unusual way to end a love cycle. Never had the Elizabethans been entertained by so violent a conclusion to a sonnet sequence, totally out of harmony with the frustrated but genteel conclusions of Sidney and Shakespeare or the marital satisfaction of Spenser and Habington.

Barnes's next opus is totally different in character: while traveling in France in 1594, he began writing spiritual sonnets (according to the dedication to Dr. Toby Matthew) and published them as *A Divine Century of Spiritual Sonnets* in 1595. In the first poem he says he will turn away from the "lewd lays of lighter loves." Then he gives the reader thirty-seven sonnets on aspects of the Holy Trinity and sixty-two on his own spiritual dryness. The sequence ends with a long poem about the Trinity. If one can believe Barnes, he felt that these religious

THE DIVILS CHARTER:
A TRAGÆDIE

Conteining the Life and Death of *Pope* ALEXANDER *the sixt.*

As it was plaide before the Kings Maiestie, vpon Candlemasse night last: by his Maiesties Seruants.

But more exactly reuewed, corrected, and augmented since by the Author, for the more pleasure and profit of the Reader.

AT LONDON
Printed by G. E. for *Iohn Wright*, and are to be sold at his shop in New-gate market, neere Christ church gate. 1607.

Title page for Barnabe Barnes's play about Pope Alexander VI and the Borgias

poems were more important than his earlier love poetry.

In 1598 Barnes found himself in deep trouble for trying to kill John Browne with a poisoned lemon. Fortunately, Browne did not eat the lemon, but the relentless Barnes then tried to put mercury in Browne's wine at a tavern. Suspecting the drink, Browne went to get a constable, and Barnes fled. He was caught but escaped to the north. His motivation, as biographer Mark Eccles deduces it, was generated by his involvement with the Scottish border feuds. He was probably acting for Lord Eure, warden of the Middle Marches. From 1598 to 1606 Barnes's life is a mystery, except he seems to have settled in Durham, where he testified in court for his brother Timothy in 1599 and witnessed a will in 1605. He probably lived in the parish of Saint Mary-le-Bow, where he was buried in December 1609.

Of his minor works, two survive. A dull prose treatise on governmental offices (210 pages) appeared in 1606, organized into four sections to correspond to the four cardinal virtues of temperance, prudence, justice, and fortitude. A play, *The Devil's Charter,* was performed for the king on Candlemas 1607 as the final play of the Christmas holiday season (which had begun with Shakespeare's *King Lear*). The play concerns the machinations and death of Pope Alexander VI, his son Cesare Borgia, and his daughter Lucrezia. A second play, *The Battle of Hexham,* was probably produced between 1607 and 1609, but a copy was last seen at an 1807 auction where it was sold for one shilling. (That price would seem low except, as Eccles points out, the book was probably only a fragment or in very poor condition.)

In his own day reaction to Barnes was negative. He was satirized with three epigrams by Campion in *Observations in the Art of English Poetry* (1602) for telling tall tales and for being a cuckold. Campion also attacked him in *Poemata* (1619) with an epigram on sonnet 63 of *Parthenophil and Parthenophe.* Eccles believes Barnes was also the butt of extended satire by Sir John Harington and Thomas Middleton, the former by way of epigrams, the latter in a pamphlet called *The Black Book* (1604). Later critics continued the abuse. William John Courthope in the *History of English Poetry* (1895–1910) calls Barnes an idiot, and the *Dictionary of National Biography* finds his sonnets suffer from conceits.

Although C. S. Lewis notes Barnes's colorful use of varied meters, he offers scant praise for the poet's overall talent. *Parthenophil and Parthenophe* uses a sonnet in alexandrines and in madrigal 4 even the "broken-backed line of Lydgate," but Barnes is little more than a minor voice. In him, a "Golden" conceit can lose its quality because it lacks phonetic beauty, as in the line "Rest's mist with silver cloud had closed her sun." Some poems show classic influence (madrigal 13 falls in the erotic tradition of Ovid and Propertius), and the ode "On the plains" follows Pierre de Ronsard. Overall, concludes Lewis, "If he were our only English sonneteer we should probably praise him."

In his discussion of sixteenth-century "Golden" poetry, Lewis singles out "Simpsonian rhyme"

as an aspect of metrics that modern ears find jarring. He defines it as a "rhyme on the second syllable of a disyllabic word where metre forbids that syllable to carry the stress," and he instances Barnes twice for its use. In sonnet 4 Barnes rhymes "fróm thee" with "to mé," and in sonnet 49 he rhymes "inextricáble" with "impórtable." Attributing Simpsonian rhyme to a poor poetic ear and noting that even major poets such as Shakespeare use it, Lewis concludes that Renaissance readers and listeners were less affected by strict stress in pronunciation than today's audience. Thus, although scholars now more readily associate Simpsonian rhyme with satire or comic verse, Barnes is not effecting a comic device in the two sonnets mentioned.

Victor A. Doyno, in the most recent edition of *Parthenophil and Parthenophe,* finds Barnes often reaches the excellence of Samuel Daniel and Michael Drayton. Eccles finds him a treasure for collecting examples of bad poetry (bathos, punctuation-mark conceits, a passion for apostrophe, excessive use of feminine rhyme) and a "parade of intimacy with the best families on Olympus"; but he praises Barnes for breaking away from worship of Petrarch and writing, when he was barely twenty-two, poems steeped in "a confused richness of sensuous imagery." The most detailed analysis of both the secular and the divine poems has been done by Thomas P. Roche, who reads the two sequences numerologically.

References:

Mark Eccles, "Barnabe Barnes," in *Thomas Lodge and Other Elizabethans,* edited by Charles J. Sisson (Cambridge, Mass.: Harvard University Press, 1933), pp. 165–241;

C. S. Lewis, *English Literature in the Sixteenth Century Excluding Drama* (Oxford: Clarendon, 1954);

Thomas P. Roche, *Petrarch and the English Sonnet Sequences* (New York: AMS, 1989);

Hallett Smith, *Elizabethan Poetry: A Study in Conventions, Meanings, and Expression* (Cambridge, Mass.: Harvard University Press, 1952).

George Buchanan

(circa 1 February 1506 - 28 September 1582)

Steven Berkowitz

Fu Jen University, Taipei

BOOKS: *Jephthes* (Paris: G. Morel, 1554);

De Caleto nuper ab Henrico II Francorum Rege invictiss. recepta (Paris: R. Estienne, 1558);

Franciscanus. Varia eiusdem authoris poemata (Basel? or Paris?, 1566) — also includes *Somnium* and *Epigrammata,* an early version of *Fratres Fraterrimi* (1568);

Elegiarum Liber I, Sylvarum Liber I, Endecasyllabon Liber I (Paris: R. Estienne, 1567) — occasional poems assembled by Pierre Daniel;

Franciscanus et fratres (Basel: T. Guarinus, 1568) — completes the *Fratres* with the *Palinodiae,* includes the three previously published plays and translations of Greek poems, adds a new iambic to the Latinist Walter Haddon and a few epigrams, and reprints substantially the three collections in the Daniel edition;

De Maria Scotorum regina, . . . plena, & tragica planè, historia, anonymous (London?: John Day?, 1571?) — includes what will be called *Detectio Mariae Reginae Scotorum* and *Actio contra Mariam Scotorum Reginam,* once attributed to Buchanan; *Detectio* translated and expanded as *Ane detectioun of the duinges of Marie quene of Scottes* (London?: John Day?, 1571?);

Ane Admonitioun Direct to the trew Lordis maintenaris of Iustice, and obedience to the Kingis Grace (Stirling: R. Lekprevik, 1571);

Baptistes, sive calumnia tragoedia (London: T. Vautrollier, 1577);

De iure regni apud Scotos, dialogus (Edinburgh?, 1579);

Rervm Scoticarvm historia (Edinburgh: A. Arbuthnot, 1582);

Franciscanus et Fratres (Geneva?, 1584) — expanded edition of *Franciscanus et fratres* (Basel, 1568) adds *Iambon Liber, Epigrammaton Liber I, II* (*Iusta* and *Icones*), *III* (*Strenae, Pompae,* and *Valentiniana*), and a fragment of *Sphaera;*

Sphaera . . . quinque libris descripta (Herborn: C. Corvinus, 1586) — books IV and V were never finished by Buchanan; F. Morel printed books I and II (Paris, 1585);

George Buchanan (portrait by an unknown artist; Edinburgh University)

De prosodia libellus (Edinburgh: R. Waldegrave, 1595?);

Vita ab ipso scripta (Rostock, 1595) — authorship disputed;

Poemata omnia innumeris penè locis ex ipsius autographo castigata & aucta, edited by John Ray (Edinburgh: A. Hart, 1615) – despite Ray's claim of first printing *Miscellaneorum Liber,* several of these poems had appeared in *Selectorum carminum ex doctissimis poetis collectorum . . . libri quatuor* ([Geneva]: Israel Taurinus [Jacobus Stoer], 1590), a Huguenot anthology that also printed for the first time Buchanan's *Satyra* directed against the cardinal of Lorraine, a poem not included by Ray.

Editions and Collections: *Fratres Fraterrimi, Three Books of Epigrams, and Book of Miscellanies,* translated by Robert Monteith (Edinburgh: Heirs of Andrew Anderson, 1708);

Opera Omnia, 2 volumes, edited by Thomas Ruddiman (Edinburgh: R. Freebairn, 1715) – the folio standard complete works, includes biography and bibliography;

Opera Omnia, 2 volumes, edited by Pieter Burmann (Leiden: J. A. Langerak, 1725) – the quarto standard complete works, based on the 1715 edition;

Paraphrase of the Psalms, translated by Andrew Waddel (Edinburgh: J. Robertson, 1772);

The Franciscan Friar, translated by George Provand (Glasgow: Brash & Reid, 1809);

The History of Scotland, 4 volumes, translated and continued by James Aikman (Glasgow: Blackie, Fullarton, 1827);

Vernacular Writings, edited by P. Hume Brown (Edinburgh: William Blackwood, 1892) – includes *Opinion Anent the Reformation of the Universitie of St. Andros, Ane Admonitioun,* and the *Chamaeleon;*

George Buchanan: A Memorial, 1506–1906, edited by D. A. Millar (Saint Andrews: W. C. Henderson, [1907]) – includes translations of selected poems;

Vita, translated by James M. Aitken in his *The Trial of George Buchanan before the Lisbon Inquisition* (Edinburgh: Oliver & Boyd, 1939);

De iure regni apud Scotos, in *The Powers of the Crown in Scotland,* translated and introduced by Charles Flinn Arrowood (Austin: University of Texas Press, 1949);

The "Sphera" of George Buchanan, translated, with an introduction and commentary, by James R. Naiden (N.p.: Privately printed, 1952);

The Tyrannous Reign of Mary Stewart: George Buchanan's Account, translated and edited by W. A. Gatherer (Edinburgh: Edinburgh University Press, 1958) – includes *Detectio, Ane Admonitioun,* and passages from *Rerum Scoticarum Historia;*

"George Buchanan's *Elegies* and *Silvae* Translated, with Introduction and Commentary," by David Henry Sabrio, Ph.D. dissertation, University of South Carolina, 1980;

Miscellaneorum Liber, translated by Philip J. Ford and W. S. Watt in Ford's *George Buchanan: Prince of Poets* (Aberdeen: Aberdeen University Press, 1982);

George Buchanan: Tragedies, edited by P. Sharrat and P. G. Walsh (Edinburgh: Scottish Academic Press, 1983) – includes *Medea, Alcestis, Baptistes,* and *Jephthes,* the last two translated;

A Critical Edition of George Buchanan's "Baptistes" and of the Anonymous "Tyrannicall-Government Anatomized," edited by Steven Berkowitz (New York: Garland, 1992).

OTHER: *The Chamaeleon,* in *Miscellanea Antiqua* (London: W. Taylor, 1710);

Opinion Anent the Reformation of the Universitie of St. Andros, in David Irving, *Memoirs of the Life and Writings of George Buchanan* (Edinburgh, 1817).

TRANSLATIONS: Thomas Linacre, *Rudimenta grammatices Thomae Linacri* (Paris: C. Wechel, 1533);

Euripides, *Medea* (Paris: M. Vascosan, 1544);

Euripides, *Alcestis* (Paris: M. Vascosan, 1556);

Psalmorum Davidis paraphrasis poetica (Paris?: H. & R. Estienne, 1565?) – first complete edition of the psalm paraphrases.

The Scotsman George Buchanan was acknowledged the foremost Latin poet of his age. He also became well known as an educator, historian, and political propagandist. Although a satirist of Roman Catholic orders, a victim of the Inquisition, and eventually a convert to the Protestant side, Buchanan was not, like his contemporary John Knox, an impassioned reformer of church customs and doctrines. Rather, he was "of gud religion, for a poet," according to Sir James Melville of Hallhill, and his own fortuitous career came to represent a pattern for the literary entrepreneur, necessarily engaged in the theological and political conflicts of his day, but following the path of neither priest nor lawyer. Ornamental and instrumental in court for his linguistic knowledge and art, the poet was also a *vates* who revealed hidden truths to the secular world. Sir Philip Sidney numbered Buchanan among the "piercing wits" and praised his Latin tragedies, which "bring forth a divine admiration"; John Milton honored him as a true poet and hater of tyrants; and Samuel Johnson, who despised his politics, freely admitted Buchanan to be "a great poetical genius."

Scotia fi Vatem hunc gelidam produxit ad arcton,
Credo equidem gelidj percaluere polj :

Engraving of Buchanan from Jean Jacques Boissard's Icones *(1597)*

Buchanan was born near Killearn, Stirling-shire, circa 1 February 1506, the youngest son of Thomas and Agnes Heriot Buchanan. After he flourished under the solid training available in local schools, an uncle, James Heriot, funded his Latin studies at the University of Paris. Two years later, in 1522, the young man's ill health, along with the death of his patron, caused his return to Scotland. In 1523 Buchanan joined the Regent Albany's brief foray into England. After another bout with illness he studied logic (or "sophistry," as the autobiographical *Vita* [1595] terms it) with the aged schoolman John Mair at Saint Andrews, receiving his B.A. in 1525. He then returned with Mair to Paris, where, overcoming hardship, he studied Greek, earned his M.A. (1528), and at last became an instructor at the Collège de Sainte-Barbe. *Quam misera sit conditio docentium literas humaniores Lutetiae* (*Elegiarum Liber I* [1567]), although not necessarily com-posed at this time, records in dispiriting detail how the day-to-day drudgery of teaching drives the man of letters to forsake the Muses. From circa 1531 to 1536 Buchanan tutored Gilbert Kennedy, Earl of Cassillis, to whom he dedicated *Rudimenta Grammatices* (1533), a Latin translation of Thomas Linacre's grammar.

In 1534 or 1535 Buchanan returned to Scotland with Cassillis, later becoming the tutor to James V's bastard James Stewart (died 1558). At this time, perhaps frustrated by the clerical corruption that made a religious career repugnant, he found himself satirizing the Franciscan order. His *Somnium* (1566) is based on William Dunbar's dream vision "How Dunbar was desyrit to be ane frier." Next, at James V's behest, Buchanan composed two sarcastic *Palinodiae* (1568) and then *Franciscanus* (1566), an ingeniously protracted cata-logue of hypocrisy written to satisfy the king, who deemed the earlier attacks too mild. Buchanan's continued hostility to depraved religions is recorded in the collection *Fratres Fraterrimi* (1568) and later epigrams. In 1539, assisted by the king, Buchanan fled to England to escape Cardinal David Beaton's persecution.

But English politics and religion were too confused and dangerous for Buchanan's taste, and he sailed to Paris. Thinking himself still pursued by Beaton, he accepted André de Gouveia's invitation to join the faculty of the Collège de Guyenne in Bordeaux. There his skill at encomiastic verse was soon enlisted to welcome Charles V on his way to the Low Countries. At the Collège (1539–1543?) Buchanan prepared student-performance Latin translations of Euripides' *Medea* (1544) and *Alcestis* (1556) and two original biblical tragedies, *Baptistes* (1577) and *Jephthes* (1554), in all of which he tried to draw his pupils away from popular dramatic forms and to instill classical models. In his *Essais*, Michel de Montaigne later recalled with pride that as a young student at the Collège he acted the major roles in these plays.

Toward the end of 1543 Buchanan was again in Paris, at the Collège du Cardinal Lemoine. In the years that followed he strengthened associations with leading humanists, poets, and patrons, such as Théodore de Bèze, Adrien Turnèbe, Lazare de Baïf, Mellin de Saint-Gelais, Jean de Gagnay, Cardinal Jean de Lorraine, and Cardinal de Guise. He also wrote occasional verse and tended to the 1544 publication of his *Medea* by Michel Vascosan. During the years 1545–1547 he revisited Bordeaux, again teaching at the Collège de Guyenne.

In 1547, perhaps (as he says in the *Vita*) to escape wars in Europe, Buchanan traveled to Portugal with a band of scholar friends, led by de Gouveia, to help found the Real Colègio das Artes in Coimbra. Sadly, the college fell victim to sordid academic dissension, culminating in a formal investigation into the religious convictions of its faculty. Accused of eating meat in Lent, of doubting the reality of the Eucharist, and, in general, of harboring Lutheran tendencies, Buchanan was arrested by the Lisbon Inquisition in August 1550. His astute testimony during trial, which came to light only in the 1890s, is now a valuable source of information concerning his beliefs and acquaintances. As penance he was confined during July–December 1551 to the monastery of San Bento, where he found the monks "neither unkindly nor lacking in general culture" — though "wholly ignorant of religious truth" (according to the James M. Aitken 1939 translation of *Vita*). While interned, Buchanan translated many of the biblical psalms into Latin verse, paraphrases that he completed and published to immediate acclaim in the mid 1560s. More than technical exercises – Buchanan himself suffered the "exile and unjust oppression" explored in psalms 88, 114, and 137, according to John Wall – the psalm paraphrases were prized especially for their metrical virtuosity and were reprinted well into the nineteenth century.

After his release in February 1552 Buchanan traveled to London, but he soon returned to Paris. There he taught at the Collège de Boncourt, possibly with Marc-Antoine Muret, and resumed friendships with members of the Pléiade, especially Joachim du Bellay. Buchanan's earlier erotic verse on the tawdry courtesan Leonora and the intractable nymph Neaera (*Epigrammatum Liber* 1) may have been a fashionable, neo-Catullan response to the Petrarchan tradition. Showing loftier influences of the Pléiade is the beautiful Horatian ode "Calendae Maiae," which transforms a transient pastoral into the promise of eternity (*Miscellaneorum Liber* 11):

> Salve fugacis gloria seculi,
> Salve secunda digna dies nota,
>   Salve vetustae vitae imago,
>   Et specimen venientis aevi.

(Hail, glory of a fleeting age, hail, day worthy of a favorable mark, hail, picture of a former life, and token of an age to come.)

Despite his apparent ease within high Catholic circles, scholars have questioned Buchanan's religious loyalties at this stage in his life. His own statements are inconclusive, since they are either defenses before the Inquisition or recollections from the refuge of Calvinist Scotland. There is evidence that in 1553–1554 absolution was obtained from the pope for Buchanan, who perhaps wished to repair the damage of his Lisbon experience, according to I. D. McFarlane in *Buchanan* (1981). In 1554 he published *Jephthes,* in which the keeping of vows and the offering of sacrifices are debated. But the play evidences Euripidean irony more than heresy. Also pointing to Buchanan's orthodoxy, Charles du Cossé, Comte de Brissac – the magnanimous soldier to whom *Jephthes* was dedicated – retained Buchanan as tutor to his son Timoléon. Nevertheless, the Huguenot intellectual Hubert Languet believed that at the time of his engagement by the *maréchal* (marshal), probably 1554, Buchanan was openly professing his Protestant faith, according to Languet's *Epistolae Secretae* (1699). In the *Vita* Buchanan says only that while serving Brissac in France and Italy, he had opportunity to give serious study to current theological issues. In any case he experienced no difficulties with French authorities and enjoyed no risky reputation as a reformer. Nor was he a radical in astronomy. His didactic poem *Sphaera* (1585-1586), begun during these years and addressed to the promising Timoléon, defends the centrality and immobility of Earth, while rejecting the revolutionary schemes of Copernicus and, in passages added later, of Tycho Brahe.

Buchanan continued to cultivate the French court. The 1556 Paris printing of his translation of *Alcestis* bore a laudatory preface to Marguerite de France, protectress of the Pléiade. In 1558 he published the ode *De Caleto . . . recepta,* celebrating the fall of Calais to François, Duc de Guise (revised and reprinted as *Miscellaneorum Liber* 1). In the same year he commemorated the marriage of Mary Stuart and the Dauphin François in an epithalamium distinguished more for expressions of Scottish nationalism than for any particular praise of the couple's virtues (*Silvae* 4).

After the death in 1560 of the queen regent, Mary of Lorraine, power in Scotland quickly settled into the hands of Knox and the Protestant lords. The next year Mary Stuart, now a young widow, returned from France to claim her native land. Buchanan also came home and soon joined the Church of Scotland, while adorning Mary's court as tutor, translator, and poet. His aulic verse included New Year gift poems (*Strenae*), masques, and encomiums, among them an epigram in which he dedicated his psalm paraphrases to the queen of Scots.

In 1565 Mary married Henry Stewart, Lord Darnley, a Catholic, but also a Lennox man, a clan to which Buchanan could claim tenuous kinship. Buchanan celebrated the dubious marriage in verse (*Miscellaneorum Liber* 35; *Pompae* 2), and, for the birth of their son James in 1566, he composed a "Genethliacon" (*Silvae* 7) remarkably lacking in the usual flattery; rather, it is replete with prescient exhortations and admonitions. Buchanan foresaw that only if the prince were educated to serve his people could he rule peacefully over Scotland and England; if brought up in the traditions of Catholic absolutism, James would be set against his subjects. Buchanan here departs from the conventional birthday poem to develop the voice of seer and humanist counselor, a voice heard most clearly in the three dedicatory epistles addressed to James VI in the 1570s. Meanwhile, the aging humanist made one last, brief visit to Paris in 1565-1566 and, urged by friends who had been circulating and collecting his

manuscripts for more than ten years, began to cooperate in the revision and printing of his psalm paraphrases and secular poems.

Political and educational posts in Scotland, however, hampered the increasingly retrospective work of the poet. Buchanan was a member of the General Assembly from 1563 to 1567, serving as moderator in 1567. He seems to have written his *Opinion Anent the Reformation of the Universitie of St. Andros* (1817), which recommends a rigorous preliminary program of classical languages, as a consequence of having been selected for a commission established in 1563 to improve the university. In 1566 Mary's half brother, the earl of Moray, also a member of the 1563 commission and the dedicatee of the published *Franciscanus,* nominated Buchanan to the principalship of Saint Leonard's College.

The murder of Darnley and the ensuing deposition of Mary in 1567 made Buchanan the premier propagandist of the Lennox faction. Accordingly, in 1568-1569 he accompanied Regent Moray to England for the conferences held to investigate the queen's conduct. In London he once again enjoyed court society, penning epigrams to Queen Elizabeth and Lady Cecil and dining with Roger Ascham. The contentious years subsequent to his return to Scotland in 1569 produced *Detectio Mariae Reginae Scotorum* (1571?), reiterating crimes itemized in the English hearings; *Ane Admonitioun Direct to the Trew Lordis* (1571), warning of the threat posed by the Hamiltons to James VI after Moray's assassination in January 1570; and the *Chamaeleon* (1710), a bitingly clever satire on the intriguing William Maitland of Lethington, lately allied with the disgraced queen's party: "Thair is a certane kynd of beist callit chamaeleon, engenderit in sic cuntreis as ye sone hes mair strenth in yan in this yle of Brettane the quhilk albeit it be small of corporance noghtyeless it is of ane strange nature the quhilk makis it to be na les celebrat and spoken of than sum beastis of greittar quantitie." Had he written more in his vigorous Scots, Buchanan would have been canonized among the founders of national literatures. Also as an aftermath of Moray's murder, the Privy Council directed Buchanan to resign from Saint Leonard's in order to take charge of the young king's education. Later in 1570 Regent Lennox appointed him director of Chancery and then keeper of the Privy Seal.

The publication in 1577 of Buchanan's early school drama *Baptistes,* on the execution of John the Baptist, was made opportune by the addition of an epistle to his pupil James VI, advising him pointedly of the torments suffered by tyrants. A similar dedi-

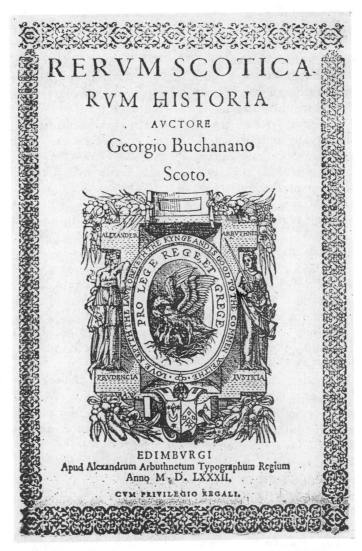

RERVM SCOTICA-
RVM HISTORIA
AVCTORE
Georgio Buchanano
Scoto.

EDIMBVRGI
Apud Alexandrum Arbuthnetum Typographum Regium
Anno M. D. LXXXII.
CVM PRIVILEGIO REGALI.

*Title page for Buchanan's longest work, an account of Scottish history
intended to guide James VI of Scotland (later James I of England)*

cation prefaces a more notorious work originating in the turbulent late 1560s. *De iure regni apud Scotos* (1579) is written as a dialogue between Buchanan and Thomas Maitland (William's younger brother) in which Buchanan defends the right of the Scottish people to resist tyranny. Set against the current absolutist doctrine, which was based on Scripture, Buchanan's theory of popular sovereignty — unlike the religious opposition of the Marian exiles Knox and Christopher Goodman (and of his own tragic hero Joannes Baptista) — appeals to natural law and civic history. As with Buchanan's works generally, *De iure regni* was neither deep nor essentially new (novelty was not a sixteenth-century disputant's boast), but was an articulate amalgam, sufficiently persuasive to be perceived as radical. Although the dialogue circulated in manuscript, it was not printed

until 1579 to avoid offending Queen Elizabeth when her favor was most needed. In 1584 the Scots Parliament condemned the treatise, and in 1683 it was publicly burned by Oxford University. Yet Buchanan's ideas, assimilated, for example, by Milton in his *Tenure of Kings and Magistrates* (1649), fortified Anglo-American political discourse.

In March 1579, after receiving a copy of *De iure regni* in London, Thomas Randolph, who had become Buchanan's friend while serving as Elizabeth's agent at the Scottish court, wrote to Peter Young, James VI's pedagogue: "callinge to mynde the notable actes of [Buchanan's] lyfe, his studie, his travayle, his danger, his wisdome, his learninge, and to be short, as muche as could be wished in a man; I thought the kinge . . . more happie that had Buchanan to his maister, then *Alexander the Great,* that had *Aristotell* his instructor" (from P. Hume Brown's *George Buchanan: Humanist and Reformer,* 1890). But the dream of Protestant liberals, such as Randolph, that Buchanan might raise a philosopher king soon evaporated, and the dedicatory epistle to Buchanan's longest and most maligned work, *Rerum Scoticarum Historia* (1582), could only pretend to hope that the political and moral lessons drawn from Scottish history would guide James VI where his tutor had failed. James Melville, Andrew Melville's nephew, records that in 1581, weakened by years of illness but still defiant, Buchanan was warned that his account of Mary's royal reinterment of David Rizzio would offend the king. He responded, "Tell me, man, giff I have tauld the treuthe?" Told "yis," Buchanan concluded, "I will byd his fead [enmity], and all his kins', then" (from *George Buchanan: Humanist and Reformer*). Published the next year, reprinted surreptitiously, banned and burned with *De iure regni,* inaccurate and biased, the *Rerum Scoticarum Historia* is the last great humanist history. Buchanan died 28 September 1582. His burial at Edinburgh's Greyfriars was well attended, but the location of the grave has long been uncertain.

On the Continent and in Britain, Buchanan's fame as a poet rested firmly on his undisputed gifts. When it concerned his politics, however, his reputation ranged from apostle of liberty to "raskal" (according to George Chalmers in a letter to David Laing, 6 March 1817) and opportunistic trimmer. Samuel Johnson's backhanded tribute – "the only man of greatness his country ever produced" – brings to mind the melancholy mix of achievement and regret that fashioned the Scotsman's life and times. Not quite forgotten in this century, the once-celebrated Latinist's accomplishments were commemorated by a spate of publications honoring the quatercentenary of his death. More promising, current investigations by Renaissance scholars into the relationship between belles lettres and power may again make Buchanan the subject of learned controversy.

Letters:

Epistolae, edited by James Oliphant (London: D. Brown & W. Taylor, 1711);

"Een Onuitgegeven Brief Van George Buchanan aan Philips van Marnix van Sint-Aldegonde," edited by Aloïs Gerlo, in *Mededelingen van de Kroninklijke Academie voor Wetenschappen, Letteren en Schone Kunsten van België, Klasse der Letteren, Academiae Analecta,* 45 (1983): 66–76.

Bibliographies:

David Murray, "Catalogue of Printed Books, Manuscripts, Charters, and Other Documents," in *George Buchanan: Glasgow Quatercentenary Studies, 1906,* edited by George Nielson (Glasgow: James Maclehose, 1907), pp. 393–542;

J. Maitland Anderson, "The Writings of Buchanan," in *George Buchanan: A Memorial, 1506–1906,* edited by D. A. Millar (Saint Andrews: W. C. Henderson, [1907]), pp. 166–185;

I. D. McFarlane, "Preliminary Check-List," in his *Buchanan* (London: Duckworth, 1981), pp. 490–518.

Biographies:

George Chalmers, *The Life of Thomas Ruddiman, A.M. . . . to Which Are Subjoined New Anecdotes of Buchanan* (London, 1794);

David Irving, *Memoirs of the Life and Writings of George Buchanan* (Edinburgh, 1817);

P. Hume Brown, *George Buchanan: Humanist and Reformer* (Edinburgh: David Douglas, 1890);

David MacMillan, *George Buchanan: A Biography* (Edinburgh: Morton, 1906);

James M. Aitken, *The Trial of George Buchanan before the Lisbon Inquisition* (Edinburgh: Oliver & Boyd, 1939);

I. D. McFarlane, *Buchanan* (London: Duckworth, 1981).

References:

James W. L. Adams, "The Renaisssance Poets: (2) Latin," in *Scottish Poetry: A Critical Survey,* edited by James Kinsley (London: Cassell, 1955), pp. 68–98;

James Boswell, *Boswell's Life of Johnson,* 4 volumes, edited by George Birbeck Hill, revised by L. F. Powell (Oxford: Clarendon, 1934);

Leicester Bradner, *Musae Anglicanae: A History of Anglo-Latin Poetry, 1500–1925* (New York: Modern Language Association, 1940);

J. H. Burns, "The Political Ideas of George Buchanan," *Scottish Historical Review,* 30 (April 1951): 60–68;

John Durkan, "George Buchanan: New Light on the Poems," *Bibliotheck,* 10, no. 1 (1980): 1–9;

Philip J. Ford, *George Buchanan: Prince of Poets* (Aberdeen: Aberdeen University Press, 1982);

Carl Fries, "Quellenstudien zu George Buchanan," *Neue Jahrbücher für das klassische Altertum, Geschichte und deutsche Litteratur und für Paedagogik,* 6 (1900): 177–192, 241–261;

W. Leonard Grant, "The Shorter Latin Poems of George Buchanan, 1506–1582," *Classical Journal*, 40 (March 1945): 331–348;

R. P. H. Green, "The Text of George Buchanan's *Psalm Paraphrases*," *Bibliotheck*, 13, no. 1 (1986): 3–29;

Hubert Languet, *Epistolae Secretae* (Halle, 1699);

Raymond Lebègue, *La Tragédie religieuse en France. Les débuts (1514–1573)* (Paris, 1929);

James MacQueen, "Scottish Latin Poetry," in *The History of Scottish Literature*, volume 1, edited by R. D. S. Jack and Cairns Craig (Aberdeen: Aberdeen University Press, 1988), pp. 213–226;

Roger A. Mason, "Rex Stoicus: George Buchanan, James VI, and the Scottish Polity," in *New Perspectives on the Politics and Culture of Early Modern Scotland,* edited by John Dwyer (Edinburgh: Donald, 1982), pp. 9–33;

I. D. McFarlane, "George Buchanan's Latin Poems from Script to Print: A Preliminary Survey," *Library*, fifth series 24 (December 1969): 277–332;

McFarlane, ed., *Acta Conventus Neo-Latini Sanctandreani: Proceedings of the Fifth International Congress of Neo-Latin Studies (1985)* (Binghamton, N.Y.: Medieval & Renaissance Texts & Studies, 1987);

D. A. Millar, ed., *George Buchanan: A Memorial, 1506–1906* (Saint Andrews: W. C. Henderson, [1907]);

John Milton, *Pro Populo Anglicano Defensio Secunda,* edited by Eugene J. Strittmatter, in *The Works of John Milton,* volume 8, edited by Frank Patterson (New York: Columbia University Press, 1933);

Michel de Montaigne, *Essais,* edited by Albert Thibaudet (Paris: Gallimard, 1950);

[George Nielson, ed.], *George Buchanan: Glasgow Quatercentenary Studies, 1906* (Glasgow: James Maclehose, 1907);

David Norbrook, "*Macbeth* and the Politics of Historiography," in *Politics of Discourse: The Literature and History of Seventeenth-Century England,* edited by Kevin Sharpe and Steven N. Zwicker (Berkeley: University of California Press, 1987), pp. 78–116;

James E. Phillips, "George Buchanan and the Sidney Circle," *Huntington Library Quarterly,* 12 (1948–1949): 23–55;

Sir Philip Sidney, *A Defence of Poetry,* in *Miscellaneous Prose,* edited by Katherine Duncan-Jones and Jan van Dorsten (Oxford: Clarendon, 1973), pp. 59–121;

D. F. S. Thomson, "George Buchanan: The Humanist in the Sixteenth-Century World," *Phoenix,* 4 (1950): 77–94;

H. R. Trevor-Roper, *George Buchanan and the Ancient Scottish Constitution, English Historical Review,* supplement 3 (1966);

John Wall, "The Latin Elegiacs of George Buchanan," in *Bards and Makars: Scottish Language and Literature: Medieval and Renaissance,* edited by Adam J. Aitken (Glasgow: University of Glasgow Press, 1977), pp. 184–193.

Papers:

Buchanan materials are at the British Library, Bibliothèque Nationale, National Library of Scotland, Bodleian Library, Edinburgh University Library, and in other research collections. I. D. McFarlane's *Buchanan* (1981) includes a checklist.

Sir John Cheke

(16 June 1514 – 13 September 1557)

Albert J. Geritz
Fort Hays State University

BOOKS: *The hurt of sedicion howe greueous it is to a commune welth,* anonymous (London: Printed by John Day, 1549; enlarged edition [London or Cambridge]: Printed by John Day & W. Seres, 1549);

De obitu doctissimi et Sanctissimi theologi Doctoris Martini Buceri, Regii in Celeberrima Cantabrigiensi Academia apud Anglos publice sacrarum literarum prelectoris epistolae duae (London, 1551);

De Pronvntiatione Graecae potissimum linguæ disputationes cum Stephano Wintoniensi Episcopo (Basel: Per Nicol. Episcopium juniorem, 1555).

Editions: "Letter to Edward VI," in *Nugae Antiquae: Being a Miscellaneous Collection of Original Papers in Prose and Verse, Written in the Reigns of Henry VIII, Edward VI, Mary, Elizabeth, James I,* edited by Sir John Harington (London: W. Frederick, 1769), pp. 71–74;

The Gospel According to Saint Matthew and Part of the First Chapter of the Gospel According to Saint Mark Translated into English from Greek, with Original Notes by Sir John Cheke, edited by James Goodwin (London: W. Pickering, 1843);

"Sir John Cheke's *The Hurt of Sedition:* A Critical Edition," 2 volumes, edited by Joan Eileen Mueller, Ph.D. dissertation, Ohio State University, 1959;

De Pronuntiatione Graecae Linguae, selected and edited by R. C. Alston (Menston, U.K.: Scolar Press, 1968);

The Hurt of Sedition, facsimile edition (Menston, U.K.: Scolar Press, 1971).

TRANSLATIONS: Saint John Chrysostom, *D. Joannis Chrysostomi, Homilae Duae, nunc Primum in lucem editatae, et ad Serenise Angliae Regem latinae factae* (London, 1543);

Leo V, *Leonis Imperatoris, De Bellico Apparatu Liber* (Basel, 1554).

Learning, politics, and religion – forces that combined in the decade of his birth to produce in

Sir John Cheke (portrait by an unknown artist; from Paul Johnson, Elizabeth I: A Study in Power and Intellect, *1974)*

Cambridge the revival of classical learning of which Sir John Cheke was to become the acknowledged leader – combined as well to determine his fate. Ironically, what renown Cheke earned resulted not from his official and public duties at court, but from the impact of his teaching and personality in his earlier days at Saint John's College. As a humanist teacher called to serve the king, Cheke exemplified the Ciceronian ideal that Renaissance humanists from Thomas More to John Milton held in so much esteem. His knowledge and appreciation of the classics for their wisdom, style, and literary excellence, his views about using native English words rather than borrowing from foreign tongues, and his emphasis upon simplicity and naturalness in writing – whether classical or English – constitute the legacy he left as a translator, critic, and author.

The oldest child and only son of Peter and Agnes Cheke, he was born in the parish of Saint Mary the Great in Cambridge during the year Desiderius Erasmus completed his lectures in Greek at the new college of Saint John's, which Cheke was to make famous as a center of learning in the first half of the sixteenth century. As the son of a professional official of the university, John Cheke was, if only indirectly, exposed to the school's activities. Reputed to have had a grammatical education under John Morgan, M.A., he was, at the age of fifteen, admitted to Saint John's College in 1529.

Cheke's aptness for learning soon attracted the attention of George Day, master of Saint John's, and he took his B.A. in 1530 and his M.A. in 1533. Sometime in those early years he gained the patronage of Dr. William Butts, who may have brought him to the notice of Henry VIII, who chose Cheke and Sir Thomas Smith (one of Cheke's most important friends) to be his scholars.

During his years at Saint John's, Cheke was chiefly responsible for improving the state of classical learning, particularly Greek, in his college. Fundamental to his thinking was his notion of the core of learning all men should possess. As Roger Ascham, one of his pupils, writes in *The Schoolmaster* (1570):

> I have heard worthy Master Cheke many times say: I would have a good student pass and journey through all authors both Greek and Latin, but he that will dwell in these few books only – first, in God's holy Bible, and then join with it, Tully in Latin, Plato, Aristotle, Xenophon, Isocrates, and Demosthenes in Greek – must needs prove an excellent man.

Clearly, these seven recommendations for reading were not made to encourage a single philosophy or writing style, but primarily for their wisdom, for the public and private virtues they extol. Fostering a Christian existence bolstered by the wisdom of antiquity, this list epitomizes humanist training for the good life. At the same time Cheke's list is diverse, providing an array of philosophical themes, precepts with examples, and various types of eloquence. These materials will contribute to making an "excellent man." In addition Cheke had definite views on how these materials should be used, ideas as to how the most good could be obtained from

these "few books," and the remaining concepts he taught deal largely with these methods.

Of Cheke's theories concerning techniques, perhaps the most famous is imitation, the details of which Ascham sets out in book 2 of *The Schoolmaster*. The idea of imitation was nothing new; what is new in Cheke's view is not which or how many models should be followed; that, as Ascham notes, has been too much the preoccupation. Cheke's new emphasis is on method: by analyzing parallels or by imitating passages found in the classics, the student may derive the principles from which a classical writer worked and then be guided by them in writing well himself, whether in a learned or his native tongue. Other elements of imitation include comparing the writer's precepts and examples, for the goal of imitation was not merely cultivating writing styles, but understanding and appreciating literature itself.

Such attitudes cannot be separated from another point about which Cheke felt strongly: developing an ear for language by hearing it read properly and by becoming skilled in its correct pronunciation. He read aloud from the Greek classics, a practice he valued and continued throughout life. Because of his concern for developing sensitivity to and appreciation of a writer's manner as well as his matter, he (and Smith) became involved in the controversy over the correct pronunciation of Greek at Cambridge in 1542. Published years later in Basel, his *De Pronuntiatione Graecae potissimum linguae* (1555) presents his position in this dispute with Stephen Gardiner, bishop of Winchester. Although Gardiner stopped Cheke's reformation of the English pronunciation of Greek, his method – based on how the ancients had probably pronounced this language – ultimately prevailed and is now used by modern scholars of Greek, a fact affirming his judgment.

Cheke recommended models, emphasized imitation, defined types of eloquence, and insisted upon correct pronunciation not only for the appreciation of classical languages and literature, but also for the sake of English and English writing styles. Indeed, his constant concern to teach sensitivity to kinds of language, types of rhetoric, levels of eloquence, and appropriateness of vocabulary led him to formulate his most distinguished, original conceptions regarding language and literature.

One of these conceptions, Cheke's realization that only "natural" language could produce vitality and endurance in writing, undoubtedly guided him to his position in favor of "pure" English, for which he is perhaps best remembered today. Thirteen years after he left Cambridge he most concisely ex-

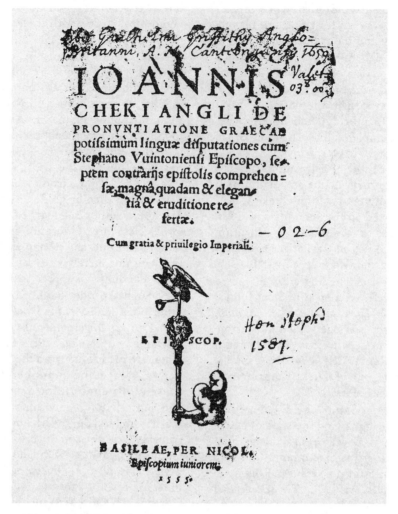

*Title page for Cheke's guide to the pronunciation of Greek, written in reaction to a 1542
dispute at Cambridge*

pressed this attitude in a letter (dated 16 July 1557) to Thomas Hoby and subsequently appended to Hoby's 1561 translation of Baldassare Castiglione's *Courtier:*

> I am of this opinion that our own tongue should be written clean and pure, unmixed and unmangled with borrowing of other tongues, wherein if we take not heed by time, ever borrowing and never paying, she shall be fain to keep her house as bankrupt. For then does our tongue naturally and praisably utter her meaning, when she borrows no counterfeitness of other tongues to attire herself withal, but uses plainly her own, with such shift as nature, craft, experience, and following of other excellencies does lead her unto, and if she want at anytime (as being imperfect she must) yet let her borrow with such bashfulness that it may appear that, if either the mold of our own tongue could serve us to fashion a word of our own, or if the old denisoned words could content and ease this need, we would not boldly venture of unknown words.

Although Cheke's own scholarly writing was done exclusively in Latin, enabling it to reach a wider, frequently Continental, scholarly audience, he was at the same time aware of the necessity to strengthen the fabric of vernacular writing. His use of "natural" language and his skill in writing English prose can be seen in his only extensive English work, *The Hurt of Sedition* (1549), and his personal correspondence. In the rising battle between sixteenth-century theories for enriching the English language, Cheke's stand was outspokenly for English "unmixed and unmangled" and, when absolutely unavoidable, for judicious borrowing from other languages, but against conscious efforts to introduce foreign coinages, such as those of Thomas Elyot and other inkhornists.

Then, too, at about this same time, Cheke further indicated his stand on the adequacy of the vernacular by starting a translation of the New Testa-

ment in "pure" English, completing the Gospel of
Saint Matthew and a portion of Saint Mark's. Although the fragment was not published until 1843,
it is interesting as another example of his efforts to
enrich English, not from foreign sources but, as he
stipulates, from "the mold of our own tongue."
Comparing the vocabulary and style of Cheke's
translation of Matthew's Gospel with those of John
Wycliffe, William Tyndale, and the Authorized
Version shows how scrupulously he avoided borrowed words and how closely his version approxi-
mated "the actual speech of the common people,"
for whom this emphatically vernacular translation
was intended, according to Hugh Sykes Davies.
Cheke's pervasive directness and simplicity and his
use of common English words are illustrated in his
translation of Matthew 6:19–21:

> Hord not yourself up greet hoords on the earth, wheer
> nother moth nor rust can wast them, and wheer theeves
> mai dig unto them and steel them. But hoord yourselves
> hoords in heaven, wheer nother moth nor rust can wast
> them, and wheer theves can not dig unto them nor steel
> them. For wheer your treasur is theer be your harts.

Similarly incidental to Cheke's stature as a
theorist is the fact that this translation is written in a
revised orthography that he and Smith devised in
an attempt to standardize the then-chaotic state of
English spelling. Generally Cheke felt that letters
without sound should be thrown out and that letters
should be added to make words express their
sounds more accurately. Therefore, he doubles long
vowels (*taak* for *take*), discards the final *e* (*wast* for
waste), and always uses *i* for *y*. Although "it is not
our system or that of most of his contemporaries . . . it is a system and he observed it," Albert C.
Baugh states in *History of the English Language* (1957).

These central conceptions – study of the classics for wisdom, for stylistic models, and for an appreciation of literature; and emphasis upon simplicity and naturalness in writing and speech, whether
classical or vernacular – preoccupied Cheke at
Cambridge from 1529 to 1544, and these constitute
the legacy he left, with the inspiration of his teaching, to his followers there. By his thirtieth year
Cheke had succeeded in cultivating and bringing to
fruition the seeds of humanism planted in England
by earlier humanists, such as William Grocyn, John
Colet, Thomas Linacre, Erasmus, More, and John
Fisher. His good husbandry did not go unnoticed.
On the foundation of the Regius Professorships in
1540, he was nominated to the Greek chair he continued to occupy until October 1551. About the beginning of 1544 he was elected public orator of the

university; and on 6 May 1544 he was awarded
from the court a grant of the canonry and prebend
at King's College (now Christ Church), Henry
VIII's college at Oxford.

Such recognitions from university and court,
however, only foreshadowed greater recognition
soon to come, and they marked the end of a successful academic era and the beginning of involvement
in public life. In early July 1544 the regency (established by Henry VIII to rule at home during his absence in France) under Queen Catherine (Parr), an
ardent reformer, appointed Cheke to tutor Prince
Edward. The honor and position he received with
this appointment did not come uninvited. In 1543
he had dedicated to Henry VIII a Latin translation
of two Greek homilies by Saint John Chrysostom,
the first work of the young scholar to appear in
print and reputedly the first book to be printed
using Greek type in England. About the same time,
he was working on a Latin translation of Leo V's
Greek books on war policies, similarly dedicated to
the king, as was his translation, again from Greek to
Latin, of Plutarch's "On Superstition." Cheke never
lost Henry's good grace, and his retention as
Edward's tutor at the young king's accession in January 1547 shows that the avidly Protestant Seymour protectorate endorsed his influence upon Edward. In his only extant writing to Edward, Cheke
exhibits his attitudes about his responsibility for
and his philosophy of the education of governors;
he also stresses his deepest convictions about blending classical and Christian virtues. As Milton's sonnet so aptly declares, "Sir John Cheke . . . taught'st
Cambridge, and King Edward Greek" ("Sonnet XI:
On the Detraction Which Followed upon My Writing Certain Treatises").

Cheke's other activities during these years
suggest that he filled an increasingly powerful and
consequently hazardous position. Pertinent records
begin with May 1547, when he married Margaret,
daughter of Richard Hill, who had been sergeant of
the wine cellar to Henry VIII. In October 1547 he
sat in the House of Commons for the Borough of
Blechingly, Surrey. In January 1548 Ascham urged
William Cecil to promote the new learning by rec-
ommending Cheke as a candidate for provost of
King's College, Cambridge. In February 1548 Ascham wrote Cheke asking him to do what he could
to secure for him the tutorship of Princess Elizabeth. Evidence of Cheke's growing importance in
public matters may also be found in lists of official
commissions, where his name begins to appear frequently. For instance, in November 1548 he was
one of seven dignitaries serving on a commission to

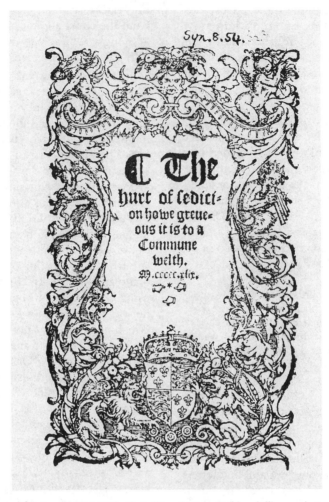

Title page for Cheke's plea for public order, prompted by rebellions against the protectorate government of Edward VI

visit Eton College and Cambridge University to execute certain instructions and appoint separate colleges at Cambridge for the study of civil law and medicine.

Circumstances of Cheke's life from January 1549 until his death in 1557 cannot be separated from political unrest and upheaval during the last years of Edward's reign and following Mary's accession. Although records show little about his activities in these years, the implications for him and his work in the times' occurrences are clear, and the few facts about his life are greatly elaborated when set against the background of the period's religious, economic, and political strife. As early as 1547, when he represented the protectorate in the Commons by sitting for Blechingly in the first Edwardian Parliament, Cheke's life became complicated with politics. From 1549 on, he lived uneasily between crises and successes.

Apparently the year 1549 began well, with Cheke among the favored to whose servants the king gave New Year's rewards, but January held many fates in the balance, Cheke's among them. According to his own statement, 11 January was a day of disgrace and near loss of office. He gives no reasons, but in that month the protector's brother, Thomas Seymour, lord high admiral, was imprisoned for dishonesty and recalcitrance, having attempted, among other alleged crimes against the realm, to influence the young king for his own gain and power. In subsequent testimony against Admiral Seymour, Cheke was many times mentioned as having been considered by Seymour as a ready way to Edward's affections. Seymour himself is reported to have tried to purchase influence in the royal household by means of gifts, including one to Cheke, who refused to take it. Cheke, in a declaration of 20 February 1549, stated that the lord admiral had indeed tried to persuade him to use his influence with the king in order to procure power for Seymour from the House of Lords. Cheke refused to cooperate and, according to Edward's testimony against Seymour, implied that the king also did right not to be influenced by Seymour. In addition to the suspicion cast upon him by Seymour's machinations, Cheke had other problems at court at this time. In a letter to the wife of the protector, the duchess of Somerset, Cheke asked her to forgive his wife for some offense she had given the duchess at court. It is impossible to say which of these events, if either, led to Cheke's temporary disgrace and withdrawal from court.

In June 1549 came the first serious popular protest against protectorate governmental policies. Insurrections began in Devon and Cornwall and spread from the southwest to the northeast, common people rising first for religious, then for economic reasons. By midsummer the political situation was grave and provoked Cheke, probably from Cambridge, to write *The Hurt of Sedition,* his vernacular plea to the common people for order. A first-hand account of the rebellion from his Cambridge friend Matthew Parker may have moved him to write it. Since the tract was written for the emergency, the shorter of the two 1549 texts may well have been sent from Cambridge to John Day's shop in London, where it was hastily set up to be distributed to rebelling commoners. Cheke, possibly from Cambridge or London, may have overseen the second 1549 edition, with its enlarged and cleaner text. If he wrote the treatise purely from personal conviction, if he felt he was doing the state a service adequate to reinstate him at court, or if he had both these motives or others, he may well have been called back to London at the request of the same powers he had earlier offended. On the other hand, he may have been commissioned from the beginning to write the treatise, or urged by friends at court, such as Thomas Cranmer, archbishop of Canterbury, to employ his rhetorical abilities to argue the case against rebellion.

The treatise presented the philosophy of civil obedience that most religious and political thinkers of Cheke's day embraced; and, whether or not it was officially commissioned, it functioned as propaganda for the Crown. While it is unlikely that the tract in any way was instrumental in halting the rebellion, it played its part in Cheke's own situation, for its contribution to the cause of peace was probably helpful in reinstating him at court. The significance of the rebellions to the state of English politics is, however, clear, and Cheke's fortunes were im-

plicitly tied to the attitudes and activities of vying powers behind the throne. The main result of these rebellions was to discredit Somerset and to exalt John Dudley, Earl of Warwick.

As the work's subtitle, "The True Subject to the Rebel," implies, the tract was designed as an address in which Cheke successfully employed the formal classical oration in a popular plea for the godly order of quiet. Although it was never delivered as such, it provided Cheke's successors with a rhetorical model through which traditional arguments for reasonable, peaceful political action could be applied. Old and new themes – from the Great Chain of Being and moderation to civil disobedience and Protestantism – are met in it. Cheke also tried to analyze the rebel mind and to treat rebellion in itself as a causal factor. That he should have approached his subject this way is not surprising. By training a humanist scholar, he was one of those public-spirited individuals who felt obligated to understand the forces at work in society in hopes that, through understanding them, change might take place.

Following Aristotle's *Rhetoric, The Hurt of Sedition* uses the design of the seven-part oration to prove what ought or ought not to be. Logical, pathetic, ethical, and nonartistic proofs are employed with subtlety, and each word has been carefully calculated to have its effect. As Aristotle is the classical theorist whose precepts Cheke chose to follow, so Demosthenes is the classical orator whose practice he extols. Like Demosthenes, he presents his insight into the political situation in clear, plain, simple speech so the common man might see the point and feel the urgency of the case. Cheke not only avoids learned language, he consciously chooses to use colloquial diction and purposely selects homely and natural images. Ideas about the dangers that civil disorder inflicts upon a person and images about the body and disease permeate the work. This question about the number of vagabonds who will roam the country after the civil war vividly exemplifies Cheke's rhetorical skills.

> Is it not then daily heard how men be not only pursued but utterly spoiled, and few may ride safe by the king's way except they ride strong, not so much for fear of their goods . . . but also for danger of their life, which every man loves?

Such examples could be multiplied, and almost every page of *The Hurt of Sedition* develops logically and emotionally in terms of constructions embodying the ideas and style that define Cheke.

Woodcut depicting the demise of a rebel, in the first edition of The Hurt of Sedition

During the next two years – from Somerset's overthrow in October 1549 through his four-month imprisonment in the Tower, his release, and his uneasy return to power shared with Warwick – Cheke became increasingly concerned with ecclesiastical reforms. In October 1549 he was one of thirty-two commissioners named to examine old ecclesiastical laws and to suggest revisions. He is listed among the "divines" Cranmer appointed to the commission; and, at the commission's renewal in February 1552, he is again listed among the divines. (Apparently Cheke had taken orders sometime prior to selection of the first commission's members.) In January 1550 he was named to a commission with divines, such as Cranmer, Nicholas Ridley, Hugh Latimer, and John Ponet, to investigate heresies, to arrest heretics, and to punish those opposed to the *Book of Common Prayer*.

Cheke was a friend of foreign reformers living in England, such as Martin Bucer, regius professor of divinity at Cambridge in 1549, and Peter Martyr, divinity professor at Oxford in 1548. At Bucer's death early in 1551, he edited a collection of memorials written for him, including letters from Cheke to Martyr and Walter Haddon about Bucer as a great Protestant thinker, entitled *De obitu doctissimi . . . Doctoris Martini Buceri . . . epistolae duae*. At the same time, he tried to secure the dead theologian's library for the king's collection. In May 1551 his work on the king's behalf was rewarded with extensive grants in Suffolk, Essex, Norfolk, and Lincolnshire. In other records Cheke is mentioned in a minor court quarrel, reformation activities abroad, and involvement in the ecclesiastical commission charged with the reform of canon law. On 11 October 1551 his service was again rewarded, for on that day he was knighted.

Circumstances surrounding Cheke's knighthood implicate him with the political clique Warwick headed. In a move to overthrow Somerset, Warwick found it expedient to remove courtiers sympathetic with the protector's policies and to surround himself with powerful friends. To this end he raised his relatives and friends to knighthood and peerage, and he himself, without valid claim to the title, was made duke of Northumberland. Among the friends knighted was Cheke, and it is difficult not to conclude that his rise, coincident as it is with the fall of his first patron, Somerset, suggests timeserving; but perhaps his Protestantism and devotion to the humanist ideal of service to the state blinded him to Northumberland's treachery.

On 2 June 1553 Cheke was appointed one of the secretaries of state and sworn in as a member of the Privy Council because Northumberland desired to strengthen the council's Protestant element. On 6 July 1553 Edward VI died; the news was kept secret for three days in order to give the council time to complete the plan and, if possible, to capture Mary. On the tenth a declaration made Lady Jane Dudley queen and ladies Mary and Elizabeth illegitimate. To zealous Protestants such as Cheke, any means were acceptable for preventing the return to Catholicism that Mary's accession clearly meant. For Cheke even treason was justified in order to make Protestantism victorious.

On 11 July, Mary's challenge, requiring the council to proclaim her title, arrived; they replied (Cheke reputedly drafted the answer) with defiance. Throughout the kingdom opposition to Northumberland grew, while Mary fast won support. Within a week Northumberland was undone, and on 19 July, Mary was proclaimed queen in the presence of court dignitaries, Cheke included. On 28 July, his property already being inventoried and his servants removed, Cheke followed Northumberland to the Tower. Thus, his political career ended; ironically, the man who had written an outspoken denunciation of rebellion ended his service to the state legally guilty of treason.

After two months of imprisonment Cheke was released, and on 13 September 1553 the queen gave him a gift of one hundred pounds. At this time she and her government placed no pressure on Cheke to renounce his Protestantism. Fortunately he was not retained in the Tower longer, for Mary's popularity declined rapidly and she reacted with unbending single-mindedness against her religious and political opponents.

From his manor of Stoke near Clare, Suffolk, Cheke implored the kindness of Lord William Paget. Perhaps out of compassion Paget was instrumental in obtaining travel privileges and may have helped to secure the official pardon of 28 April 1554. Cheke's reasons for leaving England are clear: not only was it unsafe for him to remain within the increasingly intolerant queen's reach, but abroad he could be active with reformers there. Although his wife was sick, he felt that his family could gain little by his staying, so he asked his wife's stepfather, Sir John Mason, to care for her and their children.

After his stay in Calais, Cheke traveled to Basel, one refuge of Marian exiles, and later went to Padua, where he joined Hoby and other Englishmen. In spite of letters asking for leniency and assistance for his family, he was probably not interested in returning home to launch a more direct plea, for reformers had become anathema to Mary. In spring 1555, however, he decided to go north to Caldero, where he joined Hoby and continued his journey north. By October 1555 he had arrived in Strasbourg, a city second only to Geneva as a stronghold of Protestantism on the Continent. On 12 March 1556 he was still (or again) in Strasbourg, but within the week he was betrayed into a trap, kidnapped, and returned to England and the Tower.

From all sides came accusations; and, under pressure to recant, Cheke began to break, for the alternative to recanting was the heretic's punishment – death at the stake. By 15 July he had been won, for on that day he made a written statement of his belief in the real presence in the Eucharist and accompanied it with a plea that this document should stand as adequate indication that he had complied. He was not removed from the Tower immediately but was kept there into September, perhaps until early October, writing and rewriting his recantation until it embraced all materials that Cardinal Reginald Pole, John Feckenham (dean of Saint Paul's), and the queen demanded, including admissions that his most grievous offense was teaching his erroneous views to King Edward and other youths.

His vast properties had been gradually granted to others, and in return he was given land in Somersetshire and an out-of-the-way manor in Devon. Perhaps authorities hoped he would leave London for the remote West Country, where he would be safely out of touch with those sympathetic to reform. Cheke did not oblige such hopes; in fact, he might have been able to get word to his friends on the Continent that his faith was bent, not broken. He remained in London, where he died on 13 September 1557 at the age of forty-three.

Cheke's influence is difficult to estimate. As a humanist scholar he was obviously responsible for bringing the value of the classics to the attention of his students and a wider audience; this he did through his philosophy, methods of teaching, and Latin translations of Greek words. In fact, he was one of the chief forces in moving English scholars away from major concern with Latin writers to concern with Greek authors. His impact as an educator lived on in his students and others, such as Thomas Wilson, who acknowledged their debt to him. Although he wrote little in English, his views about using native English words rather than borrowing from foreign tongues epitomized "purist" opinions upon which direction the vernacular should take during those years of so much linguistic and literary change. These notions passed on to Edmund Spenser to find one of their fullest expressions in the preface to *The Shepheardes Calender* (1579), which reveals a nationalistic love of the mother tongue that incenses the poet against borrowed, foreign expressions. To the extent that elements of Henrician and Edwardian politics and religion with which he was involved had impact on Elizabethan and later politics and religion, he shared in those developments. With such significant roles in the learning, politics, and religion of his times, it is surprising that Sir John Cheke has not received more attention in the study of sixteenth-century England.

Biography:

John Strype, *The Life of the Learned Sir John Cheke, Knight, First Instructor, Afterwards Secretary of State to King Edward VI. A New Edition, Corrected by the Author* (London: J. Wyat, 1705; reprinted, New York: Burt Franklin, 1974).

References:

Roger Ascham, *English Works,* edited by William Aldis Wright (Cambridge: Cambridge University Press, 1904);

Charles Barber, *Early Modern English* (London: Deutsch, 1976), pp. 90–93, 114–115;

Albert C. Baugh, *History of the English Language* (New York: Appleton-Century-Crofts, 1957), pp. 250–251, 260–261, 276–277;

Baldassare Castiglione, *The Book of the Courtier . . . Done into English by Sir Thomas Hoby anno 1561,* edited by Ernest Rhys (New York: Dutton, 1928);

Hugh Sykes Davies, "Sir John Cheke and the Translation of the Bible," *Essays and Studies,* new series 5 (1952): 1–12;

Arthur B. Ferguson, *The Articulate Citizen and the English Renaissance* (Durham: Duke University Press, 1965), pp. 274–278;

Robert Bruce Florian, "Sir John Cheke, Tudor Tutor," Ph.D. dissertation, West Virginia University, 1973;

Anne Drury Hall, "Tudor Prose Style: English Humanists and the Problem of a Standard," *English Literary Renaissance,* 7 (Autumn 1977): 267–296;

Edward E. Halle, Jr., "Ideas on Rhetoric in the Sixteenth Century," *PMLA,* 18, no. 3 (1903): 424–444;

Richard Foster Jones, *The Triumph of the English Language: A Survey of Opinions Concerning the Vernacular from the Introduction of Printing to the Restoration* (Stanford: Stanford University Press, 1953), pp. 102–145;

W. K. Jordan, *Edward VI: The Threshold of Power: The Dominance of the Duke of Northumberland* (London: George Allen, 1970), pp. 406–409;

Jordan, *Edward VI: The Young King* (Cambridge, Mass.: Harvard University Press, 1968), pp. 41–45;

John N. King, *English Reformation Literature: The Tudor Origins of the Protestant Tradition* (Princeton: Princeton University Press, 1982), pp. 23–25, 138–139, 171;

C. S. Lewis, *English Literature in the Sixteenth Century, Excluding Drama* (Oxford: Clarendon, 1954), pp. 210, 236, 276, 282–284;

David Loades, *The Tudor Court* (London: B. T. Batsford, 1986), pp. 120–125;

Gerard Longbain, ed., *The Foundation of the University of Cambridge, with a Catalogue of the Principal Founders and Special Benefactors of All the Colleges, and Total Number of Students, Magistrates, and Officers Therein Being* (London, 1651);

John F. McDiarmid, "Sir John Cheke's Protestant Ciceronianism and Its Background," *Proceedings of the PMR Conference: Annual Publication of the Patristic, Mediaeval, and Renaissance Conference,* 10 (1985): 113–125;

Herbert Merritt, "The Vocabulary of Sir John Cheke's Partial Version of the Gospels," *Journal of English and Germanic Philology,* 39 (1940): 450–455;

John Milton, *Complete Poems and Major Prose,* edited by Merritt Y. Hughes (New York: Odyssey, 1957), p. 143;

Walter Ludwig Nathan, *Sir John Cheke und der englische Humanismus* (Bonn: Rheania-Verlag, 1928);

Alvin Vos, "Humanistic Standards of Diction in the Inkhorn Controversy," *Studies in Philology,* 73 (October 1976): 376–396;

Shoichi Watanabe, "On Sir John Cheke," *Renaissance Bulletin,* 9 (1982): 1–4.

Papers:

The manuscript for Cheke's translation of Plutarch's "De Superstitione" is at the Bodleian Library.

Thomas Churchyard

(1520? – April 1604)

Carmel Gaffney
Northern Territory University, Australia

BOOKS: *Dauy Dycars dreame* (London: Printed by R. Lant, 1552?);

A myrrour for man where in he shall see the myserable state of thys worlde (London: Printed by T. Raynald for R. Toye, circa 1552);

The contention bettwyxte Churchyeard and Camell, vpon Dauid Dycers dreame (London: Printed by O. Rogers for M. Loblee, 1560);

Churchyardes farewell (London: Printed for E. Russell, 1566);

Churchyardes lamentacion of freyndshyp (London: Printed by T. Colwell for Nicolas Wyer, 1566);

A farewell cauld, Churcheyeards, rounde. From the courte to the cuntry growND (London: Printed by W. Gryffith, 1566);

A greatter thanks, for Churchyardes welcome home (London: Printed by A. Lacy for A. Pepwel, 1566);

Come bring in Maye with me: A discourse of rebellion (London: Printed by W. Griffith, 1570);

The epitaphe of the honorable earle of Penbroke (London: Printed by W. Gryffith, 1570);

The firste parte of Churchyardes chippes, contayning twelue seuerall labours (London: Printed by T. Marshe, 1575);

A discourse of the queenes maiesties entertainement in Suffolk and Norffolk (London: Printed by H. Bynneman, 1578);

A lamentable, and pitifull description, of the wofull warres in Flaunders (London: Printed by H. Bynnemann for R. Newberie, 1578);

A prayse, and reporte of maister M. Forboishers voyage to Meta Incognita (London: Printed by J. Kingston for A. Maunsell, 1578);

A generall rehearsall of warres, called Churchyardes choise (London: Printed by J. Kingston for E. White, 1579);

The miserie of Flaunders, calamitie of Fraunce, misfortune of Portugall (London: Printed by J. Kingston for A. Maunsell, 1579);

The moste true reporte of James Fitz Morrice death, with a brief discourse of rebellion (London: Printed by J. Kingston for E. White, 1579?);

A light bondell of liuly discourses called Churchyardes charge, presented as a newe yeres gifte to the earle of Surrie (London: Printed by J. Kingston, 1580);

A plaine or moste true report of a daungerous seruice, by English men, & other soldiours, for the takyng of Macklin (London: Printed by J. Kingston for J. Perin, 1580);

A pleasaunte laborinth called Churchyardes chance, framed on fancies (London: Printed by J. Kingston, 1580);

A warning for the wise. Written of the late earthquake in London the .6. of April 1580 (London: J. Allde and N. Lyng, 1580);

A Scourge for Rebels: Wherin are many notable seruices truly set out, and thorowly discoursed of, with euerie particular point touching the troubles of Ireland (London: Printed by T. Dawson for T. Cadman, 1584);

The epitaph of sir Phillip Sidney (London: Printed by G. Robinson for T. Cadman, 1586);

The worthines of Wales: wherein are more then a thousand seuerall things rehearsed (London: Printed by G. Robinson for T. Cadman, 1587);

A sparke of frendship and warme goodwill (London: Printed by T. Orwin, 1588);

A reuyuing of the deade by verses that foloweth: by the examples of king Henry the eight (London: Printed by E. Allde for E. White, 1591);

A feast full of sad cheere (London: W. Holme, 1592);

A handeful of gladsome verses, giuen to the queens maiesty at Woodstocke (Oxford: J. Barnes, 1592);

Churchyards challenge (London: J. Wolfe, 1593);

A pleasant conceite penned in verse. Presented on new-yeeres day last, to the queenes maiestie. 1593. (London: Printed by R. Warde, 1593);

A musicall consort of heauenly harmonie called Churchyards charitie (London: Printed by A. Hatfield for W. Holme, 1595);

Thomas Churchyard's coat of arms

The honor of the lawe (London: Printed by A. Hatfield for W. Holme, 1596);

A pleasant discourse of court and wars: with a replication to them both (London: Printed by A. Hatfield for W. Holme, 1596);

A sad and solemne funerall, of sir F. Knowles (London: Printed by A. Hatfield for W. Holme, 1596);

Welcome home of the noble and worthie earle of Essex, as a new-yeres gift (London: Printed by E. Bollifant for M. Lownes, 1598);

A wished reformacion of wicked rebellion (London: Printed by T. Este, 1598);

The fortunate farewel to the most forward and noble earle of Essex (London: Printed by E. Bollifant for W. Wood, 1599);

Churchyards good will. Sad and heavy verses, in the nature of an epitaph, for the archbishop of Canterbury (London: Printed by S. Stafford, 1604);

Sorrowfull verses made on the death of our lady queene Elizabeth (London, 1604?).

Editions and Collections: *How Thomas Wolsey Did Arise . . . and How He Fell down into Great Disgrace,* in *The mirour for magistrates,* edited by

John Higgins (London: Printed by H. Marsh for T. Marsh, 1587);

A Sad and Solemne Funerall of the Right Honorable Sir Francis Knowles, Knight, edited by Thomas Park, *Heliconia,* 2 (1815) — includes *Churchyard's Good Will;*

Churchyard's Chips concerning Scotland, edited by George Chalmers (London: Longman, 1817);

Churchyard's Misery of Flanders, edited by Henry W. Adnitt (Shrewsbury: Adnitt & Nauton, 1876);

The Worthiness of Wales, Publications of the Spenser Society, no. 20 (Manchester: C. E. Simms, 1876);

Tragedy of Cardinal Wolsey, in George Cavendish, *The Life of Cardinal Wolsey* (London: G. Routledge & Sons / New York: Dutton, 1885);

The Siege of Edinburgh Castle and *Morton's Tragedy,* in *Satirical Poems of the Time of the Reformation,* edited by James Cranstoun, Scottish Text Society, no. 24, appendixes 1 & 2 (Edinburgh: W. Blackwood & Sons, 1891–1893);

The First Part of Churchyard's Chips (Menston & London: Scolar, 1973);

Thomas Churchyard's Thunder on the Right, edited by Franklin B. Williams, *English Literary Renaissance,* 3 (Winter 1973): 380–399;

Lamentable and Pitiful Description of the Woeful Wars in Flanders, English Experience, no. 790 (Amsterdam: Theatrum Orbis Terrarum / Norwood, N.J.: W. J. Johnson, 1976);

A Sparke of Frendship and Warme Goodwill, facsimile edition (London: Wynkyn de Worde Society, 1978).

With its preoccupations of war, propaganda, and moral exhortations, Thomas Churchyard's poetry and prose won him few tributes from his contemporary writers; but from 1575 to his death his dedications read like a "Who's Who" of Elizabethan nobles and influential people: even Queen Elizabeth I accepted them. In the past four hundred years only an occasional voice has been raised in his defense, but such praise is not substantiated by close textual analysis. What fascinates the reader, then, is not Churchyard's literary skill, but the manner in which he managed to survive as a minor writer in Renaissance England. His search for patronage, his patriotism, imperialism, flattery, and prejudices — together with his extraordinary life adventures — make him vulnerable and knowable. Probably the most accurate (though not the kindest) assessment of his literary talents is Edmund Spenser's in *Colin Clouts Come Home Againe* (1595):

And there is old *Palemon* free from spight,
Whose carefull pipe may make the hearer rew:
Yet he himselfe may rewed be more right,
That sung so long untill quite hoarse he grew.

The poet's character ("free from spight"), his incessant complaints about his poverty ("carefull pipe"), and the reader's reaction to his overwhelming publications("That sung so long untill quite hoarse he grew") echo many a response to Churchyard.

Churchyard was born sometime between 1520 and 1525 during the reign of Henry VIII, and he died in April 1604, during the reign of James I. From Churchyard's writings one learns that his life as a soldier spanned forty years (1540s–1580s), and he saw service on many occasions in the Netherlands, Scotland, and Ireland. His war exploits, the subject of many of his works, present him as a resourceful soldier and engaging prisoner who managed to charm his captors and noble ladies into assisting him make his escapes. His descriptions of his accomplishments as conscripted leader of the Protestants in Antwerp in 1566 and his subsequent miraculous escape disguised as a priest seem more romantic than factual. Sometime in the mid 1570s Churchyard married, and the unhappiness that followed is mentioned in his autobiographical poems. Life as a soldier brought him little remuneration, and for fifty-two years he published tirelessly, trying to gain the patronage of the great. In 1593 Elizabeth awarded him a pension of eighteen pence a day, which she increased to twenty pence in 1597. During his long life Churchyard managed to remain at court; but as he constantly informs the reader, his amiability brought him few monetary rewards.

Churchyard began his writing career with *A Mirror for Man* (circa 1552) and *Davy Dicar's Dream* (1552?), in the reign of Edward VI, probably soon after his return from service in France, where he was captured and spent a short time in prison. *Davy Dicar's Dream,* in using mutability and *contemptus mundi* themes, offers Christian living as a solution to England's social and economic ills; it also implies that prosperity will follow the king's eradication of vice. Both poems demonstrate Churchyard's facility in using conventional themes, or topoi, such as the fall of princes and the wheel of fortune, to express his dissatisfaction with society. Fourteeners, alliterative lines, and a heavy reliance on proverbs and homiletic rhetoric make Churchyard's verse indistinguishable from the works of other minor poets of the period.

While *Davy Dicar's Dream* seems in content and style as uncontroversial as *A Mirror for Man,* and de-spite the fact that England's poverty is referred to in both, Thomas Camel took issue with its implied criticism of the king. A debate in verse between Camel and Churchyard ensued; it was augmented by other poets and published as *The Contention betwixt Churchyard and Camel upon David Dicar's Dream* (1560). It is apparently these early poems to which Churchyard refers in *The Fortunate Farewell* (1599) as the ones which caused him trouble with the Privy Council in the 1550s.

Before his departure for Antwerp in 1566, again to serve as a soldier, Churchyard published three court satires – *A Greater Thanks for Churchyard's Welcome Home, Churchyard's Farewell,* and *A Farewell Called Churchyard's Round* – plus a denunciation of friends' betrayals, *Churchyard's Lamentation of Friendship* (all 1566). The poems refer to a particular event that occurred after Churchyard's return from the siege of Leith (and that he describes again in *The First Part of Churchyard's Chips* [1575] in "A Tragical Discourse of the Unhappy Man's Life"), yet the personal experience fails to make the poems memorable. The same subjects, the denunciation of sycophantic courtiers and friends, and the proverbs and hortatory rhetoric make the poems almost indistinguishable.

It was a short literary distance, at least in style, for Churchyard to move from the previous eighteen years of moralizations in his satires to epitaphs with generalizations on goodness. The form also offered Churchyard, the frequently impoverished soldier and part-time writer, the opportunity to seek patronage by flattering the families of the recently deceased. His first work in this form (many followed in the next thirty-three years), *The Epitaph of the Honorable Earl of Pembroke* (1570), honors the subject with classical allusions and encomiums of prudence and grace that scarcely reflect the opportunistic Pembroke. Churchyard apparently knew the earl, since he mentions his lack of schooling (John Aubrey remarks that he was illiterate) and recalls him as a leader in "O manly Pembroke yet me think, I see thee march upright" (Pembroke was a captain in Flanders in 1557). His choice of Pembroke as the subject of his first published epitaph is puzzling, for Pembroke was associated, at least in name, with the rebellions in the north at the time Churchyard was vociferously condemning them in verse. It is also unusual to find him praising Pembroke, who in 1551 betrayed Edward Seymour, Duke of Somerset – Churchyard's patron in the *Davy Dicar's Dream* episode, and to whose family he always remained loyal. Perhaps the choice of Pembroke for his first

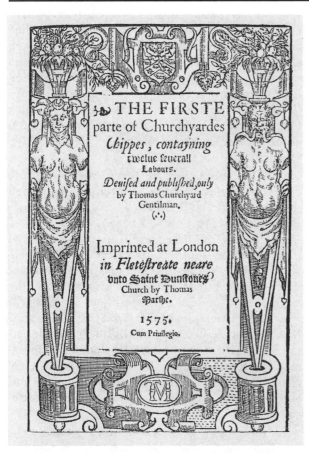

Title page for Churchyard's 1575 collection of eleven poems and one prose piece, "The Road Made by Sir William Drury"

epitaph shows Churchyard's desperate poverty and the ruthless demands of seeking patronage.

"Come bring in May with me" begins the four-line epigraph to a *Discourse of Rebellion* (1570), Churchyard's first overtly patriotic work. Using Old Testament–style prophecies of destruction and plagues as punishments, the poet warns Englishmen against the revolt in the north led by the earls of Northumberland and Westmoreland. Churchyard persists in the style of his early works, using disparate images, homely proverbs, and irrelevant examples. Here and in subsequent words of propaganda, he enlists God on the side of the monarch; and if he knew of the concept of a just war, he associated it with one of the reigning prince's prerogatives.

A short pause in Churchyard's career as a soldier between 1572 and 1575 seems to have provided him time for writing and organizing material for the eleven poems and one prose piece in *The First Part of Churchyard's Chips*. War, patriotism, and flattery of the great are the subjects of two poems, "The Siege of Leith" and "The Siege of Edinburgh Castle," and the prose piece, "The Road Made

by Sir William Drury." The description of the skirmishes may faithfully record the events, but it slows down the narrative pace and shows Churchyard's inability to organize his material. Seven of the remaining nine poems demonstrate his penchant for homiletic literature and hortatory rhetoric. Among them, "A Doleful Discourse of Two Strangers, a Lady and a Knight" is of some historical interest, as it seems to be a thinly disguised account of Lady Katherine Grey's marriage to Edward Seymour. Also interesting for its autobiographical material is "A Tragical Discourse of the Unhappy Man's Life," which also warrants comment for the manner in which it typifies Churchyard's frequent method of composition. Inconsistencies in theme and sudden narrative shifts suggest that he wrote without a plan and revised little. For example, he begins with eight stanzas of lamentations, then shifts to forty-four stanzas of factual narration – including accounts of miraculous escapes that undercut the opening's misery motif – and then moves to reflections on chance and Providence that give place inexplicably to court satire. He ends with one of his many farewells.

Within this group of poems in the *Chips,* "A Tale of a Friar and a Shoemaker's Wife" offers a welcome relief with its humor. The situational comedy of the friar tricking the shoemaker into measuring his wife for a pair of shoes as she hides beneath the sheets – "She thrust her leg out of the bed / but hid fast under clothes" – displays Churchyard's witty handling of the first climax of the story. The second incident – the gulling of the tricky friar by the shoemaker's wife, who locks him in a trunk and then persuades her husband to break it open for her medicine – also shows a competent use of humor: "The chamber shaked, the friar he quaked / and stonk for fear and woe." "Churchyard's Dream" and "The Whole Order How Our Sovereign Lady Queen Elizabeth Was Received into the City of Bristow" complete the poetry of the *Chips.* The eulogistic report of the queen's progress shows Churchyard constantly active in his search for advancement.

With six publications between 1578 and 1579, Churchyard's output can only be described as prodigious; and whatever one may think of his literary skills, his tireless efforts for preferment through patriotic propaganda enable the reader to understand something of the wars and the life of the Elizabethan soldier. Two of the prose works from this period, *A Praise and Report of Master Martin Frobisher's Voyage to Meta Incognita* (1578) and *The Most True Report of James Fitzmaurice's Death with a Brief Discourse of*

Rebellion (1579?), demonstrate Churchyard's methods in this mode of writing. Here he attempts to embody his patriotism in narrative events, but in each text the skeletal story is only an excuse to draw attention to his commitment to England's imperialistic expansion. Both texts are marred by digressions: "gain and glory" for England by colonial expansion in the Frobisher voyage, and condemnation of rebellion (in views already expressed in the 1570 *Discourse*) in the Fitzmaurice account. In most historical texts Churchyard stresses his accurate reporting and seldom resorts to storyteller's techniques; so when he writes that some stories about Fitzmaurice "are bruted abroad (to affirm it for truth I cannot)," the reader knows that history gives place to romance for propagandistic purposes.

War is Churchyard's subject in three major pieces: *A Lamentable and Pitiful Description of the Woeful Wars in Flanders* (1578); *The Misery of Flanders, Calamity of France, Misfortune of Portugal* (1579); and *A General Rehearsal of Wars* (*Churchyard's Choice*, 1579), as well as in three minor pieces from the *Choice:* "A Mirror for Rebels to Look into," an untitled account of Sir Henry Sidney's rule of Ireland, and "A Small Rehearsal of Some Special Services in Flanders." Themes in the three major works include English patriotism and the unknowable ways of Providence; but in *The Misery of Flanders,* Providence and patriotism are one and English. There is some attempt in the opening lines of *A Lamentable . . . Description* to suggest that one of the themes will be disorder and rebellion through wealth and ease, but Churchyard leaves this idea undeveloped. The longer prose works on Flanders reveal those limitations of style that characterize Churchyard's work. For instance, abrupt transitions – introduced by such phrases as "Now it is to be understood," "It was to be wondered at: the manner whereof followeth," "I must leave off this speech and follow another humor," "I had forgotten," and "Now having further causes to treat of " – show the author's lack of a comprehensive plan. It cannot be said, however, that Churchyard makes no attempt to organize his work, since the nut/kernel metaphor gives a little shape to *The Misery of Flanders,* and the rise of Nicholas Malaby from common soldier to governor of Connaught provides an extremely loose framework for *A General Rehearsal.* Churchyard is most successful in structuring autobiographical material; in *A Lamentable . . . Description* his account of his conscription by the people of Antwerp as their leader against the Spaniards (an event first described in the *Chips*) has a clear linear develop-

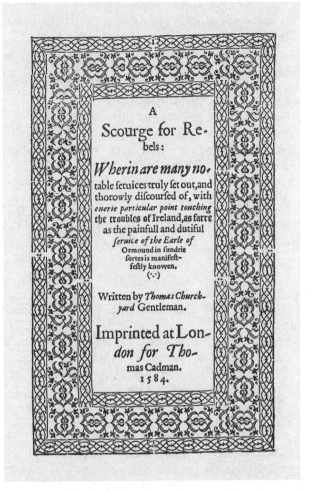

Title page for one of Churchyard's many works about war and rebellion

ment, a focus on the main event, an absence of digressions, and a brisk narrative pace.

Churchyard's frenetic writing and search for patronage continued into 1580 with few changes in topics and developments in style. *A Pleasant Labyrinth Called Churchyard's Chance* (1580) gives an insight into his literary position at the time. His assessment of his limitations – "many words" and "small learning and capacity" – is not helped by his adopting a self-deprecatory stance that exceeds the demands of the *humilitas* topos. He also reveals his enjoyment of court and acquaintance with the great: "my chance is to be in Court well known and much made of, though smally considered or advanced." The seventy-one poems in *Churchyard's Chance* continue his use of court satires, epitaphs, and the praise of virtue and condemnation of vice. There is some attempt to incorporate into his style such contemporary poetic practices as myths and personification of abstract ideas, but these are simply added to established practices.

"A Story Translated out of French," an autobiographical poem that occurs in *A Light Bundle of Lively Discourses Called Churchyard's Charge* (1580), continues Churchyard's success in this mode as the narrative moves rapidly and the subject matter sustains the reader's interest. Another 1580 publication, *A Warning for the Wise,* successfully describes the earthquake of 6 April 1580; Churchyard's compartmentalizing of moralizations in separate essays markedly improves his organization here. In confining himself exclusively to a description of the events in "The Report of the Said Earthquake," he writes succinctly and convincingly of the happenings in London.

A cessation to this pattern of steady publication and vigorous search for patronage occurred suddenly in 1580. It seems Churchyard fled to Scotland after slaying a man and on his return in 1581 was imprisoned until 1584. He recommended his writing career with his preoccupations of war and rebellion in *A Scourge for Rebels* (1584). He then resumed life as a soldier for a short period under Robert Dudley, first Earl of Leicester, in the Low Countries in 1585 and in 1586 probably toured Wales to gather information for his next publication, *The Worthiness of Wales* (1587). In the preface to this work Churchyard argues unconvincingly (for he is continually self-seeking) that his departure from war themes and his excursus into travel are due to his love of Wales and the various humors that take man's fancy. The book reveals some marked changes in Churchyard's preoccupations and style. His descriptions of pleasant scenes show an awareness of the *locus amoenus* tropes, and in the descriptions of mountains his sensitivity to prospect is evident. Many sections, such as his Arthurian sources, are carefully organized and follow logically from his introduction. His insistence on truth and eyewitness accounts, a common feature of his writings, is frequent and convincing. Digression had, however, become a habit of mind. Once illness and fatigue began to dog him, he took every opportunity to introduce topoi of mutability to sustain the descriptions and innovatively used invocations to the Muse to support them.

Churchyard's final publication of the 1580s, *A Spark of Friendship and Warm Good Will* (1588), an extravagant prose tribute to Sir Walter Ralegh, includes "A Description and Plain Discourse of Paper," in which Churchyard returns to the themes of patriotism and imperialism reminiscent of Frobisher's voyage. In these sections he gives an accurate historical account of papermaking at Spillman's mill in Dartford. Moralizations and conceits are distracting, and Churchyard loses all sense of balance when he compares the mill's hammering to the removal of vice from "cankered kind." Yet the style in those verses that actually describe the mill's activities recalls the brief descriptive account of Churchyard's earthquake report.

A return to the publication of two books of epitaphs on the famous, *A Reviving of the Dead* (1591) and *A Feast Full of Sad Cheer* (1592), as well as *A Handful of Gladsome Verses Given to the Queen's Majesty at Woodstock* (1592), suggests a desperate attempt by Churchyard to gain monetary assistance. His plight was pathetic, and there is an ever-increasing emphasis in his last years on his poverty and on his contemporaries' disregard of his works. Unfortunately, his constant demeaning of himself in comparisons more humorous than decorous must have caused amusement rather than pity for one who likened himself to a horse, an ox, and a bee.

A marked but short-lived change in Churchyard's attitude came in 1593 with the queen's granting him a pension, which he celebrated in *A Pleasant Conceit Penned in Verse* (1593). Here, within a year of his farewells, he unabashedly announces the recommencement of his publications: "The book I called of late *My dear adieu* / Is now become my welcome home most kind." Probably no one took any notice of Churchyard's farewells, for while he was making them he was also giving advance notices in his 1592 publication of his *Challenge,* which appeared in 1593. This extensive publication consists of many reprints. Of the twenty-three pieces, four are from the *Chips,* three from the *Choice,* and one, "The Tragedy of Shore's Wife," from the 1563 *Mirror for Magistrates.* With the exception of "Shore's Wife," the changes to the reprints are minor and for autobiographical reasons not artistry.

Churchyard enlarged "Shore's Wife," he tells the reader, to prove to his contemporaries who spoke of the "shallowness" of his "head" that he was capable of "the fathering of such a work." The poem makes an interesting relief from Churchyard's frequent mining of his war experiences and is the most impressive tragedy he wrote. Jane Shore narrates her own story in the *Mirror* manner, and Churchyard's empathy with the heroine precludes his often admonitory tone and homiletic passages. The longest sequence of moralistic comparisons, eight stanzas against the world's fickleness, does not seem inappropriate when one of the topics is human ingratitude. He introduces complexity into the story by suggesting that a variety of causes — beauty, the impact of majesty and power on the sensi-

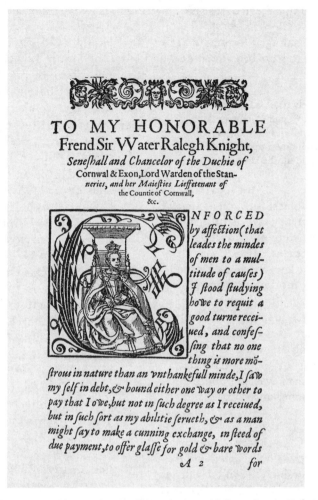

TO MY HONORABLE
Frend Sir Water Ralegh Knight,
*Seneshall and Chancelor of the Duchie of
Cornwal & Exon, Lord Warden of the Stan-
neries, and her Maiesties Lieffetenant of
the Countie of Cornwall,
&c.*

NFORCED *by affection (that
leades the mindes
of men to a mul-
titude of causes)
J stood studying
howe to requit a
good turne recei-
ued, and confes-
sing that no one
thing is more mō-
strous in nature than an vnthankefull minde, I saw
my self in debt, & bound either one way or other to
pay that I owe, but not in such degree as I receiued,
but in such sort as my abilitie serueth, & as a man
might say to make a cunning exchange, in steed of
due payment, to offer glasse for gold & bare words*

A 2   *for*

Page from the dedication to A Spark of Friendship and Warm Goodwill (1588)

bilities of a commoner, and the unhappiness of Jane's forced marriage to an apprentice — were responsible for her downfall. By making her wise, prudent, and generous in her role as Edward IV's mistress, Churchyard shows that Richard III's imposition of a public penance on her was unjust. Even in her curses against Richard, Churchyard places the emphasis on Richard's villainy rather than on the victim's revenge.

Only short works were published between 1596 and 1604; they indicate that time, age, and perhaps the critics' barbs had taken their toll on Churchyard. As he grew older, he became more sensitive to criticism, and in *A Pleasant Discourse of Court and Wars* (1596) he refers to Spenser's assessment of him in *Colin Clouts Come Home Againe.* His sorry plight and lack of self-esteem are epitomized in *A Musical Consort of Heavenly Harmony* (1595):

My breath but bores a hole within the air,
My date near done calls for a shrouding sheet

....

Mine eyes can scarce look to my stumbling feet.

A Sad and Solemn Funeral of Sir Francis Knowles (1596) names all the captains, bishops, and leaders who died that year; and for once the memento mori trope gains immediacy as the poet includes himself as one "who will follow fast / the steps to death." *The Fortunate Farewell to . . . Essex* (1599) shows him still courting the famous and condemning rebels, but at the same time undercutting any effect his words might have by drawing attention to the inadequacies of his "fruitless pen," which "makes many to gaze and few to consider well and regard." His last epitaph, *Churchyard's Good Will* (1604), with its many adages and frequent alliteration, continues the habits of a lifetime; but his sense of decorum, always a weakness, now shows a marked deterioration as tragedy gives place to comedy when the late archbishop of Canterbury tumbles "under board / like lump of lead to lose life, goods, and grace."

Although Churchyard managed to remain at the court of James I, he seems to have become something of a laughingstock:

Mr. Churchyard the poet is lately dead, and not past a fortnight before his death being in a pair of loose gaskins [trousers], being hard by the maids of honor he shot off his piece, and all the powder ran down upon his stockings, drove away the maids, and all the company was faint to be carried out.

Nineteenth-century scholarship, such as that by George Chalmers and Henry W. Adnitt, accounts for most of the knowledge of Churchyard. Twentieth-century journal articles, often the result of postgraduate research, have kept his name before readers, but there are few modern editions of his works. This is regrettable, for a selection of Churchyard's works in accessible texts would help modern readers appreciate the lives of those forced to earn their living by courting the wealthy, and by fighting their countries' wars for so long that they came to believe that patriotism was the endorsement of the state's greed for imperialistic expansion.

References:

Henry W. Adnitt, "Thomas Churchyard," *Transactions of the Shropshire Archaeological and Natural History Society,* 111 (Shrewsbury, 1880): 1–88;

John Aubrey, *Aubrey's Brief Lives,* edited by Oliver Lawson Dick (Harmondsworth, U.K.: Penguin, 1987);

Barbara Brown, "A Note on Thomas Churchyard's Bibliography," *Notes & Queries,* new series 27 (April 1980): 137–138;

Brown, "Sir Thomas More and Thomas Churchyard's *Shore's Wife,*" *Yearbook of English Studies,* 2 (1972): 41–48;

Brown, "Thomas Churchyard and *The Worthines of Wales,*" *Anglo-Welsh Review,* 18 (February 1970): 131–139;

Philip Gawdy, *Letters of Philip Gawdy of West Harling, Norfolk, and of London, to Various Members of His Family, 1576–1616,* edited by I. H. Jeayes (London: J. B. Nicholas & Sons, 1906);

Roger A. Geimer, "A Note on the Birthdate of Thomas Churchyard," *Notes & Queries,* new series 14 (December 1967): 452–454;

Merrill H. Goldwyn, "A Note on Thomas Churchyard's Pension," *Notes & Queries,* new series 21 (March 1974): 89;

Goldwyn, "Notes on the Biography of Thomas Churchyard," *Review of English Studies,* 17 (1966): 1–15;

Goldwyn, "Some Unpublished Manuscripts by Thomas Churchyard," *Studies in Philology,* 64 (April 1967): 147–158;

Goldwyn, "Thomas Churchyard's 'Marriages,'" *Notes & Queries,* new series 14 (December 1967): 454–456;

James Harner, "Churchyard's Shore's Wife," *Explicator,* 40 (1982): 11–12;

J. E. Jackson, "Thomas Churchyard," *Notes & Queries,* fifth series 8 (October 1877): 331;

Stanley J. Koziskowski, "Wyatt's 'They Flee from Me' and Churchyard's Complaint of Jane Shore," *Notes & Queries,* new series 25 (October 1978): 416–417;

Charles A. Rather, "Some Notes on the Career and Personality of Thomas Churchyard," *Notes & Queries,* new series 7 (June 1960): 211–215;

William Schutte, "Thomas Churchyard's 'Dolfull Discourse' and Death of Lady Katherine Grey," *Sixteenth Century Journal,* 15 (Winter 1984): 471–487;

Charles Shirley, "Alliteration as Evidence in Dating a Poem of Thomas Churchyard: An Exploratory Computer-aided Study," *Modern Philology,* 76 (May 1979): 375–377;

Franklin B. Williams, "Thomas Churchyard's Thunder on the Right," *English Literary Renaissance,* 3 (Winter 1973): 380–399.

John Colet

(1467 – 16 September 1519)

Daniel T. Lochman
Southwest Texas State University

BOOKS: *Oratio habita a D. Joanne Colet ad clerum in conuocatione* (London: Printed by Richard Pynson, 1512?);

Joannis Coleti theologi, olim decani diui Pauli, æditio. una cum quibusdam (London, 1527) – includes a proheme to *Cathecyzon* [catechism] and Articles of Admission to Saint Paul's School;

The sermon of doctor Colete, made to the conuocacion at Paulis (London: Printed by Thomas Berthelet, [1530?]) – a translation of the *Oratio*;

A ryght frutefull monycion, concernyng the ordre of a good chrysten mannes lyfe (London: Printed by Robert Copland for John Byddell, 1534).

Editions and Collections: *De Sacramentis Ecclesiae*, edited by J. H. Lupton (London: Bell, 1867);

Super Opera Dionysii, edited and translated by Lupton (London: Bell, 1869) – comprises commentary on the *Celestial Hierarchy* and *Ecclesiastical Hierarchy* of Dionysius the Areopagite;

Enarratio in Epistolam S. Pauli ad Romanos, edited and translated by Lupton (London: Bell, 1873) – comprises the complete commentary on Romans;

Enarratio in Epistolam Primam S. Pauli ad Corinthios, edited and translated by Lupton (London: Bell, 1874);

Opuscula quaedam Theologica, edited and translated by Lupton (London: Bell, 1876) – comprises *Letters to Radulphus on the Mosaic Account of Creation, On the Composition of Christ's Holy, Mystical Body, the Church,* and the fragmentary *Exposition of St. Paul's Epistle to the Romans, I–V*;

Commentary on First Corinthians, edited and translated by Bernard O'Kelly and Catherine A. L. Jarrott (Binghamton, N.Y.: Medieval & Renaissance Texts & Studies, 1985);

On the Sacraments, edited and translated by John B. Gleason, in his *John Colet* (Berkeley: University of California Press, 1989), pp. 270–333.

Debate still surrounds the reputation of John Colet. Recent scholars have questioned earlier claims of his pivotal role in the development of English humanism and the Reformation, but he emerges nonetheless as an important ecclesiast and educator linked to the rising middle class and the Tudor court, as well as one of the earliest English writers to exhibit the influence of Italian humanist themes and Latin style.

Colet's parents represented the nobility and merchant class of late-fifteenth-century London. His father, Henry, moved from a rural area in Wendover, Buckinghamshire, to London, where he thrived financially and politically. By 1466 Henry had increased his status sufficiently to marry Dame Christian Knevet, a nobly connected, literate woman some sixteen years younger than her husband. They moved to Budge Street in Saint Anthony's parish, where John was born in 1467, the only one of twenty-two children to live to middle age. Nothing is known of John's early character or education, although he may have studied at Saint Thomas Acon's, a school linked to the Mercers' Company.

Despite the dreary succession of deceased siblings, Colet's childhood home was probably a lively one. Erasmus praises the good cheer of his mother even in her old age. By the time John turned three or four, his sociable father was already a warden of the Mercers and an alderman of London. When John entered grammar school around 1473, his father was building influence in the community; and as his son turned thirteen, Henry began the first of five terms as master of the company, a position providing important contacts with municipal leaders and royalty. After John began university studies in 1480, his father gained political influence culminating in a term as lord mayor of London in 1486.

Henry's rise in the mercantile and political spheres contrasts with his son's more cerebral interests. Polydore Vergil was probably correct in stating that John studied at Cambridge and Oxford, apparently completing his B.A. and M.A. at Cambridge before moving to Oxford to study divinity. After completing the B.A. he received the first of

Bust of John Colet by Pietro Torrigiano (Collection of the Mercers' Company, London)

several benefices, that of Dennington, Suffolk, on 6 August 1485. In 1488 a "John Colet" recorded in Cambridge's Grace Books took the title of "inceptor" given to masters. From 1488 to 1490 he likely served as "necessary regent," a position as lecturer required of all new masters. In 1490 he became rector of Thurning, Huntingdonshire, holding that position until 1494, when he received preferments at York and Botevant.

Colet capped his arts program with a late-fifteenth-century version of the Continental tour. He stayed in Rome, writing a letter to Christopher Urswick from there in 1492 and enrolling his family in a fraternity at Rome on 13 March 1493. On 3 May he signed as a member of Rome's English hospice, a house run by English clergy as a charity and residence for Englishmen touring Italy. There is no other evidence of his stay in Italy, though speculation persists that he traveled to Flo-

rence to meet Giovanni Pico della Mirandola, Marsilio Ficino, and others from the Florentine Academy. Some suggest that he discovered there the preaching zeal of the sober Fra Girolamo Savonarola.

Colet could have discovered humanist influence at Rome. The Curia in the late fifteenth century supported clergy with humanist training. Humanists close to the papacy advocated a program of modest ecclesiastical reform and discussed heterodox opinions without condoning them. In the letter to Urswick, Colet says he will forward to England a copy of the *Historia Bohemica* by the humanist Aenius Silvius Piccolomini, later Pope Pius II. This work expresses regret for the harshness – if not the fact – of the punishment meted out to John Huss and his followers, all deemed heretical by Rome. Erasmus's letter to Jodocus Jonas (13 June 1521) confirms Colet's mildly humanist and strongly religious motives for travel; he went to Italy, Erasmus says, to refine his preaching and study sacred authors. Along the way he no doubt encountered works by humanists such as Piccolomini and philosophers such as Ficino.

Probably during his travels Colet obtained a volume of Ficino's *Epistolae* (1495) that he later annotated and inscribed with two letters from Ficino. Because the letters and annotations are not dated, they do not clarify Colet's itinerary. They do, however, suggest his reaction to Ficino: one letter from Ficino addresses a question of great import to Colet – the relative value of reason and will. On this issue Ficino upheld the preeminence of intellect in opposition to Colet, who, following Paul, favored the superior power of will.

Colet left Italy by 1495, apparently pausing in Orléans to study – presumably law – with the young legist François DeLoynes. He returned to London in 1496 or 1497 to find his industrious father serving a rare second term as lord mayor and obtaining the favor of Henry VII by guaranteeing London's cooperation in a controversial trade agreement with the Netherlands.

By 1497 Colet was studying theology at Oxford. During the winter of 1499–1500 Erasmus observed that he had lectured at Oxford for three years. Supported by new preferments, including a canonry at Saint Martin-le-Grand in London and the prebendary of Goodeaster, both held until 1504, Colet was ordained deacon in 1497 – probably after completing the B.D. – followed by ordination as priest in 1498. In 1499, the same year he met Erasmus, he was named vicar of Stepney.

The encounter with Erasmus was probably not the watershed event once claimed, but the two did develop a rich, complex, and extended relationship. The flattery of their early correspondence reveals mutual respect but betrays mercenary and personal interests. When in 1499 they half-seriously undertook an epistolary duel on the agony of Christ, seemingly trivial questions loomed more important, particularly when the theologian and grammarian employed arguments culminating in differing views of Christ. Erasmus argued that Christ's agony was a product of natural human weakness through which the Son feared the death he foreknew. In opposition, Colet asserted that Christ suffered because he foreknew the weak and sinful nature of the men who would betray him; he could have no human weakness or fear.

Their complex relationship is colored by Erasmus's sometimes less-than-flattering epistolary por-

traits of Colet. In October 1499, for instance, he wrote to Johannes Sextinus of a dinner involving Colet. In Erasmus's account Colet presented and defended a view that set Cain's violation of a natural field by plowing against Abel's pastoralism; this position elicited attacks from Erasmus and another unnamed guest. Erasmus mischievously describes Colet's impassioned rebuttal as a "holy frenzy." Erasmus's ambivalence appears even in the posthumous encomium of Colet written in 1521: he presents Colet as an example of holy living but notes defects including parsimony and sometimes overbearing assertiveness.

Whatever his standing with Erasmus, Colet thrived in his career. By 1502 he was appointed canon of Salisbury and prebend of Durford, apparently to support work toward his doctorate in divinity although he held these offices until his death. He completed his doctorate around 1504 and left Oxford for London, perhaps with a deanship already in view. He may have temporarily replaced the absent dean of Saint Paul's, Robert Sherborne, as early as 1503, perhaps before completing his degree. At the end of 1504 Erasmus wrote to praise Colet's doctorate and advancement. By the time of his father's death on 1 October 1505, Colet was securely established and held several livings to augment his father's substantial legacy.

The deanship led Colet away from academic studies. While Erasmus enthusiastically pursued Greek literature and theology and in 1505 shamelessly described himself as a leading Greek scholar, Colet remained nonproficient in Greek despite his association with those who were: Thomas Linacre, William Grocyn, William Lily, and Thomas More, in addition to Erasmus. Though he possessed antique Greek manuscripts of the New Testament, prescribed Greek for study at Saint Paul's School, toyed with Greek words in his writings on Paul and Dionysius, and attempted to learn the language in his last years, he seemingly never became a fluent reader or translator.

Colet's writing is that of a Latinist with strong ecclesiastical and theological interests. He eschewed what he considered the barbarism of medieval Latin, but his own Latin derived from no pure classicism. He favored a personal, expressive style using exhortatory and epideictic strategies together with complicated rhetorical figures of apposition, balance, and suspension to elucidate theological principles such as the Incarnation, as in *Enarratio in Epistolam S. Pauli ad Romanos* (1873):

Hic filius Dei et hominis, Deus et homo, qui grece *the-onthropon* dicitur, Jesus est Christus, mediator Dei et hominum, in se ipso utrumque extremum mire copulans; ut hoc ineffabilii medio commode et gratiose extrema inter se illa copularentur. Verbum caro factum est, et Deus filius hominis, ut caro ad verbum habeat accessum, et homo divinitatem indueret. Deus induit humanitatem, ut homo divinitatem exaltaretur. In Christo humanitatis et divinitatis unitio, ut homines cum Deo co-unirentur. O extremum medium mirabile et mirificum, omni cultu colendum et adorandum!

(This is the son of God and man, himself God and man (called *theanthropos* in Greek), Jesus Christ, mediator between God and man, marvelously uniting in himself each of two extremes so that this ineffable median couples those limits. The Word became flesh, and God the son of man so the flesh could find access to the Word and so humanity should put on divinity. God clothed himself in humanity so that mankind could be raised to divinity. In Christ [is] a conjunction of humanity and divinity, with the consequence that mankind may be co-united with God. O marvelous and miraculous limit and median, to be worshiped and adored at every devotion!)

Yet Colet's Latin lacks the effervescence, polish, and simple grace of Erasmus's and More's. The *Statutes* for Saint Paul's School assert that "laws and statutes" are needed to maintain "good order," but Colet was generally suspicious of legalism in all forms, even rules of Latin grammar and style. Erasmus describes his written violations of the rules of language as being "of the kind ... blamed by the critics." One need not look far in Colet's works to find errant grammar and syntax; yet, as Erasmus affirms, his Latin works possess a range and power derived from natural and nurtured eloquence.

In 1508 Colet's pedagogical interests became visible: construction began on a new school at Saint Paul's Churchyard, and in the *Statutes* he asked the Mercers' Company to "have all the cure and charge, rule and governance." By 12 April 1510 a committee in the company accepted the dean's proposal to reestablish Saint Paul's School. On 17 April, Colet rented a house for the school's master; in 1512 he petitioned Rome, apparently successfully, to transfer legal authority for the school from the cathedral's chancellor to the Mercers. He first asked Linacre then his headmaster, Lily, to write a grammar to help students learn a purified Latin; to this Colet added a preface and sought Erasmus's thorough revision, the whole apparently completed about 1514.

Although a school had existed at Saint Paul's before Colet's tenure, the old school was reorganized under new statutes and new governance.

Saint Paul's was not the first English school supervised by lay trustees, yet the situation was unusual in that the lay-governed school was closely connected to a church. Colet's curriculum in Latin and Greek seems something less than the "true Latin speech" promised in the *Statutes:* in addition to his catechism, Latin grammar, and Erasmus's *Institutes of a Christian Man* and *Copia,* he suggests Lactantius, Prudentius, Proba, Juvencus, and Johannes Baptista Mantuanus as examples for imitation and study. He omitted secular writers – Virgil, Cicero, Seneca, and Ovid – whom he had earlier praised as models of the "true Roman tongue." Still, Colet granted his master room to determine Latin texts "in particular," offering his list only for illustration. An ecclesiastical social climate opposed to classicism may have tempered his examples: perhaps their "chaste eloquence" sought to forestall clerical objections like those in fact raised against the operating school. Conservative opposition to Saint Paul's curriculum and the humanist training of students such as Richard Pace, Thomas Lupset, and Richard Starkey suggest that Colet was not as opposed to a secular Latin curriculum as the *Statutes* imply. As for Greek texts, he left the choice entirely up to the master and surmaster, deferring to their "wit" so long as they banish all "that filthiness and all such abusion which the later blind world brought in which ... may be called blotterature rather than literature."

Colet's school was remarkable for its size and the specificity of its statutes. Although it lacked dining room and dormitory, it offered free education to 153 boys, compared to the 70 scholars and several choristers then resident at either Eton or Westminster. The *Statutes* provide insight into Colet's interests in founding the school. He observes that nothing can "continue long and endure without laws and statutes," so he carefully specifies the privileges and responsibilities of his well-paid master; the duties of the surmaster and chaplain; procedures concerning everything from eating (none allowed in the school) to cockfights, the Child Bishop's sermon (delivered annually as an inversion of usual authority on Childermas Day, 28 December, to commemorate Herod's slaughter of the innocents), holidays, the use of wax candles, the place for urinating (a space between the buttresses of old Saint Paul's Cathedral), and a poor scholar's duty to clean up. He lists the properties whose incomes he assembled to endow the school, and he establishes guidelines to permit future trustees and teachers to adapt to new situations.

Establishing a school, especially one of such a relatively large size, required much energy as well

151

Capud XVI

Jesus noster christus resurrexit q̄ visus est [strikethrough] ē

a plurimis homines ergo in illo omnes resurgent

ille primitie est vita iam ipsa vivificans reliquos

alioqui christiani miserabiliores sunt omnibus generali

quorum professo ē mala pati temporali ut bonum

agant regni eterni. Seri enim mortales

ut suo tempore vivificati erigant nomi q̄

immortales varii per meriti q̄ claritate q̄

perfectione. Suo tamen in genere perfectum erit quodq̄

et tale quidem qualis homo ille celesti cui

ut scribit Ad philippenses reformabit corpus

humilitatis nostre configuratum corpori clari

tatis sue. secundum operationem quam thiam

possit subiicere omnia. Mysterium est resur

gent omnes: sed non omnes omnes immutabit

immutabuntur in melius q̄ in forma [strikethrough]

soli veri christiani [strikethrough] imperi no resurget

Page from Colet's commentary on 1 Corinthians (Cambridge University Library, Gg. iv. 26, fol. 151r)

as income. Still, as dean, Colet faced other ecclesiastical, administrative, and political issues. His appointment to deliver the sermon to convocation in 1510 – the one work certainly printed during his lifetime (in Latin, 1512?) – offers a glimpse into his rise in the structure of the church. Much has been made of this challenge to the clergy, sometimes stated forcefully, to abandon this world and reform their lives by adhering to existing laws against profligate ordination, simony, nonresidence of curates and bishops, improper investiture, and misuse of temporal goods. Moreover, Colet encourages the clergy to hold frequent general and provincial councils, execute existing laws, and serve as examples for the rest of the church. Although he seeks no doctrinal reform and reacts more to perceived than actual corruption, his crisply structured sermon apparently had a strong effect, leading to its preservation, printing, translation, and reprinting in the sixteenth century.

In the second decade of the century, issues of ecclesiastical reform and behavior came dramatically to the fore in London through a series of conflicts involving alleged heretics and rivalries between church and state. Old wounds from clerical assertion of privileges and immunities and royal claims of praemunire opened again in cases such as that of Richard Hunne, an unfortunate commoner who objected to mortuary fees assessed at the death of his child; Hunne paid for his intransigence with a stay in prison that ended in his mysterious death. In a series of countersuits testing the relative authority of state and church, Colet's onetime friend Richard Kidderminster was called upon by the bishop of London, Ralph Fitzjames, to defend the rights of clergy in the face of rising lay discontent.

Colet too may have felt the bishop's enmity, since William Warham, a former ally of Colet and still archbishop of Canterbury and chancellor, seems to have silenced him in 1513. Colet apparently incurred the wrath of his "diocesan," Fitzjames, who charged that the dean opposed the worship of images, the obligation of Paul's "hospitality," and Fitzjames's own method of reading sermons from notes. The bishop's enmity could explain Colet's later relations with Thomas Wolsey, an ecclesiast rising like Colet from the urban middle class: on 18 November 1515 Colet preached in Westminster at Wolsey's installation as cardinal. In 1516 Henry VIII appointed Colet to a commission of five inquiring into a dispute involving Warham; subsequently, Warham was removed as chancellor and succeeded by Wolsey. On 5 June 1516 Erasmus wrote to Andrea Ammonio to record his satisfaction

with Warham's removal and his admiration of Colet's "truly Christian spirit" in bringing this about. Early in 1517 Colet worked with Wolsey on Henry VIII's Privy Council and solicited Wolsey's support for Saint Paul's surmaster.

By 1517 Colet seems to have dispelled whatever clouds lingered from an earlier, potentially damaging exchange with Henry VIII. Erasmus's letter to Jonas recounts Colet's triumph over assembled though unnamed enemies, possibly including Fitzjames or members of Colet's own chapter at Saint Paul's. Despite Warham's fall in 1516, Fitzjames refused to give up, citing as additional incriminating evidence Colet's alleged opposition to just wars. Erasmus suggests that Fitzjames assembled Minorites to speak against Colet's pacifism and accuse him of being a "poet" (a charge Erasmus heartily denies). According to Erasmus, Henry – apparently familiar enough to speak to Colet privately – encouraged the cleric to continue preaching despite opposition from "bishops." When Colet preached on 25 March 1513 that "military" support should be offered to Christ rather than earthly monarchs – less than a month before Henry's expedition to France on 20 April – the king's concern for the morale of his troops led to another private discussion, to the delight of Colet's enemies. Colet seemingly emerged with only a minor check and a promise to clarify the difference between a just war (Henry's) and a merely worldly one. As Erasmus describes the scene, a "crowd of courtiers" anticipating Colet's fall were crestfallen because of his success and horrified to see the king embrace the dean, saying, "To every man his own teacher, and let each man back up the teacher of his choice. This is the teacher for me."

On a trip to Exeter College, Oxford, in 1519, an enfeebled Colet dined with his old friend Grocyn. He died on 16 September 1519, apparently from dropsy related to a third bout of the sweating sickness. His last will fixed the endowment to the school and named gifts to friends; it was proved 5 October 1519.

Colet did not leave a large corpus; indeed, the only works published during his life are contributions to the dispute with Erasmus (1503), the Latin text of the *Convocation Sermon* (circa 1512), possibly an introduction to Lily's grammar (earliest extant copy 1527), and possibly the devotional treatise *A Right Fruitful Monition* (earliest copy 1534). His other writings – the largest and most important part – did not appear in print until J. H. Lupton edited them in the late nineteenth century. These include two commentaries on Dionysius's *Hierarchies*; a treatise on the sacraments; three expositions of Colet's favorite topic, Paul's epistles; a fragmentary exposition on the heptameron or seven days of Creation; and a treatise on the mystical body. Also extant are documents concerning Saint Paul's School, together with miscellaneous correspondence, marginalia, and legal documents. The chronology of Colet's works remains a vexed issue.

The commentaries on the Dionysian hierarchies are usually placed early in his career, since both Grocyn and Erasmus came to doubt the supposed authorship of the hierarchies by the Areopagite mentioned in Acts 17:34. Colet seems ignorant of or unaffected by these doubts, since he routinely refers to Dionysius as a saint and makes the principle of hierarchy essential to the *Convocation Sermon*, the treatises, and even the Pauline commentaries. Colet thinks of the human hierarchy even when he considers Dionysius's angelic hierarchies. His introductory note to the comment on the *Celestial Hierarchy* identifies Dionysius's essential point:

> Quicquid aliunde accepimus boni, id benigniter deinceps impartiamus aliis et communicemus; hoc imitati inestimabilem Dei bonitatem, qui largiter se et ordine communicat universis.

> (Whatever goods we receive from another we should graciously impart and communicate to others in succession, in this way imitating the inestimable goodness of God, who abundantly communicates himself and [his] order to all.)

Neoplatonic cosmic hierarchy links human participation to divinity; it helps Colet describe a divine entelechy whose overflowing love and grace inspire Christians individually and communally to respond to and propagate God's love.

Of special interest to Colet in Dionysius's *Ecclesiastical Hierarchy* are descriptions of the sacraments and ecclesiastical offices in the supposedly primitive church. These seemingly fed Colet's desire to reinvigorate the clergy and sacraments with spiritual significance. His most striking digressions in this work concern the proper functions, obligations, and spiritual meaning of ecclesiastical offices; the appropriate roles of orders and laity within a Christian "republic"; and the lapse of the clergy from moral purity and the consequent degradation of sacraments from their pure forms in the apostolic age.

Closely related to Colet's commentary on the *Ecclesiastical Hierarchy* is his *De Sacramentis* (translated as *On the Sacraments*, 1989), a treatise that attempts to harmonize the three rites named by Dionysius and the traditional seven sacraments. Paul's supposed

disciple had identified only baptism, consecration of oils, and the Eucharist. Although Colet could discern elements of other sacraments, such as holy orders and extreme unction, within these rites, disturbing gaps between early and current practice remained. Because Dionysius says nothing about a rite for marriage, Colet devotes considerable attention to defining marriage as a form of priesthood wherein laity, like the clergy, should transcend the flesh by achieving a spiritual principle of unity. Although he extends a kind of priesthood to the married laity, he implies a sternly idealistic antipathy for the flesh and physical procreation.

Colet linked Dionysian principles of order and action to his favorite subject: the faith and charity espoused by Paul. Although his commentaries on Paul cannot be dated accurately, they seem to be revisions of earlier lectures or sermons. In a letter likely written between 1498 and 1504 to Kidderminster (during the period he would have been offering his well-attended Oxford lectures on Paul), Colet expresses his lifelong love for Paul, especially his epistle to the Romans. The letter records his effort to derive as many sententiae as possible from the introductory verses of this epistle. He sometimes adopts a similar style to generate sententious propositions and maxims in his commentaries. Yet the Pauline commentaries – the fragmentary *Exposition* on Romans written for an unidentified "Edmund" and the fuller commentaries on Romans and 1 Corinthians – reveal a sophisticated, coherent, though nonsystematic theology as well as an expressive Latin prose.

His style in the commentaries ranges from laconic terseness to expansive exhortation. Predominant is a loose expository style echoing the homiletic practice of Saint John Chrysostom but lacking the latter's systematic pattern of exposition followed by moral application. Colet breaks nonsystematic paraphrase and interpretation of the Vulgate text to insert sometimes lengthy reflective, admonitory, epideictic, exhortatory, or speculative digressions. In commenting on 1 Corinthians 14:2, he moves from the verse to consideration of context and interpretation of Paul's views on language and intellect:

> Quocirca velit Paulus vel in hoc quoque munere linguarum Corinthii ad spiritalia contendant. Spiritus loquitur mysteria [1 Corinthians 14:2]; prophitia et spiritalis interpretatio docti et sapientis, Spiritu prophetali, et Deo loquitur et hominibus, et ecclesiam edificat, maxime si re ipsa et effectu prestat, examploque et actione, quod intelligens loquitur.

Sir William Segar's portrait of Colet, with a watercolor depiction of Colet's tomb in Old Saint Paul's Church, which was destroyed in the Great Fire of London (1666). This design is on the vellum cover of the statutes of Saint Paul's School, a circa 1518 transcription of the original statutes.

Ut enim intellectus vita sermonis est, ita actio intellectus. Quapropter intellige quod loqueris; ora ut intelligas; quod intelligis age; ut actio vivificet intellectum, intellectus illustret sermonem.

(Even in the gift of tongues itself, therefore, Paul wishes the Corinthians to strive for the things that are spiritual. The Spirit speaks mysteries; and the prophecy and spiritual interpretation of a learned and wise man, by the Spirit of prophecy, speak both to God and to men; and they build up the Church, especially if in fact and effect the speaker displays, by example and by deed, what he says with understanding.

For just as understanding is the life of speech, so action is the life of understanding. Understand, then what you speak, pray, that you may understand; what you understand, do; so that action may give life to your understanding, and understanding may give light to your speech.)

Often Colet considers such rhetorical or historical circumstances of a text, leading to discussion of authorial intent rather than grammar. The effect is a thoughtful, probing, but unsystematic exposition, alternately emotive and intellectual as it attempts to articulate Paul's meaning, language, and feeling. Too much has been made of the revolutionary method of Colet's exegesis, yet it is distinctive in its rhetorical power and intellectual pursuit of divine harmonies.

Colet's intellectual achievement has been too little recognized. Woven into exposition and commentary is a coherent view of human nature, salvation, and the ecclesiastical ideal. Fundamental to his thought are the notions that will is superior to intellect in matters pertaining to faith and that justification comprehends spiritual progress from hope to faith and charity. In the *Exposition* on Romans, Colet inverts the traditional order of Paul's cardinal virtues to distinguish two types of faith: one rooted in trust and the other in cognitive belief. The former he links to hopeful expectation of salvation exemplified by Old Testament covenants: this expectant faith he identifies with justification. From this "trust" grows an intellective "faith" in the Incarnation of Christ and the church. In his longer commentary on Romans, Colet, like Augustine, argues that Christ's grace offers a means to re-form the mind and soul corrupted at the Fall. Christ possesses a tripartite soul including "spirit" together with intellect and being; through Christ's redemption, Christians may regain this spiritual part of the "mind."

In the commentaries on Romans and 1 Corinthians and a treatise on the mystical body, Colet links the psychology of the justified individual to the corporate structure of the church, whose "body" is properly motivated by the Spirit as its life-giving "soul." He insists that humanity since Christ has had a *potential* for perfection individually and socially based on Christ's model. The justified reflect divine love both to God and others through the action (*operatio*) of charity. Divine love makes God's ministers "cocreators" in a regenesis of the world insofar as each member voluntarily extends the Spirit's power to all within the precincts of salvation.

Colet's interest in society may explain his persistent interest in governance, law, and education. His political involvements in his final years contradict his intention, expressed as early as 1514, to seek private reflection and study in his secluded home at Shene. Yet his interactions with the intellectual and political leaders of the time ensured that his reputation would survive. Praised by friends and contemporaries such as Polydore Vergil, Erasmus, and More, and seen as a model by Lupset, Pace, and Starkey, Colet gained a strong reputation for integrity, countered later in the century by those who saw his involvement in ecclesiastical courts as reactionary support of Catholic authority.

Despite Lupton's publication of Colet's works in the last decades of the nineteenth century, scholars still disagree about his thought and place in English humanism; however, most see in his life and works a glimpse at a transitional moment in English history and culture. His writings record a peculiar marriage of humanist and theological thought and style, and they stand independent of, though in close relation to, the humanism of his contemporaries.

Bibliographies:
Sears Jayne, *John Colet and Marsilio Ficino* (Oxford: Oxford University Press, 1963), pp. 149–159;

J. B. Trapp, "John Colet, His Manuscripts, and the Ps.-Dionysius," in *Classical Influences of European Culture, A.D. 1500–1700,* edited by R. R. Bolgar (Cambridge: Cambridge University Press, 1976), pp. 205–221.

Biographies:
Samuel Knight, *The Life of Dr. John Colet, Dean of St. Paul's* (London, 1724; Oxford: Clarendon, 1823);

J. H. Lupton, *A Life of John Colet* (London: Bell, 1887);

John B. Gleason, *John Colet* (Berkeley: University of California Press, 1989).

References:
P. S. Allen, "Dean Colet and Archbishop Warham," *English Historical Review,* 17 (1902): 303–306;

Desiderius Erasmus, *Collected Works,* volume 8, translated by R. A. B. Mynors (Toronto: University of Toronto Press, 1988);

Erasmus, *Opus Epistolarum D. Erasmi,* 12 volumes, edited by P. S. Allen (Oxford: Clarendon, 1906–1958);

John B. Gleason, "The Birth Dates of John Colet and Erasmus of Rotterdam: Fresh Documentary Evidence," *Renaissance Quarterly,* 32 (Spring 1979): 73–76;

W. Robert Godfrey, "John Colet of Cambridge," *Archiv für Reformationsgeschichte,* 65 (1974): 6–17;

André Godin, *Erasme: Vies de Jean Vitrier et de John Colet* (Angers: Editions Moreana, [1982]);

Walter M. Gordon, "The Religious Edifice and Its Symbolism in the Writings of Erasmus, Colet, and More," *Moreana,* 22 (November 1985): 15–23;

Christopher Harper-Bill, "Dean Colet's Convocation Sermon and the Pre-Reformation Church in England," *History,* 73 (1988): 191–210;

W. H. Herendeen, "Coletus Redivivus: John Colet – Patron or Reformer?," *Renaissance and Reformation / Renaissance et Réforme,* 24 (1988): 163–188;

C. A. L. Jarrott, "Erasmus's Annotations and Colet's Commentaries on Paul: A Comparison of Some Theological Themes," in *Essays on the Works of Erasmus,* edited by Richard L. DeMolen (New Haven: Yale University Press, 1978), pp. 125–144;

Peter Iver Kaufman, *Augustinian Piety and Catholic Reform* (Macon, Ga.: Mercer University Press, 1982);

Kaufman, "John Colet and Erasmus' *Enchiridion*," *Church History,* 46 (September 1977): 296–312;

Kaufman, *The "Polytyque Churche": Religion and Early Tudor Political Culture, 1485–1516* (Macon, Ga.: Mercer University Press, 1986);

Arthur F. Leach, "St. Paul's School before Colet," *Archaeologia,* 62, no. 1 (1910): 191–238;

Daniel T. Lochman, "Colet and Erasmus: The *Disputatiuncula* and the Controversy of Letter and Spirit," *Sixteenth Century Journal,* 20 (Spring 1989): 77–87;

Jean-Claude Margolin, "The Epistle to the Romans (Chapter 11) According to the Versions and/or Commentaries of Valla, Colet, Lefèvre, and Erasmus," translated by John L. Farthing in *The Bible in the Sixteenth Century,* edited by David C. Steinmetz (Durham: Duke University Press, 1990), pp. 136–166;

Leland Miles, *John Colet and the Platonic Tradition* (La Salle, Ill.: Open Court, 1961);

H. C. Porter, "The Gloomy Dean and the Law: John Colet, 1466–1519," in *Essays in Modern English Church History in Memory of Norman Sykes,* edited by G. V. Bennett and J. D. Walsh (London: Black, 1966), pp. 18–34;

Eugene Rice, "John Colet and the Annihilation of the Natural," *Harvard Theological Review,* 45 (1952): 141–163;

Frederic Seebohm, *The Oxford Reformers* (London: Longmans, 1867);

J. B. Trapp, "John Colet and the *Hierarchies* of the Ps.-Dionysius," in *Religion and Humanism,* edited by Keith Robbins (Oxford: Blackwell, 1981), pp. 127–148.

Papers:

Colet's commentaries and treatises are found in manuscripts at Cambridge University Library (MS Gg.iv.26); Emmanuel College, Cambridge (MS III.III.12); Corpus Christi College, Cambridge (Parker MS 355); the British Library (Add 63853); and Saint Paul's School. Trinity College, Cambridge (MS 0.4.44), holds a commentary on Peter and brief extracts questionably attributed to Colet. Sears Jayne lists manuscript locations of correspondence, documents, and marginalia in *John Colet and Marsilio Ficino.*

William Cornish

(circa 1465 – circa 1524)

W. R. Streitberger
University of Washington

EDITIONS AND COLLECTIONS: "Pleasure it is," in *Twenty Songs* (London, 1530);

"A treatise between Truth and Information," in John Skelton, *Pithy, pleasant and profitable workes of maister Skelton* (London: Printed by Thomas Marshe, 1568);

"Bow you down," edited by J. P. Collier in his *History of English Dramatic Poetry*, volume 1 (London, 1831), pp. 68–70;

"A treatise between Truth and Information," *Anglia*, 14 (1892): 467–471; *Archiv für Studium der neueren Sprachen und Literaturen*, 120 (1908): 421–426;

"O mischievous M, first syllable of thy name," in *The Great Chronicle of London*, edited by A. H. Thomas and I. D. Thornley (London, 1938), pp. 344–347;

"Salve Regina," in *Musica Britannica*, volume 10, edited by F. Harrison (London: Stainer & Bell, 1973), p. 116;

"Stabat Mater," in *Musica Britannica*, volume 11, edited by Harrison (London: Stainer & Bell, 1973), p. 137;

"Ave Maria," "Gaude Virgo," and "Gaude Flore," in *Musica Britannica*, volume 12, edited by Harrison (London: Stainer & Bell, 1973), pp. 57, 59, 161;

"Fa la sol," "Adieu, mes amours," "Adieu, adieu," "My love," "Ah, the sighs," "Blow thee this horn," "Adieu, courage," "Trolly lolly," "You and I," "Ah Robin," "Whiles life or breath," and "Consort VII," in *Musica Britannica*, volume 18: *Music at the Court of Henry VIII*, edited by J. Stevens (London: Stainer & Bell, 1973), pp. 7, 12, 17, 23, 25, 29, 32, 33, 38, 40, 46;

"Woefully arrayed," "Ay, beshrew you," and "Hoyda, hoyda," in *Musica Britannica*, volume 36: *Early Tudor Songs and Carols*, edited by Stevens (London: Stainer & Bell, 1975), pp. 92, 128, 132.

PLAY PRODUCTIONS: *St. George and the Dragon* (pageant-disguising), Westminster, 6 January 1494;

Entertainments for the wedding of Prince Arthur and Catherine of Aragon (pageant-disguisings), Westminster, 19–28 November 1501;

Unnamed plays or interludes, performed before the king with the Players of the Chapel in the Januarys of 1505, 1506, 1507, 1510, and 1511; February 1512; and June 1512;

Entertainments for the betrothal of Princess Mary and Archduke Charles (play), Richmond, 25 December 1508;

The Golden Arbor in the Orchard of Pleasure (pageant-disguising, play), Westminster, 13 February 1511;

The Fortress Dangerous (pageant-disguising), Greenwich, 1 January 1512;

The Rich Mount (pageant-disguising), Greenwich, 6 January 1513;

Venus and Beauty (interlude and morris dance), Richmond, 6 January 1514;

The Pavilion in the Place Perilous (pageant-disguising, tourney), Richmond, 6 January 1515;

Maying Festival (music, singing, tournament), Greenwich, May 1515;

Troilus and Pandarus (comedy, pageant-disguising, barriers), Eltham, 6 January 1516;

Entertainments for Margaret, Queen of Scots (jousts, play), Greenwich, 19–20 May 1516;

Unnamed plays and interludes, performed before the king with the Children of the Chapel on 4 January 1517, 24 February 1517, 1 January 1519, 7 March 1519, 25 December–6 January 1519–1520, 1 April 1520 (2 interludes), 6 January 1521;

In the fleete made by me VVilliam Cornishe otherwise called Nyshewhete chapelman vvith the molte famose and noble Kyng Henry the V I I. his Reygne the. X I X. yere the moneth of Iuly A treatife bitæene Trouth, and Information.

A. B. of. C how. C. for. C. was. P. in. P
Prologue.
The hoole content.
The knowlege of God, paffyth comparifon
The deuill knowith all il thing, cofented or done
And man knoweth nothing, faue only by reafon
And reafon in man, is diuerfe of operation
How can then man be parfite of cognicion
For reafon fhall fo reafon that fomtyme among
A man by informatió may ryghtewifly do wróg
Gofpell.
The auctorifed gofpel and reafó holdeth theriõ
Whofe litterall fence agreith to the fore feyng
Qui ambulat in tenebris nefcit quo vadit
Now moralyfe ye farther & peyfe the contriuyng
I meane, bytwene trowth and fotele conueyngæ
Who gothe in the darke, muft ftumble amongæ
Blame neuer a blynd man, thou he go wronge.
Fxample.
A Iuge to the Iury nedes muft geue credence
Now what yf they purpofe fals maters to cópafe
The

First page of "A Treatise Between Truth and Information" (from John Skelton, Pithy, Pleasant, and Profitable Works of Master Skelton, 1568)

The Garden of Esperance (pageant–disguising), Greenwich, 6 January 1517;

Entertainments for the imperial ambassadors (jousts, pageants), Greenwich, 7 July 1517;

A merry supplication unto the king's grace (impromptu mock petition), progress from Reading to Abingdon, March 1518;

Pegasus, Report, and *The Rock of Amity* (political allegory, pageant-disguising, tourney), October 1518;

Summer, Winter, Moon, Sun, Rain, and Wind ("pastime," double masque), Newhall, 3 September 1519;

Entertainments at the Field of Cloth of Gold (musical arrangements, pageants), June–July 1520;

Château Vert (pageant-disguising), York Place, 2 March 1522;

Friendship, Prudence, and Might (political allegory), Windsor, 15 June 1522.

William Cornish belongs to the generation of men who created the spectacular entertainments that helped to earn the courts of Henry VII (1485–1509) and Henry VIII (1509–1547) their reputations for magnificence. The multitalented Cornish could compose in a variety of genres, and his fame in his own time rested on songs, musical arrangements, and singing performances as well as on poetry, drama, and dramatic performances. As a composer he was ranked with Robert Fairfax, as a poet with John Skelton, and as a deviser of court revels with Sir Henry Guildford; but as the innovator of dramatic performances by the Children of the Chapel, he stood alone at the beginning of a tradi-

Musical setting by Cornish for Sir Thomas Wyatt's "A Robyn, joly Robyn," which is sung by Feste in William Shakespeare's Twelfth Night
(British Library, Add. MS 31922 f 53b)

tion carried on through the century by William Crane, Richard Bower, and Richard Edwards. Today he is regarded as one of the most important composers and influential devisers of court entertainments in the early sixteenth century.

Cornish's career is well documented from 1504 until his death circa 1524. The details of his early life, particularly between 1502 and 1504, are difficult to sort out. There were many individuals named Cornish flourishing in this period, several of them composers (John and Thomas, for example), and there were no fewer than three men named William Cornish living in or near London, including the composer and one of his sons, along with another who died circa 1500–1502. Evidence needed to place the biographical documents in context is lacking; consequently, confusions surface in all scholarship on the subject – worse still, in standard reference sources.

A William Cornish became the first master of the song school at Westminster Abbey in 1479, a post he held until 1490–1491. Most scholars identify him with the William Cornish who received a substantial reward from King Henry VII in 1493. On 12 November 1493 Cornish received another reward for presenting a prophecy at court, and on 6 January 1494 he appeared in the lead role as Saint George in the king's disguising. Cornish interrupted a play in progress by the King's Players by riding into Westminster Hall on horseback accompanied by a virgin who led a fire-spouting pageant dragon. He then delivered a speech before the king in rhyme royal and sang an anthem of Saint George with the Gentlemen of the Chapel before departing.

In 1494 he also began to receive grants of property, which suggests favor at court. Cornish is first associated with the Chapel Royal, the choral organization of the royal household, in 1494, confirmed in a Chamber payment in 1496 and in another reward in 1500. He was also responsible for producing at least one disguising and at least three pageants for the wedding celebrations of Prince Arthur and Catherine of Aragon in November 1501.

One group of scholars holds that this William Cornish was the famous composer. However, conflicting evidence survives from the years 1502–1504. The accounts of Saint Margaret's parish, Westminster, show that a William Cornish died in 1500–1502, and another group of scholars holds that this William was choirmaster at Westminster Abbey (1479–1491), Gentleman of the Chapel (1493–[1500–1502]), and father of William the composer. Part of the evidence comes from the Fairfax Manuscript (circa 1500), in which some songs are ascribed to William Cornish "jun.," and from Henry VIII's Manuscript (circa 1510–1520), in which some songs are ascribed to William Cornish. While it is attractive to imagine that his father was named William – it would explain the use of "jun." in the Fairfax Manuscript – there is no evidence to prove that William Cornish (died 1500–1502) was a member of the Chapel Royal or that he was the father of William the composer. Furthermore, payments continued to be made to Cornish at court during this period. In December 1502 he received a reward from Queen Elizabeth for setting a carol to music, and Chamber payments were made to him on 31 December 1503 and 13 January 1504.

In July 1504 "A treatise between Truth and Information" was written "In the Fleet made by me William Cornish otherwise called Nysshewhete Chapelman with the most famous and noble King Henry the VIIth." (*Nysshewhete* is a pseudonym that plays on Cornish's name by reversing the syllables and substituting *wheat* for *corn*.) The poem, written in seven-line rhyme-royal stanzas (*ababbcc*), consists of four introductory verses that complain that a man may be convicted by false information. This is followed by sixteen stanzas of "A parable between Information and Music," which argues by musical metaphors that the author had been wrongfully accused. The poem has been of interest to music historians for its references to contemporary instruments and to the four colors of musical notation.

In his article on Cornish for the *Dictionary of National Biography*, W. B. Squire suggests that Cornish was imprisoned for writing a satire against Sir Richard Empson, Henry VII's chief collector of fines, at the instigation of Richard Grey, Earl of Kent, and that the rubric that begins the poem, "A. B. of E. how C. for T. was P. in P.," can be read as "A Ballad of Empson, how Cornish for Treason was Put in Prison." Squire's suggestion cannot be supported. While the pseudonym *Nysshewhete* suggests that Cornish may have written other abusive satires, it could not have been the one he wrote for the earl of Kent, "O mischievous M, first syllable of thy name." Both John Stow, who attributed this satire to Cornish, and the writer of *The Great Chronicle of London*, who copied the poem into his text, date the work early in the reign of Henry VIII. This twenty-stanza poem in rhyme royal attacks Empson, his wife ("that foul sow's image"), and his son before presenting examples of contemporary and classical criminals who ended their lives in prison for corruption. The poem is in part abusive satire and in part a speculum in which Empson is encouraged to recognize the inevitable result of his crimes.

That Cornish was well known in his own time as a poet is clear from an anonymous satire in *The Great Chronicle of London* on John Baptist Grimald, one of Empson's deputies, entitled "O most cursed caitiff, what should I of thee write." Cornish is there mentioned as a poet of the caliber of his sometime associate Skelton, as well as of Sir Thomas More, and even of Geoffrey Chaucer, "if he were now in life."

Whatever the reason for his imprisonment, Cornish was released probably by late 1504 and certainly by 25 December 1508, when he was paid along with others of the chapel for performing before the king at Richmond. In November 1509 Cornish succeeded the noted composer William Newark as master of the Children of the Chapel Royal, although some evidence indicates that he had acted in that capacity as early as 1508. There are many Chamber payments to him for the diets of the children, including those associated with the trip to France from 29 May to 31 July 1520 for the entertainments at the Field of Cloth of Gold. Like other masters of the children, Cornish had a commission to recruit talented boy singers. Chamber payments show reimbursements for such activities, and two letters in the State Papers from 1518 record his successful attempt to take one such boy from Cardinal Wolsey's chapel.

Cornish's main business was to compose and arrange music, to teach some of the children to play the organ, and to teach all of them to sing at Mass, in court ceremonies, and in secular entertainments. Some of his religious music is preserved in the Eton Choir Book, the Caius Choir Book, and the Fairfax Manuscript. His secular songs and music are preserved in the Fairfax Manuscript and in Henry VIII's Manuscript, along with the king's own compositions and those of other noted composers of the period. Their work as a group is considered transitional from the more rigid, number-dominated compositions of the late Middle Ages to the expressiveness of post-Reformation music, which was suited to the natural accentuation of words. Cornish was a composer of the highest sophistication who was capable of a wide range of musical styles, from the most serious formal settings in multiple parts for devotional music to the lightest songs for recreation.

Several of his secular songs are associated with court entertainments. "Whiles life or breath" was a carol sung on behalf of Queen Catherine on an occasion when Henry VIII had a particularly good day in a tournament, such as the great tournament at Westminster in February 1511. "Trolly lolly" is a Maying song, such as may have been used in the Royal Maying entertainment of 1515.

"You and I and Amyas" was associated with the pageant-disguising *Château Vert* in March 1522, and J. P. Collier ascribes "Bow you down" to the interlude of *Venus and Beauty,* produced by Guildford for Twelfth Night 1514. One of Cornish's songs, "Hoyda, hoyda, jolly rutterkin," is mentioned in Skelton's play *Magnificence,* and "Ah Robin, gentle Robin" is an earlier setting by Cornish of the poem, better known in the later version by Sir Thomas Wyatt.

A letter from Richard Pace to Thomas Wolsey of 26 March 1518 suggests that Cornish's wit was an established part of even casual court entertainments. When Cornish accompanied the king on progress from Reading to Abingdon, where it was feared provisions might run short, he made an impromptu "merry supplication unto the king's grace for a bottle of hay and an horseloaf." Cornish's reputation as a performer and composer also extended beyond court circles. When his services were not required by the king, he was permitted to take outside engagements. Cornish's performances, some with the Gentlemen of the Chapel, are recorded at churches in London and Westminster, and one of his compositions, "Pleasure it is," was selected for inclusion in the first printed songbook in England, *Twenty Songs* (1530).

The traditional involvement of the chapel in court ceremonials, coupled with the interdependence of music, poetry, and drama in the early Tudor period, made the movement of the chapel into the court's secular entertainments a natural step. The formation of some of the Gentlemen of the Chapel, and eventually of the Children, into acting companies occurred during Cornish's career. The Gentlemen Players of the Chapel first appeared at court in 1505 and continued to give performances until 1512. By 1517 Cornish had organized the Children into an acting company and initiated a tradition of royal performances by them that continued into the reign of Elizabeth I.

No texts of any of Cornish's plays survive, and only a few titles can be associated with the Children of the Chapel. They were paid for a play on 7 March 1519, the same day on which the first known comedy by Plautus was acted in England, but it is not certain that they performed it. While the children were trained to sing in Latin, Cornish was not a classicist.

The revels on which he collaborated from 1494 to 1522 share similar characteristics. They almost all employ allegorical pageants that are used as scenic devices for dramatic action: assaulted castles, pavilions in perilous places, gardens of pleasure,

Music and lyrics for one of Cornish's court songs (from John Stevens, ed., Musica Britannica, *volume 18, 1962)*

and symbolic mounts or rocks. Most of these revels employ a three- or four-part structure consisting of a play as prologue, a pageant-disguising with dramatic action or martial exhibition thematically connected to the play, and a concluding disguised dance. Several of them use a presenter or prologue – often played by Cornish himself – who interprets the allegorical import of the revel. All employ music and song, and all draw their inspiration from medieval literature, particularly from romance. Most are linked to the chivalric ideal and, like most of his surviving songs, to the courtly-love tradition.

By 1516, and probably beforehand, Cornish was writing and producing his own texts for his plays and speeches for pageant-disguisings as well as composing his own songs. A distinctive feature of these revels, one that particularly suited them to the king's diplomatic and political purposes, was the adaptation of extensive dramatic action to the pageant-disguising. This occurred as early as 1494, when Cornish "interrupted" the King's Players performance with his

pageant-disguising, thus structurally and thematically combining two forms of entertainment.

Cornish retired from the chapel by the spring of 1523. In August of that year he received the grant of the manor of Hylden, Kent, and, in addition to the one he owned at Malmesbury, a corody at Thetford Priory. He died before 14 October 1524, the date his will was proved. He wished to be buried in the Chapel of the Rood in East Greenwich and left money for a tomb of brick with a stone border to be built over him. He left his property to his wife, Joan, and at her death to his eldest son, Henry. He also made bequests to his son William.

Cornish's music and songs have been most carefully studied in their social contexts by John Stevens. Sydney Anglo provides the most detailed description of Cornish's revels and the most thorough analysis of their political contexts. Important interpretive disagreements remain about Cornish's biography, but few linger about the significance of his music and his contribution to the development of court revels. While it is excessive to claim, as

C. W. Wallace does, the role of "Octavian Shakespeare" for Cornish, the evidence indicates that he was one of the most important innovators in court entertainments of the period, creating a unique blend of drama, music, song, poetry, and spectacle. Between 1509 and 1522 all of the musical performances by the Children of the Chapel, about one-third of the revels, and about half of the plays produced at court bore the stamp of his style.

References:

Sydney Anglo, "The Evolution of the Early Tudor Disguising, Pageant, and Mask," *Renaissance Drama,* new series 1 (1968): 3–44;

Anglo, *Spectacle, Pageantry and Early Tudor Policy* (Oxford: Clarendon, 1969), pp. 98–206;

Anglo, "William Cornish in a Play, Pageants, Prison, and Politics," *Review of English Studies,* new series 10, no. 40 (1959): 347–360;

J. P. Collier, *History of English Dramatic Poetry,* volume 1 (London, 1831), pp. 64–65;

H. N. Hillebrand, "The Child Actors," *University of Illinois Studies in Language and Literature,* 11 (1926): 40–64;

Ian Lancashire, *Dramatic Texts and Records of Great Britain: A Chronological Topography to 1558* (Toronto: University of Toronto Press, 1984);

John Stevens, *Music and Poetry in the Early Tudor Court* (London: Methuen, 1961);

W. R. Streitberger, "Henry VIII's Entertainment for the Queen of Scots, 1516: A New Revels Account and Cornish's Play," *Medieval and Renaissance Drama in England,* 1 (1984): 29–35;

Streitberger, "William Cornish and the Players of the Chapel Royal," *Medieval English Theatre,* 8 (July 1986): 3–20;

C. W. Wallace, *The Evolution of the English Drama up to Shakespeare* (Berlin: Georg Reimer, 1912), pp. 13–60.

Papers:

No texts of Cornish's plays or revels survive. Narrative evidence is found in Edward Hall's *The Union of the Two Noble and Illustrious Families of Lancaster and York* (London, 1548) and *The Great Chronicle of London* (London, 1938). Documentary evidence is found in the Revels accounts, the Chamber accounts, the State Papers, and various other official records. Cornish's music and songs are in B. L. Add. MS. 5465 (The Fairfax Manuscript); B. L. Add. MS. 31922 (Henry VIII's Manuscript); B. L. Harleian MS. 1709, fol. 63b; the Eton Choir Book; and Gonville and Caius MS. 667 (Caius Choir Book). "A treatise between Truth and Information" is in B. L. Royal MS. 18.D.II, fols. 163a–164a and B. L. Harleian MS. 43, fols. 88a–91a (imperfect). "O mischievous M" is in the Guildhall Library, London, Guildhall MS. 3331, fols. [320v–323v].

Thomas Cranmer

(2 July 1489 – 21 March 1556)

John N. Wall
North Carolina State University at Raleigh

BOOKS: *An exhortation vnto prayer . . . to be read in euery church afore processyons. Also a letanie with suffrages to be said or song in the tyme of the said processyons* (London: Printed by T. Berthelet, 1544);

Certain sermons, or homilies, appoynted by the kynges maiestie, to be declared and redde, by all persones, vicars, or curates, euery Sonday in their churches, where thei haue cure, by Cranmer and others (London: R. Grafton, 1547);

The order of the communion (London: R. Grafton, 1548);

The booke of the common prayer and administracion of the sacramentes, and other rites and ceremonies of the Churche: after the vse of the Churche of England (London: E. Whitchurch, 1549);

A defence of the true and catholike doctrine of the Sacrament of the Body and Blood of Our Savior Christ (London: R. Wolfe, 1550);

An answere against the false calumniacions of D. Richarde Smyth, who hath taken vpon hym to confute the Defence (London: R. Wolfe, 1551?);

An answer of . . . Thomas archebyshop of Canterburye, vnto a crafty cauillation by S. Gardiner. Wherin is also, answered places of the booke of D. Rich. Smyth (London: R. Wolfe, 1551);

The boke of common prayer, and administracion of the sacramentes, and other rites and ceremonies in the Churche of Englande (London: E. Whitchurch, 1552);

A confutation of vnwritten verities, both bi the holye scriptures and moste auncient autors (Wesel?: J. Lambrecht?; 1556?);

All the submyssyons, and recantations of T. Cranmer, truely set forth both in Latyn and Englysh (London: J. Cawood, 1556);

The recantation of Thomas Cranmer . . . tr. faythfully out of Latin (London: Printed by W. Copland for W. Riddell, 1556);

The copy of certain lettres sent to the quene, and also to doctour Martin and doctour Storye, by T. Cranmer who suffrd martirdome in Marche. 1556. (Emden: E. van der Erve, 1556?);

The lamentacion of England. . . . (A declaracion of T. Cranmer [against] the reporte, that he should sett vp the masse at canterbury 1553) (Germany?, 1557).

Editions and Collections: *The Remains of Thomas Cranmer, D.D., Archbishop of Canterbury,* edited by H. Jenkins (Oxford: Oxford University Press, 1833);

Writings and Disputations of Thomas Cranmer, Archbishop of Canterbury, Martyr, 1556, Relative to the Sacrament of the Lord's Supper, edited by J. E. Cox (Cambridge: Parker Society, 1884);

Miscellaneous Writings and Letters of Thomas Cranmer, Archbishop of Canterbury, Martyr, 1556, edited by Cox (Cambridge: Parker Society, 1846);

The First and Second Prayer Books of Edward VI (London: Dent, 1910);

The Work of Thomas Cranmer, edited by G. E. Duffield (Appleton, Wis.: Sutton Courtenay Press, 1964);

The Book of Common Prayer 1559, edited by John E. Booty (Charlottesville: University Press of Virginia, 1976);

Certain Sermons or Homilies (1547) and A Homily against Disobedience and Wilful Rebellion (1570), edited by Ronald B. Bond (Toronto: University of Toronto Press, 1987).

TRANSLATIONS: *The determinations of the moste famous vniuersities of Italy and Fraunce,* possibly translated by Cranmer (London: Printed by T. Berthelet, 1531);

Cathechismus, that is to say, a shorte instruction into christian religion, translated by Cranmer (London: Printed by N. Hill for G. Lynne, 1548);

Marten Micron, *A short and faythful instruction, for symple christianes, whych intende worthely to receyue the holy supper,* translated by Cranmer (Emden: E. van der Erve, 1556?).

Thomas Cranmer, 1545 (portrait by Fliccius; from Jasper Ridley, Thomas Cranmer, *1962)*

Thomas Cranmer is remembered chiefly because his work as a liturgist during the reign of Edward VI was recovered in the Elizabethan Settlement of Religion and over time became the standard form of Christian worship for the English-speaking world. As a result he must be viewed, after the translators of the English Bible, as the most influential prose stylist in English letters. Having overcome Roman resistance to the use of English in worship and survived Reformed Church opposition to written prayers, Cranmer's liturgical texts in his Book of Common Prayer have entered the realm of oral culture. It now seems inevitable that a Christian wedding service of whatever tradition should begin "Dearly beloved," or that a burial service should summarize human life as a passage from "earth to earth, ashes to ashes, dust to dust." On a more literary level the tone and rhythm of Cranmer's prayers and liturgies form part of the inescapable background for poets as diverse as George Herbert or John Dryden; William Wordsworth or Dante Gabriel Rossetti; Alfred, Lord Tennyson, or T. S. Eliot.

Little in Cranmer's early years suggests the significant role he would play in the history of English literary or religious history. Cranmer found the opportunity to play a major role in the great religious and social revolution of the mid sixteenth century only after a less-than-stellar undergraduate career at Cambridge and a brief detour into matrimony. According to the most reliable sources, the future archbishop of Canterbury and liturgist of the Church of England was born on 2 July 1489, the second son of Thomas and Agnes Hatfield Cranmer. The senior Cranmer was the squire of the village of Aslockton in Nottinghamshire. Young Thomas had an older brother, a younger brother, and at least five sisters. His father was a gentleman of Norman ancestry who could claim possession of a coat of arms, yet he was not so wealthy that he stood in the way of one daughter's marriage to a miller.

As in the case of so many younger sons in Tudor England, both Thomas and his younger brother, Edmund, went to university and later became priests of the church. It is significant that Cranmer's basic education, both at the local and the university level, came prior to the humanist educational revolution sparked by Desiderius Erasmus's 1511 lectures at Cambridge University. Cranmer thus participated in the traditional curriculum of Latin grammar, rhetoric, and logic (the trivium), followed by arithmetic, geometry, music, and astronomy (the quadrivium), and large doses of scholastic philosophy, probably taught by masters prone to instruction by rote memorization and the occasional flogging. When Cranmer encountered the "new learning," his strongest perception of it would have been in terms of its contrast with the "old learning" and the value that the "new learning" placed on education for the enrichment of the moral life and on training in rhetoric for effectiveness in persuading people to pursue that moral life.

Cranmer attended a local grammar school until he was fourteen. In 1503 he was sent to Jesus College, Cambridge, where he spent the next eight years. Yet for one who would so shape the language of English religion and culture, his academic record was not outstanding. When he was awarded his B.A. degree in 1511, he was graduated thirty-second in a class of forty-two students. Hugh Latimer, Cranmer's future colleague in the reformation of the Church of England, also took his B.A. that year, finishing a more distinguished eighth on that year's list of graduates.

Nevertheless, Cranmer was to remain at Jesus College for three more years of study in classical and biblical languages and literatures, for which he received his M.A. in 1514. During this time his prospects for an academic and clerical career must have improved, for he was named a fellow of Jesus College. The years of his postbaccalaureate study were also coincidentally years in which Erasmus was in residence for long periods at Cambridge as professor of Greek and Lady Margaret professor of Divinity. Erasmus lectured there on biblical languages, worked on his edition of the Greek New Testament (1516), and prepared to write *Education of*

a Christian Prince (1515). This was the time of Erasmus's greatest popularity – the years after publication of his *Manual of Christian Warfare* (1501) and *Praise of Folly* (1509), when his attacks on Scholasticism and abuses of the medieval church and his vision of the Christian life as one of good works grounded on the reading of Scripture, eucharistic sharing, and godly conversation were the talk of progressive Europeans.

The extent of Cranmer's contact with Erasmus is uncertain, but his later career is unthinkable without the influence of the great Dutch humanist and philologist. For example, in the preface to his Greek New Testament of 1516, Erasmus argues that the Bible should be "translated into all the languages of all Christian people" so "that the farm worker might sing parts of them at the plough, that the weaver might hum them at the shuttle, and that the traveller might beguile the weariness of the way by reciting them." Cranmer expanded on Erasmus's image twenty years later when he wrote the preface to the 1540 edition of the Great Bible, the first official English translation: "Here may all manner of persons: men, women; young, old; learned, unlearned; rich, poor; priests, laymen; lords, ladies; officers, tenants, and mean men; virgins, wives, widows; lawyers, merchants, artificers, husbandmen, and all manner of persons ... learn all things."

But that was in a perhaps wished-for but as yet unimaginable future in 1515, when Erasmus left Cambridge and Cranmer was married. Conceivably because of the contrast between the images of learning for the active life offered by Erasmus and the traditional scholastic curriculum still in place in Cambridge, Cranmer turned from the prospect of more study in preparation for ordination and with it vows of poverty and chastity. In 1515 he married one Joan, perhaps daughter of the proprietor of the Dolphin Inn in Bridge Street; she soon became pregnant. Resigning his fellowship at Jesus College (a position available only to celibates), Cranmer became common reader at Buckingham (later Magdalene) College and sought other means of income to support his family.

This change in state of life was to be temporary, however. Joan died in childbirth; shortly after, Cranmer was restored to his fellowship at Jesus College. Immersing himself in religious studies, following a curriculum influenced by Erasmus's models, he was by 1520 ordained to the priesthood and granted license to function as university preacher, and in 1521 he was awarded the degree of bachelor of divinity. After five more years of study, he was awarded the doctor of divinity degree in 1526. During this period Cranmer's scholarly reputation also grew, for in 1525 he was awarded a post at the newly formed Cardinal College at Oxford. He declined, deciding instead to remain at Jesus College; his loyalty was rewarded the next year when he was named examiner in divinity for Cambridge University.

At this time many of Cranmer's fellow students and faculty at Cambridge were eagerly reading the works of Martin Luther and debating the new ideas coming out of Germany, Switzerland, and France. Some were rushing into print with attacks on the medieval church or plunging into projects to produce the Bible in English. But the future architect of the Church of England prepared for his as-yet-unglimpsed role of reformer by immersing himself in study, after an Erasmian plan. A contemporary said of his theological education that after returning to Jesus College on the death of his wife, Cranmer "gave himself to Faber, Erasmus, good Latin authors . . . unto the time that Luther began to write [around 1519–1520] and then he, considering what great controversy was in matters of religion . . . bent himself to try out the truth [and] applied his whole study three years unto the [Holy] Scriptures, [then] he gave his mind to good writers both new and old."

As a result of his studies, Cranmer probably came to the conclusion that there was substance in at least some of the Lutheran Reformers' charges against the authority of the papacy. The English had always resisted the more extreme papal claims to local authority; certainly recent popes were hardly promising candidates for the leader who would promote the kinds of church reform called for by Erasmus and his followers. Yet Cranmer was never one to move precipitously in theological matters; independent of mind, he resisted absorption into any Continental reform movement. The formularies of the faith in which he had a hand (the Ten Articles of 1536, the Bishops' Book of 1537, and the Articles of Religion of 1553), while clearly nonpapal, always took a stand distinct from either contemporary Lutheranism or an emerging Calvinism on essential matters of justification, salvation, faith, and works. Cranmer's mature thought on the matters at issue in the Reformation controversies would, for example, affirm justification by faith, but only as the beginning of a lifelong process of charitable action needed for salvation; his view on predestination was pragmatic, affirming the comfort it could give to the believer but rejecting its negative corollary for the unbeliever.

Whatever his developing beliefs about the Lutheran Reformation, Cranmer would not have much of a role in the rapidly changing religious scene until the end of the 1520s, and then for quite different reasons than the advocacy of church reform. By then the support of the papacy displayed by King Henry VIII during the early years of its controversy with the Reformers had begun to show signs of retreat. Pope Leo X had awarded Henry the title Defender of the Faith in 1521 because of the king's attack on Luther's position on the sacraments. Yet his successor, Pope Clement VII, politically captive to King Charles I of Spain, would not look so kindly on Henry's desire by 1527 to divorce Queen Catherine.

By the end of the decade, the king's frustration was heightened by delays in papal proceedings, and he was eager for new perspectives. One soon came from an unexpected source. Cranmer in 1529 apparently happened to meet with two members of Henry's court – Stephen Gardiner, the king's secretary, and Edward Fox, the king's almoner – while they were all staying at the home of a Master Cressy of Waltham, who was related to Cranmer by marriage. Cranmer had known both men at Cambridge and felt free to discuss with them the king's "Great Cause." He suggested that Henry would be more successful in his efforts to secure support for his divorce if he defined the issue as a theological, not a legal, one and consulted university-trained theologians on the subject. Later that year at Cambridge, the king's marriage was the subject of a debate at which Cranmer argued successfully in support of divorce.

As a result Cranmer was summoned to an audience with the king in late October 1529 and charged with writing a book in support of Henry's desire to divorce Catherine. Thus Cranmer entered the list of English authors with a work of pivotal interest for the historical record. Its power and persuasiveness were substantial, for it contributed to the decision of the Cambridge University faculty in theology, delivered in March 1530, that Henry's marriage to Catherine was against divine law. It may have contributed to the similar decisions of the faculties of Oxford, Orleans, and Angers reached in May 1530. Cranmer's proposal for resolving Henry's marital dilemma therefore was off to a successful start, yet it was halted in May 1530, when Pope Clement prohibited further discussion of the divorce by any university.

The text of Cranmer's arguments for Henry's divorce is not known to survive. On the basis of his later writings, one can surmise that it gave careful review of the arguments, marshaled copious evidence for its case, and treated its opponents with

Letter from Cranmer to Thomas Cromwell, 17 April 1534, in which the archbishop asks the king's minister to allow Thomas More and John Fisher not to swear to the whole contents of the Act of Succession (British Library Cleopatra, E VI, fol. 175 recto and verso)

either of a wilfulnes will not, or of an indurate
and indurtible conscience can not, altre fro their
opinions of the kinges first pretensed mariage (wherein
thay have ones said their myndes, & peraps have a
pswasion in their headps, yt if thay sholde undo [vary]
therfrome their fame & estimation were disteyned
for euer) or ellps of the autoritie of the Busshopp
of Rome: yet if at the reaulme no one accorde hold
apprehende the said succession, in my ingement it is
a thynge to be amplected & imbraced. Which thing
although I trust surely in god yt it shal be brought
to passe, yet herunto might not a litle avayle
the consent and othes of theis two psonps the
Busshops of Rochest and maist agore to their adhe
rentp or rather confederatp. And if the kinges
pleasure so were, their said othes might be suppressed
but shall and wigore
~~~~~~~~~~~ his highnes might take some como
dite by the publisshynge of the same. Thus our
lorde have you en in his conservation. ffro my man[er]
at Croydon the xxvi day of April.

yor own assured ...
Thomas Cantuar

Woodcuts depicting the Pharisee and Publican and Christ healing a man (from Catechism, *1548)*

courtesy and respect. Yet by the time it was put to use in Cambridge, Cranmer was in Italy and Germany serving as Henry's agent in the cause of the divorce.

Cranmer spent much of 1530 in Italy seeking support for Henry's cause. Part of his agenda was encouraging the theological faculties of other universities to follow the lead of Cambridge in finding for Henry in his claims about the invalidity of his marriage to Catherine of Aragon. Many in fact did so. Following Cranmer's return to England in the fall of 1530, *The Determinations of the Most Famous Universities of Italy and France* was published. This work lays out arguments for Henry's side in his divorce case, together with citations of support from scriptural, patristic, and medieval sources. The favorable opinions of eight foreign universities serve as a preface.

The Determinations was originally written in Latin and published in the spring of 1530; Fox, with whom Cranmer had spoken about the king's divorce in the summer of 1529, is listed as one of the authors. According to one tradition, Cranmer translated this work for its English edition. The relationship, if any, between *The Determinations* and the book he wrote in support of Henry's divorce prior to the debates among the theological faculty at Cambridge is problematic, yet it is plausible to conjecture that Cranmer's work served as one source for its form and perhaps for its substance.

Cranmer's journeys to Germany in 1532 gave him direct experience of worship in the Reformed Lutheran church and the opportunity to learn more about its developing theology from conversations with Lutheran clergy. The extent of his adopting distinctly Lutheran theological positions remains controversial, since the fullest evidence dates from fifteen years later. In his Homily on Justification in the Book of Homilies (1547), Cranmer articulates a position on justification that displays clear Lutheran affinities: "we be justified by faith only, freely, and without works." Yet he would go on to distinguish salvation from justification, affirming that the faith that justifies is a "quick or lively faith" that reveals itself in good works (Homily on Faith) and that such works are what "lead faithful men unto eternal life" (Homily on Good Works). Unlike the Lutheran position, in which faith is not only the sole ground of justification but provides all that is necessary for salvation, or the Calvinist position, in which the ability to do good works becomes a sign of one's eternal election to salvation by God, Cranmer's mature position retains Erasmus's call to the life of active charity in imitation of Christ as the chief concern of Christian proclamation.

Yet while in Germany, Cranmer certainly came to affirm the Lutheran acceptance of a married clergy, for during this visit he married for the second time, one Margaret, niece of the Lutheran divine Andrew Oisander, who performed the marriage ceremony. Cranmer would remain married to Margaret for the rest of his life, refusing to renounce her even when it would have been politically advantageous to do so. The marriage was not made public until 1549; in the interim were periods in which Margaret lived in England secretly (1533–1539 and 1543–1549) and periods in which she was sent home to Germany for her own personal safety. They had two children, Thomas and Margaret.

In the fall of 1532 the course of Cranmer's life was irrevocably changed. Summoned by Henry VIII to return to England, Cranmer learned that he had been chosen by the king to succeed William Warham as archbishop of Canterbury. With his divorce proceedings bogged down in the church courts, with pressures brought to bear on Pope

Clement proving ineffective, and with mounting domestic pressure to resolve the matter (including Anne Boleyn's pregnancy), Henry took matters into his own hands. Cranmer was consecrated archbishop on 30 March 1533; after a brief hearing on the matter, he declared on 23 May that Henry's marriage was invalid and that Henry was free to remarry; on 28 May he declared that Henry's marriage to Anne Boleyn (which had taken place the previous January) was valid.

Cranmer's claim to the ability to act independently of the papacy in the resolution of the king's "Great Cause" was based on the argument that Henry, not the pope, was head of the Church in England. This position was soon enacted into law through a series of parliamentary measures. By depriving the pope of authority over religious matters in England, Henry and Cranmer also created the opportunity for more-extensive religious reform, which Cranmer would promote for the remainder of his life. The archbishop's support for the royal supremacy, which was established in Henry's reign through a series of acts by Parliament and submissions by clergy and laity, brought opportunity for reform; it also linked the pace and character of reform to the personal and political aims of the monarch. During the late 1530s and early 1540s in Henry's reign, power lay with Cranmer and Thomas Cromwell, whom Henry put in charge of exercising his supremacy in regard to the church. Movement toward reform included adoption of the Bible in English, abolition of monasteries, and promulgation of statements of doctrine that rejected abuses of the cult of the saints and the doctrine of purgatory. Cautious revisions of theological position were put forward in the Ten Articles and a commentary on the Ten Articles known as the Bishops' Book.

In the mid 1540s, however, Henry needed alliances with more-conservative forces; Cromwell was executed, and Cranmer had to withstand attacks from conservative bishops such as Gardiner. What has been called the "Tudor Reaction" led to the Six Articles (1539), a theological statement that, while reasserting royal supremacy, supported more traditional positions on such matters as the Real Presence of Christ in the Mass, clerical celibacy, private masses, and reception of the bread only by the laity. Cranmer again dueled with Gardiner; on this occasion he held his position as archbishop through Henry's loyalty and the support of Henry's last queen, Catherine Parr.

While preserving his position – if not his power – through Henry's intervention, Cranmer prepared the texts necessary for the next stage of reformation. These display his excellence as a writer of English prose. Landmark occasions in the progress of reform in which his literary hand is clearly evident include the authorization and publication of an official English version of the Bible (1539), republished with his preface the following year; his *Catechism* (1548); the beginnings of liturgy in English with the publication of the English Litany (1544) and the Order of Holy Communion (1548); the establishment of an official collection of sermons to be read every Sunday and holy day "in such order as they stand in the book" (the Book of Homilies); the publication of an official guide to the interpretation of the New Testament (Erasmus's *Paraphrases* of the Gospels and Acts in 1548); and the first complete liturgy in English (the Book of Common Prayer, 1549) and its first revision (1552).

As the dates make clear, most of these works were published during the reign of Edward VI, Henry's son, who succeeded him to the throne in 1547. The product of Henry's marriage to Jane Seymour, Edward represented the success of Henry's program for resolving his marital and dynastic problems by taking control of the church. The doctrine of royal supremacy, which Cranmer accepted when he cooperated with Henry in securing his divorce from Catherine of Aragon, made possible such a sweeping and comprehensive program of religious reform. Reformation of the church through use of new texts in public worship could be mandated quickly once the support of the monarch could be secured.

Cranmer's reforming efforts were controversial, provoking armed rebellion as well as vigorous polemic. In 1549 rebels in Devon and Cornwall demanded the return of the Mass in Latin, finding Cranmer's English rite to be "a Christmas game." Gardiner, Cranmer's own bishop of Winchester, joined other writers in attacking such fundamental departures from the liturgical discipline of the Middle Ages. Rebellion was put down by the monarchy; Cranmer himself responded to the polemic in a series of texts, most notably his *Defense of the True and Catholic Doctrine of the Sacrament of the Body and Blood* (1550), his *Answer . . . unto a Crafty Cavillation by Gardiner* (1551), and his *Confutation of Unwritten Verities* (1556). As a controversialist Cranmer was certainly no worse a rhetorician, or perhaps no better, than his opponents; his polemical works have been praised for their utilitarian clarity and their effective articulation of officially sanctioned positions but not for their subtlety or delightfulness. Although he was a prolific writer, his work is most often treated

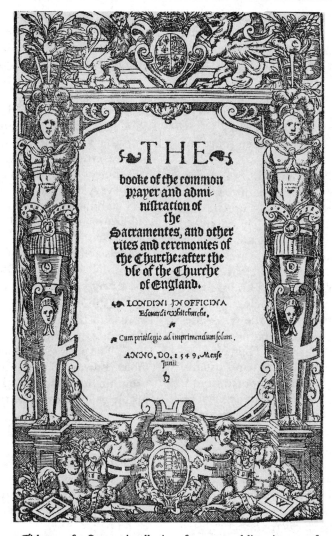

Title page for Cranmer's collection of prayers and liturgies, one of the most influential works in English letters

under the categories of the historical, the theological, or the liturgical rather than the literary.

Even in regard to his liturgical writings, many studies of sixteenth-century prose describe Cranmer's distinction more in terms of his skill at translation than his creativity in original composition. The argument for his literary distinction must begin with the point that he produced two kinds of writing. The first and most significant includes such works as the Book of Common Prayer and the Book of Homilies, texts for use in public worship that constitute the heart of Cranmer's reform program for the Church of England. The second includes such texts as *Defense of the True and Catholic Doctrine of the Sacrament* and *Answer . . . unto . . . Gardiner,* occasional works instigated by specific political, social, or religious controversies he was called to address. Cranmer's distinction must rest on the basis

of the first category, for, as a liturgist and crafter of prose for use in public worship, he has no peer.

Yet even this claim is further complicated by the fact that of the works most closely associated with his name it is uncertain which parts are Cranmer's and which are actually the work of other members of the English episcopate or anonymous members of their staffs. It is known, for example, that the Book of Homilies was a collaborative effort; of its twelve sermons, three and perhaps four are Cranmer's, but the rest were contributed by other bishops and priests of the church. The Book of Common Prayer is too massive an undertaking to imagine as the exclusive effort of a single person, especially one so responsible for the day-to-day life of the Church of England as its spiritual leader. Cranmer had advice and help from a variety of sources in the preparation of his two editions of the prayer book, probably including the text-drafting help of a committee.

Yet if one acknowledges that Cranmer worked toward the completion of his liturgical projects over two decades and played a decisive and shaping part in their final form — and if one broadens the categories of the literary to include more than the romantic notion of the isolated imagination in solitary communication with the inspiring muse — then one may see Cranmer's achievements in a clearer light. The reader needs to value as literary the work of one who at a critical moment in the history of the English language was able to shape disparate elements of language — whether received from the past or from other participants in a corporate effort — into a distinctive stylistic voice working toward a unified rhetorical purpose. In these terms Cranmer may certainly lay claim to major significance as a writer of English prose. Certainly, based in the duration and scope of his popularity, he can justly be held the second most influential prose stylist in the history of English letters.

On such grounds pride of place must still be given to William Tyndale, Miles Coverdale, and the host of lesser-known translators responsible for the succession of official English-language Bibles, from the Great Bible of 1535 to the Authorized Version of 1611. Their prose renderings of the Hebrew and Greek Scriptures achieved a scope of audience and a duration of popularity unparalleled among English writers. Indeed, in the consciousness of many, the King James translation continues to serve as the Bible itself, supplanting in the functioning of the mind the ancient Hebrew and Greek texts.

But Cranmer's liturgical writings, most notably the Book of Homilies and two Books of Common Prayer, inaugurated the use of English as a language for official public worship and established standards for style in formal discourse that persist wherever member churches of the Anglican Communion are to be found. The 1662 revision of the Book of Common Prayer remains the official prayer book of the Church of England, and more recent revisions of Cranmer's original texts — such as the so-called "Rite One" texts of the American Episcopal Church's 1979 Book of Common Prayer — continue in wide use, even where contemporary-language rites have been officially adopted.

Cranmer himself might well be surprised by the endurance of his liturgical style and by the energy many have invested in its preservation. Among the goals he sought in the reformation of worship was — according to his preface to the first Book of Common Prayer — to have "nothing . . . read,

but . . . in such a language and order, as is most easy and plain for the understanding, both of the readers and hearers." The traditional liturgy, for Cranmer, was of course "the service . . . read in Latin to the people," with the result, in Cranmer's view, that the people "understood not, so that they have heard with their ears only; and their hearts, spirit and mind, have not been edified." Whether Cranmer's liturgical style can still be said to meet his own criteria of being "easy and plain," his prayer book established through constant use over the centuries a widely admired and imitated standard for formal uses of language, especially at occasions in which deep personal experiences of joy, grief, and other powerful emotions are publicly observed. Like the Reformation translations of the Bible, the texts of Cranmer's prayer book became part of the received tradition of English letters, their words and phrases woven into the fabric of daily discourse, marking the passage of seasons and holidays and the major events of human life.

Opportunity for beginning the transformation of worship into the vernacular came in 1544, when Henry sought to rally public support for his foreign policy through public processions. Cranmer's response was an English litany for use in procession in which the distinctive style of the Book of Common Prayer can be glimpsed. Cranmer's originality in liturgical composition has been documented by James A. Devereux, and his distinctive style has been aptly described by Janel M. Mueller as the joining of the successiveness of native English prose with the suspensiveness of liturgical Latin to produce a hybrid enrichment of the vernacular. Thus the doubling and parallelism of such petitions in the litany as "Remember not, Lord, our offenses, nor the offenses of our forefathers, neither take thou vengeance of our sins" anticipates the later style of such prayers as the Collect for the Second Sunday after Epiphany: "Almighty and Everlasting God, which dost govern all things in heaven and earth: mercifully hear the supplication of thy people, and grant us thy peace all the days of our life."

Cranmer drew on vernacular oral forms appropriate for texts intended to be read aloud, enriching them with repetitions and redundancies in words, phrases, and clauses, which were often arranged in binary, correlative form. The result is a powerful balancing of language that holds together a sense of the agency of both God and his people. The Reformation crisis over the relationship between divine grace and the freedom of human agency is here resolved in a dynamic sense of cooperation: God enables through grace the doing

Cranmer in old age, with the beard he began to grow in 1547 in memory of Henry VIII (portrait by an unknown artist; Collection of the Archbishop of Canterbury)

of good works that humans are called to desire freely.

This vision of participatory action, articulated in the very style of Cranmer's prayer book, is embodied in all of his official liturgical writings. It is an Erasmian vision, in which the functioning of the Godly Feast as reading and exposition of Scripture and sharing of eucharistic bread and wine, leading to charitable work in the world, is made the model of human endeavor on the parish, community, and national level. God's grace, conveyed through the Sacraments of the church, enables faith that reveals itself in good works. Salvation comes to those who engage in a life of good works, enabled by grace through faith and nurtured through the public worship of the church. The goal of Christian living is the building up of the true Christian commonwealth, achieved through charitable action toward one's neighbor.

In his sermons in the Book of Homilies, Cranmer argues that the faith that justifies is a "true and lively faith" that reveals itself in good works of active charity that lead one to salvation. Cranmer's prayer book organizes the regular public reading of the Bible into an annual cycle of texts used at daily morning and evening prayer. His Eucharist, to be celebrated on Sundays and holy days, entails the proclamation and interpretation of the Word and celebration and reception of the sacramental bread and wine, leading to the discovery that worshipers are "very members incorporate in [Christ's] mystical body," enabled by grace to "do all such good works, as [God] hast prepared for us to walk in." Cranmer's rites for baptism, marriage, ministry to the sick, and burial all work to bring private events in life into the context of the worshiping community, where they are to find their meaning and significance.

Cranmer sought to move the focus of theological interpretation in the Eucharist away from the objects of consecration (and the medieval development of adoration for them) toward the action of the Eucharist, what he calls in *An Answer . . . unto . . . Gardiner* the "due ministration of the Sacrament according to Christ's ordinance and institution" in which Christ is present and through which "all benefits of his passion" are conveyed. Cranmer's 1552 revision of the prayerbook of 1549 was made in part to clarify this point, for Gardiner had claimed that he could interpret the 1549 Eucharist in terms of medieval understandings of "real presence." Cranmer wished to assert the active working of Christ in the world, promoting the reign of charity and building the Christian commonwealth, not the isolation of Christ in objects and in rites that turned people away from their neighbors.

Cranmer believed the commonwealth that he sought could be promoted through liturgical uniformity in England; where "there hath been great diversity in saying and singing in churches within this realm," he proposed that "all the whole realm shall have but one use." Bringing all Englishfolk to use one prayer book must have contributed significantly to the development of a standard dialect of English, as well as to the spread of literacy and the esteem of learning. The work of promoting the Reformation in England through preparation of public documents such as the prayer book and the Book of Homilies – and through defense of their use in such controversial writings as *An answer . . . unto . . . Gardiner* – occupied Cranmer from the mid 1530s until the early 1550s.

All of Cranmer's reforming aspirations and efforts came to a sudden halt with the death of Edward VI in 1553. With the accession of Mary, he was imprisoned in the Tower; because he had supported the coronation of Lady Jane Grey rather than the succession of Mary, he was tried for treason, convicted, and sentenced to be executed. According to the normal course of things, he would have been beheaded early in 1554. But Mary's government and the new archbishop of Canterbury, Reginald Pole, had other things in store for the deposed archbishop. After being held in the Tower of London for six months, he was taken to Oxford and made to face charges of heresy. Convicted, he was excommunicated by Pope Paul IV in December 1555, and on 14 February 1556 he was publicly humiliated by being first dressed in the clothing of the episcopacy and then stripped of all signs of his church office.

Cranmer then faced the most challenging days of his life, and the most painful ones for his admirers. Scheduled for execution by being burned at the stake on 21 March 1556, he on six occasions recanted his actions as archbishop and his belief in the tenets of the Reformation. His motivation for this remains unclear. He may have thought to survive this crisis – as he did earlier ones during Henry's reign – by giving just enough to get by, so as to live and fight another day. Or he could have been overcome by fear and the humiliation of his constant degradation at the hands of Mary's and Pole's inquisitors. Many historians have faulted him for these actions, but none of them has ever had to face the collapse of his life's work so thoroughly and without recourse as Cranmer, nor have any faced the certainty of death by bonfire.

On the morning of 21 March, Cranmer was led through the rain into Saint Mary's Church to face yet one more public humiliation. Dressed in a ragged gown and an old square cap to cover his head, which had been shaved during his degradation, he heard a sermon declaring that his execution was an act of vengeance for the deaths of Thomas More and Cardinal Fisher. He was then forced to stand on a raised platform and called upon to read another statement of recantation.

Cranmer, however, surprised his persecutors. His last act as a writer dramatically reasserted his stance as a reformer; he departed from a text that had been approved for his use prior to his execution. Instead of proclaiming his allegiance to the pope and affirming the doctrine of transubstantiation, he read from another text declaring that he repudiated his recantations, describing the pope as "Christ's enemy, and Antichrist" and confirming his belief in the doctrine of the Eucharist as "taught in my book against the Bishop of Winchester [Gardiner] . . . so true a doctrine of the Sacrament, that it shall stand at the last day before the judgement of God." To signal the authenticity of this final position, he promised to hold the hand that had signed the recantation into the fire so that it would burn before the rest of his upper body.

Pulled quickly from the platform, Cranmer was hurried to the stake. The forces of Counter-Reformation silenced him in his sixty-seventh year; his ashes were left in a ditch outside the wall of Oxford, and his memory was subjected to a campaign of vilification. Yet his final affirmation of the Reformed church would inspire resistance to Mary's reign and help insure that upon her death his goddaughter Elizabeth would restore the independence of the Church of England.

The burning of Tharchbishop of Cant. D. Tho. Cranmer in the town dich at Oxford, with his hand first thrust into the fyre, wherwith he subscribed before.

Engraving of Cranmer's execution in Oxford, showing him holding the hand with which he had signed his recantation into the fire (from Acts and Monuments of These Latter and Perilous Days, *1563)*

The Elizabethan Settlement of Religion was based on the use of revised versions of Cranmer's Book of Common Prayer (revised, 1559), his Book of Homilies (revised, 1559), the English Bible (Great Bible; reprinted, 1560; revised as the Bishops' Bible, 1569), the English Primer (revised 1559), and the Articles of Religion (revised 1562). In most cases these revisions reflect efforts either to make Cranmer's prose more "understanded of the people" or to bring it into line with an imagined notion of Tudor style created by continuous use of that prose. With changing circumstances faced by the church, Cranmer's work other than his prayer book has become mostly of historic interest. Yet respect for his liturgical style has perpetuated his influence; use of liturgies crafted from his originals is so widespread that his texts must exceed even William Shakespeare's in frequency of performance.

Study of Cranmer is generally confined to liturgical and theological circles, where the heritage of the archbishop is sought by partisans of different schools of Anglicanism. Cranmer revised his 1549 liturgies almost immediately; the Church of England has continued to do so, although modern traditional-language liturgies are still claimed as the work of Cranmer, or at least to be authentically Cranmerian. In literary circles commentary beyond the merely appreciative is rare, limited to a few excellent analyses of Cranmer's style. Studies of influence are handicapped by the difficulty of grasping the effect of constant repetition by generations of English-speaking Christians, and these are usually limited to pointing out potential isolated echoes of this or that passage. Future studies may well attend to the different spiritualities that have been sustained by Anglican worship and the differing literary responses to them. Also, understanding of prayer book use can be a guide to the experience of the Bible and of major life events by English writers through the centuries. Reflection on Cranmer's liturgical achievement can be a reminder that religion is for most people not a system of thought but a lived experience, shaped at least for Anglicans as much by the rhythms of his prose as by the vision of worship structured by that prose.

Biographies:

A. F. Pollard, *Thomas Cranmer and the English Reformation, 1489–1556* (London: Putnam, 1926; Hamden, Conn.: Archon, 1965);

F. E. Hutchinson, *Cranmer and the English Reformation* (London: English Universities Press, 1951);

G. W. Bromiley, *Thomas Cranmer, Archbishop and Martyr* (London: Lutterworth, 1956);

T. Maynard, *The Life of Thomas Cranmer* (London: Staples Press, 1956);

Jasper Ridley, *Thomas Cranmer* (Oxford: Clarendon, 1962);

Peter Newman Brooks, *Cranmer in Context* (Minneapolis: Fortress, 1989).

References:

John Booty, John N. Wall, and David Siegenthaler, *The Godly Kingdom of Tudor England: Great Books of the English Reformation* (Wilton, Conn.: Morehouse, 1981);

G. W. Bromiley, *Thomas Cranmer: Theologian* (New York: Oxford University Press, 1956);

Stella Brook, *The Language of the Book of Common Prayer* (New York: Oxford University Press, 1965);

James A. Devereux, S. J., "The Primers and the Prayer Book Collects," *Huntington Library Quarterly,* 32, no. 1 (1968–1969): 29–44;

A. G. Dickens, *The English Reformation* (New York: Schocken, 1964);

G. R. Elton, *Reform and Reformation: England, 1509–1558* (Cambridge, Mass., Harvard University Press, 1977);

Elton, *Reform and Renewal: Thomas Cromwell and the Common Weal* (Cambridge: Cambridge University Press, 1973);

Whitney R. D. Jones, *The Mid-Tudor Crisis, 1539–1563* (London: Macmillan, 1973);

Jones, *The Tudor Commonwealth, 1529–1559* (London: Athlone, 1970);

John N. King, *English Reformation Literature* (Princeton: Princeton University Press, 1982);

James K. McConica, *English Humanists and Reformation Politics* (Oxford: Clarendon, 1965);

Janel M. Mueller, *The Native Tongue and the Word: Developments in English Prose Style, 1380–1580* (Chicago: University of Chicago Press, 1984);

J. A. Muller, *Stephen Gardiner and the Tudor Reaction* (New York: Macmillan, 1926);

Maurice Powicke, *The Reformation in England* (New York: Oxford University Press, 1941);

John N. Wall, "The Book of Homilies of 1547 and the Continuity of English Humanism in the Sixteenth Century," *Anglican Theological Review,* 58 (January 1976): 75–87;

Wall, "History, Culture and the Changing Language of Worship: The Case of the Books of Common Prayer," *Anglican Theological Review,* 73 (Fall 1991): 403–429;

Wall, "The Reformation in England and the Typographical Revolution," in *Print and Culture in the Renaissance,* edited by Gerald P. Tyson and Sylvia S. Wagonheim (Newark: University of Delaware Press, 1986), pp. 208–221;

Wall, *Transformations of the Word: Spenser, Herbert, Vaughan* (Athens: University of Georgia Press, 1988).

Papers:

Cranmer's manuscripts are at the Public Records Office, London; the Lambeth Palace Library; the British Library; and the libraries of Oxford and Cambridge Universities.

Gavin Douglas
(1476 – September 1522)

Priscilla Bawcutt
Liverpool University

BOOKS: *The palice of honour* (Edinburgh: Probably printed by Thomas Davidson, circa 1535) – fragments survive of this early edition;
The palis of honoure compyled by Gawyne Dowglas (London: Printed by William Copland, 1553?);
Heir beginnis ane treatise callit the Palice of honour (Edinburgh: Printed by John Ross for Henry Charteris, 1579).

Editions and Collections: *Virgil's Aeneis* (Edinburgh: Andrew Symson & Robert Freebairn, 1710);
Select Works of Gawin Douglass (Perth: R. Morison, 1787);
The Poetical Works of Gavin Douglas, 4 volumes, edited by John Small (Edinburgh: William Paterson, 1874);
Virgil's Aeneid Translated into Scottish Verse by Gavin Douglas, 4 volumes, edited by David F. C. Coldwell (Edinburgh: Blackwood, 1957–1964);
Selections from Gavin Douglas, edited by Coldwell (Oxford: Clarendon, 1964);
The Shorter Poems of Gavin Douglas, edited by Priscilla Bawcutt (Edinburgh: Blackwood, 1967);
The Palis of Honoure, facsimile of 1553 edition (Amsterdam: Theatrum Orbis Terrarum / New York: Da Capo, 1969).

TRANSLATION: Virgil, *The .xiii. bukes of Eneados of the Famose Poete Virgill Translatet out of Latyne Verses into Scottish metir* (London: Printed by William Copland, 1553).

Gavin Douglas was one of several distinguished poets who flourished at the court of James IV of Scotland (1488–1513). He is most famous for *The Eneados* (1553), his excellent translation of Virgil's *Aeneid,* which long predates those by Henry Howard, Earl of Surrey, and Richard Stanyhurst. The prologues to each book of this work not only give a valuable insight into the critical ideas and principles of translation of the first great Renaissance translator but also contain fine and original poetry. Douglas's other works include *The Palice of Honour* (circa 1535), an impressive dream vision, which forms an important link in the tradition of courtly allegorical poetry that stretches from Geoffrey Chaucer to Edmund Spenser.

Douglas was a younger son of Archibald Douglas, fifth Earl of Angus, and Elizabeth Boyd Douglas. Little is known of his childhood, except that he was born in East Lothian, possibly at Tantallon Castle. He was well educated, graduating from Saint Andrews University in 1494, and may possibly have later studied in Paris. Douglas was designed from his youth for the church, and the fact that he belonged to a powerful aristocratic family undoubtedly aided his career. He rapidly acquired several minor benefices and by 1503 was provost of Saint Giles, Edinburgh, a well-endowed collegiate church. All of Douglas's known poetry belongs to the early part of his life in the reign of James IV; indeed, he dates the completion of *The Eneados* precisely on 22 July 1513. But on 9 September 1513 James died, and his army was routed at the disastrous battle of Flodden.

Flodden seems to have been a turning point for Douglas; politics, which previously competed with poetry for his attention, seems to have become all-important from that point. His fortunes thenceforth were closely involved with those of his nephew, Archibald Douglas, sixth Earl of Angus, who had married James's widow, Margaret Tudor, and was to become a prominent figure in the troubled minority of James V. Douglas aspired first to be archbishop of Saint Andrews, and then to be bishop of Dunkeld; a letter to one of his agents, dated 18 January 1515, clearly reveals his ambition: "my self and frendis thinkis nedful I be promouit to that Seyt quhilk now is vacand

and but pley [unencumbered by litigation], and an rycht gud Byschopry of rent and the thryd Seyt of the realm."

But Douglas did not obtain Dunkeld easily. He incurred the hostility of John Stewart, Duke of Albany – governor of Scotland in the minority of James V – who feared that the Douglases were becoming too powerful. Charged with infringing the laws regulating the purchase of benefices at Rome, Douglas was briefly imprisoned in Edinburgh Castle. The turbulence of this period is well illustrated by his later difficulty in gaining physical possession of Dunkeld Cathedral; Alexander Myln, an eyewitness, reports how the retainers of a rival candidate refused to let him enter: "then shooting began from the steeple and the episcopal palace, and the nobles who were with the bishop disposed themselves for his defense." At the peak of his career Douglas was a member of a Scottish embassy to France (1517); but when Albany returned to Scotland in 1521, the earl of Angus fled to the Borders and Douglas was dispatched to London in an attempt to enlist English support against Albany. He was accused of treason by the lords of council and died in exile at London in 1522.

There is some uncertainty as to the precise nature of Douglas's canon. Later writers, such as Sir David Lindsay and John Bale, make vague references to his other works, and Douglas himself, in the "Mensioun . . . of hys pryncipall warkis," speaks of having in his youth translated something mysteriously entitled "Of Lundeys Lufe the Remeid." In view of his evident familiarity with Ovid, this has most plausibly been interpreted as a garbled reference to Ovid's *Remedium Amoris. The Maitland Folio Manuscript* (circa 1570), an important Scottish poetry miscellany, also contains two attributions to Douglas: "Conscience," a brief satirical attack on the corruption of the church, is probably his; "King Hart," a subtle homiletic allegory with affinities to *Everyman* and other morality plays, is a longer and more ambitious piece, but there are stylistic and linguistic grounds for doubting Douglas's authorship.

There is no reason to doubt Douglas's claim to *The Palice of Honour* – his earliest surviving work – listed in the "Mensioun" of his own writings. This long and complex allegorical poem, composed of more than two thousand lines, was written around 1501; its dedication to James IV contains a clear plea for his favor and was followed by Douglas's appointment to Saint Giles, a benefice in the king's patronage. *The Palice of Honour* has no obvious source, although it abounds in allusions

Gavin Douglas's coat of arms

to Douglas's favorite poets, such as Chaucer and Ovid, and also to a Latin treatise on classical mythology and geography by Giovanni Boccaccio. It is also indebted more generally to the medieval tradition of dream poetry that originated with *Le Roman de la Rose* (thirteenth century).

Douglas treats a theme very fashionable in the early sixteenth century: the nature of honor and the ways of attaining it. The dreaming poet encounters three processions led by Minerva, Diana, and Venus, who are seeking the Palace of Honor; he himself is allowed to join a fourth procession, that of the Muses, but is eventually instructed that true Honor is won by virtue and must be distinguished from earthly "gloir," which is vain and transient. In describing the Muses, Douglas gives priority to Calliope, who inspires epic poets to write of heroes and is also the dreamer's guide. Honor is termed "a god armypotent" (line 1921), and the inmost court of his palace is peopled with heroes of both sexes. It is clear that Douglas attributes highest value to honor of a particular kind: heroic honor, won by courage and martial prowess. The earlier sections of the poem abound in stories of "knichtlie" deeds, tournaments, and "battellis intestine." Such themes were likely to be congenial to James, a king famed for his love of chivalry and participation in tournaments.

The self-portrait of the dreamer in *The Palice of Honour* is partly shaped by literary convention, yet

Dunkeld Cathedral, where Douglas was installed as bishop in 1516

there are striking correspondences to Douglas's real-life personality. The figure who here vigorously disputes with Venus in a trial scene where he is charged with "blasphemy" against love has much in common with Douglas — a litigious churchman who repeatedly engaged in legal controversy, on either his own or his family's behalf. This poem also tells much about Douglas's approach to poetry. Despite the climactic position reserved for Honor, the central and most interesting section — book 2 — is dominated by the Muses and their train. It includes writers of all kinds but is led by Homer and ends with the famous English trio of Chaucer, John Gower, and John Lydgate, and three Scottish poets, one of whom is William Dunbar. Douglas sees vernacular poets as inheriting the rich tradition of ancient poetry; compared to the multitude of Latin poets their number is pathetically small, yet they too are followers of the Muses. Douglas also places himself in the procession but implies, half-seriously, half-comically, that he is a novice with much to learn. There follows a marvelous aerial journey, implying that a poet's imagination takes flight when favored by the Muses; but it also suggests a kind of literary initiation or apprenticeship. At the beginning of his career Douglas thus repre-

sents poetry as his own personal road to lasting honor and makes clear his aspiration to write in the elevated, "courtly" style that Chaucer introduced to Britain.

Much in Douglas's approach is highly traditional: he sees the poet's office as to teach and delight, envisages rhetoric and poetry as closely interrelated, and displays the usual admiration for elevated diction, or polished "terms," and skillful patterning, or "rethorik colouris fine" (line 819). Not surprisingly, the style of *The Palice of Honour* is ornate and highly rhetorical. There is much use of antithesis, anaphora, and other figures of speech, and a striking taste for catalogues of all kinds — whether sages, virgins, lovers, or musical instruments. Honor's palace well illustrates Douglas's descriptive technique: it is highly idealized, glistening with precious metals, its beauty surpasses Troy or the Temple of Solomon, and it is characterized by many small, modish architectural features, "Pinnakillis, fyellis [finials], turnpekkis [spiral staircases] mony one" (1,432). There are other vivid set pieces of description, some conventionally beautiful, such as the paradisal garden in May with which the poem opens; some grotesque, such as the contrasting landscape to which the dreamer is then transported – a monstrous wilderness, with a stream "Like till Cochyte the river infernall," in which yelling fish shout like elves. There is much comedy and irony in the poem, often self-directed; in one passage, clearly inspired by Ovid, the dreamer fears that Venus in her anger will metamorphose him into "a beir, a bair [boar], ane oule, ane aip," and anxiously inspects his hand and face: "oft I wald my hand behald to se / Gif it alterit, and oft my visage graip" (743–744).

Douglas had a varied and learned circle of friends that included the historian Polydore Vergil and several distinguished churchmen, such as the head of the Scottish Dominicans, John Adamson, and the theologian John Major. The translation of the *Aeneid* was commissioned by his kinsman Henry, Lord Sinclair, whom he characteristically portrays as a bibliophile and "fader of bukis." Douglas himself was a widely read man, and his works abound in references to other writers. He vividly communicates his likes and dislikes, whether enthusiasm for the "mysty" poetry of Virgil ("Directioun," 105) or scorn for the "febil proys" of William Caxton (Prol. 5:51). He criticizes Chaucer for his treatment of the Dido and Aeneas story yet perceptively styles him "evir . . . womanis frend" (Prol. 1:449). Douglas displays an impressive awareness of new publications, consulting recently printed editions of Ovid and Virgil. According to his own testimony in 1515, he had traveled widely in "Ingland, France and Rome" and was familiar with the scholarly debates that were taking place on the Continent. He had much in common with humanists, such as Lorenzo Valla and Desiderius Erasmus; he shared their antipathy to Scholasticism and their belief in the high importance of the ancient classical authors. In translating the *Aeneid* he was fired by a double purpose: to convey to his countrymen an intimate knowledge of Virgil's great poem and also to transfer to his native "Scottis" tongue something of the "forth," or linguistic richness, of Latin, which – as he said – "knawyn is maste perfyte langage fyne" (Prol. 1:382).

In the early 1500s no major classic had yet been translated into English. Douglas's *Eneados* was thus a pioneering work; what is more, it was not just an abridgment or free paraphrase, but a close and careful translation based directly on Virgil's text. Douglas was very conscious that he was an innovator and proclaimed this to his readers; he voiced pithy criticisms of certain other writers who purported to be translators. He complained that a work recently published by Caxton, for instance, was no more like the *Aeneid* "than the devill and

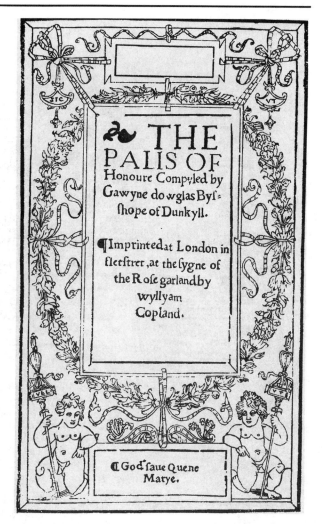

Title page for Douglas's allegory about honor, published circa 1553

Sanct Austyne" (Prol. 1:143). Douglas proudly asserts his own fidelity to Virgil's text; and if one takes into consideration the imperfect editions that he used, this boast is largely justified. There is one apparent inconsistency – his decision to translate the so-called Thirteenth Book, written by the Italian humanist Maffeo Vegio – but here too one should recall that most editions of Virgil, even as late as the seventeenth century, also included this work as a kind of supplement to the *Aeneid*.

The scholar in Douglas attempted to give his readers a taste of the Virgilian scholarship of his age, which was otherwise available only to those who could read Latin. Many things in *The Eneados* that might seem extraneous are closely related to the layout, contents, and apparatus of contemporary editions of Virgil. The marginal "Comment" that accompanies book 1 is directly indebted to the commentaries of Servius and Ascensius; elsewhere

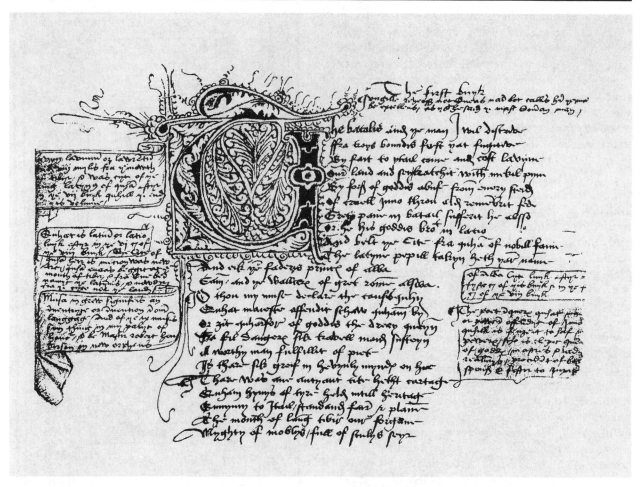

Page from a scribal copy of Douglas's translation of the Aeneid, *with marginal notes in Douglas's handwriting (Trinity College, Cambridge, Gale's MSS. O.3.12)*

Douglas incorporates into the text some of the shorter, explanatory glosses provided by these Virgilian commentators. This pedagogic zeal partly accounts for the undoubted diffuseness of his translation, compared with Surrey's. In his desire to convey the full implications of Virgil's "sentence," or inner meaning, he tends to be overexplicit. He thus often sacrifices the compression of his original and simplifies what is daring in Virgil's handling of language.

Douglas seems much better at rendering some aspects of the *Aeneid* than others: those passages that he perhaps found particularly affecting, such as the story of Dido, or that deal with supernatural or timeless experience, such as Aeneas's visit to the Underworld. He is responsive to Virgil's pathos – to the grief of Dido or the babes weeping on the threshold of the Underworld. He is also successful with invective, more so than with the great oratorical speeches. He excels at rendering passages of vigorous activity, such as

the hunt in book 4 and the many battle scenes, and descriptions of the natural world, as in the famous similes and the storms of books 1 and 3. He excels also at portraiture, catching the beauty of Venus in disguise (1.6.25–27):

As scho had bene a wild hunteres,
With wynd waving hir haris lowsit of tres,
Hir skyrt kiltit til hir bair kne

(As if she had been a wild huntress, with the wind waving her loosened hair, and her skirt caught up, like a kilt, to her bare knees)

and the strange, uncanny aspect of Charon (6.5.9–12):

Terribil of schap and sluggart of array,
Apon his chyn feil cannos harys gray,
Lyart feltrit tatis; with burnand eyn red,
Lyk twa fyre blesys fixit in his hed.

116

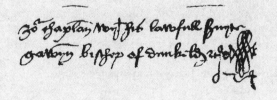

Letter written by Douglas in 1522, in which he offers his services to Cardinal Thomas Wolsey (State Paper Office, Wolsey Correspondence, IV, 71.)

(Terrible of form and slovenly of dress, upon his chin many hoary, gray hairs, in grizzled and matted tufts; with glowing red eyes, like two firebrands fixed in his head.)

At his best – as in these extracts – Douglas transmits not only the sense but also the tone or emotion latent in Virgil's words.

It is illuminating to compare what Douglas, Surrey, and John Dryden make of a brief but vivid passage in Virgil. Dido is preparing to go to the hunt (*Aeneid*, 4:133–139, edited by R. A. B. Mynors [1969]):

> reginam thalamo cunctantem ad limina primi
> Poenorum exspectant, ostroque insignis et auro
> stat sonipes ac frena ferox spumantia mandit.
> tandem progreditur magna stipante caterua
> Sidoniam picto chlamydem circumdata limbo;
> cui pharetra ex auro, crines nodantur in aurum,
> aurea purpuream subnectit fibula uestem.

(The queen lingered in her own room, while the noblest among the Carthaginians awaited her at the doors. Her spirited horse, caparisoned in purple and gold, pawed the ground and champed a foaming bit. At last she came, stepping forth with a numerous suite around her and clad in a Sidonian mantle with an embroidered hem. Golden were her quiver and the clasp which knotted her hair, and golden was the brooch which fastened the purple tunic at her neck.)

Douglas renders it thus (4.4.8–20):

> Nobillys of Cartage, hovand [lingering] at the port [gate],
> The queyn awatys that lang in chawmyr [chamber] dwellys;
> Hyr fers [fierce] steyd stude stampyng, reddy ellys,
> Rungeand [gnawing] the fomy goldyn byt gynglyng;
> Of gold and pal wrocht hys rych harnasyng.
> And scho at last of palyce yschit [proceeded] owt,
> With huge menye [retinue] walking hir abowt,
> Lappyt [dressed] in a brusyt [embroidered] mantill of Sydony,
> With gold and perle the bordour al bewry [adorned],
> Hyngand [hanging] by hir syde the cays with arowis grund [sharpened];
> Hir bricht tressis envolupyt [entwined] war and wond [wound]
> Intil [within] a quayf [cap] of fyne gold wyrin [wire] threid;
> The goldyn button claspyt hir purpour weid[;]

Surrey thus (4:170–178, edited by Emrys Jones [1964]):

> And at the threshold of her chaumber dore
> The Carthage lords did on the quene attend.
> The trampling steede with gold and purple trapt,

Chawing the fomie bit, there fercely stood.
> Then issued she, awayted with great train,
> Clad in a cloke of Tyre embradred riche,
> Her quyver hung behinde her backe, her tresse
> Knotted in gold, her purple vesture eke
> Butned with gold[;]

and Dryden thus (4:188–199, edited by James Kinsley [1958]):

> The Tyrian Peers, and Officers of State,
> For the slow Queen, in Anti-Chambers wait:
> Her lofty Courser, in the Court below,
> (Who his Majestick Rider seems to know)
> Proud of his Purple Trappings, paws the Ground;
> And champs the Golden Bitt; and spreads the Foam around.
> The Queen at length appears: on either Hand
> The brawny Guards in Martial Order stand.
> A flow'rd Cymarr, with Golden Fringe, she wore;
> And at her Back a Golden Quiver bore:
> Her flowing Hair, a Golden Caul restrains;
> A Golden Clasp the Tyrian Robe sustains.

All these poets translate fairly closely (one should recall that in line 138 most sixteenth-century editions of Virgil had *humero* not *auro*), but of the three Surrey is characteristically the most succinct. All convey the visual magnificence of this occasion, although Dryden's "Officers of State" and "Anti-Chambers" make Dido's court more grandiose than it is in Virgil. Douglas inserts small extra details – the jingling bit, the pearls on Dido's mantle – but he alone catches the scene's rich sensuousness and mood of expectation. "He makes the world of the *Aeneid* seem almost contemporary; Virgil's characters might be just round the corner; they are young and glowing," according to R. G. Austin in *Some English Translations of Virgil* (1956).

Douglas provided each book of the translation, including the thirteenth, with a prologue and placed at the end of the whole work six different pieces of verse, in which, among other things, he takes a leisurely farewell of Aeneas and Venus, Virgil, his readers, and also his critics. These prologues and epilogues are an unusual feature; there is no parallel to them in contemporary translations. They are extremely varied, both in metrical form – which includes rhyme royal, alliterative verse, and the five-beat couplet that is used for the translation itself – and also in tone and theme. The first six prologues and a few of the later ones may be seen as introductions to their respective books, but others, notably numbers 8, 10, and 11, seem to roam far from the *Aeneid*. Earlier critics indeed treated them virtually as self-contained, independent poems; more-recent ones have sought to place them within some underlying scheme, thematic or chronological.

The prologues essentially have two functions, expository and creative. They are designed, in the first place, to introduce Virgil to the reader and to explain Douglas's methods of translation. But they also reveal the poet's desire to make a work of his own, which leads Douglas away from the self-effacement of many translators. In these prologues he invokes the Muses for assistance, projecting himself as creator and the act of translation almost as momentous an enterprise as the *Aeneid* itself. In the "Exclamatioun agaynst detractouris" (4:192–193) he thus says:

> Now throw the deip [deep sea] fast to the port I mark [proceed],
> For heir is endyt the lang disparyt [depaired of] wark.

He proudly commends his "vulgar [vernacular] Virgill" to a varied audience:

> Now salt thou with every gentill [noble] Scot be kend [understood],
> And to onletterit [illiterate] folk be red on hight [read aloud],
> That erst [formerly] was bot with clerkis [scholars] comprehend.

One of the most persistent themes, appearing in almost every prologue, arises from the tension in Douglas between admiration for a great poet and the scruples of a Christian and a priest at translating a pagan author. Prologue 1 opens with a magnificent eulogy of Virgil, "of Latyn poetis prynce," but the phrase is later self-consciously remodeled so that it becomes part of a prayer to God: "Thou prynce of poetis, I the mercy cry / I meyn thou Kyng of Kyngis, Lord etern" (452–453).

Three of these prologues (7, 12, and 13) have long been particularly admired. They contain vivid and detailed passages of seasonal description, depicting, respectively, December at the winter solstice, a May morning, and a June night. It has sometimes been claimed that they spring solely from Douglas's direct observation of nature. In fact they belong to the tradition of the *chronographia* employed by ancient and medieval poets, and they have many conventional features. They also owe much to Douglas's reading of a wide range of works, from Virgil's *Georgics* to the storm scenes in medieval English alliterative poetry. Yet this does not diminish Douglas's originality. No earlier English or Scottish poet described the natural world so perceptively or

with such an accumulation of minute details, ranging from the fluffy down upon a dandelion and flowers "depart [divided] in freklys red and quhite" of spring (Prol. 12) to mountain peaks "slekit [made smooth] with snaw" and roads "Full of floschis, dubbis, myre and clay [pools, puddles, mud and clay]" of winter (Prol. 7).

Douglas's aim in these prologues, however, was rarely to describe nature solely for its own sake. The twelfth is perhaps the most wholeheartedly devoted to celebrating "dame Nature"; it is unified by the splendid image of the sun as a monarch, making a royal progress and receiving the homage of his subjects (35–40, 251–258):

> Furth of hys palyce ryall ischit [issued] Phebus,
> With goldyn croun and vissage gloryus,
> Crysp [curling] haris, brycht as chrisolyte or topace,
> For quhais hew mycht nane behald hys face,
> The fyry sparkis brastyng [bursting] from hys eyn [eyes],
> To purge the ayr and gilt [gild] the tendyr greyn.
> . . . .
> And al smail fowlys syngis on the spray:
> "Welcum the lord of lycht and lamp of day,
> Welcom fostyr [fosterer] of tendir herbys grene,
> Welcum quyknar of floryst flowris scheyn [beautiful],
> Welcum support of every rute [root] and vayn,
> Welcum confort of alkynd fruyt and grayn,
> Welcum the byrdis beild [sustainer] apon the brer [briar],
> Welcum master and rewlar [ruler] of the yer."

Prologue 7, which is the most realistic and the most "Scottish" of the three, opens with a wide, panoramic landscape within which the activities of men and animals are paralleled, but it ends with a vignette of Douglas himself in his chilly bedroom (87–96, 105–108):

> The callour [fresh] ayr, penetratyve and puyr [pure],
> Dasyng [congealing] the blude in every creatur,
> Maid seik warm stovis and beyn [comforting] fyris hoyt [hot],
> In dowbill garmont cled and wily coyt [extra underclothing],
> With mychty drink and metis confortyve [nourishing],
> Agane [against] the stern wyntir forto stryve.
> Repatyrrit [refreshed] weil and by the chymnay bekyt [warmed],
> At evin [evening] be tyme [early] doune a bed I me strekyt [stretched myself],
> Warpit [wrapped up] my hed, kest on clathis thrynfald [three times as many],
> Fortil expell the peralus persand cald.
> . . . .
> Hornyt Hebowd [the barn owl], quhilk we clepe the nycht owle,

> Within hir cavern hard [heard] I schowt and yowle
>   [howl].
> Laithly [loathsome] of form, with crukyt camscho beke
>   [crooked, deformed beak]
> Ugsum [terrifying] to heir was hir wild elrich screke [un-
>   canny shriek].

This prologue embroiders a common literary topos — the poet weary of his task but resuming his labors — and marks the halfway stage in the translation.

Prologue 13 contains a particularly beautiful description of a summer night, but this is the poem's frame rather than its center, the symbolic setting for a visionary experience: at its beginning Douglas prepares to rest, his translation of the *Aeneid* accomplished, but at its end dawn brings a resumption of labor for all creatures, the poet included. Maffeo Vegio appears and rebukes the dreamer for devoting so much time to Virgil, yet ignoring his work: "Quhy schrynkis thou with my schort Cristyn wark?" Douglas eventually yields, persuaded more by force than by arguments (147–152):

> Syne to me with hys club he maid a braid [sudden
>   movement],
> And twenty rowtis [blows] apon my riggyng [back] laid,
> Quhill "Deo, Deo, mercy," dyd I cry,
> And be my rycht hand strekit [stretched] up in hy [haste],
> Hecht [vowed] to translait his buke, in honour of God
> And hys Apostollis twelf, in the number od.

This subtle and humorous dramatization of Douglas's doubts as to the propriety of including the thirteenth book is one of his most accomplished pieces of writing.

Douglas has many stylistic registers: in prologue 1 he ranges from the rhetorical formality of the opening eighteen-line panegyric of Virgil to the slangy colloquialism of his "flyting" attack on Caxton. But undoubtedly the most striking and persistent feature of his style is the "fouth," or copiousness, of his vocabulary. The different strands in his diction give some idea of the different poetic traditions to which he was indebted. His taste for long, sonorous, Latin neologisms — "Placis of silence and perpetuall nycht" or "the comete stern sanguynolent" — was clearly influenced by his reading of Virgil, but also by the vogue among other early-sixteenth-century writers for such "aureate terms." The importance to Douglas of Chaucer and his courtly English followers, such as Lydgate, is evident not only in direct imitation (more obvious in the prologues than the translation) but also in two closely inter-

*Douglas's seal while he served as bishop of Dunkeld,
1516–1520*

related features of his style, anglicisms and archaisms. The frequent use of verbal forms no longer current in the Scottish vernacular — for example, the past participle with prefixed *y*, such as *ybaik* (baked) or *yberyit* (buried) — produces the effect of an artificial and poetic diction that is closer to Spenser than Chaucer.

Douglas also draws upon another important native tradition, that of the medieval Scottish "epics" celebrating heroes such as Robert Bruce and William Wallace, particularly when he renders Virgil's battle scenes (11.12.41–44):

> Thai meit in melle with a felloun rak,
> Quhill schaftis al to-schuldris with a crak;
> Togiddir duschis the stowt stedis atanys,
> That athyris contyr fruschyt otheris banys.

> (They engage in hand-to-hand fighting with a great clatter, while spears splinter with a cracking noise; the strong horses rush together all at once, with the result that the breast of one smashes the bones of another.)

Such verse is often, as here, strikingly alliterative and characterized by formulaic words and phrases — for example, "douchty dint," "burnyst brand," "hors and harnes," "blude and brane." Douglas's use of these expressions, which were often of great antiquity, contributes much of the stylistic vigor that his critics have often praised. Alliteration is also used elsewhere for a mimetic purpose, as in the effective characterization of birdcalls in prologues 7 and 12.

In his "Conclusio," Douglas audaciously echoes Ovid's proud assertion that his poetry will be immortal:

Throw owt the ile yclepit [named] Albyon
Red sall I be and sung with mony one.

There is no doubt that Douglas was indeed famous in his lifetime and throughout the sixteenth century. In Scotland *The Palice of Honour* was praised and imitated by several lesser poets, such as John Bellenden, John Rolland, and Patrick Hume of Polwart. In England, although this poem was available in print and is likely to have been read by Spenser, it was Douglas's translation of the *Aeneid* that was best known and that influenced some Tudor poets, notably Surrey and Thomas Sackville. In later centuries Douglas continued to have a high reputation when his fellow Scottish poets, Dunbar and Robert Henryson, were virtually forgotten; association with the great name of Virgil helped to keep his name alive, and his language was of great interest to antiquarians and lexicographers.

In the twentieth century Douglas has received somewhat eccentric praise from Ezra Pound – who called him better than Virgil because "he had heard the sea" – and more balanced but equally enthusiastic appraisals from other critics, especially C. S. Lewis, who considered his translation superior to Dryden's. There is no doubt as to the historical and cultural importance of *The Eneados;* it was the first translation of a great classical work into any form of English. Today, however, there is increasing awareness that Douglas was not just a good translator but an original poet with a distinctive, lively, and humorous voice, remarkable descriptive powers, and great "fouth" of language.

Letters:

Included in "Biographical Introduction," *The Poetical Works of Gavin Douglas,* volume 1, edited by John Small (Edinburgh: William Paterson, 1874).

Bibliographies:

William Geddie, *A Bibliography of Middle Scots Poets* (Edinburgh: Scottish Text Society, 1912);

Florence Ridley, "Middle Scots Writers," in *A Manual of the Writings in Middle English, 1050–1500,* volume 4, edited by A. E. Hartung (New

Haven: Yale University Press, 1973), pp. 961–1060, 1123–1284;

Priscilla Bawcutt, "Middle Scots Poets," in *The New Cambridge Bibliography of English Literature,* volume 1, edited by George Watson (Cambridge: Cambridge University Press, 1974), pp. 651–664;

Walter Scheps and J. Anna Looney, *Middle Scots Poets: A Reference Guide to James I, Robert Henryson, William Dunbar and Gavin Douglas* (Boston: G. K. Hall, 1986).

References:

A. J. Aitken, "The Language of Older Scots Poetry," in *Scotland and the Lowland Tongue,* edited by J. D. McClure (Aberdeen: Aberdeen University Press, 1983), pp. 18–49;

Mark Amsler, "The Quest for the Present Tense: The Poet and the Dreamer in Douglas' *The Palice of Honour," Studies in Scottish Literature,* 17 (1982): 186–208;

Elizabeth Archibald, "Gavin Douglas on Love: The Prologue to *Eneados,* IV," in *Bryght Lanternis: Essays on the Language and Literature of Medieval and Renaissance Scotland,* edited by McClure and M. R. G. Spiller (Aberdeen: Aberdeen University Press, 1989), pp. 244–257;

R. G. Austin, *Some English Translations of Virgil* (Liverpool: Liverpool University Press, 1956);

Priscilla Bawcutt (Preston), "Did Gavin Douglas Write *King Hart ?," Medium Aevum,* 28, no. 1 (1959): 31–47;

Bawcutt, "Douglas and Surrey: Translators of Virgil," *Essays and Studies,* 27 (1974): 52–67;

Bawcutt, *Gavin Douglas: A Critical Study* (Edinburgh: Edinburgh University Press, 1976);

Bawcutt, "Gavin Douglas and Chaucer," *Review of English Studies,* new series 21 (November 1970): 401–421;

Bawcutt, "Gavin Douglas and the Text of Virgil," *Edinburgh Bibliographical Society Transactions,* 4, no. 6 (1973): 213–231;

Bawcutt, "The Library of Gavin Douglas," in *Bards and Makars,* edited by Aitken and others (Glasgow: Glasgow University Press, 1977), pp. 107–126;

Charles Blyth, "Gavin Douglas's Prologues of Natural Description," *Philological Quarterly,* 49 (1970): 167–177;

Bruce Dearing, "Douglas' *Eneados:* A Reinterpretation," *PMLA,* 67 (September 1952): 845–862;

John Dryden, *The Poems,* edited by James Kinsley (Oxford: Clarendon, 1958);

Lois Ebin, "The Role of the Narrator in the Prologues to Gavin Douglas's *Eneados,*" *Chaucer Review,* 14 (Spring 1980): 353–365;

Alastair Fowler, "Virgil for Every Gentill Scot," *Times Literary Supplement,* 22 July 1977, pp. 882–883;

Denton Fox, "The Scottish Chaucerians," in *Chaucer and Chaucerians,* edited by D. S. Brewer (London: Nelson, 1966), pp. 164–200;

C. D. Gordon, "Gavin Douglas's Latin Vocabulary," *Phoenix,* 24 (Spring 1970): 54–73;

C. S. Lewis, "The Close of the Middle Ages in Scotland," in *English Literature in the Sixteenth Century, Excluding Drama* (Oxford: Clarendon, 1954), pp. 66–119;

A. K. Nitecki, "Gavin Douglas's Rural Muse," in *Proceedings of the Third International Conference on Scottish Language and Literature,* edited by R. J. Lyall and F. Riddy (Stirling & Glasgow: University of Glasgow Press, 1981), pp. 383–395;

John Norton-Smith, "Ekphrasis as a Stylistic Element in Douglas's *Palis of Honour,*" *Medium Aevum,* 48 (1979): 240–253;

Florence Ridley, "Did Gawin Douglas Write *King Hart?,*" *Speculum,* 34 (July 1959): 402–412;

Ridley, "Surrey's Debt to Gawin Douglas," *PMLA,* 76 (March 1961): 25–33;

Penelope Starkey, "Gavin Douglas's *Eneados:* Dilemmas in the Nature Prologues," *Studies in Scottish Literature,* 11 (1973–1974): 82–98;

Henry Howard, Earl of Surrey, *Poems,* edited by Emrys Jones (Oxford: Clarendon, 1964);

Ronald E. Thomas, " 'Ere he his Goddis brocht in Latio': On Pound's Appreciation of Gavin Douglas," *Paideuma,* 9 (Winter 1980): 509–517;

Virgil, *Opera,* edited by R. A. B. Mynors (Oxford: Clarendon, 1969);

Launchlan M. Watt, *Douglas's Aeneid* (Cambridge: Cambridge University Press, 1920).

Papers:

No manuscript is extant of *The Palice of Honour.* Five survive of *The Eneados,* of which the earliest and most authoritative is that in Trinity College Library, Cambridge University (MS O.3.12); two others are in the Library of Edinburgh University. Douglas's letters are in the British Library and the Public Record Office; his will is in the Scottish Record Office, Edinburgh.

William Dunbar

(1460? – 1513?)

Elizabeth Archibald
University of Victoria

BOOKS: *The ballade of ane right noble lord Barnard Stewart* (Edinburgh: W. Chepman & A. Myllar, 1508);

Here begynnys ane litil tretie intitulit the goldyn targe (Edinburgh: W. Chepman & A. Myllar, 1508).

Collections: *The Poems of William Dunbar,* 3 volumes, edited by John Small, with W. Gregor and A. J. G. Mackay, Scottish Text Society (Edinburgh & London: Blackwood, 1884–1893; reprinted, Hildesheim & New York: G. Olms, 1973);

The Poems of William Dunbar, edited by W. Mackay Mackenzie (London: Faber & Faber, 1932; revised, 1960);

The Poems of William Dunbar, edited by James Kinsley (Oxford: Clarendon, 1979).

William Dunbar is one of the most important writers of late-medieval Scotland; compared with his near contemporaries Robert Henryson and Gavin Douglas, he is the most varied and the most enigmatic. The eighty-odd poems that can be confidently attributed to him are for the most part quite short (references here, both titles and numbers, are to *The Poems of William Dunbar* [1979]; translations are based on the notes and glossary of the editor, James Kinsley). The longest, "The Tretis of the Tua Mariit Wemen and the Wedo" (K14: The Tale of the Two Married Women and the Widow), is only 530 lines; "The Flyting of Dunbar and Kennedie" (K23) is somewhat longer, but half is by Walter Kennedy. Yet they offer an extraordinary range of language, meter, style, tone, and content: aureate allegory and ferocious flyting, begging poems and devout prayers, dream visions and celebrations of court occasions, rhyming couplets and alliterative verse, formal English, colloquial and colorful Scots, and even Latin refrains or macaronic insertions.

Although many of these poems seem extremely personal, remarkably little is known about Dunbar. There are few William Dunbars in the Scottish records of the time, but one cannot be sure that any of the references do indeed relate to the poet. He may have been the William Dunbar listed as studying at Saint Andrews University in the late 1470s, graduating perhaps in 1479. Since it was usual to enter university at about fifteen, this Dunbar would probably have been born about 1460. According to Kennedy, Dunbar's adversary in "The Flyting," the poet was born in the year of the great eclipse: there was an eclipse in 1460 – but also in several other years between 1448 and 1465. There is no reference to university life in Dunbar's surviving poems, but it would have been a conventional education for a future cleric. He frequently reiterates his desire for a benefice (in the poems addressed to the king), yet it is not clear when he became a priest. The records note that ten pounds was given to him for his first Mass in 1504; this seems a long time after his graduation. His name appears as a witness to a 1509 legal document concerning property, and he is described as a chaplain. Demands for money are regular features of his poems to the king; in 1500 he was granted a pension of ten pounds a year until such a time as he should have a benefice worth forty pounds. In November 1507 this pension was doubled, and in August 1510 it was quadrupled to eighty pounds, a very substantial sum.

In 1501 Dunbar seems to have been in England, perhaps in connection with the impending marriage of James IV of Scotland to Margaret, daughter of Henry VII. The English Privy Purse records note two payments in this year to "the Rhymer of Scotland," though it is not certain that this was Dunbar. The last entry for Dunbar in the Scottish records is in 1513, not long before the disastrous battle of Flodden Field. He may have lived for some years after this – perhaps he finally received his benefice, or perhaps all pensions were cut in this gloomy time; but it seems unlikely in view of the lack of reference to him in any document after 1513. He must have been dead by 1522, the year of Douglas's death, since Sir David Lindsay, a fellow Scot, names them both in a passage lamenting de-

*Title page for Dunbar's allegorical dream poem in which Beauty
battles Reason*

ceased poets in *The Testament of the Papyngo* (printed in 1530).

Since it is impossible to group Dunbar's poems chronologically, most editors arrange them by content. The results can be controversial, but this practice does demonstrate the range, variety, and idiosyncrasy of his work. Where Geoffrey Chaucer experiments with the frame of *The Canterbury Tales,* exploiting the conscious and unconscious prejudices of his pilgrims, Dunbar's different voices are all apparently his own. Particularly striking is his "eldritch quality" (noted by C. S. Lewis), a voice that can be clearly heard in "Fasternis Evin in Hell" (K52: Shrove Tuesday in Hell), a dream (or nightmare) vision in which the Seven Deadly Sins and Satan celebrate carnival in Hell, and in "The Flyting of Dunbar and Kennedie." The latter is a lively battle of rhetoric and invective with a contemporary

poet in a genre well known in Continental and Gaelic literary tradition:

> Muttoun dryver, girnall ryver, ȝadswyvar — fowll
>   fell the;
> Herretyk, lunatyk, purspyk, carlingis pet,
> Rottin crok, dirtin dok — cry cok, or I sall quell the.
> *Quod Dumbar to Kennedie*
> ("Flyting," 11. 246–249)

(Driver of dead sheep, granary plunderer, marebuggerer, may evil strike you down; heretic, lunatic, pickpocket, old wives' pet, rotten old ewe, filthy arse — admit defeat, or I will destroy you.)

Kennedy's attacks on Dunbar have been mined by biographers, but all information offered in the poem should be treated with great caution, given the polemical and caricaturing nature of the genre. It has also been mined by lexicographers: Dunbar's colloquial works are full of neologisms, or at least first-recorded literary usages. The alliterative and often assonant verse lends itself to the accumulation of invective, in Latin and the vernacular.

At the other extreme Dunbar sometimes uses elaborate, aureate vocabulary (polysyllabic Latinate words, linked by patterns of alliteration and assonance), a style associated with Chaucer by admiring fifteenth-century poets and used by James I for *The Kingis Quair*. Dunbar adopts this formal style for his allegorical dream visions "The Golden Targe" (K10: The Golden Shield) and "The Thrissil and the Rois" (K50: The Thistle and the Rose, written to celebrate the wedding of James IV and Margaret of York in 1503). These poems clearly owe something to Chaucer's dream visions, though they differ from them considerably in both style and content. At the end of "The Goldyn Targe," Dunbar salutes Chaucer as "rose of rethoris [orators] all" and praises his "fresch anamalit termes celicall" (fresh, enameled, heavenly terms); next he invokes "morall Gower and Lydgate laureate," whose "sugurit lippis and tongis aureate" (sugared lips and golden tongues) have illuminated the rude language of Scotland. Chaucer never used the sort of "anamalit termes" in which Dunbar evokes a spring morning in "The Goldyn Targe"; but Dunbar may have borrowed from John Lydgate, whose influence is evident in other parts of his work. In praising Chaucer, Dunbar refers to him as "of oure Inglisch al the lycht [light]"; clearly he thinks of himself as writing in the same language (Douglas was the first Scots writer to distinguish his literary language from that used south of the border, in the prologue to his *Eneados* of 1512–1513).

In "The Goldyn Targe" the dreamer witnesses a gathering of divinities including Nature and Venus in a landscape of such beauty that neither Homer nor Cicero could have done justice to it: "Your aureate tongis both bene all to lyte / For to compile that paradise complete" (11. 71–72: your golden tongues are both too slight to describe that perfect paradise). At Venus's command the dreamer is threatened by Beauty and other allegorical figures familiar from *The Romance of the Rose:* "Fair Having wyth hir went, / Fyne Portrature, Plesance, and Lusty Chere" (11. 149–150: Fair Demeanor went with her, Fine Appearance, Delight, and Pleasing Countenance). Reason defends the dreamer with a golden shield but is blinded, and the dreamer yields to Beauty. But Disdain hands him over to Dejection, the deities hurry on board their ship at a blast

from Æolus's bugle, and the poet wakes on a fine May morning, lamenting his inadequate poetic talent.

In "The Thrissil and the Rois" the dreamer witnesses a gathering of all birds, beasts, and plants before Nature, who crowns the lion king of beasts and the eagle king of birds, instructing them both to rule justly:

> Exerce justice with mercy and conscience,
> And lat no small beist suffir skaith na skornis
> Of greit beistis that bene of moir piscence....
>
> (11. 106–108)

(Exercise justice with mercy and conscience, and do not let any small beast suffer harm or insults from large beasts which are more powerful....)

She crowns the thistle (emblem of Scotland) king of plants, with a warning to love only the rose (emblem of England). The poem is, at one level at least, advice to the king, a notorious philanderer, about good kingship and good behavior in marriage. In each poem the fantastic situation is framed in a nature description of great elaboration and artifice:

> The cristall air, the sapher firmament,
> The ruby skyes of the orient
>   Kest beriall bemes on emerant bewis grene;
> The rosy garth depaynt and redolent
> With purpur, azure, gold and goulis gent
>   Arayed was by dame Flora the quene
>   So nobilly that joy was for to sene....
>
> ("The Goldyn Targe," 11. 37–43)

(The crystal air, the sapphire firmament, the ruby skies of the orient cast sparkling beams on emerald green boughs; the rosy garden, colored and fragrant with purple, azure, gold, and fine vermilion, was adorned so splendidly by Dame Flora that it was a joy to see....)

Aureation is put to very different use in "Ane Ballat of our Lady" (K2), where Dunbar celebrates the Virgin in a virtuoso display of Latinate language and elaborates the traditional Marian imagery. Elsewhere he often uses Latin refrains, for instance to celebrate the Resurrection in "Surrexit Dominus de sepulchro" (K4: The Lord has risen from the tomb) and, more melancholically, to lament human mortality, and especially the deaths of so many brother poets, in the remarkable "Lament for the Makaris [makers, poets]" (K62, sometimes cited as "I that in heill wes and gladnes"). The chilling refrain of this poem is "*Timor mortis conturbat me*" (The fear of death distresses me), a much-quoted phrase from the Office of the Dead, also used by Lydgate in "So as I lay this other night." Dunbar lists twenty-four poets

Ryght as the stern of day begouth to schyne
Quhen gone to bed war vesper and lucyne
I raise and by a rosere did me rest
Up sprang the goldyn candill matutyne
With clere depurit bemes cristallyne
Glading the mery foulis in thair nest
Or phebus was in purpur cape reuest
Up raise the lark the hevyns menstrale fyne
In may/in till a moro my:thfullest

Full angellike thir birdis sang thair houris
Within thair courtyns grene in to thair bouris.
Apparalit quhite and rede wyth blomes suete
Anamalit was the felde wyth all colouris
The perly droppis schake in silvir schouris.
Quhill all in balme did branch and leuis flete
To part fra phebus did aurora grete
Hir cristall teris I saw hyng on the flouris
Quhilk he forlufe all drank up wyth his hete

For mirth of may wyth skippis and wyth happis
The birdis sang vpon the tender croppis
With curiouse note as venus chapell clerkis
The rosis yong new spreding of thair knopis
War powdit bry with hevinly beriall droppis
Throu bemes rede birnyng as ruby sperkis.
The skyes rang for schoutyng of the larkis
The purpur hevyn our scailit in silvir sloppis
Our gilt the treis branchis left barkis

Doun throu the ryce a ryuir ran wyth stremys
So lustily agayn that lykand lemys
That all the lake as lamp did leme of licht.

Page from the 1508 edition of The Golden Targe

by name, starting with Chaucer, "of makaris flour" (the flower of poets); he includes some otherwise unknown Scots poets and ends with his "Flyting" rival, Kennedy, who was apparently dying at the time of writing:

> Gud Maister Walter Kennedy
> In poynt of dede lyis veraly –
> Gret reuth it wer that so suld be:
> *Timor mortis conturbat me.*
>
> Sen he has all my brether tane
> He will naught lat me lif alane;
> On forse I man his nyxt pray be:
> *Timor mortis conturbat me.*
>
> (11. 89–96)

(Indeed, good Master Walter Kennedy lies at the point of death; it is a great pity that is should be so: *The fear of death distresses me.*

Since he has taken all my brothers, he will not allow me alone to survive; of necessity I must be his next victim: *The fear of death distresses me.*)

But his use of Latin is not always so serious. In "The Testament of Maister Andro Kennedy" (K38), he uses alternate lines of Scots and Latin to create a mock will reminiscent of the Archpoet and of François Villon, with its satirical bequests and urgent request that the dying man should be buried within reach of a drink:

> A barell bung ay at my bosum
>   Of warldis gud I bad na mair.
> *Corpus meum ebriosum*
>   I leif on to the toune of Air. . . .
>
> (11. 33–36)

(The stopper of a barrel always at my breast – I desired no other worldly goods. I leave my drunken body to the town of Ayr. . . .)

In the "Dregy" (K22: Dirge) Dunbar mockingly urges the king to return from the purgatory of his religious retreat in Stirling to the heavenly delights of Edinburgh, parodying the Office of the Dead – first in English and then in Latin – and also the Paternoster:

> Et ne nos inducas in temptationem de Strivilling:
> Sed libera nos a malo illius.
> Requiem Edinburgi dona eiis, Domine,
> Et lux ipsius luceat eiis.
>
> (11. 97–100)

(And lead us not into the temptation of Stirling, but deliver us from its evil. Give them the peace of Edinburgh, Lord, and may its light shine upon them.)

Unlike the work of his literary heroes Chaucer, Lydgate, and John Gower, much of Dunbar's poetry consists of short occasional verses intimately linked to his life at court, some of them begging poems addressed to the king. In one he characterizes himself as an old horse, deserving of recognition at Christmas but shouldered aside by less worthy horses (K43: "To the King"); in the manuscripts this poem is immediately followed by lines attributed to the king himself. They maintain the metaphor and grant Dunbar new clothes; many editors accept them as James IV's own work. Dunbar's tone in addressing both king and queen is often intimate and comic: he teases and cajoles the king, and he also laughs at himself, for instance in the pair of poems describing his relations with the keeper of the queen's wardrobe, one James Dog. In a poem complaining of Dog's refusal to give him a promised doublet, Dunbar's refrain is "Madame, ye heff a dangerous dog!" (K29: "Of James Dog, Kepair of the Quenis Wardrep"). Clearly the poet got the doublet in the end, though, for in a companion piece his refrain is "He is na dog; he is a lam" (K 30: "Of the said James, quhen he had plesett him" [Of the said James, when he had pleased him]). "Ane Dance in the Quenis Chalmer" (K28: A Dance in the Queen's Chamber) describes the queen's entourage in irregular meter reminiscent of dance music; Dunbar himself joins the dance, with other historical members of the court. In "Schir Thomas Norny" (K27) Dunbar gently mocks the court fool in a parody of Chaucer's romance parody *Sir Thopas*. But in other poems he also criticizes the corruption around him, for instance in "Aganis the Solistaris in Court" (K20: Against the Petitioners at Court), "Thir Ladyis fair that in the Court ar kend" (K71: These Fair Ladies who are known at Court), and "Tydingis hard at the Sessioun" (K74: Tidings heard at the Court of Justice).

A curiosity among the court poems is "Ane Blak Moir" (K33: A Blackamoor), a mock eulogy to a black woman who apparently presided over tournaments at the Scottish court in 1507 and 1508. The refrain of this poem is "My ladye with the mekle lippis" (My lady with the large lips). In the first line Dunbar claims that he has written often about fair ladies, but in fact very few of his extant poems are concerned with love. "In Prays of Wemen" (K72) is a very conventional piece. More original, and writ-

Musical setting of Dunbar's "Welcum to Margaret Tudor as Queen of Scotland," sung at the dinner following the marriage of Margaret Tudor to James IV of Scotland, 8 August 1503 (British Library; Royal MSS., No. 58)

ten with much more relish, are two eavesdropping poems in which courtly ideals are caricatured. "In Secreit Place" (K13) is a debased *pastourelle,* a conversation between two knowing and lowborn lovers, overpacked with colloquial terms of endearment:

> Quod he, My claver, my curledoddy,
> My hony soppis, my sweit possoddy,
> Be nocht our bustious to ȝour billie. . . .
>
> (11. 29–31)

(Said he, "My clover, my ribwort plantain [wild scabious?], my bread dipped in honey, my sheep's head broth, don't be too harsh on your friend. . . .")

"The Tretis of the Tua Mariit Wemen and the Wedo" is altogether more sinister. On Midsummer Eve, the narrator eavesdrops on three women discussing marriage and love over their wine in a beautiful garden. They look elegant and noble but turn out to be close relatives of Chaucer's Wife of Bath, though with none of her redeeming features. Each describes her husband (or husbands) in the most pe-

jorative terms, gloats over her success in extracting money from him, and boasts of her lovers. The alliterative verse changes rapidly from the aureate opening description of the summer evening to the avalanche of colloquialisms with which the women crush their men:

> I have ane wallidrag, ane worme, ane auld wobat carle,
> A waistit wolroun na worth bot wourdis to clatter,
> Ane bumbart, ane dron bee, ane bag full of flewme. . . .
>
> (11. 89–91)

(I have a slovenly fellow, a contemptible worm, a hairy old caterpillar, an exhausted boar good for nothing but chattering, a lazy fellow, a drone, a bag full of phlegm. . . .)

Innocently the narrator asks at the end which of the three ladies the gentlemen in his audience would choose to marry, but this is a deeply misogynistic poem.

It is hard to know whether Dunbar really held the view that prevails in his debate poem "The Merle and the Nychtingall" (K16: The Blackbird and the Nightingale), that "all luve is lost bot upone

128

God allone" (all love is wasted except on God alone). The world-weary persona of many of his moralizing poems seems strangely at odds with both the aureate elegance and the colloquial comedy of the court poems. Dunbar's character and views cannot be safely reconstructed from his poems; but it can be said with confidence that here is a most original and powerful voice, writing in a much more subjective mode than his supposed master Chaucer, not only adapting traditional genres and themes but putting an unmistakably personal stamp on them.

Very little is known about the early reception of Dunbar's poems; but there must have been some demand for them, for three were published in 1508 by Walter Chepman and Andrew Myllar, the first printers in Scotland who were granted a royal patent (1507), and three others by another printer, as yet unidentified (in Rouen, according to some scholars, though Priscilla Bawcutt argues for a Scottish origin in a 1991 study). The poems preserved in these early prints testify to the variety of Dunbar's oeuvre and, apparently, its popularity: an allegorical dream vision about love ("The Goldyn Targe"); the energetic and satiric "Flyting" and "Testament"; "The Ballade of Barnard Stewart Lord Of Aubigny" (K35), a eulogy of a Frenchman of Scots extraction who came on an embassy to Scotland in 1508; the bawdy "Tretis of the Tua Mariit Wemen and the Wedo"; and the melancholic dance of death and catalogue of dead poets, "The Lament for the Makaris." The other poems are preserved in sixteenth- and early-seventeenth-century English and Scots manuscript collections of verse, again in combinations that emphasize Dunbar's multifarious talent. Some attributions rest only on the evidence of a single manuscript and have occasioned considerable debate among modern scholars. (Some editions include in an appendix poems of doubtful attribution, though Kinsley's does not; in a 1981 article Bawcutt criticizes his edition on this and other grounds. She will shortly publish her own edition.)

Dunbar's repeated expressions of admiration for Chaucer have led many critics to refer to him (with Henryson and Douglas) as a "Scottish Chaucerian." One of many powerful reasons for objecting to this label is that the three poets linked by it are so unlike in style and themes, as well as being very different from Chaucer. The trend in recent criticism has been to move away from the "Scottish Chaucerian" label and to consider them as original Scots poets rather than imitators, in the context of Scottish language and culture at the court of James IV, at a time when literature and learning were flourishing in Scotland (Dunbar himself names twenty-one Scots poets in the "Lament for the Makaris," and three universities were founded in the course of the fifteenth century). Considerable attention has also been paid to Dunbar's use of language, his aureate terms, his bawdy colloquialisms, and his imagery; these studies have been much aided by the publication of the *Dictionary of the Older Scottish Tongue* (1937–), now nearing completion. Dunbar's attitudes toward women continue to arouse interest, as they have for many years: a fascinating 1981 study by Elizabeth Roth of the reception of "The Tretis of the Tua Mariit Wemen and the Wedo" charts a surprising range of critical comment over the past two centuries. Critics today also are interested in the problem of subjectivity: is Dunbar's use of the first personal conventional, or can one reconstruct his views and personality on the basis of his poems? As Bawcutt remarks in *Dunbar the Makar* (1992), "He speaks with almost too many voices"; his many styles and personae, from eldritch to aureate, from beggar to satirist, from devout Christian to wild reveler, offer a constant challenge to the modern reader.

Bibliographies:
Florence H. Ridley, "Middle Scots Writers," in *A Manual of the Writings in Middle English, 1050–1500,* volume 4, edited by A. E. Hartung (New Haven, Conn.: Archon, 1973), pp. 1005–1060;

Jean-Jacques Blanchot, "Dunbar and His Critics: A Critical Survey," in *Scottish Language and Literature, Medieval and Renaissance,* edited by D. Strauss and H. W. Drescher (Frankfurt: Peter Lang, 1986), pp. 303–336;

Walter Scheps and J. Anna Looney, *Middle Scots Poets: A Reference Guide to James I of Scotland, Robert Henryson, William Dunbar, and Gavin Douglas* (Boston: G. K. Hall, 1986).

Biography:
J. W. Baxter, *William Dunbar: A Biographical Study* (Edinburgh: Oliver & Boyd, 1952; New York: Books for Libraries Press, 1971).

References:
Priscilla Bawcutt, "Aspects of Dunbar's Imagery," in *Chaucer and Middle English Studies in Honour of Rossell Hope Robbins,* edited by Beryl Rowland (London: Allen & Unwin, 1974), pp. 190–200;

Bawcutt, *Dunbar the Makar* (Oxford: Oxford University Press, 1992);

Bawcutt, "The Earliest Texts of Dunbar," in *Regionalism in Late Medieval Manuscripts and Texts: Es-*

says *Celebrating the Publication of "A Linguistic Atlas of Late Medieval English,"* edited by Felicity Riddy (Cambridge: D. S. Brewer, 1991), pp. 183–198;

Bawcutt, "The Text and Interpretation of Dunbar," *Medium Aevum,* 50, no. 1 (1981): 88–98;

W. A. Craigie and A. J. Aitken, eds., *Dictionary of the Older Scottish Tongue: From the Twelfth Century to the End of the Seventeenth* (Chicago: University of Chicago Press, 1937–1971; vols. 5ff. published by Aberdeen University Press);

Denton Fox, "The Chronology of William Dunbar," *Philological Quarterly,* 39 (October 1960): 413–425;

Fox, "The Scottish Chaucerians," in *Chaucer and Chaucerians,* edited by D. S. Brewer (London & Edinburgh: Nelson, 1966), pp. 164–200;

Gregory Kratzmann, *Anglo-Scottish Literary Relations, 1430–1550* (Cambridge: Cambridge University Press, 1980);

C. S. Lewis, "The Close of the Middle Ages in Scotland," in his *English Literature in the Sixteenth Century, Excluding Drama* (Oxford: Oxford University Press, 1954), pp. 66–119;

R. J. Lyall, "Politics and Poetry in Fifteenth and Sixteenth Century Scotland," *Scottish Literary Journal,* 3, no. 2 (1976): 5–29;

Edwin Morgan, "Dunbar and the Language of Poetry," *Essays in Criticism,* 2 (April 1952): 138–158; reprinted in his *Essays* (Manchester: Carcanet, 1974), pp. 81–99;

Edmund Reiss, *William Dunbar* (Boston: Twayne, 1979);

Ian Simpson Ross, *William Dunbar* (Leiden: E. J. Brill, 1981);

Elizabeth Roth, "Criticism and Taste: Readings of Dunbar's *Tretis,*" *Scottish Literary Journal,* supplement 15 (1981): 57–90;

Tom Scott, *Dunbar: A Critical Exposition of the Poems* (Edinburgh: Oliver & Boyd, 1966).

Papers:

Manuscripts for Dunbar's poems are at the Town House, Aberdeen (Aberdeen Burgh Sasine Register); National Library of Scotland (Asloan and Bannatyne MSS.); British Library (Arundel MS. 285); Pepysian Library, Magdalene College, Cambridge (Maitland Folio); and Cambridge University Library (Reidpeth MS.).

John Foxe

(1517 – 18 April 1587)

John N. King
Ohio State University

BOOKS: *De non plectendis adulteris consultatio* (London: Hugh Singleton, 1548);

De censura siue excommunicatione ecclesiastica rectoque eius vsu (London: Printed by Robert Toy, 1551);

Commentarii Rerum in Ecclesia Gestarum (Strasbourg: Wendelin Richelius, 1554);

Christus Triumphans (Basel: Joannes Oporinus, 1556); translated by Richard Day as *Christ Jesus Triumphant* (London: John & Richard Day, 1598);

Rerum in Ecclesia Gestarum (Basel: Nicolaus Brylinger & Joannes Oporinus, 1559);

Actes and monuments of these latter and perillous dayes, touching matters of the church [the "Book of Martyrs"] (London: Printed by John Day, 1563; revised and enlarged to two volumes, 1570; revised, 1576, 1583); abridged by Timothy Bright (London: Printed by John Windet, 1589);

A sermon of Christ crucified, preached at Paules Crosse (London: Printed by John Day, 1570); translated into Latin as *De Christo Crucifixo Concio* (1571);

De oliua euangelica. Concio, in baptismo Judæi (London: Christopher Barker, 1578); translated in part by Bishop James Bell as *A sermon preached at the christening of a certaine Jew* (London: Christopher Barker, 1578);

Papa confutatus, anonymous (London: Printed by Richard Sergier, 1580); translated by Bell as *The pope confuted* (London: Printed by T. Dawson for Richard Sergier, 1580);

Eicasmi seu meditationes, in sacram Apocalypsin, edited by Samuel Foxe and Abraham Fleming (London: Printed by George Bishop, 1587).

Editions and Collections: *Acts and Monuments of John Foxe,* 8 volumes, edited by Stephen R. Cattley (London: Seeley & Burnside, 1837–1841; revised, 1843–1849; New York: AMS, 1965); revised by Josiah Pratt (London: Seeleys, 1853–1868); abridged by George A. Williamson (Boston: Little, Brown, 1966);

John Foxe (National Portrait Gallery, London)

"John Foxe on Astrology," edited by John Hazel Smith, *English Literary Renaissance,* 1 (Autumn 1971): 210–225;

Christus Triumphans, translated and edited by Smith, in *Two Latin Comedies: "Titus and Gesippus" and "Christus Triumphans"* (Ithaca, N.Y.: Cornell University Press, 1973), pp. 199–371;

The English Sermons of John Foxe, edited by Warren W. Wooden (Delmar, N.Y.: Scholars' Facsimiles & Reprints, 1978).

OTHER: *The gospels of the fower euangelistes tr. in the olde Saxons tyme out of Latin into the vulgare toung of the Saxons,* edited by Foxe (London: Printed by John Day, 1571);

The whole workes of W. Tyndall, John Frith, and Doct. Barnes, edited by Foxe (London: Printed by John Day, 1573).

TRANSLATIONS: Martin Luther, *A frutfull sermon of the moost euangelicall wryter M. Luther, made of the angelles* (London: Hugh Singleton, 1548?);

Joannes Œcolampadius, *A sarmon, of Ihon Oecolampadius, to yong men, and maydens* (London: Printed by H. Powell & sold by Hugh Singleton, 1548?);

Urbanus Regius, *An instruccyon of christen fayth howe to be bolde vpon the promyse of God* (London: Hugh Singleton, 1548?).

John Foxe is renowned as the compiler of one of the most widely read, popular, and influential works of the Elizabethan Age: *Acts and Monuments of These Latter and Perilous Times.* In 1563 John Day published the first of four editions that appeared in Foxe's lifetime. From the beginning it has been known popularly as Foxe's "Book of Martyrs." It contains scores of highly charged, polemical accounts of the martyrdom of Christians whom Foxe alleges maintained faith with the "true" church of Christ as opposed to the "false" church of Antichrist said to be under the leadership of the pope in Rome. The narratives concerning persecutions during the reign of Mary I, the Catholic queen who ruled England from 1553 until 1558, are charged with the nationalistic fervor that supported the reestablishment of Protestant theological doctrine in the Church of England under Elizabeth I. Foxe's emotionally exciting stories stirred up intense hostility against the papacy and Roman Catholicism. It became a truism to state that if a Protestant household of England or New England contained no more than two books, they would have been the English Bible and some version of Foxe's "Book of Martyrs." Methodical reading from these "holy" books was a standard practice in sixteenth- and seventeenth-century English-speaking Protestant families.

The few facts that are known about the parents or family background of Foxe have been summarized in Warren W. Wooden's *John Foxe* (1983). He was born in Boston, Lincolnshire, in 1517. The death of his father led to his mother's marriage to Richard Melton, to whom Foxe later dedicated his translation of *An Instruction of Christian Faith* (1548?), a tract by the Lutheran reformer Urbanus Regius. Impressed by Foxe's aptitude for learning, some res-

idents of Boston underwrote his enrollment as a sixteen-year-old student at Brasenose College, Oxford. After receiving the B.A., he became a fellow of Magdalen College in 1538.

He became a Protestant while at Oxford and moved within a circle of religious reformers who included Alexander Nowell, Hugh Latimer, and Robert Crowley. He gave up his fellowship in 1545 – the same year he proceeded to the M.A. – in line with his opposition to the clerical vow of celibacy and the entry into religious orders that was required of permanent fellows. After an interval of employment as tutor to the children of William Lucy, who resided at Charlecote in Warwickshire, Foxe married Agnes Randall in 1547. The children resulting from this union included Christiana, Dorcas, Samuel, Rafe, Mary, and Simeon. Foxe moved to London in 1547 and caught the attention of Mary Fitzroy, Duchess of Richmond, a notable patroness of Protestant reformers. The peeress not only gave him lodging in her London household, where Foxe forged a long-standing acquaintance with his fellow resident John Bale, but she also arranged for him to tutor the offspring of her brother, the poet Henry Howard, Earl of Surrey, who had recently been executed.

Foxe arrived in London soon after the accession of Edward VI, during whose minority a thoroughgoing program of ecclesiastical reform was implemented by the Protestant lords in control of the government. The Privy Council and Parliament reversed the policy of religious reaction that marked the last years of Henry VIII. The extraordinary freedom of expression that Protestants enjoyed during Edward's reign provided a climate hospitable to Foxe's first efforts as a theologian and chronicler of church history. It was at Mountjoy House, the London home of the duchess of Richmond, and at the Reigate household where Foxe tutored the Howard offspring that he completed *De Non Plectendis Adulteris Consultatio* (1548), a tract opposed to the execution of adulterers. This work testifies to his unconventional and long-standing opposition to capital punishment. *De Censura sive Excommunicatione Ecclesiastica* (1551) called for the use of excommunication in order to punish religious and social infractions. Foxe's religious convictions may also be noted in his translations of tracts by Martin Luther and his coreligionists Joannes Oecolampadius and Urbanus Regius. Foxe's ordination as deacon in 1550 enabled him to transmit reformist ideology through the preaching of sermons. Soon afterward he began the historical research that would become his life's work and result in the increasingly massive

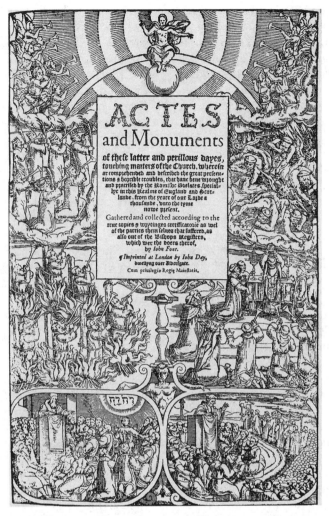

ACTES
and Monuments
of thefe latter and perillous dayes,
touching matters of the Church, wherein
ar comprehended and defcribed the great perfecu-
tions & horrible troubles, that have bene wrought
and practifed by the Romifhe Prelates. Special-
lye in this Realme of England and Scotlande. from the yeare of our Lorde a
thoufande, vnto the tyme
nowe prefent.

Gathered and collected according to the
true copies & wrytinges certificatorie as wel
of the parties them felues that fuffered,as
also out of the Bifhops Regifters,
which wer the doers therof,
by Iohn Foxe.

¶ Imprinted at London by Iohn Day,
dwellyng ouer Alderfgate.
Cum priuilegio Regiæ Maieftatis.

*Title page for Foxe's collection of narratives on Protestant martyrs,
one of the most popular and influential works of the Elizabethan Age*

editions of the "Book of Martyrs" that appeared during his lifetime.

When a period of Catholic reaction ensued upon the accession of Mary I, Foxe fled with his wife from England to the Continent. They took haven in Strasbourg, where Wendelin Richelius printed the first Latin installment of his history of the martyrs: *Commentarii Rerum in Ecclesia Gestarum* (1554). This work deals with events that took place before 1500, focusing on those whom Foxe regards as forerunners of the Lutheran Reformation: John Wycliffe, the Lollards, and Jan Hus. Foxe soon moved on to Frankfurt, where he lodged with Anthony Gilby, later an active Puritan clergyman, and sided with John Knox in favor of liturgical reform that went beyond the second Edwardian *Book of Common Prayer* (1552). At the defeat of Knox's party, Foxe departed for Basel. He spent the remainder of his exile in that Swiss city, where he joined Lau-

rence Humphrey, an associate from Magdalen College, and his friend Bale. He and Bale resided in the household of Joannes Oporinus, a prominent Protestant printer, before they joined other exiles resident in a dissolved convent, Klarakloster. While Foxe earned a living as a proofreader for Oporinus, he worked on a variety of historical and theological projects.

The onset of Mary I's persecution of Protestants, about three hundred of whom were burned alive from February 1555 onward, left an indelible imprint upon Foxe's career. Manuscript accounts of their persecutions and transcripts of the final testimonies of the martyrs who were smuggled out of England came into Foxe's hands. Many of these documents were passed on to him by his fellow exile Edmund Grindal, later archbishop of Canterbury under Elizabeth I; he urged Foxe to chronicle the Marian persecutions. As Foxe collected these materials with the intention of incorporating them into his forthcoming martyrological history, he published *Christus Triumphans* (1556), a Latin closet drama in five acts that he terms an "apocalyptic comedy." The work is "comic" in the sense that it enfolds the individual "tragic" sufferings of "true" Christians within the overarching trajectory of providential history. Although the original version of this work may have dated back to his university days, the printed work dramatizes the Marian persecutions as part of the unfolding of the history of the church as Foxe believed it to have been prophesied in Revelation.

The fifth act of *Christus Triumphans* alludes to a recent cause célèbre, the double execution of Hugh Latimer and Nicholas Ridley by burning at Oxford University, under the guise of the martyrdom of preachers named Hierologus and Theosebes. Foxe presents their suffering under Dynastes (Mary I) as the culminating example of the succession of "wondrous tragedies" of the elect faithful following the loosing of Satan after his imprisonment of one thousand years. As a manifestation of Antichrist, Pope Pseudamnus invests ecclesiastical primacy in Pornapolis (whorish city [Rome]), whose identification as the Whore of Babylon (*meretrix Babylonica*) associates her with the visually splendid "false" church. By contrast, Ecclesia (the "true" church that remains invisible) is cast in the role of the Woman Clothed with the Sun, who takes flight into the wilderness to await Christ's return. The concluding epithalamium and chorus of the virgins prophesy the resolution of the apocalyptic conflict with Christ's victory and the descent of the New Jerusalem. Ecclesia's designation as the Spouse of Canticles carries with it intense apocalyptic expectation, as the play concludes immediately prior to the promised double catastrophe that will follow upon the union of Christ the Bridegroom and his Spouse. In a dramatization of the song sung at the Marriage of the Lamb (Rev. 19:6–8), the epithalamic chorus celebrates the anticipated return of Christ in the high comic mode of divine praise. This vision of apocalyptic conflict between the invisible church of "true" apostles and the visible church of Roman corruption is aligned with Bale's influential commentary upon Revelation in *The Image of Both Churches* (1545?).

When Queen Mary died in 1558, the accession of Elizabeth I allowed for the homecoming of the Protestant exiles and the renewal of expectations for the reforms of the English church. Shortly before returning to his homeland, Foxe published *Rerum in Ecclesia Gestarum* (1559), the sequel to his *Commentarii.* These works provided the foundation for the "Book of Martyrs." *Rerum in Ecclesia Gestarum* focuses on the persecution of "true" believers from the time of the Lollards through the early years of the Marian persecutions. Soon after his return to England, Foxe was ordained as a priest in 1560 by Grindal. He later received a prebendary at Salisbury that was in the gift of Bishop John Jewel, as well as patronage from John Parkhurst, bishop of Norwich. Nevertheless, Foxe's opposition to the wearing of ecclesiastical vestments during the first outbreak of Puritan controversy in the 1560s appears to have blocked him from further advancement in the ecclesiastical hierarchy.

Four years after his return Foxe produced the first edition of his "Book of Martyrs" under the auspices of Day, the zealously Protestant printer with whom he worked for the remainder of his life. He collaborated with Day in turning that text into one of the best-illustrated books of its age. Like the text that they illustrate, these woodcuts appeal to a broad popular audience. The woodcut images tend to be of three kinds, as noted in the introduction to George A. Williamson's abridgment of *The Book of Martyrs* (1966). Small stereotyped figures of martyrs recur randomly throughout the collection. Larger and more realistic scenes may have been designed from eyewitness accounts as illustrations for specific martyrdoms; these narrative woodcuts function as direct illustrations for the text because they carefully incorporate details mentioned by Foxe, and their banderoles quote words that he attributes to the martyrs. Finally, a small number of large-scale illustrations, such as the pictures of Henry VIII and Elizabeth I triumphing over the pope, introduce real persons into allegorical scenes. In the popular imagination the "Book of Martyrs" is remembered for the lurid images of the "roasting" of Sir John Oldcastle, the hangings of Lollards, and the seemingly countless burnings of Protestant martyrs. Because the author's extensive printed commentary contains many cross-references and specific page references to the body of his history as a guide to interpreting the visual scenes, Foxe clearly joined Day in designing the woodcut series. These pictures served as visual arguments that could be understood even by the illiterate.

The first edition of the "Book of Martyrs" begins with a calendar of holy days and martyrdoms, a dedication in Latin to Jesus Christ ("Ad Dominum Jesum Christum"), a dedication to Queen Elizabeth I, a Latin preface "Ad doctum Lectorem" ("To the Learned Reader"), a polemical address "To the Persecutors of God's Truth, Commonly Called Pa-

Part of the dedication page in the 1563 edition of Actes and Monuments

pists," and "A Declaration concerning the Utility and Profit of This History." Although Foxe came under attack from radical Protestants who argued that his calendar merely disguised the old calendar of saints, he pointedly omits those traditional saints whose careers lack scriptural authority. Foxe's calendar supplants the host of later saints honored by the Church of Rome with the names of historical individuals who underwent martyrdom for the sake of their religious beliefs, for example, Wycliffe and William Tyndale; the text describes their careers in detail. The execution dates of the Protestants who had been burned alive during the reign of Mary I receive a place of prominence both in the calendar and in ensuing accounts of their lives and deaths.

Foxe designed the "Book of Martyrs" to supplant medieval legends of saints, which celebrated their subjects' alleged ability to work miracles, cures, and magical feats. Foxe claims that his martyrologies differ from old-fashioned saints' lives that are unable "to abide the touch of history" because they are mingled with "untrue additions and fabulous inventions of men." His preface "To the Learned Reader" specifically attacks the most famous medieval collection of saints' lives, Jacobus de Voragine's *Golden Legend* (thirteenth century), for containing lying "fables." In place of alleged examples of saintly intercession, healing, and prophecy, Foxe substitutes instances of providential intervention to deliver the faithful or to work vengeance against their opponents. He participates in the Protestant conception of martyrdom as an act of witnessing to religious faith. The suffering experience of saints is a common element in Protestant and Catholic accounts, but Foxe and his coreligionists insist that sainthood inheres in risking even life itself to testify on behalf of Christ, rather than in the marvelous elements emphasized in late-medieval saints' legends. Instead of the older belief that saints are exceptional individuals who possess the power to intercede on behalf of sinners, Protestants believed that the divine imputation of faith was a necessary part of sainthood, one that is accessible to any elect Christian. In place of the famous miracle workers of medieval tradition, Foxe celebrates the little-known artisans and lowly workers who died for their faith under Mary I.

Some of the best-known narratives in the collection are those that describe the death of John Rogers, the first of the Marian martyrs; the suffering of John Hooper, bishop of Gloucester; and the recantation, reaffirmation of faith, and burning of Thomas Cranmer, archbishop of Canterbury, at Oxford University. Perhaps the most poignant of these narratives is the description of the double execution of the Protestant heroes Nicholas Ridley and Hugh Latimer.

Many of Foxe's narratives follow a "three-stage pattern," according to Wooden. The first part of this conventional sequence focuses on the apprehension of a Protestant believer by unjust authorities, who resort to punishment or torture in an effort to break the martyr's will to testify to faith in Christ. The heroic action of this opening section leads to interrogation by ecclesiastical authorities that stresses doctrinal argument rather than exciting action. The final section glorifies the martyr's refusal to recant in opposition to antagonists, who may include a divine assigned to preach on a symbolic scriptural text from a portable pulpit near the martyr's pyre. This closing scene often incorporates an eloquent testimonial of faith moments before the lighting of the heretic's pyre.

Foxe's narrative account of the burning of Latimer and Ridley in the 1563 edition provides a stirring example of the concluding sequence. Upon arrival at the site of their immolation in a ditch to the north of Balliol College, Oxford, Ridley is alleged to have delivered words of comfort that are justifiably famous as a rallying cry in favor of the English Reformation: " 'Be of good heart, brother, for God will either assuage the fury of the flame or else strengthen us to abide it.' With that went he to the stake, kneeled down by it, kissed it, most effectuously [earnestly] prayed, and behind him Master Latimer kneeled, as earnestly calling upon God as he." Master Smith opens the day's proceedings with a homily on 1 Corinthians 13:3: "If I yield my body to the fire to be burned, and have not charity, I shall gain nothing thereby." The narrator then idealizes the martyrs' testimonials of faith and refusal to recant at the end of what is termed a "wicked sermon":

"Well," quod Master Ridley, "so long as the breath is in my body, I will never deny my Lord God and his known truth; God's will be done in me." And with that he rose up and said with a loud voice: "Well, then, I commit our cause to Almighty God, which shall indifferently [objectively] judge all." To whose saying Master Latimer added his old poesy [motto or verse], "Well, there is nothing hid but it shall be opened." And he said he could answer Smith well enough, if he might be suffered [permitted]. Incontinently [immediately] they were commanded to make them[selves] ready [for death], which they in all meekness obeyed.

The narrative emphasizes Latimer's patient suffering as a martyr who goes to the stake wearing a funerary shroud that appears to confer upon him moral strength and dignity that contradict his physical decrepitude as a man of great age: "And being stripped into his shroud, [he] seemed as comely a person to them that were there present as one should lightly [readily] see. And whereas in his clothes he appeared a withered and crooked silly [pitiable] old man, he now stood bolt upright, as comely a father as one might lightly behold." The aged reformer demonstrates his scorn for death all the more with the symbolic gesture of donning his burial shroud for the occasion.

A woodcut of the kind that characteristically illustrates death scenes provides a visual supplement to the narrative account of this execution. Banderoles that extend from the mouths of Latimer and Ridley contain their respective dying prayers: "Father of heaven receive my soul" and "In manibus tuas domine . . ." ("Into your hands, Lord, [I give my soul]"). Like other realistic woodcuts, this picture portrays them at the center of a large crowd of hostile onlookers. Master Smith stands in the portable wooden pulpit at the rear of the scene as Cranmer looks down from the walls of Oxford, stating, "O Lord strengthen them."

Foxe had already presented the burning of Latimer and Ridley as a climactic incident in the current age of ecclesiastical history in *Christus Triumphans*. Of the five ages of Christian history that Foxe propounds in the 1563 edition of the "Book of Martyrs," he devotes most attention to the final age following A.D. 1000, an era during which a corrupt church establishment departed more and more from a state of apostolic Christian purity. The second edition (1570) goes back to the origins of the church in order to place the martyrdoms of Christian believers from the Roman persecutions onward within the context of the evolving relationship between ecclesiastical and secular authority.

Allegory of the Reformation, *a woodcut from the 1570 edition of* Actes *and* Monuments

Frances A. Yates's seminal essay "Queen Elizabeth I as Astraea" (1975) demonstrates how Foxe presents the Marian burnings as recapitulations of the persecutions of Christians by the Roman emperors. According to this scheme Emperor Constantine's designation of Christianity as an official religion of the Roman Empire was a central event in reversing the imperial policy of persecuting Christians. Foxe aligns the popes, through their claim to secular authority, and the Church of Rome with the role of persecutor once played by the tyrannical emperors. He gives particular attention to the contemporary age of the Tudor monarchs and praises Henry VIII, Edward VI, and Elizabeth I for restoring evangelical government after centuries of usurpation by papal authority.

Foxe asserts that the return to "true" religion under Elizabeth I constitutes a return to the short-lived ideal of collaboration between church and state that existed under Constantine. Thus the illustration contained within the initial capital C of the dedication to Elizabeth I in the first edition of the "Book of Martyrs" portrays the queen as a type of Constantine governing a Christian empire, just as Foxe himself plays the role of a new Eusebius in chronicling the martyrdoms of the faithful under Mary I. This iconoclastic illustration reverses the triumph of pope over emperor by portraying Elizabeth, seated on her throne and carrying the Sword of Justice, as she surmounts the toppled pope, who is entwined with demonic serpents beneath her feet. It is probable that the three men at the queen's side are, from right to left, Day, Foxe, and their likely sponsor at the royal court, Thomas Norton.

When chained copies of the 1570 edition of Foxe's "Book of Martyrs" were placed in English cathedrals under order from the Convocation, that text and its illustrations became widely known in

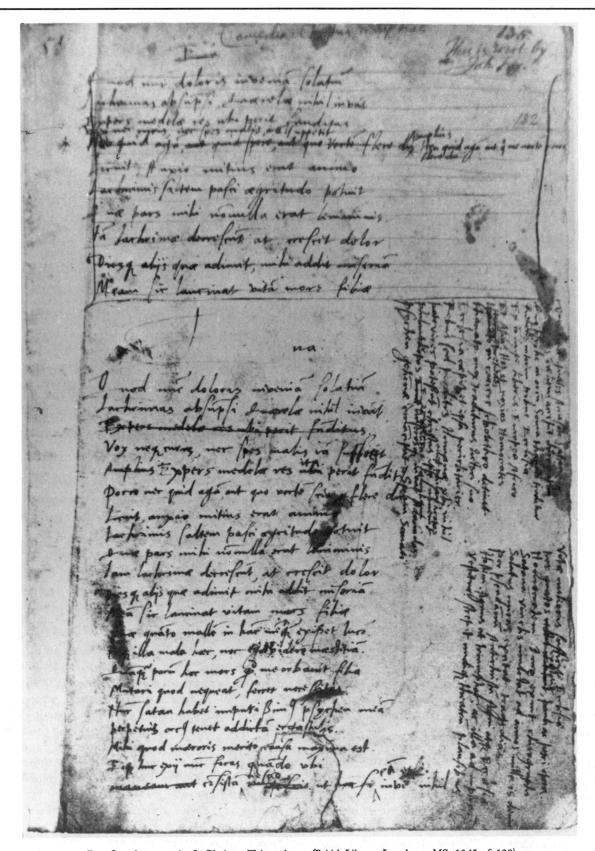

Page from the manuscript for Christus Triumphans *(British Library; Lansdowne MS. 1045, f. 132)*

Elizabethan England. Foxe revised or omitted most of the preliminary materials in the first edition, including the dedication to Elizabeth I, which now begins with Christ rather than Constantine and compares the queen not with the Roman emperor, but with the Salome present at Christ's Crucifixion. This change accommodates the division of the text into two separate volumes and contributes to the praise of Henry VIII rather than Elizabeth as Constantine redivivus, a change that honors all of the Protestant Tudors rather than the queen alone. Accordingly, the second volume of the 1570 edition begins with Henry's reign and the reimposition of royal authority over the church. According to Foxe this action anticipated the renewal of reform that is praised in the climactic account of Elizabeth, which emphasizes the suspicion and danger of death that she suffered as princess during the reign of her half sister, Mary I. The construction and reconstruction of the reformed Church of England therefore define the formal limits of contemporary British history in the revised edition.

The years during and after publication of the second edition of the "Book of Martyrs" saw Foxe immersed in a variety of other projects. His pulpit defense of Queen Elizabeth against Pope Pius V's bull of excommunication ("Regnans in Excelsis") was published by Day as *A Sermon of Christ Crucified* (1570). Foxe edited the Anglo-Saxon text of the four Gospels with a parallel text from the Bishops' Bible under the patronage of Matthew Parker, the first Elizabethan archbishop of Canterbury. For the publication of this volume in 1571, Day employed a font of Anglo-Saxon type that he had already cut under Parker's auspices. The work represented a contribution to the effort of antiquaries such as Bale and Robert Crowley to reconstruct and rehabilitate "pure" English alternatives to the literary and religious tradition of the Church of Rome. Foxe also compiled an edition of the writings of three heroes of the English Reformation, *The Whole Works of William Tyndale, John Frith, and Doctor [Robert] Barnes* (1573), to which he attached biographies of those famous Protestant martyrs. Day published Foxe's second revised edition of the "Book of Martyrs" in 1576. A well-attended homily that Foxe delivered at the conversion and baptism of a Sephardic Jew was published in 1578, both in Latin, as *De Oliva Evangelica,* and in Bishop James Bell's translation into English, *A Sermon Preached at the Christening of a Certain Jew. Papa Confutatus* (1580) contained yet another attack against the papacy and was translated by Bell as *The Pope Confuted* (1580). Day published Foxe's final revision of the "Book of Martyrs" in

1583. Shortly before the martyrologist's death on 18 April 1587, his extended commentary on Revelation 1–17, *Eicasmi seu Meditationes in Sacram Apocalypsin* (1587), was edited by his son Samuel and Abraham Fleming.

The increasingly massive editions of the "Book of Martyrs" that appeared during the compiler's lifetime were followed by Timothy Bright's 1589 abridgment, the first of many modifications of Foxe's great work that would appear during ensuing centuries. Two-volume editions of the complete "Book of Martyrs" that appeared in 1596, 1597, and 1610 were followed by a three-volume version in 1632. Archbishop William Laud's alleged refusal to permit publication of a new edition in 1638 fueled the Puritan attack against the regime of Charles I. The second volume of the 1641 edition contains a biography of Foxe that is attributed to his son Samuel. An ever-increasing degree of textual corruption entered into the many abridged and unabridged editions of the "Book of Martyrs" that appeared in ensuing centuries.

The reliability of Foxe's massive work came under attack soon after the appearance of the first edition. Robert Parsons, a Jesuit priest, was one of many early Catholic readers who claimed that the "Book of Martyrs" was filled with an extraordinarily large number of falsifications and errors. Although examination of surviving documents indicates that Foxe did not alter his sources, he clearly selected partisan narratives to which he attached inflammatory comments. His comment about Bishop Stephen Gardiner, who organized the persecutions under Queen Mary, provides a good example:

> I will not here speak of that which hath been constantly reported to me touching the monstrous making and misshaped fashion of his feet and toes, the nails whereof were said not to be like to other men's, but to crook downward, and to be sharp like the claws of ravening beasts.

He weighted his text in favor of Protestant heroes such as Latimer, Ridley, and Cranmer and against Catholic "villains" such as Gardiner and Edmund Bonner, whom he defamed as ringleaders of the Marian persecutions. He calls Gardiner a "bloody tyrant," for example, and exults in describing his painful death as a "spectacle worthy to be noted and beholden of all such bloody burning persecutors."

The attack against Foxe's truthfulness once again came to the fore following publication of Stephen R. Cattley's eight-volume version (1837–1841) of the fourth edition. That editor incorporated corrections into his 1843–1849 edition in response to arguments by S. R. Maitland that were published in the *British Magazine* (1837-1847). More recent scholarship, notably William Haller's *The Elect Nation: The Meaning and Relevance of Foxe's "Book of Martyrs"* (1963), has redirected attention away from questions of historical accuracy and toward Foxe's masterful manipulation of his subject matter into a providential design of apocalyptic history. Even though Haller overestimates the role of England as an "elect nation" within Foxe's grand design, his thesis remains influential as it undergoes qualification in more recently published work by Richard Bauckham, Katharine R. Firth, and others. The continuation of controversy over the validity of Foxe's work shows how difficult it is for scholars and general readers to be neutral about Foxe's "Book of Martyrs," even to the present day.

Bibliographies:

George Watson, ed., *The New Cambridge Bibliography of English Literature,* volume 1 (Cambridge: Cambridge University Press, 1974), p. 2207;

Warren W. Wooden, "Recent Studies in Foxe," *English Literary Renaissance,* 11 (Spring 1981): 224-232.

References:

Richard Bauckham, *Tudor Apocalypse* (Appleford: Sutton Courtenay Press, 1978);

Paul Christianson, *Reformers and Babylon: English Apocalyptic Visions from the Reformation to the Civil War* (Toronto: University of Toronto Press, 1978);

Katharine R. Firth, *The Apocalyptic Tradition of Reformation Britain, 1530-1645* (Oxford: Clarendon, 1979), pp. 32-68;

William Haller, *The Elect Nation: The Meaning and Relevance of Foxe's "Book of Martyrs"* (New York: Harper & Row, 1963);

John N. King, *English Reformation Literature: The Tudor Origins of the Protestant Tradition* (Princeton: Princeton University Press, 1982);

King, *Tudor Royal Iconography: Literature and Art in an Age of Religious Crisis* (Princeton: Princeton University Press, 1989), pp. 131-164;

S. R. Maitland, *Six Letters on Fox's "Acts and Monuments," Addressed to the Editor of the British Magazine and Re-Printed from that Work with Notes and Additions* (London: J. G. & F. Rivington, 1837);

Maitland, *Six More Essays on Fox's "Acts and Monuments," Originally Published in the British Magazine in the Years 1837 and 1838* (London: J. G. & F. Rivington, 1841);

J. F. Mozley, *John Foxe and His Book* (London: Society for Promoting Christian Knowledge, 1940);

V. Norskov Olsen, *John Foxe and the Elizabethan Church* (Berkeley: University of California Press, 1973);

Helen C. White, *Tudor Books of Saints and Martyrs* (Madison: University of Wisconsin Press, 1963), pp. 132-195;

Warren W. Wooden, *John Foxe* (Boston: Twayne, 1983);

Frances A. Yates, "Foxe as Propagandist," *Encounter,* 27 (October 1966): 78-86;

Yates, "Queen Elizabeth I as Astraea," in her *Astraea: The Imperial Theme in the Sixteenth Century* (London: Routledge & Kegan Paul, 1975), pp. 29-87.

Papers:

Foxe's manuscripts, which include many documents and transcripts that he collected, are preserved among the Harleian and Lansdowne manuscripts at the British Library.

Barnabe Googe

(11 June 1540 – February 1594)

Judith M. Kennedy
Saint Thomas University

BOOKS: *Eglogs epytaphes, and sonettes. Newly written* (London: Printed by T. Colwell for Rafe Newbery, 1563);

A newe booke called the shippe of safegarde (London: Printed by W. Seres, 1569) — includes two tales versified from Rufinus's Latin version of Eusebius's *Ecclesiastical History:* "The Death of St. Polycarpus" and "A Priest of Apollo Strangely Converted."

Editions and Collections: *Eglogs, Epytaphes, and Sonettes. 1563,* edited by Edward Arber, English Reprints no. 30 (London, 1871; London: A. Constable, 1895); republished, with an introduction by Frank B. Fieler (Gainesville, Fla.: Scholars' Facsimiles & Reprints, 1968);

The Popish Kingdome; or, Reigne of Antichrist, Written . . . by T. Naogeorgus and Englyshed by B. Googe, 1570, edited by R. C. Hope (London: W. Satchell, 1880); republished, with an introduction by Peter Davison (New York: Johnson Reprint, 1972);

The Zodiake of Life by Marcellus Palingenius Translated by Barnabe Googe, introduced by Rosemund Tuve (Delmar, N.Y.: Scholars' Facsimiles & Reprints, 1947);

Selected Poems, edited by Alan Stephens (Denver: Swallow Press, 1961);

Fovre Bookes of Husbandry (New York: Da Capo Press, 1971);

"The Overthrow of the Gout" and "Three Renaissance Scientific Poems," edited by Robert Schuler, *Studies in Philology,* 75, no. 5 (1978): 67-107;

"A Critical Annotated Old-Spelling Edition of Barnabe Googe's Translation of Marcellus Palingenius's *Zodiake of Life* (Books I–VI)," edited by Roland Stephen Marandino, Ph.D. dissertation, Columbia University, 1981;

Eclogues, Epitaphs, and Sonnets, edited by Judith M. Kennedy (Toronto: University of Toronto Press, 1989);

The Overthrow of the Gout and A Dialogue Betwixt the Gout and Christopher Ballista, edited, with an introduction, by Simon McKeown (London: Indelible, 1990).

OTHER: "Let rancour not you rule," prefatory poem in Nilus Cabasilas, *A briefe treatise, conteynynge a playne declaration of the popes vsurped primacye,* translated by Thomas Gressop (London: Printed by H. Sutton for R. Newbery, 1560);

"To my very loving friend Captain Barnabe Rich," commendatory epistle in Barnabe Riche, *Allarme to England, foreshewing what perilles are procured, where the people liue without regarde of martiall lawe* (London: Printed by C. Barker, 1578).

TRANSLATIONS: Marcellus Palingenius, *The firste thre bokes of the most christian poet M. Palingenius, called the zodyake of lyfe* (London: Printed by J. Tisdale for R. Newbery, 1560); enlarged as *The firste syxe bokes . . .* (London: Printed by J. Tisdale for R. Newbery, 1561); enlarged as *The zodiake of life . . . wherein are conteyned twelue bookes* (London: Printed by H. Denham for R. Newbery, 1565); revised and annotated by Googe (London: Printed by H. Middleton for R. Newbery, 1576; Printed by R. Robinson, 1588);

Thomas Kirchmeyer, *The popish kingdome, or reigne of Antichrist. By T. Naogeorgus* (London: Printed by H. Denham for R. Watkins, 1570) — includes Kirchmeyer's "The spirituall husbandrie";

Conrad Heresbach, *Foure bookes of husbandry, Collected by Mr. Conradus Heresbachius,* translated "and increased" by Googe (London: Printed by R. Watkins, 1577; reprinted, 1578, 1586, 1596, 1600, 1614); revised by G. Markham as *The whole art of husbandry* (London: Printed by T. Cotes for R. More, 1631);

Christopher Balista, *The ouerthrow of the gout, written in Latin verse* (London: Printed by J. Allde for A. Veale, 1577);

Iñigo Lopez de Mendoza, *The prouerbes of . . . sir James Lopez de Mendoza with the paraphrase of P. Diaz* (London: Printed by R. Watkins, 1579);

Andrew Bertholdus, *The wonderfull and strange effect and vertues of a new terra sigillata found in Germanie* (London: Printed by R. Robinson for R. Watkins, 1587).

Barnabe Googe is important for his original poetry, for his translations, and for his position as a representative literary figure of his age. *Eclogues, Epitaphs, and Sonnets* (1563) is the first volume of English personal poetry published in the modern era by a gentleman poet during his lifetime, the eclogues (together with Alexander Barclay's) providing the earliest example of the form in English. The writings for which Googe was most highly praised in his own lifetime, however, and those which doubtless he most valued, were the translations he engaged in for the spiritual and material betterment of his less well educated compatriots. In everything he did he showed himself intensely aware of the duties and responsibilities of his privileged social status.

Googe's parents, Robert Goche (variously spelled Gouche, Gougge, and other ways) and Margaret Mantell, were married at Bekesbourne near Canterbury on 18 June 1539, and Barnabe was born 11 June 1540 – Saint Barnabas's Day – probably in Kent. His mother died 24 July 1540. He was educated at Cambridge, matriculating at Christ's College in May 1555, and then at the Inns of Court. His father owned extensive property in Nottinghamshire, in Lincolnshire, and in and around London, a goodly portion of which was left to Barnabe upon his father's death in 1557. Barnabe became a ward of the court, being allowed to purchase his wardship on favorable terms when his great kinsman Sir William Cecil (later Lord Burghley) became master of the wards in 1561. However, Barnabe did not gain full control of his inheritance until the death in 1587 of the wealthy widow his father had married in 1552, and he was often short of money to support his wife, Mary Darrell, and their nine children.

Barnabe Googe's coat of arms (from the 1565 edition of The Zodiac of Life)

In his will Barnabe's father enjoined that he "study and apply his learning in the law," and as a condition of inheritance "on my blessing that he never take penny or any manner of reward for his counsel, but to give the same to all men without taking any things." It seems to have been in this spirit of free counsel that Googe first undertook in 1558 or 1559 the translation of Marcellus Palingenius's *Zodiacus vitae,* after much encouragement from family and friends, publishing the first three books in 1560. In the dedication to his grandmother Lady Hales, at whose home in Canterbury he evidently spent many of his younger days, he announces his intention "to finish the rest, as shortly as I may. In which doing I trust I shall do no less profit to my country than service to God." The next installment of *The Zodiac of Life* appeared in 1561, the whole work in 1565, and a revised and annotated edition in 1576. All these editions were dedicated to Cecil, who remained a major influence on Googe's literary and political career.

This sprawling allegorical, philosophical, scientific, satiric epic poem by an early-sixteenth-century Italian doctor recommended itself to early Elizabethan reformers not least because it was placed on the index of prohibited books in 1558, and because its author's bones were exhumed and burned following a posthumous heresy trial. The descriptive title pages of the 1565 and 1576 editions give a good indication of what appealed to readers. The "most lively" depiction of such fascinating topics as the "wicked vices of our corrupt nature," the "perfect pathway unto eternal life," and "the mysteries of nature" promoted the Latin poem to the status of school text, perhaps helped by the popularity of Googe's fluent translation, which was highly praised by contemporaries. The commonplace that the pleasures of the soul transcend those of the body, and that the lower sensual experiences of taste and touch draw humanity close to bestial nature, finds vivid expression in the description of the lion and the horse in pursuit of food and sex ("meat . . . and gendering act"):

> When the lion fierce doth spy
> In fields by chance a cow, he leaps and lifts his mane
>   on high
> And twines and twirls his twisting tail, desirous of his
>   prey;
> Or when the foamy horse beholds the gadding mare
>   astray,
> With haughty head upheld he runs, and here and there
>   he kicks,
> And leapeth hedge and ditch abroad, while lusty guts
>   him pricks,
> And causes all the skies above with hinnying noise to
>   shriek.

The image of the world as a stage play or pageant in which individuals act successive parts culminates in the delineation of "wrinkled age":

> Body fades, the strength abates, the beauty of his face
> And color goes, his senses fail, his ears and eyes decay,
> His taste is gone, some sickness sore frequenteth him
>   alway;
> Scarce chaws his meat his toothless chaps, scarce walks
>   with staff in hand
> His crooked old unwieldy limbs, whereon he scarce
>   may stand.
> The mind likewise doth feel decay, now dotes he like a
>   child,
> And through his weak and aged years is wisdom quite ex-
>   iled.

Shakespeare's errant horse in *Venus and Adonis* (1593) and his brilliant conclusion to Jaques's "Ages of Man" speech in *As You Like It* (1599), "second childishness, and mere oblivion, / Sans teeth, sans eyes, sans taste, sans everything," are greater variations on the same themes. In these and in many other passages, it is not surprising that modern scholars have discerned the influence of Palingenius's poem, in both Latin and English dress, upon Shakespeare, Edmund Spenser, John Milton, and others.

Googe had much to occupy him besides translation in the early 1560s. In November 1561 he traveled across France to Madrid in the train of the new ambassador to Spain, returning to England by sea in June 1562. Upon his return he discovered that friends had taken steps to publish his poems, and rather than put the printer to unnecessary expense by stopping publication, he hastily completed the dream-vision allegory "Cupido Conquered," added material drawn from his recent experiences abroad to the eclogues and lyrics, and allowed his personal poems to be shared with the general public.

The eight eclogues present a warning against the grief and pain of being enslaved by sensual love and a promise of blessedness for those who "leave Cupido's camp" and "remove Dame Venus" from their eyes and instead "love and fear the mighty God that rules and reigns on high." The suicidal fates of Dametas and Claudia in the second and fifth eclogues (together with Dametas's minatory voice from the grave in the fourth) reinforce the message, as do the reasoned arguments for the conquest of love in the sixth and seventh. The third eclogue turns from the topic of love to that of the contrast between urban vice and pastoral contentment. This conventional theme is given life by Googe's indignation in his references to the Marian persecutions, an indignation spurred perhaps by the memory of his stepgrandfather, Sir James Hales, who had been hounded to madness and suicide in 1554.

The epitaphs and "sonnets" memorialize and praise contemporary English military leaders, reformers, and writers and provide a glimpse of mid-sixteenth-century society by recording exchanges with family and friends, as when he ruefully admits his own giddiness in "To George Holmedon of a running head" or berates his "cursèd hand" for not finding his own beloved's name in the game of drawing lots for valentines. Sometimes the poems offer variations on moral commonplaces, but Googe is also capable of wittily reversing conventional wisdom, as when he chooses money over friendship because "Fair face show friends, when riches do abound, / Come time of proof, farewell, they must away . . . / Gold never starts aside, but in distress / Finds ways enough to ease thine heaviness." The last and longest poem in the volume puts the medieval amatory genre of dream vision to the purposes of moral allegory, as Diana's champion Hippolytus, "the unspotted pearl of pure virginity," with his captains Continence, Abstinence, and Labor, conquers Cupid and his allies "drowsy Idleness" and "vile Excess, / A lubber great . . . / Much nosèd like a turkey cock, with teeth as black as jet, / A belly big, full trussed with guts, and pistols two, like posts."

Most of these poems had been written by the time Googe was twenty-one, and in many ways they smack of the schoolroom. The eclogues show the strong influence of Mantuan (Giovanni Battista Spagnolo) and of Ovid's *Remedy of Love,* the shorter poems are in the vein of *Tottel's Miscellany* (1557), and "Cupido Conquered" draws upon the much-admired Geoffrey Chaucer. But new influences from Spain, particularly in the translations from Jorge de Montemayor's best-selling pastoral romance *Diana* (circa 1559), point forward to Sir Philip Sidney and Spenser's fusing of native and Continental models to achieve writings that seductively please as well as worthily instruct.

Googe's apparent hostility to Cupid did not extend to "his own dear mistress," Mary Darrell; the stormy progress of their love in the summer of 1563 is the very stuff of romantic comedy. Darrell's parents, wishing her to marry a richer suitor, forced her to write Googe to abandon his suit "if ever any true love or goodwill you have borne toward me." Her kinsmen and her suitor complained of Googe's threats, "hot head," and "sick brain"; he complained of "the martial furniture that hath been prepared against me, and the Italian inventions that have been menaced against me." The happy outcome of their marriage on 5 February 1564 was achieved only by the intervention of Archbishop Matthew Parker of Canterbury and Cecil. Bad feelings did not persist: the young couple settled close to Mary's parents on the border of Sussex and Kent, Googe engaged in land transactions with her kinsmen, and in 1569 he dedicated a book of poetry to two of her sisters.

Googe's own experience did not, however, induce him to write of romantic passion or to moralize faithful loves. He first wrote "The Counterfeit Christian," on the contrast between the hypocrisy of modern Christians and the glorious virtue of "the

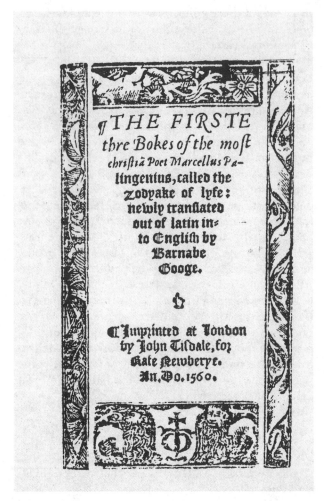

Title page for Googe's translation of the first three books of Palingenius's Zodiacus vitae

first and ancient professors of Christ." This manuscript having "by ill-favored misfortune perished," he offered two stories of the early church and *The Ship of Safeguard* (1569), which (despite his deprecatory references to its being "but rudely furnished, and God knows simply rigged . . . wanting both strength of timber and comeliness of proportion") is an entertaining satiric allegory of the voyage of life, often calling to mind Spenser's *The Faerie Queene* (1596), especially Acrasia's bower and the approach to it. Like Spenser, Googe venerated "Chaucer that gem of poetry," celebrating him in this poem by quoting the description of "Popeholy" from the Chaucerian translation (early 1360s) of *The Romance of the Rose.* In 1602 *The Ship of Safeguard* attracted the attention of Anthony Nixon, who brazenly presented it to Archbishop John Whitgift as his own work, though even his title, *The Christian Navy,* is drawn from Googe's description of "the Navy fair of Christianity" being wrecked on the "woeful rock" of Heresy. Apart from some omitted passages, Nixon's major change was to alter Googe's ottava rima to rhyme royal; although some telling phrases are lost, the ease with which he reduced the stanza length reveals the expansiveness of Googe's style.

One of Googe's earliest appearances in print was a poem condemning "that haughty whore / That boasts herself for God" (the Church of Rome), contributed to Thomas Gressop's translation of Cabasilas's *Brief Treatise . . . of the Pope's Usurped Primacy* (1560). In 1570, the year in which Queen Elizabeth was excommunicated and deposed by the pope, he dedicated to his "redoubted sovereign Lady" a translation of a "brief description of your grace's greatest adversary," Thomas Kirchmeyer's *The Popish Kingdom; or, Reign of Antichrist.* The mock-epic manner and sarcastic tone are as congenial to Googe as the matter: in a dedicatory epistle to Cecil (1565) he was already inveighing against "the corrupt and unchristian lives of the whole college of contemptuous cardinals, the ungracious overseeings of bloodthirsty bishops, the paunch-plying practices of pelting priors, the manifold madness of mischievous monks, with the filthy fraternity of flattering friars."

The fourth book of Googe's zestful translation of Kirchmeyer appeals to modern readers – in ways that probably neither author nor translator intended – in its detailed descriptions of folk customs and superstitions connected with religious feasts such as Christmas, New Year's, Candlemas, Whitsun, and saints' days. After a useful "Table of the principal matters contained in this book," Googe added his earlier translation of two books of Kirchmeyer's "Spiritual Husbandry," instructions in the right methods of cultivating the true faith. This most recent profession of his religious and political beliefs must have made him a congenial colleague to like-minded friends and acquaintances in the Parliament of April and May 1571, during which he was the member for Aldborough, Yorkshire. Googe was probably named to the riding by Cecil, with whom he seems to have been particularly closely associated during the 1570s and early 1580s. Cecil was created Lord Burghley in 1571; and when he feasted the queen at his new mansion, Theobalds, in 1572, he assigned Googe to be first server to Her Majesty at the first table.

It was on an assignment from Burghley that Googe paid his first visit to Ireland in 1574, and his letters, quoted extensively by William Pinkerton in "Barnaby Googe" (1863), provide images of Ireland even more graphic than his sketches, though his head of Turloch Luineach O'Neill is quaintly gripping. In his letter of 7 April 1574 Googe himself says of it: "I have therein disclosed the counterfeit of Terlough Lenogh rudely by me drawn, but assure your Lordship greatly resembling him." Googe was extremely sick with dysentery for his first two months in Ireland and was naturally appalled by the filthy conditions he found, but he was still contemptuous of the English missionary clergymen, "belly-fed ministers" who, "at the first touch of sickness and a miserable hard diet, ran home again, and left all more meet for the gallows than for the church." For the summer months Googe was in the front lines of the military and diplomatic maneuvers, comporting himself so as to win Walter Devereux, first Earl of Essex's "friendly report" for "his good desert" when he returned to England in July. Four years later, in his commendatory epistle to his friend Barnabe Riche's *Alarm to England,* he writes with feeling of the need to provide for good soldiers, "such virtuous minds as are contented with the expense of their blood to benefit their country."

Googe's recognition of the contrast between the miseries of war and the peacefulness of English country life is evident in his dedication of his next major work, *Four Books of Husbandry* (1577), to Sir William Fitzwilliam, lord deputy of Ireland from 1571 to 1575, whom Googe praises for his "charge given upon the O'Neill at Monham, in the rescue of your miserably distressed and slaughtered companions," seeing "the benefit of a quiet and contented life at home" as the "condign reward" for such service. The work itself is basically a translation of Conrad Heresbach's *Rei rusticae libri quattuor* (1570), although, as Googe says, "I have altered and increased his work with mine own readings and observations, joined with the experience of sundry my friends." The work is full of practical details on what to look for in buying a farm, what kind of soil is best for which crops, how to care for livestock, and even (against the advice of some of his friends) how to grow vines, since from his own experience Googe knows that good grapes can be produced in England and claims that the poor showing of English vineyards "is rather to be imputed to the malice and disdain peradventure of the Frenchmen that kept them, than to any ill disposition or fault of the soil." Copious annotations in surviving copies of the many editions indicate the practical usefulness of Googe's work, but farmers and estate managers were also presumably refreshed and elevated by the interspersed translations from Virgil's *Georgics* and other classical poetry.

At this period Googe was also occupied with revising his translation of Palingenius and with two new translations: a curious poem on the gout, dedicated to Dr. Richard Master, who was physician both to the queen and to Burghley; and the *Proverbs* of Iñigo Lopez de Mendoza, dedicated to Burghley. "The noble and worthy Spanish soldier" the marquis of Santillana had written his hundred rhyming proverbs of glorious doctrine and fruitful teaching for the heir apparent of Castile. Googe presents his translation of the brief verse proverbs, the prose commentary of Peter Diaz, and a life of the author as suitable "guides in good demeanor, to every man of what degree soever he be," who seeks to be trained "to honesty and virtuous life."

Despite his many activities shortage of money drove Googe to seek office in Ireland, and in December 1582 he was appointed provost marshal in the province of Connaught and Thomond, at which time he met Geoffrey Fenton (who gave him a horse) and probably also Spenser and Lodowick Bryskett. Separated from his wife and children, forced to hire servants likely to cut his throat, and engaged in uncongenial work, Googe was most unhappy. Affairs in England were also troublesome, taking him from his Irish duties from September 1583 to March 1584; even the death of his stepmother at this time did not relieve him from care, since he had to disengage himself from his Irish commitments. This was not achieved until April 1585, when the family was reunited on his patrimonial estate of Alvingham in Lincolnshire, where he died in February 1594. Apart from his letters the only literary product of these years is the 1587 translation of a pamphlet describing a wonder drug, again dedicated to Dr. Master, and to another of the queen's physicians, Dr. Bayley.

In his lifetime Googe was most frequently praised for his translation of Palingenius (often mentioned together with Arthur Golding's Ovid [1565–1567]) and for his agricultural handbook. But not only kinsfolk and friends enjoyed his original poetry for its "pleasant framèd style" and found it worthy to be mentioned with Chaucer's. Richard Stephens, who contributed commendatory verses in Greek and Latin to the 1565 edition of Palingenius, had never set eyes on Googe but had seen many times "your pretty epigrams, and these equal the skilled writings of old Chaucer," and the translation, "all of which things you yourself have written beautifully . . . things worthy of the sacred office of poets." Toward the end of the century, Gabriel Harvey, surveying the literary scene from Richard Grafton and John Heywood to Samuel Daniel and

Woodcut from Eclogues, Epitaphs, and Sonnets *(1563)*

Saint Robert Southwell, placed Googe among those in whom "many things are commendable, divers things notable, some things excellent."

Googe's translations continued to be read into the seventeenth century, but his *Eclogues, Epitaphs, and Sonnets* disappeared from view until rediscovered by eighteenth-century literary historians, who seemed more struck by the rarity of the volume than by its contents. In 1863 Pinkerton believed him best known for the curiosities of *The Popish*

Drawing (1575) by Googe of Turloch Luineach O'Neill, a contestant for the rule of Ulster, Ireland, in the late 1560s (Public Record Office; State Papers, Ireland, Elizabeth, S.P. 63/45, 60 [II])

Kingdom but thought it worth exploring "the life of an author of considerable note in his day, and whose name must ever find a place in the history of English literature." In 1871 Edward Arber placed him among "the early streamlets of a mighty river" of Elizabethan literature, one of "the heralds, the forerunners, the teachers of Spenser, Shakespeare, and Johnson, and their glorious phalanx of contemporary poets." Through the twentieth century his importance in the history of English pastoral poetry and the influence of his translation of Palingenius have frequently been recognized; and, since the appearance of Yvor Winters's "The 16th Century Lyric in England" (1939), Googe's achievement in the plain style of lyric has increasingly been praised. Mark Eccles confidently refers to him as the "first significant Elizabethan lyric poet."

Googe had no doubts about the function of poets: "I think verily, the almighty God hath ordained them in all ages to extol virtue, and rebuke vice." As kinsman and servant of Lord Burghley, he shared his great patron's ambitions for reform of religion, education, and government and used his talents in poetry and prose not to win fame and fortune for himself, but to serve God and his neighbor. The last words of the 1565 edition of Palingenius are "Non nobis Domine, sed nomini tuo" (Not for us O Lord, but for thy name); the second of the *Four Books of Husbandry* ends "Soli Deo laus et gloria, per Christum Jesum" (To God alone praise and glory, through Christ Jesus), which after the third book becomes "Soli Deo honor et gloria" and finally "Soli Deo." He was proud of his ancestry and his family relationships, as can be seen in the prominent display of coats of arms in his publications, but that pride was fully conscious of Christian humility and responsibility. His initials boldly flank the mailed fist grasping a dragon's head on his crest, but the motto gives all praise to God. Googe was, as Sir Nicholas Malby, governor and president of Connaught, called him, "an honest, learned, and virtuous gentleman."

References:

J. D. Alsop, "Barnabe Googe's Birthdate," *Notes & Queries,* new series 38 (1991): 24;

Marc Allan Beckwith, "A Study of Palingenius' *Zodiacus Vitae* and Its Influence on English Renaissance Literature," Ph.D. dissertation, Ohio State University, 1983;

Mark Eccles, "Barnabe Googe in England, Spain, and Ireland," *English Literary Renaissance,* 15 (Autumn 1985): 353–370;

Gabriel Harvey, *The Works of Gabriel Harvey,* 3 volumes, edited by Alexander B. Grosart (London: Privately printed, 1884–1885; reprinted, New York: AMS, 1966);

Elizabeth and Michael Klaassen, "Latin Poems in Praise of Googe's Palingenius" (1991);

Brooke Peirce, "Barnabe Googe: Poet and Translator," Ph.D. dissertation, Harvard University, 1954;

Douglas L. Peterson, *The English Lyric from Wyatt to Donne: A History of the Plain and Eloquent Styles* (Princeton: Princeton University Press, 1967);

William Pinkerton, "Barnaby Googe," *Notes & Queries,* third series 3 (1863): 141–143, 181–184, 241–243, 301–302, 361–362;

William E. Sheidley, *Barnabe Googe* (Boston: Twayne, 1981);

Yvor Winters, "The 16th Century Lyric in England: A Critical and Historical Reinterpretation" [1939], in *Elizabethan Poetry: Modern Essays in Criticism,* edited by Paul J. Alpers (New York: Oxford University Press, 1967), pp. 93–125.

Lady Jane Grey

(October 1537 – February 1554)

Carole Levin
State University of New York College at New Paltz

BOOKS: *An epistle of the ladye Jane to a learned man of late Falne from the truth of Gods word. Whereunto is added the communication that she had with master Feckenham. Also another epistle to her sister, with the words she spake vpon the scaffold* (London?: Printed by J. Day?, 1554?);

The life, death and actions of the lady Jane Gray. Containing foure discourses written with her owne hands (London: Printed by G. Eld for John Wright, 1615; republished, 1629, 1636).

Editions and Collections: Thomas Bentley, *The monument of matrones: conteining seuen seuerall lamps of virginitie, or distinct treatises* (London: Printed by H. Denham, 1582), pp. 98–102;

Sir Nicholas Harris Nicolas, *Memoirs and Literary Remains of Lady Jane Grey* (London: Henry Colburn & Richard Bentley, 1832);

John Foxe, *Acts and Monuments,* volume 4, edited by the Reverend Stephen Reed Cattley (London: R. B. Seeley & W. Burnside, 1837–1841), pp. 415–425.

Even though she died at the age of only sixteen and left behind a relatively small body of work — some carefully crafted letters, a prayer, a theological debate, and a dying speech — Lady Jane Grey is one of the best-known women of sixteenth-century England. Sometimes called the "nine days' queen," she is best known for her political position in the dynastic struggle of 1553 and for her steadfast Protestantism. But she is also known today — and was known in her own century — for her writings that expressed that vehement faith. Grey accomplished most of these writings in the last six months of her life, while a prisoner in the Tower of London for her unwilling part in the attempted coup of John Dudley, Duke of Northumberland, to replace Mary Tudor on the throne with Grey herself. In February 1554 Grey was executed. Her writings demonstrate her concern with what constituted an appropriate religious life and how one could battle despair and prepare for a tranquil death.

Jane, born in October 1537, was the daughter of Henry Grey and Frances Grey, whose mother was Henry VIII's younger sister, Mary. Jane was a cousin of the Tudor monarchs Edward VI, Mary I, and Elizabeth I, and her close position to the throne led to her political importance — especially given the insecure succession, since Henry had only one son. Before his death in 1547 Henry VIII made a will, sanctioned by Parliament, ignoring the Stuart line of his older sister, Margaret, and placing the Grey line in the succession if none of his children had heirs.

Grey was known as one of the best-educated women of her day and the hope of many reformers. She corresponded with some of them, such as Heinrich Bullinger. Her education stood out as an especially remarkable one, even in an age when humanists argued for highly educated upper-class women. Because of Grey's potential to become queen, her parents, Henry and Frances Grey, duke and duchess of Suffolk, assured her the finest education possible, as fine as one an aristocratic male of the time would have received. By the time she was seven, Jane's tutor Master Harding had begun instructing her in Greek and Latin as well as at least a smattering of Spanish, Italian, and French. She was also well trained in biblical study and given a theological background suitable for a grandniece of Henry VIII born after the break with Rome. As an aristocrat, she was also trained in music and dancing.

Her education was augmented by her stay, beginning in 1547, in the household of the dowager queen Catherine Parr, who after only a few months of widowhood married Thomas Seymour, lord admiral and uncle to Edward VI. Seymour, who would be executed for treason in 1549, promised Grey's parents that he would negotiate a marriage between the boy king and his cousin Jane, but he was unsuccessful. While such a prospect excited Henry and Frances Grey, for Jane herself the significance of the time she spent in the Seymour household was the dowager queen's influence on her reli-

Lady Jane Grey (from Henry Holland, Herwologia Anglica, *1620)*

gious development. Catherine, a humanist with strong sympathy for Reformers, believed reading the Scriptures was central to Christian devotion. While she did not exclude good works that grew out of faith, Catherine did emphasize the importance of justification by faith in her own writings. In her prayers and letters Grey would later advocate these same doctrines, central to Protestant belief. She was a member of the household until Catherine's death due to complications from childbirth in August 1548. At the funeral Grey, not quite eleven, was the chief mourner.

Grey's education, particularly its religious emphasis, was clearly important to her and shaped how she regarded herself and what she wrote. This is especially apparent in her interchange with Roger Ascham late in Edward VI's reign – one of the most famous descriptions of Grey, published in Ascham's *The Schoolmaster* (1570). He had stopped at the Grey home of Bradgate before leaving for the Continent. The rest of the household was out

hunting deer, but Ascham was told Jane was home: "I found her in her chamber reading Phaedon Platonis in Greek." He asked her why she was not out enjoying herself with the others. She told him that they, "good folk, they never felt what true pleasure meant." Ascham asked Grey how she learned the nature of this pleasure. In her much-quoted response she did nothing to spare her parents:

> One of the greatest benefits that ever God gave me is that he sent me so sharp and severe parents and so gentle a schoolmaster. For when I am in presence either of father or mother, whether I speak, keep silence, sit, stand, or go, eat, drink, be merry or sad, be sewing, playing, dancing, or doing anything else, I must do it . . . even so perfectly as God made the world, or else I am so sharply taunted, so cruelly threatened . . . that I think myself in hell till time come that I must go to Master Aylmer, who teacheth me so gently, so pleasantly, with such fair allurements to learning, that I think all the time nothing while I am with him. And when I am called from him, I fall on weeping because whatsoever I do else

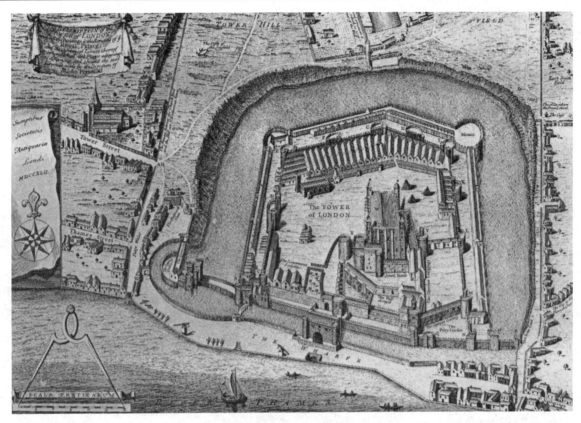

The Tower of London as seen in a 1597 survey by Hayward and Gascoyne. Grey spent the last six months of her life there.

but learning is full of grief, trouble, fear, and wholly misliking unto me.

Ascham does not analyze why Grey's parents treated her so harshly or why she was so free with the information. Yet her criticism of her parents did not cause him to think any less of her, "that noble and worthy lady." He wrote *The Schoolmaster* with a clearly didactic purpose and some years later, which might cause one to wonder how accurate a portrait it really is of the fourteen-year-old Grey. Ascham's earlier accounts, however, are consistent with his later judgment. In 1550 he recounted finding Grey reading Plato, adding that she was "so thoroughly understanding it that she caused me the greatest astonishment."

In the spring of 1553, as Edward VI was dying, neither Grey's education nor her piety made her important to John Dudley, Duke of Northumberland, the real ruler of England since the fall of Edward Seymour, Duke of Somerset, two years earlier. Northumberland arranged with the Greys for Jane and his youngest son, Guilford, to marry. Edward VI, whether it was first suggested by Northumberland or not, made a will excluding both his sisters in favor of Grey. But this attempt to overturn the succession failed; throughout the country that July, as soon as news of Edward's death was out, people proclaimed Mary queen. Northumberland had no following. Grey was already in the Tower awaiting her coronation; instead she stayed there as a prisoner. In February 1554, as part of the reprisals after Thomas Wyatt's revolt against Mary's proposed Spanish marriage, Mary ordered Grey's execution. Most of Grey's writings were produced during these last months of her life. These include a letter to a friend newly fallen from the faith (probably her first tutor, Harding); a prayer written within a few weeks of her death; letters to her father, Henry, also to be executed, and to her sister, Katherine, which Jane composed the night before she died; and the speech she gave from the scaffold. A few days before her execution Grey debated theology with Dr. John Feckenham, Mary's confessor, within the confines of the Tower in the presence of Tower officials. This debate was recorded and is included in collections of her works.

The most influential book of the sixteenth century to discuss the significance of Grey's life and to present her own writings is John Foxe's *Acts and Monuments* (1563). Foxe emphasizes her education and steadfast religion and praises her as being "in learning and knowledge of the tongues" superior to

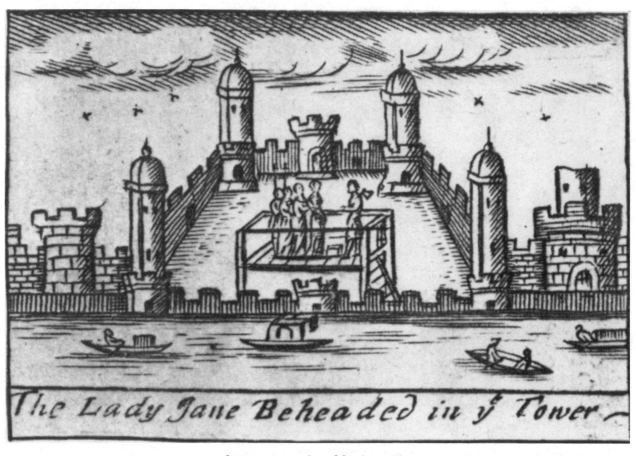

The Lady Jane Beheaded in ÿ Tower.

Contemporary woodcut of Grey's execution

her cousin Edward. He is also significant in popularizing her own work, which he included in his discussion of her history and martyrdom. Some of her writings had been published by Protestants abroad in 1554, soon after her death. Foxe, however, gave them a wider audience. His second edition (1570) identifies the recipient of her letter to one newly fallen from the faith as her first tutor, Master Harding, an identification for the most part accepted. Foxe applauds her "sharp and vehement" letter since it came from "an earnest and zealous heart." In her letter Grey does not spare Harding; for betraying the true faith, she calls him "the deformed imp of the devil . . . the unshamefaced paramour of Antichrist" and declares he was now "in the stinking and filthy kennel of Satan." For acting thus, he must be a "wretched and unhappy man." This was not simply a rhetorical strategy; she strongly believed in what she said. She also had nothing but contempt for Northumberland when she heard that he had recanted and accepted the Catholic faith: "As his life was wicked and full of dissimulation, so was his end thereafter. I pray God, I, nor no friend of mine, die so."

Foxe gives a full transcript of the religious debate between Grey and Feckenham, whom Queen Mary had sent to attempt to convert Jane before her death. In the public debate with Feckenham, Grey was assured in her belief and expressed a clearly Protestant theology, emphasizing the importance of faith rather than works, and the Mass taken in commemoration: "I affirm that faith only saveth: but it is meet for a Christian, in token that he followeth his master Christ, to do good works; yet may we not say that they profit to our salvation." Grey describes the Sacrament of the Lord's Supper as "but bread and wine which . . . put me in remembrance how that for my sins the body of Christ was broken, and his blood shed on the cross." She is clear that her faith came not from the church; instead, "I ground my faith upon God's word."

This assurance wavers in the last prayer she wrote, though she must have recognized that she was crafting it for public consumption as well as her own use; yet the sixteen-year-old woman, about to die and dealing with that fear, also is evident behind the carefully shaped language. Grey's greatest fear was the sin of despair, from which she was, she begged God, "craving thy mercy and help." She needed to feel God's presence: "How long wilt thou be absent? for ever? . . . Shall I despair of thy mercy, O God?" Grey begged that God "arm me . . . that I may stand fast."

It appears that her prayer was answered. The night before her death she demonstrated an appreciation of her situation without despair or self-pity in the letters she wrote to her father and sister. While these are personal, like her prayer and her scaffold speech, they also are carefully shaped public assertions of faith, to be read as autobiographical statements. She would have known that her statements would have a potentially large public distribution, and she would have shaped them accordingly.

Grey's letter to her father expresses her understanding that his direct actions were leading to her own death. Yet she also expresses compassion toward him, having heard he was not only "bewailing" his "own woe" but "especially, as I hear, my unfortunate state." He need not, she claims, since "I may account myself blessed." For her, "nothing . . . can be more welcome than . . . to aspire to that heavenly throne." While she did not want to excuse her father or mitigate his culpability, she did want both of them to go to their deaths comforted.

The same resignation, even joy, at meeting her death is present in the letter Grey wrote her sister, Katherine. Although it contains advice, the letter is also a statement about her own life and self-knowledge. It is written in the back of the New Testament, a book, she assures Katherine, that "shall teach you to live, and learn you to die." The night before her execution at the age of sixteen, Grey was all too aware that being young did not secure one's life: "And trust not that the tenderness of your age shall lengthen your life, for as soon (if God call) goeth the young as the old." Katherine also would face an early death, at the age of twenty-eight, after years of imprisonment for her imprudent marriage to Edward Seymour, Earl of Hertford.

Foxe describes Grey's behavior on the scaffold; he was especially impressed by her serene courage. Grey believed herself guiltless of the treason for which she had been condemned: "The fact against the queen's highness was unlawful, and the consenting thereunto by me: but touching the procurement and desire thereof by me . . . I do wash my hands thereof in innocency before God." But she perceived of herself as a sinner: "This plague and punishment is happily and worthily happened unto me for my sins." Yet her God "of his goodness . . . hath thus given me a time and respite to repent." Her Protestant theology did not waver, and she wanted this publicly known in the last moments of her life. Believing prayers for the dead to be blasphemy, she concludes by asking those witnessing her execution, "While I am alive, I pray you assist me with your prayers."

In the decades following her death, Grey was known as one of the most steadfast Protestant women of her time, a quality demonstrated in her writing and one that Foxe's *Acts and Monuments* presented widely. At the end of the sixteenth century and into the next, this interest in Grey began to shift. The innocent martyr replaced the stalwart Protestant, and seventeenth-century church historians, such as Peter Heylin and Bishop Gilbert Burnet, offered a much meeker, milder, and more romantic Lady Jane Grey to their reading public. But her own words speak for Jane Grey, now as then, depicting a strong-minded and courageous Protestant woman.

Biographies:
Richard Davey, *The Nine Days' Queen, Lady Jane Grey, and Her Times* (London: Methuen, 1901);
Hester Chapman, *Lady Jane Grey* (London: Cape, 1962);
David Mathew, *Lady Jane Grey: The Setting of the Reign* (London: Methuen, 1972);
Mary Luke, *The Nine Days' Queen: A Portrait of Lady Jane Grey* (New York: Morrow, 1986);
Alison Plowden, *Lady Jane Grey and the House of Suffolk* (New York: Watts, 1986).

References:
Roger Ascham, *The Schoolmaster,* edited by Lawrence V. Ryan (Ithaca, N.Y.: Cornell University Press, 1967);
Ascham, *The Whole Works,* 2 volumes, edited by J. A. Giles (New York: AMS, 1965);
Gilbert Burnet, *History of the Reformation of the Church of England,* 4 volumes, edited by the Reverend E. Nares (London: J. F. Dove, 1830);
Peter Heylin, *Ecclesia Restaurata; or, The History of the Reformation of the Church of England,* edited by James Craigie Robertson (Cambridge: Cambridge University Press, 1849);
Carole Levin, "Lady Jane Grey: Protestant Queen and Martyr," in *Silent but for the Word: Tudor Women as Patrons, Translators, and Writers of Religious Works,* edited by Margret P. Hannay (Kent, Ohio: Kent State University Press, 1985), pp. 92–106;
John Gough Nichols, ed., *The Chronicle of Queen Jane by a Resident in the Tower of London* (New York: AMS, 1968).

Edmund Grindal

(1519 or 1520 – 6 July 1583)

Robert Lane
North Carolina State University

BOOKS: *A Profitable and Necessary Doctrine with Certain Homilies Adjoined Thereunto* (London: John Cawood, 1555);

Sermon at the Funeral Solemnity of the Most High and Mighty Prince Ferdinandus, the Late Emperor of Most Famous Memory, Holden in the Cathedral Church of St. Paul in London, the Third of October, 1564 (London: Printed by John Day, 1564).

Edition: *The Remains of Edmund Grindal,* edited by the Reverend William Nicholson (Cambridge: Cambridge University Press, 1843).

Edmund Grindal (portrait by an unknown artist; from Patrick Collinson, Archbishop Grindal, 1519–1583: The Struggle for a Reformed Church, *1979)*

Archbishop Edmund Grindal is remembered for his refusal to obey Queen Elizabeth I's orders to limit the number of preachers in the English church and to suppress the preaching conferences called "prophesyings." The themes that mark his disobedience are foreshadowed, however, in the style and substance of those few of his earlier works that survive. A pervasive Scripturalism, a tendency to antithesis, and the moral intensity of life lived in the face of death are vital ingredients of Grindal's challenge, but they also point to broader impulses integral to progressive, reform-oriented Protestantism in sixteenth-century England. Grindal's career itself encapsulates the fluctuating prospects of this branch of Protestantism during his life.

Born in 1519 or 1520 of a poor tenant farmer in provincial Saint Bees, Cumberland, Grindal distinguished himself through his academic pursuits. He was conferred a B.A. by Pembroke Hall, Cambridge, in 1538, an M.A in 1540, and a B.D. in 1549, the same year he became vice-master of the college. His theological erudition and rhetorical skills were further evidenced by his appointment in 1550 as Lady Margaret preacher and by his selection that same year to present the Protestant side in a Cambridge disputation on the question of transubstantiation. His advance in official circles was further demonstrated by his appointment as chaplain to the bishop of London, Nicholas Ridley, and

as royal chaplain, both in 1551, and as prebendary of Westminster in 1552.

On the death of Edward VI, Grindal went into exile at Strasbourg, where his contacts with influential Continental Protestants, first initiated at Cambridge, deepened. While in Germany he collaborated with John Foxe in preparing the "Book of Martyrs," a work that included his statement of the Protestant position on Communion, "A fruitful dialogue between Custom and Verity Declaring These Words of Christ: 'This is my Body.' "

This work demonstrates not only Grindal's erudite facility in theological interpretation and argu-

Grindal's birthplace, Cross Hill, in Saint Bees, Cumberland

ment but also his deep commitment to Scriptural authority, even as he expounds the symbolic, as opposed to the literal, meaning of the words of Jesus instituting Communion. The dialogic structure further reveals a polemical bent in presenting as irreconcilable the Protestant and Catholic understandings of the Lord's Supper: "Christ's body is food, not for the body but for the soul, and [should be received] with the instrument of faith appointed thereunto, not with . . . teeth or mouth."

On his return to England, Grindal accepted appointment as bishop of London (1559), his doubts about the Crown's economic exactions against church lands overcome by the need he felt to prevent control of the church lands overcome by the need he felt to prevent control of the church falling to "semi-papists." While bishop he showed his rhetorical skill in his sermon at the memorial service for Emperor Ferdinand I, published in 1564. Capitalizing on the occasion, Grindal organized his oration around the exhortation to his audience "to prepare to die," admonishing them that "the true preparation to die well is to live well." Foreshadow-

ing a theme that would resurface in his challenge to the queen, he subordinated the emperor's authority to that of God, declaring that "though he were the greatest and honorablest of all earthly kings, [Ferdinand] hath as a subject obeyed the irrevocable statute of the heavenly emperor." After an ongoing struggle with nonconformist clergy over vestments, and the effort to repair Saint Paul's after a 1561 fire, Grindal was appointed archbishop of York (1570), where he undertook to remove the significant vestiges of Catholicism, primarily by upgrading the clergy. In 1576 he was promoted to archbishop of Canterbury.

Before his challenge to the Crown, all the signs indicated that Grindal was a team player and resolute in opposing nonconformity. He was selected to preach at Saint Paul's when the new Prayer Book was introduced in 1559 and repeatedly offered to include in his sermons matters the government wanted covered. In 1570 he urged the Privy Council to silence Thomas Cartwright and his adherents in schools and pulpits, and he actively enforced the regime's command mandating clerical

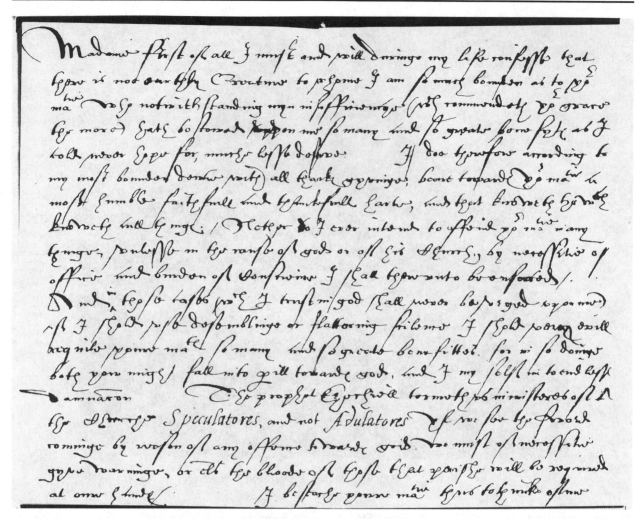

Page from a scribal copy of "Book to the Queen," the letter to Elizabeth I in which Grindal refuses to obey her orders concerning the Church of England (British Library)

vestments. But it was his commitment to the supremacy of the Word of God as essential spiritual nourishment for the people that was at the heart of his disobedience of Elizabeth. Thinly disguised as the shepherd "Algrind," Grindal is celebrated for just this trait – his pastoral concern for the people – in Edmund Spenser's *Shepheardes Calender* (1579). Though "great in [de]gree" himself, this figure extols the model "first shepherd," "Humble, and like in eche degree, / The flocke, which he did keepe."

Grindal's letter setting out the grounds for his disobedience, known to his contemporaries as his "book to the queen," was dated 8 December 1576 but probably not delivered to her until 20 December. In it Grindal opposed the queen's order to ration preachers to "three or four . . . a shire," citing the "plain" Scriptural injunction "that the gospel of Christ should be plentifully preached." Not only was preaching the primary "mean and instrument

of the salvation of mankind" – "the food of the soul" – it also "planted [due obedience] in the hearts of subjects. . . . Where preaching wanteth, obedience faileth." He considered preaching superior to reading the *Homilies* (1547, 1563), preferred by the queen, because it could speak more directly to a specific audience and its situation. He pointedly reminded her that the *Homilies* were only a stopgap, necessitated by the diversion of the church's wealth to the Crown's lay clients, itself the subject of persistent complaints by Grindal and other church reformers.

In defense of the prophesyings, Grindal cited "the great and ancient authority" warranting them, especially that of "the primitive church," and the salutary effects they engendered in the education of the clergy and the more "edifying of the unlearned" lay audience. It was precisely this audience, however, that prompted Elizabeth's denunciation of these exercises: they "aired disputations, and new devised opinions, upon points of divinity, far and unmeet of unlearned people." They squarely contradicted her policy of unity through religious uniformity because they "schismatically divided [the people] into a variety of dangerous opinions . . . and manifestly thereby encouraged [them] to the violation of our laws, and to the breach of the common order." She viewed the diversity of interpretations offered to the common people at the prophesyings as inherently subversive, implying as it did a role for their judgment on important religious questions. But Grindal endorsed the variety of perspectives the exercises presented, citing the same among "the ancient fathers" as "all to the good of the church." Because of "the benefit that groweth . . . to the hearers," he flatly rejected a compromise offered by William Cecil that the conferences continue without the common people.

Seeing his role in terms of Ezekiel's prescription for ministers as "*speculatores* [watchmen] . . . not *adulatores* [flatterers]," he lectured the queen on her attitude, comparing her to the pope:

> When you deal in matters of faith and religion, or matters that touch the church of Christ . . . [I petition that] you would not use to pronounce so resolutely and peremptorily . . . as ye may do in civil and extern matters; but always remember, that in God's causes the will of God, and not the will of any earthly creature, is to take place. It is the antichristian voice of the pope, *Sic volo; stet pro ratione voluntas* [So I will have it; so I command: let my will stand for a reason].

In his conclusion, adopting the role of pastoral counselor to the queen, Grindal reiterates the theme of his funeral sermon for Ferdinand, quoting Saint Ambrose's words to Emperor Theodosius to suggest that in this matter her immortal soul was in peril:

> Look not only . . . upon the purple and princely array, wherewith ye are apparelled; but consider withal, what is that that is covered therewith. Is it not flesh and blood? Is it not dust and ashes? Is it not a corruptible body, which must return to his earth again, God knoweth how soon?

Grindal's letter stylistically enacts what it preaches in ways that reveal the fault lines of conflict between reformist Protestantism and the Crown. Most obvious are the references to the Bible and church fathers that permeate the letter. His reliance on this tradition is unrelenting, its sanction taken as compelling. More striking is the way in which Grindal increasingly weaves this authority into his own language, gradually merging his own voice with those of the religious tradition. Declaring "I say with Ambrose," he incorporates the language of this eloquent spokesperson for the church's autonomy from the state to such an extent that Grindal's biographer Patrick Collinson concludes, "Grindal *was* Ambrose, and Elizabeth Theodosius." Not merely a rhetorical device for dramatizing the contemporary bearing of "ancient authority," this merger measures the extent to which reformist Protestants saw themselves as reenacting the tradition they espoused, the degree to which personal identity was shaped and individual action motivated by that tradition. Grindal's claim of individual conscience was imbued with a religious heritage whose authority was so formidable it could warrant disobedience of a direct royal command.

The sense of his individual soul imperiled ("Bear with me . . . Madam, if I choose rather to offend your earthly majesty, than to offend the heavenly majesty of God") is reinforced throughout the letter by the stylistic device of juxtaposing antithetical elements, often in the form of "not . . . but," as in "*in causa fidei . . . episcopos solere de imperatoribus Christianis, non imperatores de episcopis judicare* [in the cause of faith . . . bishops were wont to judge concerning Christian emperors, not emperors of bishops]." The repeated eliciting of oppositions evokes the image of warfare so common to church reformers, combat that poses the need to choose between two mutually exclusive conditions, one ordained by the tradition, the other precluded by it. The construction echoes Grindal's "fruitful dialogue" over the interpretation of the Lord's Supper, with the striking difference that the same chasm he earlier saw as separating God's word and Catholicism is here applied to the policies of the Crown. Conspicuous by its absence is the mediation of *adiaphora*, things indifferent and thus within the royal prerogative. Grindal had earlier relied on this principle in prosecuting nonconformists for their refusal to wear the prescribed vestments, declaring that where "God neither commandeth nor forbiddeth . . . princes have authority to order or to command . . . [such things] may be used for order and obedience' sake."

The challenge Grindal articulated made plain that for reformist Protestants the authority of the religious tradition superseded that of the monarchy itself, providing an independent and compelling basis from which to critique, and to resist, royal commands. He courageously owned up to the implications of his disobedience of the queen, articulating a groundbreaking conception of the church's

Letter (15 October 1563) from Grindal to William Cecil, secretary to Elizabeth I, in which Grindal suggests a cure for Cecil's persistent backache (British Library, MS. Lansd. 6, no. 77, fol. I)

autonomy from civil power. Invoking the model of Ambrose, who had rigorously defended the church's prerogative in ecclesiastical affairs, he declared simply that these matters "are things to be judged . . . *in ecclesia* . . . *non in palatio* [in the church . . . not in the palace]." The primacy thus accorded the religious institution over the political regime in matters of faith entailed nothing less than the repudiation of the Crown's religious supremacy, the very basis of the Elizabethan settlement. At the same time, Grindal demonstrated how that religious tradition could provide the foundation for an inviolable religious conscience, free of political intrusion – later to become a bulwark of liberty, both religious *and* political.

The queen could not tolerate such a challenge from the officer she regarded as ultimately responsible for the execution of her policies in the church. In May 1577 she bypassed the archbishop altogether, declaring directly to the bishops that the prophesyings were illegal and ordering them suppressed, while Grindal was ordered sequestered in the archbishop's residence. In the ensuing struggle at court over his fate, the Crown's policies toward various religious groups, from Puritans to Catholics, played the most important role. In late 1577 Grindal made the first of many appeals to be reconciled with the queen, but no ground for compromise could be found. The sensitive character of the matter was underscored by popular interest, one councillor describing the people as "addicted" to it. A stalemate persisted for some years until failing health and despair over the possibility of reinstatement led Grindal to contemplate resignation, but he died on 6 July 1583.

Because Grindal's career serves as a kind of "ideological index" (as Collinson states) of the role of religion in the English state and society, it is not surprising that scholarly opinion of him is diverse. Though some earlier scholars deprecated him, according to Collinson, as "possessing a natural incapacity for government," a man "infirm of purpose," even a "false son of the church . . . a perfidious prelate," he has had supporters dating from his contemporaries to the present. In addition to Spenser's af-

firmation, John Milton called him "the best" of the Elizabethan bishops, and William Prynne regarded him as "a grave and pious man." The most recent scholarship by Collinson gives a much fuller, but still positive, view. He acknowledges that "Grindal's immediate failure was nearly total" but maintains that he "was important as a symbol of all that was best and of so much that might have been in the episcopal leadership of the English Church and Reformation."

Biographies:

John Strype, *The Life and Acts of the Most Reverend Father in God, Edmund Grindal* (Oxford: Oxford University Press, 1821);

Patrick Collinson, *Archbishop Grindal, 1519-1583: The Struggle for a Reformed Church* (London: Cape, 1979).

References:

Patrick Collinson, "The Downfall of Archbishop Grindal and Its Place in Elizabethan Political and Ecclesiastical History," in *Godly People: Essays in English Protestantism and Puritanism* (London: Hambledon, 1983), pp. 371-397;

S. E. Lehmberg, "Archbishop Grindal and the Prophesyings," *Historical Magazine of the Episcopal Church*, 34 (1965): 87-145;

Edmund Spenser, *Poetical Works*, edited by J. C. Smith and Ernest de Selincourt (Oxford: Clarendon, 1912; London: Oxford University Press, 1969).

Papers:

Grindal's letter to Elizabeth I and other manuscripts are located in the British Library (primarily in the Harleian and Landsdowne Manuscripts), the Bodleian Library, and the Lambeth Palace Library. There are also letters from him in the Public Records Office. Records from his tenure as bishop of London are in the Guildhall Library, London, and records from his archepiscopacy in York are in the Borthwick Institute of Historical Research at the University of York. There are many annotations in his hand in the volumes of the library that he bequeathed to Queen's College, Oxford.

Edward Hall

(1497 – April 1547)

D. R. Woolf
Dalhousie University

BOOK: *The Vnion of the Two noble and illustrate fame-lies of Lancastre & Yorke* (London: Richard Grafton, 1548); second edition, with tables (London: Richard Grafton, 1550).

Editions: *Hall's Chronicle,* edited by Henry Ellis (London: J. Johnson, 1809; reprinted, New York: AMS, 1965; reprinted, Menston, Yorks.: Scolar Press, 1970).

Edward Hall was one of the leading historical writers of the early sixteenth century, a chronicler whose work has remained of great importance both as an eyewitness source for the events of Henry VIII's reign and as an early example of the development in the sixteenth century of an English vernacular tradition of historical writing. This tradition drew on its medieval chronicle antecedents but was also strongly influenced by humanist notions of the civic usefulness of history, of the historian's duty to criticize and evaluate his materials, and of the need to write about the past in a style that was plain and clear but also entertaining and persuasive. While retaining the annalistic framework of a medieval chronicle, Hall nevertheless provided an important bridge between the urban chronicles of his fifteenth-century predecessors and the humanist political histories of the late sixteenth and early seventeenth centuries.

Hall (or Halle, as his name would be spelled in his will) was born in the parish of Saint Mildred, Poultry, London, the son of John and Katherine Hall. His ancestors originated in Northall, Shropshire. John Hall had for some time been a successful grocer who had served as warden of his company from 1512 to 1513. Among the elder Hall's apprentices was a son of the late-fifteenth-century London chronicler Robert Fabyan, and this connection may have helped to turn the young Edward's mind to historical writing. Edward was schooled at Eton and then at King's College, Cambridge (1514–1518), where he became junior fellow in 1517–1518 and received his B.A. the following year. The tale related by the seventeenth-century biographer Anthony à Wood – that Hall was among several young scholars who migrated to Oxford to hear lectures founded by Thomas Wolsey in 1518 – is without solid evidentiary foundation.

On leaving Cambridge, Hall returned to London and was admitted as a student at Gray's Inn. It may be that he started taking notes on events at this time, since his chronicle is fullest from about 1520 to 1540. He may have been a member of Parliament, perhaps for a Shropshire borough, in 1523, though this cannot be documented. He was, however, certainly a member for the borough of Much Wenlock in the Reformation Parliament of 1529 (perhaps being among those reelected at the king's request in 1536), and he sat for an unknown constituency, perhaps Wenlock once again, in 1539. In the last two Parliaments of Henry VIII's reign, held in 1542 and 1545, Hall was member for the Shropshire borough of Bridgnorth. His sitting for Shropshire ridings demonstrates both his debt to the court (the Council of the Marches in Wales was active in Bridgnorth) and his family's continued connection with the county; there were various relatives of the Halls in the parish of Kinnersley (in which Northall was located). Shropshire was also, significantly for Hall, the home of the Grafton family, and it was one of their number, Richard, who would become Hall's friend and literary executor, ultimately bringing his chronicle to the press after Hall's death in 1547.

As a young lawyer in London, Hall was expected to fulfill certain obligations within his society and within the city. The former he fulfilled by serving as autumn reader in 1533 and Lent reader in 1540. London he would serve first in the capacity of common serjeant from 17 March 1533 to 2 June 1535, at which date he was appointed the city's undersheriff at the king's request, a position he retained until his death. In these capacities and as an M.P. he also provided service to the Crown, supporting government bills and generally siding with royal authority.

Hall had absorbed something of the anticlericalism that was common in early Tudor England, whether from his London upbringing or his education at Cambridge. His hostility toward overmighty prelates such as the "crafty" Cardinal Lorenzo Campeggio, the "archtraitor" Reginald Pole, and especially the king's minister Wolsey is evident in the chronicle, for instance in his account of Wolsey's career: "a good philosopher, very eloquent and full of wit, but for pride, covetous, and ambition, he excelled all others." This anticlericalism, which applied particularly to adherents of the old religion, also emerges from his careful but sympathetic comments on Thomas Cromwell's fall and execution late in the chronicle. Much of Hall's dislike of Wolsey may have derived from the cardinal's frequent financial exactions on the city. The same venom does not attach to reformed bishops such as Archbishop Thomas Cranmer and other "learned men" who helped bring about the Henrician reformation. Hall admired Cromwell, and it may have been through the latter's patronage that he acquired offices such as that of undersheriff.

In 1539, having adhered to the Reformation since its inception, Hall was placed in the uncomfortable position of speaking in the Commons in favor of the bill that became the so-called Act of Six Articles, which dramatically increased the persecution of "heretics" and those of more advanced Protestant opinions. It is clear from Hall's speech that he unhesitatingly supported the theocratic kingship of Henry VIII and conceded the king's ultimate control over both doctrine and practice: in discussing such matters as auricular confession, made mandatory by the act, he stressed the evidence that chronicles provided of monarchs' traditional power to command obedience in such matters. This speech has been labeled "Hobbesian"; but if it is an anticipation of anything, it is of the Erastian doctrine of the autonomy of the laity and its freedom to legislate on confessional issues.

As a loyal spokesman and servant of the Crown, Hall was a natural candidate for the commission established in 1541 to enforce the Six Articles in London and to take oaths from the mayor and city officials. Although he was named both to this commission and a subsequent, Edwardian one, it is nevertheless clear that his obedience to the Crown was creating conflict with his doctrinal beliefs. His ambivalence arose less from the law itself than in the manner in which it was being enforced: he comments in the chronicle that it had brought "many an honest and simple person to their deaths" because of its reliance on the simple testimony of

Woodcut from Edward Hall's Union of the Two Noble and Illustrate Families of Lancaster and York

two witnesses who, he says, were often put up to testifying against innocent men and women by the clergy. He particularly blames the conservative bishop of Winchester, Stephen Gardiner, for trumping up the charges of heresy that would bring the reformers Robert Barnes, Thomas Gerard (or Garrard), and William Jerome to the stake at Smithfield in 1540.

While it is virtually certain that Hall was collecting material and writing observations of events as they unfolded in London in the 1520s and 1530s, the chronicle as it was ultimately finished was crafted, rewritten, and turned into a unified whole at some later date, likely in the early 1540s. Grafton indicates in his edition that Hall left much of the material for the period after 1532 in an inchoate form, which Grafton himself was obliged to revise; the extent of these revisions is open to question, but there can be little doubt that the vast majority of the work remains Hall's.

Hall owes his reputation to this famous chronicle (a title that he did not give it). *The Union of the Two Noble and Illustre Families of Lancaster and York* (1548) is a work of interest on several levels. To the historian it is a valuable source for the events of Henry VIII's reign as recorded by an acute observer of and minor participant in events. To the literary scholar it is of significance primarily as an early instance of the flowering of humanist and vernacular historical writing, and of related genres such as the historical drama, which would fully flower in the late sixteenth century. William Shakespeare would draw indirectly but extensively from Hall's account of the fifteenth century, through the medium of Raphael Holinshed's enormous *Chronicles* (1577). Many of the principal themes of Shakespearean drama and of Elizabethan and early-Stuart historical prose writing were first enunciated in English by Hall.

Despite its familiar name, the *Union* is a much more complex work than it might at first appear. Hall saw events from the vantage point of a prosperous Londoner, and he wrote within the same tradition as Fabyan, his predecessor by two generations, whose own chronicle was first published in 1516. In many important ways, however, Hall's work stands apart from Fabyan's and the other urban chronicles of the fifteenth and early sixteenth centuries. More carefully designed and tightly crafted than its precursors, it has a firm historical beginning in recorded time, a middle, and an end. Most of all it has an argument, a central theme that the author is out to demonstrate, namely the providential delivery of England from the anarchy of civil war in the first instance and, more cautiously, from the tyranny of papal/clerical rule in the second. In that regard it anticipates John Foxe's *Book of Martyrs* (1563), which frequently relies on Hall's version of events as much as on Holinshed's *Chronicles*.

Like medieval monastic chroniclers, Hall precedes the story of his own times with material about the more remote past drawn from other writers, Fabyan among them. Unlike them, however, he does not commence with Brutus, the legendary founder of Britain – nor even with the foundation of the city of London – but with an event that loomed large in the political mind of the Tudor era, the deposition and murder of Richard II in 1399–1400 by Henry Bolingbroke, Duke of Lancaster, and the appalling consequences of that act for England in the following century. In the fashion of a city chronicler, Hall retains the annal, or regnal year, as a unit for organizing his material, but he goes beyond this to link these building blocks together under the reigns of each of the kings from Henry IV to Henry VIII. Moreover, he does so in such a way as to make the whole of his chronicle a single story (with many tales, subplots, and digressions within its frame) running from the "unquiet" time of Henry IV through the "victorious acts" of Henry V, the "troublous" season of Henry VI, the "prosperous" (but still unstable) rule of Edward IV, the "pitiful life" of his short-lived heir, Edward V, the "tragical doings" of Richard III, and the "politic governance" of Henry VII. The climax of the work, and indeed its focal point, comes in a kind of secular telos, the eponymous "union" of the two houses of York and Lancaster in Henry VII and the Yorkist heiress Elizabeth, daughter of Edward IV. As Hall puts it in his dedication to Edward VI, apparently written just before Hall's death, "as King Henry the Fourth was the beginning and root of the great discord and division, so was the godly matrimony the final end of all dissensions, titles, and debates."

As his list of sources reveals, Hall was thoroughly conversant with the vernacular chronicles of England as well as with Latin clerical chronicles, and he would become acquainted with what is arguably the first humanist history to be written in and about England, Polydore Vergil's *Anglica Historia* (first published at Basel in 1534, covering the period up to 1509; extended to 1538 in the third edition of 1555, also published at Basel). It is largely to Vergil's Latin model that Hall owed the design and style of his own chronicle, which is in many places closer to a Continental humanist history than his Elizabethan successor, Holinshed, would ever get. According to Foxe, Hall had the assistance not only of Grafton but of John Bettes, a miniatures painter who executed some engravings for the work, and a man named Tyrell, who assisted with royal pedigrees or "vineats."

In particular Hall wished to supplement and extend two fifteenth-century works, Fabyan's chronicles of England and France, and "one without name," the so-called Great Chronicle of London, which may also have been by Fabyan. The manuscript of this, which Hall (who called it his "Cronica cronicarum") would bequeath in his will to the city of London, may have come to him from Fabyan's son, who had been Hall's father's apprentice; or he may simply have had access to it in his capacities as common serjeant and undersheriff. While Hall regarded both these chronicles as useful fonts of information, he declared them to be "far shooting wide from the butt of an history." Although his own book does not entirely escape their influence and

The victorious actes Fo. xxxiii.
of Kyng Henry the fifth.

ENry Prince of wales, sonne The.i.yere. and heire to kyng Hery the .iiii. borne at Monmouth on the Riuer of Wye, after the obsequies of his noble parēt solēply celebrate and sūpteously fini-shed, toke vpon him the high power & regiment of this realme of Englande the. xx. daie of Marche in the yere af-ter that Christ our sauior had entered into the immaculate wōbe of the holy Uirgin his naturall mother a thou-sande foure hundred and .xii.and was crouned the.ix.date of Aprill then next ensuyng, and proclaimed kyng by the name of kyng Henry the fifth. Before whiche royall possession so by hym obteined, diuerse noble men and honorable personages did to hym homage,liege and sware dewe obeisance(whiche thyng had not been before experimēted)as to hym in whom thei conceiued a good ex-pectacion bothe of his verteous beginnynges and also of his fortunat successe in al thynges whiche should be attempted or begonne duryng the tyme of his prosperous reigne and fortunate Empire .

THIS kyng, this man was he, whiche (accordyng to the olde Pro-uerbe) declared and shewed that honors ought to change maners, for incontinent after that he was stalled in the siege royall,and had recei-ued the croune and scepter of the famous and fortunate region, deter-mined with hymself to put on the shape of a new man , and to vse ano-ther sorte of liuyng,turnyng insolencie and wildnes into grauitie and sobernes,and waueryng vice into constant vertue.And to thētent that he would so continue without goyng backe,& not therunto bee allured by his familier cōpaignions,with whom he had passed his young age and wanton pastime & riotous misorder (insomuche that for imprison-mente of one of his wanton mates and vnthriftie plaisaiers he strake the chiefe Justice with his fiste on the face . For whiche offence he was not onely committed to streight prison, but also of his father put out of the preuy counsaill and banished the courte, and his brother Thomas

Page from Hall's chronicle of English history

lacks both Vergil's style and his foreign perspective on events in England, it is not notably inferior, and on domestic matters it is frequently more informative simply because of Hall's greater familiarity with English politics. Though it has long been established that Hall drew from Vergil a very large portion of his treatment of the fifteenth century, and particularly that of Henry VII (in the absence of Fabyan), it is going too far to say that his chronicle is, except at certain points, merely a translation of the *Anglica Historia*. It is nevertheless indisputable that the finished version of the chronicle draws from Vergil the Italian's conception of the purpose of history as an instrument for recording the deeds of the famous in order to rescue them from oblivion, and a sense of the need to evaluate one's sources critically.

Like some of the courtly writers, medieval and humanist, after whom he patterned his work, Hall also intended his chronicle as a practical and educational treatise. Far from being a simple record of events, the chronicle is consistent throughout in its efforts to assign blame, assess character, weigh up the implications of actions, and point to moral examples; consequently, it would provide a ready source of material in the 1550s for the authors of *A Mirror for Magistrates* (1559). Hall's didacticism is also betrayed in an oratorical and even conversational style which implies that, like such earlier aristocratic chroniclers as Jean Froissart, he intended his work to be read both privately and, on occasion, aloud to courtly audiences, both for their entertainment and edification. Yet Hall also fattened the work with documents, treatises, reports of civic and courtly feasts and other occasions, and lists of officials that break up the narrative and make the book as much a work of reference as an entertainment. Many may have been inserted by Grafton from Hall's papers, and while they are often of great value to the historian, they make the chronicle suffer as narrative literature.

The work nowhere resembles a traditional chronicle more than in the second half of its account of Henry VIII's reign, where the sheer abundance of information (and Hall's apparent lack of leisure to polish the work to the degree that he had for the years prior to 1532) causes a certain narrowing of vision and a tendency simply to report events, especially those in London, with a less acute sense of their relative significance. Although its information is often very useful, it is here that Hall (unlike Vergil, whose account stops in 1538) experienced some difficulty in keeping his material fully under control and in perspective. He had completed much of his work, according to Grafton, by the twenty-fourth year of Henry VIII's reign (1532), but the extensive use of Vergil (first published in 1534) indicates that however unfinished the later sections were, Hall had at least continued to work on them to a much later date, though the pressure of civic affairs gave him less time for historical endeavors.

Having sat for a final time in the Parliament of 1545, Hall made his will in 1546 or early 1547. This document, reproduced by A. F. Pollard in 1932, indicates that his religious views were those of the Reformation: he entrusted his soul not to saints or the Virgin but exclusively to "her maker and redeemer by whose passion and not by my deserts I trust only to be saved." He wished to be buried in the Church of the Grey Friars, with a plate on the wall to commemorate him, but he would in fact be buried in Saint Benet Sherehog Church. Among the beneficiaries was one Mr. Warren (possibly Sir Ralph Warren [1486?–1553], lord mayor of London in 1536–1537 and 1544), who received Hall's "charts." His English and French books were left to his brother, William, and a collection of pedigrees to a former servant. Hall left his chronicle to Grafton on the clear understanding that he would edit and publish it. On 31 March 1547 Hall was named to a new commission for the administration of the Six Articles in the city, but he had already been gravely ill for several weeks. He was dead by 25 May, on which date his will was proved. The actual date of his death, while unknown, may with reasonable certainty be pushed back into mid April, since Hall's successor as undersheriff, Thomas Atkyns, was appointed to that post on 19 April, on which day a second Six Articles commission was announced with Hall's name removed. In addition to his brother, he was also survived by his mother, named as the will's overseer, who was buried in Saint Benet Sherehog Church in 1557. The will's reference to his mother but not his fa-

ther renders it virtually certain that the John Hall and his wife whom Foxe mentions as imprisoned for Protestant beliefs in 1555 were not the parents of Edward the chronicler.

Grafton's first edition of the chronicle appeared in 1548. The evidence for a 1542 edition, printed by Thomas Berthelet and supposedly almost completely destroyed by order of Queen Mary, is weak, and bibliographical authority has generally recognized the 1548 edition as the first. A second edition appeared from Grafton, with the addition of tables, in 1550. In both cases Grafton, finding the job too vast for him alone when combined with his position as king's printer, farmed out some of the printing to others, including John Mychell and, subsequently, the Dutchman Steven Mierdman. Further sheets of various portions were printed at later dates and inserted into early editions to make up incomplete sets, and this has led to much of the bibliographical confusion surrounding the work and its dates, which the revised *Short-Title Catalogue* (1991) has now largely sorted out. The Marian proclamation unsuccessfully commanded that "the book commonly called Hall's chronicle" – the last mentioned in a long list of authors including Martin Luther, John Calvin, Ulrich Zwingli, and most of the major Continental reformers – be called in and destroyed because of its Protestant sympathies and its favorable depiction of the divorce of Henry VIII and Catherine of Aragon and its aftermath.

Hall was a significant English author on several counts. His chronicle was based on a more scrupulous and careful assessment of the surviving medieval chronicles than its many predecessors and was, with Sir Thomas More's shorter life of Richard III, among the earliest works of English historiography to combine a sense of the national past with some of the literary methods of humanism. Although supplanted in terms of length and scope of time by Holinshed's *Chronicles,* its Elizabethan successor, Hall's work (together with Vergil's) provided one of the staples for Holinshed's book. Because of its unique formulation of the period from 1399 to the accession of Henry VIII as a historical whole, invested with providential significance (from the point of view both of the reestablishment of stable government and of the beginnings of the Reformation under Henry VIII), it had a highly significant role in the shaping of later-Tudor and early-Stuart historical consciousness.

Biographies:

A. F. Pollard, "Edward Hall's Will and Chronicle," *Bulletin of the Institute of Historical Research,* 9 (1931–1932): 171–177;

Alan Harding, "Hall, Edward," in *The History of Parliament: The House of Commons, 1509–1558,* volume 2, edited by S. T. Bindoff (London: History of Parliament Trust, 1982), pp. 279–282.

References:

Joseph Foster, *Register of Admissions to Gray's Inn, 1521–1889* (London: Privately printed, 1889), p. 9;

John Foxe, *The Acts and Monuments of John Foxe,* 8 volumes, edited by George Townsend (New York: AMS, 1965);

F. S. Fussner, *Tudor History and the Historians* (New York: Basic Books, 1970);

Antonia Gransden, *Historical Writing in England, II: circa 1307 to the Early Sixteenth Century* (Ithaca, N.Y.: Cornell University Press, 1982);

Denys Hay, *Polydore Vergil: Renaissance Historian and Man of Letters* (Oxford: Clarendon, 1952);

Henry A. Kelly, *Divine Providence in the England of Shakespeare's Histories* (Cambridge, Mass.: Harvard University Press, 1970);

F. J. Levy, *Tudor Historical Thought* (San Marino, Cal.: Huntington Library, 1967);

Graham Pollard, "The Bibliographical History of Hall's Chronicle," *Bulletin of the Institute of Historical Research,* 10 (1932–1933): 12–17;

J. and J. A. Venn, *Alumni Cantabrigienses,* part 1, volume 2 (Cambridge: Cambridge University Press, 1922), p. 285;

Anthony à Wood, *Athenae Oxonienses,* volume 1, edited by Philip Bliss (London: F. C. & J. Rivington, 1813–1820), pp. 164–166.

Papers:

The manuscript of Hall's chronicle does not survive. His will is in the Public Record Office, London (reference PCC 36 Alen).

Stephen Hawes

(1475? – before 1529)

A. S. G. Edwards
University of Victoria

BOOKS: *The example of vertu* (London: Printed by Wynkyn de Worde, 1504; reprinted, 1509?, 1530);

The passetyme of pleasure (London: Printed by Wynkyn de Worde, 1509; reprinted, 1517);

The conuercyon of swerers (London: Printed by Wynkyn de Worde, 1509);

A joyfull medytacyon to all Englonde of the coronacyon of our moost natural souerayne lorde kynge Henry the eyght (London: Printed by Wynkyn de Worde, 1509);

The comforte of louers (London: Printed by Wynkyn de Worde, 1515).

Editions and Collections: *The Pastime of Pleasure,* edited by W. E. Mead, Early English Text Society, no. 173 (London: Oxford University Press, 1928);

The Minor Poems, edited by Florence W. Gluck and Alice B. Morgan, Early English Text Society, no. 271 (London: Oxford University Press, 1974);

The Works of Stephen Hawes, introduction by Frank J. Spang (Delmar, N.Y.: Scholars Facsimiles & Reprints, 1975).

Stephen Hawes was an early-sixteenth-century poet whose verse enjoyed some popularity during the first half of the century. His writings are of particular interest for their efforts to employ medieval literary forms and conventions to new purposes. Little can be established with much certainty about Hawes's life. He may have attended Oxford University, and one mid-sixteenth-century account claims that he also studied in Scotland and France. Various records of payments, the earliest dating from 1503, describe him as groom of the chamber to Henry VII. One of these payments, in 1506, is specifically for a "ballet" for the king.

His major works, *The Example of Virtue* (composed between August 1503 and August 1504) and *The Pastime of Pleasure* (composed between August 1505 and August 1506), belong to this period of Hawes's life, although the latter was apparently not published until 1509, the year that also saw the publication of two short poems, *The Conversion of Swearers* and *A Joyful Meditation,* the latter celebrating the accession of Henry VIII. His last surviving work, *The Comfort of Lovers,* was apparently written between April 1510 and April 1511, although the only edition now extant dates from 1515. It is uncertain whether Hawes remained in the court circle after Henry VIII's accession. Some very cryptic passages in *The Comfort of Lovers* suggest that he had fallen from favor in the new reign. The date of his death is unknown, but he was certainly dead before 1529, when he is so described in a poem published in that year.

The Example of Virtue and *The Pastime of Pleasure* share common elements. *The Example of Virtue* is the shorter (2,129 lines, nearly all in rhyme-royal stanzas). The dreamer (who is named first as Youth and then as Virtue) is taken in his dream by a guide, Lady Discretion, to an island where he listens to Dame Justice arbitrate a debate among Nature, Fortune, Hardiness, and Wisdom. Justice concludes that all these qualities are essential to human well-being: "And you of him shall be copartners / Both of his life and of his manner" (lines 1,035–1,036). After this the dreamer goes on a quest for the lady Cleanness, whom he rescues from a dragon and marries. The poem then concludes with the death of the hero/narrator, a description of his visions of both hell and heaven, and final praise for the future Henry VIII.

The Pastime of Pleasure, Hawes's longest poem (5,816 lines in rhyme royal and couplets), combines some of the same elements in *The Example of Virtue* but in a greatly expanded and somewhat modified

Here begynneth the passe tyme of pleature.

Frontispiece for the 1517 edition of Stephen Hawes's longest poem

form. The narrator and protagonist, Grand Amor, is confronted initially with a choice between the active and contemplative lives. He chooses the former and is then sent to study at the Tower of Doctrine, where he receives instruction in the Seven Liberal Arts. Following this and an encounter with La Belle Pucelle, with whom he falls in love, Grand Amor is given further instruction at the Tower of Chivalry before embarking on a quest.

The quest is interrupted by an encounter with a dwarf, Godfrey Gobelieve, the embodiment of antifeminist and anticourtly attitudes. After recounting the fates of Aristotle and Virgil (both depicted as dupes of women), Godfrey is chastised by Dame Correction, who exhorts Grand Amor to constancy in his love: "Look that your heart, your word, and countenance / Agree all in one withouten variance" (4,252–4,253). He continues on his quest, overcoming a series of opponents — first a three-headed, then a seven-headed giant, and finally a dragon composed of seven metals — before winning La Belle Pucelle. After their marriage the narrative moves quickly to Grand Amor's death: "For though the day be never so long, / At last the bells ringeth to evensong" (5,479–5,480). The poem concludes with the protagonist's visions of the Seven Deadly Sins, the Nine Worthies, and Eternity, this last through which (5,785–5,788):

Time past with virtue must enter the gate
Of Joy and bliss with mine high estate
Without time for to be everlasting
Which God grant us at our last ending.

167

Woodcut from The Pastime of Pleasure: *"Eternity in a fair white vesture . . . And on her head a diadem right pure / With three crowns of precious treasure."*

Hawes's next-longest poem, *The Comfort of Lovers* (938 lines in rhyme royal), is his last. It is a work that is particularly hard to interpret, since many of its allusions seem to refer to contemporary events and circumstances that cannot now be confidently identified. But it does seem to contain an autobiographical element. For example, it specifically identifies the protagonist, Amor, as the author of *The Pastime of Pleasure* ("Of late I saw a book of your making / Called *The Pastime of Pleasure,* which is wondrous" [785–786]) and even repeats lines from that poem. This figure appears as a solitary lover, lamenting the loss of his beloved, a loss that is directly related to his difficulty in writing. He is directed by a lady to a tower where he sees three magic mirrors. After this he meets his lady love, Pucell. Their dialogue concludes with Pucell's resolution that Venus and Fortune must settle the fate of their love (911–915):

> I do now submit
> My will and thought to the lady Venus
> As she is goddess and doth true love knit

Right so to determine the matter between us
With assent of fortune.

After this the dreamer awakes.

There are obvious similarities between all these poems. All are cast in the form of allegorical dream visions in the course of which the dreamer/protagonist receives instruction and undertakes a quest connected with his beloved. But all these educative and amatory elements exist in a rather inert relationship that gives only limited structural or thematic coherence to the work as a whole.

Hawes's two remaining poems are briefer and reflect more-limited concerns. *The Conversion of Swearers* (366 lines mainly in rhyme royal) is a complaint against the use of oaths in society. It concludes with the injunction: "And ye kings and lords of renown, / Exhort your servants their swearing to cease" (353–354). The poem clearly struck a responsive chord in sixteenth-century audiences: four separate editions survive from between 1509 and

Woodcut from Hawes's A Joyful Meditation *depicting the coronation of Henry VIII and Catherine of Aragon*

the 1550s, the decade that saw the last reprintings of Hawes's works. *A Joyful Meditation* (217 lines in rhyme royal) celebrates the accession of Henry VIII in 1509, alluding, perhaps not with the greatest tact, to the greed of his father, Henry VII: "Our late sovereign his father excellent / I know right well some hold opinion / That to avarice he had entendement" (70–72).

The limitations of Hawes's achievements are perhaps more obvious than his merits. In *The Pastime of Pleasure* he looks back to medieval literary tradition and singles out for praise the fifteenth-century poet John Lydgate, particularly for his rhetorical skills, some features of which are reflected in Hawes's own writings. His use of aureate diction (a polysyllabic, Latin-derived vocabulary) appears to have come from his reading of Lydgate's works. He praises Lydgate for having created "The depured [purified] rhetoric in English language / To make our tongue so clearly purified" (1,164–1,165), and he seeks to reflect this in passages such as the following with its (italicized) Latinate, polysyllabic diction (5,264–5,268):

Her *redolent* words of sweet *influence*
Degouted *vapor* most *aromatic*
And made *conversion* of my *complacence*
Her *depured* and her lusty *rhetoric*
My courage *reformed* that was so *lunatic.*

It is likely that Lydgate also provided Hawes with an example of a moral poet, one concerned with the relationship between poetry and proper conduct, as is most of Hawes's own poetry. Such a preoccupation, accompanied by a stylistic and linguistic debt to poetic traditions that were beginning to lose their vitality, inevitably limits the possibility of sympathetic engagement with his works. In some respects they were perceived to be incipiently old-fashioned soon after they were written. Wynkyn de Worde even undertook a revision of *The Example of Virtue* after Hawes's death, often changing his vocabulary to make it more accessible to contemporary audiences.

But Hawes's merits are nonetheless real and substantial. His was the earliest attempt in England to combine allegory with the romance form,

Title page for The Comfort of Lovers, *showing the lady Pucelle
offering her lover, Amour, a ring*

to create a literary hybrid that sought to adapt old forms to new purposes. His recurrent preoccupations with instruction and education and their importance to conduct and morality seek to give allegory a direct, contemporary relevance, consistent with emergent humanist tendencies in early-sixteenth-century England. His deployment of late-medieval motifs and topics in such new ways is seen in part in the self-referentiality of his writings. The autobiographical element emerges with growing explicitness in his poems so that his personal preoccupations and fate become part of their design. In all these ways, Hawes can be seen as a transitional poet, looking back to fifteenth-century literary traditions yet employing such traditions in new ways.

In addition Hawes's works are unusual for their careful attempts to integrate text and image through the use of woodcuts made specifically to illustrate de Worde's editions of *The Example of Virtue* and *The Pastime of Pleasure*. These attempts suggest Hawes's direct involvement in the preparation of his texts to an extent that seems highly unusual for the period. Indeed, his relationship with the printer seems to have been an unusually close one.

All the first editions of his works were printed by de Worde, who reprinted them and seems also to have had an interest in his posthumous reputation. Praise of, or allusions to, Hawes's works appears in some of de Worde's publications. Finally, Hawes's accomplishments as a prosodist in an age of very erratic versification are worthy of comment. His verse reflects a degree of metrical regularity significantly higher than the norm for the early sixteenth century.

Hawes's influence was not great. There is some evidence that he had a circle of admirers during the early decades of the sixteenth century. Both *The Example of Virtue* and *The Pastime of Pleasure* were reprinted several times after his death, and a few selections from his writings were made in contemporary manuscripts. It has been argued that he was an influence on Edmund Spenser's *The Faerie Queene* (1590–1596), and he earned the approbation of some distinguished later critics. Thomas Warton acclaimed him as "the restorer of invention" (*Observations on "The Fairy Queen" of Spenser*, 1754), and Elizabeth Barrett Browning admired the "passages of thoughtful sweetness and cheerful tenderness" in *The Pastime of Pleasure* (*The Greek Christian Poets and* the English Poets, 1863). He has also been discussed sympathetically by such demanding twentieth-century critics as John Churton Collins and C. S. Lewis.

References:

Lois Ebin, *Illuminator, Makar, Vates: Visions of Poetry in the Fifteenth Century* (Lincoln: University of Nebraska Press, 1988);

A. S. G. Edwards, "Poet and Printer in Sixteenth Century England: Stephen Hawes and Wynkyn de Worde," *Gutenberg Jahrbuch* (1980): 82–88;

Edwards, *Stephen Hawes* (Boston: Twayne, 1983);

Arthur B. Ferguson, *The Indian Summer of English Chivalry* (Durham, N.C.: Duke University Press, 1960);

Alastair Fox, "Stephen Hawes and the Political Allegory of *The Comfort of Lovers*," *English Literary Renaissance*, 17 (Winter 1987): 3–21;

John N. King, "Allegorical Pattern in Stephen Hawes's *The Pastime of Pleasure*," *Studies in the Literary Imagination*, 11 (Spring 1978): 57–67;

Tsuyoshi Mukai, "Wynkyn de Worde's Treatment of Stephen Hawes' *Example of Vertu*," *Studies in Medieval English Language & Literature*, 5 (1990): 57–74;

Fitzroy Pyle, "The Barbarous Metre of Alexander Barclay," *Modern Language Review*, 32 (July 1937): 353–373.

Papers:

There are no authoritative manuscripts for any of Hawes's works. A manuscript of *The Pastime of Pleasure*, now no longer extant, was recorded in the seventeenth century; see Andrew G. Watson, *The Manuscripts of Henry Savile of Banke* (London: The Bibliographical Society, 1969), p. 64, no. 248. There are, however, a few manuscript selections that indicate contemporary interest in his poems. Eight stanzas from *The Conversion of Swearers* appear in British Library MS. Harley 4820, f. 80. And selections from *The Pastime of Pleasure* and *The Comfort of Lovers* are incorporated into several of the poems in Bodleian Library MS Rawlinson C. 813; for full details see Sharon L. Jansen and Kathleen H. Jordan, eds., *The Welles Anthology: A Critical Edition*, Medieval and Renaissance Texts and Studies 75 (State University of New York at Binghamton: Center for Medieval and Early Renaissance Studies, 1991), Appendix B, pp. 300–302.

Henry VIII of England

(28 June 1491 – 28 January 1547)

Peter C. Herman
Georgia State University

BOOK: *Assertio septem sacramentorum aduersus M. Lutherum* (London: Richard Pynson, 1521); translated as *The Defense of the Seven Sacraments* (London: N. Thompson, 1687).

Editions and Collections: *The Defense of the Seven Sacraments,* edited by Louis O'Donovan (New York: Benziger Bros., 1908);

Songs, Ballads and Instrumental Pieces Composed by King Henry the Eighth, edited by Lady Mary Trefusis (London: Roxburghe Club, 1912);

Miscellaneous Writings of Henry the Eighth, edited by Francis Macnamara (Waltham, Mass.: Golden Cockerel Press, 1924) — includes the *Defense,* love letters to Anne Boleyn, songs, a letter to Emperor Charles V, two proclamations, and Henry's will;

The King's Book; or, A Necessary Doctrine and Erudition for Any Christian Man, edited by T. A. Lacey (London: Church Historical Society, 1932);

John Stevens, *Music and Poetry in the Early Tudor Court* (Lincoln: University of Nebraska Press, 1961) — appendix includes Henry's lyrics;

Musica Britannica, volume 18: *Music at the Court of Henry VIII,* edited by John Stevens (London: Stainer & Bell, 1973).

OTHER: *A necessary doctrine and erudition for any christen man, sette furthe by the Kynges maiestie,* preface by Henry VIII (London: Printed by Thomas Berthelet, 1543).

King Henry VIII once confessed to Cardinal Thomas Wolsey that "writing is to me somewhat tedious and painful," and his scanty literary remains testify to this aversion: a handful of seemingly crude poems and song lyrics produced during the first decade of his reign; assorted diplomatic letters; several short love letters to Anne Boleyn in English and French; the *Assertio Septem Sacramentorum* (1521; translated as *The Defense of the Seven Sacraments,* 1687), a theological polemic written in answer to Martin Luther's *On the Babylonian Captivity* (1520);

and a short preface to a 1543 book setting forth the official religion. There were also one or two works that were never completed and are now lost, such as a tragedy on Boleyn and a book justifying his divorce. Nevertheless, Henry VIII's centrality to the development of sixteenth-century English literature cannot be doubted.

First, his patronage of humanists contributed to the adoption of the humanist curriculum in English letters and education. Second, even though his lyrics scarcely qualify as masterpieces, the very fact that he wrote at all deeply influenced the future course of Renaissance poetry. For a commoner or even a courtier to write a love lyric, heartfelt or conventional, is no great matter; but once the king does so, no matter what the quality or the quantity of the product, then the poem takes on political resonances. Third, Henry exerted a tremendous influence on English Renaissance literature through his activities as an instigator of literary endeavors. Under his sponsorship the Italian masque became a regular part of courtly life, and his presence shaped the imaginations of such famous courtly poets as Sir Thomas Wyatt and Henry Howard, Earl of Surrey. Finally, the usual distinctions between fact and fiction do not apply to Henry VIII, for even though he rarely put quill to parchment, he used literary motifs, in particular chivalric romances, as models for his foreign and domestic policies.

Henry Tudor, born on 28 June 1491, was the second son of King Henry VII and Queen Elizabeth. Because he occupied the unthankful position of younger brother to the heir apparent, Arthur, the records contain relatively little about his early years other than the dates upon which he received various titles. Like other members of the royal household and the upper class, he received a broad humanist education at the hands of several tutors, including John Skelton, who later boasted that he introduced the young prince to the classics. Some of his schoolbook exercises are preserved in the Folger Shakespeare Library.

Henry VIII (portrait attributed to Joos van Cleve; Collection of Her Majesty the Queen)

A public letter written in 1523 by the famous humanist Desiderius Erasmus shows that Henry's career as a patron began sometime during the summer of 1499. Erasmus was staying at the Greenwich country house of his former pupil and then-patron, William Blount, Lord Mountjoy. Thomas More dropped by one day and invited his friend to take a walk to the nearby village of Eltham. Without first warning Erasmus, More led his friend to Eltham Palace, which served as the royal nursery. Prince Arthur had been dispatched to Wales for his apprenticeship in statecraft, and so everyone's attention was focused on the eight-year-old Prince Henry, Duke of York. More, who had prepared for the occasion by bringing a small literary gift, bowed to the young prince and presented his offering. Erasmus, caught entirely unawares and not a little peeved at More for this surprise, mumbled his excuses and promised to remedy the omission another time. However, during the meal Erasmus received a note from Henry "challenging something from his pen." The eminent humanist complied several days later with an exceedingly tedious panegyric to Henry, the king, England in general, and a great deal else besides.

This anecdote says a great deal about its author, about More, and about Henry VIII. It shows that the prince, doubtless encouraged by Skelton (who might have sparked the prince's challenge), liked the company of the learned, thereby prefiguring his patronage of humanist endeavors. The letter also prefigures Henry's role as an instigator of writing, both as patron and as subject. More ominously, this anecdote also shows how even as a child, Henry injected an element of threat into his literary doings. It was not enough for the young prince graciously to accept Erasmus's apologies and promises; instead, he imperiously challenged – that is to say, he *commanded* – Erasmus to come up with something, and the flustered guest clearly understood the note as much more than a child's whim. Twenty years later Erasmus would interpret the incident as a prediction of Henry's future glory, writing that even as a child he had "already something of royalty in his demeanor, in which there was a certain dignity combined with a singular courtesy." But Erasmus also spent three days slaving over Henry's demand, and the event so traumatized him that he neither wrote nor read poetry again (which, given his poem's dreariness, may have been a good thing). Power figures as an abiding concern in nearly all of Henry's literary writings and doings.

This incident would never have been recounted had not Prince Arthur died in April 1502. Two results ensued from Arthur's premature demise. The first is obvious – Henry would become king. The second was less obvious but no less momentous. Five months before he died, Arthur had married Catherine of Aragon, daughter of King Ferdinand II of Aragon, although it remains unclear whether they ever consummated the marriage (Catherine always insisted that Arthur was too sickly). Almost immediately after he became king (for reasons best known to himself, since he was certainly under no diplomatic imperative to do so), Henry chose to wed Catherine despite the fact that marrying his brother's widow was considered incest and therefore required a papal dispensation. One or two important clergymen hinted that such a marriage might not be a good idea, but in 1509 this scruple, so crucial to later developments, was barely noted.

Henry VII died on 29 April 1509, and Henry VIII was crowned on 24 June. His accession received almost universal acclaim because the English were generally tired of the late king's tight-fisted manner and his dour court. In the last installment of *The Book of the Courtier* (1528), Baldassare Castiglione has Signor Ottaviano – one of the lords of Urbino participating in the debate over what constitutes the perfect courtier – quote a letter from "Castiglione," their ambassador in England, who praises Henry as a humanist dream come true: "It seems that nature chose to show her power in this lord by uniting in a single body excellences enough to adorn a multitude." The new king certainly appeared to fulfill most of the conditions the court of Urbino prescribed for the perfect courtier: he was a gifted athlete, had an excellent pedigree, danced well, jousted superbly, played several instruments quite well, dabbled in poetry, and generally valued letters as much as military affairs (but not more). In sum, the new king's youth, energy,

and vitality promised a new dawn – a new beginning politically, artistically, and intellectually.

The festivities that greeted the new king seemed to continue practically unabated for the first decade of his rule. The Spanish ambassador Luis Caroz, for example, reported that "he is young, and doesn't care to occupy himself with anything but the pleasures of his age"; Richard Foxe, bishop of Winchester, perhaps in keeping with the gravity of his position, put the matter more tartly: "All other offices he neglects." In *The Union of the Two Noble and Illustrate Families of Lancaster and York* (1548), Edward Hall reports that the king daily exercised:

> shooting, singing, dancing, wrestling, casting of the bar, playing at the recorders, flutes, virginals, and in setting of songs, making of ballads; and [he] did set two goodly masses, every of them in five parts, which were sung oftentimes in his chapel, and afterwards in diverse other places. And when he came to Woking, there were kept both jousts and tourneys; the rest of this progress was spent in hunting, hawking, and shooting.

When Hall wrote that the "king being lusty, young, and courageous, greatly delighted in feats of chivalry," he not only meant that Henry enjoyed playing military games; he also wanted to emphasize how the king's entertainments were consciously patterned after chivalric literature. The king and his courtiers frequently entered the list or participated in pageants in which they adopted the roles of Fame, Renown, Sir Gallant, and Sir Loyal Heart. Caroz also reported that the king's jousts were "instituted in imitation of Amadis and Lancelot, and other knights of olden times, of whom so much is written in books."

Henry's penchant for dancing and chivalric disguisings also led to the introduction of a literary form that Ben Jonson and Inigo Jones would perfect during the Stuart era – the masque:

> On the day of the Epiphany at night, the king with eleven others were disguised, after the manner of Italy, called a masque, a thing not seen afore in England: they were apparelled in garments long and broad, wrought all with gold, with visors and caps of gold; and after the banquet done, these masquers came in, with six gentlemen disguised in silk, bearing staff torches, and desired the ladies to dance; some were content, and some that knew the fashion of it refused, because it was not a thing commonly seen. And after they danced and commoned together, as the fashion of the masque is, they took their leave and departed, and so did the queen and all the ladies.

Anne Boleyn (portrait by an unknown artist; National Portrait Gallery, London)

Hall's description of the Epiphany masque reveals a chief characteristic of the Tudor masque: the incorporation of the monarch into a spectacle designed to confirm his power. Thus these entertainments, which at first blush appear as purely apolitical diversions, became under Henry vehicles for expressing the hierarchy of the court and reinforcing the power of the monarchy.

Clearly, in Henry's court the distinction between fact and fiction was frequently blurred, and nowhere more so than in his use of chivalric legends as the guiding principles for his foreign policy. Henry VII had assiduously kept England out of foreign quarrels, not so much because he disapproved of militarism but because war cost too much. His son, on the other hand, inflamed by the Arthurian legends of derring-do, knights-errant, and chivalry that he had read as a child, made it abundantly clear from the moment he be-

came king that he intended to act out these roles on both the dance floor and the battlefield. In other words, Henry wanted to live his own chivalric adventure by restarting the Hundred Years' War and invading France in July 1513.

Not surprisingly, his attempt to bring a chivalric romance to life by invading France had disastrous results. At least partially because Sir Thomas Malory and Chrétien de Troyes did not allow unchivalric contingencies into their narratives, Henry simply did not count on unreliable allies, poor supply lines, bad weather, disease, and grumbling, mutinous soldiers. To their credit the English did achieve one victory, the Battle of the Spurs, so called because of how the French "spurred" their horses in ignominious retreat. But Henry wasted many lives and came very close to bankrupting the country, and the victory achieved nothing either strategically or diplomatically. Furthermore, this skirmish pales in comparison to the genuinely important victory achieved over the Scots on 9 September 1513 in the Battle of Flodden Field, during which the Scottish king James IV himself was killed by an army led by Queen Catherine. About twenty years later Henry would blame the French wars on the advice of evil councillors; however, the true culprit was his desire to write a chivalric romance with real soldiers.

Henry VIII's lyrics date from the first decade of his reign, and they also illustrate this melding of poetry and politics. Even though it is impossible to determine their exact chronology, their generally light tone and occasional references to Queen Catherine indicate that Henry must have penned them sometime between 1510 and 1520. Two anonymous early Tudor songbooks contain the entirety of Henry's lyric output. The first is known as *Henry VIII's Manuscript* ("H") because its compiler, evidently someone close to the court, included all the king's lyrics ("Pastime with Good Company" is the first vocal composition) along with many of his musical compositions. This manuscript, beautifully written on vellum, also includes songs by William Cornish, John Dunstable, and others interspersed with instrumental compositions and songs popular in the king's court. The second, called *Ritson's Manuscript* after its nineteenth-century owner, clearly originates from the provinces, perhaps Exeter.

Taken strictly as aesthetic artifacts, the lyrics have little to recommend them; consequently, they have been uniformly ignored by literary critics. Doubtless, such trifles as H24 ("The thoughts within my breast / They grieve me passing sore, / That I cannot be pressed / To serve you evermore") yield few rewards. But Henry's lyrics, like some of Wyatt's, were intended for singing, not for silent reading, probably accompanied by a lute, in a room with "many ladies present" (as C. S. Lewis dismissively and with no little sexism puts it). Actually, with the appropriate music they are quite charming, and one, "Pastime with Good Company," otherwise known as "The King's Ballad," became something of a standard in the sixteenth century. Preachers were even known to incorporate it into their sermons.

The king's lyrics derive from the tradition of courtly love that in England more or less begins with Geoffrey Chaucer, continues through the anonymous poems of the fifteenth century, and culminates in Wyatt. Despite his attachment to humanism, Henry's efforts show no Renaissance influence at all in either form or content. Most of his lyrics repeat with little variation the standard pose of the courtly lover swearing eternal fealty to his lady: "As the holly groweth green / And never changeth hue, / So I am, ever hath been, / Unto my lady true" (H33), or "Thus am I fixed without grudge, / Mine eye with heart doth me so judge" (H51). Their emphasis on fidelity may also be explained by their immediate audience, since many lines appear to refer overtly to Queen Catherine, such as "I hurt no man, I do no wrong / Love true where I did marry" (H66).

Henry VIII's lyrics become more interesting texts when looked at as interventions in the cultural poetics of the early Tudor court. First, the language of courtly love, no matter how lamely versified, carried political connotations. From its inception in France among the troubadors and trouvères, *fin amour* – with its emphasis on service, suits, hope, jealousy, and rejection – constituted a means of talking about courtly ambition as well as erotic concerns. Consequently, Wyatt, coming to the end of his ambassadorship in Spain, could send Henry an epigram about returning to the court that concludes: "My king, my country, alone for whom I live, / Of mighty love the wings for this me give." And if courtiers could use erotic language to talk about politics, then so could the king; Henry VIII may actually have been the first "courtly maker" (to borrow George Puttenham's phrase describing Wyatt and Surrey) to use poetic conventions as a means of covertly talking about political power.

The first three lines of "Pastime with Good Company," for example, sound like a mere declaration of high spirits:

Pastime with good company
I love and shall until I die;
Grudge so will, but none deny.

But the fourth line – "So God be pleased, this life will I" – transforms the song into a vehicle by which Henry establishes his independence, "this life will I" reminding one and all that these are the king's desires. The line, then, functions as a claim to power and independence. No matter how frivolous the circumstances of performance, it would be hard for any courtier or lady mindful of the few practical limitations on royal power to miss the overtone of threat vibrating in the last line of the burden:

For my pastaunce [pastime]
Hunt, sing, and dance;
My heart is set
All goodly sport
To my comfort:
Who shall me *let?* [prevent; emphasis added]

*Illustration from Henry VIII's psalter, showing the king playing a harp
while his fool, Will Somers, listens*

Similarly, in H92, Henry uses a song that superficially appears to be an apologia for sowing wild oats to emphasize once more his royal independence:

> For they would have him his liberty refrain,
> And all merry company for to disdain;
> But I will not so whatsoever they say,
> But follow his mind in all that we may.

"Who will stop me from doing whatever I choose to do?" the king asks. The question, of course, is rhetorical. However, Henry's songs are not the assured assertions of a firmly established king; rather, they are part of the process by which he established his independence. In reading these seemingly confident lyrics, one needs to remember that between 1510 and 1520 or so, Henry's profligate spending and his foreign policies, especially his decision to restart the Hundred Years' War by invading France, provoked criticism from many quarters, including the councillors left over from his father's government and such important humanists as Erasmus and More.

Consequently, some of Henry's lyrics radiate a curious defensiveness. H66 represents the most

overt example of his using a parlor song as a vehicle for simultaneously rebutting and reassuring his elders. The song begins in a defensive, if not apologetic, mood:

> Though some say that youth ruleth me,
> I trust in age to tarry;
> God and my right and my duty,
> From them shall I never vary:
> Though some say that youth ruleth me.

He ends this lyric with a strategically placed revelation of the author's name and, most important, his title:

> Then some discuss that hence we must;
> Pray we to God and Saint Mary
> That all amend; and here an end,
> Thus sayeth the king, the eighth Harry:
> Though some sayeth [that youth ruleth me].

More than "Pastime with Good Company," this song deserves the title of "The King's Ballad" because it would be inconceivable for anyone other than Henry VIII to perform it. And for that reason this is the most deeply political of his lyrics. What begins as a somewhat sheepish defense harkening back to the conventional youth/age debates of medieval poetry becomes a not-very-subtle assertion of royal power and prerogative. It is the *king* – and the eighth of that name to sit on England's throne, a position that gives him the collective authority of the previous seven (not the least being Henry V) – who issues this defense of his life. By including this self-referential allusion to his position and his name's history, Henry VIII forcefully reminds his listeners that if youth rules the king, the king rules everyone else.

While not jousting, dancing, or making war in France, Henry also did as much as he could to promote the cause of humanism in England. "Without knowledge," Henry told Blount, "life would not be worth our having," and Henry gave much more than lip service to the New Learning. He lavished patronage upon such significant humanists as Erasmus, More (who wrote a poem celebrating Henry's accession), Juan Luis Vives, and Thomas Linacre (who translated the medical works of Galen). Henry's sympathy for the New Learning also set the standard for those immediately below him in power. Queen Catherine, for example, materially assisted the establishment of a humanist college at Cambridge, Saint John's; and Richard Pace, in *The Benefits of a Liberal Education,* praises Cardinal Wolsey as having been blessed with "nature's fairest gift, namely a love for all learned men. . . . He patronizes them so admirably that he seems to have no greater care than to advance them to high places." Consequently, through a kind of trickle-down effect, humanists found supporters and patrons in nearly every level of government.

Henry supported the introduction of a public Greek lecture at Cambridge in 1517, and he twice publicly defended the study of Greek. In the first incident, he heard about a preacher at Oxford who, in the middle of a sermon, inveighed against Greek studies; according to Erasmus, Henry "declared that those who wished should be welcome to follow Greek." Henry was a little more forceful the next time, partially because his antagonist was a little more foolish. After a court preacher put forward a diatribe against Greek studies in 1518, he found himself summoned to debate the point further with More. Erasmus's account of the incident illustrates Henry's familiarity with humanists and humanist thought:

> The king was pleased to be present at the disputation; and when More had spoken fluently and at length and the preacher's reply was awaited, he fell on his knees and contented himself with begging for forgiveness, extenuating what he had done with the plea that as he was preaching he was carried away by some spirit to make this attack on Greek. "Well," said the king, "that was

not the spirit of Christ; it must have been folly." Then he asked the man whether he had read anything by Erasmus; for it had not escaped the king's notice that he had directed some shafts at me. He said no. "That shows," said the king, "what a fool you are, if you condemn what you have not read." "I have read something," the theologian said; "it was called the Folly [*The Praise of Folly*, 1511]." Here [Richard] Pace interrupted with "And a very suitable subject, too, may it please your Majesty." Then the divine thought up another argument to palliate his offense: "I am not all that much against Greek," he said, "only because Greek is derived from Hebrew." The king was amazed at the man's extraordinary stupidity and told him to go, but on condition that he never appear again to preach at Court.

Even though Henry did all he could to promote humanism, his enthusiasm for good letters needs to be kept in perspective. While he genuinely supported the New Learning and liked to surround himself with courtiers schooled in the classics, he used humanism and humanists for his own ends, not the other way around. If a conflict ever arose between the demands of policy and the ideals of humanism, the latter gave way, not the former. On Good Friday 1513, for example, at the same time that Henry's ships were about to set off to invade France, John Colet preached before him and his court a sermon inveighing against war. Henry then went to Colet's residence, where he had a private conference with him. Colet backed down, declared Henry's cause just, and Henry dismissed the dean of Saint Paul's with this equivocal toast: "Let every man have his own doctor. This is mine." Similarly, the king may have befriended Thomas More; but when William Roper congratulated his father-in-law on the king's favor, More replied with a shrewd and prophetic assessment of Henry's priorities: "I have no cause to be proud thereof. For if my head would win him a castle in France . . . it would not fail to go."

The years 1520–1521 mark a watershed in Henry's reign because this period included the ultimate combination of chivalric playacting and politics: the Field of the Cloth of Gold and Henry's entry into the arena of religious polemic with the publication of his anti-Luther tract, *Assertio Septem Sacramentorum.* After 1521 the tone of his reign begins to darken, and marital/religious controversies dominate the rest of his rule.

A meeting between the French and English monarchs had been in the works since the peace of 1514. For a variety of reasons – including the death of the French king Louis XII and the ascension of his heir, François I – nothing much was done. The idea resurfaced in 1518 as part of a batch of treaties

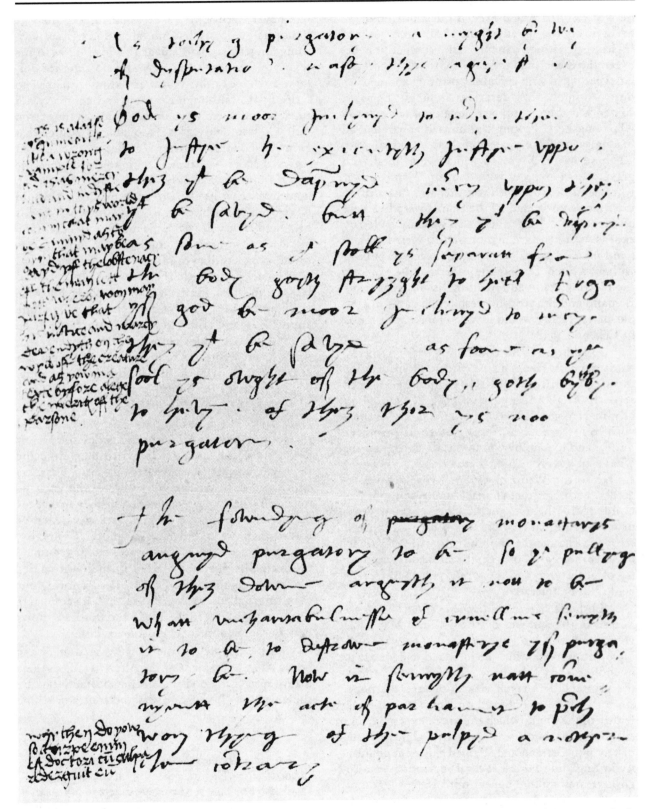

Page from a manuscript in which Hugh Latimer argues for the dissolution of the English monasteries, with Henry VIII's comments in the left margin (British Library, Cotton, Cleopatra, E V, fol. 142)

on a variety of Anglo-French questions, and the event finally transpired in June 1520: three weeks of feasting, jousting, dancing, and competition between the French and the English. It was a spectacular event, filled with chivalric posturing and marvelous costumes. Hall describes it in his *Chronicle:* "Then was there another company of ten lords in which maskery the king was himself apparelled all in long garments of estate all pale rich cloth of gold; all these had rich gowns which were lined with green taffeta and knit with points of Venice silver wherewith the rich cloth together was fastened on their face's visor, and all the beards were fine wire of ducket gold." The event also was horrendously expensive, a logistical nightmare that Henry's right-hand man, Cardinal Wolsey, managed to pull off without a hitch. Despite the effort and the expense, the meeting resolved few of the issues separating England and France; and despite the oaths to eternal amity, Henry would invade France twice more, in 1523 and 1543.

In addition to his consuming passion for chivalric pursuits, Henry also considered it his mission to safeguard the church. He invited Erasmus to settle in England in part because he wanted an ally in reform: "It has been and is my earnest wish to restore Christ's religion to its primitive purity, and to employ whatever talents and means I have in extinguishing heresy and giving free course to the Word of God . . . you and we together, with our joint counsels and resources, will build again the Gospel of Christ." Henry approved of humanist religious reform because it strove to change the church from within; Luther, on the other hand, overtly threatened the authority of both pope and monarch, and therefore he could not be tolerated.

Luther's *Babylonian Captivity of the Church* appeared in the summer of 1520, and in May 1521 Henry sent word to Pope Leo X that he was working on a response which he intended to dedicate to his holiness. By July the work was finished and at the printers. The result clearly pleased the pope, since that fall he conferred on Henry the title Defender of the Faith (which the king never gave up). Although the book was translated almost immediately into German and attained sufficient popularity in England to merit several reprintings, an English version did not appear until 1687, suggesting that Henry's intended audience was not the native English reader but the international diplomatic community.

Whether Henry VIII actually wrote the *Defense* or whether he merely assigned his name to it has never been entirely determined. On the one hand, he evidently had no talent for writing anything longer than half a page (his love notes to Boleyn are frequently shorter) and no time for sustained composition. Nor were kings expected to write books (although Erasmus and company did think it incumbent upon them to support those who did). Consequently, it is reasonable to assume that Henry used a ghostwriter – critics most often put forward More – or that a committee produced the work under his name. However, More always denied that he wrote the *Defense,* even when it would have been in his interest to claim the work for his own, and Henry did have the intellect and the training to come up with the arguments by himself. Furthermore, according to More's biographer Richard Marius, the Latin style is clearly not More's. In all likelihood, then, Henry wrote the book, but with considerable help from his more theologically astute councillors, including More. Perhaps he laid the groundwork, told his councillors the general outline – even wrote short drafts of the chapters – and then they filled in the details, which were subject to the king's revisions.

The *Defense* has nine chapters. The first defends the pope's authority to grant indulgences, and the second defends his authority generally. Henry devotes the remaining chapters to defending the seven sacraments (the eucharist, baptism, penance, confirmation, marriage, holy orders, and extreme unction). Theological disputation usually makes for dull reading, and the *Defense* fares no better or worse than most other such tomes. Generally, Henry employs the following pattern of argumentation: he begins by isolating Luther's novelties and proceeds to refute them by first pointing out their internal contradictions; second, he compares Luther's assertions to the Bible; and third, he shows how Luther contradicts Christian tradition.

For example, in the longest section of the book, "The Sacrament of the Altar," Henry begins his defense of the doctrine of transubstantiation by showing "how Luther staggers and contradicts himself":

"For," he says, "the sin consists in the priests taking the liberty of one kind from the laity." If anybody should ask him here how he knows that custom to have been practiced against the people's will, I believe, he cannot tell it. Why then does he condemn the whole clergy for having taken the laity's right from them by force, seeing he cannot by any testimony prove that this was forcibly done?

Henry VIII (portrait by Hans Holbein; National Gallery, Rome)

In the next section Henry rebuts his antagonist's arguments over what exactly Christ meant when he said *Hic est sanguis meus* (the pronoun *hic* is the wrong gender) by making the humanistically informed point that deriving doctrine from Latin points of grammar, as Luther does, makes no sense, since the Latin is but a translation of the Greek, which in turn is a translation of the Hebrew. Finally, Henry relies on Christian tradition to prove Luther wrong: "the opinions of the holy fathers are against him, as also the canon of the Mass, with the custom of the Universal Church, confirmed by the use of so many ages, and the consent of so many people."

From 1521 onward Henry focused more and more of his attention upon the vexing issue of Queen Catherine's inability to produce a male heir. By the early 1520s their marriage had grown cold, partially because of Henry's amorous restlessness (the queen was in her forties, practically old age in

the sixteenth century, while Henry was still a virile young man), but also because of their inability to produce a living male child, which of course Henry blamed on Catherine. The queen had given birth to six children, all but one stillborn or dead within a short time; the only child to survive was a girl, Mary, who would later become Renaissance England's only Catholic queen. Over the years Henry discreetly had a variety of mistresses, including Boleyn's sister. In 1516 one Mistress Bessie Blount managed to produce a surviving male child, christened Henry Fitzroy. But even though illegitimacy did not carry the same stigma that it would later on in England's history, the clear preference was for the heir to be born to married parents.

It is important to remember that Henry was not driven to infidelity exclusively by lust (his weakness was more for food than for women), but by dynastic concerns. The Tudor claim to the throne was weak, powerful counterclaimants existed, and the civil strife of the previous century, collectively known as the War of the Roses, was fresh in everyone's mind. By 1522 Henry's attention was drawn to Anne Boleyn; but Anne – unlike Henry's other mistresses, including Anne's sister – for a while refused to sleep with Henry until he married her. This resistance, ambition, or moral fiber – whatever one chooses to call it – apparently only raised Anne in Henry's estimation. By 1527 the disintegration of Henry's marriage was common knowledge, and divorce was an open topic of conversation.

Henry put forward two arguments for divorce. First, he said that the original dispensation to marry his brother's widow was invalid from the start because of a technical irregularity in the bull itself. Second, he argued that his marriage could not be valid, since marrying his brother's widow contradicted two passages in Leviticus: "Thou shalt not uncover the nakedness of thy brother's wife: it is thy brother's nakedness" (18:16), and "if a man shall take his brother's wife, it is an unclean thing: he hath uncovered his brother's nakedness; they shall be childless" (20:21). Henry thus concluded that his dynastic problems resulted from a forbidden union, and the pope did not have the authority to override biblical injunctions. Therefore, to appease God, his conscience, and the state, he and Catherine had to part ways. The problem with the "Great Matter" of Henry's divorce is that Deuteronomy 25:5 contradicts Leviticus and makes levirate marriage an obligation: "If bretheren dwell together, and one of them die and have no child, the wife of the dead shall not marry without unto a stranger: her husband's brother shall go in unto her, and take her to him to wife, and perform the duty of an husband's brother unto her." For Henry to succeed, he had to resolve the contradiction in his favor, and his case was not a strong one. The established principle of biblical exegesis regulating such problems called for harmonizing the clashing passages, and so the bulk of canon law reconciled the two by saying that Leviticus did not apply if the brother had died leaving the widow childless, which of course describes Catherine's situation.

The weakness of Henry's case notwithstanding, matters probably would have gone smoothly had Pope Clement VII been cooperative; but he was in the power of Charles V, Holy Roman emperor, who was Catherine's nephew and did not sympathize with Henry. At first the king tried to prove his point by drafting a "galaxy of Greek and Hebrew scholars, Christian and Jew, of theologians and canonists, of religious houses and universities, first in England and then on the Continent," to provide evidence on his behalf, as biographer J. J. Scarisbrick puts it. For their part Charles and Catherine called upon another horde of scholars and humanists, including Bishop John Fisher and Vives, to prove their point. This exegetical war produced a mountain of polemical *libelli,* most of which remains unread today. Even Henry tried to add another book to the pile. In a note to Boleyn written in July 1528, he excuses his brevity because "my book maketh substantially for my matter, in writing whereof I have spent above four hours this day, which caused me now to write the shorter letter to you at this time, because of some pain in my head, wishing myself (specially an evening) in my sweetheart's arms, whose pretty ducks [breasts] I trust shortly to kiss." Henry's effort, however, assuming that he ever finished it, is lost. The legal battle continued. Clement artfully delayed, Henry grew increasingly frustrated, Boleyn grew increasingly demanding, Catherine's popularity among the populace continued to grow, and there was still no male heir to the throne.

In 1529 Henry's struggle with Rome over the divorce began to change course. Until then he had taken the position of a loyal son of the church appealing to Rome for justice, but in the fall of 1529 he began taking an anticlerical position. The late summer of 1530 marks the decisive moment, for then Henry announced that in addition to being king of England, he also claimed an imperial status that meant refusing to acknowledge his subservience to anyone on earth, including, if not especially, the pope. That year also marks the beginning of his attack on the clerical estate within his realm. In sum, Henry was not only asking the pope to dissolve his marriage to Catherine; he also threatened him with schism if the pope refused. Matters came to a head in January 1533, when Boleyn discovered that she was pregnant. Henry could no longer afford to dally, since gestating inside his mistress might be the male heir that he so desperately wanted. They were secretly married on 25 January, and on 7 September, Boleyn gave birth to a girl, who was named Elizabeth. Despite Henry's disappointment, the Reformation in England continued apace; and in 1534 Parliament passed the Act of Royal Supremacy, which established Henry as the unconditional head of the English church.

Ironically, by the time Henry could enjoy his marriage to Boleyn without impediment, the union had grown cold and he wanted out of it. He had the marriage annulled on the amazing ground that his earlier adultery with Anne's sister rendered the marriage void from the beginning. Anne was exe-

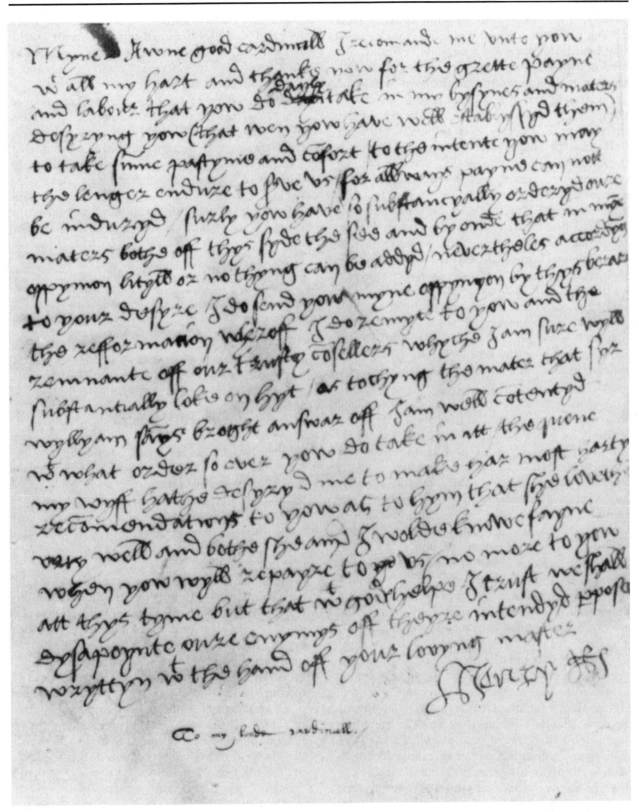

Letter from Henry VIII to Cardinal Thomas Wolsey, in which the king expresses his gratitude for Wolsey's devotion (British Library)

cuted in 1536 for treasonous adultery, which she probably did not commit; soon after Anne's execution he married his third wife, Jane Seymour. She died not long after giving birth to Henry's much-awaited male heir, the future Edward VI. Three years later, as part of an attempt to forge an alliance with the Protestant princes of Germany, Henry married Anne of Cleves, even though he knew her only through Hans Holbein's portrait. However, the king found her so unappealing that he could not consummate the marriage. It was annulled in 1540, and immediately thereafter he married his fifth wife, Catherine Howard, who was thirty years his junior. At first the union seemed to revivify Henry, but his new wife began committing adultery within a short time. Her infidelities were discovered, and Catherine, along with most of her lovers, was executed in 1542. In 1543 Henry married his sixth and final wife, Catherine Parr, who outlived her husband. Navigating the complicated shoals of Henry's marital history has been made easier through this rhyme describing the fate of his six wives: "Divorced, beheaded, died; divorced, beheaded, survived."

During the 1530s and 1540s Henry continued to patronize humanists; but in place of supporting learning for its own sake, he now hired writers for the specific purpose of supporting and defending the government. During the uprising known as the Pilgrimage of Grace (1536–1537), his chief minister and Wolsey's successor, Thomas Cromwell, employed Thomas Starkey and Richard Morison to write tracts against the rebels. Cromwell did most of the actual work of patronage, but Henry supervised his activities and had the final say on the content of these tracts. Furthermore, Henry's subjects had to be informed of the break with Rome and convinced that their king was right, which was no easy task. To that end he and Cromwell deployed a small army of propagandists drafted from the ranks of the humanists to write tracts against the evils of popery. Cromwell also turned to the popular drama as a medium for declaring the perfidy of Rome. Again, Henry's patronage was indirect, but there is no doubt that his ministers took their cue from their master and encouraged such playwrights as John Bale to produce anti-Rome propaganda. Although Henry left off writing poetry, he continued to use literary motifs for political purposes. The chivalric imagery of the first decade of his reign, however, was replaced by explicitly religious iconography. On the title page of the Great English Bible (1540), for example, Henry – not the pope – is shown as the supreme head of the church. The religious and the literary meld toward the end of his reign, when he was frequently depicted as the psalmist David. His personal investment in this role is suggested by an illustration in his personal psalter that places a harp in the king's hands.

Henry's interest and skill in theology also led him to oversee the drafting of an official statement of the new English church's doctrines, and he contributed a preface himself. Like his earlier *Assertio*, *The King's Book* (1543), as this work came to be known, was intended to combat heresy. But having split from Rome and allowed some reform into the church, Henry now found it difficult to control the spread of Protestantism, as seen in *A Necessary Doctrine*:

> Perceiving that in the time of knowledge the Devil . . . hath attempted to return again . . . into the house purged and cleansed . . . we find entered into some of our people's hearts an inclination to sinister understanding of Scripture, presumption, arrogancy, carnal liberty, and contention; we be therefore constrained, for the reformation of them in time and for avoiding of such diversity in opinions . . . to set forth with the advice of our clergy such a doctrine and declaration of the true knowledge of God and his word.

However, Henry's attempt at imposing religious conformity from above failed, as the shifts in emphasis and even allegiance throughout the Renaissance amply demonstrate.

From the 1530s onward the optimism of Henry's earlier years faded into a pervasive sense that he was a tyrant "more cruel than Nero," as one subject put it. Catherine of Aragon had been a popular queen, and Henry's subjects resented his treatment of her. The rest of his matrimonial affairs did little to endear him to his people. In addition, his heavy-handed enforcement of the Reformation also caused his popularity to drop precipitously. More's beheading in 1535 led to a great "murmuration" both at home and abroad, and less-celebrated executions also fueled the mounting discontent. The rise of court factions, the king's suspiciousness (if not paranoia), the uncertain succession, the fall of two princesses, Cromwell's judicial murder, and the rebellions and their brutal suppression – all contributed to Henry's malign reputation during the latter half of his reign. "If the king knew every man's thought," one subject was overheard to say, "it would make his heart quake."

The uncertainty and danger of life in Henry's court shaped the poetry produced by his literary courtiers, who made the unpredictable king their chief subject. Both Wyatt and Surrey, for example, used poetry to criticize the king and to talk about the corruption of the court. Sometimes the literary protest was done obliquely, as in Wyatt's highly charged sonnet "Whoso list to hunt," his paraphrases of the seven penitential psalms, and Surrey's biblical paraphrases. Occasionally, however, the criticism was overt, as in Wyatt's satires. One of the most interesting examples of how Henry dominated the literary imagination of his court is found in the Devonshire manuscript, a private commonplace book of verse that was owned by Mary Shelton. In this manuscript Shelton and her friends, including Wyatt, recorded their poems for their own pleasure; but the striking parallels between the verses and the lives of the many contributors suggest how Shelton and her collaborators, through their careful manipulation of courtly tropes, manage to transform erotic verse into a form of protest literature. Thus, even though Henry wrote no verse after the first decade of his reign, his malign presence significantly shaped the literary production of his court.

Even though Henry's actual literary output was quite slight, both in quantity and in quality, he had an incalculably huge influence on contemporary and future literary production. He was instrumental in the adoption of humanism in English intellectual life. He led the way in using the conventions of lyric poetry as a vehicle for talking about politics, a practice of which Wyatt and Surrey would take full advantage in their own works. He also presided over the appropriation of seemingly innocent entertainments for the purposes of consolidating royal power and disseminating the ideology of the court, a device that later monarchs would also use for their own ends. Finally, his contribution to Reformation literature, scanty though it may be in its own right, began a veritable avalanche of polemical books, poems, pamphlets, and plays. He instigated another eruption of prose when his divorce and break with Rome gave rise to two pamphlet wars: one on the king's "Great Matter," the second on the question of royal supremacy. Indeed, even though his works account for barely one short volume, King Henry VIII accurately may be called the presiding genius of early Tudor literature.

Letters:

The Letters of King Henry VIII, edited by Muriel St. Clare Byrne (London: Cassell, 1936);

The Love Letters of Henry VIII, edited by Jasper Ridley (London: Cassell, 1988).

Title page for a 1521 manuscript of Henry VIII's tract against Martin Luther (Biblioteca Apostolica Vaticana, MS. Vat. Lat. 3731)

Biographies:

A. F. Pollard, *Henry VIII* (London: Longman, 1905; reprinted, 1951);

J. J. Scarisbrick, *Henry VIII* (Berkeley: University of California Press, 1968);

Lacey Baldwin Smith, *Henry VIII: The Mask of Royalty* (London: Cape, 1971);

Carolly Erickson, *Great Harry* (New York: Summit, 1980);

Jasper Ridley, *Henry VIII* (New York: Viking, 1985).

References:

Sydney Anglo, *Spectacle, Pageantry, and Early Tudor Policy* (Oxford: Clarendon, 1969);

Baldassare Castiglione, *The Book of the Courtier*, translated by Charles Singleton (Garden City, N.Y.: Anchor, 1959);

Maria Dowling, *Humanism in the Age of Henry VIII* (London: Croom Helm, 1986);

Desiderius Erasmus, *The Correspondence of Erasmus: Letters 842–992, 1518–1519,* translated by R. A. B. Mynors and D. F. S. Thomson, annotated by Peter G. Bieterholz, and *The Correspondence of Erasmus: Letters 1252 to 1355, 1522–1523,* translated by Mynors, annotated by James M. Estes, in the *Collected Works of Erasmus,* volumes 6 and 9 (Toronto: University of Toronto Press, 1982, 1989);

Alistair Fox, *Politics and Literature in the Reigns of Henry VII and Henry VIII* (London: Blackwell, 1989);

Stephen J. Greenblatt, *Renaissance Self-Fashioning: From More to Shakespeare* (Chicago: University of Chicago Press, 1980);

Alexandra Halasz, "Wyatt's David," *Texas Studies in Language and Literature,* 30, no. 3 (1988): 320–344;

Edward Hall, *The Union of the Two Noble and Illustrate Families of Lancaster and York* (London: Richard Grafton, 1548); edited by Henry Ellis as *Hall's Chronicle* (London: J. Johnson, 1809; reprinted, New York: AMS, 1965);

Peter C. Herman, "Rethinking the Henrician Era," in *Rethinking the Henrician Era: Essays on Early Tudor Texts and Contexts,* edited by Herman (Champaign-Urbana: University of Illinois Press, forthcoming);

Skiles Howard, "Ascending the Riche Mount: Performing Hierarchy and Gender in the Henrician Masque," in *Rethinking the Henrician Era: Essays on Early Tudor Texts and Contexts,* edited by Herman (Champaign-Urbana: University of Illinois Press, forthcoming);

C. S. Lewis, *English Literature in the Sixteenth Century, Excluding Drama* (Oxford: Oxford University Press, 1954);

Richard Marius, *Thomas More* (New York: Vintage, 1985);

Sir Thomas More, *"The History of King Richard III" and Selections from the English and Latin Poems,* translated and edited by Richard S. Sylvester (New Haven & London: Yale University Press, 1976);

Richard Pace, *The Benefits of a Liberal Education,* translated and edited by Frank Manley and Richard Sylvester (New York: Ungar, 1967);

Paul G. Remley, "Mary Shelton and Her Tudor Literary Milieu," in *Rethinking the Henrician Era: Essays on Early Tudor Texts and Contexts,* edited by Herman (Champaign-Urbana: University of Illinois Press, forthcoming);

William Roper, *The Life of Sir Thomas More,* in *Two Early Tudor Lives,* edited by Richard S. Sylvester (New Haven: Yale University Press, 1962), pp. 197–254;

David Starkey, *The Reign of Henry VIII: Personalities and Politics* (London: George Philip, 1985).

Papers:

Henry VIII's letters to Anne Boleyn are in the Vatican Library. Both *Henry VIII's Manuscript* and *Ritson's Manuscript* are in the British Library along with another manuscript of Henrician music, the *Fairfax Manuscript.* Henry VIII's diplomatic correspondence, as well as many other documents relating to his reign, can be found in *Letters and Papers, Foreign and Domestic, of the Reign of Henry VIII, 1509–47,* 21 volumes, edited by J. S. Brewer, R. H. Brodie, and James Gairdner (London: Her Majesty's Stationery Office, 1862–1910).

Thomas Hoby

(1530 – 13 July 1566)

Kenneth R. Bartlett
Victoria College, University of Toronto

TRANSLATIONS: Martin Bucer, *The gratulation of the mooste famous clerke M. Martin Bucer vnto the churche of Englande* (London: Printed by Steven Mierdman for Richard Jugge, 1549);

Baldassare Castiglione, *The Covrtyer of Count Baldessar Castilio diuided into foure bookes* (London: William Seres, 1561).

Editions: *"The Book of the Courtier" of Count Baldassare Castiglione,* introduction by Sir Walter Ralegh (London: David Nutt, 1900);

The Travels and Life of Thomas Hoby, Knight, of Bisham Abbey, Written by Himself, 1547–1564, edited by E. Powell, Camden Miscellany 10, series 3, no. 4 (London: Camden Society, 1902);

The Book of the Courtier (London: Everyman's Library, 1928).

Thomas Hoby is today celebrated exclusively as a translator – a reputation, moreover, that rests upon a single work: his brilliant rendering into English of Baldassare Castiglione's *Il libro del Cortegiano* (1528), one of the most influential texts of the Renaissance. However, Hoby's genius as an author extended beyond his special gift for translation. He was also an important early travel writer whose journal (although not printed until this century) represents a significant insight into the growing mid-sixteenth-century English appreciation of Continental, especially Italian, models of culture. The journal also furnishes a reflection of a mind striving for self-knowledge and understanding, laying thereby the foundations of autobiography.

Hoby was the son of William Hoby of Leominster, Herefordshire, by his second wife, Katherine Forden Hoby. Thomas was thus the half brother of Sir Philip Hoby, a courtier, diplomat, and ambassador to the emperor Charles V. Thomas entered Saint John's College, Cambridge, where he matriculated in 1545. At Cambridge he came to know Sir John Cheke, the celebrated Greek scholar and Protestant, and Roger Ascham, who was to re-

mark on the young man's skill in languages in *The Schoolmaster* (1570).

Hoby did not take a degree but rather in 1547 set out for a lengthy tour of the Continent. This period of travel was, however, to be a formative part of his education. By October 1547 he was resident in Strasbourg in the house of the Reformer Martin Bucer, with whom he studied divinity. In addition, he followed the lectures of Peter Martyr Vermigli in theology, Johannes Sturm in litterae humaniores, and Paul Fagius in Hebrew. Hoby notes in his journal that in 1548 he made the acquaintance of William Thomas, author of *The History of Italy* (1549) and the *Italian Grammar* (1550), while Thomas was returning from Italy to England. Hoby also writes that Sir Thomas Wyatt the Elder passed through Strasbourg en route to Italy, perhaps stimulating Hoby's interest in Italian culture and literature.

It was at Bucer's residence that Hoby produced his first printed work, a translation of his host's contributions to the events of the English Reformation as well as Bucer's response to letters concerning clerical marriage written by Stephen Gardiner. *The Gratulation of the most Famous Clerk, Master Martin Bucer* (1549) was a youthful piece of translation, a linguistic exercise as much as a public statement of his Reformed confessional beliefs. Unlike his later translations from Italian, this early work is an English version of a Latin text for which there were many models to emulate and a continuous tradition to follow. Consequently, it is an unexceptional but clear and accurate reflection of Bucer's argument and their pedagogical relationship. Hoby sent the translation to Sir Philip (a courtier of Edward VI with a reputation for zeal in Reformed religion), who had the piece published in London.

Hoby left Strasbourg in August 1548 for Italy. Reaching Venice he stayed briefly in the house of Edmund Harvel, the English factor (unofficial ambassador) in the Venetian Republic, but soon departed for the great university of Padua, where he continued his studies, although in an informal way,

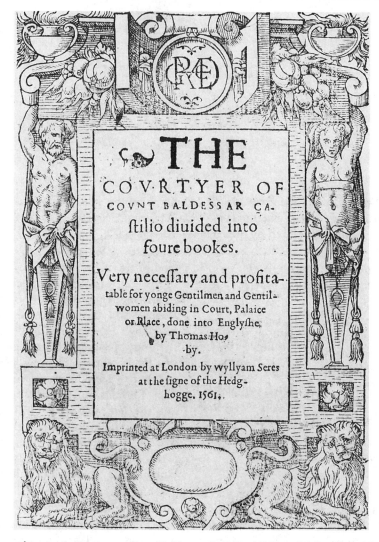

Title page for Hoby's translation of Baldassare Castiglione's Il libro del Cortegiano

since there is no evidence of his registration with the rector of the arts or law faculties. Hoby records that at Padua he attended the lectures of Lazaro Bonomico – a celebrated professor of humanities and successor to Niccolò Leonico – probably to perfect his Greek and Latin. He also spent some time in informal studies with the other luminaries of the university: Mantuanus (Marco Mantova) in civil law, Bernardino Tomitano in logic, and Claudio Tolomei in Italian. Indeed, one of the purposes of Hoby's residence in Padua was to polish his Italian, an accomplishment that was later to serve him in his translation of Castiglione's *Cortegiano*.

On 7 June 1549 Hoby left Padua for a grand tour of the peninsula. He visited Ferrara and Bologna before entering Florence and Siena. From Siena he rode with some fellow English travelers to Rome, where they explored the ancient and modern

monuments. In February 1550 he visited Naples, which he describes in great detail, especially the ancient monuments, Mount Vesuvius, and the countryside surrounding the city. That month he also went to Sicily – an extremely unusual voyage for an Englishman at the time and one that illustrates particularly well Hoby's contribution to travel literature. He records what he sees, hears, and knows. Ancient literature is placed in the context of modern history, geography, and even folklore: never is he judgmental or superior, regardless how fanciful the story he records. Unlike so many English Protestant travelers, Hoby wished to learn and understand the nature of the places and the cultures he encountered rather than compare them to some unexamined model of truth.

Hoby's trip to Sicily says much about him, then, as a traveler and a linguist. The reasons for his journey were to see the island and "to absent myself for a while out of Englishmen's company for the tongue's sake" – that is, to be forced to function in Italian (indeed, what must have often been local dialect) in an area that saw few English travelers. The journey itself was described at some length, including Messina; he remarks on the fountain there recently completed by the Florentine sculptor Giovanni Angelo Montorsoli, a pupil of Michelangelo. This is one of the few mid-sixteenth-century descriptions of Italian Renaissance sculpture by a foreign traveler and perhaps the inspiration for the fountain Hoby was to erect on his estate at Bisham in 1563. He seems, however, to have been less interested in the description of landscape, given that he remarks upon the ruins in Taormina but not the celebrated view. After a harrowing journey back across the straits of Messina, Hoby rejoined his English companions at Naples and returned with them to Rome on 30 April 1550, only to set out for Siena on 6 May.

This second sojourn in Siena was significant, since it probably saw the very beginning of Hoby's translation of Castiglione's *Cortegiano*. In his journal Hoby records that he reached the city on 9 May and "settled myself somewhat to my book" – certainly a reference to his work on *The Courtier*. It is important to note that in Siena he frequented the company of the small English community, including Henry Parker (quite probably the son of Henry Parker, Lord Morley, who had made the first translation of Petrarch's *Triumphs* into English and who recommended the works of Niccolò Machiavelli to Thomas Cromwell) and William Barker, the other great translator of Italian works during Hoby's generation. It is interesting to imagine these two Italianate Englishmen – Barker, the translator of Lodovico Domenichi and Giovanni Battista Gelli, and Hoby, the translator of Castiglione – discussing their shared enthusiasm for Italian culture and perhaps their principles of translation, despite their wide divergence in religion.

In Siena, Hoby received word from his brother, then ambassador to the emperor at Augsburg, that he was to leave Italy and join him at the imperial court. While attending on his brother in Augsburg, Hoby records that he completed another translation from the Italian, *The Tragedy of Free Will*, which he dedicated to William Parr, Marquis of Northampton. This Italian morality play by F. Negri Bassanese was printed in 1546 as *Tragedia di F.N.B. intitolata, Librio Arbitrio*. Unfortunately, Hoby's text does not survive, but it is interesting to note that the English translation printed circa 1589

as *A Certain Tragedy Written First in Italian by F.N.B. Entitled Freewill* was attributed to Henry Cheke, eldest son of Hoby's former teacher and friend Sir John Cheke. It might be suggested, therefore, that the version printed under Henry Cheke's name corresponded closely to Hoby's.

The Hobys returned to London in December 1550, and Thomas entered the service of the marquis of Northampton, serving on his mission to France and later at court. While in Northampton's service he also continued substantial work on his translation of the *Cortegiano* at the request of the Marchioness Elizabeth. He describes the inception of the project: "I returned again to London the 26 of April [1552], after I had been rid of mine ague, where I prepared myself to go into France and there to apply my book for a season. . . . After I had conveyed my stuff to Paris and settled myself there, the first thing I did was to translate into English the third book of the Courtisan [which discusses the ideal court lady], which my lady marquess had often willed me to do and for lack of time ever deferred it."

At the same time, Hoby notes that he sent another courtier, Sir Henry Sidney, an epitome of the Italian tongue "which I drew out there for him." The implication is that this was an original Italian grammar, perhaps a version of the *Italian Grammar* by his acquaintance William Thomas, or perhaps a completely new book. Again, there is no evidence that this work survives; nevertheless, it provides additional proof of Hoby's importance as a vehicle for spreading Italian Renaissance culture in England.

Hoby did not complete his translation of Castiglione at this time. He had to wait until another period of enforced leisure, after the death of Edward VI and the accession of Mary deprived Protestants of their places at court. On 21 May 1554 the Hobys left England for Italy to join the English exile community in Padua. It was probably in February 1555 that Hoby finished his *Book of the Courtier*, before his return to England in January 1556.

After his repatriation Hoby lived quietly on his brother's estate of Bisham Abbey, which he soon inherited. He also contracted a marriage with Elizabeth, one of the remarkable daughters of Sir Anthony Cooke. Despite the ascension of Queen Elizabeth in November 1558, he continued for a time to live in the country, often ill and perhaps polishing his translation of Castiglione, because on 5 November 1560 he traveled to London, staying twelve weeks, presumably to supervise the printing of *The Courtier of Count Baldessar Castilio* by William Seres, whose shop stood in Saint Paul's Churchyard. In

1561 the book was in print, complete not only with the full text of Castiglione's work but containing a letter from Sir John Cheke (since deceased), a sonnet by Thomas Sackville, and Hoby's own dedication to Henry, Lord Hastings, Earl of Huntingdon, whom he had met on his journey back to England and who was a descendant of the lord who had been host to Castiglione during his visit to England.

Hoby's version of the *Cortegiano* is one of the monuments of Tudor translation, not only for its style but also for its making available to his fellow countrymen one of the most influential texts of the Italian Renaissance. Hoby's journal reflects well his deep knowledge of and respect for Italian culture and his facility in the language that he both studied formally at Padua and polished through his travels in the peninsula. Moreover, he had already practiced the art of translation in his youthful rendering of the *Gratulation* and in his lost *Tragedy of Free Will.*

Hoby, it must be remembered, attended Saint John's, the Cambridge college of Cheke and Ascham, whose influence remained powerful. Indeed, it is probable that Cheke's views on the use of "pure" English greatly affected Hoby as he completed his translation in Padua in 1554–1555, accounting for the letter from Cheke praising Hoby's vocabulary that was appended to the first printing. This obsession with avoiding neologisms and "borrowings of other tongues" clearly made Hoby's work more difficult and, on many occasions, unclear or even incorrect in its rendering of the Italian. "Stoutness of courage" is a poor translation of *magnaminità,* as is "palmastrers" of *fisionomi.* Nevertheless, there is generally, with some exceptions, a kind of rigorous exactitude to the translation. Hoby follows the Italian with great care, converting each passage into his vigorous, solid English, according to the Italian original: he does in fact translate, not paraphrase, as in this sample from Bembo's celebrated speech on love in the fourth book:

> For since a kiss is a knitting together both of body and soul, it is to be feared, lest the sensual lover will be more inclined to the part of the body than of the soul: but the reasonable lover woteth well that although the mouth be parcel of the body, yet it is an issue for the words that be the interpreters of the soul, and for the inward breath, which is also called the soul.

There are naturally some errors – but relatively few, given the complexity of the original and the lack of a lengthy tradition of English translation from Italian to provide models. The book was an enormous success, identified as a milestone in the development of English courtly culture. The reign of Elizabeth saw four printings of the work (1561, 1577, 1588, and 1603); and even Ascham, who was not sympathetic to Italy, given the propensity to vice he claims to have seen in his nine days in Venice, recognized the significance of the translation.

Hoby's literary significance rests almost altogether on his translation of Castiglione. However, it is equally important that his journal be recognized for what it represents: one of the most important mid-sixteenth-century autobiographical travelogues in English. The single manuscript is altogether in Hoby's hand and is preserved in the British Library. Entitled by the author *A Book of the Travels and Life of Me, Thomas Hoby,* it begins in 1547 when Hoby was just seventeen years old and continues until 1564, two years before his death. However, the entries after 1555 are schematic at best, occasionally comprising only a few lines. The great part of the book, then, is the record of Hoby's travels on the Continent during the reigns of Edward VI and Mary.

It is as a travel journal that Hoby's book is most significant. It records almost every aspect of his journeys, not only the sights seen, monuments sought, people met, and adventures experienced, but also the folklore of the local inhabitants, exact distances between towns, literary (especially classical) allusions, historical – both ancient and contemporary – events, gossip, and topography, as well as many other things of interest to Hoby.

In addition to being a travel record, there are elements of the commonplace book about Hoby's journal. Like many humanistically educated young gentlemen, Hoby transcribed ancient inscriptions, quoted appropriate passages from classical authors, and sought monuments of the ancient world described in Latin literature. There are also descriptions of royal entries, lists of French princes and great nobles with their retinues, and short pieces on contemporary political situations and events, even if these are not directly relevant to his itinerary – for example, material relating to the execution of Lady Jane Grey. Significantly, similar texts of the last words of Lady Jane are also found in John Foxe's 1563 *Acts and Monuments* (begun in Basel), although with slight differences, indicating that Foxe and Hoby had access to the same information while abroad.

Besides elements of historical interest, Hoby includes in the journal extended descriptions of baths and their various medicinal properties. Furthermore, there are lengthy, largely classical, inscriptions copied into Hoby's journal, again linking him with Barker, whose *Epitaphia et inscriptiones lugubres* was first printed in 1554. Another significant feature of Hoby's journal is its reflection of the author's open, learned, and searching personality, evident from his youth. Hoby was curious about the world and wanted to experience it firsthand. He avoided the company of his fellow Englishmen in Sicily; he inquired into popular beliefs and practices, not to make superior judgments but to learn. Despite his rather advanced Protestantism, he is not overly critical of Roman Catholic and papal practices in Italy as he observed them. He exhibits a real knowledge of and interest in current political events and, more unusual, contemporary Renaissance culture, illustrated by his description of Montorsoli's fountain in Messina. It is appropriate, in fact, to propose Hoby as the prototype of the English grand tourist.

Hoby's preferment by Elizabeth was exceptional, not only because of his loyalty to the Crown but also because of his remarkable skill at languages and knowledge of foreign affairs. He was made a knight in 1566, the same year he was appointed ambassador to France. He died in Paris on 13 July 1566, almost immediately after assuming his post.

Lady Elizabeth Hoby, his widow, had an elegant monument with a Latin inscription raised to both Sir Thomas and Sir Philip at Bisham. Hoby had two sons, Edward and Thomas Posthumous, as well as two daughters, Anne and Elizabeth, who died young in 1571. Lady Hoby took as her second husband Lord John Russell, son of Francis Russell, second Earl of Bedford, who had himself been a traveler to Italy during Mary's reign.

References:

K. R. Bartlett, "The Courtyer of Count Baldassar Castilio: Italian Manners and the English Court in the Mid-Sixteenth Century," *Quaderni d'Italianistica,* 6 (1985): 249–258;

Bartlett, *The English in Italy, 1525–1558: A Study in Culture and Politics* (Geneva: Slatkine, 1991);

J. William Hebel and Hoyt H. Hudson, eds., *Tudor Poetry and Prose* (New York: Appleton-Century-Crofts, 1953), pp. 1307–1308;

Steven J. Masello, "Thomas Hoby: A Protestant Traveler to Circe's Court," *Cahiers elisabéthains: Etudes sur la Pré-Renaissance et la Renaissance Anglaises,* 27 (1985): 67–81;

Mary Augusta Scott, "The Book of the Courtyer," *PMLA,* 16 (1901): 475–502.

Papers:

A Book of the Travels and Life is in the British Library (Egerton MSS, 2148, fol. 5–182). Many letters, dispatches, and documents relating to Hoby's diplomatic service under Elizabeth are preserved in the State Papers, Public Records Office, London.

Richard Hooker
(April 1554 – 2 November 1600)

Lee W. Gibbs
Cleveland State University

BOOKS: *Of the lawes of ecclesiasticall politie. Eyght bookes* (London: Printed by John Windet, [1593]) – includes the preface and books 1-4;

Of the lawes of ecclesiasticall politie. The fift booke (London: Printed by John Windet, 1597);

The answere of Mr. Richard Hooker to a supplication preferred by W. Travers to the Privie Counsell, edited by Henry Jackson (Oxford: Printed by Joseph Barnes, sold by John Barnes, 1612);

A learned and comfortable sermon of the certaintie and perpetuitie of faith in the elect, edited by Jackson (Oxford: Printed by Joseph Barnes, sold by John Barnes, 1612);

A learned discourse of justification, edited by Jackson (Oxford: Printed by Joseph Barnes, sold by John Barnes, 1612; revised and enlarged edition, 1613);

A learned sermon of the nature of pride, edited by Jackson (Oxford: Printed by Joseph Barnes, sold by John Barnes, 1612);

A remedie against sorrow and feare, delivered in a funerall sermon, edited by Jackson (Oxford: Printed by Joseph Barnes, sold by John Barnes, 1612);

Two sermons upon part of S. Judes epistle, edited by Jackson (Oxford: Printed by Joseph Barnes, 1614);

Certayne divine tractates (London: Printed by William Stansby for Henry Fetherstone, 1618) – first collected edition of *Tractates,* published with the 1616–1617 reprint of Books 1-5 of *Of the lawes of ecclesiasticall politie;*

Of the Laws of Ecclesiastical Polity: The Sixth and Eighth Books . . . Now Published According to the Most Authentic Copies (London: Printed by Richard Bishop, sold by John Crook, 1648) – first edition of books 6 and 8, the latter incomplete [omits chapters 7 and 9].

Editions and Collections: *The Works of Mr. Richard Hooker . . . in Eight Books of Ecclesiastical Polity, Now Completed, as with the Sixth and Eighth, so with the Seventh . . . out of His Own Manuscripts, Never before Published,* 3 volumes, edited and prefaced with *The Life and Death of Mr. Richard*

Richard Hooker (from Michael Foss, Tudor Portraits: Success and Failure of an Age, *1973)*

Hooker [the first biography of Hooker] by John Gauden (London: Printed by J. Best for Andrew Crook, 1662) – includes the first edition of book 7; reprinted with Izaak Walton's *Life* [1665] substituted for Gauden's (London: Printed by Thomas Newcomb for Andrew Crook, 1666);

The Works of . . . Mr. Richard Hooker, with an Account of His Life and Death by Isaac Walton, 3 volumes, edited by John Keble (Oxford: Clarendon,

1836); revised by R. W. Church and F. Paget (Oxford: Clarendon, 1888; reprinted, New York: Burt Franklin, 1970);

Book I: Of the Laws of Ecclesiastical Polity, edited by R. W. Church (Oxford: Clarendon, 1866);

Confession and Absolution: Being the Sixth Book of the Laws of Ecclesiastical Polity by That Learned and Judicious Divine Mr. Richard Hooker, edited by John Harding (London: Charles Murray, 1901);

Of the Laws of Ecclesiastical Polity: The Fifth Book, edited by Ronald Bayne (London: Macmillan, 1902);

Of the Laws of Ecclesiastical Polity: Books 1–5, 2 volumes, edited by Bayne, with a revised introduction by Christopher Morris (London: Dent / New York: Dutton, 1907; revised edition, 1954);

Hooker's Ecclesiastical Polity: Book Eight, edited by Raymond Aaron Houk (New York: Columbia University Press, 1931);

Of the Lawes of Ecclesiasticall Politie: Books 1–5 (1594–1597) (Menston, U.K.: Scolar Press, 1969) — facsimile of the first editions of Books 1–5;

Two Sermons upon Part of Saint Jude's Epistles, facsimile edition (Amsterdam & New York: Da Capo, 1969);

Of the Laws of Ecclesiastical Polity: An Abridged Edition, edited by Arthur Stephen McGrade and Brian Vickers (London: Sidgwick & Jackson, 1975);

The Folger Library Edition of the Works of Richard Hooker, 6 volumes, edited by W. Speed Hill and others ([volumes 1–5] Cambridge, Mass. & London: The Belknap Press of Harvard University Press, 1977–1990; [volume 6] Binghamton, N.Y.: Medieval & Renaissance Texts & Studies, 1993) — volume 5 includes "Three Sermon Fragments on Matthew 27:46, Hebrews 2:14–15, and Proverbs 3:9–10;

Of the Laws of Ecclesiastical Polity: Preface, Book 1, Book 8, edited by Arthur Stephen McGrade (Cambridge & New York: Cambridge University Press, 1989).

OTHER: *A Sermon of Richard Hooker . . . Found in the Study of the Late Learned Bishop Andrewes,* appendix to *The Life of Dr. Sanderson, Late Bishop of Lincoln,* by Izaak Walton (London: Richard Marriott, 1678).

Richard Hooker was an Elizabethan of the greatest importance. He is remembered today almost exclusively for *Of the Laws of Ecclesiastical Polity: Eight Books* (1593–1662), his magnum opus. In the composition of this monumental treatise, primarily written to defend the Elizabethan church against the attacks of the English Presbyterians at the end of the sixteenth century, but always with careful secondary attention given to the refutation of what he and his Anglican contemporaries perceived to be the "errors" of the Church of Rome, Hooker decisively helped to shape that via-media way of thinking and making moral decisions that has so dominated Anglican thought and the Church of England from his own day forward. Hooker is also commemorated for the lofty grandeur of his Latinate, English prose style — a style that is now recognized to be inseparable from the method and content of his thought as a whole. Finally, because he so luminously exposited the Elizabethan worldview of a hierarchically ordered universe, and because he so elegantly set forth the ethical, political, and religious assumptions of his age, Hooker still engages the interest of scholars from many different disciplines. Theologians correlate his practical principle of "all things in measure, number, and weight" with his dynamic balancing of the respective authority of Scripture, tradition, and reason. Philosophers study him as the author of the first major treatise in English on political theory, noting particularly his teachings about "the nature and kinds of law" and the role of consensus in a constitutional monarchy. Intellectual historians place Hooker in the joint context of the Reformation and Renaissance humanism, and students of English literature compare the intricacies of his literary style with that of his contemporary, William Shakespeare, and that of his great Puritan successor in the following century, John Milton.

Richard Hooker was born in or near Exeter in Devonshire in April 1554. His family, although socially prominent in that locality, was of moderate financial means. Therefore, when the schoolmaster in the grammar school at Exeter recommended that the promising young scholar be further educated at one of the universities, he was introduced by an uncle, John Hooker, to John Jewel. Jewel, the bishop of Salisbury who had published in 1562 the first major defense of the Church of England against attacks made by supporters of the Church of Rome, became Hooker's patron.

With Jewel's support Hooker matriculated at Corpus Christi College, Oxford, probably in the fall of 1569. He received his B.A. in 1574 and his M.A. in 1577, whereupon he was appointed instructor in logic. He was ordained deacon on 14 August 1579. That same year he was made a full fellow of his college and appointed to deliver the annual Hebrew lecture, a task that he continued to fulfill until his departure from Oxford.

On 9 October 1580 Hooker was expelled from Oxford, along with three other fellows and his former tutor and lifelong friend, John Rainolds. The expulsion occurred because he and his friends had supported Rainolds's candidacy for the office of president of Christ College. All were restored on the following 4 November after Rainolds, who was known to have strong Calvinist-Presbyterian sympathies, had assumed the presidency. This incident may reflect not only Hooker's early friendship with Rainolds but perhaps also certain youthful tendencies toward Calvinist nonconformity.

During his tenure at Oxford, Hooker made two other very influential contacts that were to bear fruit in later friendship and joint cooperative efforts. He became the tutor of George Cranmer, who was a great-nephew of the martyred archbishop of Canterbury, and also of Edwin Sandys, whose father was the archbishop of York and Hooker's patron after the death of Bishop Jewel in 1571.

Hooker was ordained to the priesthood in 1581. Around the time he left Oxford, during the fall of 1584, he delivered a sermon at Paul's Cross, the preaching station outside of Saint Paul's Cathedral, London. This sermon has not survived, but later testimony affirms that some of the Puritan Reformers who heard it were offended because it attacked certain features of the Calvinist doctrine of predestination.

On 16 October 1584 Hooker was presented with the living of Drayton Beauchamp in Buckinghamshire, but there is no evidence that he ever took up residence there. Instead, upon leaving Oxford he moved into the household of John Churchman, a distinguished London merchant who would later be elected master of the Merchant Taylors' Company and city chamberlain. Hooker continued to reside with the Churchmans until 1595, during which time he was assisted in his literary efforts by Benjamin Pullen, a family servant who made fair copies of his manuscripts for the press. On 13 February 1588 he married John Churchman's daughter Joan, whose handsome dowry of seven hundred pounds provided financial security for her husband and their growing family.

On 17 March 1585 Queen Elizabeth I appointed Hooker as master of the Temple in London, one of the principal centers of legal studies in England. He had not been the first choice for the position. The favored candidate was Walter Travers, whose *Full and Plain Declaration of Ecclesiastical Discipline* (1574) was the leading exposition of the Presbyterian system of church government over the regime of bishops. At the time of Hooker's appointment, Travers was reader of the Temple and had the support of lawyers and the lord treasurer of England, William Cecil, Lord Burleigh. The archbishop of Canterbury, John Whitgift, preferred Nicholas Bond, an elderly chaplain to the queen, but was willing to accept Hooker as a compromise candidate.

Immediately after Hooker arrived at the Temple, a dispute broke out with Travers that prompted the new master to conceive the writing of a major treatise on the laws of ecclesiastical polity. Travers initiated the argument by openly advocating his Presbyterian principles, by encouraging Hooker to submit his royal appointment to congregational approval, by promoting liturgical changes supported by Nonconformists, and by proposing the conversion of traditional churchwardens and overseers into ruling lay elders and deacons. Hooker firmly rejected all such efforts to presbyterianize the Temple.

Travers countered by using the pulpit as a public platform from which to challenge the orthodoxy of Hooker's teachings. He would respond critically on Sunday afternoons to sermons that Hooker had delivered earlier the same mornings. The major doctrinal issues at stake between the antagonists included what Travers perceived to be Hooker's too lenient attitude toward the spiritual status and authority of the Church of Rome, a faulty understanding of the relation of the nature of God's grace to the divine will, and interpretations of the related doctrines of predestination, justification, and assurance that he considered to be at odds with the teachings of the "best" Church Fathers and Protestant Reformers.

The public controversy continued for almost a year until suddenly, in March 1586, Archbishop Whitgift silenced Travers. Travers appealed in a *Supplication* that he addressed to the queen's Privy Council. Hooker replied by writing an *Answer to the Supplication,* which he addressed to Whitgift. (Both of these were not published until 1612.) Although Travers's appeal fell on deaf ears, he stayed on for some time at the Temple, where his faction continued its harassment.

Hooker did not publish any of the sermons that he delivered at the Temple. Yet several have survived, primarily because after his death some of his friends were committed to preserving and publishing as many as they could find of his lesser works. *A Learned and Comfortable Sermon of the Certainty and Perpetuity of Faith in the Elect* (delivered 1585–1586; published 1612) is the earliest of the surviving sermons that provoked the controversy with Travers. Travers was put off by Hooker's teaching that "that which we see by the light of grace, though it be indeed more certain, yet is it not to us so evidently certain, as that which sense of the light of nature will not suffer a man to doubt of."

The tractate printed under the title *A Learned Discourse of Justification* (1612) actually comprises three sermons delivered at the Temple at different times during 1585–1586. These sermons adjudicate the agreements and disagreements between Rome and the Church of England on the crucial point of the necessity of good works as opposed to justification by faith. *A Learned Sermon of the Nature of Pride* also belongs to the series delivered during Hooker's first year at the Temple. The version first published in 1612 was only its first part; John Keble more than trebled its length in his 1836 edition by using the manuscript copy at Trinity College, Dublin.

All of the other five surviving sermons or sermon fragments that can be dated were written before the *Laws*. The *Two Sermons upon Part of Saint Jude's Epistle* (1614) are the earliest works that remain from Hooker's pen; their tone is strongly anti-Catholic and reflects the political climate of 1582 or 1583, when there was still good cause to fear the resurgence of Roman Catholicism in England. There is no way of discerning when *A Remedy against Sorrow and Fear* (1612) was delivered; all that is known is that it was given at the funeral of "a virtuous gentlewoman" with whom Hooker was acquainted.

A few remaining sermons or fragments have now been published that were not included in the collection published in 1618 under the title *Certain Divine Tractates*. In 1678 Izaak Walton first published *A Sermon of Richard Hooker Found in the Study of the Late Learned Bishop Andrewes* on Matthew 7:7. This sermon on petitionary prayer gives no hint as to when it was written or under what circumstances it was delivered. The same is true of the three sermon fragments (printed for the first time in *The Folger Library Edition of the Works of Richard Hooker,* volume 5 [1990]) on Matthew 27:46 (concerning "dereliction of probation and reprobation"), on Hebrews 2:14–15 (concerning the death of death by means of Christ's death and of the salvation that ensued), and on Proverbs 3:9–10 (concerning the nature of divine providence).

All of these early sermons and tractates are of singular importance, for they reveal that the most important characteristics of Hooker's later work in the *Laws* were already present by the time of the Temple controversy with Travers. These include his patient quest to base the exposition of complex issues upon their philosophical foundations or "first causes"; his confidence in the persuasive force of ra-

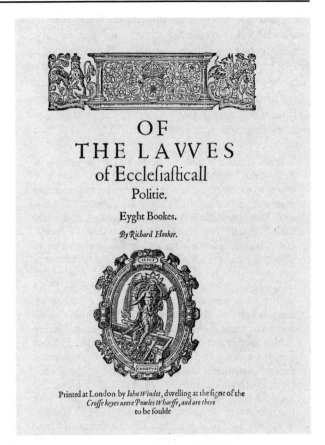

Title page for the first installment (1593) of Hooker's treatise on theology

tional inquiry and logical demonstration; his charity and forbearance; his wide reading; and his keen sense of tension between tradition and custom on the one hand, and the changes demanded by new historical circumstances on the other.

These sermons and tractates also demonstrate that Hooker had by 1585 already achieved the most distinctive contours of his literary style. He was most distinctively known and remains best remembered as a writer of copious sentences. Nevertheless, though less frequently noted, he also had a gift for the epigram, which he frequently employed to focus attention, to summarize a general truth, or to balance opposites: "We cannot examine the hearts of other men, we may our own" (*Two Sermons upon Part of Saint Jude's Epistle*), "Charity does always interpret doubtful things favorably" (*A Learned Discourse of Justification*); "Diseases that come of fullness, emptiness must remove" (*A Learned Sermon of the Nature of Pride*).

The following passage from *A Learned and Comfortable Sermon of the Certainty and Perpetuity of Faith in the Elect* reveals the most distinctive characteristics of Hooker's literary style, namely his use of rhetorical question; his grave and chastened Ciceronianism, marked by inversion of order and periodicity of structure but counterbalanced at times by an epigram; his mastery of the figures of thought and diction; his ordered and balanced grouping of forces about a central point of stability; and his slow but deliberate unfolding of an argument in such a way that its conclusion appears inexorable:

> Is it not thus? Yet if we could reckon up as many evident, clear, undoubted seals of God's reconciled love towards us as there are years, yea days, yea hours passed over our heads; all these set together have not such force to confirm our faith, as the loss, and some times the only fear of losing a little transitory goods, credit, honor, or favor of men, a small calamity, a matter of nothing to breed a conceit, and such a conceit as is not easily again removed, that we are clean crossed out of God's book, that he regards us not, that he looks upon others, but passes us like a stranger to whom we are not known. Then we think, looking upon others, and comparing them with ourselves: Their tables are richly furnished day by day, earth and ashes are our bread; they sing to the lute and they see their children dance before them, our hearts are as heavy in our bodies as lead, our sighs beat as thick as a swift pulse, our tears do wash the beds wherein we lie; the sun shines fair upon their foreheads, we are hanged up like bottles in the smoke, cast into corners like the sherds of a broken pot; tell not us of the promises of God's favor, tell such as do reap the fruit of them; they belong not to us, they are made to others. The Lord be merciful unto our weakness, but thus it is.

This style already clearly carries within itself the authority and intellectual tautness that were later to characterize his much longer treatise on ecclesiastical polity.

Although Hooker's great treatise on the *Laws* had its inception in the Temple controversy with Travers, his major opponent soon became Thomas Cartwright, former Lady Margaret professor of theology at Cambridge. Hooker left the Temple in 1591 with Archbishop Whitgift's blessing so that he might bring to a conclusion the case of the Church of England in a public debate that had broken out some years earlier between Cartwright and Whitgift.

The dispute had its beginning in 1572 with the anonymous publication of *Admonition to Parliament* — a Puritan manifesto that not only attacked all existing ecclesiastical and university dignitaries but also demanded a Presbyterian constitution for the English church. Whitgift had replied with his *Answer to the Admonition* (1572), to which Cartwright responded in *A Reply to an Answer Made of Master Doctor Whitgift* (1574). Whitgift's final contribution to the

debate was his mammoth *Defense of the Answer* (1574). Cartwright, however, had gone on to publish two further treatises: *The Second Reply against Master Whitgift's Answer* (1575) and *The Rest of the Second Reply of Thomas Cartwright against Master Doctor Whitgift's Second Answer* (1577), both of which had remained unanswered.

In 1591, in order to expedite Hooker's literary efforts, Whitgift presented him with the living as rector of Boscombe in Wiltshire; he also made him at this time subdean of Salisbury Cathedral and prebendary of Netheravon. There is no evidence that Hooker or his family ever lived at Boscombe, but records indicate that he did spend a prescribed amount of time each year at Salisbury, working at the cathedral library and conferring with the dean, John Bridges. Significantly, Bridges had by that time already published his own massive diatribe against the Puritans, the *Defense of the Government Established in the Church of England for Ecclesiastical Matters* (1587).

During the early years of writing the *Laws,* Hooker's primary residence remained the home of his father-in-law, John Churchman. Here he consulted frequently with his two former students, Sandys and Cranmer. Sandys was by then a lawyer, a member of the Inns of Court, and a member of the House of Commons. Cranmer had become a secretary, first to William Davidson, secretary of state, and later to Sir Henry Killigrew, an ambassador to France. Both Sandys and Cranmer read early drafts of the *Laws,* criticizing them and urging Hooker to deal less with general principles of philosophy and theology and more with a point-by-point refutation of the specific Puritan demands for reform. In response to their critique Hooker revised and expanded his initial drafts to address the Puritans and their arguments more directly.

The preface and first four books of the *Laws* were published in 1593. Hooker had not been able to find a printer who was willing to undertake such a large and financially risky publishing venture. Sandys, who was participating actively in the Parliament of 1593, wanted the first installment of the *Laws* published as support for his legislative efforts to have Puritans and other Protestant Nonconformists included under recusancy laws that had previously applied only to Roman Catholics. Sandys therefore volunteered to subsidize the printing of the first books of the *Laws,* but only after persuading Hooker to append in chapters 8 and 9 of the preface several last-minute additions that associate reforms demanded by the Elizabethan Puritans with the excesses of Thomas Münzer and certain other Continental Anabaptists.

The preface of the *Laws* is a historical account of the Genevan and English Reformed Movement; it assaults the spiritual credentials and socially subversive implications of sixteenth-century Presbyterianism. Book 1, on the other hand, is an intricate elaboration of the idea of law as the first principle of Hooker's philosophical theology. He intended that this survey of "laws and their several kinds in general" would rationally demonstrate that there are more norms or laws guiding individual and social behavior than those invoked by the zealous Reformers from their exclusivistic interpretation of the Bible.

Books 2–4 continue along the lines set out in book 1. In book 2, Hooker argues against the position that "Scripture is the only rule of all things which in this life may be done by men." In book 3 he proceeds against the assertion that "in Scripture there must be of necessity contained a form of church polity, the laws whereof may in no wise be altered." Having in books 2 and 3 rejected what he takes to be the major affirmative principles of the Reform movement, he argues in book 4 against what he regards to be the movement's chief negative principle, anti-Romanism. He asserts that conformity with Roman usage is insufficient reason for the English church to abandon otherwise wholesome devotional forms.

In 1595 Hooker was presented by the queen with the living at Bishopsbourne in Kent, where he moved from London with his family. While he was there, book 5 of the *Laws* was completed and published in 1597, again with Sandys's financial sponsorship, and with extensive revisions that nearly trebled the length of an earlier draft. Book 5 is a skillful defense against Puritan attacks upon the legally prescribed forms of public worship as set forth in the Elizabethan Book of Common Prayer (1559).

Book 5 was the last book of the *Laws* to be published during Hooker's lifetime. His response to an event that occurred shortly before his death reveals how anxious he remained during his final days concerning the unfinished and unpublished manuscripts still in his possession. According to Walton in *The Life of Mr. Richard Hooker* (1665), after being informed that his house had been robbed, Hooker immediately asked, "*Are my books and unwritten papers safe?* and being answered *that they were*; his reply was, *then it matters not, for no other loss can trouble me.*"

At the time of his death at Bishopsbourne on 2 November 1600, he was preparing a rebuttal to *A Christian Letter of Certain English Protestants* (1599), an anonymous Puritan treatise that had attacked him and all five books of the *Laws* then in print. Only fragments of his answer remain, including one that constitutes his most substantial treatment of grace

and predestination, along with his own copy of the tract heavily interspersed with autograph notes that provide a most intimate view of the man. He was also still at work revising and expanding earlier drafts of the last three books of the *Laws*. Books 6 and 8 were not published until 1648, and book 7 only in 1662.

There has been a problem concerning the authenticity of these posthumous books that has been bound up with fallacious rumors about Hooker's domestic life – rumors that have been in circulation since Walton's *Life of Mr. Richard Hooker*. In an appendix to the *Life* that deals with the *Laws*, Walton implies that Joan Hooker was largely responsible for the lengthy disappearance and supposed mutilation of Hooker's unpublished literary remains. He qualifies his statement that Hooker lived to finish the last three books by adding: "whether we have the last three as finished by himself, is a just and material question."

Then Walton tells a story that he claims was related to him some forty years past. He says that about a month after Hooker's death, Archbishop Whitgift sent one of his chaplains to Mrs. Hooker to inquire about the unpublished books, and that she either would not or could not give any account of them. Three months later Whitgift summoned her to London, where the day before she was to have been examined by some of the queen's Privy Council she told him at Lambeth that "one Mr. Charke and another minister that dwelled near Canterbury came to her, and desired that they might go into her husband's study and look upon some of his writings; and that there they two burned and tore many of them, assuring her that they were not fit to be seen." The next morning she was found dead in her lodging on King Street, Westminster. Walton, after observing that there appear to be both omissions and additions in the last three books, concludes his efforts to call into question the authenticity of the last three books by stating that King Charles I, who was a devoted reader of Hooker, doubted that they were Hooker's.

Twentieth-century scholarship has fully vindicated Hooker's widow from the charges of irresponsibility or collusion leading to the corruption of the texts or the delay in publication of the last three books. Perusal of parish records has established that Joan Hooker lived well beyond the time specified by Walton. These documents indicate that she was remarried at Bishopsbourne to Edward Neversole of Canterbury on 23 March 1601, some five months after Hooker's death, and that she was not buried at Saint Peter's in Canterbury until 18 February 1603.

A Christian Letter

8.

It feemeth to vs that naturall light, teaching morall virtues, teacheth thinges neceffarie to faluation, whiche yet is not perfect
without that which fupernaturall knowledge in holy Scripture
reveileth. Heere wee pray you to explane your owne meaning,
whether you thinke that there be anie naturall light, teaching
knowledge of things neceffarie to faluation, which knowledge
is not contayned in holy fcripture: if you thinke, no: How then
fay you before: Not the fcripture feverallie, but nature and fcripture iointlie, be compleate vnto euerlafting felicitie. If you fay
yea: how then agree you with the beleef of our Church: which
affirmeth, that holy fcripture contayneth all thinges neceffarie
to falvation ? And here we pray you to fhew vs, whether nature
teach anie thing touchinge Chrift, whether without or befide
him any thing be neceffarie: whether that in him
we be not [a] copleate. Laftlie, whether you meane   a Coloff.1.10.
that the knowledge of humane wifedome con-
cerning God, haue anie thinge not expreffed in
Scripture, or that morall virtues are any where
rightlie taught but in holy fcriptu. or that wher-
foeuer they be taught, they be of fuch neceffitie,
that the wante of them exclude from falvation,
and what fcripture approueth fuch a faying, or
that cafes and matters of falvation bee determi-
nable by any other lawe then of holy fcripture.
And then tell vs howe you vnderftande thefe
places following, and howe they agree with this
your pofition of the light of nature and morall
virtues : [b] *A man is iuftified by faith without the*   b Rom.3.27.
workes of the law. [c] *Neither is there falvation in*   c Act.4.12.
anie other. For there is no other name which is gi-
uen vnder heauen amongft men by which we muft
be faued. [d] *The naturall man perceaueth not the*   d 1 Cor.2.14.
thinges of the fpirit of God, for they are foolifhnes
vnto him.&c. [e] *Except a man be borne againe, hee*   e Ioh.3.3.
can not fee the kingdome of God.

4. Holy fcript-
ure aboue the
Church.

The Reverend Fathers of our church, to avouch
our forfaking of the Antichriftian finagogue of
Rome,

Page from A Christian Letter of Certain English Protestants *(1599), an anonymous Puritan attack on Hooker's* Of the Laws of
Ecclesiastical Polity. *Hooker made notes in the margins in preparation for a response, of which only fragments survive*
(Corpus Christi College, Oxford, MS 215b)

The most important evidence to appear on Joan Hooker's behalf was published in 1940, when C. J. Sisson made public the results of his research into the archives of the Court of Chancery. He discovered there records concerning a series of legal suits brought against various defendants, and especially Sandys, by guardians of Hooker's surviving children. The two sons born to the Hookers, Richard and Edwin, had died in infancy, so the suits were brought on behalf of his four daughters, Alice, Cecily, Jane, and Margaret. The substance of these charges concerned the deprivation of Hooker's daughters because of negligence on the part of his literary executors in publishing the three last books of the *Laws*. The depositions taken for the trials, which ran their course in Chancery between January 1610 and April 1624, undercut the veracity of many of the details and some of the most important overall impressions conveyed by Walton in his account of Hooker's life.

For instance, trial testimony establishes what did in fact happen to Hooker's unpublished manuscripts. In his will Hooker had nominated as overseers of his literary estate his father-in-law, John Churchman, and his friend and patron, Edwin Sandys. On 26 November 1600, a short time after Hooker's death, Churchman sent a servant to Bishopsbourne to collect all the manuscripts that could be found in Hooker's house. The servant put all the writings he could find into a "cloak bag" and then returned with them to London. Churchman subsequently called together several of Hooker's former friends and colleagues to examine the manuscripts that had been recovered, namely Sandys, Henry Parry (bishop of Worcester), and John Spenser (president of Corpus Christi College, Oxford). Lancelot Andrewes (bishop of Winchester) was later added to this group.

During the litigation hearings of 1613–1614, Spenser described in sworn testimony what was found in the cloak bag. Books 6 and 7 were among the manuscripts, "though not fully perfected." There were "diverse tracts and discourses scatterdly written but no coherent body" of book 8. There were also some sermons and the partly written answer to *A Christian Letter*.

These literary remains were later divided. Spenser was allotted the last three books of the *Laws,* Andrewes was given the sermons, and Parry received the rest of the fragments, with the understanding that each man was to make ready the material in his care for publication. Spenser testified under oath that he had "taken some pains in the fitting and perfecting of those three last books and

hath brought two of them, viz. the sixth and seventh, to some reasonable perfection though not yet thought fit for the press." These manuscripts that Spenser describes as having been made ready for the press immediately following Hooker's death are regarded by the editors of the Folger Library edition of Hooker's *Works* as essentially the surviving holographs that were used as copy texts.

Depositions from the Chancery Court also fix the blame for the delay in publication of the last three books squarely upon the literary coadjutors of Hooker's will. Spenser intimates in his testimony that publication of these books had been abandoned because a difference of opinion arose between Sandys and Andrewes over "the inserting of a tract of confession . . . into the said books." Sisson identifies that part of book 6 that has traditionally since 1648 been published as book 6 as the particular "tract of confession" that fell under dispute. Sandys, who had with Cranmer seen an earlier and now lost draft of book 6 that dealt specifically with the designated topic of refuting the Presbyterian office of ruling lay elders, was reluctant to see published as book 6 what appeared to be in large part a diatribe against the Roman church's teaching that private penance is a sacrament. The High Churchman Andrewes, on the other hand, favored Hooker's emphasis here on the pastoral and sacramental functions of the church. With the emergence of such doctrinal and ideological differences, the publication of the last three books foundered, and the literary executors of Hooker's estate eventually turned their attention to other concerns.

Any differences that might have arisen between Sandys and Andrewes over book 6 were greatly extenuated by the content of book 7, where Hooker argues for the authority of bishops on grounds of historical precedent and practical expediency rather than a divine-right theory of apostolic succession, and of book 8, where he argues for royal supremacy over church as well as state on grounds of consensus of the people rather than a divine-right theory of monarchy. Hooker's teaching in these last two books would not have been well received by Queen Elizabeth, and it would have been even less palatable to seventeenth-century supporters of emerging divine-right theories concerning the apostolic succession and the royal supremacy that were expounded in the royal theology of Stuart ideology and in the Caroline church of Archbishop William Laud and the Restoration.

The ironic conclusion to this whole matter concerning the authenticity of the last three books was anticipated by Samuel Taylor Coleridge in the nineteenth century. Previously, under Walton's influence it was thought that the finished manuscripts for books 6–8 were destroyed or so mutilated by Puritans that they could not be accepted as Hooker's own work. It now appears most likely, however, that High Churchmen espousing divine-right theories concerning the episcopacy and royal sovereignty disliked and feared what Hooker had written, and therefore deliberately ignored and successfully suppressed publication of the manuscripts for nearly fifty years after his death.

The eventual publication of books 6 and 8 in 1648 and book 7 in 1662 is thus now regarded as having occurred against the wishes of the hierarchy of the church. Book 8, on royal power and jurisdiction, supports a moderate constitutional view of monarchy restricted by the rule of law; it appeared just as the monarchy was falling. Book 7, which presents a moderate view of episcopacy, was published at the time when prelates of the Restoration were taking a more strident position.

When John Gauden, a strenuous advocate of the Restoration church, published the first complete edition of the *Laws* in 1662, he prefaced his edition by writing *The Life and Death of Mr. Richard Hooker*. This initial biography is marred by many historical inaccuracies, and it often tends to present Hooker the man in a rather unfavorable light. More important, however, Gauden endorsed the three posthumously published books of the *Laws* as "legitimate progeny," although, he continued, "they have not that last polish that their author is so customarily recognized for."

The posthumous publication of books 6–8 prompted a certain segment of the recently reestablished ecclesiastical hierarchy to discredit their authenticity. To accomplish this, Gilbert Sheldon, elevated to the throne of Canterbury in 1663, immediately commissioned Walton to write a new and officially authorized life that would not only correct Gauden's errors and other shortcomings but also discredit the genuineness of books 6, 7, and 8. Walton's *Life*, which prefaced all subsequent editions of the *Laws* through the end of the nineteenth century, has tended to prejudice readers' minds to resist doctrines set forth in the last three books by representing them not as the thought of the great apologist of the English church, but rather as the corruptions and interpolations of her enemies.

David Novarr has demonstrated how Walton fulfilled his official commission not only by perpetrating the story of Hooker's widow cooperating with Puritan conspirators who stole, burned, or interpolated the manuscript copies of the last three books (which, Walton claims, had been completed or "perfected"), but also by presenting a hagiographical picture of Hooker as a judicious, mild-mannered, brilliant person who yearned for domestic tranquillity but was vexed by a shrew of a wife. According to Walton, Joan Churchman was an ugly and ill-tempered woman who was forced upon the shy, shortsighted Hooker by her anxious, scheming mother.

Walton also speaks about the misery of Hooker's marriage, wherein the long-suffering scholar was plagued by a sharp-tongued wife who imprisoned her husband in a routine of menial, domestic chores. In one of the most memorable of these fanciful accounts, Walton relates how Hooker's former students, Sandys and Cranmer, once visited him at Drayton Beauchamp, where they found him reading the odes of Horace while tending sheep. In Walton's narrative they watch in dismay as Joan Hooker orders her husband away from their company to rock the baby's cradle. This story cannot be true, however, for Hooker never took up residence at Drayton Beauchamp, and he was not married at the time when he might have been there.

In short it is now recognized that Joan Churchman was not forced upon Hooker at all. The marriage was of great advantage to Hooker, providing him with financial stability and an entrance into a prosperous and influential London family. Further, he had no need to be occupied with household chores. In the first three years of the marriage, he was busy researching and writing the early books of the *Laws* while enjoying the benefits of a household replete with an efficient staff of servants.

Moreover, books 6–8 are now accepted as representing Hooker's own mind on the subjects with which they deal. A portion of book 6 attacking the Roman church's teaching that repentance is a private sacrament is extant, although an earlier and longer manuscript of it dealing more specifically with the delegated topic of Presbyterian lay elders was lost before 1600. This lost part of book 6 has been largely reconstructed on the basis of extensive notes written about it by Cranmer and Sandys between 1593 and 1596 (first discovered and published by Keble in 1836) and of other controversial writings by Hooker's contemporaries.

Hooker left book 7, on episcopacy, in near-readiness for the press. Book 8, on royal supremacy, survives in pieces, each coherent in itself but unfinished. It is, however, possible to put the pieces together and to reconstruct most of this last book. Today there is general scholarly consensus that readers now have most of Hooker's *Laws* as he conceived it from the beginning.

Of particular significance in confirming the authenticity of these last books and their consistency with what had been written before was the 1974 discovery at Trinity College, Dublin, of some fifteen folios of Hooker's working notes for books 6 and 8. These notes were printed for the first time in the Folger Library edition of Hooker's *Works* and should finally lay to rest any lingering suspicion that someone else wrote or substantially altered the posthumous books.

The story of the reception of the *Laws* and its influence on later thought has unfolded in a very significant, wavelike fashion, for this treatise has, more than most texts, been summoned to bolster a variety of diverse doctrinal postures. There was, to start with, an upsurge of interest in Hooker's *Laws* during the seventeenth century, as reflected by the several reprintings of his writings between 1611 and 1639. After the period of the Commonwealth, supporters of the Restoration extolled Hooker as the great defender of the established church and its Book of Common Prayer against all the charges aimed at both by Roman Catholics and Protestant Nonconformists. Yet Restoration Royalists found some of his ideas too radical for their tastes. Particularly suspect was book 8, which, read in conjunction with book 1, chapter 10, seemed to attribute the virtues of the English constitution to an initial communal decision to erect constitutional safeguards. Such teachings were incompatible with the desire of many Restoration leaders to elevate monarchy in terms of divine-right theory.

Restoration antipathy to Hooker's political doctrine was reinforced by its incorporation into a theory of parliamentary sovereignty, for his authority was also evoked by anti-Royalist propagandists of the Civil War to support the right of the community to protect itself during a constitutional emergency by acting through Parliament without assistance from the king. Such sentiments and arguments were still in vogue during and after the Restoration, when John Locke cited Hooker as an authority in his *Two Treatises on Government* (1689). In these essays, published anonymously to justify the Glorious Revolution of 1688, Locke deliberately exploits Hooker's reputation in order to support revolutionary arguments based upon philosophical grounds that were very different from those of Hooker himself — in Locke's case, a voluntarist conception of law concealed by repetitive appeals to reason.

For more than two centuries Hooker's political philosophy was largely interpreted through the distorting lens of Locke's *Second Treatise*. Whig historians in the eighteenth and nineteenth centuries perpetrated the Lockean interpretation, thereby creating the general impression that Hooker's views were, in all essentials, those of Locke, namely that he was an exponent of the social-contract theory of the origin of government, and that he advocated a theory of individual rights grounded in natural law. Some of the more radical Whigs inferred from this "ardent contractualism" that Hooker had licensed the deposition of arbitrary and tyrannical monarchs, either through resistance or by just war — a position that the more conservative Hooker certainly never advocated.

There was during the eighteenth century a lingering Tory suspicion of Hooker's political views that continued to express itself in repeated doubts concerning the authenticity of the posthumous books of the *Laws*. A more accurate and balanced interpretation was further hindered during the nineteenth century because of hagiographical distortions introduced by Anglicans writing from a High Church perspective. For example, as edited in 1836 by Keble, a leader of the Oxford movement, Hooker became the arch-defender of catholic Christianity against the menace of extreme Protestantism. Even secular historians of the nineteenth century continued to accept Walton's image of the "dove-like," "hen-pecked" Hooker, along with the accepted Anglican view of the noble, irenic hero whose mind transcended the bitter and ephemeral party conflicts of his own time.

The primary thrust of Hooker scholarship in the twentieth century has been to break away from the stereotypical thinking of earlier centuries. The traditional Whig interpretation of Hooker as a forerunner of Locke was in part corrected during the 1930s by the writings of Alessandro Passerin D'Entrèves. D'Entrèves emphasizes Hooker's indebtedness to Thomas Aquinas and medieval scholasticism, and he argues that it is anachronistic to interpret Hooker's commentary on consensus and natural law in terms of Locke and the seventeenth century.

Then the quality of Hooker's achievement as a theologian and political thinker was sharply called into question by three important studies. A short but provocative essay by H. F. Kearney (1952) not only argues that Hooker was "too much caught up in the ephemeral problem of his time to be considered great" but also that there was a fundamental inconsistency in his argument, arising from his failure to reconcile the dichotomy between a "rationalist" and a "voluntarist" conception of law. According to Kearney, Hooker begins by discussing law in terms of reason, as Aquinas does, but ends by virtually identifying it with the will of the Crown, as does Marsilius of Padua.

Manuscript pages for the beginning of Hooker's fragment on the sacraments and the beginning of his fragment on predestination (Trinity College, Dublin, MS 121, fols. 55ʳ and 57ʳ)

The tenth Article touching predestination.

57

To make up your first decade of Articles, you cast yourself headlong into a Gulfe of bottomless depth. Gods unsearchable power urgeth his eternall predestination and will moue as you pretend thereunto, by words of mine concerning in generall inclination in God towards all mens safetie, and yet an occasioned determination of the contrarie to some, meere everlasting perdition and woe, wherein how strange your proceedings are, I willingly forbeare to lay open before you, till it be first made manifest touching mans eternall condition of life and death not only that there is in the will of God that verie different which you in noe wise can digest: but further allsoe how the same distinction doth as a ground sustaine and passe as a strong principle throughout all the parts of that doctrine, which deliuereth rightly the predestination of Saints, whereinto because you compell mee, to enter I may not in a cause of soe great moment spare any requisite labour and paine: but Gods most gratious Spirit assisting mee, declare to the uttermost of my slender and poore skill what I thinck is true.

To beginne therefore with that groundation which must here be laid for as much as the nature of the matter in question is contingent, neyther can be understood as it ought unlesse, wee foreconceiue the difference betweene things contingent and such as come necessarilie to passe, lett it be first of all considered what the trueth is in this point.

Wee haue not for the course of this World any one more infallible rule, then that besides the highest cause wherein all dependeth, there are inferiour causes from which since the first creation all things (miraculous euents excepted) haue had their being. The nature of which inferiour causes is exprest in the nature of their effects, for if the cause be uniforme and constant in operation, the effects of that cause are founde allwayes like themselues, if it be variable they alter and change. And by this wee are ledd to distinguish things necessarie from contingent respecting howe diuersly they issue from their true immediate peculiar and proper causes. Of which causes wee haue perfect sensible experience, wee knowe and see in what sorte they worke, and wee are thereby out of doubt that all things come not necessarily to passe, but those effects are necessarie which can be noe other then they are, by reason that their next and neerest causes haue butt one only waye of working; from which as it is not in their power to varye, soe they are not subject to any impediment by opposition, nor unto change by addition of any thing which may befall them more at one tyme then at another, nor to defect by losing any such habilitie or complement as serueth to further them in that they doe. On the other side, those contingent which in regard of the verie principall inferiour causes whereupon they depend, are not allwayes certaine, in as much as the causes whereof they come, may diuers wayes varie in their operation. Things apt to suffer, are allwayes least certaine in that they doe. Againe whatsoeuer hath any thing contrarie unto itselfe, the same when it meeteth therewith is euermore subject to suffring, and soe in doing consequentlie hindered. For the more subject that causes are to impediment or lett the further their effects are of from the nature of things necessarie. And apparent it is, that some things doe bring forth perpetually the same effects, whereby it appeareth they are neuer hindered, some things the same effects commonly, yet not allwayes. Some things doe that att one tyme or other, which they neuer or verie seldome doe againe, some things all at all tymes, are equallie uncertaine what their issue or euent will be, till they come to passe. Els which varietie of contingents that which altereth not often differeth but little, from that which perilie cannot alter. The greatest part of things in this world, haue a mixture of causes necessarie and the contingent: soe that where both kindes concurre unto any one effect the effect doth followe the weaker side and is contingent: in as much as the nature of euerie effect is according to the nature of those causes totally presupposed which doe giue it being, and therefore if the causes be in part contingent, the effect through their uncertainty, is likewise made doubtfull. whereupon some considering how farre this made contingencie of cause reacheth, haue imagined all things in the world to be casuall. other on the contrarie part, because they did onelie see how inuariable and uniforme

Peter Munz reaches a similar conclusion in an independent study (1952). Munz also concludes that Hooker's argument was flawed because he was unable to reconcile his initial theory of church and state, based upon the principles of Aquinas, with the realities of the Tudor political situation. Therefore, Munz agrees with Kearney in holding that Hooker ended in self-contradiction as a disciple of Marsilius.

Gunnar Hillerdal (1962) makes a third major attack upon the logical consistency and overall coherence of Hooker's thought, arguing that he was not successful in reconciling his Aristotelian-Thomist concept of reason with his Protestant theology of grace and predestination. In fact, Hillerdal concludes, the *Laws* is constructed around two basically inconsistent conceptions of grace and reason.

These negative critiques of Hooker's thought are especially important, for they provoked a series of enlightened and persuasive essays by Arthur Stephen McGrade (1963, 1968, 1978), Egil Grislis (1964), and W. D. J. Cargill Thompson (1980). These three authors each convincingly argue on internal and external grounds that Hooker saw his treatise on the *Laws* as a coherent whole from the very beginning, and that there is in fact a basic consistency in the major phases of his argument that can be discerned throughout the *Laws* as a whole. McGrade in particular argues that in the first four books, published in 1593, Hooker is chiefly concerned with necessary or universally recognized philosophical and theological first principles, while the more specific topics dealt with in the last four books are dependent on the system of general principles developed in the earlier books.

Twentieth-century scholarship has also corrected the traditional interpretation of Hooker as a gentle, irenic person who transcended the brutal religious polemics of his day. He is now often presented as a deeply engaged controversialist who used every resource at his disposal to defend an existing power structure against the demand for revolutionary changes, whether those demands were made by Roman Catholics or Protestant Nonconformists. It is now readily admitted that Hooker took sides, that he was often unfair to his opponents, and that he was not beyond using smear tactics to undermine their credibility. Take, for example, the ad hominem argument that he makes against the Presbyterians' individualism and trust in private judgment when they refuse to obey laws made for the common good to which the whole society has consented: "Yea, I am persuaded, that of them with whom in this cause we strive, there are those whose betters among men would hardly be found, if they do not live among men, but in some wil-

derness by themselves." Even the elevated search in book 1 for first principles and final causes is now regarded as having a controversial point to make: the hierarchical universe so exquisitely depicted herein is now seen to reflect that Elizabethan love for order that made it dangerous to risk any social disruption which might be caused by disobedience or nonconformity.

Nevertheless, when Hooker's work is compared with that of his sixteenth-century contemporaries, the uniqueness of his breadth of vision and of his generally irenic tone continues to stand out. Even though the critic rightly perceives that his repetitive appeals to reason are themselves part of the style of a skilled rhetorician, the fact remains that Hooker chose this rhetorical persona far more frequently than any of his theological contemporaries. Moreover, he was indisputably master of vast intellectual resources in his attempt to place the most divisive issues of his day in a larger, less-divisive historical and doctrinal context. That which most distinguishes the style and content of Hooker's thought from those of his colleagues and adversaries is this repeated movement from the particular to the general, this instinctive effort to dig beneath particular controversial issues to their philosophical and theological roots and goals. Although this habit was frustrating to his opponents, and even to some of his friends, it was not one that he could break, for it was an inherent part of his personal identity.

It was Hooker's greatness to combine in coherent fashion this speculative breadth with partisan polemics. Admittedly, the fraternal tone in which he addresses his opponents is always at least in part rhetorical device, but it cannot be dismissed as mere pretense. By comparison with his contemporaries, both his language and the manner in which he conducts his argument are commendably temperate. He never descends to the sort of vituperation that disfigures so much sixteenth-century literature. He is at times irenic, at other times ironic, and sometimes sarcastic and angry. From his perspective the English law that he defends does not merely request, it demands obedience. He realizes, however, that in the final analysis the movement from "sound reason" to a "willing acceptance" of the ecclesiastical laws of the land is better grounded upon voluntary participation in a given communal order than upon coercion. Accordingly, Hooker's appeal is always at the end to a judgment of conscience.

Hooker did not write a Thomist *Summa Theologiae* or a Calvinist *Institutes of the Christian Religion*. By the standards of medieval scholasticism or systematic Reformation theology, his thought as explicated in the *Laws* often seems loose and undeveloped. For example, in spite of all of his emphasis upon "the law of reason" in book 1, one searches in vain for a full discussion of "conscience" in terms of the traditional scholastic notions of *suneidesis* or *synteresis.*

This lack of exhaustive explication and apparent lack of intellectual rigor are due in part, at least, to considerations of audience and purpose. Hooker wrote for readers ready to appreciate learning but not necessarily ready to follow sustained abstract argumentation. But the relative superficiality of the *Laws,* including the lofty search for first principles in book 1, is not merely a concession to the limitations of Hooker's readers; it is also warranted by his paramount aim in writing, which has both a negative and a positive dimension.

Hooker is not rendering a serene reflection upon a peaceful situation but is rather a man grappling with severe problems. He is refuting attacks made by powerful opponents, while at the same time seeking to interpret constructively an establishment that can by no means be taken for granted. For instance, in book 7, Hooker openly criticizes many abuses associated with the episcopacy and calls for their reform. To understand and appreciate the constructive aspects of his work, the severe difficulties inherent in the Anglican position must be recognized, along with his positive effort to overcome or correct them as part of his attempt to put down his enemies.

In the short run Hooker must be judged to have failed in his primary undertaking. By placing the defense of the established regulations of the English church in a broader normative context, he had hoped to win over the Reformers and their followers, not merely to refute them. But the relatively moderate Elizabethan Puritans, who were neither satisfied nor pacified, were only driven underground, soon to reappear and unite with even more radical Nonconformists in a bloody revolution that would displace the Book of Common Prayer and see the executions of an archbishop of Canterbury and a king of England.

Hooker must also be judged to have failed in persuading his immediate colleagues and successors to accept his views concerning the necessity of consensus and constitutional limitations of governmental power by the rule of law. When Richard Bancroft, William Laud, and their Restoration successors began to assert the apostolic succession of bishops, thus tending to place them altogether outside the realm of positive human law, their teaching was antithetical to Hooker's basic position. Hooker was equally unsuccessful in persuading Queen Elizabeth

and her Stuart successors about the need for curbing royal despotism by a legal constitutionalism that is reflected in the common-law tradition of England.

Hooker attempted to defend the liturgy and the polity of the Church of England in a way that did not fully satisfy partisans of the left or the right. He was a man little understood in his own time, whose successors used him to buttress theologies and political theories that were antithetical to his own. The record of this qualified acceptance and checkered response demonstrates how difficult it is to achieve and then to hold the delicate balance of Hooker's distinctive "Middle Way" of thinking, acting, and living in the world.

It is in no small measure this delicate balance and complexity of thought that have made Hooker since his death in November 1600 the most widely and consistently read of all theologians of the English church, for he more than any other set the general tone and stance of Anglican theology for his own and all subsequent centuries. Nevertheless, a new combination of circumstances, scholarship, and texts is now making a new approach to his works not only possible but necessary. For instance, a reexamination of his relation to the natural-law and social-contract theories of Locke is now in order, as is a comprehensive new study that evaluates how successful he was in reconciling his irenic appeal to reason and first principles on the one hand with his self-conscious intent to marshal all of his immense learning in the defense of a particular religious establishment on the other.

Some of the most troubling ambiguities that are resurfacing in the study of Hooker's life and work would undoubtedly be clarified by a fuller investigation of his training as a Renaissance humanist. His allegiance to the established church, for example, along with his conservative respect for tradition and disdain for "innovation" or "originality," is certainly related to the humanistic ideal of looking to the past as a guide to the present. And his reputation as a stylist needs to be reinterpreted in light of the humanist recovery and advocacy of that classical Ciceronian ideal of uniting wisdom and eloquence in service of the active life. Reemphasis upon Hooker's commitment to this ideal unity of substance and style should establish once and for all that his virtues as a stylist may no longer be isolated from, or regarded as irrelevant to his predominant roles as theologian, political theorist, and apologist for the English church.

Bibliographies:

W. Speed Hill, *Richard Hooker: A Descriptive Bibliography of the Early Editions, 1593–1724* (Cleveland

& London: Press of Case Western Reserve University, 1970);

Egil Grislis and Hill, eds., *Richard Hooker: A Selected Bibliography* (Pittsburgh: Clifford E. Barbour Library, Pittsburgh Theological Seminary, 1971);

P. G. Stanwood, "Richard Hooker," in *The New Cambridge Bibliography of English Literature,* volume 1, edited by George Watson (Cambridge: Cambridge University Press, 1974), cols. 1949–1958;

John Lawry, "A Working Bibliography of Studies of Richard Hooker," *English Renaissance Prose,* 4 (Fall 1990): 33–38.

Biographies:

C. J. Sisson, *The Judicious Marriage of Mr. Hooker and the Birth of "The Laws of Ecclesiastical Polity"* (Cambridge: Cambridge University Press, 1940);

Frederick E. Pamp, Jr., "Walton's Redaction of Hooker," *Church History,* 17 (1948): 95–116;

David Novarr, *The Making of Walton's "Lives"* (Ithaca, N.Y.: Cornell University Press, 1958), pp. 197–298;

John E. Booty, "The Quest for the Historical Hooker," *Churchman,* 80 (1966): 185–193.

References:

Christopher F. Allison, *The Rise of Moralism: The Proclamation of the Gospel from Hooker to Baxter* (New York: Seabury / London: S.P.C.K., 1966);

Rudolph P. Almasy, "The Purpose of Richard Hooker's Polemic," *Journal of the History of Ideas,* 39, no. 2 (1978): 251–270;

Almasy, "Richard Hooker's Address to the Presbyterians," *Anglican Theological Review,* 61, no. 4 (1979): 462–474;

Almasy, "Richard Hooker's Book VI: A Reconstruction," *Huntington Library Quarterly,* 42, no. 2 (1979): 117–139;

Stanley Archer, *Richard Hooker* (Boston: Twayne, 1983);

Richard Bauckham, "Hooker, Travers and the Church of Rome in the 1580s," *Journal of Ecclesiastical History,* 29, no. 1 (1978): 37–50;

John E. Booty, "Contrition in Anglican Spirituality: Hooker, Donne, and Herbert," in *Anglican Spirituality,* edited by William J. Wolf (Wilton, Conn.: Morehouse-Barlow, 1982), pp. 25–48;

Booty, "An Elizabethan Addresses Modern Anglicanism: Richard Hooker and Theological Issues at the End of the Twentieth Century," *Anglican Theological Review,* 71 (Winter 1989): 8–24;

Booty, "Hooker's Understanding of the Presence of Christ in the Eucharist," in *The Divine Drama in History and Liturgy: Essays Presented to Horton Davies on His Retirement from Princeton University,* Pittsburgh Theological Monographs, 10, edited by Booty (Allison Park, Pa.: Pickwick, 1984), pp. 131–148;

Booty, "The Judicious Mr. Hooker and Authority in the Elizabethan Church," in *Authority in the Anglican Communion,* edited by Stephen W. Sykes (Toronto: Anglican Book Center, 1987), pp. 94–115;

Booty, "Richard Hooker," in *The Spirit of Anglicanism: Hooker, Maurice, Temple,* edited by William J. Wolf (Wilton, Conn.: Morehouse-Barlow, 1979), pp. 1–45, 189–195;

Daniel C. Boughner, "Notes on Hooker's Prose," *Review of English Studies,* 15 (1939): 194–200;

Brendan Bradshaw, "Richard Hooker's Ecclesiastical Polity," *Journal of Ecclesiastical History,* 34, no. 3 (1983): 438–444;

George Bull, "What Did Locke Borrow from Hooker?," *Thought,* 7 (1932): 122–135;

W. D. J. Cargill Thompson, "The Philosopher of the 'Politic Society': Richard Hooker as Political Thinker," in *Studies in the Reformation,* edited by C. W. Dugmore (London: Athlone, 1980), pp. 131–191;

Samuel Taylor Coleridge, "Richard Hooker," in *Coleridge on the Seventeenth Century,* edited by Roberta Florence Brinkley (Durham, N.C.: Duke University Press, 1955), pp. 140–152;

William Covel, *A Just and Temperate Defense of the Five Books of Ecclesiastical Polity against an Uncharitable Letter of Certain English Protestants* (London: Printed by P. Short for Clement Knight, 1603);

Hardin Craig, "*Of the Laws of Ecclesiastical Polity* – First Form," *Journal of the History of Ideas,* 5 (January 1944): 91–104;

Richard A. Crofts, "The Defense of the Elizabethan Church: Jewel, Hooker, and James I," *Anglican Theological Review,* 54, no. 1 (1972): 21–30;

E. T. Davies, *The Political Ideas of Richard Hooker* (London: S.P.C.K., 1946);

Horton Davies, *Worship and Theology in England from Cranmer to Hooker, 1534–1603* (Princeton: Princeton University Press, 1970);

Dionisio De Lara, "Richard Hooker's Concept of Law," *Anglican Theological Review,* 44 (1952): 380–389;

Alessandro Passerin D'Entrèves, *Political Thought: Thomas Aquinas, Marsilius of Padua, Richard Hooker* (Oxford: Oxford University Press, 1939; reprinted, New York: Humanities Press, 1959);

Cletus F. Dirksen, *A Critical Analysis of Richard Hooker's Theory of the Relation of Church and State* (South Bend, Ind.: University of Notre Dame Press, 1947);

Edward Dowden, "Richard Hooker," in *Puritan and Anglican: Studies in Literature* (London: Kegan Paul, 1900; New York: Henry Holt, 1901), pp. 69–96;

C. W. Dugmore, *Eucharistic Doctrine in England from Hooker to Waterland* (London: S.P.C.K. / New York: Macmillan, 1942);

Robert Eccleshall, "Richard Hooker and the Peculiarities of the English: The Reception of the *Ecclesiastical Polity* in the Seventeenth and Eighteenth Centuries," *History of Political Thought*, 2, no. 1 (1981): 63–117;

Eccleshall, "Richard Hooker's Synthesis and the Problem of Allegiance," *Journal of the History of Ideas*, 37, no. 1 (1976): 111–124;

Robert K. Faulkner, "Reason and Revelation in Hooker's Ethics," *American Political Science Review*, 59, no. 3 (1965): 680–690;

Faulkner, *Richard Hooker and the Politics of a Christian England* (Berkeley: University of California Press, 1981);

Arthur B. Ferguson, "The Historical Perspective of Richard Hooker: A Renaissance Paradox," *Journal of Medieval and Renaissance Studies*, 3, no. 1 (1973): 17–49;

Albert W. Fields, "Emerson and Hooker: From the Footstool of God," *Xavier Review*, 7, no. 1 (1987): 11–20;

Paul E. Forte, "Richard Hooker's Theory of Law," *Journal of Medieval and Renaissance Studies*, 12 (Fall 1982): 135–141;

Lee W. Gibbs, "Richard Hooker," in *The Middle Way: Voices of Anglicanism* (Cincinnati: Foreward Movement Publications, 1991), pp. 11–28;

Gibbs, "Richard Hooker's *Via Media* Doctrine of Justification," *Harvard Theological Review*, 74, no. 2 (1981): 211–220;

Gibbs, "Richard Hooker's *Via Media* Doctrine of Repentance," *Harvard Theological Review*, 84, no. 2 (1991): 59–74;

Gibbs, "The Source of the Most Famous Quotation from Richard Hooker's *Laws*," *Sixteenth Century Journal*, 21, no. 1 (1990): 77–86;

Gibbs, "Theology, Logic, and Rhetoric in the Temple Controversy between Richard Hooker and Walter Travers," *Anglican Theological Review*, 65 (April 1983): 177–188;

Vivian H. H. Green, "Richard Hooker," in *From St. Augustine to William Temple: Eight Studies in Christian Leadership* (London: Latimer House, 1948), pp. 103–125;

Egil Grislis, "Richard Hooker's Image of Man," *Renaissance Papers 1963*, edited by S. K. Heninger, Jr. (The Southeastern Renaissance Conference, 1964), pp. 82–84;

Grislis, "Richard Hooker's Method of Theological Inquiry," *Anglican Theological Review*, 45 (1963): 190–203;

Grislis, "The Role of *Consensus* in Richard Hooker's Method of Theological Inquiry," in *The Heritage of Christian Thought: Essays in Honor of Robert Lowry Calhoun*, edited by Robert E. Cushman and Grislis (New York: Harper & Row, 1965), pp. 64–88;

Sarah Gustafson, "A Semiotic Inquiry: Exegesis by More, Tyndale, and Hooker," in *Semiotics 1989*, edited by John Deel (Lanham, Mass.: USA Press, 1990), pp. 68–76;

Anne D. Hall, "Richard Hooker and the Ceremonial Rhetoric of 'Silly Sooth'," *Prose Studies*, 11, no. 2 (1988): 25–36;

William P. Haugaard, "Richard Hooker: Evidences of an Ecumenical Vision from a Twentieth-Century Perspective," *Journal of Ecumenical Studies*, 24 (Summer 1987): 427–439;

Haugaard, "The Scriptural Hermeneutics of Richard Hooker," in *This Sacred History: Anglican Reflections for John Booty*, edited by Donald S. Armentrout (Cambridge, Mass.: Cowley Publications, 1990), pp. 161–174;

Haugaard, "Towards an Anglican Doctrine of Ministry: Richard Hooker and the Elizabethan Church," *Anglican and Episcopal History*, 56, no. 3 (1987): 265–284;

W. Speed Hill, "The Authority of Hooker's Style," *Studies in Philology*, 67 (July 1970): 328–338;

Hill, "Doctrine and Polity in Hooker's *Laws*," *English Literary Renaissance*, 2 (Spring 1972): 173–193;

Hill, "Hooker's *Polity*: The Problem of the Last Three Books," *Huntington Library Quarterly*, 34 (August 1971): 317–336;

Hill, ed., *Studies in Richard Hooker: Essays Preliminary to an Edition of His Works* (Cleveland & London: Press of Case Western Reserve University, 1972);

Gunnar Hillerdal, *Reason and Revelation in Richard Hooker* (Lund: C. W. K. Gleerup, 1962);

Philip Edgcumbe Hughes, *Faith and Works: Cranmer and Hooker* (Wilton, Conn.: Morehouse-Barlow, 1982);

S. R. Jackson, "Richard Hooker: An Approach to the Renaissance," *Manitoba Arts Review*, 2 (Spring 1940): 22–33;

H. F. Kearney, "Richard Hooker: A Reconstruction," *Cambridge Journal*, 5 (February 1952): 300–311;

W. J. Torrance Kirby, *Richard Hooker's Doctrine of the Royal Supremacy* (Leiden & New York: E. J. Brill, 1990);

Kirby, "*Supremem Caput*: Richard Hooker's Theology of Ecclesiastical Dominion," *Dionysius*, 12 (1988): 69–110;

Josef Koennen, *Die Busslehre Richard Hookers: Der Versuch einer anglikanischen Bussdisziplin* (Freiburg im Breisgau: Herder, 1940);

Peter Lake, "Richard Hooker," in *Anglicans and Puritans? Presbyterianism and English Conformist Thought from Whitgift to Hooker* (London: Unwin Hyman, 1988), pp. 145–238;

Olivier Loyer, *L'Anglicanisme de Richard Hooker*, 2 volumes (Lille: Université de Lille / Paris: Librairie Honore Champion, 1979);

Loyer, "Contrat Social et Consentement chez Richard Hooker," *Revue des Sciences Philosophiques et Théologiques*, 59 (July 1975): 369–398;

Loyer, "Hooker et la doctrine eucharistique de l'église anglicane," *Revue des Sciences Philosophiques et Théologiques*, 58, no. 2 (1974): 213–241;

John K. Luoma, "Restitution or Reformation? Cartwright and Hooker on the Elizabethan Church," *Historical Magazine of the Protestant Episcopal Church*, 46, no. 1 (1977): 85–106;

Luoma, "Who Owns the Fathers? Hooker and Cartwright on the Authority of the Primitive Church," *Sixteenth Century Journal*, 8, no. 3 (1977): 45–59;

Michael T. Malone, "The Doctrine of Predestination in the Thought of William Perkins and Richard Hooker," *Anglican Theological Review*, 52 (1970): 103–117;

John S. Marshall, *Hooker and the Anglican Tradition: An Historical and Theological Study of Hooker's Ecclesiastical Polity* (Sewanee, Tenn.: University Press at the University of the South, 1963);

Marshall, "Richard Hooker and the Origins of American Constitutionalism," in *Origins of the Natural Law Tradition*, edited by A. L. Harding (Dallas: Southern Methodist University Press, 1954), pp. 48–68;

Henry R. McAdoo, "Richard Hooker," in *The English Religious Tradition and the Genius of Anglicanism*, edited by Geoffrey Rowell (Oxford: Ikon, 1992), pp. 105–125;

Richard McCabe, "Richard Hooker's Polemic Rhetoric," *Long Room*, 37 (1986): 7–17;

Arthur Stephen McGrade, "The Coherence of Hooker's *Polity*: The Books on Power," *Journal of the History of Ideas*, 24 (April–June 1963): 163–182;

McGrade, "Constitutionalism Late Medieval and Modern – *Lex Facit Regem*: Hooker's Use of Bracton," in *Acta Conventus Neo-Latini Bononensis*, edited by McGrade and R. J. Schoeck (Bologna, 26 August to 1 September 1979), pp. 116–123;

McGrade, "The Public and the Religious in Hooker's *Polity*," *Church History*, 37 (December 1968): 404–422;

McGrade, "Repentance and Spiritual Power: Book VI of Richard Hooker's *Of the Laws of Ecclesiastical Polity*," *Journal of Ecclesiastical History*, 29, no. 2 (1978): 163–176;

John T. McNeill, "Richard Hooker: The Laws of Ecclesiastical Polity," in his *Books of Faith and Power* (New York: Harper, 1947), pp. 61–88;

Gottfried Michaelis, *Richard Hooker als politischer Denker: Ein Beitrag zur Geschichte der naturrechtlichen Staatstheorien in England im 16. und 17. Jahrhundert* (Berlin: Emil Ebering, 1933; reprinted, Vaduz: Kraus, 1965);

Marianne H. Micks, "Richard Hooker as Theologian," *Theology Today*, 36 (January 1980): 560–563;

Peter Milward, "Hooker and Bacon," *English Literature and Language*, 25 (1988): 3–17;

Angel Facio Moreno, "Dos notas en torno a la idea de derecho natural en Locke: Hooker en el segundo tratado de gobierno civil," *Revista de Estudios Politicos*, 190 (1960): 159–164;

Christopher Morris, *Political Thought in England: Tyndale to Hooker* (London: Oxford University Press, 1953);

Peter Munz, *The Place of Hooker in the History of Thought* (London: Routledge & Kegan Paul, 1952; reprinted, New York: Greenwood, 1970);

F. S. C. Northrup, "Richard Hooker and Aristotle," in *The Meeting of East and West: An Inquiry Concerning World Understanding* (New York: Macmillan, 1946; reprinted, New York: Collier, 1966), pp. 171–181;

Robert R. Orr, "Chillingworth versus Hooker: A Criticism of Natural Law Theory," *Journal of Religious History,* 2 (December 1962): 120-132;

J. R. Parris, "Hooker's Doctrine of the Eucharist," *Scottish Journal of Theology,* 16 (1963): 151-165;

Alfred Pollard, *Richard Hooker* (London: Longmans, Green, 1966);

Malcolm M. Ross, "Ruskin, Hooker, and 'The Christian Theoria,' " in *Essays in English Literature from the Renaissance to the Victorian Age* (Toronto: Toronto University Press, 1964), pp. 283-303;

Paolo Rossi, "Francis Bacon, Richard Hooker e le leggi della natura," *Rivista Critica di Storia della Filosofia,* 32 (1978): 72-77;

F. J. Shirley, *Richard Hooker and Contemporary Political Ideas* (London: S.P.C.K., 1949);

J. P. Sommerville, "Richard Hooker, Hadrian Saravia, and the Advent of the Divine Right of Kings," *History of Political Thought,* 4, no. 2 (1983): 229-246;

M. R. Sommerville, "Richard Hooker and His Contemporaries on Episcopacy: An Elizabethan Consensus," *Journal of Ecclesiastical History,* 35, no. 2 (1984): 177-187;

Vernon Staley, *Richard Hooker* (London: Masters, 1907);

P. G. Stanwood, "The Richard Hooker Documents," *Long Room,* 11 (Spring/Summer 1975): 7-10;

Stanwood, "Stobaeus and Classical Borrowing in the Renaissance, with Special Reference to Richard Hooker and Jeremy Taylor," *Neophilologus,* 59 (January 1975): 141-146;

Stanwood and Laetitia Yeandle, "Richard Hooker's Use of Thomas More," *Moreana,* 35 (1972): 5-16;

Stanwood and Yeandle, "Three Manuscript Sermon Fragments by Richard Hooker," *Manuscripta,* 21, no. 1 (1977): 33-37;

M. Stephanie Stueber, "The Balanced Diction of Hooker's *Polity*," *PMLA,* 71 (September 1956): 808-826;

Paul Surlis, "Natural Law in Richard Hooker (c. 1554-1600)," *Irish Theological Quarterly,* 35 (1968): 173-185;

Norman Sykes, "Richard Hooker," in *The Social and Political Ideas of Some Great Thinkers of the Sixteenth and Seventeenth Century,* edited by F. J. C. Hearnshaw (London: George C. Harrap,

1926; New York: Barnes & Noble, 1949), pp. 63-89;

Henry O. Taylor, "The Anglican *Via Media:* Richard Hooker," in *Thought and Expression in the Sixteenth Century,* volume 2 (New York: Macmillan, 1920; revised edition, New York: Frederick Ungar, 1959), pp. 159-182;

Elizabeth Tebeaux, "Donne and Hooker on the Nature of Man: The Diverging 'Middle Way,' " *Restoration Quarterly,* 24, no. 1 (1981): 29-44;

Elbert N. S. Thompson, "Richard Hooker among the Controversialists," in *Renaissance Studies in Honor of Hardin Craig,* edited by Baldwin Maxwell (Stanford: Stanford University Press, 1941), pp. 262-272;

Lionel S. Thornton, *Richard Hooker: A Study in His Theology* (London: S.P.C.K. / New York: Macmillan, 1924);

H. R. Trevor-Roper, "The Good and Great Works of Richard Hooker," *New York Review of Books,* 1 November 1977, pp. 48-55; republished as "Richard Hooker and the Church of England," in *Renaissance Essays* (Chicago: University of Chicago Press / London: Fontana, 1985), pp. 103-120;

John N. Wall, "Hooker's 'Faire Speech,' " in *This Sacred History: Anglican Reflections for John Booty,* pp. 125-143;

Basil Willey, "Humanism and Hooker," in *The English Moralists* (New York: Norton / London: Chatto & Windus, 1964), pp. 100-123;

Richard H. Wilmer, "Hooker on Authority," *Anglican Theological Review,* 33 (1951): 102-108;

Sheldon S. Wolin, "Richard Hooker and English Conservatism," *Western Political Quarterly,* 6 (1953): 28-47;

Yeandle and Stanwood, "An Autograph Manuscript by Richard Hooker," *Manuscripta,* 18, no. 1 (1974): 38-41;

Samuel A. Yoder, "*Dispositio* in Richard Hooker's 'Laws of Ecclesiastical Polity,' " *Quarterly Journal of Speech,* 27 (1941): 90-97.

Papers:
The major collections of Hooker's manuscripts and letters are in Trinity College, Dublin; Corpus Christi College, Oxford; the Bodleian Library, Oxford; and the Archepiscopal Library, Lambeth. There are also important holdings at the British Library, London; Gonnvile and Caius College, Cambridge; Dr. Williams's Library, London; and Queen's College, Oxford.

John Knox

(circa 1514 – 24 November 1572)

Peter Auksi
University of Western Ontario

BOOKS: *A confession & declaration of praiers vpon the death of king Edward the VI* (Rome [Wesel?], 1554);

A percel of the .vi./Psalme expounded (London?: John Day?, 1554); revised as *An exposition vpon the syxt psalme of David, wherein is declared hys crosse, complayntes and prayers* (Wesel?: Printed by Hugh Singleton?, 1556?); revised as *A fort for the afflicted* (London: Printed by Thomas Dawson, 1580);

An admonition or warning that the faithful Christians in London, Newcastel Barwycke & others, may auoide Gods vengeaunce (Wittenberg [London?]: N. Dorcaster [John Day?], 1554); republished as *A godly letter sent too the fayethfull in London, Newcastell, Barwyke, and to all other within the realme of Englande, that loue the comminge of oure Lorde Iesus* (Rome [Wesel?], 1554; revised, 1554);

A faythful admonition made by Iohn Knox, vnto the professours of Gods truthe in England (Emden: E. van der Erve, 1554);

A Vindication of the Doctrine That the Sacrifice of the Mass Is Idolatry (Wesel?: Printed by Hugh Singleton?, 1556);

A Letter of Wholesome Counsel Addressed to His Brethren in Scotland (Wesel?: Printed by H. Singleton?, 1556);

The copie of a letter, sent to the ladye Mary dowagire, regent of Scotland, in 1556. Here is also a sermon (Wesel?: Printed by Hugh Singleton?, 1556; revised, Geneva: J. Poullain & A. Reboul, 1558);

The first blast of the trumpet against the monstruous regiment of women, anonymous (Geneva: J. Poullain & A. Reboul, 1558);

The appellation of John Knoxe from the cruell sentence pronounced against him by the false bishoppes and clergie of Scotland, published with *Letter to the Commonalty of Scotland* (Geneva: J. Poullain & A. Reboul?, 1558);

The copie of an epistle sent vnto the inhabitants of Newcastle, & Barwike. In the end wherof is added a briefe exhortation to England (Geneva, 1559);

An answer to a great nomber of blasphemous cauillations (Geneva: J. Crespin, 1560);

The Book of Discipline (Edinburgh: Printed by John Scotte, 1561);

The coppie of the ressoning which was betuix the Abbote of Crosraguell and John Knox (Edinburgh: Printed by Robert Lekpreuik, 1563);

A sermon preached by Iohn Knox in the publique audience of the church of Edenbrough, the .19. of August .1565. For the which the said I. Knoxe was inhibite preaching for a season. To this is adioyned an exhortation for the reliefe of ministers (London: Printed by Henry Denham?, 1566);

To his louing brethren whome God ones gathered in the church of Edinburgh (Stirling: Printed by Robert Lekpreuik, 1571);

An answer to a letter of a Iesuit named Tyrie (Saint Andrews: Printed by Robert Lekpreuik, 1572);

The Troubles at Frankfort (Geneva?, 1575);

The first book of the history of the reformation of religion within the realm of Scotland (London: Printed by Thomas Vautrollier, 1587).

Editions and Collections: *The Works of John Knox,* 6 volumes, edited by David Laing (Edinburgh: Wodrow Society, 1846–1864; New York: AMS, 1966);

John Knox's Genevan Service Book, 1556, edited by William D. Maxwell (Edinburgh: Oliver & Boyd, 1931);

John Knox's "History of the Reformation in Scotland", 2 volumes, edited by William C. Dickinson (London: Thomas Nelson, 1950).

OTHER: Sir Henry Balnaves, *The confession of faith, conteining how the troubled man should seeke refuge at his God,* edited by Knox (Edinburgh: Printed by Thomas Vautrollier, 1949).

Even after four centuries, when lesser personalities and greater theologians have disappeared from accounts of the Reformation, the name and figure of the Scottish historian and religious orga-

John Knox (portrait by an unknown artist; National Portrait Gallery, London)

nizer John Knox have remained in the popular imagination. Schools, churches, and seminaries bearing his name — especially in countries where successive waves of Scottish immigrants have shaped religious institutions and cultural values — are testimonies to his forceful personality, and their power in celebrating an almost mythic name has been augmented by scholarly accounts of his reforming efforts on an international scale — in England, France, and chiefly Scotland. His infamous *First Blast of the Trumpet against the Monstrous Regiment of Women* (1558) has also guaranteed him a place in the vanguard of those prepared to be incautiously bold or imprudent on behalf of the Reformed religion in the sixteenth century. The subsequent anger of Elizabeth I no doubt magnified its object, who kept up a vituperative dialogue with another famous member of the "monstrous regiment," Mary, Queen of Scots. Contributing similarly to Knox's reputation are his moral austerity and his powers of "prophecy." His sermons against "vanities" such as

dancing and extravagant dress are always convenient targets for satirists of religious excess in any century, and his influence in creating a community in Edinburgh during the 1560s where moral transgressions were punishable by law under an austere code gives to him, no less than to John Calvin in Geneva, a certain notoriety in moral engineering. That he could also foresee or predict how his enemies would die — as many apocryphal anecdotes claim — adds a bizarre twist to his contemporary status as a messenger of God.

In physical person he was short, broad-shouldered, and vigorous; his hair was black, and he appears in his portraits with a long beard. Three portraits share a claim to his likeness, but the one appearing in Theodore Beza's *Icones* (1580) — sketches of the lives of the most influential Reformers — offers the greatest likelihood of verisimilitude; Beza's text offers as well some pertinent data for reconstructing the Scottish Reformer's life. To this as a source may be added Knox's letters (more than a

211

hundred survive; twenty-nine are to Mrs. Elizabeth Bowes) and his *History of the Reformation of Religion within the Realm of Scotland* (1587). The first edition was not published in Knox's lifetime; rather, it was published in London by certain Puritans, or published in part (the original text has only pages 17–560), and was said to have been stopped and suppressed by Archbishop John Whitgift's order. Much of a sense of Knox's life, in fact, comes from this *History*, which was completed in 1566. Curiously, the author refers to himself consistently as "John Knox," in the third person, though the book clearly casts a retrospective look back over his life. It is not a diary or confessional account, but there are many insights into, and comments about, the intersection of private life and public event. One may read the *History* for autobiographical details available nowhere else, remembering the selective nature of partisan memory and the tendency of hindsight to reconstruct complete or malicious motives where they did not exist originally. Because of its narrative flair, sense for human drama, and skillfully manipulative rhetoric, the *History* still merits belletristic attention.

Some accounts place Knox's birth in 1505, but the modern consensus appears to be for a date in 1513 or, more probably, in 1514. The hamlet of Giffordgate, next to the town of Haddington, is the most likely birthplace. Very little is known of the Reformer's family or parents. In his poem "A Brief Commendation of Uprightness" (1573), the poet John Davidson states that his friend and master "descended but of lineage small," an assertion that appears to argue for ancestry remote from gentility. Knox's father and merchant brother were both named William, and the mother's surname, Sinclair, was used by Knox as a pseudonym. Haddington Grammar School in all probability gave him his earliest formal education. Some biographers have written that he went to Glasgow University, but Beza states that he went to Saint Andrews University, probably around 1529, studying theology at Saint Salvator's College in 1531–1532. Having persuaded the university and King James V to give him a dispensation to be ordained a priest at age twenty-two instead of the canonical twenty-four, he underwent the ordination ceremony on 15 April 1536. Unable to procure a benefice he began acting, around 1540, as a "notary apostolic," or minor lawyer, near Haddington. In 1543–1544 he adopted the vocation of tutor, teaching Latin and theology to the sons of minor gentry in Samuelston and Longniddry.

Knox's spiritual evolution, however, had commenced fifteen or sixteen years earlier, when he had witnessed with outrage the burning of a so-called Protestant heretic, Patrick Hamilton, in February 1528. His conversion, effected silently, occurred in 1543, when he heard one Thomas Gwilliam, a former monk from Inverness, preaching Protestant doctrines. The popular effect of such preaching in a disaffected country was predictably unsettling, and in August 1543 crowds attacked friaries in Dundee, Angus, and Fife. The decisive figure in Knox's early religious evolution was George Wishart, a Scot who had recently returned from England and whom Knox met in Leith in December 1545. Wishart, "that blessed martyr of God" and "a man of such graces as before him were never heard within this realm," appears to have mesmerized Knox, who subsequently became a member of the armed bodyguard escorting Wishart on his proselytizing rounds. Wishart preached against ceremonies and the veneration of images and saints, influencing Knox as much by his invective style as his now unremarkable matter. In January 1546 Wishart was seized, tried as a heretic, and then strangled and burned. In his *History*, Knox writes passionately that "men of great birth avowed, that the blood of the said Master George should be revenged." The revenge was inflicted on the dominant governor of Scotland, Cardinal David Beaton, who was murdered on 29 May 1546. Knox describes this murder "merrily" in his *History*, ironically satirizing the bishops involved in the business of dealing with a corpse in hot weather. To him the murder was one of the "works of God" to be understood but not cosmetically disguised.

Knox's livelihood during these years of increasing turbulence depended upon the teaching of languages and divinity to genteel pupils, but he appears to have been of necessity an itinerant tutor, moving from the household of one Protestant lord to that of another simply to avoid arrest for associating with the heretical Wishart. A renewed drive from March 1547 on against suspected heretics doubtless drove him to consider the safety of exile in England or Germany, but his first recourse was to Saint Andrews Castle, to whose safekeeping he took his young pupils in April 1547. Here he was asked to preach in the castle's parish church; at first unwilling, he slowly accepted the task before the citizens of Saint Andrews who came to hear him. In June 1547 Henri II, the new king of France, sent twenty or more galleys to Scotland to lay siege to Saint Andrews Castle, which fell on 30 July. About one hundred captives, Knox among them, were put on prison ships for France; in mid August he was in Rouen with some expectation of freedom. In fact

Scottish nobles were imprisoned and the lowly made galley slaves – "miserably entreated," as he writes in his *History*.

Knox does not dwell on this dramatic episode, but his treatment and life were undoubtedly harsh: he was chained, the food was poor, the toil deadening, and corporal punishment conventional. In June 1548 he saw Scotland again from a French ship attacking the forces of Edward Seymour, Duke of Somerset; his health deteriorated seriously; and he spent a second winter in France as a galley slave. During this winter he summarized the Lutheran text of Sir Henry Balnaves, a fellow Scottish prisoner, on justification by faith; those two-dozen pages, first published in 1584, are his earliest surviving work.

In February or March 1549 the French and English exchanged some prisoners, Knox among them. In England he received a small reward for his suffering and stayed there for two years. In later years there are few references to the "torments of the galleys," as he termed them, but the experience probably strengthened his sense of deliverance from evil as one of the elect, now freed to do God's work.

In England, Knox was appointed a preacher at Berwick, a few miles south of Scotland. The position implies that he was given the status of some kind of English citizenship; certainly he learned to speak the English dialect of his chosen country and to write in English, not in Scottish. For four years he ably and prudently preached a religion whose prescribed forms in some measure did not match his own ideals. He instructed his congregation in Berwick, for example, to receive the Communion sitting, and not kneeling, as was the traditional practice of the Church of England. Radicals such as John Hooper had spoken for a similar act. Knox's sermons were partly against the doctrine of the real presence in the sacrament – though it is difficult to schematize his views on the sacrament – and partly against the Mass, which he ridiculed with great skill. In April 1550 Cuthbert Tunstall, the aged bishop of Durham, had Knox appear before him for these attacks on the Mass. Knox published his speech before Tunstall as *A Vindication of the Doctrine That the Sacrifice of the Mass Is Idolatry* (1556), but it is not a learned or scholarly text dependent upon patristic citations; characteristically, Knox is concerned more with use and misuse than with theory. His point to Tunstall was one of his central tenets: if not found in Scripture, all ceremonies are illegal. "The express Word of God" was for Knox, perhaps more than for any other Reformer in the first generation, the touchstone of true practice. In the sum-

mer of 1551 he also traveled regularly to Newcastle, about sixty miles from Berwick, where he preached to Scots in exile as an unofficial prophet of reform, to the consternation of his English hosts.

In the summer of 1552 Knox traveled south to London with the power broker John Dudley, Duke of Northumberland, who planned to use the preaching of the Scottish firebrand as a tool against the moderate archbishop Thomas Cranmer before the king at court. In August at Windsor and in October at Hampton Court, Knox did preach before Edward VI. In October 1552 he refused the bishopric of Rochester (which had been arranged by Northumberland) and returned to northern England, in good measure because he was unwilling to lose touch with his reform-minded compatriots and congregations.

During his stay in London, Knox left his mark on one liturgical action. The second edition of the Book of Common Prayer (1549), published in March 1552, had specified that believers should receive the Communion kneeling. Knox declared that this was idolatrous, as it signified, in effect, a belief in the real presence. The view of Knox and others was that the real presence was not in the bread and wine. The result was the "black rubric," a term applied to the loose sheets (probably drafted by Cranmer but popularly attributed to Knox) inserted into the Book of Common Prayer after its printing, specifying that the act of kneeling implied no adoration of the host.

Personal reasons also drew Knox once more to northern England. While in Berwick he had met Elizabeth Bowes and her daughter Marjory, who became his wife. The twenty-nine letters to Mrs. Bowes (and the one extant to Marjory) attest to an unusually warm and intimate relationship. Mrs. Bowes, in fact, lived with Knox and her daughter, and with Knox even after Marjory's death. Although Catholic foes made scurrilous fun of the domestic arrangement, Knox's letters to Mrs. Bowes show that he was her serious spiritual counselor, addressing her fears, errors, and hesitation with understanding and kindness. If it appears to be an unconventional kind of closeness, it is not without parallels in the letters of Calvin and Martin Luther. Certainly the relationship provided Knox with an occasion to unburden himself of his shortcomings. In a letter of 1553 to Mrs. Bowes, for example, he speaks frankly of "a spiritual pride which is not hastily suppressed in God's very elect children," adding, "I can write to you by my own experience." After her death he wrote in July 1572 that "she was to me and mine a mother," though the next few

Portrait of Knox from Theodore Beza's Icones *(1580)*

words – "yet it was not without some cross" – hint at the cost and burden of his ministrations to a demanding mother-in-law. The letter to Marjory is dated 1551–1552, at least before their betrothal. By 1553 Knox speaks of Marjory as his wife, though a formal marriage was not celebrated until 1555, when they were together in Scotland. Like William Shakespeare, Knox may have been joined to his spouse by a precontract, which had, before witnesses, the force of a civil marriage.

Flight to the north was not without its immediate political cause either. While Knox was in Buckinghamshire, Edward VI had died (6 July 1553); in August, Mary I was in London. To avoid the fate of his associates Hugh Latimer, Miles Coverdale, Hooper, and Cranmer, now in prison, Knox moved from place to place, writing a treatise on prayer, *A Confession and Declaration of Prayers upon the Death of King Edward the VI* (printed in July 1554). While hid-

ing in London he may also have written, for Mrs. Bowes, *An Exposition upon the Sixth Psalm* (1554) and started work on *An Admonition or Warning That the Faithful . . . May Avoid God's Vengeance* (1554), which was republished as *A Godly Letter Sent to the Faithful in London* (1554).

In many ways the *Godly Letter* succinctly represents Knox's gifts as a writer. Because he could not reach the people by preaching or conversation, he composed this consolatory epistle – increasingly a Reformation genre – filled with advice, warnings, and judgment. Although the *Letter* can be warm and personal when he addresses his "beloved brethren" in England or when he engages in the question-and-answer format of the classical rhetorician (*anthypophora,*) it is equally fierce and magisterial in using a mass of scriptural citations to illustrate how God can punish kingdoms and visit plagues upon them. Knox regards himself as a biblical prophet, forced –

like John Milton in the 1640s – to use his talents for the regeneration of a backsliding nation:

> For so zealous is God over his gifts that if we labor not to employ them to the glory of God and to the profit of the others his creatures, He will, according unto the threatening of Jesus Christ, take the talent from us and will give it to him that will labor thereupon.

Here the slight inversion ("zealous is God"), unobtrusive parallelism ("of God . . . of the others"), and the iambic and trochaic rhythms of the phrases – made possible, as in William Tyndale's translation of Scripture, by the strategically inserted monosyllables – raise the prose to the level of artistic composition. Knox is always artful in his appeals (note the force of "us" in his application of the parable), masterful with both affective pathos and the clear, ordered intelligibility of his argument, through which he wishes to alert and forearm the unwary mind. The "warning" was warranted by the imminent collapse of the Reformation in England and of Knox's hopes; in December 1553 the Mass was reintroduced by Parliament.

A month later Knox fled to Dieppe, where there was a colony of Scottish merchants, and then at the end of January 1554 moved on to Switzerland, meeting Calvin in Geneva and Heinrich Bullinger in Zurich. He had fled to the Continent without Marjory or her mother; Marjory's father, Richard Bowes, may well have refused to allow the precontract to be solemnified in marriage. Being without Marjory – "that which of earthly creatures is most dear unto me," as he describes her in a 1554 letter – Knox turned his thoughts to the condition of those who had not been able to escape, writing two letters from Dieppe, *An Epistle to His Afflicted Brethren in England* (10 May) and *A Comfortable Epistle Sent to the Afflicted Church of Christ* (31 May). These were followed in July by a second, revised version of his *Letter to the Faithful in London, Newcastle, and Berwick* and a soon-notorious tract, *A Faithful Admonition unto the Professors of God's Truth in England,* often referred to as his *Admonition to England.*

The *Admonition* startled and alarmed many, not only for its unprecedented invective against Mary as monarch, but also for its open suggestion that "Had [Mary] . . . been sent to hell before these days, then should not their iniquity and cruelty so manifestly have appeared to the world." The espousal in print of a prudent, preventive assassination shocked many. It was one implication of the larger theory that he was developing in the summer of 1554, namely, the justification of revolution, es-

pecially for the subjects of a Catholic governor, where only armed revolution could return religious reform. This doctrine alone would have earned Knox a place in the evolution of Renaissance political theory.

In November 1554 the Frankfurt émigrés invited Knox to be their pastor. On Calvin's urging, he agreed. Three months later he and four English colleagues produced an order of service that became, after 1560, the Book of Common Order of Scotland. Knox had always been able to accept the Church of England's Book of Common Prayer, except where kneeling for Communion and expressions of belief in the real presence were asserted, and the liturgical roots of this new "Order of Geneva" grew moderately out of conservative soil. Still, many of the English congregation were ultraconservative and liturgically faithful to the oldest rites of the Anglo-Catholic tradition. Their intrigues forced the Frankfurt authorities to ask Knox to leave in March 1555. In Geneva, where many eventually followed him, he wrote a cool account, *The Troubles at Frankfort* (1575), and again met Calvin, who wrote to the émigrés in Frankfurt on Knox's behalf. The reply was that he had uttered "atrocious and horrible calumnies against the Queen of England."

Knox's four months in Frankfurt were followed by four in Geneva, where the Calvinist doctrines and social experiment entered his daily life and imagination. The Genevan stay was, however, a short one, as he had by now decided to return to Scotland, where the new faith appeared to be tolerated tacitly. Equally important, perhaps, was the presence in Edinburgh of Marjory and Mrs. Bowes. After their flight from England, Knox joined them in September 1555 and formally married Marjory. The next few months were spent in organizing Protestant unrest and spreading regenerate doctrine. "Be assured," he wrote to Mrs. Bowes on 4 November 1555, "that God stirs up more friends than we be ware of." Knox's "Answers to Some Questions Concerning Baptism" was probably written during this period of his life; never published, it circulated among those families and houses that he visited in the spring of 1556, celebrating Communion. On 15 May he was summoned to Edinburgh to answer a charge of heresy. He had done his popular work well, however, and the danger of violence in the streets caused the charge to be withdrawn. Regardless, he characteristically came to preach.

In July 1556 Knox left Scotland and returned to Geneva, partly to find religious peace and partly out of a sense of obligation to his congregation of émigrés. Before he left, he drew up *A Letter of Wholesome Counsel Addressed to His Brethren in Scotland* (1556), a handbook outlining the need for certain spiritual exercises, such as daily reading of Scripture. From Dieppe he also sent to Scotland a few letters as "John Sinclair" – using his mother's surname – since the political climate, particularly in Edinburgh, where he had been burned in effigy as a heretic, was increasingly hostile. Having joined his growing English congregation in Geneva at summer's end, Knox found himself once again, in December, elected as their minister for the coming year. His first child, Nathaniel, was born during this period of relative calm, on 23 May 1557.

By the autumn of 1557, however, the fear of persecution for religious beliefs in Scotland had lessened substantially, and Knox remained for several months in Dieppe awaiting a clear invitation from sympathetic backers and patrons. The summer of 1557 had been eventful, as French Protestants had been attacked in Paris in August, and some were burned in the autumn. Still in Dieppe, Knox translated but never published a French account of those persecutions, "Apology for the Protestants Holden in Prison at Paris." And as a letter of his to the Scottish lords, dated 27 October 1557, makes clear, he was – perhaps in the light of the French violence – meditating on the duty of nobles to compel princes to undertake religious reformation. Their "office and duty," he writes, "is to vindicate and deliver . . . subjects and brethren from all violence and aggression." He then adds that "the reformation of religion and of public enormities doth appertain to more than to the clergy, or chief rulers called kings." Such activist counsel and the entire question of resistance to unjust or unregenerate authority startled many, including Calvin, from whom Knox took much of his inspiration on matters of social morality and ecclesiastical structure. Also in Dieppe he probably started composing his most notorious treatise, *The First Blast of the Trumpet against the Monstrous Regiment of Women.* It was against both the law of God and nature, argued Knox, for a woman to govern a kingdom – ostensibly Mary in England. Lacking a specific invitation from Scotland, he left Dieppe and returned to Geneva in February 1558. Here he produced six works in one year of creative energy.

Knox's *First Blast of the Trumpet,* published anonymously in Geneva in 1558, was an appeal to the English nation to overthrow Queen Mary violently. Here he regards England and Scotland as one Protestant state committed to one spiritual renewal. Where his earlier polemic had been proudly

personal, this fiery invective advances under the protective shield of anonymity, challenging the orthodoxy of Christian obedience and calling Mary a "wicked traitress" and "bastard." His letter of July 1558 to Mary of Lorraine, the queen regent of Scotland, clarifies the considered nature of his challenge: "Only they which to the death resist such wicked laws and decrees are acceptable to God, and faithful to their princes." In his subsequent *Appellation* (1558), Knox explains, in fact, that "it is . . . blasphemy to say that God hath commanded kings to be obeyed when they command impiety." The opposite is true: "God . . . hath approved, yea, and greatly rewarded such as have opposed themselves to their ungodly commandments and blind rage."

The First Blast proceeds out of this conviction. Many of its "proofs" are traditional and patristic (Tertullian, Saint Basil, Saint John Chrysostom); others are scriptural and represent Knox's reading of Old Testament history, where God's people are chastised for not resisting evil rulers violently. In July 1558 Knox addressed two revolutionary texts to Scotland, published together: one was *The Appellation of John Knox from the Cruel Sentence Pronounced against Him by the False Bishops and Clergy of Scotland;* the other was a more startling and populist *Letter to the Commonalty of Scotland.*

The First Blast was explosively unsettling, as Knox had probably gauged it would be. "My rude vehemency and inconsidered affirmations," he explained to John Foxe on 18 May 1558, "I do not excuse." Calvin, Beza, and the English émigrés in Europe maneuvered themselves cautiously away from Knox's subversive undermining of Christian Europe's social order, while England announced through a royal proclamation the penalty of death for anyone who did not burn heretical or treasonable books. Through a masterpiece of mistiming Knox had, of course, wounded not Mary but Elizabeth, whose weak position was now further weakened. Their subsequent relations confirm the monarch's unforgiving enmity toward the Scottish Reformer's dramatic imprudence. In exile Knox was out of touch with national affection for Elizabeth and probably ignorant of her carefully veiled Protestant sympathies.

Knox's second son, Eleazar, was christened on 29 November 1558 in Geneva; Coverdale was the godfather. Two other publications conclude Knox's second period on the Continent. *A Brief Exhortation to England for the Speedy Embracing of Christ's Gospel* (January 1559) chastises England for sinfully embracing the idolatry of Mary's reign. Knox's longest text, more than 160,000 words, was pub-

AN ADMONITION
or vvarning that the faithful
Chriſtiãs in London, Newcaſtel, Barwycke & others, may auoide Gods vengeaũce, both in thys life and in the life to come. Com= pyled by the Seruaunt of God John Knokes.

Crueltye   Trueth   Tyrannye

The Perſecuted ſpeaketh.

I fear not for death, nor paſſe not for bands:
Only in God put I my whole trust,
For God wil requyre my blod at your hands,
And this I know, that once dye I must:
Only for Christ, my lyfe if I gyue;
Death is no death, but a meane for to lyue.

Title page for Knox's 1554 consolatory epistle to the Protestant faithful in England, written while he was in exile on the Continent during the reign of the Catholic queen Mary I

lished in Geneva in 1560: *An Answer to a Great Number of Blasphemous Cavillations.* This elaborate production cites heavily from Calvin and Scripture, especially biblical exempla; but in language, technique, and thought it is relatively clear and simple. An Anabaptist adversary is quoted, and then Knox's "Answer" is given lucidly, often monosyllabically, and sometimes in homely fashion, as in this accessible and partly poetic exposition:

The will of God, plainly revealed in his Holy Scriptures, we do not only follow as a bright lantern shining before us, for the directing of our paths, walking in the darkness of this mortality, but also we affirm it to be of such sufficiency, that if an angel from the heaven, with wonders, signs, and miracles, would declare to us a will repugning to that which is already revealed, persuading us upon that to ground our faith, or by that to rule the

actions of our lives, we would hold him accursed and in no wise to be heard.

In this periodic thought there is no confusion: Knox always directs his sentences with rhetorical discipline and flair. Nor is he afraid to be creative with what one character "might have said" in all probability or in directing readers, through jabbing glosses, to note "the hypocrisy of the Anabaptists" or "the saying of a blasphemous mouth." Though the subject matter to Knox is, of course, the crucial part, technique here receives an attention that many have not noted fully in their eagerness to explain the Reformer's fears and larger agenda. Politically, predestination was a doctrine that could be used to battle those speaking for libertarianism and religious toleration, in which zealous sectarians saw a substantive threat. At the time of the composition of

An Answer to a Great Number of Blasphemous Cavillations, Knox had received a letter inviting him back to England. In January 1559 he left his wife and mother-in-law in Geneva and by February was once again in Dieppe, ministering to its Protestant émigrés. He did not, however, receive permission from an angry English monarch to travel through England to Scotland. "To me it is written," he complained, "that my *First Blast* hath blown from me all my friends in England."

Knox waited no longer for permission but sailed to Scotland, arriving on 2 May to a country in tumult. Citizens had attacked the friaries in Perth, but massive confrontations were avoided, partly because Knox had persuaded the nobles to support the popular revolt. Still, Protestant and Catholic forces were always in danger of a direct clash as monasteries came under attack. The Abbey of Scone and the bishop's palace, for example, were looted and burned to the ground. Though Knox had at times encouraged the destruction of the old priestly nesting places, even he was dismayed by that act of violence and condemned it. He doubtless recognized that the only way to a Protestant victory lay through negotiations with the English for military assistance, but permission to visit England would always be denied — as it was in 1559 — to a violent zealot. At Knox's urging, William Cecil, first Baron Burghley, had convinced Elizabeth of the wisdom of ridding Scotland of French troops, but negotiations over the amount and nature of aid to the Scottish Protestants were always circuitous and inconclusive. On 20 July 1559 Knox even wrote to Elizabeth directly, asking for assistance.

That summer the Edinburgh congregation elected Knox its minister; soon his wife and mother-in-law joined him from Geneva. Personal incidents, however, paled beside the adventure of secret travel and negotiations with England. In August 1559 France had sent more troops to Scotland, and Knox was convinced that unless the English were "more forward in this common action" they would "utterly discourage the hearts of all here." In November, French troops chased the Protestant forces out of Edinburgh; Knox rallied the dispirited Protestants, but few seemed committed to direct confrontation, especially since another contingent of French soldiers had arrived in December. In March 1560 about ten thousand English soldiers entered Scotland, and events grew well out of Knox's hands. His influence on the English leadership was minimal, and he used his enforced absence from public events and politics to pursue literary, liturgical, and doctrinal projects, chief among them his *History of*

the Reformation of Religion within the Realm of Scotland. With other church leaders he also composed for the Scottish church *The Book of Discipline* (1561), which deals with a host of crimes and punishments in a regenerate society.

By the terms of the Treaty of Edinburgh (6 July 1560), the French withdrew from Scotland, which now abolished papal authority and declared the Mass illegal. After Knox and others had presented a confession of faith to the Parliament — a confession clearly but not polemically Calvinist — Scotland officially became a Protestant country on 24 August 1560. In January 1561 *The Book of Discipline* was presented to Parliament; it divided Scotland into ten diocesan districts, allowed local congregations to elect their ministers, forbade Communion in private houses, and in educational matters was inventive and farsighted. Every child, for example, was to go to school, and even the university syllabus was revised to include modern physics and economics in the place of dated theology. Though universal education came to Scotland more than a century after Knox's death, he was a primary force in its inception.

At age forty-six Knox, as the minister of the congregation of Edinburgh, may well have anticipated a more settled life. However, a personal tragedy occurred in December 1560: Marjory died at age twenty-four or twenty-five, leaving him with two young sons, Nathaniel (age three) and Eleazar (age two). Mrs. Bowes eventually helped him to look after them, but a more critical historical event occurred on 19 August 1561: Mary, Queen of Scots, devoutly Catholic, arrived by sea from France. Knox gave a sermon denouncing her and met her in private interview on 4 September. "In communication with her," he subsequently wrote to Cecil in a letter of 7 October, "I espied such craft as I have not found in such age." The relations between them quickly went from bad to worse, as both sensed the paradoxical quandary: Mary was a Catholic queen in a Protestant country, favoring the disestablished church of her faith, which was unable publicly to celebrate its major rites, while Knox represented the Scottish Protestant church, which was influential in the population but deprived of property and income.

One of Knox's public disputations with Catholic defenders was published in 1563 as *The Reasoning Which was Between the Abbot of Crossraguell and John Knox.* During the first few years of Mary's reign, he functioned as a moralistic vigilante of her court, denouncing its frivolities, luxury, and excesses. A ball that she held in October 1562 at Holyroodhouse was in December denounced by his sermon against the vanities of dance. Aware of her enemy's power, Mary held many conferences — or rather clashes — with him. At one of these she burst into tears, and Knox recalls it in a dramatic reenactment:

> Madam, in God's presence I speak: I never delighted in the weeping of any of God's creatures; yea, I can scarcely well abide the tears of my own boys whom my own hand corrects, much less can I rejoice in your Majesty's weeping.

Rarely does he reveal so much of his own emotional life in commentary, but he was unremittingly caustic and unforgiving with a spiritual enemy. Between them there were constant arguments, problems, and tension, and Knox on several occasions found himself summoned before the queen and council.

On 25 March 1564, at age fifty, Knox married his second wife, Margaret Stewart, age seventeen and of noble blood. A more eventful wedding occurred in July 1565: Mary married Henry Stewart, Lord Darnley, to the consternation of the nation's Protestants, who now feared a consolidation of monarchic power. One manifestation of this renewed power was a prohibition of Knox's preaching whenever the regal pair was in Edinburgh. The Scottish Reformer characteristically replied, in a sermon on 19 August 1565, with the caustic observation that kings "have not an absolute power in their regiment what pleaseth them; but this power is limited by God's Word." A Protestant uprising against Mary in the same month came to nothing.

Anger, resistance, and conspiracies rose to a height in the winter of 1566; Knox must have been aware of the many, and sometimes unsavory, forms which that activity assumed. One troubling act occurred on 9 March, when a group of men violently entered Holyroodhouse and slew Mary's secretary, David Riccio, an Italian musician. Why this member of Mary's staff was murdered remains a mystery. That he was a papal agent or political power broker seems implausible. Perhaps the simplest answer involves the jealousy of Darnley, who was among the first to stab Riccio, but the political motives behind the slaying remain unclear.

In his *History,* Knox praises the murderers; he was possibly a party to the conspiracy, in whose planning his role remains problematic. He probably agreed to the crime in some form because its aftermath would loosely assist the Protestant cause, but the whole affair must constitute a moral nadir in Knox's career. Riccio's murderers fled or were per-

mitted to go into hiding. Knox himself moved to Ayrshire in the summer of 1566 to work quietly, or secretly, on his history of the Reformation in Scotland. Little is known of his whereabouts from December 1566 to June 1567: he may have returned to Edinburgh in the wake of Mary's pardon of the murderers, or he may have visited his sons, under the care of Mrs. Bowes in Northumberland. He may also have come into contact with English Puritans seeking his counsel and guidance, but Knox was invariably moderate and cautious with reform-minded zealots seeking his imprimatur.

Scottish events, in any case, were coming to a head. Three months after Darnley's own sensationalized murder, Mary married James Hepburn, fourth Earl of Bothwell, a Protestant and one of the alleged assassins of Darnley, and in June of the same year the Catholic nobility rose up in revolt against her. To them she surrendered. In June, Knox also returned to Saint Giles, preaching the new faith assertively and demanding Mary's death unequivocally. Following Mary's signing of a deed of abdication and imprisonment, James VI was crowned on 29 July 1567. At the coronation in Stirling, Knox preached the sermon.

The Scottish Parliament of December 1567 signaled the triumph of Knox and the renewed church. Of the ninety-two statutes enacted into law, nineteen dealt with religion and established solidly the Protestant religion as "the only true and holy Church." In 1568 Knox was fifty-four; he preached regularly in Saint Giles, still played a significant part in church affairs, and supervised unofficially the spiritual life of several dioceses, but his health was weakening. In 1570 he suffered an apparent stroke, losing the power of speech and then recovering it. He was able to preach, but less strenuously and frequently than before.

In April 1571 there was an assassination attempt against Knox. The shot fired through his residence window missed its intended target, but for reasons of safety Knox left Edinburgh for Fife and then, three months later, for Saint Andrews, where he stayed for more than a year, actively preaching, though now old and weak. In July 1572 he published his last pamphlet, *An Answer to a Letter of a Jesuit Named Tyrie,* which had been composed five or six years earlier. It not only attacked the universality of the Catholic church, but also satirized violently the lives of vice enjoyed by the popes. Later that summer Knox returned to Edinburgh, preaching almost inaudibly. When the Saint Bartholomew's Day Massacre took place on 24 August 1572 in Paris, Knox condemned the events, but

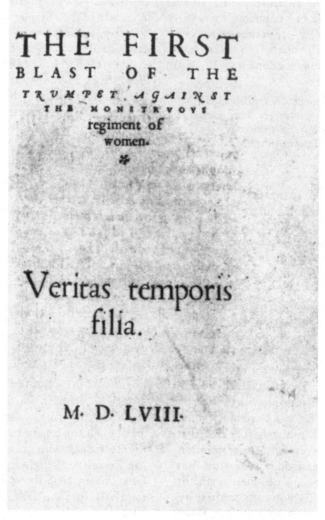

THE FIRST
BLAST OF THE
TRVMPET AGAINST
THE MONSTRVOVS
regiment of
women.
✻

Veritas temporis
filia.

M· D· LVIII·

*Title page for Knox's 1558 tract against Mary, Queen of Scots; her
mother, Marie de Guise; and Mary Tudor, all of whom opposed
the Reformation*

stronger voices were already being heard. Three months later, on 24 November, he died peacefully in his bed during the night, at age fifty-eight.

He left a wife who was twenty-five when he died and three young daughters, Martha, Margaret, and Elizabeth. The death of such a powerful religious force did not, strangely, redirect or clearly influence Scottish church history. In his last years Knox had not been influential in national politics, though replies to the *First Blast* were an almost annual event in the last half of the sixteenth century. And, as a form of church government, Presbyterianism did not really develop until some years after Knox's death. His liturgical influence was far more immediate and long-lasting, as the Scottish church service still uses the Order of Geneva and features a Communion that is received sitting. Above

all, Knox determined that the theology of Calvin, rather than the eclectic system of the Church of England, should replace the Church of Rome.

Knox was not an innovative theologian. Much of his polemic and preaching attacks the conventional topoi of the Reformation warrior. His claim that the Church of Rome is Antichrist and his diatribes against fasting laws, pilgrimages, clerical celibacy, and the Mass are echoed in many controversialists, as is his anger against tithes and his championing of the naked Scripture, a text to be read and discussed in every home. He shared Calvin's interest in predestination but also championed Luther's clear sense of man's justification by faith alone. He was opposed to private baptism (to save an unbaptized child) and held that the offspring of excommunicated persons should not receive baptism until the parents had repented, but such questions were not as central to the Reformation in the British Isles as in, for example, Switzerland. And even on the matter of bishops, which vexed the Puritans, Knox was not exemplary, as he tolerated them but more actively supported a populist system of elected ministers and diocesan superintendents.

In the larger history of ideas, he occupies a mythic place as a champion of the struggle – perhaps even a duty to fight – for human freedom and human rights. While Calvin certainly had justified theoretically the doctrine of resistance to Catholic governors, Knox developed independently the whole idea of violent resistance to ungodly rulers, even to the point of discarding doctrines of passive Christian obedience to monarchs after skeptical inquiry and iconoclastic rejection.

Without his literary skills, however, Knox might well have remained a part of the chorus or a supporting actor in the Scottish Reformation. *The History of the Reformation of Religion within the Realm of Scotland* displays Knox's powers of sarcastic invective and ironic description; it is also a superbly dramatic narrative, cleverly shaped and engagingly told by a self-conscious artist. Knox creates lines, dialogue, and whole speeches for his cast of characters, attributing and imputing motives (especially in sarcastic glosses), inserting metaphors ("led by the cruel beast, the Bishop of Saint Andrew"), and peppering the surface of his account with pointed jabs and epithets – "these pestilent Papists," "a poor, aged matron," "the flatterers of the Court," and "such pleasures as were meet to provoke the disordered appetite." He is a first-rate chronicler, reproducing letters and giving a mass of times, dates, and places, but he is also a teacher, intent on interpreting doctrine or on providing for unknowing readers *The Book of Discipline* between books 3 and 4 of the *History*. As a dramatist he plays skillfully with the persona of a "John Knox" in the third person, orchestrates growing arguments among characters, and pushes the narrative forward with immense artistry as different historical figures arrive and depart with great suddenness.

Knox is especially good at seeing the "craft" of his enemies with their hypocrisies and elaborate pretenses and in evaluating the interplay between public event and private character. He honestly confesses his limits at times – "what communication was between them, it is not certainly known" – but then can also, having inserted a lively debate into a certain scene, turn to the "good Reader" (whom he addresses frequently) to pose a polemical, editorializing, and partisan question, such as "But did God

approve any part of this obedience?" Nor have Knox's skills as a savage, often comic ironist in the *History* been much appreciated. One lover of Mary, for example, is executed to prevent scandal. "He lacked his head," observes Knox with grim wit, "that his tongue should not utter the secrets of our Queen." The sense of struggling opposites in the accounts – of light against darkness and of uprightness against corruption – indicates something of the epic dimension that this masterly *History* had for Knox. It repays literary scrutiny. Obscured by infamy, *The First Blast* equally merits fuller rhetorical analysis.

The First Blast blends scholastic argument and affective diatribe in unnerving manner. Knox has a clear and orderly tripartite division of his proofs (*divisio*), creates a tissue of biblical texts and allusions (*oraculum,* quoting God's commandments), and brings in classical allusions (Circe, the Sirens). However, the effect of these conventional devices becomes lost among the more fiery and exaggerated technique that he takes from the diatribe in its classical and hellenized, patristic Christian forms. Knox also asks savagely rhetorical questions (*erotesis*), seeks the opinion of readers (*anacoenosis*), indulges in bitter taunts of Mary (*sarcasmus*), uses highly rhythmic doubling of witty and grotesque epithets (*synonymia*), utters imprecations (*ara*), and frequently explodes in indignant exclamations (*ecphonesis*). To these may be added particularly characteristic stimulations of pathos in the heavy use of imagery (blindness, thirst, pits, fire) and a delightfully perverse use of logic ad absurdum, replete with false ergos. And as a prose stylist Knox is a master of clever word order, employing inversions and sudden bluntness after hypotactic structures or creating rhythm and balance through arch repetition and mocking refrains (*epimone*). He is a formidable rhetorician in the *First Blast,* almost overwhelming his contemporary target with polemical technique. There is less overtly manipulative prose in *The History of the Reformation of Religion within the Realm of Scotland,* but it too is at times a rhetorical showpiece. Among Reformation polemicists Knox stands in the front rank.

His literary range is considerable. He is quite capable of a disarming sincerity and affective warmth in his letters, where there is also at times a grimly self-effacing and ironic humor. He is equally at home with earthy, simple instructions and narrative; and when the occasion presents itself, he can be a political pugilist, somewhat in the tradition of Tyndale and Latimer. Knox's ebullient force in caricature and sarcasm gives a memorable energy to

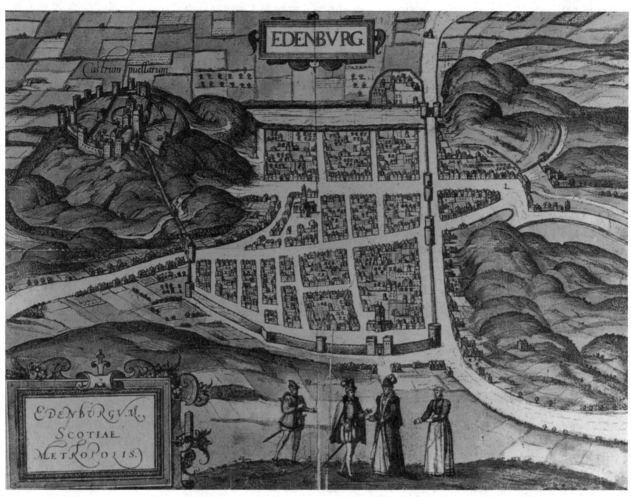

Plan of Edinburgh, circa 1582 (National Library of Scotland). Knox lived in the city from 1560 to 1572.

his anger. Most modern readers are unsettled by the collocation of this force and power with a sensitive and imposing religious sensibility, or they are at least not prepared at one moment for the wily aggressiveness of the serpent, followed at another by expressions of piety and religious feeling more appropriate to the dove. Among the other Reformers, Luther alone – and possibly also Calvin in controversy – can reveal the unresolved tensions and paradoxes of the spiritual warrior that one finds in Knox. It is one measure of his complex and cosmopolitan being that Knox is both willing and able to reveal the shifting and contradictory states of his spiritual pilgrimage with such expressive skill.

Bibliography:

Ian Hazlett, "A Working Bibliography of Writings by John Knox," in *Calviniana: Ideas and Influence of Jean Calvin,* edited by Robert V. Schnucker (Kirksville, Mo.: Sixteenth Century Journal Publishers, 1988), pp. 185–193.

Biographies:

Peter H. Brown, *John Knox: A Biography* (London: A. & C. Black, 1895);

Andrew Lang, *John Knox and the Reformation* (London: Longmans, 1905);

Eustace S. Percy, *John Knox* (London: Hodder & Stoughton, 1937);

Marjorie Bowen, *The Life of John Knox* (London: Watts, 1949);

Elizabeth Whitley, *Plain Mr. Knox* (London: Skeffington, 1960).

References:

John W. Allen, *A History of Political Thought in the Sixteenth Century* (New York: Barnes & Noble, 1957);

Theodore Beza, *Icones* (Geneva, 1580); translated into French as *Les Vrais Pourtraits des hommes illustres* (1581);

Charles Bourgeaud, "Le 'Vrai Portrait' de John Knox," *Bulletin de la Société de l'Histoire du Protestantisme français,* 84 (1935): 11–36;

J. H. Burns, "John Knox and Revolution, 1558," *History Today,* 8 (1958): 565–573;

V. E. D'Assonville, *John Knox and the Institutes of Calvin* (Durban: Drakensberg, 1969);

Donald Davidson, "Influence of English Printers on the Scottish Reformation," *Records of the Scottish Church History Society,* 1 (1926): 75–87;

William C. Dickinson, *Andrew Lang, John Knox, and Scottish Presbyterianism* (Edinburgh: Thomas Nelson, 1952);

Dickinson, *The Scottish Reformation and Its Influence upon Scottish Life and Character* (Edinburgh: Saint Andrew Press, 1960);

Gordon Donaldson, *The Scottish Reformation* (Cambridge: Cambridge University Press, 1960);

Katharine R. Firth, *The Apocalyptic Tradition in Reformation Britain, 1530–1645* (Oxford: Oxford University Press, 1979);

David H. Fleming, *The Reformation in Scotland* (London: Hodder & Stoughton, 1910);

John R. Gray, "The Political Theory of John Knox," *Church History,* 8 (1939): 132–147;

Richard L. Greaves, *Theology and Revolution in the Scottish Reformation: Studies in the Thought of John Knox* (Grand Rapids, Mich.: Christian University Press, 1980);

G. D. Henderson, "John Knox and the Bible," *Records of the Scottish Church History Society,* 9 (1946): 97–110;

Pierre Janton, *Concept et sentiment de l'Eglise chez John Knox* (Paris: Presses Universitaires de France, 1972);

Janton, *John Knox, l'homme et l'œuvre* (Paris: Didier, 1967);

Maurice Lee, Jr., "John Knox and His *History,*" *Scottish Historical Review,* 45 (1966): 79–88;

Paul M. Little, "John Knox and English Social Prophecy," *Journal of the Presbyterian Historical Society of England,* 14 (1970): 117–127;

Peter Lorimer, *John Knox and the Church of England* (London: H. S. King, 1875);

Geddes MacGregor, *The Thundering Scot: A Portrait of John Knox* (London: Macmillan, 1958);

John MacRae, "The Scottish Reformers and Their Order of Public Worship," *Records of the Scottish Church History Society,* 3 (1929): 22–30;

William D. Maxwell, *A History of Worship in the Church of Scotland* (New York: Oxford University Press, 1955);

James S. McEwen, *The Faith of John Knox* (Richmond, Va.: John Knox Press, 1961);

William McMillan, *The Worship of the Scottish Reformed Church, 1550–1638* (London: James Clarke, 1931);

Adrien Mezger, *John Knox et ses rapports avec Calvin* (Montauban: Imprimerie Coopérative, 1905);

Edwin Muir, *John Knox: Portrait of a Calvinist* (Port Washington, N.Y.: Kennikat, 1972);

David D. Murison, "Knox the Writer," in *John Knox: A Quatercentenary Reappraisal,* edited by Duncan Shaw (Edinburgh: Saint Andrew Press, 1975), pp. 33–50;

W. Stanford Reid, "John Knox and His Interpreters," *Renaissance & Reformation,* 10 (1974): 14–24;

Reid, "John Knox's Attitude to the English Reformation," *Westminster Theological Journal,* 26 (November 1963): 1–32;

Reid, *Trumpeter of God* (New York: Scribners, 1974);

A. M. Renwick, *The Story of the Scottish Reformation* (London: Inter-varsity Fellowship, 1960);

Jasper G. Ridley, *John Knox* (New York: Oxford University Press, 1968);

Robert Louis Stevenson, "John Knox and His Relations to Women," in his *Familiar Studies of Men and Books* (New York: Dodd, Mead, 1887), pp. 307–366;

John Strype, *Annals of the Reformation* (London: J. Wyat, 1709);

Wesley J. Vessey, "The Sources of the Idea of Active Resistance in the Political Theory of John Knox," Ph.D. dissertation, Boston University, 1961;

Hugh Watt, *John Knox in Controversy* (London: Thomas Nelson, 1950).

Papers:

An autograph fragment of *An Exposition upon the Sixth Psalm of David* is in the British Library (Harleian MSS, no. 416, fol. 40–45), along with some of his letters (Harleian MSS, no. 7004). Other letters are in the Public Record Office, London, and the Library of the Faculty of Advocates, Edinburgh.

William Latymer

(1498 – August 1583)

Maria Dowling
University of London

BOOK: *A Brief Treatise or Chronicle of the Most Virtuous Lady Anne Bulleyne, Late Queen of England,* edited by Maria Dowling, Camden Miscellany 30 (London: Royal Historical Society, 1990).

William Latymer was the author of an important early biography of Anne Boleyn, whom he served as chaplain. The treatise, addressed to Elizabeth I, is an eyewitness account of Anne; and though due allowance must be made for Latymer's loyal and Protestant bias, it goes far to confirm Anne's role in the Reformation and also shows the hopes placed in her royal daughter by Protestant Reformers.

Latymer (who is not to be confused with the classical scholar and friend of Desiderius Erasmus) was born in 1498 into a gentry family of Freston in Suffolk. A member of Corpus Christi, Cambridge, which was the college of Matthew Parker, another of Anne's chaplains, he was graduated M.A. in 1536. In that year he was already in Anne's service: Archbishop Thomas Cranmer entrusted him and Hugh Latimer (not a relation) with the examination of a book presented to Anne. This was Tristram Revell's translation of Lambertus's *Farrago Rerum Theologicarum,* and it proved far too unorthodox for her to accept. When Anne was arrested in the spring of 1536, Latymer was in Flanders buying illicit religious books for her. He was arrested at Sandwich, Kent, on his return to England and, learning that Anne was in the Tower, provided the mayor of Sandwich with a list of the books he had purchased abroad. He did not suffer in the coup that destroyed Anne and the chief members of her political faction.

For all his reform-mindedness Latymer was notable as a pluralist. Early in 1536 King Henry VIII gave him the living of Stackpole in Saint David's diocese, Wales. In 1538 he received the benefices of Witnesham, Suffolk, and Speldhurst, Kent; and the king made him master of the college of Saint Laurence Pountney, London, vacant by the death of the humanist scholar Thomas Starkey. This last appointment gave him several college livings. As master of Saint Laurence Pountney, he clashed with Edmund Bonner, bishop of London, ostensibly over ecclesiastical taxation, though religious differences most probably played a part. Latymer was accused of dubious transactions over college land, lead from the roof, and other property; of omitting to appoint curates to fulfill his duties in two benefices; and of failing to provide sacks of coal for the poor, as laid down in the college charter.

Saint Laurence Pountney was dissolved in 1547, and Latymer received the handsome pension of £28 13*s.* 4*d.* In that year he sat in convocation as one of the proctors for Norwich diocese and voted in favor of clerical marriage. He was married about this time, though there is no documentary proof of the date. In 1549 the chance for revenge on Bonner came, and he joined John Hooper in accusing the bishop of popery. Latymer's religious temper can be gauged by Bonner's counteraccusations that he was a notorious heretic and sacramentary and that he held conventicles and preached heresy openly in London and its suburbs.

On the accession of Mary I in 1553, Latymer lost all his preferments because of his marriage. Deprived by the rehabilitated Bishop Bonner, he lived for a time on his pension from Saint Laurence Pountney. However, a serious shortage of clergy in Ipswich led the Marian regime to employ him and other scarcely desirable churchmen, and by 1556 he was incumbent of the parishes of Saint Laurence and Saint Stephen in that town. He seems to have been in good standing with his parishioners, despite the fact that he continued to see his wife.

Elizabeth's accession in 1558 improved the fortunes of Latymer as of many Protestant clerics. He was restored to his living of Saint Mary Abchurch, London, and in April 1559 received from the queen the benefice of Saint George, Southwark. In 1560 he was appointed dean of Peterborough and obtained a canonry at Westminster, being styled "Archdeacon of Westminster" in some documents. As a member of convocation, he signed the Thirty-Nine Articles in 1563. He resigned his livings in London and Southwark and became the queen's chaplain and clerk of her closet. In August 1564 he accompanied Elizabeth to Cambridge and was created D.D. in the royal presence. He was one of the Lent preachers at court in 1565, and he apparently held two livings in Suffolk, Kirkton and Shotley. Whether the favors and patronage he received from Elizabeth were connected with his composition of the *Chronicle* for her – how far they were the fruit of the queen's loyalty to her mother's old clients and servants – cannot be known.

It must be admitted that Latymer's *Chronicle* is not among the finest flowers of sixteenth-century English literature. The work was not published until the twentieth century. The only existing version of the text is a working manuscript rather than a presentation copy, and it might be a draft submitted to the authorities for approval. The manuscript has many scratches through words and interlineations with carelessly placed carets, and parts of it are difficult to make sense of grammatically. These faults notwithstanding, the work is a structured and harmonious whole, and it fulfills Latymer's double purpose of rehabilitating Anne Boleyn as a Protestant heroine and champion of the English Reformation, and of advising Elizabeth as to what course that Reformation should take.

Latymer begins his account of Anne precisely on 12 April 1533, when she was proclaimed queen; he ends it in a tactful and imprecise way by alluding to the "sudden departing of so good a princess." No mention is made of the rather sordid business of the royal divorce, nor – overtly at least – of Anne's predecessor, Catherine of Aragon. Equally, Anne's sudden fall and execution as a criminal are omitted. Latymer's concern is to show Anne as a Protestant prince (the impression is given throughout that she, not Henry VIII, was the ruling monarch) who demonstrates by her speeches and actions the policies a godly magistrate should pursue.

In a speech to her councillors and household officers, Anne praises God for raising her to her high estate and orders them to keep the court orderly and free from immorality and extravagance. She gives her chaplains a similar charge, telling them to admonish her if they suspect she might "decline from the right path of sound and pure doctrine, and yield to any manner of sensuality." They must also instruct her household people to pursue virtue and avoid vice, and above all "to embrace the wholesome doctrine of Christ's gospel."

Anne is shown as having especial concern for relief to the poor, and instances of her munificence are cited. She is generous to English "upholders of the gospel" and provides a safe haven for refugees from popish tyranny in France. She is bountiful, too, to the two universities and to individual scholars, and she hopes to use the revenues of the monasteries for endowment of education and relief to the poor. She promotes godly men in the English church and hierarchy and combats superstition in religious practice. In her private life she keeps an English Bible in her chamber, gives her maids books of devotions, and imports scriptural and salutary works from France and Flanders. In short she is a perfect example of Plato's philosopher-king, and Latymer does not hesitate to say so: "The notable philosopher Plato in his book *De Republica* showeth that the manifest token of the prosperous commonwealth is where wisdom hath made the prince her fellow or companion." As was the mother, so should the daughter be.

Latymer's work compares interestingly with other Tudor biographies. His *Chronicle* is closest to two contemporary treatises, George Wyatt's *Extracts from the Life of the Virtuous, Christian, and Renowned Queen Anne Boleyn* and William Forrest's *History of Griselda the Second,* a portrait of Catherine of Aragon composed for her daughter, Mary I. Wyatt's Elizabethan work, like Latymer's, is Protestant and sympathetic to its subject, though there are two crucial differences: Wyatt was not a contemporary of Anne, so he relied on evidence from those who knew her; and a large part of his purpose was to exonerate his grandfather, the poet Sir Thomas Wyatt, from the imputation of having been Anne's adulterous lover.

Forrest's life of Catherine (completed 1558) is much different from Latymer's *Chronicle;* it is a semi-allegorical poem depicting the queen as "patient Griselda." However, there are vivid parallels in the two authors' treatment of their respective heroines. Both Catherine and Anne are presented as examples of piety and virtue for their daughters; both love to read Scripture and other good works; both are charitable to the poor, and their organizations of relief are strikingly similar; and both are patrons of learning. The two accounts are so alike that it is tempting to speculate that Latymer might have imitated Forrest directly so as to show Anne outshining Catherine in virtue and religious devotion. However, his account of Anne's good deeds and support of reformed religion can be substantiated from other sources.

Latymer died in August 1583 and was buried in Peterborough Cathedral. His will of "25 July 25 Elizabeth" mentions his wife, Ellen, and sons, Edward and Joshua. Some of the will's provisions echo the concerns of Anne as he depicted them in his *Chronicle*. He left money for preaching at Peterborough, 10*s* for his funeral sermon and 6*s*. 8*d*. each for two other sermons; he showed charity to the poor, leaving general alms of £3 6*s*. 8*d*. and 40*s*. "to the poor whose houses were lately burned"; and he stipulated that all servants dismissed by his wife after his death should receive a quarter's wages.

Latymer's *Chronicle* is useful both as historical material about Anne Boleyn and as an unusual specimen of the *speculum principis* genre of writing (which gave advice and virtuous examples to rulers). As Latymer declares in his dedicatory preface, Elizabeth "as in a mirror or glass might behold the most godly and princely ornaments of your most gracious and natural mother; not a little to your highness' comfort . . . to the honor of your crown, to the comfort of your most humble subjects, and to the enlarging of your realm."

References:

Maria Dowling, *Humanism in the Age of Henry VIII* (London: Croom Helm, 1986);

E. W. Ives, *Anne Boleyn* (Oxford: Basil Blackwell, 1986);

Diarmaid MacCulloch and John Blatchly, "Pastoral Provision in the Parishes of Tudor Ipswich," *Sixteenth Century Journal,* 22 (Fall 1991): 457–474;

Arthur Slavin, "The Tudor Revolution and the Devil's Art," in *Tudor Rule and Revolution: Essays for G. R. Elton from His American Friends,* edited by Delloyd J. Guth and John W. McKenna (Cambridge: Cambridge University Press, 1982), pp. 3–23.

Papers:

The sole manuscript of Latymer's *Chronicle* is in the Bodleian Library, Oxford (MS Don. C.42, fols. 21–33). His will is in the Public Record Office, London (Prob. 11/66/27, fols. 214–215).

William Lily

(circa 1468 – 10 December 1522)

Louis V. Galdieri
Massachusetts Institute of Technology

BOOKS: *Rudimenta grammatices* (London?, 1509?); revised as *Libellus de constructione octo partium orationis,* anonymous, edited by Desiderius Erasmus (London: Printed by Richard Pynson, 1513); revised as *Rudimenta . . . nuper impressa & correcta* (York: Printed by Ursyn Mylner, 1516?);

Progymnasmata (Basel: Froben, 1518) – printed with Thomas More's *Utopia;*

Antibossicon (London: Printed by Richard Pynson, 1521);

Epigrammata (London: Printed by Wynkyn de Worde, 1521);

Of the tryumphe, and the v'ses that Charles themperour, & kyng of England, Henry the .viii. were saluted with, passying through London (London: Printed by Richard Pynson, 1522) – contains Lily's *Acclamatio* and pageant verses.

De generibus nominum, ac verborum præteritis & supinis regulæ (Southwark: Printed by Peter Treveris, 1528?).

Edition: *Progymnasmata,* translated by Leicester Bradner and Charles A. Lynch, revised by Clarence Miller, in *The Complete Works of Thomas More,* volume 3, part 2, edited by Miller, Bradner, Lynch, and Revilo P. Oliver (New Haven: Yale University Press, 1984).

William Lily was Tudor England's most famous grammarian. His Latin grammar, developed while he was master at Saint Paul's School, became England's national grammar. Shakespeare learned his small Latin from Lily's grammar, and he makes quibbling references to it in *Love's Labor's Lost* (performed circa 1595) and *Twelfth Night* (performed 1601); generations of English writers after him learned how to make sentences from Lily's syntax. Polydore Vergil exaggerated when he styled Lily the first to bring Latin eloquence from Italy to England, but he was not alone in his opinion. In Tudor England, Lily's Italian learning set him apart; abroad, he was known for his poetic wit, his knowledge of Greek, and his abilities as a translator.

Lily was born at Odiham in Hampshire, probably in 1468. Virtually nothing is known of his youth before 1486, when he was admitted demy (or foundation scholar) of Magdalen College, Oxford. The Magdalen of Lily's day has been called the home of the Renaissance in Oxford; there John Anwykyll, William Grocyn, and John Stanbridge taught such students as John Colet and William Horman. Although there is no evidence of Lily's having taken a degree at Magdalen, Anthony à Wood supposes that he took "one degree in arts" before "giving a farewell to the university"; Lily's son George simply says that a youthful wanderlust took hold of his father. Sometime in the late 1480s Lily went on pilgrimage to Jerusalem. He then visited Rhodes, where the Knights of Saint John held their splendid fortress against the Turks. If he left for Italy with Grocyn in 1488 and from there took the pilgrim galley to Jerusalem, it is hard to believe George Lily's assertion that in his studies at Rhodes – which could have lasted one year at most – William Lily thoroughly acquired the rudiments of Latin and Greek. For the humanist, the rudiments of Latin were acquired only after long years of intensive study; at Rhodes, Lily probably continued to study and practice the figures and classical forms. As for Greek, he may have begun to study grammar at Magdalen under Grocyn's tutelage; Rhodes may have inspired him to improve.

In 1489 or early 1490 Lily quit Rhodes for Rome, where he stayed until 1492. In Rome he belonged to a learned English circle that included Christopher Bambridge, Colet, John Kendall, Thomas Linacre, and William Warham. He attended the Academia Pomponiana, where he may have seen plays by Terence and Plautus performed. It is known only that he heard the lectures of the humanists Joannes Sulpicius and Giulio Pomponio Leto. Leto had studied Latin with Lorenzo Valla and Greek with Theodore Gaza; in his house on the

Quirinal, he led discussions of poetry, rhetoric, philology, and antiquities. In the grammarian Sulpicius, Lily may have found a champion: Horman informed John Bale that Sulpicius had Lily crowned poet laureate. The irascible Filippo Buonaccorsi may also have taken an interest in Sulpicius's talented young English disciple. A Barberini Library manuscript of Buonaccorsi's writings contains two poems ascribed to "Lylius"; these may be the work of Lily or of Lilio Gregorio Gyraldi. The first poem addresses the beautiful Fannia, a relative of Archbishop Gregory Sanochi; the second treats envy. Through Sulpicius, Lily may also have become acquainted with the work of the grammarian and educator Ognibene Bonisoli (Omnibonus Leonicenus). Bonisoli was the most faithful disciple of Vittorino da Feltre; there can be little doubt that Lily made himself the rightful English heir to da Feltre's legacy.

A William Lily was presented with the living at Holcot on 24 May 1492. If this is the grammarian, he probably did not spend much time in the South Midlands; Northamptonshire could not have held him after his travels in Italy. In 1495 Richard Nichols took the living; Lily went to London, where he taught grammar and gained some reputation for his Latin verse. In 1503 he wrote an epitaph for Queen Elizabeth, wife of Henry VII. A storm of 15 January 1506 occasioned a second poem. Philip the Handsome, Duke of Burgundy, was headed for Spain from Flanders, but the storm forced him to the beaches of Cornwall. According to Edward Hall, Henry VII saw an occasion for profit in Philip's unexpected landing and called for an impromptu reception and ceremony for Philip and his demented queen, Joanna. Lily wrote Latin verses of welcome for the occasion. He noted that Philip took the eagle as his insignia and that the storm had blown the big eagle weather vane off the steeple of Saint Paul's; it landed on a bookbinder's sign, the sign of the eagle, at the east end of the cathedral. Lily made this auspicious state of affairs his central conceit.

In London, Lily also found a congenial group of friends: Colet, Desiderius Erasmus, Linacre, and Thomas More. Lily married a woman named Agnes. More may have been following suit or setting an example when he married Jane Colt in 1504. Lily apparently shared More's views on the education of women; his daughter Dionysia was known for her learning and is said to have written the tragedy of Dido acted before Cardinal Thomas Wolsey in 1527. His literary collaboration with More began around 1503, when Lily translated

William Lily

Lorenzo Spirito's *Libro della Fortuna* from Italian to English at More's request; More wrote his *Verses for the Book of Fortune* to accompany the moralizing parlor game. From about 1503 to 1508 More and Lily produced rival versions of Greek epigrams from the *Planudean Anthology* and other sources. These treat themes such as miserliness, luck, extravagance, self-indulgence, and false friends; there are epigrams on Sappho, on a philosophical dilemma from Aulus Gellius, and on the neat paradox of Niobe's statue:

Ex vita saxum Dii me fecere: sed ipse
Ex saxo vitam denuo Praxiteles.

(The gods deprived me of life and turned me to stone. But it was Praxiteles who from stone restored me to life.)

Woodcut from Lily's Antibossicon *(1521), showing Bossus the Bear being torn apart by "Lily" dogs, a representation of the pamphlet war between Richard Whittinton (Bossus) and Lily over the instruction of Latin grammar*

Although Lily and More occasionally had difficulty with the Greek, they also proved themselves capable of vivid and inventive translation that approaches poetic imitation. Lily's version of an epigram on a Spartan soldier is especially memorable; in the "hair-raising speech" of a "maddened" Spartan mother, it produces a dramatic effect not found in the Greek and has a poetic integrity of its own. Finally, "On a Man Both Lame and Stupid" shows the biting, witty concision of which Lily was capable:

Tardus es ingenio, ut pedibus: natura enim dat
Exterius specimen, quod latet interius.

(You are as slow in your wits as you are afoot, for your outward appearance gives a sample of what lies hidden within.)

Eighteen such epigrams were collected and published in March 1518 under the title *Progymnasmata;* they appeared with More's *Utopia.* In a prefatory epistle addressed to Willibald Pirkheimer, Beatus Rhenanus justly praises Lily for his learning, his familiarity with Greek authors, and his knowledge of Greek customs, which he had gained while traveling in Rhodes.

On 27 July 1510 Lily was appointed first master of Colet's new school of Saint Paul's and was awarded all the privileges of the master of the old school, including a stall in the choir. His grammatical writings date from this period; they are chiefly the product of his collaboration with Colet. In 1509 Colet dedicated his *Aeditio* to Lily. *Aeditio* deals with accidence, that is, with the eight parts of speech and primarily with the declension of nouns and the conjugation of verbs. To *Aeditio* Lily contributed prefatory verses and a syntax, *Rudimenta grammatices,* which teaches how to make sentences from the eight parts of speech. In 1513 Erasmus revised Lily's work and without naming Lily as author published

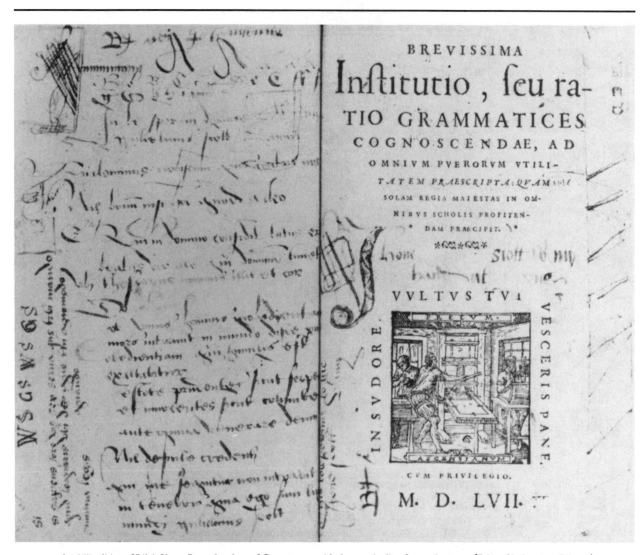

A 1557 edition of Lily's Short Introduction of Grammar, *with the marginalia of an early owner (Folger Shakespeare Library)*

it for the first time under the title *Libellus de constructione octo partium orationis*. In most subsequent editions Lily's syntax is followed by his very popular *Monita paedigogica* or *Carmen ad discipulos de moribus*. Like Sulpicius's *De moribus puerorum carmen juvenile*, Lily's *Carmen . . . de moribus* contains precepts for the schoolboy's cultivation of learning and practice of virtue. These materials, along with his *De generibus nominum* and *De verborum praeteritis,* went through many editions, revisions, and amplifications; they gradually metamorphosed into "Lily's Grammar," made the official grammar of the realm in 1540. Especially noteworthy is the edition of 1529, a republication of Lily's *Rudimenta* for use at Ipswich; the volume named Cardinal Wolsey as its author and included prefatory matter from Wolsey's pen.

As schoolmaster of Saint Paul's, Lily wrote commendatory verses for Horman's *Vulgaria* (1519)

and a prefatory *tetrastich* for Colet's *Aeditio*. His prefatory poem in Linacre's *Progymnasmata grammatices vulgaria* (1512) defends Linacre against charges of plagiarism; other verses commend Linacre's *Rudimenta grammatices* (not published until circa 1525) to Princess Mary. He corresponded with fellow humanists, sometimes in verse. One poem thanks Vergil for a gift of fish; another accompanied Lily's New Year's gift to him. A 1517 epigram addressed to More at Calais celebrates Quentin Metsys's diptych of Erasmus and Peter Giles. In another poem Lily praises the Seven Wise Men of Greece. They are distant figures; a more genuine praise of wisdom may be found in the epitaph he wrote for Colet in 1519. The schoolmaster was not above flattery, and he wrote some careful lines in which he longs for the day when Wolsey will become pope. In May 1522 the aldermen of London commissioned Lily to write Latin verses for

Charles V's entry into London. He composed an *Acclamatio* in praise of Charles and poems of greeting for pageants along Charles's route. The poems combine classical, Christian, and Arthurian imagery; they pay tribute to Charles's powers and express the vain hope that Charles and Henry VIII will reign together in peaceful amity.

Lily also found himself embroiled in controversy. Like Erasmus and Colet, the grammarian favored getting his students to the study of Latin literature as quickly as possible; in humanist parlance, he advocated learning by imitation. In the grammarians' war of the 1520s, he sided with Horman, whose *Vulgaria* or Latin grammar he used at Saint Paul's. Horman's chief opponent, Richard Whittinton, charged that Lily and Horman taught students how to ape the ancients without first providing them with a thorough knowledge of the rules of Latin grammar. The pamphlet war began around 1520, when Whittinton, poet laureate and author of a *Vulgaria* (1520), tacked an epigram to the door of Saint Paul's attacking Lily and Horman. He signed the epigram "Bossus," turning to bad Latin the sobriquet that Lily and Horman had given him after Whittington's boss, a Billingsgate water tap in the shape of a bear's head, popularly called "Bossa."

Lily responded in a collection of epigrams and short poems, *Antibossicon* (1521; not to be confused with Horman's work of the same name), which lambastes the puffed-up Whittinton in three books. Lily celebrates in mock-epithalamium the nuptials of Bossus and Bossa, the Billingsgate bear; he derides Whittinton's Latin and scoffs at his laurels, which are, he points out, most unlike the ivy the Romans used to crown their poets. Woodcuts in the *Antibossicon* depict a bear being torn apart by dogs, but they are tame in comparison to Lily's verse: "stupor" overwhelms Lily's Bossus. Perhaps he is not worthy of his beloved: while Bossa spouts "pure," cleansing water from her mouth, her lover Bossus spews forth "filth" and defiles all who come in touch with him. Bossus wishes to debauch and besmirch the wits of London youths, writes Lily; he should repent and retire in shame. In response, Whittinton wrote an *Antilycon* (1521); when the poet John Skelton joined the fray, Lily attacked him in verses, of which only a fragment remains. To his credit, in "Speak, Parrot" Skelton refrains long enough from ad hominem attack to frame the issues:

> Plautus in his comedies a child shall now rehearse,
> And meddle with Quintilian in his *Declamations*,
> That *Petty Cato* can scantly construe a verse,

> With *'Aveto'* in *Graeco,* and such solemn salutations,
> Can scantly the tenses of his conjugations.

The end of the medieval preceptive tradition is apparent in this heated controversy. At its edges are the Oxford battle over the study of Greek and the ongoing sixteenth-century debate over the imitation of Cicero.

The virulence of *Antibossicon* did not detract from Lily's great contemporary reputation for learning, wit, and eloquence; indeed, it may have added to it. His death from the plague in the winter of 1522 brought "great grief" to "learned men," according to Wood, but his fame endured. Around 1570 Sir NicholasBacon placed Lily's portrait next to those of Servius, Donatus, and Priscian in his Trimalchian banqueting house at Gorhambury. In 1610 William Camden spoke of an inscription too difficult even for Lily to read. And in 1789 Benjamin Franklin's press printed *Carmen de moribus* at Philadelphia. Early literary biographers speak of him in glowing terms, but his poetry was forgotten long ago. Intellectual historians and bibliographers have fruitfully studied his grammar; literary historians remember him as the grandfather of dramatist John Lyly. His writings remain scattered; they await a patient editor.

References:

C. G. Allen, "The Sources of 'Lily's Latin Grammar': A Review of the Facts and Some Further Suggestions," *Library,* 9 (June 1954): 85–100;

Sydney Anglo, *Spectacle, Pageantry, and Early Tudor Policy* (Oxford: Clarendon, 1969), pp. 187–189;

John Bale, *Index Brittaniae Scriptorum. John Bale's Index of British and Other Writers,* edited by Reginald Lane Poole and Mary Bateson (Cambridge: D. S. Brewer, 1990), pp. 132–133;

C. R. Baskerville, "William Lily's Verse for the Entry of Charles V into London," *Huntington Library Bulletin,* 9 (April 1936): 1–14;

J. W. Binns, *Intellectual Culture in Elizabethan and Jacobean England* (Leeds: Francis Cairns, 1990), pp. 270–306;

Albert Feuillerat, *John Lyly: Contribution à l'Histoire de la Renaissance en Angleterre* (Cambridge: Cambridge University Press, 1910), pp. 3–10;

Vincent Joseph Flynn, "The Grammatical Writing of William Lily, ?1468–?1523," *Papers of the Bibliographical Society of America,* 37, no. 2 (1943): 85–113;

Flynn, *The Life and Works of William Lily, the Grammarian,* Ph.D. dissertation, University of Chicago, 1939;

Hubertus Schulte Herbruggen, "Sir Thomas Mores Fortuna Verse," in *Lebende Antike: Symposion für Rudolf Suhnel* (Berlin: E. Schmidt, 1967), pp. 155–172;

G. K. Hunter, *John Lyly: The Humanist as Courtier* (London: Routledge & Kegan Paul, 1962);

A. F. Leach, "St. Paul's School before Colet," *Archaeologia,* 62, no. 1 (1910): 191–238;

Damian R. Leader, "Professorships and Academic Reform at Cambridge: 1488–1520," *Sixteenth Century Journal,* 14 (1983): 215–227;

George Lily, *Elogia,* in *Descriptio Britanniae, Scotiae, Hybernia, et Orchadum,* edited by Paulus Jovius (Venice: Zilletti, 1539);

James K. McConica, *English Humanists and Reformation Politics under Henry VIII and Edward VI* (Oxford: Oxford University Press, 1965);

James J. Murphy, *Rhetoric in the Middle Ages* (Berkeley: University of California Press, 1974);

William Nelson, *John Skelton, Laureate* (New York: Columbia University Press, 1939), pp. 148–157;

G. B. Parks, *The English Traveler to Italy,* volume 1 (Stanford: Stanford University Press, 1954);

Hastings Rashdall, *The Universities of Europe in the Middle Ages,* volume 3, edited by F. M. Powicke and A. B. Emden (Oxford; Oxford University Press, 1969);

Izora Scott, *Controversies over the Imitation of Cicero* (Davis, Cal.: Hermagoras, 1991);

John Skelton, *The Complete English Poems,* edited by John Scattergood (New Haven: Yale University Press, 1983);

J. B. Trapp, "William Lily," in *Contemporaries of Erasmus,* edited by Peter G. Bietenholz (Toronto: University of Toronto Press, 1985–1987);

Anthony à Wood, *Athenae oxonienses,* edited by Philip Bliss (London: For Rivington and J. Parker, Oxford, 1813–1820);

Vladimiro Zabughin, *Giulio Pomponio Leto: Saggio Critica,* 2 volumes (Grottaferrata: Tipografia Italo-Orientale "S. Nilo," 1910–1912).

Papers:
Manuscript copies of Lily's poems are at the British Museum (Harleian MS. 540) and Vatican (Barberini Latini MS. 2031, xxx. 104, fol. 78v–79, including two poems questionably attributed to Lily).

Sir David Lindsay

(circa 1485 – 1555)

David Parkinson
University of Saskatchewan

BOOKS: *The complaynte and testament of a popiniay* (London: Printed by John Byddell, 1538);

The tragical death of Dauid Beaton bishoppe of sainct Andrews wherunto is ioyned the martyrdom of maister George Wyseharte (London: Printed by John Day & William Seres, 1548?);

[The Book of the Monarch] Ane dialog betuix experience and ane courteour off the miserabyll estait of the warld. And is deuidit in foure partis (Edinburgh: Printed by John Scot, 1554?) – three copies of this edition contain *The Tragedy of the Cardinal, The Testament of the Papingo, The Dream of Sir David Lindsay,* and *The Complaint of Sir David Lindsay*; Scot's second edition of *Ane Dialog* (1559) regularly contains these poems; another edition (Paris: Samuel Jascuy / Rouen: Jean Petit, 1558) contains *The Dream of Sir David Lindsay, The Testament of the Papingo,* and *The Tragedy of the Cardinal*;

The warkis of the famous and vorthie knicht-Schir Dauid Lyndesay. Newly correctit, and augmentit (Edinburgh: Printed by John Scot for Henry Charteris, 1568) – contains *The Book of the Monarch, The Testament of the Papingo, The Dream of Sir David Lindsay, The Complaint of Sir David Lindsay,* and *The Tragedy of the Cardinal,* as well as a second series of Lindsay's minor poems: "The Deploration of the Death of Queen Madeleine," "The Answer to the King's Flyting," "The Complaint of Bagsche," "A Supplication to the King's Grace in Contemption of Side Tails," "Kitty's Confession," and "The Jousting between Watson and Barbour";

The historie of ane nobil and wailzeand squyer, William Meldrum (Edinburgh: Printed by Henry Charteris, 1594);

Ane satyre of the thrie estaits (Edinburgh: Printed by Robert Charteris, 1602).

Editions and Collections: *The Poetical Works of Sir David Lyndsay of the Mount, Lion King at Arms, under James V,* 3 volumes, edited by George Chalmers (London: Longman / Edinburgh: Constable, 1806);

Sir David Lyndesay's Works, 5 volumes, edited by John Small, Fitzedward Hall, and J. A. H. Murray, Early English Text Society, original series 11, 19, 35, 37, 47 (London: N. Trubner, 1865–1871);

The Poetical Works of Sir David Lyndsay, 3 volumes, edited by David Laing (Edinburgh: William Paterson, 1879);

The Works of Sir David Lindsay, 4 volumes, edited by Douglas Hamer, Scottish Text Society, third series 1, 2, 6, 8 (Edinburgh: William Blackwood, 1931–1936);

Squyer Meldrum, edited by James Kinsley (London: Nelson, 1959);

Ane Satyre of the Thrie Estaites, edited by Roderick Lyall (Edinburgh: Canongate, 1989).

Sir David Lindsay, courtier and herald, is the most notable Scottish poet of the reign of James V (1513–1542) and the regency of James Hamilton, Earl of Arran (1543–1554). From John Barbour's national epic *The Bruce* (1376) to the achievements of Robert Henryson, William Dunbar, and Gavin Douglas, Lindsay's native literary heritage was diverse and vigorous. In the new climate of post-Reformation Scotland, he became the most palatable (certainly the most popular) representative of this tradition. Although capable of a wide satiric range from farce to irony, Lindsay wrote as an adviser, first to his prince and then to the civil and religious governors of his nation. Much of his work – light, occasional pieces as well as longer, weightier poems – is exemplary, setting up models of good and bad governance.

For generations Lindsay's family had owned an estate (called the Mount) near the town of Cupar in the county of Fife (on the east coast) and another, farther south, near Haddington in East Lothian. As an eldest son he inherited the given name of his father and grandfather; in 1507, soon after his twenty-first birthday, he was granted the Haddington estate. By

Page from the 1559 edition of Testament of the Papingo, *a satiric poem about the fall and demise of the royal parrot*

1524 he had assumed the surname "of the Mount," having come into possession of the Fifeshire land on the death of his father. Lindsay was married by 1522; his wife, Janet Douglas Lindsay, died sometime after 1542. If they had children, none survived infancy.

Lindsay's adult life centered on the court, where from the outset (he was a servant of James IV by 1507) he was involved in various kinds of entertainment and performance. In 1511 the king paid for blue and yellow taffeta for a play costume for Lindsay. Tradition places Lindsay beside James IV on the eve of James's departure for the catastrophic Battle of Flodden Field (1513), but there is no record of his accompanying the king to Flodden; instead, he was entrusted with the safekeeping of the infant Prince James. The poet recalls the prince's first words being "pa, Da Lin" (Play, David Lindsay); and indeed,

Lindsay seems to have been more than a mere usher, perhaps something of a father figure for James during the prince's first twelve years. The poet alludes to carrying the little prince, tucking him into bed, singing and playing the lute for him, dancing and playing games, impersonating demons and ghosts, and telling many stories, from the great tales of chivalry and love to popular tales of the supernatural.

This familiarity was ended when the regent, John, Duke of Albany, his policy of alliance with France and hostility to England in disrepute, departed for France in 1524. The twelve-year-old James passed under the control of the earl of Arran, who was supported by the prince's mother, Queen Margaret, sister of Henry VIII. In 1526 the queen's estranged husband, Archibald Douglas, sixth Earl of Angus, took control of the person of the new king, and thus the nation. With these changes Lindsay was dismissed and detached from James (1524-1528). Having escaped from the earl of Angus in July 1528, James became king in fact; he was only fifteen years old. Lindsay offered his services, but not as playmate. In his earliest recorded poems (the *Dream,* the *Complaint,* and the *Testament of the Papingo,* all composed during the first year or so of James's personal rule) Lindsay plays the part of royal adviser.

Lindsay begins what is probably the earliest of these poems, the *Dream* (circa 1528; in rhyme royal with a concluding section in nine-line stanzas), by describing his former association with James. The personal note of this opening epistle gives way to Lindsay's demonstration of his politically valuable learning and eloquence. The speaker of the poem moves through a wintry landscape toward a seaside cave, in which he attempts to write "some merry matter of antiquity" (line 123); depressed by his surroundings and the instability of the world, he falls asleep. Dame Remembrance appears to him and escorts him into the center of the world, where churchmen, princes, ladies, and merchants lie suffering in Hell. Describing each place as she goes, Remembrance leads the dreamer upward through the elements (earth, water, air, and then fire), past the seven planets (the moon, Mercury, Venus, the sun, Mars, Jupiter, and Saturn), toward heaven. Despite the dreamer's longing to remain there, she leads him back to Earth, the proportions, continents, and nations of which she reveals to him.

After he is shown Paradise, the dreamer requests that Remembrance bring him back to Scotland. The lesson in cosmography over, the poem enters into direct admonition. Blessed with all things necessary for prosperity, Scotland is poor because it is poorly governed, Remembrance tells the dreamer. Illustration is provided immediately by the arrival of John Commonwealth, who complains that he is banished, having been oppressed past endurance by corrupt State and greedy Church. Now that good government "is fled again in France" (947), he cannot survive. Awakened by the sound of cannon fire from a nearby ship, the poet writes his vision, concluding with an exhortation to the king to restore good government in Scotland.

Lindsay's *Dream* is more emphatically didactic and admonitory than its immediate models in the Scottish tradition, Douglas's *Palace of Honor* (composed circa 1501) and Henryson's *Orpheus and Eurydice* (composed mid-fifteenth century). In particular, Lindsay is more forthright than his predecessors in criticizing the misconduct of the church. He refers ironically to aspects of church doctrine (notably the Donation of Constantine and Purgatory, lines 232-238, 337-350). Various elements from this poem find their way into his later writings; for instance, the oppressed, banished John Commonwealth reappears in his play *The Satire of the Three Estates* (composed 1540-1554).

As in the *Dream,* Lindsay reminisces in the *Complaint* about his former intimacy with James and complains about political and religious corruption in Scotland. Now, however, his principal models are the court complaints of William Dunbar: Lindsay adopts the verse form of Dunbar's most unrestrained and "personal" complaints, the octosyllabic couplet; in the style of Dunbar, he insultingly lists various kinds of social climbers; he also assumes Dunbar's petitionary frankness. In his appeal for "reward," Lindsay recalls the corruption of the prince by the followers of his unscrupulous regent, the earl of Angus. The poet depicts himself, discarded: he hides "in a nook" to witness the gathering up of offices and privileges by the Douglas faction. Toward a vision of a kingdom revitalized by good governance, Lindsay ends with a comically exaggerated claim to the reward that gratitude owes to loyalty at court.

The balance of the jocular and the serious continues in the *Testament of the Papingo.* Neither as earnestly didactic as the *Dream* nor as wildly satiric as the *Complaint,* this poem concerns the toppling from a high perch and death of the royal parrot, a bird (like Skelton's Parrot) with the skills of a courtier: mimicry, agility, and charm (89-98). While dying this parrot makes three speeches. The first exhorts the king to learn to rule by reading exemplary books (tragedies, chronicles, and "mirrors" of advice for princes); by exercise of arms, pursuit of game, and the maintenance of sound health; and by involving the nobility in the administration of justice. The second, more openly critical, is to fellow courtiers, chronicling the miserable instability of Scottish court life and the fall of various political figures in Scotland and abroad. The last is to the clergy, in the person of three scavenging birds (a magpie, a raven, and a kite) who have opportunely arrived at the side of the dying parrot. She tells them an allegorical tale – later to be dramatized in the *Satire of the Three Estates* – about the banishment of Poverty and Chastity from the Church by Wealth and Sensuality. The parrot bequeaths her properties to the needy (and her heart to the king) and dies, only to be torn to pieces by her greedy executors. As does the *Complaint,* the *Testament of the Papingo* ends with serious criticism and advice offset by low comedy: first, in the parrot's invective against ecclesiastical greed and ambition, the scavenging birds stand for officers of the church; once the parrot dies, these scavengers become real birds who pull her apart and devour her, but who quarrel racily while they grab for choice pieces.

These poems do not seem to have hindered their author's promotion at court; having presented himself to James as a loyal friend and a frank, eloquent adviser, Lindsay was named a herald in 1530. Representing James V to the emperor Charles V in August 1531, Lindsay wrote a letter (his only extant one) in which he describes the many magnificent triumphs, joustings, and tournaments at the imperial court. Over the next five years he made four trips to France, one via England (July and August 1535) to participate in the installation by proxy of James in the Order of the Garter at Windsor Castle.

Lindsay's poems associated with the years 1531–1536 are "The Complaint and Public Confession of the King's Old Hound, Called Bagsche" and "The Answer to the King's Flyting." The first recalls the *Testament of the Papingo* in that the life of a creature at court is shown to be like a courtier's; courtly success now depends on canine aggressiveness and greed. Court life uses up the fiercest of dogs, however, and another, stronger dog is always waiting to displace him. The theme of displacement at court (exploited already in the *Complaint*) is also the mainspring of the Scottish verse entertainment called flyting. With its gestures of respect and humility, "The Answer to the King's Flyting" is not a conventional flyting, however. While responding meekly to the king's gibes, Lindsay admonishes James for his waste of prowess in "Venus' works" (26). The poet wishes he had a "tiger's tongue" (4), although he knows he is just a dog (17); the king, on the other hand, is like an elephant, a restless ram, and a bull (25, 36, 47) – but he is caught with a serving woman, the two of them wallowing like swine (58). The herald Lindsay refers to animals as emblems of increasingly uncourtly behavior.

Royal marriage negotiations with France bore fruit. Madeleine, eldest surviving daughter of Francis I, was wedded to James at Notre Dame in Paris on 1 January 1537. Triumph soon gave way to mourning, the infirm Madeleine dying on 1 July 1537 on the eve of her state entry into Edinburgh. Lindsay responded almost immediately with a "Deploration of the Death of Queen Madeleine" (July–October 1537). His poem is largely taken up with a description of the unprecedented magnificence of the preparations in Edinburgh for her royal entry, all canceled by her death. In October 1537 negotiations began for another French princess, Marie de Guise, to marry James. She arrived in Scotland on 10 June 1538 and was welcomed into the burgh of

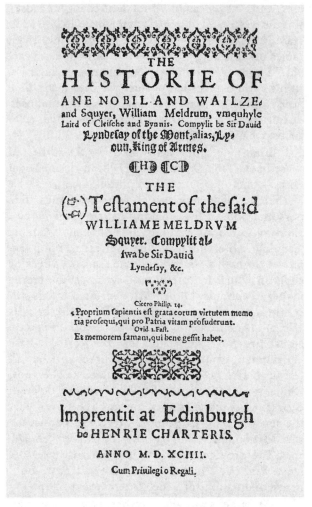

Title page for Lindsay's chivalric romance about a squire who is a model of behavior in difficult times

Saint Andrews with a pageant devised by Lindsay: an angel descended from a cloud, gave her the keys of Scotland, and recited a speech of exhortation.

Two other poems by Lindsay can be dated to the late 1530s, both of them satires of the aping of court styles and practices by common people: "The Jousting between Watson and Barbour" and "A Supplication to the King's Grace in Contemption of Side Tails" (1538–1542). Lindsay introduces his "Jousting" as the record of a mock-tournament staged for the amusement of the royal household at Saint Andrews, the combatants being two barbers at court. The second of these poems is a mock-petition to the king, requesting prohibition of women's "tails" (gowns with long trains), the queen alone exempted. While satirizing this fashion as an index of social climbing, Lindsay is also engaged in an invective against women: particular trends in costume (tails and veils) manifest inner foulness and lust.

A third poem ascribed to Lindsay and included in the 1568 edition of his works may be associated with the same period. "Kitty's Confession, Compiled (as Is Believed) by Sir David Lindsay" begins as a satirical dialogue between a rapacious rural curate and the peasant woman Kitty. Before long, however, Kitty is addressing the reader directly; she abandons her pose of naiveté and attacks the exploitation of confession by ignorant, greedy priests. In the person of Kitty, Lindsay is more outright in his condemnation of church corruption than he is in his earlier writings.

Shortly after the humiliating defeat of a Scottish army by the English at Solway Moss in 1542, James V died, not yet thirty-one. James Hamilton, third Earl of Arran, leader of those favoring ties with Protestant England, became governor of Scotland. Among those successfully opposing him were the widowed Queen Marie and Cardinal David Beaton, archbishop of Saint Andrews. Lindsay now had to balance his own wishes for reform against his official duties. Before the king's death in December 1542, he had been knighted (3 October 1542) and had become the highest-ranking herald in Scotland, the Lyon King of Arms. That year he compiled his "Armorial," a heraldic manuscript illustrating the coats of arms of the Scottish nobility and gentry, now located in the National Library of Scotland.

The tension between Lindsay's desire for reform and his official duties came to a head with the murder of Cardinal Beaton on 29 May 1546. The murderers (several of Lindsay's friends among them) had barricaded themselves inside the cardinal's residence, the Castle of Saint Andrews; on behalf of the Crown, Lindsay negotiated a truce with them on 16 December 1546. As the occupation of the castle dragged on, Lindsay became increasingly implicated. He is reputed to have attended a council in the castle, at which the occupying reformers asked John Knox to become their preacher; this took place in June 1547, a month before their surrender. These events led to the writing of *The Tragedy of the Cardinal* in 1547–1548, a *de casibus* tragedy (a story of how people of high rank or position, through either bad fortune or their own error or vice, fall from high to low estate) on the model of those in the fifteenth-century English poet John Lydgate's *The Fall of Princes* (1431–1438). The belatedly repentant cardinal confesses his crimes and, likening himself to Goliath, Holofernes, and Lucifer, describes his murder. Following Lydgate's practice Lindsay ends this work with the speaker exhorting officers of church and state to amend their prac-

tices while there is yet time; here, however, the range of political comment has contracted to the single issue of the ignorance, greed, and indolence of the bishops and the imprudence of the Crown in appointing unworthy prelates.

It would be wrong to characterize all of Lindsay's writing subsequent to the death of King James V by concern with church governance, however. In 1550–1555 Lindsay wrote *The History of a Noble and Valiant Squire, William Meldrum,* a poem that is biography in the guise of chivalric romance. He merely alludes to religious disaffection in the pendant *Testament of the Noble and Valiant Squire, William Meldrum,* in which the title character devises a festive, exclusively profane funeral. These specifications are appropriate, given the emphases of the *History,* in which the title character passes spectacularly and rapidly from martial to romantic encounter. During his exploits at the taking of Carrickfergus Castle in Ulster, Meldrum pauses to rescue a woman from two Scottish soldiers; following his brilliant victories against the English in France, Meldrum stays at the house of the widowed Lady of Gleneagles, with whom he falls hotly in love. Describing the progress of this affair, Lindsay shifts rapidly from courtly periphrasis to explicit language of sexual desire and experience. The unstable but delightful conjunction of Mars and Venus ends when Meldrum is brutally ambushed and wounded; under the surgeons' hands, forbidden to return to the Lady of Gleneagles, he passes into a new phase of life, a devotee of Mercury, patron of medicine and rhetoric. However ironically he views Meldrum's affairs, Lindsay presents his hero as a model of behavior in difficult times.

Perhaps because they did not conform to any pattern of increasing earnestness perceivable in Lindsay's output, the *History* and its pendant *Testament* were omitted from all editions of his works before the scholarly editions of the nineteenth century. So was his play *Satire of the Three Estates* (begun as early as 1540, with versions completed in 1552 and 1554), similarly diverse and disturbing in its range of topics. The centerpiece of the earlier editions of the *Works* is instead *The Book of the Monarch,* Lindsay's longest poem (6,338 lines in octosyllabic couplets, rhyme royal, and eight- and nine-line stanzas). Properly (and more informatively) entitled *A Dialogue betwixt Experience and a Courtier of the Miserable Estate of the World* (*The Monarch* was the headline title in the early editions), this poem is built on the fiction of a Maytime encounter between the narrator, who is a courtier, and an aged man named Experience, who offers him counsel. As Lindsay states

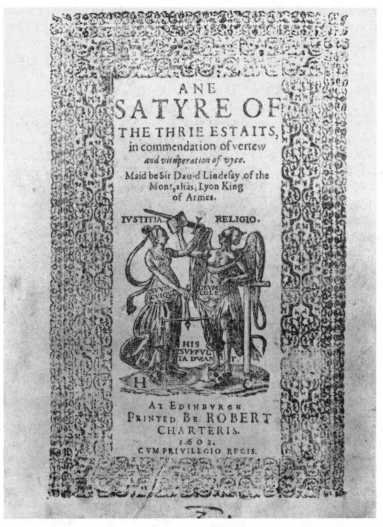

ANE
SATYRE OF
THE THRIE ESTAITS,
in commendation of vertew
and vituperation of vyce.

Maid be Sir Dauid Lindesay of the
Mont, alias, Lyon King
of Armes.

IVSTITIA.   RELIGIO.

AT EDINBVRGH
PRINTED BE ROBERT
CHARTERIS.
1602.
CVM PRIVILEGIO REGIS.

Title page for Lindsay's play attacking the abuses of church and state. Bookseller
Henry Charteris reported that a 1554 performance lasted
from "nine houris aforne noon till six houris at evin."

in his prefatory "Epistle to the Reader," this book lacks its proper audience, a king; it must be addressed instead to those looking after the civil and spiritual governance of Scotland.

The Monarch expounds on the dreadful examples history holds for Scotland in these latter days. Asked to put the woes of the realm in historical context, Experience uses the familiar epochal structure of the five Monarchies (from the prophet Daniel's interpretation of Nebuchadnezzar's dream of a statue of gold, and below it silver, brass, iron, and iron mixed with clay; Daniel 2.31–45) for his vision of human overreaching and God's retribution. Experience recounts the great acts of trespass and their consequences: the fall of Adam and Eve, the Flood, the confusion of tongues at Nimrod's Tower of Babel, the founding of the idolatrous Assyrian monarchy (by Ninus with his unnatu-

rally ambitious queen, Semiramis) and its destruction during the reign of the effeminate Sardanapalus, the burning of Sodom and Gomorrah, then (after a summary of the Persian and Greek monarchies) the Roman destruction of Jerusalem. In his description of the fifth, the "spiritual and papal monarchy," Experience catalogues the vice of the present age and foresees an imminent Judgment Day, toward which the nation drifts, unguided by its immoral, ignorant clergy. In the troubled circumstances of the 1550s, *The Book of the Monarch* brings Lindsay's work as adviser to princes to a pessimistic close.

Appealing to the sixteenth-century taste for moralizing historical surveys (such as *A Mirror for Magistrates,* 1559), Lindsay's *Monarch* was widely read and often reprinted in London, Paris, and Copenhagen, as well as Edinburgh. The poem found its way into a variety of situations, a portion of it even being recast as a song (Richard Maitland's "Ballad of the Creation of the World, Man His Fall and Redemption Made to the Tune of *The Banks of Helicon*").

In the preface to his edition of Lindsay's *Monarch*-dominated *Works* (1568), the printer Henry Charteris gives a memorable and influential portrait of the poet, whose characteristic balance between polemic and playfulness is typified thus: when Lindsay gravely requested to be appointed royal tailor, James V asked whether he had any skill at that craft; Lindsay responded, "Sir, that makes no matter, for you have given bishoprics and benefices to many standing here about you, and yet they can neither teach nor preach" (an anecdote that recalls *The Tragedy of the Cardinal,* lines 351–364). For Charteris, Lindsay may have been something of a jester, but he was also a prophet of Reformation. That characterization also occurs in *Dialogue against the Fever Pestilence* (1564), by the English physician William Bullein, in which Lindsay utters a scrap of doggerel favoring union of the Reformed Churches of England and Scotland. In his manuscript collection of Scottish verse the Edinburgh merchant George Bannatyne tends to prefer the jesting side of Lindsay's work: the Bannatyne Manuscript version of *A Satire of the Three Estates* is a selection of comic interludes from the larger play; also included is the vigorously satiric "Against Pedlar Coffs [Knaves]," ascribed to Lindsay.

Lindsay's poems remained popular long after the Reformation and the departure of James VI for an English throne. Sir Walter Scott refers frequently to the common people's proverbial familiarity with Lindsay. From another perspective, in 1774 Thomas Warton praised Lindsay's verse in *The Monarch* as "nervous, tense, and polished" – the qualities of Augustan poetry. In the past thirty years the most widely discussed of Lindsay's works have been his play *A Satire of the Three Estates, Squire Meldrum,* and the early trio of court poems (*Dream, Complaint,* and *Papingo*). This poet tends to be thought of as a follower of Henryson, Dunbar, and Douglas, less concerned than they with artistry and more with social and moral issues. To be sure, his themes and techniques are not as various as his predecessors', the topics of his early poems cropping up again in his last ones. Nevertheless, Lindsay's poems are engaging, inventive, and eminently deserving of further attention.

Bibliographies:

William Geddie, *A Bibliography of Middle Scots Poets,* Scottish Text Society, original series 61 (Edin-

burgh: William Blackwood, 1912), pp. 268–317;

Douglas Hamer, "The Bibliography of Sir David Lindsay," *Library,* 10 (June 1929): 1–42.

References:

Glenn D. Burger, "Poetical Invention and Ethical Wisdom in Lindsay's 'Testament of the Papyngo,'" *Studies in Scottish Literature,* 24 (1989): 164–180;

Sandra Cairns, "Sir David Lindsay's *Dreme:* Poetry, Propaganda and Encomium in the Scottish Court," in *The Spirit of the Court,* edited by G. S. Burgess and R. A. Taylor (Cambridge: D. S. Brewer, 1985), pp. 101–115;

C. S. Lewis, *English Literature in the Sixteenth Century, Excluding Drama* (Oxford: Clarendon, 1954), pp. 100–105;

William Murison, *Sir David Lyndsay, Poet and Satirist of the Old Church in Scotland* (Cambridge: Cambridge University Press, 1938);

Felicity Riddy, "*Squyer Meldrum* and the Romance of Chivalry," *Yearbook of English Studies,* 4 (1974): 26–36;

Thomas Warton, *The History of English Poetry,* volume 3, edited by R. Price (London: T. Tegg, 1824), pp. 125–153;

Janet H. Williams, "'Although I beir nocht lyke ane baird': Sir David Lyndsay's *Complaint,*" *Scottish Literary Journal,* 9 (December 1982): 5–20;

Williams, "David Lyndsay's 'Antique' and 'Plesand' Stories," in *A Day Estivall: Essays on the Music, Poetry and History of Scotland and England and Poems Previously Unpublished in Honour of Helena Mennie Shire,* edited by Alisoun Gardner-Medwin and Janet Hadley William (Aberdeen: Aberdeen University Press, 1990), pp. 155–166;

Williams, "'Thus Every Man Said for Himself': The Voices of Sir David Lyndsay's Poems," in *Bryght Lanternis: Essays on the Language and Literature of Medieval and Renaissance Scotland,* edited by J. Derrick McClure and Michael R. G. Spiller (Aberdeen: Aberdeen University Press, 1989), pp. 258–272.

Papers:

The Bannatyne Manuscript (1568) is in the National Library of Scotland (Advocates' Manuscripts 1.1.6), as is Lindsay's "Armorial" (1542; MS 31.4.3). The 1556 manuscript for *The Book of the Monarch* is in Lambeth Palace, London (Manuscript 332).

The *Marprelate Tracts*

(1588 – 1589)

Joseph Black
University of Toronto

BOOKS: *Oh read ouer D. John Bridges, for it is a worthy worke: or an epitome of the fyrste booke, of that right worshipfull volume, written against the Puritanes. . . . this learned epistle* (East Molesey: R. Waldegrave, 1588);

Oh read ouer D. John Bridges, for it is worthy worke:. . . . In this epitome (Fawsley: R. Waldegrave, 1588);

Certaine minerall, and metaphisicall schoolpoints, to be defended by the reuerende bishops (Coventry: R. Waldegrave, 1589);

Hay any worke for Cooper: or a briefe pistle directed to the reuerende byshopps (Coventry: R. Waldegrave, 1589; London?: R. Overton?, 1642);

Theses Martinianae: that is, certaine demonstrative conclusions. Published by Martin junior (Wolston: J. Hodgkins, 1589);

The iust censure and reproofe of Martin junior (Wolston?: J. Hodgkins, 1589);

The protestatyon of Martin Marprelat (Wolston?: R. Waldegrave?, 1589).

Collections: *The Marprelate Tracts: 1588, 1589,* edited by William Pierce (London: James Clark, 1911);

The Marprelate Tracts (1588–1589) (Menston: Scolar Press, 1967).

Notorious in their day, and until this century a byword for scurrility and invective, the seven extant *Marprelate Tracts* are now thought to be among the finest prose satires of the Elizabethan era. The pseudonymous tracts attack the established Elizabethan church, in particular church government by bishops, and defend a Presbyterian system. Their wit, irreverence, and stylistic freedom shocked contemporaries accustomed to a dignified sobriety in writings on religion, and they generated an important discussion of issues concerning language and decorum in religious controversy.

The central concerns of the *Marprelate Tracts* reflect arguments formulated by Protestant reformers over decades of opposition to the state church. The Elizabethan Settlement of 1559 had compromised between Catholic and Protestant practice, and like most compromises had failed to satisfy either extreme. Zealous Protestants – the Puritans – pushed for the elimination of what they perceived as Catholic remnants. Puritanism gained strength in the 1570s, with reformers such as Thomas Cartwright and John Field challenging the church on such issues as clerical vestments, the lack of a preaching ministry, and the legitimacy of episcopacy itself. The appointment of John Whitgift as archbishop of Canterbury in 1583, however, initiated sweeping efforts to clamp down on dissent and impose uniformity within the church. Restrictions on printing were tightened, discussion of Puritan reforms in Parliament was blocked, and church officers were given powers that even William Cecil, the queen's chief minister, described as "too much savoring of the Romish Inquisition."

The *Marprelate Tracts* protest this repression of reform. Like Cartwright and Field before, "Martin Marprelate" firmly believed that the New Testament prescribed a Presbyterian system of church government. Bishops, he thought, were unscriptural, suspiciously Catholic in origin, and, through their discouragement of a preaching ministry, active hinderers of salvation. Witty and jocular in approach, the *Marprelate Tracts* owe their power to an intense, underlying anger at a church apparently determined to ignore the blueprint divinely provided for its organization.

The identity of Martin Marprelate remains uncertain. Contemporary authorities suspected most of the more vocal reformers at one time or another, and subsequent researchers have offered additional possibilities. By far the most probable candidate is Job Throckmorton, a well-connected Warwickshire gentleman, Puritan controversialist, and Member of Parliament. Throckmorton was indicted for treason in connection with the tracts in 1590, but he was released on a legal technicality. Having a cousin who was one of the queen's ladies-in-waiting may have helped his case. But one consequence of the various

Oh read ouer D. John Bridges/for it is a worthy worke;

Or an epitome of the

fyrste Booke/of that right Worshipfull vo=
lume/ written against the Puritanes/ in the defence of
the noble cleargie/ by as worshipfull a priefte/ John Bridges/
Presbyter/Priest or elder/doctor of Diuillitie/ and Deane of
Sarum.Wherein the arguments of the puritans are
wifely preuented/ that when they come to an=
fwere M. Doctor/ they must needes
fay fomething that hath
bene fpoken.

Compiled for the behoofe and ouerthzow of
the Parfons/Fyckers/and Currats/that haue lernt
their Catechifmes/and are paft grace: By the reuerend
and worthie Martin Marprelate gentleman/and
dedicated to the Confocationhoufe.

The Epitome is not yet publifhed/ but it fhall be when
the Bifhops are at conuenient leyfure to view the fame.
In the meane time/let them be content with
this learned Epiftle.

Printed ouerfea/in Europe/within two fur=
longs of a Bounfing Prieft/at the coft and charges
of M. Marprelate/gentleman.

Title page for the first Marprelate Tract, *usually called the* Epistle, *which
attacks the episcopal hierarchy*

attempts to identify the elusive Martin has been to reveal how collective an effort the production of the tracts actually was.

The manager of the project was the Welsh reformer John Penry. He is still occasionally championed as author of the tracts, and he could certainly have had a hand in their expositions of Presbyterian arguments. The tracts were printed by Robert Waldegrave and John Hodgkins, and the presses themselves were smuggled from one sympathetic household to another. Once proofreaders, binders, distributors, and suppliers of ink and paper are included, the number of known "Martinists" is more than twenty. In an age that took the power of the printed word seriously, all risked charges of treason: to challenge authority was to challenge the queen. Except for the author himself, every one was identified by the end of 1590.

The first Marprelate production, usually known as the *Epistle,* appeared in October 1588. Informal, sarcastic, and full of puns, banter, and racy insinuations, the *Epistle* broke most of the unwritten rules of religious controversy. Its initial target was John Bridges, the dean of Salisbury, who in 1587 had published a fourteen-hundred-page *Defense* of the established church: "a very portable book," Martin writes in his second tract, "a horse may carry it if he be not too weak." With pungent wit Martin ridicules the logic and style of the *Defense,* justifying his no-holds-barred approach with the argument that a senseless book demands a similarly foolish response: "give me leave to play the dunce," he requests, "otherwise dealing with Master Doctor's book, I cannot keep *decorum personae.*"

The primary target of the *Epistle,* however, is not Bridges but the entire episcopal hierarchy – the "proud, popish, presumptuous, profane, paltry, pestilent, and pernicious prelates." While the bishops had received their share of Puritan criticism over the years, the novelty of Martin's attack lay in his willingness to descend to the personal. As Thomas Cooper, the bishop of Winchester, complained, Martin was not "contented to lay down great crimes generally, as some others have done," but chose instead to "charge some particular bishops with particular faults." A major reason for the popularity of the *Epistle* was its assortment of scandalous stories and spicy gossip involving "particular bishops." Martin's decision to forgo deference gave him a potent weapon: accurate or not, the stories helped secure attention to his general scrutiny of episcopal claims to spiritual and secular authority.

The impact of the *Epistle* was immediate and far-reaching, but not all readers were amused. By mid November Cecil could inform Archbishop Whitgift that "her Majesty has understanding of a lewd and seditious book lately printed as it should seem in secret manner, and as secretly dispersed by persons of unquiet spirits." To Elizabeth and her councillors, the *Epistle* set "a dangerous example" that might "encourage private men . . . to subvert all other kinds of government under Her Majesty's charge, both in the church and common weale." Whitgift was therefore instructed to "search out the authors . . . and their accomplices, and the printers and the secret dispersers of the same, and to cause them to be apprehended and committed." The archbishop quickly instituted a nationwide search, and the story of the remaining tracts is played out against a backdrop of informers, raids, disguises, surreptitious drop-offs, and ever-closer pursuit.

Despite the claim on its title page to have been "Printed oversea, in Europe, within two furlongs of a bouncing priest," the *Epistle* was produced at the house of Mrs. Elizabeth Crane in East Molesey, a village in Surrey a few miles west of London. With the hunt for Martin begun, the press was soon moved to the house of Sir Richard Knightley in Fawsley, just outside of Northampton, where the *Epitome* was printed in late November 1588. Martin introduces the *Epitome* by boasting of his first book's popularity: "I have been entertained at the Court; every man talks of my worship. Many would gladly receive my books, if they could tell where to find them." He mocks his pursuers by thanking them for their concern over his whereabouts. He also acknowledges the uneasiness his approach has generated, even among those sympathetic to his cause. "The Puritans are angry with me," he admits: "And why? Because I am too open. Because I jest." He defends his frankness by arguing its necessity: "I am

plain, I must needs call a spade a spade, a pope a pope." The *Epitome* continues to gibe at Bridges and derides John Aylmer, bishop of London, for an early book of his that had denounced the power and wealth of bishops. But on the whole the *Epitome* is more serious in argument than the *Epistle*.

The first official response to the Marprelate attack appeared in January 1589. Cooper's *Admonition to the People of England* was a collaborative effort that included submissions by various disputants all trying to clear their names from Martin's accusations. With its outraged rebuttals of the most bantering of comments, the *Admonition* provided Martin with an irresistible new target. The press had been moved to the house of John Hales in Coventry, and by the end of the month the Martinists had published the broadside *Certain Mineral and Metaphysical Schoolpoints*. A schoolpoint was a thesis that a student had to defend, using formal logic, against all comers; Martin offered thirty-seven points, each with its own defendant from among the contributors to the *Admonition*. The theses range from serious theological issues to clerical scandals; schoolpoint two, for example, requires the bishop of Saint David's to defend the proposition "That a Lord Bishop may safely have two wives *in esse* at once." The *Schoolpoints* was an interim publication, a parody of the official defense designed to keep readers amused until a more substantial response to Bishop Cooper could be prepared.

Hay Any Work for Cooper was finally ready in March 1589. The title echoes a popular London street call, *hay* being a contraction of *have ye,* and the bishop's name gives Martin opportunity for much wordplay. *Hay Any Work* is primarily occupied with setting forth the scriptural authorities for Presbyterian claims. But deepening Puritan opposition to his methods did prompt Martin to defend his use of satire. "I am not disposed to jest in this serious matter," he claims. But the unwillingness of men to read works that espoused "the cause of Christ's government" led him to use "mirth . . . as a covert, wherein I would bring the truth to light. The Lord being the author both of mirth and gravity, is it not lawful in itself for the truth to use either of these ways, when the circumstances do make it lawful?" With this defense Martin initiated a discussion of issues concerning language, decorum, and style that would extend well into the next century.

One person not convinced by Martin's argument was his printer, Waldegrave, who left the project, claiming that the preachers he consulted "misliked it." A new printer was recruited, the press was moved to the nearby house of Roger Wigston in

THE PROTESTATYON
OF MARTIN MARPRELAT

Wherin not wih standing the sur-
prizing of the printer, he maketh it
known vnto the world that he fear
eth, neither proud priest, Antichri
stian pope, tiranous prellate, nor
godlesse catercap: but defie: he all
the race of them by these presents
and offereth conditionally, as is
farthere expressed hearin by open
disputation to apear in the defence
of his cauf aginst them and
theirs

Which chaleng if they dare not
maintaine aginst him: then doth he al-
soe publishe that he never meaneth by
the assitaunce of god to leaue the a slaying of them and theire generation vntill they be vterly extinguised
out of our church
Published
by the worthie gentleman D. martin mar
prelat D. in all the faculties primat and
metropolitan

Page from the last Marprelate Tract, *which is less comic than the first six*

Wolston, and the *Theses Martinianae* appeared in July 1589. This collection of more than a hundred Martinist beliefs and criticisms is usually known as *Martin Junior* because it claims to be an edition by one of Martin's sons of his father's loose papers. *The Just Censure and Reproof of Martin Junior* followed a week later. Martin Senior rebukes his younger brother for publishing their father's unfinished work; he also fears that the scorn in the biting epilogue to *Martin Junior* will spur their father's pursuers to greater efforts. To illustrate his point Martin Senior presents a clever, lengthy speech in which a furious Archbishop Whitgift goads his servants in their search for Martin and his press.

With the real searchers closing in, paper and type were packed up and carted to Warrington in Lancashire, where the printer Hodgkins had his own press. Disaster struck when a box of type

spilled during unloading. Hodgkins informed bystanders that the small objects were lead shot; but word of the incident eventually reached someone who knew what type was, and in mid August 1589 the operation was raided near Manchester. The sheets of the unfinished *More Work for Cooper* were confiscated and destroyed, and judicial proceedings began. In September, in a final act of bravado, Throckmorton and Penry published their last tract, the *Protestation*. Perhaps the most personal of the tracts, the *Protestation* drops the comic tone almost entirely and analyzes the costs and benefits of the whole Martinist enterprise. Martin defends his course of action, summarizes the lost *More Work for Cooper,* and defiantly prophesies that "Martinism" – the "descrying and displaying of lord bishops" – will continue long after he has been silenced. For silenced he was. While Throckmorton was eventually released, those who had harbored the press were fined heavily and imprisoned. Waldegrave escaped to Scotland, where he became printer to James VI, but others involved in printing and distributing the tracts were put on the rack. Penry, declared an "enemy to the state" for books he had published under his own name, evaded the authorities until 1592, when he was caught and hanged.

In addition to Cooper's *Admonition* and the archbishop's investigation, the official response to the *Marprelate Tracts* included a royal "Proclamation against Certain Seditious and Schismatical Books and Libels." But the government also sponsored a parallel campaign that tried to use Martin's own style against him. More than twenty anti-Martinist works, in verse and prose, survive; only descriptions remain of the stage burlesques, which were eventually banned for indecency. The poetry is doggerel: the anonymous author of "Mar-Martin," for example, argues typically that "Martin the merry, who now is Mar-prelate, / Will prove mad Martin, and Martin Mar-the-state." Much of the prose consists of uninspired abuse; but writers such as John Lyly, Thomas Nashe, and Robert Greene have been associated with this pamphlet warfare, and the act of imitating Martin's style probably influenced the development of their own. Writers such as Francis Bacon, Gabriel Harvey, and Richard Harvey produced works that deplored the tactics of both sides. In addition to the problems they caused the bishops and the court, the *Marprelate Tracts* were also to occupy many of the most prominent literary figures of the age.

In their desire to replace bishops with presbyters, the *Marprelate Tracts* were written on behalf of a losing cause: Richard Hooker's *Of the Laws of Ecclesiastical Polity* (1593) would, in the long run, settle the question authoritatively in favor of the status quo. But they did help popularize the ideal of a free and public disputation on important matters, an ideal that in the next century would lead to discussions on freedom of conscience and religious toleration. The Marprelate persona in fact reappeared in radical pamphlets published in the 1640s during the Civil War. The *Marprelate Tracts* also helped promote the development of a racy, informal, colloquial prose, the prose of Thomas Dekker, Thomas Deloney, Nashe, and Greene. Martin Marprelate's style, with its remarkable freedom of language, would ultimately have much greater impact than his ideas on church government.

References:

Raymond Anselment, *"Betwixt Jest and Earnest": Marprelate, Milton, Marvell, Swift and the Decorum of Religious Ridicule* (Toronto: University of Toronto Press, 1979);

Edward Arber, *An Introductory Sketch to the Martin Marprelate Controversy, 1588–1590* (Westminster: Constable, 1895);

Leland H. Carlson, *Martin Marprelate, Gentleman: Master Job Throckmorton Laid Open in His Colors* (San Marino, Cal.: Huntington Library, 1981);

Carlson, "Martin Marprelate: His Identity and His Satire," in *English Satire* (Los Angeles: William Andrews Clark Memorial Library, 1972), pp. 3–53;

Ritchie Kendall, *The Drama of Dissent: The Radical Poetics of Nonconformity, 1380–1590* (Chapel Hill: University of North Carolina Press, 1986);

Donald J. McGinn, *John Penry and the Marprelate Controversy* (New Brunswick, N. J.: Rutgers University Press, 1966);

Ronald B. McKerrow, "The Marprelate Controversy," in his edition of *The Works of Thomas Nashe,* volume 5 (Oxford: Blackwell, 1958), pp. 34–65;

Peter Milward, *Religious Controversies of the Elizabethan Age: A Survey of Printed Sources* (Ilkley: Scolar Press / Lincoln: University of Nebraska Press, 1977);

William Pierce, *An Historical Introduction to the Marprelate Tracts* (London: Constable, 1908);

J. Dover Wilson, "The Marprelate Controversy," in *The Cambridge History of English Literature,* volume 3, edited by Sir A. W. Ward and A. R. Waller (Cambridge: Cambridge University Press, 1911), pp. 425–452.

Papers:

The official investigation of the Martinist press generated a large amount of manuscript material, mainly in the form of depositions, legal documents, and trial records. Most of this material is located in the Public Record Office, London, and the British Library; the most important documents are reprinted in Edward Arber's *An Introductory Sketch to the Martin Marprelate Controversy, 1588–1590* (1895). There is also an important collection of documents at the Huntington Library, San Marino, California. For a detailed listing of manuscript sources see Leland H. Carlson's *Martin Marprelate, Gentleman: Master Job Throckmorton Laid Open in His Colors* (1981).

Reginald Pole

(3 March 1500 – 17 November 1558)

Thomas F. Mayer

Augustana College

BOOKS: *Reginaldi Poli ad Henricum octavum Britanniae regem, pro ecclesiasticae unitatis defensione* (Rome: Antonio Blado, 1539?; Strasbourg: W. Rihelius, 1555; Ingolstadt: David Sartorius, 1587);

Discorso di pace di Mons. Reginaldo Polo Cardinale Legato a Carlo V. Imperatore et Henrico II. Re di Francia (1554 [possibly two editions of this year]; Venice: Nell'Accademia Veneta, 1558; Milan: G. A. degli Antonii, 1560); translated by Jacopo Pholio (Rome: Blado, 1555);

Copia delle lettere del . . . Re d'Inghilterra et de . . . Polo . . . alla Santità di . . . Julio Papa III sopra la reduttione di quel Regno alla unione della Chiesa (Milan, 1554);

Oratio . . . qua Caesaris . . . conatur . . . inflammare, ut adversum eos, qui nomen Evangelio dederunt, arma sumat . . . cum Scholiis Athanasii (Venice, 1554); translated by Fabian Wythers as *The seditious and blasphemous oration of cardinal Pole intytuled the defence of the eclesiastical vnitye* (London: O. Rogers, 1560);

Testamentum vere christianum (Dillingen: S. Mayer, 1559);

De concilio. De baptismo Constantini. Reformatio Angliae ex decretis eiusdem (Rome: Manuzio, 1562; Dillingen: S. Mayer, 1562; Venice: G. Ziletti, 1562);

De summo pontifice christi in terris vicario (Louvain: John Fowler, 1569);

A treatie of iustification, possibly by Pole (Louvain: John Fowler, 1569);

Epistola de Sacramento Eucharistiae (Cremona: Draconio, 1584).

Editions: *Epistola de Sacramento Eucharistiae,* translated by J. LeGrand in *Histoire du divorce de Henri VIII,* volume 1 (Paris: E. Martin, J. Bondot, E. Martin, 1688), pp. 289ff;

The Reformation of England, by the Decrees of Cardinal Pole, translated by Henry Raikes (Chester: R. H. Spence, 1839);

"Consilium . . . de emendanda ecclesiae" [Legal Opinion . . . on the Reform of the Church], in *Documents Illustrative of the Continental Reformation,* edited by B. J. Kidd (Oxford: Clarendon, 1911); translated in *The Catholic Reformation: Savonarola to Ignatius Loyola,* edited by John C. Olin (New York: Harper & Row, 1969); also translated in *Reform Thought in Sixteenth-Century Italy,* edited by E. G. Gleason (Chico, Cal.: Scholars Press, 1981);

De concilio. De baptismo Constantini. Reformatio Angliae ex decretis eiusdem (Farnborough, U.K.: Gregg Press, 1962);

Reginaldi Poli ad Henricum octavum Britanniae regem, pro ecclesiasticae unitatis defensione (Farnborough, U.K.: Gregg Press, 1965);

Pole's Defense of the Unity of the Church, translated, with an introduction, by Joseph G. Dwyer (Westminster, Md.: Newman Press, 1965); translated by Noëlle Marie Egretier as *Défense de l'unité de l'église* (Paris: J. Vrin, 1967);

"Vita Longolii," preface to *Christophori Longolii Orationes duae* (Farnborough, U.K.: Gregg Press, 1967);

De summo pontifice christi in terris vicario (Farnborough, U.K.: Gregg Press, 1968);

Reformatio Angliae, translated by J. P. Marmion in "The London Synod of Reginald, Cardinal Pole, 1555-6," volume 2, M.A. thesis, Keele University, 1974, pp. 1–65;

Friedenslegation des Reginald Pole zu Kaiser Karl V. und König Heinrich II. (1553-1556), edited by Heinrich Lutz (Tübingen: Niemeyer, 1981), pp. 381–403.

OTHER: "Vita Longolii," preface to *Christophori Longolii Orationes duae* (Florence: Heirs of F. Giunta, 1524).

Reginald Pole – cousin of Henry VIII, cardinal, archbishop of Canterbury, cultural conduit, and nearly successful candidate for pope – was one

Reginald Pole, circa 1543 (portrait by an unknown artist; from Philip Hughes, The Reformation in England, *volume 2:* Religio Depopulata, *1953)*

of the most important international figures of the mid sixteenth century. As the first well-known anti-Machiavellian, he has also come to play a large part in the history of political thought. Pole's role as Maecenas to a generation of both English and Italian writers, his hand in directing the creation of a saintly Thomas More, as well as his own large literary and especially biographical output (almost all of it in Latin) have contributed to increasing his importance as symbol and creator of symbols beyond even his exalted standing during his lifetime. It is not too much to say that virtually the whole European historiography of the English Reformation has depended on his views.

As the grandson of George, Duke of Clarence (brother of Edward IV), Pole might well have faced the fate of his uncle Edward, earl of Warwick, who was executed quietly by Henry VII for the White

Rose threat he posed to the new Tudor Crown. Instead both Henry VII and even more his son Henry VIII patronized Pole, providing a humanist education first in England (grammar school at the Carthusian House of Sheen, just outside London, then Oxford) and later in Padua, with a few months in Avignon as well. Pole was closely tied to the dean of Paduan humanists, Pietro Bembo, and had as his principal tutor Niccolò Leonico, a famous humanist and philosopher. While in Padua in the early 1520s, Pole made the friendship of the Flemish humanist Christoph Longueil, who had been too Ciceronian for even Roman Ciceronian humanists. This connection established Pole's literary claims, in the form of his elegant short life of Longolius (composed in 1524), his reputation for friendship, a habit of caring for dying friends in his household (whose lives he then rewrote), as well as a lifelong tie to the cultural resources of the Low Countries. Nevertheless, to judge from the expectations of Pole and his friends (including Longueil and Thomas Starkey), at least until the late 1520s Pole was preparing himself for a career in political service to his king.

Pole's first big opportunity, and a moment that became one of his favorite autobiographical subjects, came in 1529–1530 when Henry VIII asked him to help persuade the theologians of the University of Paris to render a favorable verdict on the king's divorce from Catherine of Aragon. Pole agreed enthusiastically and succeeded completely. Yet for reasons that remain obscure, he never collected his reward; instead, within six months of his return from Paris, Pole offered Henry his first inflammatory political writing (no longer extant), an opinion *against* proceeding with the king's divorce. In early 1532 Pole left England for Italy again, at the beginning of what turned out to be a twenty-year exile.

Once back in Padua, Pole slowly underwent a religious conversion, leaving him with an abiding belief in justification by faith alone, and a political one, too, as he opened technically treasonous communication with Emperor Charles V. Knowing how important a prize Pole was to his campaign to win acceptance of his divorce and the resultant new ecclesiastical order, Henry kept pressure on Pole for a public declaration of his opinion. Starkey sent Pole a steady stream of letters suggesting what that opinion should be. Pole refused the hints. In late 1535 and early 1536 he wrote Henry his most famous work, *Pro ecclesiasticae unitatis defensione* (On the Unity of the Church), known as *De unitate.*

This long work is probably most important for the paired images it created of the demonic Henry and the saintly More, John Fisher, and other "martyrs" to Henry's policy, including Pole himself. As successful as Pole was at handing on his portraits of others, *De unitate* works best in creating his own image as a consistent opponent of Henry, a view that passed directly from Pole's hands to those of his first biographers and thence to nearly all subsequent historians. *De unitate,* a thoroughly literary and rhetorical work, no matter how serious its professed purposes, caused a great deal of trouble for Pole. Although he probably never knew its full import, Henry was thoroughly annoyed by Pole's demeaning treatment of him and persistent demands that the king do penance (there was more than a distant echo of Thomas Becket here and in other of Pole's writings); but in his determination to subvert Henry, Pole appealed to the "people" (that is, the nobility) to overthrow the king (his own noble origins and standing were highlighted in several especially inflammatory passages). This doctrine angered the emperor and cost Pole crucial support from him over the next three years.

Interestingly enough, Pole's view of papal primacy did *not* offend Pope Paul III. Pole argued in favor of a charismatically grounded papacy, not an institutional monarchy, but Paul nevertheless invited him to Rome and made him a cardinal in December 1536. From that point forward Pole made his career in papal service. Associated from the first with the party of reform, the so-called *spirituali,* he contributed almost immediately to the "Consilium . . . de emendanda ecclesiae" ("Legal Opinion . . . on the Reform of the Church," 1537), which would have disassembled the financial basis of papal absolutism. In 1537 he undertook his first (unsuccessful) legation to aid the Pilgrimage of Grace against Henry and in 1539 another (more typical) legation to establish peace between the emperor and Francis I. No more successful, it nevertheless established Pole's enduring concern with peacemaking, one of his most important legacies from Desiderius Erasmus. In the course of his 1537 mission, he assisted as midwife in the reunification of the Italian and the Flemish Renaissance by bringing the painter/entrepreneur Lambert Lombard to Italy with him. Pole also shortly thereafter made his first contribution to Italian historiography, heavily influencing Paolo Giovio's narrative of the English Reformation in Giovio's *Descriptio Britanniae, Hiberniae, et Orchadum* (1548).

From 1541 until the opening of the first session of the Council of Trent, Pole governed the papal state of Viterbo, not far from Rome. While there he patronized a distinguished circle of writers and religious thinkers (among them Marcantonio Flaminio, one of the most enduringly popular of Neo-Latin poets, especially in England) who produced the most important text of the Italian Reformation, *Il Beneficio di Christo* (1543; translated as *The Benefit of Christ's Death,* 1548, by Pole's cousin Edward Courtenay, Earl of Devon). He also associated closely with the poet Vittoria Colonna, Michelangelo, and probably Michelangelo's close associate Sebastiano del Piombo, who painted the most striking portrait of Pole, now in the Hermitage.

Keeping his focus tight on the ruling order, Pole opened the Council of Trent in 1545 with a famous sermon blaming the ills of the church on the laxity of the clergy. (John Calvin would later have great fun with this text in his *Antidote to the Council of Trent.*) Although somewhat more diplomatically worded than *De unitate,* it probably helped to isolate the already somewhat eccentric Pole. While the other two legates had prepared to open the council, Pole had remained behind in Rome, writing his first major ecclesio-political statement, *De concilio* (not published until 1562, in an expurgated version). The presently available text defends papal primacy more than *De unitate* by grounding the form of a general council not in Nicaea (where the Emperor Constantine had taken a hand) but in the council of Jerusalem (where Pole also had to revise Peter's role relative to Paul). But as in *De unitate,* Pole offers a charismatic interpretation both of the council's matter – everything pertaining to faith, probably deliberately not further defined – and of its action, which depended completely on "an effusion of the Holy Spirit." It is not terribly surprising that Pole had little direct impact on Trent, as he left in the midst of the debate over justification, which ultimately led to a strongly worded repudiation of justification by faith, Pole's own position up to that point. (As obscure as were Pole's actions in this crisis, the existence of a pair of diametrically opposed opinions on justification leaves his "true" views well up in the air.)

After teaming up with the erstwhile Roman humanist and then papal secretary Blosio Palladio to refute the emperor's protest against the translation of the council to Bologna in 1548, Pole made a strong run at the papacy in the conclave of 1549–1550. His chances set by the Roman oddsmakers at ninety-five to one hundred, Pole actually came within one vote of election. Instead of campaigning he spent his time writing at least four or five versions of a dialogue (his favorite form), *De summo pontifice.* (The published text of 1569 seems not to be Pole's final intention; in addition, there are at least a half-dozen manuscripts of a completely different text, "De summo pontifice extra conclavi scripta.") The major burden of the published text is that only candidates distinguished by their Christlike humility are suited to election.

Flying once more in the face of a rapidly developing papal monarchy, Pole yet spent his last years in its service as legate first for peace (as in 1539) and then for the reconciliation of England. During the course of the first assignment, he wrote *Discorso di pace* (Discourse on Peace, 1554), in which he argues that divine providence has established the pope as the only teacher of true peace, a matter of heartfelt desire on the part of kings and emperors, rather than of political maneuverings. After his return to England in 1554, following a delay of more than a year caused precisely by political maneuverings, Pole began to oversee the reconversion of En-

gland. He had time only to hold one legatine synod, in which he placed most emphasis on the quality of the clergy, as seen in *Reformatio Angliae* (1562), a text written in the requisite legal format, to which Pole was unaccustomed.

A strong personal favorite of both Mary Tudor and her consort, King Philip, by whom he was made archbishop of Canterbury, Pole nonetheless fell afoul of Pope Paul IV, his old enemy and refounder of the Roman Inquisition. Paul accused Pole of heresy and revoked his legation. Pole died on 17 November 1558, leaving a large pile of broken monuments behind him. These included his tomb, designed by his secretary, Dominic Lampsonius, a poet, painter, biographer of artists (especially Lombard), and another important link between Pole and the Netherlands. Lampsonius may well have assisted in Anton Mor's coming to England to create his cultural and religious icons of Mary Tudor and others. With more time this offensive might have been as successful as Pole's reform of the English church looked likely to be. That reform, too, had a major literary dimension in the form of Bartolomé Carranza's catechism, which would eventually land Carranza in the hands of the Spanish Inquisition. Unquestionably Pole's greatest success stemmed from his patronage of Ellis Heywood (a member of his household in England), Nicholas Harpsfield (his archdeacon of Canterbury), and George Lily (longtime intimate and chaplain to the archbishop), through whom he directed the creation of the Catholic view of the English Reformation.

Until very recently Pole and his works have been read as saintly antidotes to the evils of the English Reformation, even if Pole himself has usually been adjudged a failure. This is true even of Dermot Fenlon's careful 1972 study of Pole's position in the Council of Trent. Of his authorship, there is even less word, apart from a minor dispute about whether he really wrote the "Vita Longolii" (1524).

Nevertheless, it is possible to treat Pole's achievement under three heads: political, religious, and literary. His political stature is only just beginning to be recognized (particularly in a 1990 study by T. F. Mayer), especially his contribution to the room for maneuver in both Rome and England characteristic of the middle of the sixteenth century. In the long term he was unsuccessful in preserving that opening, just as he was in his other major political sphere, peacemaking, as examined by Heinrich Lutz in a 1981 commentary. In both politics and religion Pole kept alive crucial Renaissance ideals in an age of increasing Counter-Reformation (as seen in studies by Massimo Firpo [1990], Paolo Simoncelli [1979], and J. I. Tellechea Idigoras [1977]). Although he seems to have made an accommodation with the new era, he had too little time to give it full shape. The same held true for his literary efforts, which have yet to attract much attention. None of them was finished, including even *De unitate*, the only major work published in his lifetime; how unfinished and how much the various manuscripts differ from one another was not recognized until the work of Thomas F. Dunn (1976), who only just began the study of the text. However, the images Pole's works create – of himself, his allies, and his opponents – have proved much more enduring than their original fate might have suggested (as seen in Peter S. Donaldson's 1989 study). According to Simoncelli (1977), the figure of Pole became at least as important after his death as a principal bellwether of the interpretation of the Reformation in England and Italy.

Letters:

Epistolarum Reginaldi Poli, edited by A. M. Quirini (Brescia, 1744–1757).

Biographies:

Ludovico Beccadelli, "Vita di Reginaldo Polo" (circa 1561), in *Monumenti di varia letteratura,* volume 2, edited by G. B. Morandi (Bologna: Istituto per le scienze, 1797–1804), pp. 277–333; translated by Benjamin Pye as *The Life of Cardinal Reginald Pole, Written Originally in Italian by Ludovico Beccadelli* (London: Bathurst, 1766);

Thomas Phillips, *The History of the Life of Reginald Pole* (Oxford: William Jackson, 1764);

Edward Stone, *Remarks upon the History of the Life of Reginald Pole* (Oxford: W. Jackson, 1766);

Gloucester Ridley, *A Review of Mr. Phillips' History of the Life of Reginald Pole* (London: J. Whiston, 1766);

Timothy Neve, *Animadversions upon Mr Phillips's History of the Life of Cardinal Pole* (Oxford: Clarendon, 1766);

Walter Farquhar Hook, *Lives of the Archbishops of Canterbury,* volume 8 (London: R. Bentley, 1869);

F. G. Lee, *Reginald Pole, Cardinal Archbishop of Canterbury* (London: John C. Nimmo, 1888);

Athanasius Zimmermann, *Kardinal Pole, sein Leben und seine Schriften. Ein Beitrag zur Kirchengeschichte des 16. Jahrhunderts* (Regensburg: F. Pustet, 1893);

Marie Hallé (as Martin Haile), *The Life of Reginald Pole* (London: Pitman & Sons, 1911);

Reginald Biron and Jean Barennes, *Un prince anglais cardinal légat au XVIe siècle, Reginald Pole* (Paris: Arthur Savaète, 1922);

Wilhelm Schenk, *Reginald Pole, Cardinal of England* (London: Longman, 1950);

Maria Teresa Dainotti, *La via media: Reginald Pole, 1500–1558* (Bologna: EMI, 1987).

References:

Salvatore Caponetto, ed., *Il "beneficio di Cristo" con le versioni del secolo XVI, documenti e testimonianze* (De Kalb: Northern Illinois University Press, 1972);

J. Crehan, "St. Ignatius and Cardinal Pole," *Archivum historicum societatis Jesu,* 25 (1956): 72–98;

Peter S. Donaldson, "Machiavelli and Antichrist: Prophetic Typology in Reginald Pole's *De unitate* and *Apologia ad Carolum quintum,*" in *Machiavelli and Mystery of State* (Cambridge: Cambridge University Press, 1989), pp. 1–36;

Thomas F. Dunn, "The Development of the Text of Pole's *De unitate ecclesiae,*" *Papers of the Bibliographical Society of America,* 70 (1976): 455–468;

Paul van Dyke, "Reginald Pole and Thomas Cromwell: An Examination of the *Apologia ad Carolum quintum,*" *American Historical Review,* 9, no. 4 (1904): 696–724;

Dermot Fenlon, *Heresy and Obedience in Tridentine Italy: Cardinal Pole and the Counter Reformation* (Cambridge: Cambridge University Press, 1972);

Massimo Firpo, *Tra alumbrados e "spirituali": Studi su Juan de Valdés e il Valdesianesimo nella crisi religiosa del '500 italiano* (Florence: Olschki, 1990);

Gigliola Fragnito, "Aspetti della censura ecclesiastica nell'Europa della controriforma: l'edizione parigina delle opere di Gasparo Contarini," *Rivista di storia e letteratura religiosa,* 21 (1985): 3–48;

Adrian Gasquet, *Cardinal Pole and His Early Friends* (London: George Bell & Sons, 1927);

Hubert Jedin, *The Struggle for the Council,* translated by Ernest Graf in *A History of the Council of Trent,* volume 1 (Saint Louis: Herder, 1957);

T. F. Mayer, "If Martyrs Are Exchanged with Martyrs: The Kidnappings of William Tyndale and Reginald Pole," *Archiv für Reformationsgeschichte,* 81 (1990): 286–308;

Mayer, "A Mission Worse than Death: Reginald Pole and the Parisian Theologians," *English*

Historical Review, 103 (October 1988): 870–891;

George B. Parks, *The Middle Ages (to 1525),* in *The English Traveller to Italy,* volume 1 (Rome: Storia e letteratura, 1954);

Parks, "The Parma Letters and the Dangers to Cardinal Pole," *Catholic Historical Review,* 46, no. 3 (1960): 299–317;

H. J. Sieben, "Eine 'ökumenische' Auslegung von Apostelgeschichte 15 in der Reformationszeit: Reginald Poles *De concilio,*" *Theologie und Philosophie,* 60 (1985): 16–42;

Paolo Simoncelli, *Il caso Reginald Pole: eresia e santità nelle polemiche religiose del cinquecento* (Rome: Storia e letteratura, 1977);

Simoncelli, *Evangelismo italiano del cinquecento: Questione religiosa e nicodemismo politico* (Rome: Istituto italiano per l'età moderna e contemporanea, 1979);

Quentin Skinner, *The Reformation,* in *Foundations of Modern Political Thought,* volume 2 (Cambridge: Cambridge University Press, 1978);

J. I. Tellechea Idigoras, *Fray Bartolomé Carranza y el cardenal Pole: Un navarro en la restauracion católica de Inglaterra (1554–1558)* (Pamplona: CSIC, 1977);

W. Gordon Zeeveld, *Foundations of Tudor Policy* (Cambridge, Mass.: Harvard University Press, 1948).

Papers:

Pole's manuscripts are scattered all over Europe. The Biblioteca Apostolica Vaticana (esp. Vaticani Latini, 5964–5972 and 5826–5827), the British Library (esp. among the Cottonian MSS), and the Public Record Office, London (many letters and the presentation copy of *De unitate,* among other documents), hold the major collections. There are also large holdings in the archive of Pole's majordomo Bartolomeo Stella in Bergamo as well as various libraries and archives in Florence, Venice (the Marciana has another manuscript of *De unitate* and a large volume of Pole's correspondence), Brescia (the Biblioteca Queriniana has that cardinal's working papers for his edition of Pole's letters), and Parma. Copies of Pole's correspondence from his last peace legation are most widespread; for these see *Friedenslegation* (1981). Other of his diplomatic correspondence is in Brussels, Simancas, and Madrid; scattered letters are to be found in anthologies in most major libraries in Europe.

John Ponet

(1516? – circa 1 August 1556)

Christopher Hodgkins
University of North Carolina at Greensboro

BOOKS: *A defence for mariage of priestes, by Scripture and aunciente wryters* (London: Printed by R. Wolff, 1549);

A notable sermon concerninge the ryght vse of the lordes Supper (London: Gwalter Lynne, 1550);

Catechismus breuis christianae disciplinae summam continens, omnibus ludimagistris authoritate regia commendatus. Huic catechismo adiuncti sunt Articuli (Zurich, 1553); translated by Ponet as *A short catechisme* (Zurich, 1553);

An apologie fully aunsweringe by scriptures and aunceant doctors, a blasphemose book gatherid by D. Steph. Gardiner, and other papists (Strasbourg, 1556);

A Shorte Treatise of Politike power, and of the true Obedience which subjectes owe to Kynges and other Ciuile Gouernours, with an Exhortacion to all true naturall Englishe men, compyled by D. I. P. B. R. W. (Strasbourg?, 1556);

Diallacticon viri boni et literati, de veritate, natura, atque substantia corporis et sanguinis Christi in Eucharistia (Strasbourg?, 1557);

A defence of priestes mariages (London: Richard Jugge, 1561?).

Edition: *A Shorte Treatise of Politike Power* (New York: Da Capo, 1972) – facsimile of the 1556 edition.

TRANSLATION: Bernardino Ochino, *A tragoedie or dialoge of the uniuste primacie of the bishop of Rome* (London: Gwalter Lynne, 1549).

John Ponet – Thomas Cranmer's chaplain, bishop of Rochester and Winchester, Marian exile, and first Protestant advocate of limited monarchy – is one of the more influential forgotten men in literary history. Actually, he is not quite forgotten: John Adams, introducing his *Defense of the American Constitutions* (1787), writes that Ponet's *Short Treatise of Politic Power* (1556) "contains all the essential principles of liberty, which were afterwards dilated upon by [Algernon] Sydney and [John] Locke." Nevertheless, apart from this striking statement from a framer of the U.S. Constitution, the rest (more or less) is silence. Sydney and Locke do not acknowledge him – nor does John Milton, who (in *The Tenure of Kings and Magistrates,* 1649) quotes Ponet's arguments for popular sovereignty and elective kingship but misattributes the quotation. So as Ponet's ideas rose in currency, his name sank into relative oblivion.

Nothing is known of Ponet's parentage, and indeed little is known of his origins at all. John Bale records that he was born in Kent about the year 1516. The first definite record comes in 1532, when he received his B.A. and became a fellow of Queen's College, Cambridge, which, along with Saint John's, had become both a humanist and Lutheran center within the university. He belonged to a circle of friends established around the promising young scholars John Cheke and Thomas Smith of Saint John's. Besides their shared Protestantism, this group was unified by the study of Greek and an interest in English as a medium for literary and learned expression. Ponet quickly earned a reputation as a great scholar. Beyond his theological and linguistic attainments, he also took a strong interest in mathematics, astronomy, and architecture.

Ponet advanced quickly in his parallel scholarly and clerical careers. He was appointed Greek lecturer and received his M.A. in 1535; then he was ordained priest in 1536, held office as college bursar from 1537 to 1539, and served as dean during 1541–1542. Ponet's speedy rise drew the attention of the powerful. Cranmer, Thomas Cromwell, and King Henry VIII all took a keen interest in him and in the entire Cambridge humanist circle. But Ponet and the young Protestants had also made a powerful enemy in Stephen Gardiner, by 1542 chancellor of Cambridge, who was particularly alarmed at their curricular proposal to de-emphasize the Schoolmen in favor of biblical and classical studies. Thus, the early 1540s saw a temporary setback for the "Cambridge circle," so that between 1543 and 1546 Ponet seems to have disappeared from university affairs, probably for active work as a parish priest. Nevertheless, some accounts place him at this time at court as chaplain to the failing king.

With Henry's death and the succession of Edward VI in 1547, the influence of the "Cambridge circle" began to be felt nationally and in earnest – since 1544 Cheke and John Cox had been tutors to the boy king, and William Grindal to Princess Elizabeth. Ponet, made doctor of divinity in 1547, had already become canon of the church at Canterbury in January 1546 and soon after emerged as chaplain to Cranmer. With the change of monarchs Cranmer sought to promote a theological consensus among Europe's Protestant factions, both through his own writings and through the encouragement of international scholarly exchange. As Cranmer's administrative duties kept him more and more from research, he relied increasingly on Ponet to abstract the necessary works from the extensive Lambeth Palace and to provide a body of authorities for citation. This was the crucial period of Cranmer's eucharistic writings and liturgical reforms, and stylistic differences between Cranmer's first and second eucharistic works – *A Defense of the True and Catholic Doctrine* (1550) and *An Answer unto a Crafty and Sophistical Cavillation* (1551) – suggest that Ponet had a substantial hand in the latter publication. Ponet's years at Lambeth also introduced him to Europe's leading Reformers, many of whom were received at the palace as "brethren" and established at the English universities as divines.

A translation of a Latin book by one such émigré, Bernardino Ochino, is probably the earliest surviving printed work in Ponet's name. *A Tragedy or Dialogue* (1549) is cast in the form of dramatic exchanges between the warring forces in Christian history as the devil and the pope are vividly overthrown by Christ and the gospelers. In making his translation Ponet probably developed his often-noted skill with biting and amusing satirical dialogue – a quality that was to draw him both praise for "merriness" and blame for flippancy with serious matters. At about this time he produced the first of his own controversial works, a brief propaganda tract called *A Defense for Marriage of Priests* (1549). After the repeal of the Henrician Act of Six Articles in 1547, the Convocation of Bishops had voted to allow clerical marriage, followed by Parliament in February 1549. Ponet's tract defends the émigré Peter Martyr from acid conservative polemics by Gardiner and Richard Smith, though with none of the ad hominem excitement of his opponents.

Having served Cranmer and the Protestant cause effectively, Ponet was at thirty-four approach-

ing the zenith of his career. As a means of grooming him for a bishopric, Cranmer appointed him, along with John Hooper, to preach the Lenten sermons of 1550 at Paul's Cross in the presence of the young king. Only one of Ponet's weekly offerings has survived: *A Notable Sermon Concerning the Right Use of the Lord's Supper* (1550). In it he takes the middle way of the Edwardine Forty-two Articles and of Cranmer's later eucharistic writings, to which he himself contributed. He argues that Christ's presence in Holy Communion is real – but spiritual, not physical. Anyone who partakes of the outward sign without inward faith not only does not receive Christ but actually brings damnation on himself. Ponet's moderating position is virtually identical with John Calvin's.

Ponet's successful sermons do not seem to have determined his elevation to a bishropric because on 8 March 1550, before he had completed the series, he had already been nominated to the see of Rochester. On 29 June he was consecrated in the Lambeth chapel, the first bishop to be elevated under the rites of Cranmer's new ordinal. So after years near the seats of power, Ponet began to occupy one himself. In January 1551 he was appointed one of thirty-one commissioners to suppress heresies and enforce administration of the Sacraments according to the new Prayer Book. He also was called on to decide – along with Cranmer and London's new bishop, Nicholas Ridley – a delicate case: whether or not Princess Mary should be allowed to hear Mass. Their conclusion – "that to give license to sin was sin; nevertheless, they thought the king might suffer to wink at it for a time" – is often attributed to Ponet, being seen by his detractors as evidence of his unscrupulousness and by his defenders as evidence of his unfanatical flexibility.

Ponet's detractors have found further occasion for blame in the circumstances surrounding his translation to the bishropric of Winchester between March and June of 1551. The charge is simony, for his preferment depended on his resigning to the Crown all the lands of the see in return for a fixed income of two thousand marks a year. No doubt Ponet appears here in a poor light; but it can be said in his defense that he was only one of many new bishops forced that year into similar bargains by hungry courtiers, that his emolument was one of the smallest, and that the practice was eventually legalized in the first year of Elizabeth's reign. Ironically, no sooner was he made bishop of Winchester than this defender of clerical marriage obtained, on 27 July 1551, a divorce. However, that Ponet was in

THE CATHECHISME. Fol.xlii.

only mercy of god, and pure grace of Christ oure Lorde: whearby we weare in hym made to thole good workes, that God hath apointed for vs to walke in . And although good workes can not deserue to make vs righteous before god: yet do thei so cleaue vnto faythe : that neither can fayth be founde without thé, nor good workes be any wheare wythout faythe.

Trewe faithe and workes vnseparate.

Master. I lyke verye well thys shorte declaration of fayth and workes: for Paul playnly teacheth the same. But canst thou yet further

G.i. Te-

THE CATHECHISME. Fol.xliii.

assured rocke Jesus Christ and vpõ trust in hym. This is that same church, which Paul calleth the piller, and vpholding stay of truth. To this church belõg the keies, whearwyth heauen is locked and vnlocked : for that is done by the ministration of the worde: wherunto properly appertayneth the power to bynde and louse : to holde for gylty, and forgiue synnes. So that whosoeuer beleueth the Gospell preached in thys church, he shal be saued : but whoso beleueth not, he shal be dãpned.

Keies to bynde and loose.

Master. Now wold I fain

G.iii. heare

Pages from John Ponet's A Short Catechism *(1553). Edward VI commanded that it be used in all English schools, but he died seven weeks after giving the order, and the book never came into wide use.*

this case the wronged party is suggested by the presence of Cranmer – who strictly opposed divorce and remarriage except for adultery – at Ponet's marriage to Maria Haymond on 23 October.

During his brief tenure at Winchester, Ponet produced his Latin *Catechismus Brevis* (1553) and its English translation, *A Short Catechism* (1553). Aside from its thoroughgoing Protestantism, this work is most notable for its dialogic form, modeled explicitly on Socrates and Apollinaris, and for its very strong statements preferring the rule of the "king and high Bishop Christ" to the "pleasure of worldly tyrants." Thus, in the waning days of Edward – the godly "young Josiah" – Ponet anticipates the antiabsolutism of his *Short Treatise.*

After Edward's death in the spring of 1553, Ponet's episcopal career came to an abrupt end. On 4 August, Gardiner, Ponet's Cambridge enemy and predecessor at Winchester, went straight from the Tower to Queen Mary's Privy Council. By September, Ponet was ejected, to be imprisoned and later degraded from the bishop's rank. After his release

from prison, little is known of his activities until the first months of 1554, when a representative for Philip of Spain arrived in London to arrange the marriage to Mary. It is then that Ponet is seen acting on his principles of resistance, which he was later to enunciate in the *Short Treatise,* by taking part in Sir Thomas Wyatt's abortive revolt. After the plot's collapse nothing is known of him until he appears in August as an exile in Strasbourg where many of the former "Cambridge circle" fled to join Peter Martyr.

Strasbourg was to be Ponet's last home, and he seems to have accepted it as such. Two sons were born to him there, and in February 1555 he applied for and received citizenship, indicating that his English property and rights had already been forfeited. On 4 September his rented house burned with the loss of four thousand crowns. Yet he seems to have borne his lot with equanimity. "What is exile?" he wrote to Heinrich Bullinger. "A thing which, provided you have wherewithal to subsist, is painful only in imagination." Still, the exile's mind was turned steadily toward his homeland, as is clear from his literary output. During these last two years of his life he produced his most important works. The Latin *Diallacticon* (1557) develops the eucharistic theology of his 1550 Lenten sermon for a learned Continental audience in a conciliatory, noncontroversial manner, and it was to become a definitive work on the subject. On the other hand, *An Apology Fully Answering . . . a Blasphemous Book* (1556) answers the ad hominem polemics of Thomas Martin with what Ponet admits is unseemly vehemence, particularly excoriating his opponent for using "filthy and unchaste" language in a work addressed to the "virgin queen" Mary.

But it was the regime of Mary that was to occasion his most influential work – *A Short Treatise of Politic Power.* By early 1556 news from England was grim: Philip seemed ready to absorb the English Crown, while Ridley, Hugh Latimer, John Hooper, Cranmer, and many other leading Protestants had been burned at the stake. So, after reading Cardinal Reginald Pole's *De Unitate* (1535) and rereading Cicero's oration in defense of tyrannicide, Ponet began to write with two purposes in mind: to prove Mary's regime unlawful and to justify active resistance against it.

Ponet's *A Short Treatise* stands at the head of a line of Protestant resistance theory that went beyond the teachings of Martin Luther and even Calvin. The Reformers had taught that because Christ is absolute head of the church, the church can have no absolute *human* head; Ponet, by a logical extension alarming to Christian kings, argues that because Christ is absolute king of the earth, there can be no absolute *earthly* king. Instead, he says, God chooses to mediate his sovereignty through the people as a whole and through their native constitutional and common-law traditions, which are subject only to scriptural law as summarized in the Golden Rule: "do unto others as you would have them do unto you." Thus the people may elect and depose their rulers as they see fit and even – as a last resort in cases of extreme and bloody tyranny – execute or assassinate them.

Besides advancing these doctrines Ponet's political thought is most notable for attacking Mary's regime not primarily as "popish," but because it violated a divinely ordained natural law common to all people, Protestant and papist. Thus, while his argument is profoundly theological, it is remarkably nonsectarian. Also remarkably, he claims that all people share in the guilt if they do not resist tyrants. This sense of corporate responsibility is reflected in the hierarchy of means that the oppressed should

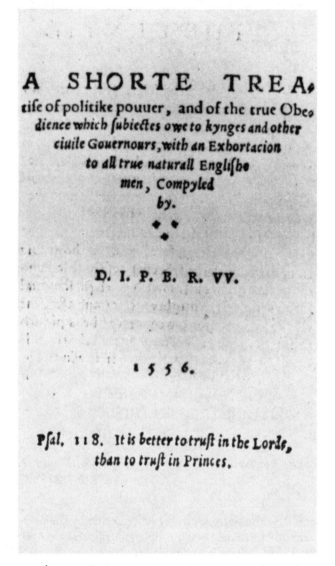

Title page for Ponet's work attacking the reign of Mary I

follow: first, an appeal to the prince's conscience; second, an appeal to the nobility and the Parliament; third, a complaint to church leaders and ministers; fourth, an appeal to the people as a whole; and fifth, a final recourse to spiritually inspired private action – that is, assassination. Ponet concludes that in England's case, the time for popular uprising has come.

Ponet's persona throughout the work is that of an Isaiah-like prophet decrying the pervasive decay of his nation from its sick head down. His style, like Isaiah's, is often satiric and witty, as in this ad hominem passage on Bishop Edmund Bonner: "But Bonner . . . stand still a while, while I rub thee. Tell me plainly, and face not out a lie, as thou art wont. . . . Once in thy life tell the truth, and shame thy master the Devil." Likewise, even in this call to action there is a lighter colloquial touch: "Remember that our countryman *Adam Afterwit* hath a great while been the lord *Forewit's* fool. . . . Say not too late: Had I wist. Thou hast sufficient warning; God give thee grace to consider it and use it." Yet in his concluding pages his language rises, like the prophet's, to an elegiac cry for repentance of the national sins that have brought this national scourge.

After completing *A Short Treatise,* Ponet survived only a few months, dying about 1 August 1556. The book was published around this time, probably in Strasbourg, but only under the initials "D. I. P. B. R. W" (for "Doctor John Ponet, bishop of Rochester and Winchester"). For this and other reasons Ponet's influence, while extensive, has been virtually anonymous. Christopher Goodman and John Knox seem to have relied on his book in writing their respective anti-Marian tracts, *How Superior Powers Ought to Be Obeyed* (1558) and *The First Blast of the Trumpet against the Monstrous Regiment of Women* (1558). However, their borrowed doctrine of tyrannicide, along with Knox's virulent misogyny, led Elizabeth to ban all three books at her accession after Mary's death in 1558, so the Marian exiles, and especially Ponet, came to be seen as seditious firebrands. Nevertheless, when the Geneva Bible appeared in 1560 (the work of William Whittingham, also an exile), the marginal glosses to Old Testament passages on kingly authority – and on the occasional kingly assassination – clearly reflected Ponet's ideas. For example, the chapter heading for Deuteronomy 17 refers to "the election of the King"; note "o" to Deuteronomy 17:20 explains that "Kings ought so to love their subjects as nature bindeth one brother to love another"; note "f" to I Samuel 8:11 denounces bad kings as unauthorized "usurpers"; and note "n" to II Kings 9:33 commends Jehu's divinely inspired assassination of Jezebel.

So Ponet's reputation has been one of paradoxically obscure fame. His early notoriety as a seditionist made his name and his book dangerous to cite, but his uncredited influence on these biblical notes ensured his ideas an astonishingly wide audience. Among other important works that show his direct or indirect influence are the last edition of Calvin's *Institutes of the Christian Religion* (1559), the Huguenot resistance tracts *Franco-Gallia* (1573) and *Vindiciae Contra Tyrannos* (1579), Richard Hooker's *Ecclesiastical Polity* (1593), Milton's *Tenure of Kings and Magistrates* (1649), and perhaps Locke's two *Treatises of Government* (1689-1690). *A Short Treatise* was republished in 1639 and finally under Ponet's name at the outbreak of the civil war in 1642. And it was "the English Bible's seditious notes," as much as any stylistic or linguistic considerations, that moved James I to commission the Authorized Version (1611). But well into the eighteenth century in New England, the unauthorized version from Geneva still reigned. So it may well be a sign of Ponet's anonymous effect that so many thousand Continentals marched to fight James's heir in 1775 under the slogan "Only God is King."

Biography:

Winthrop S. Hudson, *John Ponet (1516?-1556): Advocate of Limited Monarchy* (Chicago: University of Chicago Press, 1942).

References:

John Adams, *The Works of John Adams,* 10 volumes, edited by Charles Francis Adams (Boston: Little, Brown, 1850-1856);

A. A. Bromham, "Thomas Middleton's *Hengist, King of Kent* and John Ponet's *Shorte Treatise of Politike Power,*" Notes & Queries, 29 (April 1982): 143-145;

Barbara Peardon, "The Politics of Polemic: John Ponet's *Short Treatise of Politic Power* and Contemporary Circumstance 1553-1556," *Journal of British Studies,* 22 (Fall 1982): 35-49;

Richard Strier, "Faithful Servants: Shakespeare's Praise of Disobedience," in *The Historical Renaissance: New Essays on Tudor and Stuart Literature and Culture,* edited by Heather Dubrow and Strier (Chicago: University of Chicago Press, 1988), pp. 242-269.

Papers:

The British Library has one letter from Ponet to John Bale (29,546 f. 25).

Thomas Sackville

(1536 – 19 April 1608)

Michael Pincombe
University of Newcastle upon Tyne

See also the Sackville and Thomas Norton entry in *DLB 62: Elizabethan Dramatists.*

BOOK: *The tragedie of Gorboduc,* by Sackville and Thomas Norton (London: Printed by William Griffith, 1565); republished as *The tragidie of Ferrex and Porrex* (London: Printed by John Day, 1570).

Editions and Collections: Baldassare Castiglione, *The Book of the Courtier,* translated by Sir Thomas Hoby (London: Dent / New York: Dutton, 1928); revised edition, with an introduction by J. H. Whitfield (London: Dent, 1974);

The Complaint of Henry, Duke of Buckingham, Including the Induction; or, Thomas Sackville's Contribution to the "Mirror for Magistrates", edited by Marguerite Hearsey (New Haven: Yale University Press, 1936) — an edition of Sackville's autograph manuscript;

The Mirror for Magistrates, edited by Lily B. Campbell (Cambridge: Cambridge University Press, 1938), pp. 298–345;

Gorboduc; or, Ferrex and Porrex, edited by Irby B. Cauthen, Jr. (Lincoln: University of Nebraska Press, 1970);

"'Sacvyles Olde Age': A Newly Discovered Poem by Thomas Sackville, Lord Buckhurst, Earl of Dorset (c. 1536–1608)," edited by Rivkah Zim and M. B. Parkes, *Review of English Studies,* new series 40 (1989): 1–25.

OTHER: "The Induction" and "The Complaint of Henry, Duke of Buckingham," in *A myrroure for magistrates,* edited by William Baldwin (London: Thomas Marshe, 1559; revised, 1563);

"Thomas Sackville in Commendation of the Work," prefatory verse to Baldassare Castiglione, *The courtyer of count Baldessar Castilio,* translated by Sir Thomas Hoby (London: William Seres, 1561);

"Thomas Sackvillus, Dominus Buckhurst, Bartholomeo Clerko" [Thomas Sackville, Lord Buckhurst, to Bartholomew Clerke], prefatory letter to Castiglione, *De curiali siue aulico* [The Courtier], translated by Bartholomew Clerke (London: Printed by John Day, 1571).

Thomas Sackville was by no means a prolific poet. Only four of his poems have survived and one of those was only very recently discovered. Yet Sackville's fellows and followers in the art of poetry were in no doubt as to the quality and importance of his work. Edmund Spenser himself, the arch-poet of Elizabethan England, praised Sackville's "golden verses." Spenser was particularly impressed by Sackville's "Induction," one of the two poems he contributed to the second edition of William Baldwin's compilation *A Mirror for Magistrates* in 1563, and this is the poem that is best known and most appreciated even today as "one of the first truly great Elizabethan poems," according to scholar Alan T. Bradford.

Sackville was born in 1536 in the Sussex village of Buckhurst, from which he took the title Baron Buckhurst when Elizabeth raised him to the peerage in 1567. On that occasion she described him as her "beloved kinsman," for indeed Sackville was related to the queen through her mother, Anne Boleyn, a cousin of his father, Sir Richard Sackville. It was this royal connection and the wealth that he inherited upon his father's death in 1566 that confirmed him in his career as a courtier and statesman under Elizabeth and James I, who created Sackville earl of Dorset in 1605. It was a career for which his birth and breeding had always intended him, but as a young man — indeed, as a boy — he seems to have intended for himself the career of a poet.

Very little is known of Sackville's education, but he attended Oxford before settling, at about age seventeen, in London in 1553. The next year he was married to Cecily, daughter of Sir John Baker,

Thomas Sackville as lord treasurer, 1601 (National Portrait Gallery, London)

and a year later he was admitted to the Inner Temple, where his father was one of the governors. The Inner Temple was one of the Inns of Court, institutions that functioned both as law colleges and finishing schools for young gentlemen intending the sort of political career that Sackville was eventually to take. The Inns of Court were also the center of literary life in mid-Tudor London. Jasper Heywood, in his translation of Seneca's *Thyestes* (1560), includes Sackville among the best of the Inns of Court writers, such as Thomas North, who would translate Plutarch's *Lives* from the French version by Jacques Amyot; the poet Barnabe Googe; and Baldwin, "Whose Mirror doth of Magistrates / Proclaim eternal fame." In Heywood's work "Sackville's sonnets, sweetly sauced" are singled out for praise. These sonnets were probably amatory: in "Sackville's Old Age" the poet tells the reader that his "lusty pen" has written many a "sweet complaint of woeful lover's wrong." But none of them are now extant,

and it is on his "tragical" poetry that Sackville's reputation stands.

The idea that tragedy was a kind of drama was still a new one in mid-Tudor England. In fact it was Sackville himself, in collaboration with a fellow Inner Templar, Thomas Norton, who wrote the first neoclassical tragic drama in English, *Gorboduc,* which was performed at the Inner Temple in 1562. *Gorboduc* is an important milestone in the history of English "vernacular humanism," the enrichment of the native literary tradition by incorporating into it material and forms from classical literature, in this case the plays of the Latin tragic dramatist Seneca.

But throughout the sixteenth century the word *tragedy* was also used in its medieval sense to refer to a shortish narrative poem dealing with the fall of some great man or woman into misery. This conception of tragedy found its fullest expression in John Lydgate's translation of Giovanni Boccaccio's *De casibus virorum illustrium* as *The Fall of Princes*

(1431–1438). And it was with this kind of tragedy, and indeed this book, that Sackville's short poetic career began.

In the early part of 1555 the printer John Wayland determined to bring out a new edition of Lydgate's "Bochas" and procured Baldwin and seven others to undertake an appendix dealing with English princes. The book, which appeared in 1559, has a notoriously difficult publishing history; but it seems that the young Sackville – a lad of nineteen years or so at the time – was appointed to write the tragedy of Henry Stafford, Duke of Buckingham, one of the henchmen of Richard III. Baldwin collected nineteen tragedies, and the book went to press, but it was halted in mid print on orders from the government.

The suppression of this edition of the *Mirror* must have been due to the way in which Baldwin had shifted the emphasis of *de casibus* tragedy from a generalized contemptus mundi tradition of scorning worldly pomp to concentrate very squarely on political injustice. The *Mirror* reached the reign of Edward IV when it went to press, but Baldwin intended to extend the series of poems right up to "Queen Mary's time." Mary's Privy Council, particularly Stephen Gardiner, the lord chancellor, apparently believed that it would be imprudent to allow the publication of tragedies castigating the villainous misdeeds of political leaders whose supporters might well be still alive.

In any case the book was suppressed, and it was then that young Sackville, whose father was one of the privy councillors who had suppressed it, came up with a way to salvage the project. The original volume would now end with his own tragedy of Buckingham and go no further toward Queen Mary's time; then a second volume, going "backward even to the time of William the Conqueror," a much less controversial era, was to be written, and Sackville offered to "continue and perfect all the story himself." Moreover, he was also to write an "Induction" or general introduction to the whole series.

The "Induction" begins with a traditionally medieval description of a winter landscape, in which the poet Sackville wanders, and where, overtaken by the sudden fall of night, he muses on the mutability of fortune. It was these three stanzas that most haunted the minds of Sackville's Elizabethan followers. The opening description of a winter landscape, with its "blustering blasts," "small fowls flocking," and "naked twigs . . . shivering all for cold," is in itself entirely conventional; every detail can be traced to several earlier poems. But the skill

and sensitivity with which these details were knit together made Sackville's three stanzas the "classic" example of a "hiemal chronographia," the one that later poets imitated when they wished to write their own descriptions of winter. Spenser, for example, to take only the most prestigious of Sackville's imitators, modeled the landscape of his "January" eclogue, the first piece in *The Shepheardes Calender* (1579), on Sackville's poem.

Sackville then goes on to describe his meeting with Sorrow, and here the literary character of the poem undergoes a fundamental change as the reader steps from the late Middle Ages into the Renaissance. Sorrow certainly has her medieval antecedents, such as the Sorrow depicted in Geoffrey Chaucer's translation of *The Romance of the Rose* by Guillaume de Lorris and Jean de Meun; but first and foremost she is based on the figure of the Sibyl who acts as Aeneas's guide through the Underworld in book 6 of Virgil's *Aeneid*. From this incident onward Sackville closely models his work on Virgil's; the poet descends into the Underworld and finally meets the shade of Buckingham. It is an important moment in English literary history. Though hardly comparable, it is true, to Dante's imitation of the episode in his *Inferno,* Sackville's similar mingling of medieval and classical elements in the "Induction" is a significant contribution to vernacular humanism.

Sackville's encounter with Buckingham is also a meeting between the medieval and the early modern. Buckingham is to a large extent a concoction from old chronicles and in that sense a medieval man. But he also turns out to be remarkably well read in the classics. He has studied, for example, Plutarch's *Lives* and Valerius Maximus's *Memorable Deeds and Sayings*. This knowledge is unexpected in a late-fifteenth-century aristocrat, for the humanist program was in its embryonic stages at the time. Sackville is placing his own humanist reading in the mind of his creation.

Given the degree to which Sackville and Buckingham share a common knowledge and even common ideals, it is not surprising to find that the poet portrays his tragic protagonist more leniently than his fellow *Mirror* poets do theirs. True, in some respects he differs very little from the ruthlessly ambitious magnates of the other tragedies. Along with Richard he is "drowned in the depth / Of deep desire to drink the guiltless blood" of his victims, and he abandons his vampiric tyranny over the people of England only when his master decides to do away with the princes in the Tower. Buckingham tries to persuade the king to save them but only earns his distrust; he flees, raises a rebel army of commoners that deserts him, and is finally betrayed by an old retainer, Humphrey Bannaster.

But Sackville chooses to emphasize Buckingham's feudal loyalty to the Crown; he is content to drink the blood of English citizens, but he cannot stomach the idea of murdering the rightful heirs to the throne. Buckingham feels less remorseful at having been so wicked than resentful at having been treated so badly by the treacherous Bannaster. It is the memory of Bannaster's crime, not his own, that sends Buckingham into a seizure of "surging sorrows," "frothing at mouth," and "groveling on the ground," unable to speak for several stanzas as Sackville describes his fit in horrid detail.

Sackville's portrait of Buckingham may have been colored by the fact that it was the duke's grandson, Henry, Baron Stafford, who was responsible for reprinting the *Mirror* in 1559. But Sackville is also asking the reader to sympathize with Buckingham on aesthetic grounds, just as he does. The first appearance of the grief-stricken Buckingham causes an immediate sympathetic reaction in the poet: "My heart so molt [melted] to see his grief so great, / As feelingly, methought, it dropped away." The production of a similarly sympathetic reaction in the reader – the stimulation of tragic fear and pity – was, as far as Sackville was concerned, the real test of the quality of his writing. Sackville's praisers often single out the power and dignity of his writing. The academic playwright William Gager, dedicating his Latin tragedy *Ulysses redux* to Sackville in 1591, says of Sackville's "Complaint": "I have read nothing written in our language which is so noble and so entirely heroic, nothing so worthy of the tragic sock and of eternity itself."

But Sackville himself seems to have felt that he was not entirely successful in communicating the grief of his creature to his readers. One can see this in the unfinished epilogue that he added to his manuscript copy of the "Induction" and "Complaint." In this addition Sackville has returned to the upper world and is trying to recall to and in himself Buckingham's torments, but they are so great that not even the greatest masters of complaint could do them justice. He lists his mentors in the genre, including Virgil, Ovid, Chaucer, Sir Thomas Wyatt, and Henry Howard, Earl of Surrey – a typically humanist convocation of ancient, medieval, and modern writers. But the rehearsal of this pantheon only emphasizes his own inferiority: "least of all I, that have less than least, / May once attempt to pen the smallest part / Of those huge dolors boiling in the breast / Of Buckingham or

Sorrow's endless smart." Such a modest disclaimer of one's own talents is a common sixteenth-century poetic strategy by which a writer establishes his succession to the defunct poets he praises. But Sackville seems really to mean it. By the end of the epilogue, after a few stanzas of tediously repetitive bombast in which he tries to revive the passions of his subject and himself, he admits, "Mine eloquence is rudeness," and the poem peters out into jottings and memorandums. C. S. Lewis, borrowing Hamlet's criticism of theatrical ranting, observes of Sackville's portrait of Buckingham, "He tears passions to tatters" – and perhaps Sackville felt so, too.

After this Sackville wrote very little apart from the last two acts of *Gorboduc*. In 1561 he contributed a commendatory sonnet to Sir Thomas Hoby's translation of Baldassare Castiglione's *Book of the Courtier*. It returns to the old theme of worldly pomp that fuels the tragedies in "Bochas," and Sackville demeans the gorgeous palaces that "royal kings" erect and elevates the virtues of good courtiership: "what in Court a courtier ought to be." More important, one sees here Sackville taking up a marginal position in the literary world: a commender of other men's works who does not undertake anything considerable himself. So, for example, in 1571 he wrote a commendatory letter to Bartholomew Clerke's translation of Castiglione's book into Latin as *De curiali sive aulico*. Indeed, later poets praise Sackville for his support of literature and learning. In 1602 Thomas Campion dedicated his *Observations in the Art of English Poesy* to Sackville, calling him "the most honorable protector of all industrious learning." And in 1608 Joshua Sylvester dedicated to him part of his translation of Guillaume de Salluste, Seigneur du Bartas's *Divine Weeks and Works,* including him among the "noble host / Of learned friends to learning."

But Sackville had bade farewell to poetry long before. His last poem, written between 1566 and 1574, is the recently discovered "Sackville's Old Age." Here he returns to the theme of the transience of life (Sackville was always more attracted to the spiritual elements in the *de casibus* tragic tradition rather than the political elements that appealed to the other *Mirror* poets). He also discusses his reading habits as a younger man (he was still only in his mid thirties) and lists his favorite English authors: Chaucer, "my guide, my master"; Surrey, especially his "English Virgil"; and Wyatt's translations of the Psalms. But now, he writes, it is time to say goodbye to poetry: "O trifles past, adieu, I ye forsake." He was good to his word, and nothing else of his is extant.

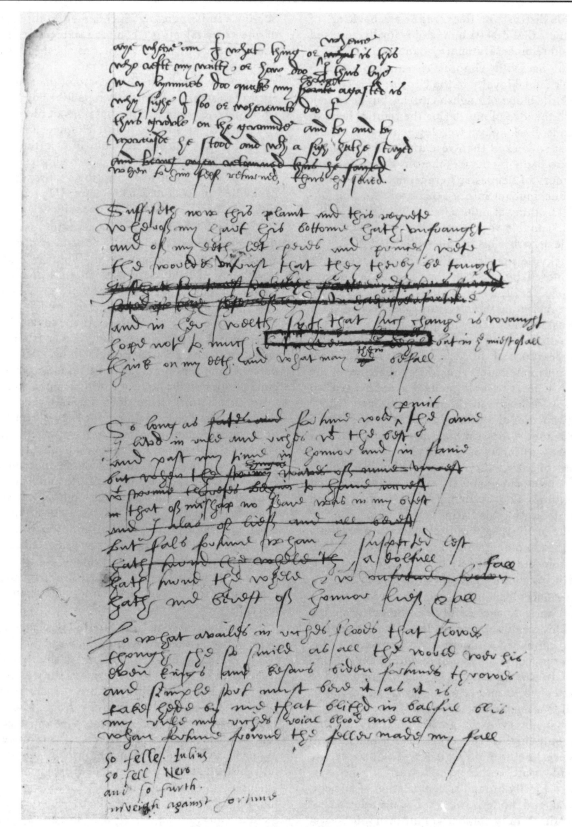

Pages from a manuscript for "The Complaint of Henry, Duke of Buckingham," from The Mirror for Magistrates *(1559). Some passages, such as the first stanza on the left-hand page, are in the hand of an amanuensis, but most of the manuscript (including all the corrections) is in Sackville's hand (Saint John's College, Cambridge, MS. L. 7 [M. R. James no. 364]).*

nor worthy wiat worthiest of them all
whom Brittain hath in later yeres furthbrought
his sacred psalmes wherin he singes the fall
of ~~x~~ Dauid dolling for the guilt he wrought
and vries deth which he so dereli bought
not his haulst vers that tainted hath the skie
for mortall domes to heventie and to hie

Not surrea he that ~~fires~~ hiest ~~in the~~ chair
of glistering fame so vay to liue and raigin
nor his proud ryme that thunders in the aier
~~Not~~ nor al the plaintes wherin he wrote ~~the~~ pain
~~the which rebil~~ when he lay fetterd in the fyry chain
of crnell loue ~~ther~~ ~~most~~ told ~~no rebil suffest~~
~~complaints in ful suffering wise~~

And lest of all I that haue les then lest
may once attempt to pen the smallest part
of those ~~sharp sorows~~ dolours boiling in the brest
of Buckingham. or sorowes endles smart
a drery sight to heuio for my hart
I want the stede wherof thei haue the store
I rather craue pdon then praise herefore.

for in my stile no sugred sawes are sownd
my songes ar not of solace or delight
of sobbes and sighes they rather yeld the sownd
and woful dities all with dolour dight
black teares alas is that wherwth I write
my mirth is mone and all my plesure pain
my swetest ioy to sorow and to plain.

Soon after, in 1574, George Turberville dedicated his *Tragical Tales* to Sackville. In a letter to the reader Turberville recalls how he had abandoned his translation of Lucan's Latin epic on *The Civil Wars* when Melpomene, the Muse of tragedy, told him the project was fit only for "noble Buckhurst's brain" (this was after Sackville's elevation to the baronage). She explains that although there is no dearth of poetic talent in England, "Lord Buckhurst is the best." Sackville could still in the mid 1570s be seen as a candidate for the poetic premiership, but by then it was too late. Sackville gave himself to statecraft, never to return to the slopes of Parnassus.

Bibliography:

Jerry Leath Mills, "Recent Studies in *A Mirror for Magistrates*," *English Literary Renaissance,* 9 (Spring 1979): 343–352.

References:

Paul Bacquet, *Un contemporain d'Elizabeth I: Thomas Sackville, l'homme et l'œuvre* (Geneva: Droz, 1966);

Normand Berlin, *Thomas Sackville* (New York: Twayne, 1974);

Alan T. Bradford, "Mirrors of Mutability: Winter Landscapes in Tudor Poetry," *English Literary Renaissance,* 4 (Winter 1974): 3–39;

Donald Davie, "Sixteenth-Century Poetry and the Common Reader: The Case of Thomas Sackville," *Essays in Criticism,* 4 (April 1954): 117–124;

C. S. Lewis, *English Literature in the Sixteenth Century, Excluding Drama* (Oxford: Oxford University Press, 1954), pp. 240–246;

Fitzroy Pyle, "Thomas Sackville and *A Mirror for Magistrates*," *Review of English Studies,* 14 (July 1938): 315–321;

Jacobus Swart, *Thomas Sackville: A Study in Sixteenth-Century Poetry* (Groningen: Wolters, 1948).

Papers:

Manuscript material by and relating to Sackville is found in various collections in the Bodleian Library. Two important manuscripts in other collections are "The Complaint of Henry, Duke of Buckingham" (including "The Induction") in Saint John's College Library, Cambridge (MS L. 7 [364]), and "Sackville's Old Age" in McMaster University Library, Hamilton, Ontario (William Ready Division of Archives and Research Collections, MS 93).

Sir Thomas Smith

(23 December 1513 – 12 August 1577)

Michael Pincombe
University of Newcastle upon Tyne

BOOKS: *An epistle or exhortacion to vnitie & peace,* attributed to Smith (London: Richard Grafton, 1548); translated as *Epistola exhortatoria ad pacem* (London: Reyner Wolfe, 1548);

An epitome of the title that the kynges maiestie of Englande, hath to the souereigntie of Scotlande, attributed to Smith (London: Richard Grafton, 1548);

De recta & emendata linguæ Græcæ pronuntiatione (Paris: Robertus Stephanus [Estienne], 1568);

De recta & emendata linguæ Anglicæ scriptione, dialogus (Paris: Robertus Stephanus [Estienne], 1568);

The offer and order giuen forth by sir Thomas Smyth, knight, and Thomas Smyth his sonne vnto suche as be willing to accompanye the sayde sonne, in his voyage for the inhabiting some partes of the northe of Irelande (London: Printed for Anthony Kitson, 1572);

A letter sent by I. B. gentleman vnto mayster R. C. esquire, of the peopling the cuntrie called Ardes, in Ireland, attributed to Smith (London: Printed by Henry Bynneman for Anthony Kitson, 1572);

A compendious or briefe examination of certayne ordinary complaints (London: Printed by Thomas Marsh, 1581);

De republica Anglorum. The maner of gouernement of England (London: Printed by Henry Middleton for George Seton, 1583).

Editions and Collections: "A Dialogue of the Queen's Marriage," edited by John Strype, in *The Life of the Learned Sir Thomas Smith, Knight* (Oxford: Clarendon, 1820), pp. 184–259;

An Epitome of the Title That the Kynges Majestie of Englande Hath to the Soveraigntie of Scotland, in *The Complaynt of Scotland,* edited by James A. H. Murray, Publications of the Early English Text Society, extra series 17 (London: Early English Text Society, 1872), pp. 247–256;

De republica Anglorum: A Discourse on the Commonwealth of England, edited by L. Alston, with a preface by F. W. Maitland (Cambridge: Cambridge University Press, 1906); edited by Mary Dewar (Cambridge: Cambridge University Press, 1982);

"The X. Commaundements," in *The Arundel Harington Manuscript of Tudor Poetry,* volume 1, edited by Ruth Hughey (Columbus: Ohio State University Press, 1960), p. 367;

Sir Thomas Smith: The Literary and Linguistic Works, 3 volumes, edited by Bror Danielsson (Stockholm: Almquist & Wiksell, 1963–1983) – volume 1 includes *Certaigne Psalmes or Songues of David Translated into English Meter by Sir Thomas Smith, Knight, Then Prisoner in the Tower of London, with Other Prayers and Songues by Him Made to Pas the Tyme There*; volume 2 includes *De recta et emendata linguæ Græcæ pronuntatione*; volume 3 includes *De recta et emendata linguæ Anglicæ scriptione*;

A Discourse of the Commonweal of This Realm of England, Attributed to Sir Thomas Smith, edited by Dewar (Charlottesville: University Press of Virginia for the Folger Shakespeare Library, 1969).

Sir Thomas Smith is chiefly remembered as a Tudor "commonwealth writer," especially as the author of the first significant study of the English state and constitution: *De republica Anglorum* (A Discourse on the Commonweal of England, 1583). Indeed, such is its importance as a constitutional classic that F. W. Maitland commented in the preface to the 1906 edition, "No one would think of writing about the England of Elizabeth's day without paying heed to what was written on that matter by her learned and accomplished Secretary of State." But two of Smith's Latin works from the 1540s, on the pronunciation of Greek and the spelling of English, may prove to be of greater significance for the understanding of sixteenth-century literature. Together they provide an illuminating insight into the attitudes and aspirations of mid-Tudor humanism.

Sir Thomas Smith (portrait by an unknown artist; from Neville Williams, All the
Queen's Men: Elizabeth I and Her Courtiers, *1972)*

Thomas Smith was born on 23 December 1513 in Walden, now Saffron Walden, in Essex. His father was a sheep farmer, and Smith's humble origins were to haunt him throughout his steady climb up the social ladder. While serving as Elizabeth's ambassador to the French court in 1564, for example, Smith quarreled violently with Sir Nicholas Throckmorton, scion of an ancient Warwickshire family and cousin to the late Queen Catherine Parr. Throckmorton, dagger drawn, accused Smith of "having come to the Court but yesterday a beggarly scholar." Smith furiously retorted that he had been spending more than two hundred marks a year long before becoming a courtier; but the insult smarted grievously, and throughout his long life he tried to conceal his obscure birth by accumulating offices and properties.

Young Thomas was a sickly child but a precociously clever one, and at the age of eleven he was sent to study at Cambridge. He was a fellow of

Queen's College by the time he was fourteen, but then ill health and poverty forced him to withdraw from the university. However, thanks to the intervention of William Butts, physician to Henry VIII, he returned to his studies and was made a king's scholar. After this his academic career flourished. By 1543, at the age of thirty, he was vice-chancellor of the university.

However, in the year immediately preceding his appointment to this eminent position, Smith had come into conflict with the chancellor himself, Stephen Gardiner, over his views on the pronunciation of Greek. Smith and his fellow king's scholar John Cheke argued that Greek should be spoken according to their idea of the way the ancient Greeks themselves spoke it, rather than in the somewhat Italian-sounding way in which it was spoken by most English scholars. Traditionalists regarded this innovation as a challenge to custom and authority and finally persuaded Gardiner to ban the pronunciation advocated by Smith and Cheke from the Cambridge lecture halls. In protest Smith addressed to the chancellor a long letter in Latin defending his position. This letter, dated 12 August 1542, was published twenty-six years later in Paris as *De recta et emendata linguæ Græcæ pronuntatione* (On the Correct and Reformed Manner of Speaking Greek).

The details of Smith's scholarship concerning the ancient pronunciation of Greek are not as significant as his arguments in favor of its restitution, which are a monument to the Tudor humanist's project to revive the glories of the classical past in his own day and age. Smith argues that there is a precedent for the restoration of ancient Greek pronunciation in the universal acceptance by scholars of the superiority of ancient or "classical" Latin over its medieval successor. Nobody doubts, he says, that correct Latin is that written by Cicero, Caesar, and other "classical authors (*classici authores*)." This form of the language perished after the fall of Rome at the hands of the barbarians and lay dead and buried throughout the Middle Ages, its place usurped by its "barbaric" medieval counterpart, until the Italian humanist scholar Lorenzo Valla "raised from the grave the first-born brother" – classical Latin – and "replaced him in his paternal estate, the proper peculiar castle and seat of his honor," the "schools and lecture rooms" of academic institutions such as Cambridge. The metaphor drawn from property and inheritance is revealing. Smith was sensitive about his status as a social upstart, and his identification of himself with the wronged but rightful heir to the "castle" of true Latinity must have appealed strongly to his sense of being snubbed by his social superiors.

But Smith failed to persuade Gardiner to lift the ban, and it was perhaps this disappointment, combined with his antiquarian interest in ancient English records, that led him to compose *De recta et emendata linguæ anglicæ scriptione* (On the Correct and Reformed Manner of Writing English), published, after some revision, in Paris in 1568. This book takes the form of a rather one-sided dialogue in which "Smithus" persuades his friend Quintus that the present way of spelling English is barbarous and proposes in great detail certain alphabetical reforms that would create a new orthography operating on strictly phonetic lines. Here, too, Smith's delight in metaphor and allegory reveals far more about himself and Tudor humanism generally than it does about the nature of the subject in hand. Smith imagines the letter *C*, for example, as a "monster or hobgoblin," a crafty, fraudulent vagabond, who has no real place in the writing of English at all and there-

fore has to cheat other letters out of what is rightfully theirs: "by such wilful impostures *C* is driving out both *S* and *K* from their houses and lands." Once again Smith indulges in fantasies of wicked usurpers and the return of the rightful heirs, in this case certain Anglo-Saxon letters he has seen in old records, now in exile, "wandering without a home." Just as Smith and the neoclassical party at Cambridge wished to restore ancient Latin to its rightful place, so Smith the spelling reformer wants to help ancient English letters expel "beggarly" upstarts such as *C* and regain their "houses and lands."

Smith no longer needed such help, for by the mid 1540s he was well established as a brilliant lecturer in law and an able and active vice-chancellor. Moreover, his legal training (he had also studied at Padua, undisputed center of civil-law studies) and his administrative skills led him eventually, as he may have always intended, to the court. In February 1547, shortly after the death of Henry VIII, Smith entered the service of Edward Seymour, Earl of Hertford and later duke of Somerset, soon to be made protector of the realm during the nonage of Edward VI. Smith began to accrue lucrative posts, such as the provostship of Eton College and the deanery of Carlisle, and started to convert these revenues into property. He soon became one of Somerset's most powerful servants and in April 1548 was appointed secretary to the king. His duties in this office were varied, and he may have been the author of two pamphlets urging the claim of Edward VI to the Scottish throne. But his most important task was advising Somerset on financial matters. Inflation rose steeply throughout the mid-Tudor period, and Smith blamed it on the successive debasements of the coinage made by Henry VIII and later Somerset too. But he was unable to make his master accept his arguments against further debasement and evidently irritated Somerset by his insistence, for the summer of 1549 saw him temporarily "exiled" from court, at Eton. It was here that Smith wrote his first major vernacular work, a dialogue on the causes of the great dearth, "A Discourse of the Commonweal of This Realm of England," posthumously printed as *A Compendious or Brief Examination of Certain Ordinary Complaints* (1581).

The dialogue takes place in an inn, where a Knight, a Merchant, a Husbandman, and a Capper are joined at dinner by a certain "Doctor Pandotheus," who puts Smith's own case for revaluation of the coinage. Pandotheus does most of the talking and proposes novel solutions to problems such as the enclosure of common land turned over to pri-

Title page for Smith's book proposing new methods for English spelling

vate sheep farming. He argues that "every man will seek where most advantage is," and if it were more profitable to grow sheep than corn, then that is what most men would be inclined to do. The answer lay not in chiding sheep farmers for being greedy and ambitious, but in making arable farming a more attractive prospect by removing restrictions in the corn trade and allowing farmers "liberty to sell it at all times and to all places." This type of thinking is fundamentally at odds with the long tradition of political dialogue stretching from Plato's *Republic* to Sir Thomas More's *Utopia* (1516), which asserts the values of a static society in which all members should be more or less satisfied with where they stand and what they have. Smith, the upwardly mobile com-

moner who would be knighted within a few months of writing "A Discourse," proposes a free-market economy where individual enterprise and ambition add to the "common wealth," rather than taking from it.

Smith's own fortunes, however, took a turn for the worse after the writing of "A Discourse." Somerset was arrested in October 1549, and Smith went with him to the Tower of London. Here he turned to astrology and poetry. He made metrical paraphrases of eleven of the Psalms and wrote eight collects in prose for the use of his fellow prisoners and three lyrics complaining of his lot. "What mean they thus to fret and fume?" he asks in the first; but his opponents had every reason to be irritated with him, for it was Smith's arrogance and greed as

Effigy of Smith in Saint Michael's Church, Theydon Mount

much as his loyalty to Somerset that had made him so unpopular.

Smith was released from prison in February 1550 and spent the next ten years in retirement on his country estates. The accession of Elizabeth in 1558 did not see him return to office immediately, but he could not resist meddling. In April 1561, when the subject of the queen's matrimonial plans was much talked of, Smith wrote a "Dialogue on the Queen's Marriage," in which "Spitewed" and "Lovealien" are put in their places by "Homefriend," the speaker in favor of the queen's marrying one of her own subjects (Smith intended him to be Robert Dudley, the queen's favorite and later earl of Leicester).

Smith's return to politics came in September 1562, when he was appointed ambassador to the court of France. It was not exactly what he wanted, for ambassadorial duties were expensive and kept him away from the court in England. His period in France was an unhappy one, for he was constantly at odds with the former ambassador, Throckmorton. But Elizabeth kept him on at the court of France, and in the spring of 1565 Smith found himself at Toulouse, recovering from a serious illness and filled with a nostalgic "yearning for our commonwealth" of England. It was here that he composed his most famous book, *De republica Anglorum,* published posthumously in 1583.

De republica Anglorum is divided into three books: the first deals with the different types of commonwealth and the particular features of the English commonwealth; the second and third books deal with the structure of judicial authority in England, from Parliament down to the village constable. The legal emphasis is only to be expected from a doctor of civil law, but the first book holds interest for students of literature, especially the chapters dealing with the various orders of society. Chapter 20, "Of Gentlemen," is particularly illuminating, since it highlights the social anxieties and pretensions of the mid-Tudor humanists, most of whom, like Smith, came from relatively humble backgrounds. Recalling, perhaps, the insults he had received from Throckmorton a mere twelvemonth before writing *De republica Anglorum,* Smith takes the side of the *novi homines* of classical Rome, who earned social esteem "for their virtues new and newly shown," in opposition to "the old smell of ancient race." Smith, of course, was one of these "new men," and he scorns gentlemen of the first generation who pay heralds to provide them with spurious genteel ancestors by the alleged "perusing and viewing of old registers."

Smith's years as an ambassador were not successful, and after his return to England he once again lived a retired life for a few years. He seems to have given up the idea of attaining high state office, for in 1571 he was casting about for other ways to make money. One was a disastrous scheme to turn iron into copper, which cost him more than one thousand pounds. He also drew up a plan for colonizing part of Ireland; his son, Thomas, was murdered while putting this plan into action. In July 1572 Smith was appointed to the principal secretaryship, but his political vigor had left him, and he seems to have spent most of his time concocting medicinal recipes (he was now in his sixties). He had always had a weak constitution, and illness forced him to retire from the court in the spring of 1576. He died on 12 August 1577.

After his death Smith was most remembered for *De republica Anglorum,* but his linguistic works were also well received. Later spelling reformers – such as John Hart in his *Orthography* (1569) and William Bullokar in his *Short Introduction or Guiding to Print, Write, and Read English Speech* (1580) – singled him out as a pioneer in the field. But the range of his interests and writings was so great that one should perhaps only sigh with the humanist Gabriel Harvey, in his funeral elegy *Smithus* (1577), that his mentor and patron was "multiscius" or "one who knew many things." Only when his many works and voluminous correspondence are available will readers be able to come to a proper estimation of his importance in the history of sixteenth-century letters.

Biography:

Mary Dewar, *Sir Thomas Smith: A Tudor Intellectual in Office* (London: Athlone, 1964).

References:

Mary Dewar, "The Authorship of the 'Discourse of the Commonweal,' " *Economic History Review,* second series 19 (1966): 388–400;

A. B. Ferguson, "The Tudor Commonweal and the Sense of Change," *Journal of British Studies,* 3 (November 1963): 11–35;

John N. King, *English Reformation Literature: The Tudor Origins of the Protestant Tradition* (Princeton: Princeton University Press, 1982), pp. 465–468;

Quentin Skinner, *The Foundations of Modern Political Thought,* volume 1 (Cambridge: Cambridge University Press, 1978), pp. 225–226;

Hallett Smith, "English Metrical Psalms in the Sixteenth Century and Their Literary Significance," *Huntington Library Quarterly,* 9, no. 3 (1946): 249–271;

Rivkah Zim, *English Metrical Psalms: Poetry as Praise and Prayer, 1535–1601* (Cambridge: Cambridge University Press, 1987), pp. 74–79.

Papers:

Smith's letters and manuscripts are preserved in many collections; a full bibliography is given by Dewar in her 1964 biography (pp. 212–213). Three important manuscripts that have yet to be published are "A Treatise on the Wages of a Roman Footsoldier" (British Library, Harleian MSS 660, and the Society of Antiquaries, London) and "Orders Set out by Sir Thomas Smith" and "Offices Necessary in the Colony of the Ardes" (both in the Essex Record Office, D/D Sh. 01/1-7).

Thomas Starkey

(circa 1499 – 25 August 1538)

Thomas F. Mayer
Augustana College

BOOK: *An exhortation to the people, instructynge thym to vnitie and obedience* (London: Printed by Thomas Berthelet, 1536).

Editions: *A Dialogue between Cardinal Pole and Thomas Lupset, Lecturer in Rhetoric at Oxford, by Thomas Starkey,* edited by J. M. Cowper, in *England in the Reign of Henry VIII,* volume 2, extra series 12 (London: Early English Text Society, 1871); edited by K. M. Burton (London: Chatto & Windus, 1948); edited by T. F. Mayer, Camden fourth series 37 (London: Royal Historical Society, 1989);

An Exhortation to the People Instructing Them to Unity and Obedience (Amsterdam: Da Capo, 1973).

Thomas Starkey's *Dialogue between Pole and Lupset* has long given him a place in the histories of both early-Tudor vernacular literature and political thought, usually as the first modern liberal and an epigone of Marsilius of Padua. Further, his pivotal role in the protracted efforts to secure his former patron Reginald Pole's opinion on Henry VIII's divorce from Catherine of Aragon produced a central, if temporary, notoriety for him in the political history of the second Tudor's reign. More recently these judgments have been revised and Starkey's "English" importance reduced; instead, he has become one of the first and most interesting of the *inglesi italianati* (Italianate Englishmen).

Born into a family of comparatively minor Cheshire gentry, Starkey may have gone to the leading grammar school in England, Magdalen College School, Oxford. In any event he took both B.A. (1516) and M.A. (1521) in that college (first as demy and then as fellow) and university. Robert Whittinton probably gave Starkey a fair amount of his early education, and it may have been at Oxford that Starkey came in contact with the ideas of John Colet, even if it took some time for him to embrace them fully. Starkey also apparently made the ac-

quaintance of his lifelong friends Edward Wotton, Thomas Lupset, and above all Pole at Oxford. Probably in company with Pole he then went to Padua, where he finished his education in natural science and in politics during the 1520s. When Pole went to Paris in 1529, Starkey accompanied him as secretary. During their leisure there, and at Sheen on their return to England in 1930, Starkey drafted his most famous work, the *Dialogue.*

Starkey's eclectic humanist education shows up clearly in his work. His well-developed rhetorical skills plus the lack of any earlier touchstone for English-language dialogues led Starkey to produce a very playful work (begun in 1529, his dialogue preceded Thomas More's first efforts in that form). For example, when defining key terms (polity or commonwealth) he offers a variety of equivalences, each a little different. Similarly, the argument often wanders off the main line, and he sometimes loses track of which character defends which position. Finally, he rested his work on the most extended use known of the metaphor of the body politic, a notoriously elastic construct. Some of the slippage in the meaning of the *Dialogue* probably also arose from a change in Starkey's intended audience. He had originally aimed his work at Pole, intending to persuade him to lead the reform of the English commonwealth. When Pole disappointed Starkey's hopes (by exactly how much remains an open question), he redirected his dialogue to the king. Pole may have seen the work, but Henry never did. It remained in manuscript and unknown until the nineteenth century.

As humanistic as the work is, it draws most of its philosophical bite directly from Aristotle. This is why Starkey had no need of Marsilius's derivatively Aristotelian ideas. Starkey agreed with Aristotle that human felicity depends on harmony of body and soul, not the dominance of one or the other, about the necessity of both friends and material

A PREFACE TO THE
KYNGES HYGHNES.

I F I HAD NOT OF longe tyme paſt concepued a ſure truſte, and great confydence, moſt noble pɜince, of your ſynguler gɝtylnes, and accuſtomed humanitie, which dayly to the great comfoɜt of al your ſeruātes & ſubiectes, your highnes declareth openly, I wolde neuer haue vſed ſuch boldnes and audacite, as to exhibyte and pɜeſent this my rude wɜitynge, vnto your gracis mooſte indifferent iudgement. Foɜ moche and longe I haue doubted with my ſelfe, whether hit ſhulde pertayne vnto me, other by woɜde oɜ by wɜityng, to touche any ſuche matters of weyght and grauyte. Foɜ as on the one ſyde, many thynges moued me to kepe ſilence, conſyderynge myn own ſtate, condition, and degre, and how late I was admytted to the ſeruyce of youre maieſtye, and howe lyttell experte I am in matters of polycie: ſo on the other ſyde, dyuers thynges ſtyɜced me, to open myne affecte and pourpoſe, vnto your grace playnly. Foɜ moued I was moche by this your great and ſpnguler humanyte, wherin amonge all other pɜincely vertues your highnes excellyth: moued I was alſo by the highe iugemente, which by the goodnes of god aboue other pɜincis is to you gyuen, in al maters of true religion and of iuſte polycy: and aboue all moued I
a.ii.   was

AN EXHORTATION TO
the people, inſtructynge theym to Unitie and Obedience.

A S IT IS TO AL OTHER creatures, by the power of God bɜought foɜth into this woɜld, naturally gͥuen by his goodnes to deſyɜe their ende and perfection, the which they be oɜdeyned vnto, ſo it is to the nature of man, who of al other here in erthe is moſte noble, and of dignitie moſte excellent, as he that is with reaſone indewed, the moſte heuenly thinge, wherof bodily creatures and erthly, may be parttakers, by the whiche as by the chiefe inſtrument, he may ſeke and inſerche al conueniēt meanes, wherby he may attayn the better to ſuche ende and perfection, as by the goodneſſe of god to hym is appoynted: and all though this deſyɜe be to all mankynde common, and euer hath bene of what religion ſo euer they be, yet we mooſte, chɜiſten people, whiche be of Chɜiſtes flocke, and lyghted with the ſpirite of god, make pfeſſion of his name, aboue al other ought to be therof moſte deſirous, as they which haue by the ſinguler benefite of god, a moɜe ſure knowlege, & a moɜe ſure groūd, to leane vnto, thē any other people in erth, foɜ we haue the expɜeſſe & manyfeſt doctrine of god, by the whiche we ar taught and inſtruct the ſtreyght and ſure waye,
to the

Pages from Thomas Starkey's An Exhortation to the People *(1536)*

goods to the fulfilled life, and most important about the superiority of a constitution composed of all three of Aristotle's pure forms – monarchy, aristocracy, and democracy – with greatest stress (as probably for Aristotle) on the second.

Even Aristotle's authority was insufficient to underpin the center of the work, Starkey's plan for collective leadership in both church and state. Drawing in part on the standard Venetian analysis of the English constitution (Starkey agreed, too, that it had been invented by those bastard Normans, even though his own family was of Norman extraction), in part on the "myth of Venice" (well espoused, just as Starkey was writing, by his friend Donato Giannotti and also by Pole's future ally Gasparo Contarini), and in part on late-medieval notions of "mixed" constitutions, Starkey argues that the government of England should be modeled on that of Venice, in which a set of councils circumscribes the doge's power. These all had some ties to Parliament, but Starkey does not make much of that political occasion (Parliament was not yet an institu-tion). He even proposes an elective monarchy in order to limit the king's power even more.

But the aristocracy of the moment was not up to the task of remedying the many problems of English society and polity. Starkey therefore designed a complete overhaul of its training in order to fit it for effective public service. Here he draws heavily on his own education, especially in civil law, which he hoped to put in the place of the barbaric common law. Its practice he would have restricted to the gentry and nobility. Dissolved monastic institutions, especially the wealthy and conveniently located Saint Albans, should serve as communal training grounds for the nobility. In the church he also defends an aristocratic constitution. Following a long conciliarist and oligarchic tradition, he limits the pope's power by means of the cardinals and general council, in the same way as he does the king's by new councils and Parliament. Here he probably made good use of his knowledge of Parisian conciliarism, gained through contact with the Paris faculty of theology at precisely the time he began to write.

(Starkey's conciliarism shows up most clearly in his plan to resolve Henry's divorce by an appeal to a general council.)

Starkey continued to work on the *Dialogue* later, putting some finishing touches to the work during his residence in the universities of Avignon in 1532–1533 and perhaps again during his final trip to Padua. In any case the work was finished (except for a few details) by 1533 at the latest. At Avignon, Starkey probably studied with the civil lawyer Gianfrancesco Sannazaro della Ripa, also a conciliarist of a sort. In Padua he continued his education in law, probably under Marco Mantova Benavides (representative of perhaps the most flourishing conciliarist tradition), and in philosophy under Marcantonio de Genova. Among Starkey's friends were Lazzaro Bonamico, prince of Ciceronians; Benedetto Lampridio, a shadowy figure until recently, but now taking on a religious complexion like Starkey's and Pole's, as well as increasing literary prominence as, for example, the composer of the program for Giulio Romano's paintings in the Palazzo del Te in Mantua; the Venetian nobleman and soon-to-be-cardinal Contarini; Giovanni Battista Egnazio, a Venetian educator and early polygrapher; and Jan van Kampen, from whom Starkey probably learned a great deal about biblical exegesis and with whom he also shared spiritual religious beliefs. This circle, together with Pole's influence, may account for the markedly more religious tone of the last part of the *Dialogue*.

Starkey had many other friends in Pole's household, among them George Lily, whom he advised to study civil law as the best preparation for political service; Bernardino Sandro, a Greek copyist and corrector for the press; Henry Cole, also a law student, who continued as a close ally of Pole, eventually preaching the sermon justifying the burning of Thomas Cranmer; and, probably superficially, Richard Morison, later a successful Henrician propagandist and Marian exile. Starkey's close ties to the unofficial English agent in Venice, Edmund Harvel, also continued.

These contacts made half of Starkey's fortune. In late 1534 he returned to England. At first he had no patron, which made his move home daring. Early in 1535 he attracted the attention of Henry's chief minister, Thomas Cromwell; Starkey fairly quickly entered the king's household (in an unknown capacity; perhaps he merely drew some kind of commons), but it apparently took a while for him to secure a royal chaplaincy. Cromwell almost immediately enlisted him to perform two functions: intelligencer for Italy – drawing especially on his friends Harvel and Sandro – and domestic propagandist. As intelligencer, Starkey entered into a protracted correspondence with Pole on behalf of Henry and Cromwell, which has been frequently reprinted. As propagandist his first assignment was to persuade the Carthusian Richard Reynolds to drop his opposition to the Royal Supremacy. Many of the themes of Starkey's suasions with both Reynolds and Pole came from the *Dialogue,* especially those about the limits of papal authority.

The constitutional views expressed in the *Dialogue* also appear in Starkey's first commissioned writing for Cromwell, composed near the beginning of his government service, perhaps in mid 1535. "What is policy after the sentence [opinion] of Aristotle" responded to a request from Cromwell, but Starkey apparently converted a high-level philosophical assignment into a display of his rhetorical talents. "What is policy" became an oration aimed at the people. As in the *Dialogue,* Starkey framed his speech on the body politic and on an Aristotelian typology of constitutions, but without the radical aristocratic innovations he had developed in the *Dialogue.*

Starkey's success continued. Although he failed with Reynolds, he did persuade Pole to write his opinion and Cromwell to give him a chance to write a large-scale piece of popular propaganda. He undertook on his own initiative his second major work, *An Exhortation to the People,* in the summer of 1535, but Cromwell soon took a close interest. In what might seem a great irony, Starkey took his breaks from writing in the garden of the executed More's close friend Antonio Buonvisi. Instead, Starkey's (and Buonvisi's) attitude merely reflects the high degree of fluidity characteristic of the middle years of Henry's reign. Starkey's remarkable letter to Henry VIII, following the fall of Anne Boleyn, reflects the same situation. Although he probably never sent it, he still intended to give the king a good deal of unsolicited advice, especially about how to use the proceeds from the dissolution of the monasteries to subvent a major reform of English education.

An Exhortation puts forward a religious case for civil obedience. Starkey's argument depends on the concept of *adiaphora:* things indifferent, which the prince could, however, command. Under Cromwell's guidance Starkey ties his adiaphorism to an insistence on the importance of pursuing the mean (a basic Aristotelian idea) that runs between popery and Protestantism, between exclusive reliance on works or on faith. A minimum definition of doctrine was much to be preferred; Starkey chose the Nicene

Creed. Nevertheless, he also develops an extended polemic against papal primacy, arguing in favor of transferring most of the pope's power to princes and "a whole congregation and perfect . . . our nation." All of this, including opposition to papal absolutism, took Starkey into the evangelical or spiritual territory that was becoming his natural habitat, even if it developed that he and Cromwell had different ideas about the apparently common language he used to describe the via media. Starkey has had a great deal of praise for his invention and development of this centrally Anglican concept, but in fact it was common coin among Henrician reformers long before *An Exhortation;* and as his correspondence with Cromwell makes plain, the inspiration for Starkey's deployment of it came from the minister. It is also significant that the printed Exhortation disappeared almost as completely as the manuscript *Dialogue*. Elizabethan Anglicans made no reference to it; and even when interest in Starkey was revived in the late seventeenth century, the work remained out of discussion.

Even as Starkey wrote, Pole was finishing his *Pro ecclesiasticae unitatis defensione* (*De unitate*), damning Henry and all his works. *De unitate* arrived in England shortly after *An Exhortation* was published. Starkey suffered in the aftermath of Pole's blast, but Cromwell allowed him to sit on the committee that digested the work for Henry. More important, Henry himself (if not Cromwell) rehabilitated Starkey by December 1536: at the same time Pole became a cardinal, Starkey took his own first major step to high ecclesiastical preferment, becoming master by royal presentation of the important collegiate church of Saint Lawrence Pountney in London.

Starkey worked on two big projects in the last two years of his life, neither of which was finished or published. Continuing the increased interest in religion manifest from the end of the *Dialogue,* he first prepared a set of notes on the Old Testament that may have been meant to underpin a defense of Pole and perhaps another criticism of Henry. These jottings were almost certainly a private exercise. Another set of notes was more clearly intended to produce a work that would rehabilitate Starkey. His comments on Albert Pighe's worrisome *Hierarchiae ecclesiasticae assertio* (1535) underpinned a sketched refutation that would "remove the foundation of [Pighe's] book."

By emphasizing the continued relevance of the prophets, the dangers in any change of the *status rei publicae,* the importance of old ways of doing things, object lessons about the assassination of tyrants (together with long discussions of princely failings), and the necessity of penance, Starkey came very close to the burden of *De unitate*. Nevertheless, in common with most English Catholics, he accepted the new order of the Royal Supremacy. Secular power must control the church; at the same time, it must not interfere in its sacramental powers. In his notes on Pighe's book, Starkey continued to adhere to his conciliarist view of the ecclesiastical constitution, just as he continued to be unimpressed by the Marsilian arguments Pighe set out to refute.

Starkey's drift toward the conservatives had gathered speed by the end of his life. As is apparent from the investigation of the so-called Exeter conspiracy, Cromwell knew of Starkey's changed opinions. Starkey's death from the plague on 25 August 1538 probably spared him indictment among the Exeter conspirators; his name was singled out in the margin of one of the records of their interrogations, and in them he figured prominently as a conduit to Pole of English plans to deal with him by foul means.

Starkey and his work disappeared almost completely for 450 years after his death. Serious interest came only in the late nineteenth century with publication of S. J. Herrtage's *Starkey's Life and Letters* (1878) and J. M. Cowper's edition of the *Dialogue* (1871). Late-Victorian Liberals proved to be Starkey's first constituency, as exemplified by the appreciative life in the *Dictionary of National Biography* by W. A. J. Archbold, whose major work treated the social impact of the dissolution of the monasteries. Starkey quickly acquired a reputation for both sympathy to the lower orders and realism in his analysis. This has remained the interpretation of Starkey as a political thinker, his usual context. Questions about his sources arose early. When F. L. Baumer in 1936 made him one of the most important heirs of Marsilius of Padua, he launched an interpretation that dominated historiography throughout Europe for fifty years.

Perhaps the largest contribution to the literature on Starkey came from W. Gordon Zeeveld's *Foundations of Tudor Policy* (1948), a study of Pole's household and its role in the Henrician Reformation. Zeeveld makes Starkey an unequivocal liberal in both politics and religion, inventor of the via media (borrowed from Philip Melanchthon) and penetrating social critic. Oddly enough for English professor Zeeveld, the literary dimensions of Starkey's work receive little attention in this study.

Given the seal of canonicity by Zeeveld, Starkey's *Dialogue* has figured in most subsequent treatments of early-Tudor political thought and literature. Although C. S. Lewis (1954) treats Starkey's literary skills as contemptuously as he does those of other "drab age" authors, he, too, praises Starkey as a political thinker. Fritz Caspari (1954) adds an important new line in linking Starkey's humanism to his gentry origins, but he also continues the misleading identification of Starkey with Neoplatonism.

Beginning in the late 1950s Starkey acquired his definitive profile as a "realistic" Reformer in the work (1965) of Arthur B. Ferguson. Yet after Zeeveld, G. R. Elton (1969) has done by far the most important work on Starkey, studying the manuscript of the *Dialogue* for the first time since Cowper (or, more likely, Cowper's amanuensis). Elton (1969 and 1973) uses Starkey's ideas to give further shape to Thomas Cromwell's reform and renewal. At roughly the same time, German students of *Anglistik*, especially Ludwig Borinski (1953), paid Starkey new attention, making him an early exponent of "bourgeois" reform. But even these students of literature continued to read Starkey's prose as a transparent medium, itself in no need of analysis.

More recently, Alistair Fox and John Guy (1986), along with Joel B. Altman (1978) and K. J. Wilson (1985), began the serious study of the form of Starkey's work and its impact on meaning. Fox treats Starkey as an empirical thinker, and barely humanist in the Renaissance sense. The work of Thomas F. Mayer (1989), by contrast, interprets Starkey's precocity and "realism" as a function of his finely honed humanist skills and his saturation in the political and linguistic agendas of Venetian and Paduan humanism in particular.

Biography:

S. J. Herrtage, *Starkey's Life and Letters,* in *England in the Reign of Henry VIII,* volume 1, extra series 32 (London: Early English Text Society, 1878).

References:

J. W. Allen, *A History of Political Thought in the Sixteenth Century* (New York: Dial, 1928; New York: Barnes & Noble, 1960);

Joel B. Altman, *The Tudor Play of Mind* (Berkeley: University of California Press, 1978);

Paul Archambault, "The Analogy of the 'Body' in Renaissance Political Thought," *Bibliothèque d'Humanisme et Renaissance,* 29 (1967): 21–52;

F. L. Baumer, "Thomas Starkey and Marsilius of Padua," *Politica,* 2 (1936): 188–205;

Ludwig Borinski, "Das politisches Denken der europäischen Humanismus," *Studium generale,* 6 (1953): 424–434;

Fritz Caspari, *Humanism and the Social Order in Tudor England* (Chicago: University of Chicago Press, 1954);

G. R. Elton, *Reform and Renewal: Thomas Cromwell and the Common Weal* (Cambridge: Cambridge University Press, 1973);

Elton, "Reform by Statute: Thomas Starkey's *Dialogue* and Thomas Cromwell's Policy," *Proceedings of the British Academy,* 54 (1969): 165–188;

Arthur B. Ferguson, *The Articulate Citizen and the English Renaissance* (Durham, N.C.: Duke University Press, 1965);

Alistair Fox and John Guy, *Reassessing the Henrician Age: Humanism, Politics and Reform, 1500–1550* (Oxford: Blackwell, 1986), pp. 9–51;

C. S. Lewis, *English Literature in the Sixteenth Century, Excluding Drama* (Oxford: Clarendon, 1954);

Thomas F. Mayer, *Thomas Starkey and the Commonweal: Humanist Politics and Religion in the Reign of Henry VIII* (Cambridge: Cambridge University Press, 1989);

Gregorio Piaia, *Marsilio da Padova nella riforma e nella controriforma: Fortuna ed interpretazione* (Padua: Antenore, 1977);

Quentin Skinner, *The Renaissance,* volume 1 of *Foundations of Modern Political Thought* (Cambridge: Cambridge University Press, 1978);

Bernard J. Verkamp, *The Indifferent Mean: Adiaphorism in the English Reformation* (Athens: Ohio University Press, 1977);

K. J. Wilson, *Incomplete Fictions: The Formation of English Renaissance Dialogue* (Washington, D.C.: Catholic University of America Press, 1985);

W. Gordon Zeeveld, *Foundations of Tudor Policy* (Cambridge, Mass.: Harvard University Press, 1948).

Papers:

The unique manuscript of Starkey's *Dialogue,* as well as most of his notes for other works, is in the Public Record Office, London (SP1/90). His letters are mainly in the Cottonian Manuscripts of the British Library.

Thomas Sternhold

(? – 23 August 1549)

and

John Hopkins

(? – October 1570)

Bradford R. DeVos
Marshall University

BOOKS: *Certayne Psalmes chosen out of the Psalter of Dauid, and drawn into Englishe Metre by Thomas Sternhold grome of the Kynges Maiesties Roobes,* by Sternhold (London: Printed by Edward Whitchurch, circa 1547);

Al such psalmes of Dauid as T. Sternehold didde in his life time draw into English metre (London: Printed by Edward Whitchurch, 1549);

Psalmes of Dauid in Metre (Wesel?: Printed by H. Singleton?, 1556?);

One and Fiftie Psalmes of David in Englishe metre, wherof .37. were made by Thomas Sterneholde: and the rest by others. Conferred with the hebrewe, and in certeyn places corrected as the text, and sens of the Prophete required (Geneva: Printed by John Crespin, 1556);

Psalmes of Dauid in Englishe metre, by T. Sterneholde and others: conferred with the Ebrue: and the note ioyned withall. Newly set fourth and allowed (London: Printed by John Day, 1560);

Foure score and seuen psalmes of Dauid in English mitre by T. sterneholde and others (London: Printed by John Day, 1561);

The Whole Booke of Psalmes, collected into Englysh metre by T. Starnhold I. Hopkins & others: conferred with the Ebrue, with apt Notes to synge them withal, Faithfully perused and alowed according to the ordre appointed in the Quenes maiesties iniunctions (London: Printed by John Day, 1562).

Editions and Collections: *English and Scottish Psalm and Hymn Tunes: ca. 1543–1667,* compiled by Maurice Frost (London: Oxford University Press, 1953) – includes unedited versions of the tunes from the Sternhold and Hopkins

psalter as each was printed in its first edition, "errors included";

The English Metrical Psalter 1562: A Catalogue of the Early Editions, an Index to Their Contents, and a Comparative Study of Their Melodies, 3 volumes, compiled by Robert Illing and others (Adelaide, 1983) – includes facsimiles of all the tunes as found in the seven earliest editions containing music.

The Sternhold and Hopkins psalter passed through more than 150 editions from its genesis in the days of Edward VI through the end of the reign of Elizabeth I. By the time of its last printing in the nineteenth century, more than 600 editions had appeared. It served as the unofficial songbook of the Church of England, falling within the allowed usage at the end of morning and evening prayer under the queen's injunctions but never receiving official sanction for use within the services themselves. Sternhold could not have foreseen the tremendous popularity of his verses which had their genesis as poetry for the court. The many editions constitute the major surviving element of the lives of the otherwise obscure authors of the metrical psalter.

Neither the place nor the date of Thomas Sternhold's birth is known. Various places have been suggested, including Southampton and Awre in Gloucestershire. Anthony à Wood notes in the *Athenae Oxonienses* that Sternhold spent some time at Oxford University but "left it without the honor of a degree." The first hard evidence about him is found in Thomas Cromwell's reorganization of the royal household in 1538, where Sternhold is listed among the "gentlemen most meet to be daily wait-

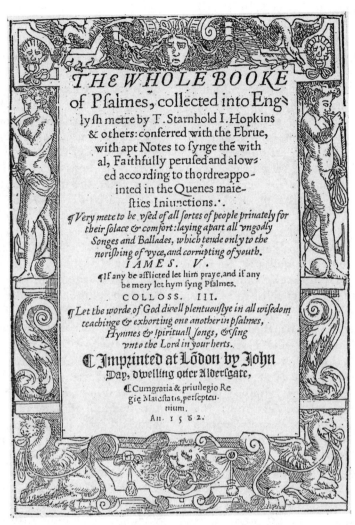

Title page for the first edition of Thomas Sternhold and John Hopkins's
complete metrical psalter

ers upon my said lord and allowed in his house."
He held various offices during the reigns of Henry
VIII and Edward VI, including groom of the king's
robes, receiver of the Court of General Surveyors,
member of Parliament for Plymouth, and master of
Saint Bartholemew's Hospital. As a supporter of the
new religion, he was imprisoned in March 1543,
along with Philip Hobby, because they had "abet-
ted, aided, favored, counseled and consented" with
one Anthony Pearson, a priest who was burned for
heresy. Sternhold and Hobby were pardoned and
returned to royal favor.

During the reign of Edward VI, Sternhold actively undertook the versification of the Psalms. A
small undated book containing nineteen Psalm versifications under the title *Certain Psalms Chosen out of
the Psalter of David and Drawn into English Meter by
Thomas Sternhold, Groom of the King's Majesty's Robes*

was printed by Edward Whitchurch and passed
through at least two editions before Sternhold's
death in 1549. In the dedication to the king,
Sternhold says that he is "encouraged to travail further in the said book of Psalms, trusting that as your
grace taketh pleasure to hear them sung sometimes
of me, so ye will also delight not only to see and
read them yourself, but also to command them to be
sung to you of others." Sternhold pledges to continue the task of versifying the Psalms, but with his
death the work passed into other hands.

*All Such Psalms of David as Thomas Sternhold Did
in His Lifetime Draw into English Meter* was published
by Whitchurch in December 1549, containing
thirty-seven Psalms adapted by Sternhold. An appendix adds seven versifications by John Hopkins.
Although Hopkins was ultimately to be the major
contributor to the complete metrical psalter, little

275

can be established with confidence as to his biography. A John Hopkins was admitted to the B.A. at Oxford in 1544 and became a schoolmaster, apparently in Suffolk, where he seems to have spent the rest of his life.

Hopkins prefaces his appendix to Sternhold's Psalms with a note stating that his Psalms should not be "fathered on the dead man, and so through his estimation be the more highly esteemed: neither for that they are in mine opinion (as touching the meter) in any part to be compared with his most exquisite doings, but especially to fill up a place, which so should have been void, that the book may rise to his just volume." Concern for the size of the volume would seem to be more of a publisher's interest than that of the versifier. Perhaps Whitchurch commissioned Hopkins's additions. No further additions were made to this collection during Edward's reign, although it was republished at least thirteen times.

What was the purpose for which this collection was originally published? Sternhold sang these verses before the king as courtly lyrics and implied that they were published because of the king's delight in them. They must have met with public response, for this collection was the only one of the many Psalm versifications during Edward's reign to have enjoyed more than one edition. There is musical evidence supporting the use of the Psalms as courtly lyrics. Fragmentary survivals of forty-eight settings (forty-four settings of Sternhold's verses and four of Hopkins's) by the Chapel Royal composer John Shepherd lend credence to Sternhold's remarks. The composer and lutenist Philip van Wilder, who had been in court service since 1529, served as a gentleman of the Privy Chamber to Edward VI in 1550. A five-voice setting of Sternhold's Psalm 128 by him is entitled "Wedding." According to the prayer books of Edward VI, this Psalm was to be sung at weddings, and this setting was probably composed specifically for such an occasion. Two anonymous settings appear in a set of experimental musico-liturgical manuscripts written about the time of the first prayer book, which may indicate a possible interest in introducing metrical psalmody into the new vernacular services.

With the death of Edward VI and the accession of Mary, the further development of the metrical psalter was carried forward among the exiles on the Continent who were attempting to maintain the Reformed English Church in the face of Mary's reinstitution of Roman Catholicism. The first Continental publication of the metrical psalter was intimately connected with the group of exiles who gathered at Frankfurt and soon came into sharp contention among themselves over the question of whether the second prayer book of Edward VI should be maintained as the standard for worship or whether there should be further reform. The background and details of the rupture between the two sides was recorded anonymously in *A Brief Discourse of the Troubles Begun at Frankfurt in the Year 1554 about the Book of Common Prayer and Ceremonies* (1575). When the first exiles arrived in Frankfurt, they were given the use of the French church for their worship. Under the leadership of William Whittingham, they used a service modified along Calvinist lines rather than that of the second prayer book. Among the changes they made was to "sing a Psalm in meter in a plain tune as was, and is accustomed in the French, Dutch, Italian, Spanish, and Scottish churches." The developments in the community and the various compromises that were attempted are recorded in the *Brief Discourse*.

Several different orders of service were drawn up and subscribed to by the constantly changing membership of the congregation. Some of these orders maintained more of the prayer-book practice, while others were more radical. The first publication of the metrical Psalms on the Continent, *Psalms of David in Meter* (1556?), seems to be directly connected with one of these orders of service. Although it is a pivotal work in the redirection of purpose of the metrical psalter, it has received inadequate attention. The only surviving copy is imperfect; Psalms 51 and 53, and the beginning of Psalm 68, are missing. This work contains all of the Psalms of Sternhold and Hopkins from the previous editions. There are also eight new metricalizations: Psalms 23, 51, 95 (misprinted "94"), 114, 115, 130, 133, and 137. All of these Psalms, as well as those of Hopkins, are integrated into a single order and are not kept separate from those of Sternhold as heretofore.

Following the Psalms is a series of metrical settings of elements of the prayer book service, including a Benedictus, a Magnificat, and several versions of the Lord's Prayer, the Creed, three settings of the Ten Commandments (two of which are in "Master Sternhold's meter"), and four metrical prayers. These prayers and one of the settings of the Ten Commandments are signed with the initials "W. S." Two of the Psalms (23 and 137) and several of the other metrical elements are signed variously "Ge." and "Gene." The rest of the new material has no indication as to author. These metrical items are succeeded by a collection of prose prayers, the first of

Page from Sternhold and Hopkins's complete metrical psalter

which is by Miles Coverdale. The final item in the book is a catechism.

This book is obviously designed as a supplement to services based on those of the prayer book. Psalm 95 is supplied with a metrical Gloria Patri, which is exactly the form in which it is found as the opening sung portion of morning prayer. The two canticles (Benedictus and Magnificat) were probably accompanied by others that were in the missing folios of the surviving copy. The rest of the metrical portions also find use in the prayer-book services. But other new elements in this book are harbingers of things to come. In earlier editions each Sternhold and Hopkins Psalm is preceded by a four-line argument, with an *8686* syllable count (later to be known as ballad stanza), such as the following from Psalm 3:

> The passion here is figured,
>   and how Christ rose again:
> So is the Church and faithful men,
>   their trouble and their pain.

The new Psalms in this book are supplied with prose arguments of a more aggressive nature, such as the following from Psalm 115:

> A prayer of the faithful oppressed by idolatrous tyrants, against whom they desire that God would succor them: for as much as there is no comparison betwixt him and their false gods or idols. Trusting most constantly that God will preserve them in this their need, seeing that he hath adopted and received them to his favor, promising finally that they will not be unmindful of so great a benefit, if it would please God to hear their prayer, and deliver them by his omnipotent power.

The two canticles and Psalm 95 have short metrical arguments of the type with the Sternhold and Hopkins Psalms, while all the rest of the new Psalms have prose arguments of the type on Psalm 115.

Another startling element is found in Hopkins's version of Psalm 30. All earlier editions read:

For why, his anger but a space,
    Doth last and slake again:
But yet the favor of his grace,
    Forever doth remain.
Though grips of grief and pangs full sore
    Do chance us over night:
The Lord to joy shall us restore,
    Before the day be light.

In this book these verses are changed:

For why, his anger but a space,
    Doth last and slake again:
But in his favor and his grace,
    Always doth life remain.
Though grips of grief and pangs full sore
    Shall lodge with us all night;
The Lord to joy shall us restore,
    Before the day be light.

Two different hands and purposes are at work here. One is preparing a book for use as a lyrical supplement to the prayer book, using as its basis the metrical Psalm of Sternhold and Hopkins supplemented with new material for use at morning and evening prayer. The second hand is preparing for further change by introducing prose arguments to the added Psalms and undertaking the revision of the earlier version of one of the Psalms. The purpose of the book has been shifted from that of private devotion and courtly lyric to that of material for use in public worship. This compromise book and the compromise liturgy for which it was prepared were both short-lived.

At Frankfurt an unbridgeable gulf opened between those under the leadership of Dr. Richard Cox, who wanted to maintain a conservative service modeled on the prayer book, and those under the leadership of John Knox and Whittingham, who wanted a more thorough reformation. The latter group withdrew to Geneva, where the next chapter in the development of the metrical psalter was written.

In 1556 the Geneva printer John Crespin published *The Form of Prayers and Ministration of the Sacraments, et cetera, Used in the English Congregation at Geneva and Approved by the Famous and Godly Learned Man John Calvin.* The second part of this volume is entitled *One and Fifty Psalms of David in English Meter, Whereof Thirty-seven Were Made by Thomas Sternhold and the Rest by Others, Conferred with the Hebrew and in Certain Places Corrected as the Text, and Sense of the Prophet Required.* The consensus is that this Psalm publication was under the editorship of Whittingham. It has exactly the same contents as *Psalms of David in Meter,* with the exception of the omission of

Psalm 95 and all the other metrical elements intended for use in the prayer-book service. This is not surprising, for the services that make up the first part of this volume are radically changed from the prayer-book services and do not allow for their use.

The Sternhold and Hopkins Psalms in this book undergo a wholesale revision. Their metrical arguments are replaced with prose arguments, and their texts are thoroughly revised in the manner of Hopkins's Psalm 30 in the former book. The Psalms that were new in the previous book are printed anonymously here without change; in later editions they are attributed to Whittingham. The fact that he was the original author accounts for their having escaped revision in this volume. Another new element in this psalter is the marginal notes commenting on the Psalms. Some of the notes are merely explanatory of the original Hebrew or point the moral to be drawn. Others are more tendentious, such as this one to Hopkins's Psalm 42:9: "The papists and infidels esteem not God, and therefore mock all such as profess his name."

This volume is the first of the series of publications in which the English reformed cause moved to the offensive. It was followed by the prose psalter, which adopted the same arguments before the Psalms as in this volume, and culminated with the Geneva Bible. This volume is also the first to include tunes. Another edition in 1558 adds nine more Psalms by Whittingham and two by John Pullain.

With the death of Mary and the accession of Elizabeth, the work on the psalter continued on two fronts. The book was brought back to England, where the printer John Day had an exclusive patent for its publication, while in Geneva further editions with additional Psalm versifications were also produced. In England an edition of 1560 added two each by Robert Wisdom and Thomas Becon and one anonymous Psalm. Another 1560 edition added twenty-five by William Kethe, who had also supplied commendatory verses to Christopher Goodman's pamphlet *How Superior Powers Ought to Be Obeyed* (1558). In 1561 Day brought out an edition with eighty-three Psalms; it is significant for the appearance of three new versifications by Sternhold and fourteen by Hopkins. Hopkins had apparently spent the reign of Mary in seclusion in England, for there is no trace of him among the Continental exiles. The source of the three additional Psalms by Sternhold, so long after his death, is unknown. Another contributor to this volume was Thomas Norton, the dramatist and translator of Calvin's *Insti-*

tutes (1536). A striking element in Day's 1561 psalm-book is the reappearance of the canticles and other metrical elements for prayer-book use from the first Continental psalter. It is typical of Day's publications that they reflect a conservative reforming tendency and that they make connection with the Edwardian church, thus the reintroduction of these prayer-book elements and the addition of further Psalms by Sternhold and Hopkins.

Finally, in 1562 the psalter was completed by the addition of thirty-nine more Psalms by Hopkins, twenty-five by Norton, and four by John Marckant. The distribution of these additions among the versifiers shows the hand of an editor – probably Day himself. In Scotland the psalter was also being completed under the order of the General Assembly. This psalter took a Genevan version of 1561 as its basis, to which were added Psalms by John Craig and Robert Pont and, for the remainder, selections from the English psalter of 1562.

The great majority of the metrical Psalms are in fourteeners, cast in what was later to be known as ballad stanzas. Sternhold used this form for all but two of his Psalms. Hopkins used the same meter but the rhyme scheme *abab* rather than *abcb*. Kethe used much more sophisticated structures; but, possibly because of this, most of his versions were left out of the completed psalter. Musical settings of prose texts for the new vernacular services reveal chaotic accentuation and syllabication, even of the same word within a single composition. For instance, *sittest, heaven,* and *spirit* (*sprite*) are treated alternately as one- or two-syllable words, *covenant* and *enemies* as two or three syllables, *magnified* as three or four syllables, and *continually* as four or five syllables. The very rigidity of the metrical settings made them attractive, for the music demanded an exact number of syllables, without deviation, in each line. This promoted an ease of singing that was impossible with prose Psalms. John Jewel attests to the great popularity of the metrical Psalms early in Elizabeth's reign when upward of six thousand gathered at Paul's Cross to sing the Psalms together. Thus what had started as private devotional lyric at court had become national, popular religious song.

Although several studies have been done on the music that accompanies the Sternhold and Hopkins psalter and two editions of that music are available, no modern edition of the word texts of the metrical Psalms has been published. What Psalms are available are found scattered through the various anthologies of Tudor poetry. Much more research has been done on the music than on the word texts. Until a modern critical edition of the psalter is available – containing all of the versifications from the various early editions as well as the original and edited versions of Sternhold and Hopkins's Psalms – a true appreciation of these verses and their place in the development of English sixteenth-century poetry is not available.

Bibliography:

William Cowan, *A Bibliography of the Book of Common Order and Psalm Book of the Church of Scotland, 1556–1664* (Edinburgh, 1913).

Biographies:

Anthony à Wood, *Athenae Oxoniensis,* volume 1, edited by Philip Bliss (London: F. C. & J. Rivington, 1813–1820), pp. 183–188;

A. B. Emden, *A Biographical Register of the University of Oxford: A.D. 1501 to 1540* (Oxford: Clarendon, 1974).

References:

Lloyd E. Berry, Introduction to *The Geneva Bible: A Facsimile of the 1560 Edition* (Madison: University of Wisconsin Press, 1969);

Herbert Byard, "A Sternhold and Hopkins Puzzle," *Musical Quarterly,* 56 (April 1970): 221–229;

A. G. Dickens, *The English Reformation* (New York: Schocken, 1964);

Edward Doughtie, *English Renaissance Song* (Boston: Twayne, 1986);

Christina H. Garrett, *The Marian Exiles: A Study in the Origins of Elizabethan Puritanism* (Cambridge: Cambridge University Press, 1938);

John Julian, ed., *A Dictionary of Hymnology* (London: John Murray, 1892; New York: Dover, 1957);

M. M. Knappen, *Tudor Puritanism: A Chapter in the History of Idealism* (Chicago: University of Chicago Press, 1939);

D. W. Krummel, *English Music Printing, 1553–1700* (London: Bibliographical Society, 1975);

Robin Leaver, *Goostly Psalmes and Spirituall Songes: English and Dutch Metrical Psalms from Coverdale to Utenhove, 1535–1566* (Oxford: Oxford University Press, 1991);

Letters and Papers, Foreign and Domestic, of the Reign of Henry VIII Preserved in the Public Record Office, the British Museum, and Elsewhere in England, 21 volumes (London: Longman, Green, Longman & Roberts, 1862–1929);

C. L. Oastler, *John Day: The Elizabethan Printer,* Oxford Bibliographical Society Occasional Publication 10 (Oxford: Bodleian Library, 1975);

Millar Patrick, *Four Centuries of Scottish Psalmody* (London: Oxford University Press, 1949);

Bernarr Rainbow, *English Psalmody Prefaces: Popular Methods of Teaching, 1562–1835* (Kilkenny, Ireland: Boethius Press, 1982);

Teut Riese, *Die englische Psalmendichtung im sechzehnten Jahrhundert,* Universitäts-Archiv anglistische Abteilung 4 (Münster: Helios-Verlag, 1937);

Hastings Robinson, ed. and trans., *The Zurich Letters, Comprising the Correspondence of Several English Bishops and Others, with Some of the Helvetian Reformers, during the Early Part of the Reign of Queen Elizabeth* (Cambridge: Cambridge University Press, 1842);

Hallet Smith, "English Metrical Psalms in the Sixteenth Century and Their Metrical Significances," *Huntington Library Quarterly,* 9 (May 1946): 249–271;

W. M. Southgate, "The Marian Exiles and the Influence of John Calvin," in *The Making of English History,* volume 1, edited by Robert Livingston Schuyler and Herman Ausubel (New York: Dryden Press, 1952), pp. 148–152;

Nicholas Temperly, *The Music of the English Parish Church,* 2 volumes (Cambridge: Cambridge University Press, 1974);

Temperly, "Psalms, metrical," in his *The New Grove Dictionary of Music and Musicians,* volume 15 (Washington, D.C.: Grove's Dictionaries of Music, 1980), pp. 347–382;

James Wrightson, *The "Wanley" Manuscripts: A Critical Commentary* (New York: Garland, 1989);

Rivkah Zim, *English Metrical Psalms: Poetry as Praise and Prayer, 1535–1601* (Cambridge: Cambridge University Press, 1987).

John Stow

(1525 – 5 April 1605)

William Keith Hall
University of North Carolina at Chapel Hill

BOOKS: *A summarie of Englyshe chronicles* (London: Printed by Thomas Marshe, 1565; revised, 1566, 1570, 1573; revised editions, London: Printed by H. Bynneman, 1574; London: Printed by R. Tottell & H. Bynneman, 1575; London: R. Newbery, 1590);

The summarie of Englyshe chronicles. (Lately collected and published) nowe abridged and continued tyl March, 1566 (London: Printed by Thomas Marshe, 1566; revised and enlarged, 1567, 1573; revised and enlarged editions, London: Printed by R. Tottell & H. Bynneman, 1579; London: Printed by R. Newbery & H. Denham, 1584, 1587; London: Printed by R. Bradocke, 1598; London: Printed by J. Harison, 1604);

The chronicles of England, from Brute vnto this present yeare 1580 (London: Printed by H. Bynneman for Ralfe Newbery, 1580);

The Annales of England, faithfully collected out of the most autenticall Authors, Records, and other Monuments of Antiquitie, from the first inhabitation vntill this present yeere 1592 (London: Printed by Ralfe Newbery, 1592; revised and enlarged, 1600, 1601; revised and enlarged edition, London: Printed by G. Eld for G. Bishop & T. Adams, 1602);

A suruay of London. Contayning the originall, antiquity, increase, moderne estate, and description of that citie (London: Printed by J. Windet for John Wolfe, 1598; revised and enlarged, 1603).

Editions: *A Survey of London,* edited by William J. Thoms (London: Whittaker, 1842); edited by Henry Morley (London: Routledge, 1890); 2 volumes, edited by Charles Lethbridge Kingsford [from the 1603 edition] (Oxford: Clarendon, 1908).

OTHER: *The workes of Geffrey Chaucer newly printed, with diuers additions, whiche wer neuer in print before,* edited by Stow (London: Printed by John Kingston for John Wight, 1561).

Effigy of Stow in the church of Saint Andrew Undershaft, London

John Stow worked at an important moment in the development of historiography and was one of the key figures in the transition from medieval to modern modes of inquiry. He is best remembered for his topographical *A Survey of London* (1598), which supports his modern reputation as a dedicated and painstaking amateur scholar whose heightened sense of historical accuracy was instrumental in setting modern historiography upon its course. However, this book was a last work, a masterpiece, composed at the end of a distinguished fifty-year career in the collection and study of English antiquities during which Stow produced several other large historical compilations in the popular form of chronicles and annals. These earlier books are, for the most part, traditional in form and content; they reproduce without challenge the accepted myths of national origin, such as the founding of Britain by survivors of the Trojan War. But Stow's later work in topography and local history gives increasing evidence of a more skeptical, interrogative sense of history. He was one of the first to question seriously the authority of traditional source authors, such as Geoffrey of Monmouth, and to work from primary source materials, such as guild, monastic, and state papers. Still, he was very much a man of his age. He retained a moralistic view of historical process, even though his work signals an important departure from the turgid and uncritical compilations of the medieval annal toward the more systematic investigation of national institutions in the post-Baconian era.

Stow had little preparation for a scholarly career. Born in London in 1525, the eldest of Thomas and Elizabeth Stow's seven children, he probably had little, if any, schooling. His father and grandfather had been tallow chandlers, but Stow served an apprenticeship to tailor John Bulley and in 1547 was made a freeman of the Merchant Taylors' Company. He continued with the company for most of his life, although he neither rose to an administrative post nor put in many appearances at public functions. Late in his life Stow received pensions from the company in recognition of his work as a scholar, not as a tailor. Near mid century he married and had three daughters, two of whom, Julian and Joan, survived him, along with his wife, Elizabeth.

Mostly self-educated, Stow read widely and attained some command of languages. His early interests included divinity, astrology, and poetry, but he later claimed that he "never esteemed" history as a worthwhile pursuit. His interest in literature led him to collect the poems of John Skelton and John Lydate, and also to edit and publish *The Works of Geoffrey Chaucer* (1561), an edition highly derivative of an earlier collection by William Thynne. Stow shared with his generation an almost total misunderstanding of Middle English metrics; therefore, as an example of his editorial skills, this edition was not promising. However, he did acquire a deep knowledge of Chaucer's time and texts that might

have made a later edition more significant, had he not been diverted to chronicle writing. While he is not remembered as a great editor of the major poems, he continues to be mentioned among Chaucerians, if only as a preservationist.

About the same time, Stow transcribed and presented to Robert Dudley, Earl of Leicester, a copy of his grandfather Edmund Dudley's *Tree of the Commonwealth*. Graciously, the younger Dudley suggested that Stow publish an original history, something he apparently was already considering upon the encouragement of others.

In 1563 London printer Richard Grafton had hastily published two editions of *An Abridgement of the Chronicles of England,* a history written, he claimed, to offset an error-ridden version of Thomas Lanquet and Thomas Cooper's *Epitome,* published in 1559 by printer Thomas Marshe. However, Grafton's book was itself highly erroneous, and Marshe, irritated by Grafton's criticism, planned to reprint Lanquet and Cooper's in better form. He approached Stow to do the editing, which Stow agreed to do without payment. Perhaps uncertain about his credentials as a scholar, Stow requested a more learned assistant. Marshe provided William Baldwin, a London parson and editor of *A Mirror for Magistrates* (1559). Baldwin died of plague before the work was well under way, but Stow continued the project on the strength of promises, never fulfilled, that Marshe would appoint another assistant.

The results of Stow's first venture into historiography, *A Summary of English Chronicles* (1565), was dedicated to Robert Dudley and printed by Marshe in octavo, a format more marketable than the larger folio and, therefore, more accessible to a public increasingly literate and interested in knowledge of the past. Written in the form of a "city" chronicle, it organizes information chronologically under the names of mayors and sheriffs. In his dedication Stow characterizes the work as a "summary of the chiefest chances and accidents that have happened in this realm, from the time of Brutus to this our age," produced, as was customary, "by the conference of many authors, both old and new." Stow used several sources but relied most upon the three he mentioned by name: Robert Fabian, Edward Hall, and John Hardyng.

Stow began to publish at a time when the majority of historical works were poorly researched and miserably written, but from the outset there was a difference in the quality of his work. In his letter to the reader, he states his principles as a historian, which are noteworthy since he often repeated them: "Diverse writers of histories write diversely"; some "pen their histories plentifully," taking in "the affairs done in foreign parts," while others "put in memory only such things as they themselves have had experience of." Stow claims a place among the latter. Although he makes use of prior chronicles, he also includes much he discovered for himself "partly by painful search, and partly by diligent experience."

Soon after the publication of the *Summary,* Stow visited Grafton. The meeting, which Stow later recorded in detail, began cordially, but the mood quickly changed when he displayed a copy of Grafton's own 1563 *Abridgement* carefully marked for errors. Stow claimed that in the *Abridgement* Grafton had not only misplaced almost all of his dates but also mangled his lists of civic officials. Grafton did not take correction kindly. Although Stow records that the interview ended with protestations of friendship, Grafton immediately took steps to sabotage Stow's career.

Grafton hastily brought out *A Manual of the Chronicles of England* (1565), a book that, without acknowledgment, uses Stow's more accurate *Summary* as its principal source. In his letter to the reader Grafton falsely claims that Stow had "counterfeited" his *Abridgement* and "made my travail to pass under his name." At the time, Stow was completing an abridgment of his own *Summary,* printed in 1566. Infuriated by Grafton's claims, he added to the second edition (1567) a dedication to the lord mayor of London that characterizes Grafton's work as "the thundering noise of empty tuns." It was, Stow claimed, "Truth's quarrel" that he laid before his patron. Heretofore (Stow clearly meant Grafton) truth had been "miserably handled . . . and such an hodgepodge made of truth and lies together, that of the ignorant in histories the one could not be discerned from the other."

Stow's work attracted notice despite Grafton's efforts to compromise Stow's reputation. Though new to the field of historical research, he developed a view of the historian's role more fully considered than that of many of his contemporaries and exhibited a concern for accuracy and locating reliable sources. He became an avid collector of manuscripts and "got into his possession as many of the ancient English writers . . . as ever he could, by money or favor," according to John Strype, an early editor of the *Survey.* Over the years Stow built a formidable personal library including many manuscripts in Latin and Old English that he made freely available to friends and fellow historians, such as William Richardson, William Camden, and Arch-

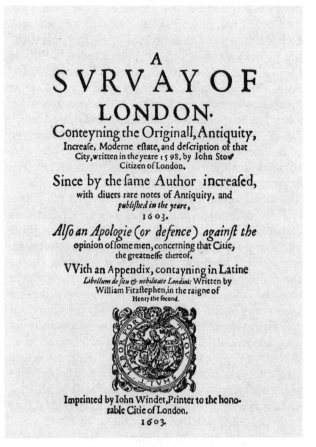

A
SVRVAY OF
LONDON.
Conteyning the Originall, Antiquity,
Increafe, Moderne eftate, and defcription of that
City, written in the yeare 1598. by Iohn Stow
Citizen of London.

Since by the fame Author increafed,
with diuers rare notes of Antiquity, and
publifhed in the yeare,
1603.

Alfo an Apologie (or defence) againft the
opinion of fome men, concerning that Citie,
the greatneffe thereof.

VVith an Appendix, contayning in Latine
Libellum de fitu & nobilitate Londini: Written by
William Fitzftephen, in the raigne of
Henry the fecond.

Imprinted by Iohn Windet, Printer to the honorable Citie of London.
1603.

Title page for the 1603 edition of Stow's scholarly history of the English capital

bishop Matthew Parker. A good many texts from Stow's library survive, some with his marginal notes. Several important registers, cartularies, and histories of dissolved London priories, which otherwise would certainly have been lost, were preserved in his collection. In at least one case, that of the *Dunmow Chronicle* of Nicholas de Bromfield, the only surviving copy is Stow's hand-copied transcript.

Occasionally, Stow's collecting got him into trouble. In 1569 a "manifesto" circulated in London that was sympathetic to Fernando Alvarez de Toledo, third Duke of Alva. The Privy Council, eager to find those responsible for its publication, called in witnesses from several of the city's guilds, including the Merchant Taylors'. When questioned, Stow confessed to having in his possession a copy that he had written out by hand. The council examined nine of Stow's fellow tailors, but none gave testimony against him, and no sentence was handed down.

Soon after this the Queen's Council received reports that Stow possessed many "foolish fabulous books" of superstition and "fantastical popish books printed in the old time." On 21 February 1569 Edmund Grindal, bishop of London, ordered a search of his house, and a list of thirty-eight "unlawful" books was drawn up and submitted to William Cecil, secretary to the queen. These included Anglo-Saxon and Latin chronicles, books of "physic, surgery, and herbs," and religious works, such as Richard Shacklock's *Hatchet of Heresies* (1565), for possession of which Stow was suspected of occultism and papist sympathies. Some were confiscated, but the council took no further action. For Stow the incident was more irritating than damaging, and it seems to have been unwarranted. There is little evidence that he was either a practicing Catholic or an active Protestant. If he had genuine sympathy for Catholicism, it was most probably informed less by religious zeal than by nostalgia for the stability and cultural continuity for which the church traditionally stood. Deeply conservative and suspicious of rapid change, Stow saw the church as an institution that revered tradition and continuity and that preserved texts and monuments of inestimable value. Beyond this it is difficult to reconstruct his religious views. Generally, his writings seem indifferent to the religious turmoils of his day. Of course, his reticence on religious issues may have been a concession to the threat of censorship.

Despite these interruptions, Stow continued collecting and writing. As his reputation grew, he formed friendships with many notable historians and scholars – John Leland, William Lambarde, Thomas Speght, Camden, and Archbishop Parker among them. Through Parker, Stow became involved in the publication of several ancient manuscripts, including the *Flores Historiarum* (1567). It was also through Parker that he became an early member of a group that in 1586 organized the Society of Antiquaries. Until its dissolution in 1607 the society met for presentations of research on the peerage, law, civic government, and topographical studies. Membership in the society put Stow in touch with men concerned with the cultural antecedents of England's institutions. Through these contacts he developed his knowledge of the social history of England and began to work with city and parish records.

In 1580 Stow published *The Chronicles of England, from Brute unto this Present Year,* which expanded the *Summary* while retaining the "civic" format. Although the quality of his data was in some respects better than that of his models and his contemporaries, he continued to work within the medieval tradition, wherein the chronicle developed by a process of "accretion," according to scholar F. J.

Levy. As more information was gathered, it was compressed into chronological format with only minor narrative connections and no sustained analysis. Motivation and causality were not systematically examined, although as humanists, historians of Stow's generation had great faith in the past as a model for present action. The study of history educated one in civic behavior, regardless of social station. As Stow states in the preface to the *Chronicles,* it is as hard to read history and not come away with "some colors of wisdom" as it is to "walk up and down in the hot parching sun, and not to be therewith sun-burned."

Still, despite the limitations of his genre, Stow's methodology was advanced for his time. To a higher degree than many other writers, he was painstaking in his transcription of manuscripts and genuinely concerned with factual accuracy. He exercised discretion in choosing between what he felt were authoritative and merely "fabulous" accounts. He often traveled to scattered parishes where he copied inscriptions, read wills and deeds, and recorded the details of monuments. One of the first to make a systematic use of public records, he used his travels and acquaintances to gain access to various sources, such as the *Liber Custumarum,* the Patent Rolls, and parliamentary records, all of which he examined and cited with care.

Stow's next major work, *The Annals of England,* was published in 1592. In the hiatus between publications, he had been at work on a much larger and more ambitious project beside which, he claimed in his letter to the reader, the *Annals* were but "an abstract." This larger work, the "History of This Island," was planned as a comprehensive history of England and would have made use of Stow's "laborious collections" of the past thirty years, had not Stow's printer, for economic reasons, insisted upon publishing annals instead.

Apparently, Stow planned the "History" as part of the "Universal History" first projected by printer Reyner Wolfe, who had conceived of a massive cosmography comprising a geography and history of the entire world. However, at Wolfe's death in 1573 the project consisted only of manuscript collections dealing with the British Isles. Wolfe's associate, Raphael Holinshed, took over the project and scaled it down to a description of England, Scotland, and Ireland. This was published in July 1578 as *Ralph Holinshed's Chronicle,* in two large folios. The book sold well enough to warrant a second edition; but Holinshed died in 1580, and his printers enlisted John Hooker to supervise revisions of the text with the aid of others. One of this editorial committee was Stow, who personally completed the history through 1587, the year of its publication. While this second edition of Holinshed's *Chronicle* was widely read and later recognized as a source for Shakespeare, Stow's vast "History" went unpublished, and the manuscript has vanished.

As a whole the *Annals* speak well of Stow's evolving sense of scholarship. In his treatment of Henry VI, he apparently used records and documents, no longer extant, that make it genuinely authoritative. Elsewhere, he gives further evidence of his concern for accuracy. In a note to the reader on "the first habitation of this island," he reasons that it is better to say little about the early inhabitants of Britain rather than to record the list of kings supplied by a surreptitious pamphlet "falsely forged, and thrust into the world" under the name of the historian Berosus. The history of England could not be grounded on so specious a source, Stow says. For his account of Britain's prehistory, he returns to Geoffrey of Monmouth, and so retains the myth of Brutus. Later, in the *Survey,* he would in turn question Monmouth and base his account of the founding of London on Caesar's *Commentaries,* a source he thought to be of "far better credit," since Caesar, unlike Monmouth, wrote of an ancient Britain he had actually seen.

On 5 July 1592 Stow presented a copy of his *Annals* to the Merchant Taylors "as a small monument given in token of his thankfulness" for remembrances from the company in the form of pensions received since 1578. This benefaction was probably the only steady income he had. Yet, at almost seventy years of age, he had neither exhausted his knowledge nor seen his best work in print. His interest in public records, monuments, and architecture accorded with a growing general interest in local history and topographical description, as exemplified by the publication of the first national atlas of England, by Christopher Saxton (1574), and Lambarde's *Perambulation of Kent* (1576). Drawing upon the abundant material collected for his never-published "History of This Island," upon his own *Summary* and *Annals,* and upon city records, Stow produced his last, most significant, and most original work, *A Survey of London.*

Originally entered at Stationer's Hall on 7 July 1598, *A Survey of London* was the "first scholarly history of an English town," according to scholar Antonia Gransden. Though not the philosophical history Bacon would later advocate, it was an exhaustive topographical "discovery," or anatomy, of the city and its institutions. Perhaps remembering Wolfe's dream of a universal cosmography, Stow expressed his hope, in his dedication to the lord mayor, that similar works might be organized into a "whole body of the English chorography."

One of the attractions of the book is that its organizational model is perfect for its purpose and content. Arranged as a "perambulation," literally a "walk around" London, the narrative proceeds chronologically within a topographical frame based on the actual layout of the city. This model structured and organized Stow's abundant material and produced a narrative that does not resemble a history as much as a form of literary cartography. Chapters on the "antiquity of London" and its walls, waters, gates, towers, schools, and customs precede a description of the city's twenty-six wards, including the suburban "liberties." Beginning in east London, in Portesoken ward, Stow provides a brief digression on each ward's name and history, describes its boundaries, and lists its principal inhabitants and notable occurrences.

Most of this material was drawn from the best documentary sources Stow could find, though he also relied upon his personal observations and memories. For example, when he writes of schools, he recalls having witnessed in his youth the annual "disputing" of schoolboys in the churchyard of Saint Bartholomew in Smithfield. There, to test his skills in logic and argument, a student stood upon a plank beneath a tree and "opposed and answered" until he was "by some better scholar overcome" and obliged to stand down. In a later section Stow remembers that the armory in Portesoken ward was during his childhood a nunnery, later "surrendered" to Henry VIII. From the farm operated by the nuns, the young Stow had "fetched many a halfpenny worth of milk . . . always hot from the kine."

Not all of Stow's memories are so sentimental. He had witnessed a great many changes to his city and did not approve of them. He remembers that Thomas Cromwell, vice regent under Henry VIII, built a sumptuous house near the residence of his father, Thomas Stow. To accommodate his garden Cromwell ordered a wall built twenty feet into Thomas's land without warning. Thomas received no compensation and had to continue paying his full rent. "Thus much of mine own knowledge have I thought good to note," Stow writes, "that the sudden rising of some men, causeth them to forget themselves."

Stow did not welcome change, yet the London he observed was a place being daily transformed from walled medieval village into crowded, preindustrial city. Overpopulation and blight were much in evidence. To accommodate newcomers,

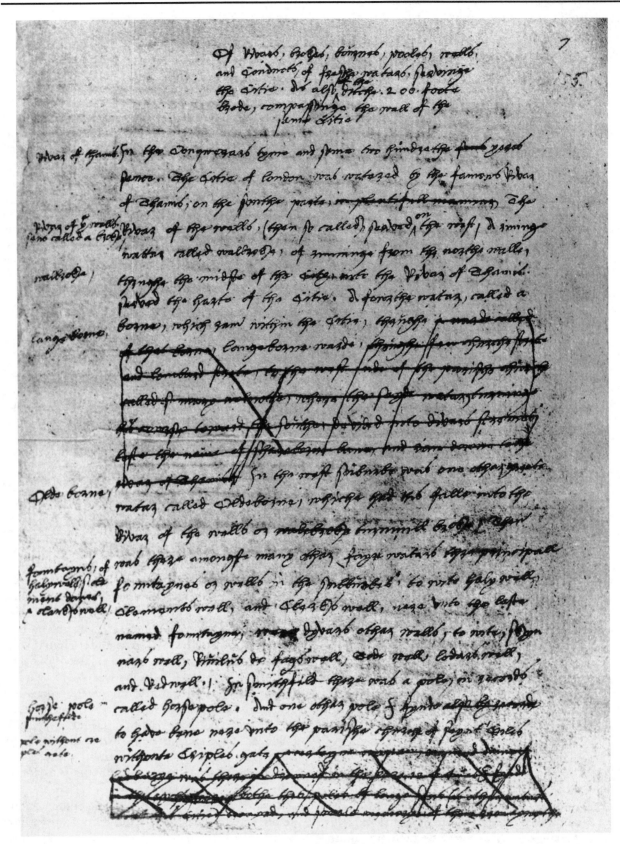

Draft for the version of "Auncient and Present Riuers" published in the 1603 revised edition of Stow's Survey of London *(Bodleian Library, Tanner MS. 464 [i]. f 155)*

abandoned monasteries were carved into apartments, and tenements were tacked onto the city walls. Opulent new homes, such as Cromwell's, sprang up at the whim of the politically favored and the suddenly rich. All of this Stow regarded with suspicion and anger. Although he was particularly annoyed by the disappearance of open spaces, gardens, and trees, some of his most vituperative passages record the destruction of church monuments as old graves were emptied to make room for the new dead. With a sense that the London he knew was disappearing before his eyes, Stow carefully recorded the condition of churches, gravestones, and landmarks, some of which literally vanished as he was writing the book.

Yet, for all that the *Survey* includes, there is much missing that would be of immense interest to the modern imagination. Stow barely mentions the activity of the city's many theaters and none of its playwrights. He also glosses over the city's role in popular uprisings, such as the Peasant's Rebellion of 1381. Similarly, due perhaps to a concern for censorship, he gives little space to the city's role in contemporary religious and political reforms, instead briefly noting occasional persecutions or memorable sermons.

Even so, the *Survey* provides a rich, reliable, first-person account of the London known to Shakespeare, Edmund Spenser, and Sir Walter Ralegh. Modern scholars continue to mine it for demographic information on Elizabethan England and to check against it names and dates found in other historical and literary works of the period. Almost immediately after Stow's death, various editors — beginning in 1614 with Edmund Howes — began to publish "continued" editions that brought the narrative up to the year of publication and corrected the more glaring of Stow's errors. While these early editions augmented Stow's work with much valuable information, some, such as John Strype's 1720 edition, took such liberties with the text that the voice of Stow is almost totally obscured. The standard modern edition, published in 1908 by Charles Lethbridge Kingsford, reprints the 1603 text and provides current scholars with the most thorough list to date of Stow's life records, correspondence, and collections.

In his entry for 18 December 1602, diarist John Manningham records a meeting with the elderly Stow. Almost seventy-eight years old but nonetheless at work on an expanded edition of the *Survey,* Stow reflected briefly upon his career as a chronicler. He told Manningham, a little defensively, "What I have written I have written," but he also proudly described an engraving he had seen of himself that bore the caption "Antiquarius Angliae." Manningham observes that Stow "thinks himself worthy of that title for his pains, for he hath no gains by his travail." The fact that he had made no money from writing was a point of honor for Stow. When Manningham met him, his chief, and perhaps only, source of income was a modest pension from his guild. The next year he would request and receive a license from James I to solicit charity. But age and poverty did not prevent Stow from denouncing the spoiling of monuments in his beloved London. He told Manningham that many "new monuments" were not mentioned in the *Survey* because their building had destroyed other, older relics. Stow believed that the spoilers of these monuments were, in effect, thieves of testimony to the nation's honor and therefore worthy "to be deprived of that memory whereof they have injuriously robbed others."

More than two years after Manningham's visit, on 5 April 1605, Stow died, and three days later he was buried in the church of Saint Andrew Undershaft in London. Though the monument that his wife had erected in his honor survives, Stow's remains suffered the same desecration he had often angrily witnessed and recorded; his grave was emptied to make way for someone else. For Stow the irony would not have been poetic. It would have been a sad testimony to the condition of his London and to the heedlessness of a new generation toward those relics of the past that he had found worthy, for their own sake, of remembrance.

Bibliography:

Charles Lethbridge Kingsford, ed., "Bibliography," in *A Survey of London by John Stow,* volume 1 (Oxford: Clarendon, 1908), pp. lxxxii-lxxxvi.

References:

Barrett L. Beer, "John Stow and the English Reformation, 1547–1559," *Sixteenth Century Journal,* 16 (Summer 1985): 257–271;

Beer, "John Stow and Tudor Rebellions," *Journal of British Studies,* 27 (October 1988): 352–374;

Charles Matthew Clode, *Memorials of the Guild of the Merchant Taylors* (London: Harrison, 1875);

E. J. Devereux, "Empty Tuns and Unfruitful Grafts: Richard Grafton's Historical Publications," *Sixteenth Century Journal,* 21 (Spring 1990): 33–56;

F. Smith Fussner, *The Historical Revolution* (New York: Columbia University Press, 1962);

Fussner, *Tudor History and the Historians* (New York: Basic Books, 1970);

Antonia Gransden, *Historical Writing in England,* volume 2: *1307 to the Early Sixteenth Century* (Ithaca, N.Y.: Cornell University Press, 1982);

William Keith Hall, "A Topography of Time: Historical Narration in John Stow's *Survey of London,*" *Studies in Philology,* 88 (Winter 1991): 1–15;

Richard Helgerson, *Forms of Nationhood: The Elizabethan Writing of England* (Chicago: University of Chicago Press, 1992);

Martin Holmes, *Elizabethan London* (New York: Praeger, 1969);

Anne Hudson, "John Stow," in *Editing Chaucer: The Great Tradition,* edited by Paul Ruggiers (Norman, Okla.: Pilgrim, 1984), pp. 53–70;

F. J. Levy, *Tudor Historical Thought* (San Marino, Cal.: Huntington Library, 1967);

Lawrence Manley, *London in the Age of Shakespeare* (London: Croom Helm, 1986);

John Manningham, *The Diary,* edited by Robert Parker Sorlien (Hanover, N.H.: University Press of New England, 1976);

May McKisack, *Medieval History in the Tudor Age* (Oxford; Clarendon, 1971);

D. R. Woolf, *The Idea of History in Early Stuart England* (Toronto: University of Toronto Press, 1990).

Papers:
The largest collection of Stow's notes, drafts, and correspondence, as well as material from his manuscript library, is in the Harley and Cotton holdings at the British Library. Of special interest is Harley 538, which comprises an original draft of *A Survey of London.* Other important manuscripts are in the Bodleian Library's Tanner and Ashmole collections.

Cuthbert Tunstall

(1474 – 18 November 1559)

Kenneth R. Bartlett
Victoria College, University of Toronto

and

Wyman H. Herendeen
University of Windsor

BOOKS: *Cutheberti Tonstalli in laudem matrimonii oratio* (London: Printed by R. Pynson, 1518);

De arte supputandi libri quattuor (London: Printed by R. Pynson, 1522);

A sermon of Cuthbert bysshop of Duresme, made vpon Palme sondaye before kynge Henry the .viii. (London: Printed by T. Berthelet, 1539);

De Veritate Corporis et Sanguinis Domini Nostri Jesu Christi in Eucheristia (Paris: M. Vascosanus, 1554);

Contra impios Blasphematores Dei praedestinationis opus (Antwerp: Withagius, 1555);

Certaine godly and deuout prayers (London: Printed by John Cawood, 1558);

A letter written by Cutbert Tunstall and J. Stokesley somtime byshop of London, sente vnto R. Pole, cardinall (London: Printed by R. Wolfe, 1560).

OTHER: *Compendium et Synopsis in decem Libros Ethicorum Aristotelis,* edited by Tunstall (Paris: Vascosanus, 1554);

Expositio Beati Ambrosii Episcopi super Apocalypsin, edited, with a preface, by Tunstall (Paris: Vascosanus, 1554).

Cuthbert Tunstall was among the first generation of England's humanist scholars, statesmen, and ecclesiastics. As such, his life and work illustrate the cosmopolitan erudition and the social and religious commitment of the time — and also its tensions, as the spirit of reform spread through Europe, often leaving behind some of its early participants, such as Tunstall, as it gained momentum and took directions unforeseen by them. As is true of others of his generation (notably Thomas More and John Fisher), his life, like his written work, was an expression of the ideals and intellectual fervor of the revival of learning as it made its way north and west to England on the eve of religious reform. Educated on the Continent and esteemed as a scholar, Tunstall dedicated himself to increasingly conflicting matters of God and country; his life reflects the Renaissance emphasis on public service. His literary achievement, including the evidence of his personal library, punctuates a career as a humanist scholar, a counselor to princes, and ultimately a theologue torn by loyalties to church and prince.

Tunstall was born in 1474, the illegitimate son of Thomas Tunstall of Thurland Castle, knight of the body to Richard III. After a period at Oxford, where his celebrated knowledge of mathematics began, and, later at Cambridge, Cuthbert was sent to the *studio* of Padua in 1499 for six years of study. In Padua his international reputation as a humanist and scholar developed fully, not only among his friends and fellow students known to him in England, such as More, John Colet, William Grocyn, and Thomas Linacre, but also among his new acquaintances on the Continent: Richard Pace, Jacques Lefèvre d'Etaples, Aldus Manutius (the printer), Niccolo Leonico Tomeo (the famous professor of philosophy and Greek), and Desiderius Erasmus. Although Tunstall was graduated doctor of laws at Padua, he must have spent much time mastering the Greek and Latin classics and acquiring a knowledge of Hebrew. This learning gave him an important role in the Erasmian reform movement that was gaining momentum in England. He was among the few Catholic humanists to survive the turbulent decades, and his qualities earned him

Cuthbert Tunstall (portrait by Burton Constable; from Charles Sturge, Cuthbert
Tunstall: Churchman, Scholar, Statesman, Administrator, *1938)*

the reputation as one of the brightest lights of
Henry VIII's court and one of the most learned men
of his generation.

Tunstall returned to England in 1505 and was
given his first cure of souls the following year. He
was ordained a subdeacon in 1509, the year the
young Henry VIII came to the throne. In 1515
Tunstall began his lifelong service as a diplomat
with his appointment as an envoy to Flanders; he
resided with Erasmus while at Brussels. His influence at the court of Henry VIII continued to grow
and can be seen in his early contribution to the reform movement, the treatise *In Laudem matrimonii oratio* (1518). Ironically, this early work on an Erasmian theme defined Tunstall's conservative position
in the later divorce issue. The following year he was
appointed master of the rolls, a position he held
until 1522. During 1520–1521 he was again in Flanders, returning to become dean of Salisbury and, in
1522, bishop of London. That same year saw the

publication of Tunstall's most successful work, his
arithmetic treatise *De Arte supputandi,* the first of its
kind in England and acclaimed throughout Europe.
From 1523 until 1530 he served as lord privy seal,
and he served abroad again, in Spain, during 1525–
1526.

The year 1529 saw Tunstall involved in
Henry VIII's divorce, but as a counselor to Queen
Catherine with John Fisher, bishop of Rochester,
and consequently in the camp of other significant
humanist figures close to Catherine's household,
including Juan Luis Vives and Sir Thomas Elyot.
Tunstall did not relish his position, finding it difficult to reconcile his sincere opposition to the
king's "great matter" with his strong sense of personal loyalty and duty to his sovereign. Despite
his difficult position, he was appointed bishop of
Durham, one of the great ecclesiastical preferments of the kingdom, a see enjoying both spiritual and palatine authority. Nevertheless, he con-

tinued his support of Catherine, protesting against the royal divorce in 1531.

Tunstall came under increasing pressure after the marriage of Henry and Anne Boleyn. His house was searched in 1534, and he was expected to share the fates of his two close friends More and Fisher. However, like Elyot, he underwent a change of heart and in 1535 recognized the royal supremacy. His Palm Sunday sermon of 1539 shows his willingness to compromise and, as far as possible, defend Henrician reform.

Henry VIII rewarded Tunstall's acquiescence by appointing him lord president of the North in 1537, an office he held until 1545. More diplomatic missions followed (to France and Calais) before the death of Henry in 1547 ended his influence and began the period of religious experimentation that saw the English church moving further away from the conservative Henrician position he had come to respect, and closer to the Continental model of the Reformation that he execrated with the full fervor of his mind and spirit.

Under the rule of the protector Edward Seymour, Duke of Somerset, Tunstall managed to steer a safe course, despite his open hostility to the religious changes represented in the English Prayer Book, which was a catalyst to radical reform directly affecting himself. The Act of Uniformity (1549) and the Act against Superstitious Books and Images (1550), intended to prepare the way for the Prayer Book, were ultimately used against him. Somerset's fall and the rise of John Dudley, Duke of Northumberland, signaled the assault, not only on the wealth and prerogatives of his see but also on the intellectual and religious positions he had so steadfastly maintained. By September 1550 Tunstall was in loose confinement, only to be sent to the Tower and eventually deprived of the see of Durham (October 1552), which was then divided, much of it taken by Northumberland himself.

The death of Edward VI in 1553 and the failure of Northumberland's plot to place Lady Jane Grey on the throne resulted in Tunstall's being restored by Mary to the bishopric of Durham. Always a conservative Henrician in policy and a Catholic in religion, Tunstall welcomed the return of the old religion. In partial reaction to earlier Edwardian reforms, his own position on certain doctrinal matters hardened, resulting, for example, in his treatise on the Eucharist (1554). During the Marian reaction, however, his irenic personality and his horror of violence were tested again. He was active in his attempts to convince Protestant divines to acknowledge the old religion and the new order, despite the

small chance of success; but he in no way participated in the burnings. Indeed, his opposition to such activities probably resulted in his being reappointed in the North to keep him away from the decisions and executions he so abhorred. It has been said that he had read so much in history and theology that he would be loath to execute anyone for heresy unless the accused rejected the most elemental truths of the Christian faith. Such an accommodating attitude was not useful to Mary or her advisers.

The death of Mary and Elizabeth's accession in 1558 resulted in Tunstall's second deprivation. He reversed his position on the oath of supremacy and in fact lectured the young queen on her duties as a daughter of Henry VIII and as a woman. Once removed from the bench of bishops, Tunstall was placed in the custody of Matthew Parker, archbishop of Canterbury, a confinement more in the sense of a houseguest than a prisoner. He died in Parker's house at Lambeth on 18 November 1559, at the age of eighty-five.

Tunstall was a product of an intellectual revolution whose political momentum overtook him. Acting as a moderating force, he brought humanist principles into the sphere of diplomacy and religious and political reform. Although he was a man of action as well as letters, Tunstall's intellectual origins, accomplishments, ambitions, and the rationale for his important place in the affairs of the Reformation can be appreciated in the light of the recent identification of the inventory of his library. The inventory appears to have been made at the time of his arrest for misprision of treason at the hands of Northumberland and his agents between 1551 and 1552. Besides using the opportunity to deprive Tunstall of his see of Durham — which the duke stripped of its palatine jurisdiction while keeping much of its landed property for himself — Northumberland seized the personal possessions of the bishop, including his library. Like Tunstall's own fate, that of his library reflects his unique place in the period of humanist reform. The product of Continental humanist interests that provided the intellectual velocity for the reform movements, the library was conscripted by others to serve the causes of controversy to which it ultimately fell victim. It was used as a research library for humanists close to Henry's and Edward's courts before it was dismantled and its contents passed into other libraries, notably that of Northumberland's agent William Cecil, who may have made the inventory and whose own collection became its home. Given its importance Tunstall's library needs to be assessed as an expression of the bishop's intellectual and literary life and achievement.

The inventory of Tunstall's library records a remarkable collection, one of the largest known from the sixteenth century, with almost five hundred titles in several languages. Reflecting a humanist library classification system in England formed in the first half of the century, the divisions are those to be expected of a humanist whose early intellectual life had been molded by the trivium and quadrivium:

1. Libri Theologici Latini (177 titles)
2. Oratores et Grammatici Latini (43 titles)
3. Philosophi Latini (42 titles)
4. Latini Poetae (20 titles)
5. Medici Latini (23 titles)
6. Historici Latini (58 titles)
7. Cosmographiae Astrologiae Greci, Latini (16 titles)
8. Jurisconsulti Latini (5 titles)
9. Libri Theologici Greci (10 titles)
10. Dictionarii Greci (6 titles)
11. Philosophi Greci (26 titles)
12. Historici Greci (11 titles)
13. Oratores Greci (10 titles)
14. Grammatici Greci (3 titles)
15. Poetae Greci (13 titles)
16. Medici Greci (4 titles)
Total: 482 titles (with some double entries not counted)

The collection is preponderantly humanist in content, integrating classical and modern authors and reflecting the practical aims of education. Unusually comprehensive in scope, its many titles on history, philosophy, and literature complement the many theological works that constitute the largest category. The principles of humanist education reveal themselves throughout in the work drawn from *bonae litterae* (ancient literature). The history section includes classical texts such as Herodotus, Thucydides, and Livy, and biographical histories such as Plutarch's *Lives,* Suetonius, and Philostratus's life of Apollonius. But classical texts were thought to be practical works and would naturally be complemented by more-modern histories, including medieval and monastic chronicles and lives that would be useful for a Catholic following the debates of his generation, as Tunstall did. Eusebius, the lives of the popes, Bede, and Nauclerus are works and authors that bring the humanist's learning into the arena of contemporary politics. "Modern" European histories in their various generic manifestations – the "historia Francorum," "Historia Bohemorum," Jean Froissart, Polydore Vergil – bring the classicism of the library into the contemporary world of letters and suggest a collector very

much in touch with the diplomatic issues of his own generation.

The sections on Greek and Latin philosophy also have a combination of classical and contemporary writings, with a predictable preference for Aristotle (although more than would be expected of anyone but a scholar). Here and throughout, the large number of Greek texts is striking and well beyond the scope of any documented collection in England at the time. Equally appropriate for a humanist accustomed to giving advice to princes – and a respected figure in coteries frequented by Erasmus, More, and Vives – is the abundance of works that deal with the training of princes and courtiers: books of conduct (broadly speaking) and education as much as philosophy. Many of these are classical models of the form (Cicero, Plutarch, and Boethius), while others (Vives's *De disciplinis* [1531], Reinard Lorichio's *De instituendo principe* [1538], and the quantities of Erasmus of every sort) would have been very current, revealing this library to be a product of its particular time and place. If, from the English perspective, the theological content suggests a person of conservative religious views, his reading was along liberal lines by sixteenth-century Continental standards and included the controversial Neoplatonists.

Unusual also for a library of the period is the extensive list of poets, mainly but far from exclusively classical, and more numerous and varied than necessary for a library designed for theological debate, as many contemporary ecclesiastics' libraries were. Whatever his position in the religious controversy of the day, the collector here did not share the more zealous Reformers' disapproval of pagan poetry, for the material included is both tolerant and democratic by most standards. Thus, not only does it contain the greats – Homer (among the Latin histories in the Mapheus edition, and also among the Greek poets) and Virgil, both with commentaries – but it also has Ovid's *Metamorphoses,* Martial, Horace, and even Ausonius. The frequency of authors having a political focus (Statius, Lucan, Claudian, the *epistolae* of Ovid) complements the didactic bent of the philosophical and historical works. The Erasmian refrain is repeated here, for many of the texts of the standard authors appear to be his editions, and others were similarly in humanist editions, perfectly chosen to round out a balanced collection representative of the Renaissance tradition: Petrarch, Giovanni Boccaccio, Giovanni Pontano, and Angelo Poliziano.

The inclusive nature of the collection, however, is suggested by the abundance of drama, both

The opening of the Parliament of 1523, with King Henry VIII (top, center).
Tunstall (to his right) delivered a speech on the events leading up to
England's 1522 declaration of war on France (Collection of Her
Majesty the Queen, Windsor Castle).

Greek and Latin: Sophocles, Aeschylus, Aristophanes, Euripides, Terence, Plautus, and Seneca. These were beginning to be classroom standards in schools such as Colet's, but they were not regularly included in the inventories of private libraries. In the case of the Greek playwrights, they would be quite modern texts. Indeed, one of the most impressive aspects of the list is the wealth of Greek material, for it was difficult to find in England and was still in its first wave of revival among printers such as Manutius on the Continent. Even rarer than Greek, however, was proficiency in Hebrew, and the presence of several Hebrew texts in the library places this collector in very select company. Of the small number of men and women in England trained in Greek, there were certainly few who

would have been able to use it for both pleasure and profit as Tunstall clearly did. Were the bishop merely engaged in controversy, another arrangement might have been designed that would have made the most useful texts more accessible and adhered less closely to the humane, liberal-arts classification used here.

The library was also used by Protestant humanists of the period, as is known from marginal notations of borrowings by Sir John Cheke, William Darrell, and Sir Anthony Cooke. It seems to have been organized as a research library rather than as a resource for purely polemical writing. The distinction may be a fine one, but it is important for creating the profile of the collection and its owner. Its contents are the sort that emerged from the revival of learning, before the major rifts that divided Protestant England. It is telling that Protestant humanists such as these were using the library at all — which is a good defense of the bishop's liberal perspective. Whatever use was made of the library, it was on an ad hoc basis: the collection seems not to have been designed for a Catholic reader fighting the tides of reform, although it might have become one. Rather, it seems to have grown out of the liberal humanist (and Catholic) milieu and then been influenced by the currents of controversy that took shape as it was being formed.

The two hundred or so Latin, Greek, and Hebrew works on theology make up the bulk of the collection and characterize the owner's humanism in important ways. When one recalls the injunctions of the Reformers against the *bonae litterae,* the Scholastics, and the exegetes, poets, and dramatists, and when one is confronted with a book list comprising five hundred titles, nearly three hundred of which are not theological, one can safely make some conclusions about the owner and his generation. The value system expressed by these categories is not one that Protestant Englishmen espoused. Even the theological texts reflect a collector whose interests were formed before it became necessary to conform, or dangerous not to do so. In this category, as in the others, the titles and authors are mainly "safe" standard figures – although less standard and less safe under Edward VI. Much of the material would have been expected of a cautious but broad-minded Catholic churchman, although only one of importance would have had so large a collection. Yet there is enough material from the period of controversy to suggest his interest in the debates, a devotion to the liberal views of Erasmus, and a tendency toward Henrician compromise. In this, the library is consistent with the views expressed in Tunstall's published prayers, his essay on marriage, and his sermons. Although the owner clearly followed the debates and maintained a hard but not fanatical Catholic point of view, the contents do not seem to suggest that the library was designed to contribute to them. There is too much of the disinterested, too much of the scholar that seems to argue against the polemicist. The combination of learning, tolerance, and firmness that is present here is certainly consistent with Tunstall, a scholar who entered clerical life relatively early in the reign of Henry VIII and reached the heights of ecclesiastical preferment and humanist reputation, only to see his Erasmian perspective crushed by the political needs and Protestant enthusiasm of Edward and Northumberland. The shift in political climate forced Tunstall into the more resistant position reflected in his treatise on the Eucharist.

On the other hand, the collection is that of a person fashioned to the ideals of learning, good taste, and a place of importance in society that were thought appropriate for a Renaissance statesman. Its rare erudition has already been noted. The collection, with its numerous folios of multivolumed *Opera* and its many representatives from the prestigious house of Manutius, was a valuable one consisting of superior editions and examples of Renaissance printing at its best. Thus, while it was a working library, it was also the library of a collector of fine books, and as such an early example of its kind in England. As a collection it also casts the long shadow of its owner, outlining his place among intellectuals and statesmen. Friends and colleagues from the international world of letters and reform are represented by Erasmus, Vives, Elyot, and others; works directly related to his own writings and his duties as counselor to kings and popes, as diplomat, scholar, as well as bishop, fill out its numbers with titles on marriage and divorce, the training of princes, and episcopal duties. If the library reveals a man made in the image of the classical tradition, its contemporaneity shows how he inscribed its ideas within his own life.

For the intellectual historian such as James K. McConica, Tunstall provides an important milestone along the path leading from European reform to English Protestantism. He was a man whose public life and literary career began as an Erasmian – bringing new learning to England and Henry's court; to prince, prelate, courtier, and congregation, he imparted the spirit of moderate reform that he shared with the humanist scholars who were his associates and whose works filled his library. But he ended his career as a Catholic theologian, forced to take a stand against Protestant policy on church images and the sacraments. As religious differences became entrenched, his own work became doctrinal and out of step with the policies of Edward and Elizabeth.

Biography:

Charles Sturge, *Cuthbert Tunstall: Churchman, Scholar, Statesman, Administrator* (London: Longmans, 1938).

References:

Kenneth R. Bartlett and Wyman H. Herendeen, "The Library of Cuthbert Tunstall, Bishop of

Durham," *Papers of the Bibliographical Society of America,* 85, no. 3 (1991): 235–296;

Maria Dowling, *Humanism in the Reign of Henry VIII* (London: Croom Helm, 1986);

Desiderius Erasmus, *The Correspondence of Erasmus,* in *The Collected Works of Erasmus,* volume 1, translated by Craig R. Thompson (Toronto: University of Toronto Press, 1974);

Sears Jayne, *Library Catalogues of the English Renaissance* (Berkeley: University of California Press, 1956);

James K. McConica, *English Humanists and Reformation Politics* (Oxford: Oxford University Press, 1965);

Reginald Pole, *Epistolarum Reginaldi Poli,* 5 volumes, edited by A. M. Querini (Brescia, 1744–1757);

Archer Taylor, *Book Catalogues: Their Varieties and Uses* (Chicago: Newberry Library, 1957).

Papers:

The most significant collections of unedited papers by and attributed to Tunstall are in the British Library. They include the library inventory in Add. MS. 40,676, fols. 110r–116r; Cotton MS Cleopatra E. V. 125 (arguments for auricular confession, 1539); and Add. MSS. 5,758, 32,647–32,648, 32,657 (letters).

William Tyndale

(*circa 1494 – 6 October 1536*)

John T. Day
St. Olaf College

BOOKS: *A compendious introduccion, prologe or preface vnto the pistle off Paul to the Romayns,* anonymous (Worms: Printed by P. Schoeffer, 1526);

The parable of the wicked mammon (Antwerp: Printed by J. Hoochstraten, 1528);

The obedience of a Christen man and how Christen rulers ought to governe (Antwerp: Printed by J. Hoochstraten, 1528);

The practyse of prelates (Antwerp: Printed by J. Hoochstraten, 1530);

The exposition of the fyrste epistle of seynt Jhon with a prologge before it (Antwerp: Printed by M. de Keyser, 1531);

An answere vnto sir Thomas Mores dialoge (Antwerp: Printed by S. Cock, 1531);

An exposicion vppon the. v. vi. vii. chapters of Mathew (Antwerp: Printed by J. Grapheus?, 1533?);

The souper of the Lorde, possibly by Tyndale or George Joye (Antwerp?, 1533);

The testament of master Wylliam Tracie esquier, expounded both by W. Tindall and J. Frith (Antwerp: Printed by H. Peetersen van Middelburch?, 1535);

A path way into the holy scripture, anonymous (London: Printed by Thomas Godfray, 1536?);

A briefe declaration of the sacraments (London: Printed by R. Stoughton, 1548?);

The whole workes of W. Tyndall, John Frith, and Doct. Barnes, 2 volumes, edited by John Foxe (London: Printed by John Day, 1573).

Editions and Collections: *Doctrinal Treatises and Introductions to Different Portions of the Holy Scriptures,* edited by Henry Walter (Cambridge: Parker Society, 1848; London: Johnson Reprint, 1968);

Expositions and Notes on Sundry Portions of the Holy Scriptures Together with the Practice of Prelates, edited by Walter (Cambridge: Parker Society, 1849; London: Johnson Reprint, 1968);

An Answer to Sir Thomas More's Dialogue, The Supper of the Lord after the True Meaning of John VI. and I Cor. XI., and William Tracy's Testament Expounded, edited by Walter (Cambridge: Parker Society, 1850; London: Johnson Reprint, 1968);

The Work of William Tyndale, edited by Gervase E. Duffield, with a preface by F. F. Bruce, The Courtney Library of Reformation Classics, volume 1 (Appleford, U.K.: Sutton Courtenay Press, 1964; Philadelphia: Fortress Press, 1965);

Tyndale's New Testament, edited by David Daniell (New Haven & London: Yale University Press, 1989) – modern-spelling edition of the 1534 translation;

Tyndale's Old Testament, edited, with an introduction, by Daniell (New Haven & London: Yale University Press, 1992) – modern-spelling edition of the Pentateuch of 1530, Joshua to 2 Chronicles of 1537, and Jonah;

The Independent Works of William Tyndale, 4 volumes, edited by Sister Anne M. O'Donnell and others (Washington, D.C.: Catholic University of America Press, forthcoming).

OTHER: William Thorpe, *The examinacion of master William Thorpe preste accused of heresye,* possibly edited by Tyndale or George Constantine (Antwerp: Printed by J. van Hoochstraten, 1530);

The praierand complaynte of the ploweman vnto Christe, possibly edited by Tyndale or George Joye (Antwerp: Printed by M. de Keyser, 1531?).

TRANSLATIONS: *The New Testament,* translated by Tyndale (Cologne: Printed by H. Fuchs [or Peter Quentel], 1525) – quarto, incomplete;

The New Testament, translated by Tyndale (Worms: Printed by P. Schoeffer?, 1526?) – octavo, complete;

The fyrst boke of Moses called Genesis [the Pentateuch], translated by Tyndale (Antwerp: Printed by J. Hoochstraten, 1530; revised edition, Antwerp: Printed by M. de Keyser, 1534);

William Tyndale

The prophete Jonas [Jonah], translated by Tyndale (Antwerp: Printed by Martin de Keyser, 1531?);

Desiderius Erasmus, *Enchiridion militis Christiani,* possibly translated by Tyndale (London: Printed by W. de Worde for J. Byddell, 1533);

The New Testament, translated by Tyndale (Antwerp: Printed by M. Emperowr, 1534; revised edition, Antwerp: Printed by H. Peetersen van Middelburch?, 1535?; revised edition, Antwerp: Printed by M. de Keyser for G. van der Haghen, 1535);

The byble, which is all the holy scripture, translated by T. Matthew [Miles Coverdale and Tyndale] (Antwerp: Printed by M. Crom for R. Grafton & E. Whitchurch, 1537).

As the first translator of the Bible into modern English, being the first to translate both the entire New Testament from the Greek and parts of the Hebrew Scriptures from their original language, William Tyndale has a justified preeminence among the first generation of English Protestants. His biblical translations – 80 percent of which survive essen-

tially unchanged in the 1611 Authorized Version of the Bible – have had an enduring effect on the understanding of the essential Christian text. They have shaped the religious language, and even the very phrasing of religious thought, of Christian believers and nonbelievers alike for more than four hundred years. In addition to the biblical translations, Tyndale wrote ten pamphlets and edited several others that set the agenda for theological controversy in England. He established a standard of verbal expression against which others would be measured, and his style was arguably unmatched, even by his principal theological opponent, Thomas More. Following but expanding upon Martin Luther, Tyndale believed that Scripture alone, properly understood, would reveal to men and women – in their own language – what they should believe and how they should live. His straightforward view of the world encompassed both religious and political life: the Christian should obey the law of God and the law of the king and all civil authority. As biblical translator, theologian, religious controversialist, political thinker, and influential prose stylist, Tyndale is an important figure of early-sixteenth-century literature, as well as the theological and historical contexts of the period.

According to John Foxe, Tyndale was born "about the borders of Wales," but exactly when and where remain uncertain: 1494 is a reasonable date, but there is little consensus about which of several villages near Berkeley Castle in western Gloucestershire has the best claim. A Tyndale family tradition states that the family emigrated from Northumberland during the War of the Roses and adopted the name Hutchins, by which William is often identified in the Oxford records and in his early publications. He came from a relatively prosperous background, as indicated by his attending Oxford and by the careers of two of his possibly four brothers: Edward was a prosperous landlord and a keeper of rents for the estate of William, Lord Berkeley, while John was a London merchant.

Little is known of the approximately thirteen years Tyndale spent at Oxford. Foxe records that he was "brought up from a child" there, presumably meaning that he attended grammar school at Magdalen Hall (now a part of Hertford College) from about the age of twelve (circa 1506); he later entered Magdalen College proper and became bachelor of arts on 4 July 1512. Foxe emphasizes two aspects of Tyndale's education important for his life's work: "the knowledge of tongues [including Latin and Greek] and other liberal arts" and "especially . . . the knowledge of the Scriptures," but the direct study of Scripture would not have been part of his formal education. Essentially unchanged for centuries, the curriculum of both Oxford and Cambridge was grounded in the trivium and quadrivium of medieval education; the students' skills were further honed through oral disputation as was consistent with scholastic approaches to learning.

Tyndale was headed for a career in the church. On 10 June 1514 he was ordained subdeacon (the lowest of the major orders) by the bishop of Hereford; the same day, his brother John was ordained acolyte (the highest of the minor orders). Ordinarily William would have been ordained deacon and then priest, but there is no record of when this occurred; in fact, he may have been dismissed from further sacred offices. After receiving his M.A. on 2 July 1515, he could have proceeded to further study; but the traditional approach to theology was apparently increasingly frustrating to him, as he later writes: "They have ordained that no man shall look on the Scripture, until he be noselled [trained or educated] in heathen learning eight or nine years and armed with false principles, with which he is

clean shut out of the understanding of the Scripture." Nonetheless, Foxe reports that Tyndale tutored students and the fellows of Magdalen College in "some parcel of divinity, instructing them in the knowledge and truth of the Scriptures." Tyndale may have tutored students using Desiderius Erasmus's brand new edition of the New Testament (printed at Basel in March 1516), which could easily have reached Oxford by the end of the year. Foxe states that Tyndale left Oxford (presumably sometime after 1516, when he would have been about twenty-two) and moved to Cambridge for four years, about which almost nothing is known.

At either or both universities, Tyndale was exposed to two new elements on the intellectual scene that would have particular effect on his life's work: the "new learning" associated with the direct study of the classics, especially in Greek, and the early manifestations of Lutheranism. At Oxford he may have experienced the impact of John Colet, later founder of Saint Paul's School, who had revolutionized the teaching of Scripture in his lectures (1497–1505) on the Epistles of Paul, notably Romans. While Tyndale may have seen Erasmus's Greek New Testament at Oxford, Erasmus had a more pronounced influence at Cambridge, where he was Lady Margaret Professor of Divinity (1510–1514). In fact a more enlightened attitude toward the new learning may have attracted Tyndale to Cambridge, but this is not known for sure.

Oxford and Cambridge both saw some of the early impact of Luther's ideas in England during these years. Luther posted his Ninety-five Theses in Wittenberg in October 1517; his books were on sale in Oxford by 1519. He was excommunicated from the Catholic church in December 1520, and his books were soon publicly burned in England, including Cambridge. As a university town and a port city in commerce with the Continent, Cambridge was a natural site for discussion of new ideas, including innovations in theology. Foxe reports that such discussions frequently took place at the White Horse Inn, contemptuously called "Little Germany." Most of the major figures of the early phases of the Reformation in England (including George Joye, Hugh Latimer, Thomas Cranmer, Miles Coverdale, and Tyndale's closest Reformer friend, John Frith) spent time at Cambridge before, during, or after Tyndale's likely stay there (circa 1517–circa 1521). But whether Tyndale knew these men there, or participated in discussions at the White Horse Inn or elsewhere, is not known.

After his stay in Cambridge, Tyndale seems to have been uncertain of his future. Rather than pursue a teaching career at the university, enter the service of the Crown, or obtain an ecclesiastical appointment – standard alternatives for a man of his time and education – he returned to Gloucestershire to take up the somewhat unusual position of tutor in the household of Sir John Walsh of Little Sodbury Manor, a man of increasing local importance. The appointment seems strange, since Walsh's oldest son, Maurice, was only seven or younger.

Tyndale may have thought that a return to Gloucestershire would provide a congenial environment for his advanced religious ideas. The new learning and the ideas of Luther – so important to his education – dovetailed with a long-standing native English tradition called Lollardism, the survival in the fifteenth century of the heretical teachings of John Wycliffe. Wycliffe had been an Oxford theologian who criticized the clergy (especially the pope and rich hierarchy), argued against the Real Presence in the Eucharist, and argued for the importance of the Scriptures – three issues taken up again by the sixteenth-century Reformers. Two early English translations of the Bible (circa 1383, circa 1386) are associated with Wycliffe's name, though the second was probably produced by his secretary, John Purvey, who worked at Bristol, not far from Tyndale's birthplace. One of the ecclesiastical counterattacks on Lollardism was the provision in the Constitutions of Oxford (1408) that forbade anyone to translate, or even to read, the Bible in the vernacular without ecclesiastical approval. This native tradition of theological dissent goes a long way to explain the ready acceptance in England of Luther's ideas as mediated and developed by Tyndale.

Tyndale's experiences in Gloucestershire, though lasting less than two years (circa 1521–July 1523), were especially formative. Both Foxe and Tyndale himself report several encounters Tyndale had with the local clergy, who found his theology unorthodox and his manner of citing Scripture to support his points objectionable. Tyndale persuaded Walsh and Walsh's wife (née Anne Poyntz) to his side of this argument by translating for them Erasmus's *Enchiridion Militis Christiani,* which among other things encourages the study of the New Testament as a guide to a good Christian life. (It is tempting to see the 1533 English translation of the *Enchiridion* as Tyndale's, but this may not be his.) Tyndale did find some support for his views from a local retired doctor and bishop's chancellor, but more typical was the response of John Bell, who (acting for the absentee Italian bishop) berated him for his opinions but did not formally charge him

with heresy. In response to an especially obdurate divine of considerable local reputation, Tyndale crystallized his opposition to a decadent clergy and settled on his life's work – translating the Scripture into English. Echoing the preface to Erasmus's New Testament, he affirmed, "If God spare my life, ere many years I will cause a boy that driveth the plough shall know more of the Scripture than thou doest."

Aware that Christendom needed an edition of the Bible in English, and with his mind set on translating it himself, Tyndale went to London around July 1523 for patronage and permission as required in the Constitutions of Oxford. Apparently well connected he arrived with a letter of introduction from Walsh to Sir Henry Guildford, the king's controller of the household. He also brought a speech of Isocrates that he had translated from Greek into English as evidence of his suitability for the task. Tyndale sought out Cuthbert Tunstall, the new bishop of London, whom Erasmus had praised in his annotations to the New Testament. Perhaps not surprisingly – in light of both Tunstall's newness as a bishop and the recent publication and subsequent condemnation of Luther's 1522 German New Testament – the interview with Tunstall was not successful: he urged Tyndale to seek other service in London.

Tyndale spent six months of his year or so in London in the household of a wealthy merchant, Humphrey of Monmouth, who was also from Gloucestershire and connected with the Poyntz family. Monmouth provided some insight into Tyndale's life in London when he had to defend himself against charges of Lutheranism to Cardinal Thomas Wolsey, lord chancellor, in 1528. Monmouth recounted having heard Tyndale preach at Saint Dunstan's-in-the-West. When Tyndale's planned attachment to the bishop of London fell through, Monmouth took him into his house, describing him as a "good priest" who "studied most part of the day and of the night at his book, and he would eat but sodden [boiled] meat . . . / nor drink but small single beer [and] never [wore] linen." Monmouth admitted circulating copies of the *Enchiridion* that Tyndale translated; however, he burned Tyndale's sermons, his later letters from Germany, and his Lutheran books. As a cloth merchant with connections in the Low Countries, he helped Tyndale emigrate when the English environment proved unsupportive of the translation project.

After conferring with his friend Frith, Tyndale came to the inescapable conclusion that not in Gloucestershire, not in the London household of a

S. Mathew.   Fo. v.

the shyppe/with Zebede their father /mendinge there nettｵ/
and called them. And they with out taryinge left the shyppe
and there father and folowed hym.

¶ And Iesus wēt about all galile/teachynge in there synago꓅
ges/ ans preachynge the gospell of the kyngdom/and healyn꓅
ge all manner of syckes / and all māner diseases amonge the
people . And hys fame spred a broade throughe out all siria.
And they brought vnto hym all sicke people/that were taken
with dyvers diseases and grypyngｵ/and them that were pes꓅
sessed with devylｵ/and those which were lunaticke/and tho꓅
se that had the palsy : And he healed thē. And there folowed
him a greate noūbre of people/from galile/ and from the ten
cetes/and from ierusalem / and from jury/and from the re꓅
gions that lye beyond iordan.

The fyfth Chapter.

When he sawe the people/ he

Lu. vi.   **W** went vp into a mountaine/and wen he was sett/
hys disciples cam vnto him / and he opened his
mouth/and taught them sayinge: Blessed are the
povre in sprete: for thers is the kyngdom of heven. Blessed
are they that mourne: for they shalbe comforted . Blessed are
the micke: for they shall inheret * the erthe. Blessed are they
which hūger and thurst for rightewesnes: for they shalbe fyl꓅
led. Blessed are the mercyfull: for they shaℓℓ obteyne mercy.
Blessed are the pure in hert: for they shall se god . Bles꓅
sed are the maynteyners of peace : for they shalbe called
the chyldren of god. Blessed are they which suffre persecucien
for righewesnes sake :·for thers is the kyngdom of heven.
Blessed are ye whē men shaℓℓ revyle you/and persecute you/
and shal falsly saye all manner of evle sayingｵ agaynst you
for my sake. Reioyce ād be gladde/for greate is youre rewar꓅
de in heven. For so persecuted they the prophettｵ which were
before youre dayes.
                                                    ꝺ

* Erth.

The worlde thi꓅
kethe too possesse
the erthe/and to
defend there aw꓅
ne/when they vse
violence ¬ power:
but christ teache꓅
th that the world
muste be possessed
with mekenes on꓅
ly/ and with oute
power and viole꓅
nce.

All these dedes
here rehearsed as
to norisshe peace/
to shewe mercy/
to suffre psecuciō/
and so forth/ma꓅
ke not a man ha꓅
ppye and blessed/
nether deserve t꓅
he rewarde of he꓅
ven : but declare
and testifie that
we archappy and
blessede and that
we shall have gr꓅
eate pmociō i he꓅
ven . and certyfy꓅
eth vs i oure her꓅
tes that we are
goddes sonnes/ ¬
that the holy go꓅
ost is in vs. for all
good thynges are
geven to vs frely
of god for christes
blouddes sake ād
his merittes

Page from Tyndale's 1525 translation of the New Testament

bishop or merchant, not in all England was it possible for him to carry out his task of translating the Bible into English. He may also have realized that the printing technology would be superior on the Continent. How much of his life's work he completed in England before his departure is uncertain, but surely some was already under way in England. In April or May 1524 Tyndale left England forever.

Since Tyndale lived the rest of his life in intentional obscurity on the Continent, it is difficult to trace his whereabouts. He apparently sailed for Hamburg, went to Wittenberg for ten months, then returned to Hamburg about April 1525. There he acquired the services of William Roye, a former Franciscan who later helped him with his translation. He returned in June to Wittenberg, where he no doubt had been developing his facility with languages, especially Greek and Hebrew. Tyndale must have been a marvelous linguist. A contemporary, taking his mastery of German for granted, observed that he was "skilled in seven tongues, Hebrew, Greek, Latin, Italian, Spanish, English, French, that whichever he speaks, you would think it was his native tongue."

Luther was, of course, a major figure at Wittenberg at this time. Until Tyndale's name was discovered in anagrammatic form in the register of the University at Wittenberg for 27 May 1524, modern scholars were reluctant to believe he ever was in Wittenberg, much less met Luther, despite the contemporary evidence, including Monmouth's understanding, Foxe's assertion, and More's accusation. Though there is no firsthand evidence affirming that Tyndale and Luther ever met, it is hard to believe they did not. In his *Answer unto Sir Thomas More's Dialogue* (1531), Tyndale denies being "confederate" with Luther; but the quality of their personal relationship is finally beside the point in light of his heavy dependence on Luther in his early works.

By the fall of 1525 Tyndale was in Cologne, where an enterprising printer, Peter Quentel (or one of his assistants, Hiero Fuchs), was preparing to print Tyndale's English translation of the New Testament. This incomplete quarto, the "Cologne fragment," has two parts that establish the two strands of Tyndale's activities during the rest of his life. The first, a "Prologue," is a theological introduction to the New Testament that provides guidance in the proper reading of the Scripture. In tone it is essentially pastoral, explaining in simple terms the basic elements of Reformed theology: "the Old Testament, the New Testament; the Law, the Gospel; Moses, Christ; nature, grace; working

and believing; deeds and faith." At first blush it appears very similar to Luther's 1522 New Testament prologue, since it follows Luther closely at points and takes over almost half of that original. But Tyndale elaborated upon Luther so that his total work is eight times larger than the corresponding parts of Luther. Some time later he further expanded the "Prologue" and printed it separately as *A Pathway into the Holy Scripture* (1536?). All of Tyndale's subsequent nonbiblical works are expansions, elaborations, tangential digressions from this seminal work.

The second part of the Cologne fragment is, of course, Tyndale's translation of the New Testament – the first modern English printed edition. The translation was incomplete because John Dobneck ("Cochlaeus"), a fiery anti-Lutheran priest in Cologne to see to the publication of his own works, plied the printer's assistants with drink; he learned that three thousand copies of "Luther's New Testament" translated into English were in press, to be published at the expense of English merchants who would convey them to England and there have them circulated. Cochlaeus used his connections with the civil authorities and had the printing stopped. Rediscovered only in 1834, the unique surviving fragment of the Cologne New Testament is printed in an elegant gothic type in quarto format in imitation of Luther's 1522 New Testament. Some other features also indicate Tyndale's use of Luther as an example: a listing of New Testament books follows Luther's order; the Gospel of Matthew is divided into paragraphs following Luther's model; and the text is accompanied by marginal notes, many of them based on Luther – some are contentious, but most are simply explanatory. The sole surviving example lacks a title page but contains a woodcut of Saint Matthew dipping his pen into an inkwell held by an angel; the text breaks off after Matthew 22:12 (modern reckoning), though more was apparently printed. Cochlaeus's informers reported that the text was set up through signature K, which would include at least parts of Mark.

With the interruption of printing of the Cologne fragment, Tyndale and Roye fled to Worms. There Tyndale quickly found a new printer, Peter Schoeffer, who printed the first complete translation of the New Testament (1526), which survives in only one complete copy (there is also one incomplete copy). Physically and visually it is a very different book, handsome in its simplicity: printed in black letter in octavo format, it lacks the prologue, marginal notes, and textual cross-references of its predecessor; it adds only a short epilogue "To the Reader" and a list of errata to the clean text; most of

Engraving from Tyndale's 1525 translation of the New Testament

the separate books of the New Testament begin with small woodcuts.

When Tyndale came to translating, he had four principal resources available to him: Erasmus's edition of the Greek text of the New Testament (third edition, 1522); Erasmus's Latin translation and elaborate apparatus, which accompanied his Greek text; the traditional Latin Vulgate; and Luther's German New Testament (third edition, 1524). Tyndale worked directly from the original, translating the ordinary Koine Greek of the first century into the everyday English of the sixteenth century; he had the simple Christian – "a boy that driveth the plough," his intended audience – clearly in mind. Stylistically, Tyndale replicates the direct vocabulary and simple structure of the original. His management of rhythm, cadence, and variation shows him to be knowledgeable of the Greek and a consummate English stylist in his own right. His style set the standard for all sixteenth-century translations to follow. Here is Matthew 5:38–42:

> Ye have heard how it is said, an eye for an eye: a tooth for a tooth. But I say to you, that ye resist not wrong.

> But whosoever give thee a blow on thy right cheek, turn to him the other. And if any man will sue thee at the law, and take away thy coat, let him have thy cloak also. And whosoever will compel thee to go a mile, go with him twain. Give to him that asketh, and from him that would borrow turn not away.

Tyndale had a good sense of what he was doing when he argued for the superiority of English over Latin as a medium for translating both Greek and Hebrew:

> They will say [the Bible] cannot be translated into our tongue, it is so rude. It is not so rude as they are false liars. For the Greek tongue agreeth more with the English than with the Latin. And the properties of the Hebrew tongue agreeth a thousand times more with the English than with the Latin. The manner of speaking is both one; so that in a thousand places thou needest not but to translate it into the English, word for word.... In the Latin [thou] ... shall have much work to translate it well-favoredly, so that it have the same grace and sweetness, sense and pure understanding with it in the Latin, and as it hath in the Hebrew.

It was not known at first that Tyndale was connected with the English New Testament, which reached England about March 1526; by the summer it had attracted the attention of the clergy; by the end of the year both Tyndale and Roye were given equal billing as the translators. Sixteenth-century English sources refer to the circulation of both the Cologne fragment ("Matthew and Mark," "the larger volume," "some with glosses") and the complete Worms New Testament ("without glosses," "unadorned," "the second print") as well as a soon-to-appear pirated edition published in Antwerp. Of these three early editions of 3,000, 6,000, and 5,000 copies respectively, only the single exemplar of the Cologne fragment, the two copies of the Worms edition, and none from the Antwerp press of Christopher van Endhoven survive.

For their part English authorities took a series of progressively more hostile steps to stop the circulation of Tyndale's New Testament. The renewed burning of Luther's heretical books had begun as early as February 1526 at a huge ceremonial conflagration presided over by Wolsey at Saint Paul's Cross in London. Wolsey was actually more tolerant than others at first but went along with Tunstall, who in October 1526 enjoined the booksellers not to import heretical books and took possession of all copies of the New Testament. William Warham, archbishop of Canterbury, followed suit. The burning of the

New Testament took place in late October or early November 1526 at Saint Paul's Cross, where Tunstall preached against the translation (which ironically Tyndale had earlier hoped Tunstall would supervise). On the Continent zealous English agents went about buying up all available copies of the translated New Testament and sent them to England to be burned. Despite these efforts the New Testament was widely distributed in London, Oxford, Cambridge, and the eastern counties, especially among the Lollards, including both men and women of humble professions.

To supplement his translation of the New Testament and to fulfill his own call for proper guidance in the reading of Scripture, Tyndale published a series of pamphlets that elaborate upon the essential Reformation beliefs. The first of these, *A Compendious Introduction unto the Epistle of Paul to the Romans* (1526), appeared shortly after the publication of the New Testament translation and was reprinted as the preface to Romans in Tyndale's revised New Testament (1534). This prologue summarizes Romans and explains the central Reformation doctrine of faith and works. Here again Tyndale follows Luther's lead, translating and paraphrasing his source, but expanding the Lutheran original (found in the 1522 New Testament) to twice its original length. Doctrinally, Tyndale begins to distinguish his thought from Luther's, seeing justification by faith as enabling a person to do good. To fill out the volume, he adds a short dialogue between God and the sinner, taken from Luther's treatise on the Lord's Prayer.

Two more substantial pamphlets appeared in 1528: *The Parable of the Wicked Mammon* on 8 May and *The Obedience of a Christian Man* on 2 October, both small books cheaply printed in octavo format. These were immensely popular works: both *Mammon* and *Obedience* were published eight times between 1528 and the appearance of Tyndale's *Whole Works* in 1573. *Mammon* is the first work to bear Tyndale's name: he refers to himself in the preface as "William Tyndale otherwise called Hychins." Apparently the burning of the New Testament and related outrages engaged a side of Tyndale not fully seen before – in *Mammon* he attacks his enemy as the Antichrist. Again he follows Luther, taking over large parts of Luther's sermon on the parable of the unjust steward (Luke 6) preached on 17 August 1522 and shortly thereafter published. About one-third of the whole treatise follows Luther closely, but in the rest Tyndale shows increasing independence. He expands the comments on the unjust steward to a full exposition of the doctrine of justification by faith, touching in a haphazard way on topics to be developed further in his later works.

Obedience, Tyndale's most important nonbiblical work, is also his first work written independent of a Lutheran original. In its preface Tyndale articulates his view of the central importance of the Bible and thus the need for vernacular translation, so that Christians would know, directly, what to believe and how to live a Christian life. Tyndale excoriates at length the abuses of the clergy, arguing that they had distorted the Bible to their own ends. The vernacular Scripture – interpreted literally, not allegorically, topologically, or anagogically – would provide the clear test of any alleged interpretation of God's word. For Tyndale, one of the primary lessons to be learned from the Bible is obedience – obedience to God's word. In response to accusations that his views encouraged civil disobedience, he argued that obedience to God required absolute submission – even by the clergy – to the temporal authority.

Henry VIII is reported to have read Anne Boleyn's copy of *Obedience* and to have said, "This book is for me and all kings to read." He had a different response to the author's next polemical work, *The Practice of Prelates* (1530), in which Tyndale continues his blistering attack on corrupt clergy, most notably on Wolsey (satirized by Tyndale as "Wolfsee"). Notably he used historical evidence from various chronicles to make his point. But unlike all other English Reformers, Tyndale opposed Henry's quest for a divorce from his first wife, Catherine of Aragon, so that he could marry Boleyn, who he hoped would bear him a much-longed-for male heir. Perhaps because he had lived outside of England for eight years, Tyndale seriously misread the political dynamics of Henry's divorce and saw it all as a clerical plot.

Tyndale's prose style in these pamphlets was profoundly influenced by his primary vocation – translating the Bible. The tone, diction, and stylistic qualities of Scripture, especially its plainness and sparing but striking use of simple figures of comparison, are evident everywhere. Whether translating a scriptural passage from Hebrew or Greek, or explaining a point of language or theology, Tyndale's style is characteristically swift, economical, clear, precise, and often pleasant. Although it is hard to convey a sense of the full variety of Tyndale's stylistic virtues in short passages, or in isolation from the often elaborate and self-consciously rhetorical style of his contemporaries, such as More, here is an instance from *The Obedience* of his more pleasing style:

> God therefore hath given laws unto all nations, and in all lands hath put kings, governors, and rulers in his own stead, to rule the world through them; and hath commanded all causes to be brought before them, as thou readest (Exodus 22). "In all causes (saith he) of injury or wrong, whether it be ox, ass, sheep, or vesture, or any lost thing which another challengeth, let the cause of both parties be brought unto the gods; whom the gods condemn, the same shall pay double unto his neighbor." Mark, the judges are called gods in the Scriptures, because they are in God's room [office, position], and execute the commandments of God. And in another place of the said chapter Moses chargeth, saying: "See that thou rail not on the gods, neither speak evil of the ruler of thy people." Whosoever therefore resisteth them, resisteth God, for they are in the room of God; and they that resist shall receive the damnation.

But Tyndale can also be witty through puns, neologisms, and striking turns of phrase. He can lampoon and be sarcastic; he is capable of nasty, almost embarrassing, violence when in the white heat of controversy — satirizing Wolsey or castigating More. In *The Obedience* he criticizes the teaching on faith and works of John Fisher, bishop of Rochester:

> I had almost, verily, left out the chiefest point of all. Rochester, both abominable and shameless, yea, and stark mad with pure malice, and so adased [stupefied, confused] in the brains with spite, that he cannot overcome the truth that he seeth not, or rather careth not what he saith; in the end of his first destruction, I would say *instruction,* as he calleth it, intending to prove that we are justified through holy works, allegeth half a text of Paul, of the fifth to the Galatians (as his manner is to juggle and convey craftily), *Fides per dilectionem operans.* Which text he thiswise Englisheth: "Faith, which is wrought by love"; and maketh a verb passive of a verb *deponent. Rochester* will have love to go before, and faith to spring out of love. Thus Antichrist turneth the roots of the tree upward. I must first love a bitter medicine (after Rochester's doctrine), and then believe that it is wholesome: when, by natural reason, I first hate a bitter medicine, until I be brought in belief of the physicians that it is wholesome, and that the bitterness shall heal me; and then afterward love it, of that belief. Doth the child love the father first, and then believe that he is his son or heir? or rather, because he knoweth that he is his son or heir and beloved, therefore loveth again? John saith, in the third of his first epistle, "See what love the Father hath shewed upon us, that we should be called his sons."

The four pamphlets published between 1526 and 1530 were second in importance to Tyndale's

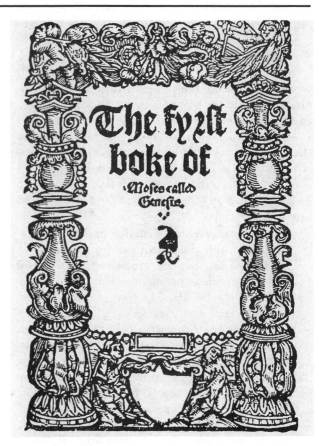

Title page for Tyndale's 1530 translation of the Pentateuch

primary work during this period: translating the books of the Hebrew Scriptures into English. Tyndale may have begun his translation from the Hebrew as early as 1527, since he likely learned Hebrew at Wittenberg. He probably stayed at Worms, which had an active Jewish community, for a year or two after the publication of the New Testament. *The First Book of Moses called Genesis* (the Pentateuch, 1530) was the first English translation of any text written in Hebrew, and thus Tyndale was the first to translate both the New Testament from Greek and the Hebrew Scriptures into English. The precise Hebrew text from which he worked is not known (the 1494 Hebrew Bible printed in Brescia is often suggested), but he had the help of Jerome's Vulgate, Luther's German Bible including his German Pentateuch (1524), and the Septuagint (a Greek text of the Hebrew Scriptures), along with Hebrew grammars and dictionaries.

Tyndale seems to have finished translating the Pentateuch ("the five books of Moses" of the Hebrew Scriptures) by 1529, after a move to Antwerp. Foxe reports that having completed Deuteronomy, Tyndale sailed for Hamburg but was shipwrecked,

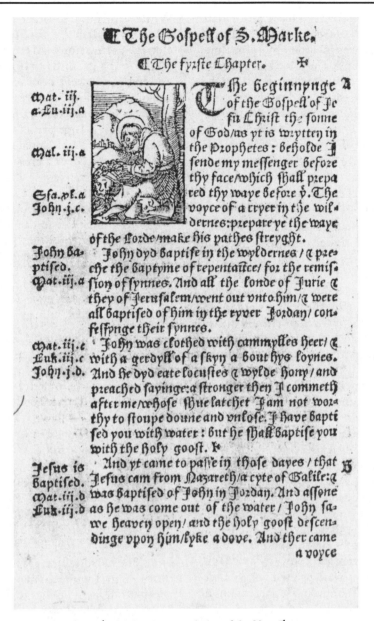

Page from Tyndale's 1534 translation of the New Testament,
his greatest achievement

lost all his work, and had to begin over again. In Hamburg, Coverdale helped Tyndale retranslate the Pentateuch between Easter and December 1529; he returned to Antwerp where the Pentateuch appeared on 17 January 1530. Tyndale's Pentateuch, with Genesis slightly revised, was reprinted in 1534.

The Pentateuch was a composite volume — two books were printed in black-letter type, three in the newer Roman type. Each of the five books (Genesis, Exodus, Leviticus, Numbers, and Deuteronomy) begins with its own title page, along with a prologue and inflammatory marginal notes, both of which are Tyndale's own, notably independent of Luther. Tyndale continued to work on translating the Hebrew Scriptures right up until the end of his life. He published a version of Jonah (May 1531?) that contains a prologue — longer than the text itself — in which he again aims to teach how to read Scripture properly. Later, he freshly translated forty extracts from the Hebrew Scriptures and several passages from the Greek Apocrypha; he appended them to his 1534 New Testament as "Epistles taken out of the Old Testament . . . after the use of Salisbury," which were prescribed for worship on specified days of the church year. Not all of Tyndale's work on the Hebrew Scriptures was published in his lifetime. He is reliably thought to have proceeded through the historical books from Joshua as far as 2 Chronicles, which work was included by John Rogers in his "Matthew's" Bible (July 1537). At about the same time that he published his Pentateuch, Tyndale is likely to have edited and published two old Lollard tracts: *The Examination of Master William Thorpe* (1530) and *The Prayer and Complaint of the Plowman* (1531?). The preface to the second work emphasizes the way these early-fifteenth-century texts criticize the church, the sacraments, and the worship of images – abuses the sixteenth-century reformers also criticized.

After the 1526 publication of the New Testament in Worms, Tyndale eluded capture by English agents and others for almost ten years. It appears that – having traveled to Hamburg, Wittenberg, Cologne, Worms (and probably to other cities, including Marburg) – he made Antwerp the center of his operations. Antwerp was a major commercial center of the early sixteenth century, and here he apparently enjoyed the patronage and protection of the English Merchant Adventurers, who had a monopoly on the cloth traded between England and the Continent. Like Monmouth, many members of the company were connected with both the international world of Lutheranism and the Lollard communities back in England. Antwerp was also well supplied with printers, many of whom were willing to work on heretical books and propaganda. It used to be thought that Tyndale left Worms for Marburg in 1527, residing there until 1530, because title pages of his books indicate that they were published by Hans Luft at Marburg in Hesse. Scholarly bibliographers of the early twentieth century have demonstrated that these works were printed not by Luft in Marburg, however, but by John Hoochstraten in Antwerp.

When condemnation, burning, and buying up New Testaments did not stem the flow of heretical books and ideas, the official response to Tyndale entered a second stage. Tunstall licensed More to read heretical works and commissioned him to respond to them. With *A Dialogue of Sir Thomas More . . . Touching the Pestilent Sect of Luther and Tyndale* (June 1529), More began an exchange with Tyndale of tomes and pamphlets that engaged the energy of two of the best theological minds and English stylists of the early sixteenth century. Using the humanistic form of a dialogue between two characters, More condemned Tyndale's vernacular translation of the Scripture and defended the authority of the church, but he ignored Tyndale's condemnation of the corrupt clergy.

While affirming in principle the possibility of a Bible in English – to be used by lay people with clerical permission – More objected to Tyndale's work on the grounds that it was a bad translation and his views were heretical. More pointed to the use of words that connote theologically innovative ideas rather than confirm traditional Christian understandings. A large part of their difference is attributable to the fact that Tyndale translated the following words from the Greek: "presbyter," "elder," or "server" (*presbuteros*), "love" (*agape*), "favor" (*charis*), "congregation" (*ekklesia*), "repentance" (*metanoia*). More insisted upon the theological correctness of rendering the corresponding words as traditionally translated from the Latin: "priest" (*presbyter*), "charity" (*caritas*), "grace" (*gratia*), "church" (*congregatio*), "penance" (*penitentiam*). Whether Tyndale was heretical or the better theologian is perhaps open to debate; but as translator, according to the tenets of the new learning that More also supported, Tyndale was clearly the better scholar.

Tyndale responded with *An Answer unto Sir Thomas More's Dialogue,* a bitter and satirical attack on More for being a pen-for-hire seeking higher political office. More joined Tyndale at the lower level of discourse and descended below him in *The Confutation of Tyndale's Answer* (1532) and *The Second Part of the Confutation of Tyndale's Answer* (1533), two lengthy works that engage in the no-holds-barred style typical of early-sixteenth-century religious controversy, but nonetheless surprising from the author of *Utopia* (1516). Tyndale wisely refrained from writing more, but More continued to pursue the same points in his *Apology* (1533) and the *Debellacion of Salem and Bizance* (1533).

The third major response of the English authorities to Tyndale consisted of efforts either to persuade him to return to England or to capture him. For a while Henry VIII, or more accurately his then-secretary Thomas Cromwell, flirted with the idea of enticing Tyndale back to England to join in the government's propaganda effort to support the "king's great matter," that is, his divorce. Cromwell, in Henry's name, commissioned Stephen Vaughan to find Tyndale. Vaughan met with Tyndale several times near Antwerp and sent back letters over the course of 1531 that give a glimpse of Tyndale's activities. According to Vaughan, at one point Tyndale considered returning to England, giving up all contentious writings, if Henry would approve "a bare text of the Scripture to be put forth among his people." But he was increasingly reluctant to consider putting himself at risk, since he had heard of the stepped-up prosecution of heretics – including the arrest and public humiliation of his own

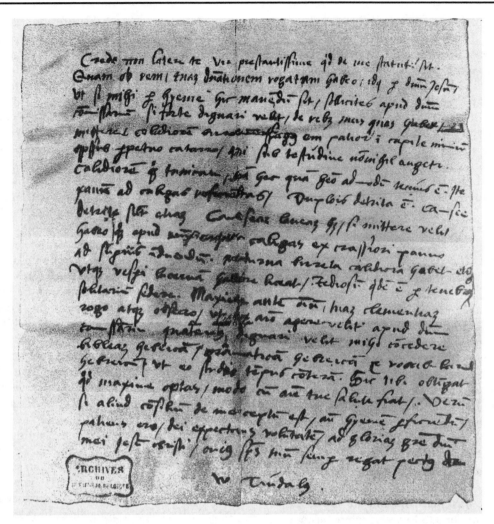

Tyndale's only holograph letter. Written in Latin while he was imprisoned near Brussels in late 1535, it requests that the prison governor provide him with some warm clothes, a lamp, and materials to continue his translation of the Bible (Archives du Royaume Belgique).

brother John – after November 1530 under the new bishop of London, John Stokesley, and the newly installed lord chancellor, More. When enticement did not work, Henry shifted strategies and commissioned Sir Thomas Elyot to go to the Continent and kidnap Tyndale, but he eluded this plot. As a final effort in the negotiations, it was suggested that Tyndale send Henry his translation of Erasmus's *Enchiridion,* but this also came to nothing.

Aside from the glimpse the Vaughan correspondence gives of Tyndale's life, not much is known about him in the early 1530s. He seems to have been increasingly isolated and to have turned again to his scriptural translations and expositions so that Reformed believers could read the Bible aright. Tyndale's works of commentary from this period include *The Exposition of the First Epistle of St. John* (1531), which develops his notion of love and

its importance in salvation: the severity of the law leads to faith in God's mercy, which in turn leads to a love of God and love of neighbor, or works, for God's sake. *An Exposition upon the V. VI. VII. Chapters of Matthew* (1533?), on Christ's Sermon on the Mount, develops another dimension of Tyndale's religious thought: the importance of a covenant made between God and believers. In 1532 he probably wrote two works found among his papers in 1535. The first was a brief commentary on the will of William Tracy, a prosperous Gloucestershire landowner and minor public official known to Walsh, the Poyntz family, and Tyndale. In this will (dated 10 October 1530), Tracy enunciated the basic Reformation tenets: he is saved by faith alone in the grace and merits of Jesus Christ, and therefore no works, including prayers that might be said for his soul after his death, were necessary for his salvation. Shortly after its promulgation the mere possession of Tracy's will became prima facie evidence of heresy. Moreover, Tracy's body was exhumed from sacred ground and burned for heresy in October 1532. Tyndale may have learned of the earlier parts of these events from his friend Frith, whom he had known at least since his London, and possibly his Cambridge, days. Frith visited England in the spring of 1531, returned to the Continent, and wrote a commentary on Tracy's will before leaving for England for the last time in July 1532. The will itself, Tyndale's commentary (perhaps written after Frith's), and Frith's commentary were published with an introduction by John Rogers as *The Testament of Master William Tracy* (1535), after Tyndale's arrest but before his death.

The second work from this period is *A Brief Declaration of the Sacraments,* the earlier extant edition of which dates from circa 1548. Even in its printed version, it reads like a draft rather than a polished piece. The theological understanding of the nature of the Lord's Supper was controversial in Tyndale's time, but he avoided sustained argument on this issue. And in one of his two extant English letters, reprinted by Foxe, he urges Frith not to make definitive statements on the subject; however, Frith was not able to avoid controversy.

When Frith returned to England in July 1532, he was arrested first at Reading and again at London, where he was imprisoned in the Tower in October 1532. From prison he wrote a brief account of his ideas about the Lord's Supper for a friend. More, having acquired this manuscript, wrote *A Letter . . . Impugning John Frith against the Blessed Sacrament of the Altar* (7 December 1532). Early in 1533 Tyndale advised Frith by letter to avoid definitive statements about the Eucharist, and Frith heeded this advice for the most part in *A Book Made by John Frith . . . Answering unto More's Letter* (1533). A second reply to More's letter, *The Supper of the Lord* (5 April 1533), however, was a strongly worded counterattack. Many, including some modern scholars, thought this anonymously published work was Tyndale's; More was not sure when he replied to it in *The Answer to the First Part of the Poisoned Book* (1534), nor was Foxe confident of Tyndale's authorship, although he included it when he edited Tyndale's *Whole Works. The Supper* is now generally thought to be by George Joye. In his second extant letter to Frith (May 1533), Tyndale encourages him not to repent but to persevere in his beliefs as he faced his by-then-inevitable execution, which came on 4 July 1533.

Tyndale brought his life's work to a kind of climax with the publication of a partial revision of the Pentateuch (1534) and a thoroughgoing revision of the New Testament (1534), his enduring masterpiece. Copies of the New Testament had been in much demand since Tyndale's 1525 Cologne quarto fragment and his 1526 Worms octavo complete translation. Some pirated editions appeared to meet this demand, produced by unsupervised Flemish printers who inadvertently introduced errors. For example, Christopher van Endhoven produced two editions (1526, 1530) of five thousand copies each; a third uncorrected edition (1534) of two thousand copies also appeared. In the "Prologue" to the Cologne fragment and in the letter "To the Reader" appended to the Worms volume, Tyndale took a modest attitude toward his own work, sought suggestions, and held out the promise of a revision. But many grew impatient. Joye, who was at Cambridge during Tyndale's probable time there and later a fellow of Peterhouse, fled to the Continent after being charged with heresy. He agreed to Endhoven's invitation to supervise and correct a fourth edition (August 1534). If Joye had limited himself to his commission of correcting typographical and other corruptions that had accumulated in the unauthorized editions, he would not have incurred Tyndale's wrath. But he also changed Tyndale's text, making alterations in style and thoroughly revising some passages. He improved the accuracy in some places but also introduced new theological ideas, substituting "life after death" for "resurrection," for example, thus begging the question about purgatory and the state of the soul after death.

With the help of Coverdale and Rogers, Tyndale worked to improve his translation from the Greek, making four thousand changes in verbal renderings and style. The new text was accompanied by cross-references and glosses. Tyndale's revised New Testament (8 November 1534) was published in a lavish octavo format. Printed in black letter with incidental use of Roman type, it includes two title pages; a preface with notes to key words, such as *repentance* and *elder;* brief prologues to the Gospels; and the second preface ("William Tyndale yet once more to the Christian Reader"), giving Tyndale's comments on Joye's work. Each of the epistles also has a separate prologue based on Luther, and the volume concludes with Tyndale's translation of the aforementioned "Epistles" of the Hebrew Scriptures.

In his second preface Tyndale argues that if Joye's practice were imitated by all, if all readers

Title page for the circa 1535 revised edition of Tyndale's 1534 translation of the New Testament

translated the text of the Scripture according to their own devices, heresy would increase. This argument is remarkably similar to More's earlier attack on Tyndale. It apparently offended Tyndale most that Joye did not take credit – and responsibility – for his changes, but made them silently and presented the whole as, ostensibly, Tyndale's revision.

The months from August 1534 until February 1535 were taken up with the acrimonious exchange with Joye and resulted in the rapid appearance of five distinct editions of the New Testament: two edited by Joye and three by Tyndale, plus three additional reprints of Tyndale's versions in 1535. Quite a bit is known about the remaining months of Tyndale's freedom because he had come to reside in the household of his final benefactor, Thomas Poyntz, a relative of Lady Anne Walsh, wife of Sir

John – Tyndale's first benefactor, in Little Sodbury, Gloucestershire. Poyntz was a member of the Grocers' Company and one of the English merchants with special privileges and immunities in Antwerp; he may have provided Foxe with the details of Tyndale's final year of freedom there, his betrayal and capture, and his execution.

Foxe gives an idyllic, hagiographic picture of Tyndale in Antwerp: on Saturdays and Mondays he tended the religious exiles from England and the poor of Antwerp; on Sundays he read from the Bible with the merchants. For the rest of the week he was devoted to his studies. But all this soon ended. On 23 May 1535 Tyndale was betrayed to the Catholic Imperial Forces of Charles V by one Henry Phillips, who had insinuated himself into Tyndale's confidence and then lured him out of the safe area of the English merchants in Antwerp. Tyndale was imprisoned in the castle of Vilvorde, six miles from Brussels. Many efforts to free him were made by the English merchants, Cromwell, and even Henry himself. Poyntz, for example, in October 1535 delivered letters from Cromwell to the Imperial authorities at Brussels on Tyndale's behalf, but he was also arrested and accused of heresy through the instigation of Phillips. During February 1536 Poyntz escaped after several months in prison.

Meanwhile, a formal inquiry into Tyndale's views was undertaken, along with efforts to convert him in his opinions where they were found to be heretical. For a year and a half he was engaged in written, and presumably oral, debate on his theological views by skilled Catholic theologians, including two native Englishmen. Tyndale's sole holograph letter, in Latin, survives from this period. Presumably in the fall of 1535 he wrote to the marquis of Bergen, the governor of the prison, requesting a warmer cap (because he suffered from a head cold), a warmer coat, and patches for his leggings. He also asked for a lamp, so that he would not have to sit in the dark in the evening, and in particular for books, "A Hebrew Bible, a Hebrew grammar, and a Hebrew dictionary so that I might pass the time in that study," that is, continuing with his self-appointed life's work, translating the Bible into English. In April 1536 Vaughan again urged Cromwell to intervene upon Tyndale's behalf. Cromwell wrote, but in vain.

By August 1536 Tyndale had been convicted of heresy. He was formally degraded from his office as priest in a ceremony designed to reverse his ordination. After two more months in his cell, he was brought to the public place of execution on 6 October 1536, strangled, and his body buried. Foxe reports Tyndale's alleged last words: "Lord, open the King of England's eyes." Ironically, after years of opposition to a vernacular Scripture, Henry gave royal approval in 1536 to Coverdale's Bible (1535) and "Matthew's" Bible (1537). All of the New Testament of both Bibles, and much of the Hebrew Scriptures in "Matthew's," are Tyndale's work.

Tyndale's literary influence is subtle but profound. As a biblical translator, he first put into English the ideas, and in many cases the verbal rhythms, of the Greek and Hebrew originals. The subsequent sixteenth-century translations are best seen as a series of revisions of his work. They introduce some improvements (based on better texts or a better understanding of them) and stylistic refinements, but the essence of Tyndale's achievement remains. If 80 percent of his original continues unchanged in the Authorized Version (1611), his influence persists through this "noblest monument of English prose." His nonbiblical prose – which he used for theological controversy, biblical exposition, and argument about the relation of church and state – shares the vigor and directness of his translations. He fostered a lively, unadorned medium that led to the "plain style" so much praised in the seventeenth century after the excesses of the several ornate modes of the sixteenth century. With the current appearance of new editions of his translations and other prose works, interest in all aspects of Tyndale's achievement is now likely to increase and may encourage new studies in biography to bring the still-valuable work of Robert Demaus and James F. Mozley up to date.

Bibliography:

Catherine Peaden, "A Working William Tyndale Bibliography," *English Renaissance Prose,* 2, no. 1 (1988): 22–43.

Biographies:

John Foxe, *The Acts and Monuments of John Foxe,* 8 volumes, edited by Stephen R. Cattley, with a life by George Townsend (London: Seeley & Burnside, 1837–1841; revised edition, 1843–1849);

Robert Demaus, *William Tindale: A Biography* (London: Religious Tract Society, 1886; Amsterdam: Gieben, 1971);

James F. Mozley, *William Tyndale* (London: Society for Promoting Christian Knowledge, 1937; Westport, Conn.: Greenwood, 1971);

C. H. Williams, *William Tyndale,* Leaders of Religion Series, edited by C. W. Dugmore (London: Thomas Nelson, 1969);

Lewis Frederick Lupton, *Tyndale: The Translator,* History of the Geneva Bible, volume 18 (London: Olive Tree, 1986);

Lupton, *Tyndale: The Martyr,* History of the Geneva Bible, volume 19 (London: Olive Tree, 1987).

References:

Peter Auksi, " 'So rude and simple style': William Tyndale's Polemical Prose," *Journal of Medieval & Renaissance Studies,* 8 (Fall 1978): 235–256;

G. D. Bone, "Tyndale and the English Language," in *The Work of William Tindale,* edited by S. L. Greenslade (London: Blackie, 1938);

F. F. Bruce, *History of the Bible in English in the Earliest Versions* (New York: Oxford University Press, 1978);

C. C. Butterworth, *The Literary Lineage of the King James Bible, 1340–1611* (London: Oxford University Press, 1941);

William A. Clebsch, *England's Earliest Protestants, 1520–1535* (New Haven & London: Yale University Press, 1964);

J. R. Coates, "Tyndale's Influence on English Literature," in *Tyndale Commemorative Volume,* edited by Richard Mercer Wilson (London: RTS, Lutherworth Press, 1939);

Norman K. Davis, *William Tyndale's English of Controversy* (London: H. K. Lewis, 1939);

A. G. Dickens, *The English Reformation* (New York: Schoecken, 1964);

Stephen Jay Greenblatt, *Renaissance Self-Fashioning: From More to Shakespeare* (Chicago: University of Chicago Press, 1980);

S. L. Greenslade, "English Versions of the Bible, 1525–1611," in *The Cambridge History of the Bible: The West from the Reformation to the Present Day,* edited by Greenslade (Cambridge: Cambridge University Press, 1963), pp. 141–174;

Gerald Hammond, *The Making of the English Bible* (New York: Philosophical Press, 1982);

C. S. Lewis, *The Literary Impact of the Authorized Version* (Philadelphia: Fortress Press, 1963);

Janel M. Mueller, *The Native Tongue and the Word: Developments in English Prose Style, 1380–1580* (Chicago: University of Chicago Press, 1984);

Rainer Pineas, *Thomas More and Tudor Polemics* (Bloomington: Indiana University Press, 1968);

Donald Dean Smeeton, *Lollard Themes in the Reformation Theology of William Tyndale,* Sixteenth Century Essays and Studies, 6 (Kirksville, Mo.: Sixteenth Century Journal Publishers, 1986);

Brooke F. Westcott, *A General View of the History of the English Bible,* revised by William A. Wright (London: Macmillan, 1868; New York: Lemma, 1972).

Thomas, Lord Vaux

(25 April 1509 – October 1556)

Michael Rudick
University of Utah

EDITIONS AND COLLECTIONS: *Songes and sonettes* (London: Printed by Richard Tottel, 1557) – nos. 9, 211, 212, and 217 attributed to Vaux;

The paradyse of daynty deuises, edited by Richard Edwards (London: Henry Disle, 1576) – nos. 8, 16, 17, 37, 71, 80, 81, 87, 89, 90, 91, 92, 113 attributed to Vaux;

Miscellanies of the Fuller Worthies Library, volume 4, edited by Alexander Grosart (N.p.: Privately printed, 1870), pp. 15–45;

The Paradise of Dainty Devices, 1576–1606, edited by Hyder E. Rollins (Cambridge, Mass.: Harvard University Press, 1927);

The Arundel Harington Manuscript of Tudor Poetry, 2 volumes, edited by Ruth Hughey (Columbus: Ohio State University Press, 1960) – no. 173 attributed to Vaux;

Tottel's Miscellany, 1557–1587, 2 volumes, edited by Rollins (Cambridge, Mass.: Harvard University Press, 1965).

Eighteen poems are all that can on reasonable grounds be attributed to Thomas, Lord Vaux. No poems are ascribed to him in extant documents before his death; scholars depend on the assignment of thirteen poems to him in the Elizabethan anthology *The Paradise of Dainty Devices* (1576) and on five more attributions found elsewhere. Vaux's is, therefore, an uncertain canon; yet if one allows that most of the attributions are reliable, he can stand as the most important of those whom literary history terms "minor courtly makers," contemporaries of Sir Thomas Wyatt and Henry Howard, Earl of Surrey, whose production and reputations fall short of theirs but whose verse emerged from the same social milieu and was to a degree enabled by their poetic innovations. It may be assumed that Vaux wrote more than has been preserved, and it is known from later allusions and imitations that his work was remembered and respected by commentators and poets through the end of the sixteenth century. This distinction did not survive the changes of taste over the following three hundred years, but the twentieth century has seen a modest revival of Vaux's reputation, recognizing him as a principal and accomplished exponent of a certain tradition in English poetry of the early Renaissance.

Thomas Vaux was born on 25 April 1509, the son of Nicholas Vaux and his second wife, Anne Green Vaux. Thomas's grandfather William Vaux was a Lancastrian loyalist whose estate was confiscated by the Yorkists after his death at the Battle of Tewkesbury in 1471. Nicholas allied himself with the Tudors, who restored the Vaux lands. In 1523 Henry VIII rewarded Vaux's long services as soldier and diplomat with a peerage, the title of baron of Harrowden, to which Thomas succeeded on his father's death in the same year. Also in that year he married Elizabeth Cheyne, his father's ward. As a still quite young man he was part of Cardinal Thomas Wolsey's entourage on an embassy to France in 1527. He sat in the House of Lords for his first Parliament in 1531. The following year found him again in France, this time with the king himself, traveling to Calais and Boulogne in the effort to enlist François I's assistance in Henry's embattled controversy with Pope Clement VII. On 1 June 1533 Vaux was created knight of the Bath at the coronation of Anne Boleyn. In January 1536 he bought an office, governor of the Isle of Jersey and the Castle of Mont Orgeuil; six months later he sold it and played no further role in national public life for twenty years.

Vaux's retirement during the remainder of Henry VIII's and all of Edward VI's reigns is easily explained: his loyalty to the Roman Catholic faith. Records of the Reformation Parliament in 1533–1534 show his attendance to have been sporadic. He presumably did not sign the Oath of Supremacy, but he was perhaps not so important a figure as to invite the extreme consequences visited on more prominent men such as Thomas More and John Fisher. He did, however, experience insecurity. In

Thomas, Lord Vaux (portrait by an unknown artist; Collection of Her Majesty the Queen, Windsor Castle)

1536 he wrote to King Henry's principal administrator, Thomas Cromwell, "Sir, I humbly require you to be good unto me. I have, as I perceive, a great many more foes than friends, and am like, your goodness reserved, to be trodden under the feet and to be made a slave." Cromwell was taking advantage of Vaux's recusancy in an effort to buy his properties in 1535 and 1536; evidently Lady Vaux's determination was more instrumental in keeping the family estate intact than was her husband's plea for relief. However, Vaux's personal life (the poetry apart) is so minimally documented that it would seem unwarranted to draw conclusions about his personal reactions in the face of his predicament as a known opponent of early Tudor religious policy.

There is, however, one notice of Vaux's later years, important in two respects: it is the only mention of him by a contemporary in a literary context, and it may say something of his temperament. In the prose preceding Thomas Sackville's "Induction" in *The Mirror for Magistrates* (1563), a tragedy narrating the deaths of King Edward IV's sons in the Tower is mentioned. William Baldwin reports, "The Lord Vaux undertook to pen it, but what he

hath done therein I am not certain." That the tragedy does not appear in any edition of the *Mirror* may mean Vaux never submitted it, perhaps never completed it. This may suggest his failure at narrative (the poet's surviving work is overwhelmingly lyric), but it may also provide a clue to his political attitudes during enforced retirement. If he was associated with the group of writers who contributed to the *Mirror* (Baldwin, Sackville, Raphael Holinshed, and others), then he probably shared with them that aloofness from or quiescence in politics that ensured them their freedom and relative fortunes while more active participants were suffering from their engagement.

The recuperation of Roman Catholicism upon Queen Mary I's accession in 1553 put an end to Vaux's stigmatized condition, but little time would be left him to enjoy the relief. He attended the queen's coronation, sat in Parliament in 1555, and died in October of the following year, a victim of plague. Loyalty to Roman Catholicism was by then an institution in the Vaux family; Thomas's eldest son, William, suffered the consequences of recusancy during the reign of Elizabeth I.

Scholars cannot speak of Vaux's development as a poet, since there is no evidence from which to arrange a chronology of his poems. It may be tempting to identify certain moments in the poetry when he might be writing out of his political experience, but there is no way to be sure. When, for instance, in "To counsel my estate" (*The Paradise of Dainty Devices,* no. 90) the poet complains about false friends and describes his estate as "abandoned to the spoil," one may infer an allusion to his troubles in 1535–1536, yet the poem's commonplace assertions permit no certain attachment to anything but the moralistic tradition that was common property to all his contemporaries. Vaux's more constant themes are reactions to instability, frustration, false pretense, and perhaps even betrayal – the same ones that mark so much of the epoch's court poetry and record at least obliquely the pressures of experience under King Henry's absolutism. What makes Vaux's work unsusceptible to precise biographical placement or interpretation is its abstraction; his expression typically reaches for the normative rather than the individualistic. His distinction in this normative, or commonplace, quality of expression – what is often called (after Yvor Winters) the "native plain style" – gives Vaux his status in the history of English poetry.

Formally, his poetry is typical of that produced in the decades after Surrey's establishment of iambic cadence in a more-or-less regular syllabic line. George Puttenham, in the 1580s, commended Vaux for "the facility of his meter," which is preponderantly, often stiffly, regular, something thought a virtue before the 1580s. Only a few poems seem to show a stress measure with variable verse length. Vaux uses the conventional lyric forms of the early sixteenth century (quatrains, sixains, and poulter's measure couplets). With these regularities comes a minimum of rhetorical ornament, as he relies overwhelmingly on plain statement supported only by the simplest figures of repetition (mainly alliteration) and a fairly traditional stock of similitudes. His syntax is straightforward, allowing for occasional inversions evidently to keep the meter regular. In subject matter one might divide the work into categories of love poems and moral poems. Recent admirers of Vaux have emphasized the latter because of a perceived congruence between the plain style and the undecorated exhibition of moral intelligence. But it should be recognized that Vaux's poems are authentically lyric rather than didactic; where they argue or assert, their matter is always the expression of a speaker caught in and aware of a problematic condition. The lyric persona may be an abstraction, but it is for that reason no less engaged in responsive analysis. The well-known "When Cupid sealed first the fort" (*Songs and Sonnets,* no. 211), praised by Puttenham for its lively "counterfeit action" (personification allegory), is in fact, for Vaux, an uncharacteristic poem, the only narrative attached to his name. Two love lyrics, "If ever man had love" and "If fraudless faith" (*Paradise,* nos. 81 and 87), are conventional enough complaints, issuing as they do in no more than pleas for pity. Beyond these, however, the categories of love poetry and moral poetry begin, in Vaux's case, to be less mutually exclusive.

An interesting example is "O temerous tauntress," a poem extant in two versions. As printed in the *Songs and Sonnets* (no. 217), it condemns a woman ("tauntress . . . depraveress . . . jestress"). In the *Arundel Harington Manuscript* text (no. 299), the object of attack is generalized ("taunters . . . depravers . . . jesters"), and the poem becomes satire instead of a lover's complaint. Which version Vaux wrote is indeterminable, but the easy adaptation of one to the other shows victimization by spite and instability to be generalizable. "What doom is this" (*Paradise,* no. 80) ostensibly depicts a lover's frustration, but it focuses not at all on a specific affair; its subject is the bafflement of a consciousness seeking to understand the paradox of love and strife and the experience of hate returned for goodwill, again not an exclusively amorous theme. The situation is similar in "The day delayed" (*Paradise,* no. 16), structured on some conventional antitheses associated with the poetry of frustration in love, and in "What grieves my bones" (*Paradise,* no. 8), which exploits the traditional physical consequences of thwarted desire. In all these, ill success in love may implicitly be one source of complaint, but it is not the only one. The poet is more concerned with a generalized condition of unhappiness, extending to life itself. When the poems evince a wish for relief, this is figured as a radical alteration of state: not a better life, but life exchanged for death or heaven. "How can the tree but waste" (*Paradise,* no. 71) is probably Vaux's most bitter expression of frustration, depicting a life amounting to death, deprived of sense, mind, and joy, where the repeated word *joy* implies rather more than its conventional signification of fulfillment in love. The speaker in "The day delayed" says he is "for no reward assigned," predicting continued loss in the pursuit of whatever satisfaction. Vaux's use of animal similitudes in this poem (horse, spider, hunted hare) evinces something of the brute frustration felt to pervade life, as though to say that *man* deserves better.

In his more uncompromisingly moral verse, love is associated with youth and the attractions of beauty in all its manifestations. As such, love seems more symptomatic than causative. In "I loath that I did love" (*Songs and Sonnets,* no. 212) Vaux explores the tension between holding on and letting go. He represents voluntary relinquishment of youth and its dispositions as the moral course, but he shows this to be inevitable in any case; the decrepitude of age leaves one no choice. Dissipated vitality causes the pain of renunciation; renunciation remains uncompensated. The poem is in one sense playful (the tone is less than altogether sober) and certainly rather more bleak than edifying. Yet more earnest an expression of the same theme is "Brittle beauty" (*Songs and Sonnets,* no. 9), comparable in its way to Shakespeare's sonnet 129. The poem may not be Vaux's, but there is no thought in it inconsistent with less disputable attributions. On much the same theme is "When I look back" (*Paradise,* no. 17), a penitential lyric whose lengthy recitation of God's benefits suggests that only a miracle, a special grace, can cancel the effects of wayward youth even upon age (this poem is almost Protestant in its despair of self and the world).

"When all is done and said" (*Paradise,* no. 89) offers a different kind of moralization. Winters admires this lyric, and Douglas Peterson singles it out as an example par excellence of the native plain style. It says, very plainly but very forcibly and economically, that because everything outside the mind is subject to decay and destruction, both ultimate virtue and ultimate happiness consist in the autonomous cultivation of thought. In isolation this poem is an unexceptionable apology for the life of the mind; placed against the other work its assertions seem the inevitable outcome of the poet's effort to find some redemptive possibility in this life. As usual with Vaux's abstractive bent, one does not learn the content of the speculation; one sees thought defined only by its contraries – all that may be "done" and "said," in effect all the experiences Vaux's other poems depict as frustrating, compromising, or destructive. It is in keeping with his generally bleak understanding of life that its highest good is more a retreat than a triumph. The voice in Vaux's poetry is more philosophically pessimistic than sentimentally elegiac.

Biography:

Godfrey Anstruther, *Vaux of Harrowden: A Recusant Family* (Newport: R. H. Johns, 1953), pp. 38–69.

References:

Lily B. Campbell, ed., *The Mirror for Magistrates* (Cambridge: Cambridge University Press, 1938; New York: Barnes & Noble, 1970);

Douglas Peterson, *The English Lyric from Wyatt to Donne: A History of the Plain and Eloquent Styles,* second edition (Princeton: Princeton University Press, 1990);

George Puttenham, *The Arte of English Poesie,* edited by Gladys Doidge Willcock and Alice Walker (Cambridge: Cambridge University Press, 1936);

Yvor Winters, "The 16th Century Lyric in England: A Critical and Historical Reinterpretation," in *Elizabethan Poetry: Modern Essays in Criticism,* edited by Paul J. Alpers (New York: Oxford University Press, 1967), pp. 93–125.

Polydore Vergil
(circa 1470 – 18 April 1555)

Louis V. Galdieri
Massachusetts Institute of Technology

BOOKS: *Proverbiorum libellus* (Venice: Christophorus de Pensis, 1498; revised and enlarged edition, Basel: Froben, 1521);

De inventoribus rerum libri tres (Venice: Cristoforo de Pensis, 1499); revised and enlarged as *De inventoribus rerum libri octo* (Basel: Froben, 1521); revised and enlarged to include *Commentariolum in Dominicam precem* (Basel: Froben, 1525);

Dialogorum de prodigiis libri tres, by Vergil and Robert Ridley (Basel: Froben, 1531);

Anglicae Historiae libri XXVI (Basel: J. Bebel, 1534); revised as *Anglicae Historiae libri viginti sex, ab ipso autore . . . recogniti* (Basel, 1546); revised and enlarged as *Anglicae Historiae libri viginti septem* (Basel, 1555);

Dialogorum libri (Basel, 1545); enlarged to include *Dialogus de prodigiis* (Basel, 1553).

Editions: *Three Books of Polydore Vergil's English History, Comprising the Reigns of Henry VI, Edward IV, and Richard III from an Early Translation Preserved among the MSS of the Old Royal Library in the British Museum* [Anglica Historia], edited by Sir Henry Ellis, Camden Society Publications 29 (London: Camden Society, 1844; reprinted, New York: AMS Press, 1968);

The Anglica Historia of Polydore Vergil, A.D. 1485–1537, edited and translated by Denys Hay, Camden Third Series 74 (London: Camden Society, 1950); *Anglica Historia* (Menston, U.K.: Scolar Press, 1972) – facsimile edition.

OTHER: Nicholas Perotti, *Cornucopiae latinae linguae,* edited by Vergil (Venice, 1496);

Gildas, *De calamitate, excidio, et conquestu Britanniae,* edited by Vergil and Robert Ridley (Antwerp?, 1525).

TRANSLATION: Saint John Chrysostom, *Comparatio regii potentatus et divitiarum* (Basel?, 1533).

Polydore Vergil

In his own day Polydore Vergil was admired chiefly for his full, easy Latin style and his knowledge of Greek. The Italian learning he displayed in his antiquarian works brought him powerful patrons and helped him advance at the English court, where he discovered his life's work: the *Anglica Historia* (1534), a history of England that, in the present day, has gained him the title of "Father of

English History." Although he wrote his history in self-conscious imitation of Livy, Sallust, and Suetonius, Vergil gave a distinctly Tudor shape to the English past. He provided the chronicler Edward Hall with a coherent vision of fifteenth-century England; and, since William Shakespeare frequently worked out of Hall, Vergil's literary achievement is not without bearing on the history of the English stage.

Vergil was born about 1470 at Urbino, Italy. Virtually nothing is known about his youth and early education. His grandfather Antonio taught philosophy at Paris; his father, Giorgio Virgilio, found favor at the court of Federigo da Montefeltro, Duke of Urbino. Of Vergil's three brothers, only Giovanni-Francesco stayed at Urbino. Girolam developed an exclusive trading concern with England. Giovanni-Matteo taught philosophy at Padua. He may have already been there when his brother Polydore arrived, probably in the late 1480s, to begin his studies. From Padua, Vergil may have gone to Bologna; he then returned to Urbino and found a patron. By 1496 he had been ordained priest and had also found a position in the chancery of Pope Alexander VI. There he practiced an elegant hand.

By the end of the 1490s Vergil had established a reputation for learning and had paved the way for his own advancement both in Italy and abroad. He published his first three works in quick succession: in 1496 he produced a new edition of Nicholas Perotti's *Cornucopiae latinae linguae;* two years later Vergil's *Proverbiorum libellus* appeared; and in 1499 he saw *De inventoribus rerum* into print. These works earned him the admiration of Adriano Castelli, who became his benefactor. The *Cornucopiae,* a grammatical commentary on the first book of Martial's *Epigrams,* no doubt appealed to Castelli's refined Latinity. Perotti's work enjoyed some of the popularity that Lorenzo Valla's *Elegantia* (composed, 1435–1444) and Desiderius Erasmus's *De copia* (1528) enjoyed. For his 1496 edition Vergil collated a previous edition of the *Cornucopiae* with the complete manuscript in the Urbino library and corrected faulty readings.

The first edition of Vergil's *Proverbiorum libellus* appeared two years before Erasmus's similar work, *Adagia.* The two authors settled the question of priority in a short epistolary exchange. Like Erasmus's work, Vergil's *Proverbiorum libellus* is a collection of classical adages, or proverbial expressions, gathered from ancient sources. In his explication of each adage, Vergil identifies its classical source, discusses its applications, and mentions classical forms of expression similar to it. Sometimes his commentary

on an adage occasions a short moral essay; but he was not prone to improvise, and his efforts in this vein never equal Erasmus's *Dulce bellum inexpertis* or *Sileni Alcibiadis* (both 1515). Both authors made their compilations not merely out of antiquarian interest but also for the sake of literary imitation; here the writer found a storehouse of classical expressions both in Latin and Greek, accompanied in the best editions by an index or table. The courtier, too, could adorn his conversation with adages; Vergil's collection circulated at Duke Guidobaldo I's court at Urbino, the setting of Baldassare Castiglione's *Courtier* (composed, 1516). The work drew the envy of Lodovico Gorgerio, who wrote an "Invectiva in Polydorum" (composed, circa 1498–1499) charging that Vergil had stolen his project, which he would have presented to Guidobaldo had it not been for his poverty.

De inventoribus rerum, Vergil's most original and most popular work, forms the perfect complement to *Proverbiorum libellus.* In humanist parlance *Proverbiorum libellus* treats words while *De inventoribus* treats matter. *De inventoribus* appeared in three books on inventors, or first begetters, of a wide variety of things. A partial list of Vergil's topics in *De inventoribus* conveys some impression of his range: the origins of mirrors, sculpture, gods, the name *God,* tragedies, comedies, time, weapons, prostitution, precious metals, labyrinths, sanctuaries, and navigation. In fashioning his accounts of these and other things and their inventors, Vergil sifts critically through biblical, classical, patristic, and medieval authorities, and he examines the claims of Greek, Roman, Egyptian, and ancient Hebrew civilization to originality and priority. There are limits to Vergil's criticism: there are no fables in his Bible; the biblical world for him is a pristine world, where Moses and his people founded the most ancient and original of the great world civilizations.

In 1502 Castelli brought Vergil to England, where his talent was much in demand. Henry VII received him courteously, as he received most learned Italians, whose literary, administrative, and diplomatic skills he turned to the good of the Tudor state. Castelli's man enjoyed Henry's beneficence: in 1503 Vergil acquired the living of Church Langston in Leicestershire; in 1507, the prebendary at Lincoln Cathedral and another at Hereford; in 1508, the archdeaconry of Wells. He was naturalized in 1510 and exempted from the usual fee. He moved in learned circles: he met William Lily (who named a son after him), Thomas Linacre, Cuthbert Tunstall, and Erasmus's English friend Sir Thomas More. In 1508 John Colet presented him along

Page from the first edition (1534) of Vergil's history of England

with William Grocyn to Doctors' Commons. He performed official and unofficial duties for Castelli. Officially Vergil had been deputed subcollector of Peter's Pence when Castelli was preferred to the see of Hereford; unofficially he was Castelli's agent in English affairs while Castelli collected his cardinal's hat.

The subcollectorship nevertheless involved him in controversy and required his vigilance. In a letter dated 12 August 1504, Pope Julius II writes to the archbishop of Canterbury and the bishop of London concerning Giovanni Paolo, merchant of Lucca, who in collaboration with an English priest falsely informed the people of London that Vergil and Castelli were not authorized to collect fruits for the camera. In 1508 Julius appointed Peitro Griffi to replace Vergil, and Griffi's *De officio collectoris in regno Angliae* (composed, circa 1508–1510) tells of

Vergil's tenacious efforts to keep his post. A threatening letter from Julius dated 26 March 1509 resolved the matter; Griffi held the post until 1512, when Vergil resumed it. Finally, upon returning to England in 1515 after a short trip to Italy, subcollector Vergil found himself imprisoned: Andrea Ammonio, who coveted the collectorship, had intercepted letters unfriendly to Chancellor Thomas Wolsey, and Vergil was ensnared. After his release from the Tower – procured by petitions to Henry VIII from Pope Leo X, Cardinal Giulio de Medici, and Oxford University – Vergil took refuge in his literary work. It may be at around this time that he began to concoct the acerbity he administers to Wolsey in the *Anglica Historia*.

Vergil began the *Anglica Historia* in 1505 at Henry VII's request. He finished a version of the history by about 1513. This version, represented by an autograph manuscript at the Vatican, takes the story of England from its beginnings to the year 1513. It celebrates the Tudor union of Lancaster and York and is dedicated to Henry VIII, "in whom the royal lines were joined." The history falls roughly into three parts: (1) books 1–7: a description of Britain and a critical account of its early history to the reign of Harold; (2) book 8: William I and William II; and (3) books 9–25: the rule of England from Henry I to Henry VIII. That in the third section of the *Historia* Vergil devotes a book to each reign is notable; for him England's monarch can be a rock of stability or a charismatic agent of historical change; a king defines the period in which he lives. More shared this idea; but Vergil never adopted his ironic, Menippean posture toward kings' games. Hall did very little to alter Vergil's understanding of English history; Shakespeare did, when he dramatized Hall.

Most remarkable are the various shapes that Vergil gives to English history in successive editions of the *Anglica Historia*. The manuscript version ends with James IV's death at Flodden Field. Vergil's Scottish king is not wholly unheroic; he is a Hotspur but a noble foe. For the first printed edition, in 1534, Vergil prudently sharpened his focus and ended at 1509, with criticism of Henry's VII's avarice. The criticism had been tolerated, perhaps even encouraged at Henry VIII's court; More made it in his *Coronation Ode*. A second edition of the *Historia* appeared in 1546. This edition shows Vergil still molding his work, bringing his English history into closer contact with Scottish, Norman, and Flemish sources and paying more attention than before to the civic history of London, the growing center of political and intellectual life in Tudor England.

In 1555, the year of Vergil's death, a third edition appeared, including an additional book on the reign of Henry VIII and carrying the story to the year 1537. Vergil's scathing portrait of Wolsey in this last book of the *Historia* betrays years of resentment, but he writes well when he writes with venom: "dragged whither his lust for wealth, his emotions, his pleasures, and above all his irresponsible whims would lead," Vergil's Wolsey is a ruthless upstart and a shameless liar. His story is a tale of overweening pride, worldly ambition, and "inordinate desires" not unlike More's story of Richard III. His triumph, like Richard's triumph, means England's tragedy: "When Wolsey attained the summit of his power, then he opened a law shop; what a Charybdis, what a whirlpool, what an abyss of every kind of plundering!" Moments such as these make More seem a master of restraint and remind

the reader that the histories of both authors are closely related to exercises in epideictic oratory.

Vergil's revisions of the *Anglica Historia* and his works of the 1520s and 1530s make it clear that he kept a finger on the pulse of contemporary events both in England and abroad. After his imprisonment he withdrew from the close circle at court but did not retire to a life of republican simplicity. In 1521 he brought out expanded editions of *Proverbiorum libellus* and *De inventoribus rerum;* the prefatory letter to *Proverbiorum libellus* flatters Wolsey and the king. Both works exhibit new motives: for the new *Proverbiorum,* Vergil gathered *Adagia sacra* from Scripture and devoted a volume of commentary to the explication of such adages as "All that take the sword, shall perish by the sword" (Matt. 26:52) and "cast lots upon my vesture" (Ps. 22:18). He pleads timidly for peace but strikes a more Erasmian chord in his criticism of nepotism, superstition, and hypocrisy. The 1521 edition of *De inventoribus rerum* takes the same tack; five additional books treat the origins of Christian rites and institutions. Vergil takes exception, again, to contemporary mores; he lauds the simplicity of the primitive church. In 1525 John Froben published a new edition of *De inventoribus;* Vergil dedicated the work to John Fisher, whose sermon against Martin Luther was already circulating, and appended a commentary on the Lord's Prayer. The dedication to Fisher gives the appearance of orthodoxy to the book's unorthodox contents; the commentary on the Lord's Prayer adopts several Erasmian readings and reiterates Vergil's criticisms of the contemporary church. Eventually, *De inventoribus* was placed on the Index of books prohibited by the Roman church.

In collaboration with Robert Ridley, Vergil edited in 1525 the sixth-century historian Gildas's *De calamitate, excidio, et conquestu Britanniae.* This is the first critical edition of an English medieval source. Vergil probably undertook the project to prepare audiences for his attack on Arthurian fables in the *Anglica Historia.* Vergil and Ridley cautiously and silently suppressed certain of Gildas's anticlerical passages. The gravity of the Luther situation may have finally become clear. In 1526 Vergil wrote *Dialogus de prodigiis,* a dialogue in which he and Ridley criticize superstition and popular belief in the supernatural; the work did not appear until 1531. When the Reformation storm hit England in the mid 1530s, Vergil kept to his work on the *Anglica Historia* and studied Erasmian equivocation. In 1531, at Erasmus's request, he translated from Greek into Latin Saint John Chrysostom's *Comparatio regii potentatus et divitiarum.* The translation, which appeared in 1533,

Title page for the 1555 revised edition of Vergil's history of England

compares the contemplative and active lives. It was an abortive effort that Erasmus did not include in his edition of Chrysostom's *Opera;* J. P. Migne echoed Erasmus's judgment when he chose Germanus Brixius's translation for the *Patrologia.*

The dialogues that followed a decade later – *De patientia, De vita perfecta,* and *De mendacio* – probably emerged from Vergil's readings in the church fathers. These take advantage of fictive settings to explore questions of human happiness. At best these dialogues bespeak an inward turn, but Vergil's tone is guarded, and his Latin is fastidious. The work is dedicated to Guidobaldo II of Urbino; apparently, Vergil was preparing to return to his native city, but he did not leave England until 1533. From Urbino he wrote to Queen Mary and completed the third edition of his history.

An eloquent witness of his own time, Vergil was not a More, not a Bishop Fisher. At times he seems a lesser Erasmus. Authors from François Rabelais to Miguel de Cervantes culled matter from his pages and poked fun at the antiquarian learning of *De inventoribus rerum;* the work lost its appeal only toward the end of the seventeenth century. The nineteenth century rehabilitated Vergil, when historians of Tudor England realized the scope of his achievement in the *Anglica Historia.* The generation that succeeds in restoring Latin literature to its rightful place in the English literary landscape will best understand Vergil and the place of his work in the story of humanism, literature, and early Tudor politics.

Bibliographies:

John Ferguson, *Bibliographical Notes on the English Translation of Polydore Vergil's work "De Inventoribus Rerum"* (Westminster, 1888);

Ferguson, *Hand List of Editions of Polydore Vergil's "De Inventoribus Rerum",* edited by John F. Fulton and Charlotte H. Peters (New Haven: Yale University School of Medicine, 1944).

Biographies:

James Dennistoun, "Polydoro Di Vergilio," in his *Memoirs of the Dukes of Urbino* (London: Longman, Brown, Green & Longmans, 1851), pp. 110–112;

Carlo Grossi, "Polidoro Virgilii," in his *Degli uomini illustri di Urbino commentario* (Urbino: G. Rondini, 1856), pp. 101–106;

E. A. Whitney and P. P. Cram, "The Will of Polydore Vergil," *Transactions of the Royal Historical Society,* fourth series 11 (London, 1928), pp. 117–136;

Brian P. Copenhaver, "Polidoro Virgilio," in *Contemporaries of Erasmus,* volume 3, edited by Peter G. Bietenholz (Toronto: University of Toronto Press, 1987), pp. 397–399.

References:

Wilhelm Busch, *England under the Tudors,* translated by Alice M. Todd (London: A. D. Innes, 1895), pp. 395–398;

Francesco Canuti, *Per il quarto centenario della morte di Polidoro Vergili, urbinate, padre della storia inglese, 1555–1955* (Urbino, 1955);

C. H. Clough, "Federigo Veterani, Polydore Vergil's *Anglica Historia,* and Baldassare Castiglione's 'Epistola . . . ad Henricum Angliae regem,' " *English Historical Review,* 82 (October 1967): 772–783;

Brian P. Copenhaver, "The Historiography of Discovery in the Renaissance: The Sources and Composition of Polydore Vergil's *De inventoribus rerum* I–III," *Journal of the Warburg and Courtauld Institutes,* 41 (1978): 192–214;

John Ferguson, "Notes on the Work of Polydore Vergil, 'De inventoribus rerum,' " *Isis,* 17 (January 1932): 71–93;

Gildas, *De calamitate, excidio, et conquestu Britanniae,* edited by Theodor Mommsen, in *Monumenta Germaniae Historica. Auctorum Antiquissimorum,* volume 13: *Chronica Minora Saeculi IV. V. VII.,* volume 3 (Berlin: Weidman, 1898);

Michael J. Haren, ed., *Calendar of Entries in the Papal Registers Relating to Great Britain and Ireland,* in *Papal Letters,* volume 18 (Dublin: Stationery Office for the Irish Manuscripts Commission, 1989);

Denys Hay, *Polydore Vergil: Renaissance Historian and Man of Letters* (Oxford: Clarendon, 1952);

Richard Koebner, " 'The Imperial Crown of the Realm': Henry VIII, Constantine the Great, and Polydore Vergil," *Bulletin of the Institute for Historical Research,* 26 (1953): 29–52;

Michele Monaco, *Il "De Officio Collectoris in Regno Angliae" di Pietro Griffi da Pisa (1496–1516),* Uomini e Dottrine 19 (Rome: Edizioni di Storia e Letteratura, 1973);

Andre Stegmann, "Le *De inventoribus rei christianae* de Polydore Vergil ou l'Erasmisme critique," in *Colloquia Erasmiana Turonensia,* edited by Jean-Claude Margolin (Toronto: University of Toronto Press, 1972), pp. 313–322.

Papers:

An autograph manuscript of Vergil's *Anglica Historia* is at the Vatican Library (Cod. Urb. Lat. MSS 497, 498). In 1844 Sir Henry Ellis edited for the Camden Society an early-seventeenth-century English translation of *Anglica Historia,* books 23–25, preserved in the British Library (MS Reg. C. VIII.IX). In his introduction Ellis describes the contents of various letters and papers relevant to Vergil's English career (preserved in Cottonian MS Vitellius B. II), and he prints Vergil's letter to Queen Mary I (from Harleian MS 6989, fol. 149).

Thomas Watson

(1545? – 1592)

Carmel Gaffney
Northern Territory University, Australia

BOOKS: *The* E'KATOMΠAΘI'A *Or passionate centurie of loue* (London: Printed by John Wolfe for Gabriel Cawood, 1582);

Amyntas (London: Printed by H. Marsh, 1585);

Compendium memoriæ localis (London: Printed by T. Vautrollier, 1585);

A gratification vnto master John Case, for his learned booke, lately made in the praise of musicke, verse by Watson, music by William Byrd (London, 1589);

The first sett, of Italian Madrigalls Englished (London: Printed by T. Este, 1590);

Meliboeus (London: Printed by R. Robinsonus, 1590);

An eglogue upon the death of sir F. Walsingham (London: Printed by R. Robinson, 1590);

Amintæ gaudia (London: Printed by P. Short for G. Ponsonbei, 1592).

Editions and Collections: *Poems,* edited by Edward Arber, English Reprints no. 21 (Birmingham, U.K.: English Reprints, 1870) – includes *Hekatompathia, Meliboeus, An Eclogue upon . . . Walsingham,* and *The Tears of Fancy;*

"Thomas Watson's *Italian Madrigals Englished,*" edited by Frederic Ives Carpenter, *Journal of Germanic Philology,* 11 (1898–1899): 323–358;

Hekatompathia; or, Passionate Century of Love, introduction by S. K. Heninger, Jr. (Gainesville, Fla.: Scholars' Facsimiles & Reprints, 1964);

Hekatompathia; or, Passionate Century of Love, Research and Source Works Series no. 150 (New York: Burt Franklin, 1967);

Amyntas, edited by Walter F. Staton, Jr., and *The Lamentations of Amyntas,* translated by Abraham Fraunce, edited by Franklin M. Dickey, in the Renaissance English Text Society (Chicago: University of Chicago Press, 1967);

Antigone, prepared, with an introduction, by John C. Coldewey and Brian F. Copenhaver, in *Renaissance Latin Drama in England,* second series 4 (Hildesheim: Zürich / New York: G. Olms, 1987).

TRANSLATIONS: Sophocles, *Antigone,* translated into Latin by Watson (London: Printed by John Wolfe, 1581);

Thebanus Coluthus, *Coluthi Thebani Lycopolitani poetæ, Helenæ raptus Latinus, paraphraste,* translated into Latin by Watson (London: Printed by John Wolfe, 1586).

Thomas Watson was admired and celebrated in his own day by such important writers as Thomas Lodge in *Phyllis* (1593), George Peele and John Lyly in the dedicatory verses to the *Hekatompathia* (1582), Christopher Marlowe in *Amintæ Gaudia* (1592), and Edmund Spenser in *The Faerie Queene* (1596). Some critics persist in identifying Watson as Amyntas in Spenser's *Colin Clouts Come Home Againe* (1595); but as Spenser revised his encomiums for those who had died after his visit to the court in 1592, it is unlikely that the reference is to him. Watson's love of music and his ability in composing madrigals meant that he enjoyed the friendship of William Byrd. It also seems his contemporaries appreciated his dramatic skills (no plays survive), for Francis Meres writes in *Palladis Tamia* (1598) that he was one of the "best for tragedy." It is not difficult to understand why Watson was honored by his contemporaries: his classical learning and his knowledge of Renaissance French and Italian writers, together with his skill in translating lucidly, were qualities that English writers of the time appreciated. His original works show his wit and imagination, and they demonstrate that he had the ability to eclipse his sources in the manner Elizabethans appreciated. It is also scarcely challenging to speculate on the reasons for Watson's neglect today, for his Neo-Latin compositions, his extensive allusions to Renaissance works that have not been translated into English, and his comprehensive knowledge of the classics create difficul-

Title page for Thomas Watson's Hekatompathia, *the first published English sonnet sequence dominated by the theme of love*

ties for readers. Moreover, many modern readers express a preference for writers who combine intellect with passion, and Watson's work is witty and imaginative rather than ardent.

Critics suggest four dates for Watson's birth: 1545, 1551, 1557, and 1561. After attending Oxford but leaving without a degree (the years are the subject of scholarly debate), Watson spent about seven and a half years in France and Italy studying poetry and law. He returned to England in 1577 and during the next fifteen years wrote works in Latin, translated foreign writers, and published three works in English: the *Hekatompathia, Italian Madrigals Englished* (1590), and *An Eclogue upon the Death of Sir Francis Walsingham* (1590). He seems to have lived an eventful life in London. He slew William Bradley in self-defense when the latter attacked him after first assaulting Marlowe; he subsequently spent five

months in prison for manslaughter (1589–1590). Watson was named posthumously in a 1593 court case by William Cornwallis, his employer at the time of the incident, as being the instigator of a plot to trick Cornwallis's daughter into signing a marriage contract with Watson's brother-in-law, Thomas Swift. Cornwallis claimed that Watson, who "could devise twenty fictions and knaveries in a play which was his daily practice and living, could draw the lies and devices of this letter." It seems reasonably certain that Watson was a Catholic, for an entry in the Calendar of State Papers refers to him in Paris in 1580 as a "great practicer" of Catholicism. Whether he continued to hold to his Catholicism in England is not known.

After Watson's return to England in 1577, he seems to have spent some time working on his Latin translation of Sophocles' *Antigone*. Gabriel Harvey's marginalia indicates that the play was performed in 1577 and 1579, but it was not published until 1581, probably after Watson's return from Paris. Watson faithfully translates the Greek into Latin but introduces to the play an argument spoken by Nature and an epilogue of four pomps and four themes that are all original compositions. (The only English translations of his additions occur in Harry Herbert Boyle's unpublished 1966 dissertation on the poet.) Although Watson imitates classical meters in the pomps and themes, the methods he adopts for their presentation are derived from Renaissance and medieval forms and suggest that both the masque and the morality play influenced him. Harvey states that the pomps were "serious and exquisite" and that the four themes were "very accurately rendered." It seems, then, that in composing the pomps and themes Watson wanted to intensify and clarify the themes by visual representations. For example, he introduces the third pomp with the proverb "To be wise and to love at the same time is scarcely given to Jove"; and Haemon's fate in the play is demonstrated by succinct comments from "Cupid, a boy with a bow and arrow," "Indiscretion, a man," "Impudence, a man of unyielding audacity," "Violence," and "Death." It also seems from the manner in which Watson uses the proverb in this pomp that he was influenced by Renaissance emblems.

The early 1580s were extremely productive for Watson, for within a year of the translation of *Antigone* he published the *Hekatompathia; or, Passionate Century of Love*. It is possible, however, that the *Hekatompathia* had been circulating in manuscript for some time, as Watson states that Edward de Vere, seventeenth Earl of Oxford, to whom the work is dedicated, had at "convenient leisures favorably perused it, being yet but in written hand." He seems to have attempted to demonstrate in this work that it was possible to incorporate classical learning into English poetry and to adapt the genres and styles of the Renaissance poets of France and Italy in their Neo-Latin compositions and use of vernaculars. Unlike Spenser – who in *The Shepheardes Calender* (1579) attempted to refashion the English language in terms of its ancient traditions – Watson, in using sixteenth-century English, shows its versatility and flexibility in accommodating foreign forms.

The *Hekatompathia* is the first published sonnet sequence in English in which one theme, love, dominates. The hundred sonnets, or passions, as Watson calls them, form two unequal sections. The first part (1–79) describes the lover's sufferings, and the second (80–100) celebrates the triumph of reason, the joy of freedom, and the cessation of suffering.

Each sonnet begins with a headnote stating the purpose and directing the reader to classical works and Renaissance French and Italian poetry. Recent work has traced all of Watson's sources, documented (but not translated) them, and thus demonstrated conclusively the poet's depth and breadth of learning in classical and Renaissance literature. Each sonnet consists of eighteen lines divided into three stanzas; as most critics have noticed, there is no feminine rhyme, and deviations from iambic pentameter are rare. Despite Watson's conservatism in rhyme and meter, his extravagant experimentation with acrostics and rhetorical patternings such as *reduplicatio* demonstrates his knowledge of contemporary trends and his desire to excel in all forms of verse. The sonnets' clarity of structure and syntax demonstrates Watson's ability to present his brilliant conceits and arguments logically and lucidly; his translations in the sequence likewise reflect these strengths.

The emphasis in the *Hekatompathia* is on the lover's emotional state, not on his actions; apart from the mistress's name, Laura, and the unstated cause of their separation, there is scarcely any narrative detail. In his introduction to the 1964 edition, S. K. Heninger, Jr., calls the sonnets more "artifice than art"; but this is only partly correct, for the witty transformations of the sources show Watson's ability to create new meanings from classical myths. For instance, in Sonnet 49 the lover in a witty conceit admits thoughts of suicide but rejects them lest Charon – fearful that his boat would be consumed by the lover's flames – would refuse to ferry him across the Styx, leaving him to suffer the fate of the unburied. Knowing that oblivion would be denied him, the lover decides to return to his present state, which differs little from the fictional fate he created for himself in the underworld. He suffers pain, but "plaints and tears" will no more move the mistress than "prayer" or "pence" would persuade Charon to take him across the Styx. Neither the beloved nor the gods survive the comic exaggerations; and it seems that Watson, in presenting both as irrational, intended to draw attention to the foolishness of allowing passion to rule reason. While his modified myths do not mock the gods' capriciousness in the manner that Marlowe's do in *Hero and Leander* (1598), they nonetheless draw attention to misrule and irrationality and prepare the reader for the triumph of reason in the last poems.

In the second section, "My Love Is Past," there is an even greater emphasis on the gods' limitations, and Watson's transformation of myths continues with even more whimsy. The all-powerful

Cupid, for example, who dominates the first section, is reduced in Sonnet 96 to a sulky boy who breaks his bow and plucks his wings because his former devotee gained independence. In this section, too, Watson aligns himself with those gods who have positive qualities. In a humorous adaptation of the Diana myth (Sonnet 84), he promises to raise the alarm should Jove appear in Diana's grove. Watson playfully suggests that a human with reason, even one smug in his newfound virtue, is superior to a lust-driven god.

Watson's witty use of tropes and conceits in the *Hekatompathia* shows his imaginative daring and cleverness and his delight in gently satirizing the lover's paradoxical state of suffering and joy. The image of the eagle testing its young by forcing them to look into the sun, for example, is used to show both positive and negative feelings. In Sonnet 21 it is used to heighten the lover's defeat by his mistress's eyes, for "No bird but Jove's can look against the sun." In Sonnet 99 a reformed lover recollects that when he was in love all thoughts, like eaglets, were tested, and if they reflected the beloved they survived; but in a state of reason he uses the same test to destroy all thoughts of her. While it may be true that there is more art than passion in these conceits, it is also true that the good-humored mocking of the lover's sufferings suggests a tolerance for the limitations of humankind.

Watson's next publication, *Amyntas* (1585), was written in Latin; but within a short time Abraham Fraunce, who saw its potential as a rich compendium of examples of elegiac pastoral images, opportunistically translated it into English. Fraunce's translation went through five editions (1587, 1588, 1589, 1591, 1596); not until the 1591 edition, where it appeared in the "Second Part" of *The Countess of Pembroke's Ivychurch,* did he acknowledge his source: "And I have somewhat altered Signor Tasso's Italian and Master Watson's Latin *Amyntas* to make them both one English." By this time Watson was not associated with the poem. He had, however, learned a costly lesson and in publishing his *Meliboeus* (1590) included a translation stating, "I interpret myself, lest Meliboeus in speaking English by another man's labor should lose my name in his change as my *Amyntas* did."

The classical and Renaissance sources of *Amyntas* suggest that Watson set out to show his mastery of the pastoral elegy in the manner that he had demonstrated his comprehensive knowledge of classical and Renaissance love poetry in the *Hekatompathia*. The elegy consists of eleven *querelae,* or lamentations (one for each day following the

death of Phyllis), each one hundred lines of dactylic hexameters (two exceptions are Eclogues 1 and 4, which are ninety-nine and ninety-eight lines respectively). The last eclogue describes the suicide and metamorphosis of Amyntas into the amaranth flower. Pastoral elegiac tropes (for example, the loss of *otium* [ease, relaxation], the invitation to Nature to mourn with the lover, the isolation of the shepherd-mourner, and apostrophes and reproaches to nymphs and deities) indicate Watson's familiarity with the classical models. Tropes usually associated with joyous pastoral activity (for example, the shepherd-singer under the beech tree, marking the bark; the activities of shepherds and shepherdesses; and descriptions of their accoutrements) are innovatively used by Watson to contrast the lover's suffering against past happiness. The many conceits that he creates from stock images and the various ways he discovers for using mortificatory tropes attest to his creativity and confidence in transforming sources. The classical myths and similes in the poem become elaborate conceits that draw attention to Watson's inventiveness rather than to the depth of Amyntas's sorrow.

In the same year as *Amyntas,* Watson produced another Latin publication, *Compendium Memoriæ Localis,* a short work of fifty-five pages on memory. Still another Latin work – a translation from Greek of *Coluthi Thebani Lycopolitani Poetæ,* "Helenæ Raptus," by a sixth-century Egyptian poet – was published the following year. Three years elapsed before Watson published another short original work, this time in English, *A Gratification unto Master John Case.* This short lyric set to music by William Byrd combines Watson's delight in music with his praise for Case. The classical allusions here, unlike those in *Amyntas* that were extravagant and distracting, work effectively to concentrate the theme in four brief stanzas.

Sometime after Watson's release from prison in 1590, he published *The First Set of Italian Madrigals Englished.* Although Watson insists on the title page that the lyrics are "not to the sense of the original ditty," Frederic Ives Carpenter (in his 1898–1899 edition) – in identifying eleven close to the Italian lyrics, three as free translations, and twelve with little relationship to the sources – argues that Watson may not have been competent in Italian. But such diversity just as readily indicates that linguistically and musically Watson felt capable of making whatever changes he thought fit.

The madrigals show not only Watson's interest in music and friendship with the composer Byrd, but also his emulation of Sir Philip Sidney (nos. 1 and 19), who shares praise with his father-in-law,

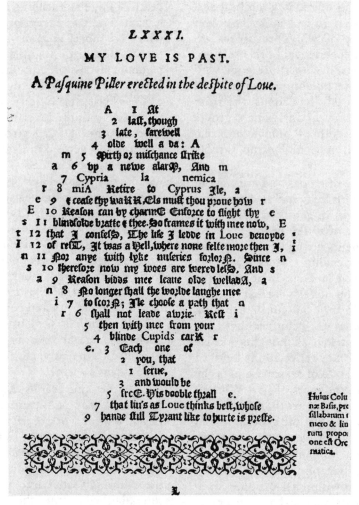

Page from The Hekatompathia

Sir Francis Walsingham (nos. 23, 24, and 27). Watson, in choosing twenty-two lyrics on love (some in a pastoral setting), continues his preoccupations of the *Hekatompathia* and *Amyntas*. Madrigal 25, a translation from Allesendro Striggio, may have suggested Watson's witty transformation of the Diana myth in *Hekatompathia* 84. Only eleven sonnets use the shepherds' names "Amarillis," "Phillis," and "Amyntas," but there appears to be no connection with shepherds of the same name in Watson's *Amyntas* or *Hekatompathia*.

Watson's second work for 1590, *Meliboeus,* an elegy for the death of Walsingham, was probably written after the madrigals, in which the lyrics on Walsingham seem hastily and inappropriately placed. Watson claims in the dedication to Lady Frances Sidney that by translating the elegy as *An Eclogue upon the Death of Sir Francis Walsingham* he hoped that more people would have an understanding of Walsingham's virtues. In the preface to the reader he makes it clear that he was also motivated by proprietorship, for he translated *Meliboeus* "not exactly to the Latin original," and he stresses that he does not want the poem appropriated in the manner that his *Amyntas* was.

Meliboeus differs from *Amyntas* in its allegory, panegyric, and restorative motifs. It shares with all of Watson's poetry a lucid style, clear organization, wit, and ingenuity. Watson uses the structure of the singing match for Corydon (Watson) and Tityrus (Thomas Walsingham) to mourn Meliboeus's passing. Arranged in what seems to be a descending hierarchy from gods to pastoral activities, the sequence takes a surprising turn when Watson concludes with a short, piscatory elegy with the conceit of Triton sounding his shell to "every shore" and with admonitions to dolphins, boys, and mermaids to cease wanton love tricks.

Christian emphases in *Meliboeus* seem to suggest that Watson may have been testing his ability to supplant pagan mythology with Christian theology. For example, in an innovative use of pastoral decorum, he presents Corydon hastily recalling his blasphemy against the gods and suggesting ingenuously that destiny should be placed in the saints' care because their "hands and hearts will always work the best." The second reference, this time to Catholic angelology, again comes from the "simple shepherd" Corydon, who gives a learned account of the nine choirs of angels, where Meliboeus has found a place.

The restorative sequence in the elegy emphasizes reason ("more than mourning reason must prevail") and recalls the similar change in the *Hekatompathia.* The movement from reason to Christian theology then follows and allows Watson to conclude with historical allegory and panegyric. Encomiums on Elizabeth I tactfully and succinctly recall Meliboeus's position of state. Using pastoral decorum again, Watson introduces the final eulogy to praise Spenser, who, Corydon claims, is more able to "set forth / such things of state," but ironically Corydon tells him what to say.

The contemporary references in *Meliboeus* suggest that Watson was aware of the interests and practices of the Sidney-Walsingham circles and perhaps through them of Elizabeth's reactions and preferences. His admiration of Spenser, while it may have been genuine, may not have been accurate in the statement of Elizabeth's preference for Spenser's poetry, since Spenser claims in *Colin Clout* that she listened to him only for Sir Walter Ralegh's sake.

Watson's final work, *Amintæ Gaudia* (1592), a Neo-Latin pastoral, was brought out posthumously by C. M. (Christopher Marlowe), who states in the dedication that Watson's dying wish was that Mary Herbert, Countess of Pembroke, should receive the poem. Consisting of ten epistles and eight eclogues totaling more than a thousand lines, the poem has been translated in full only by Boyle (1966) and in part (the first four epistles and part of the fifth) by J. T. in *An Old Fashioned Love* (1594). Analysis of Neo-Latin pastorals enables the identification of many of Watson's sources, such as eclogues of contemporary events, journeys, cryptic allegory, and dream; but it is the witty transformation of these forms and the mannered art that show Watson's extravagant imagination and technical ability.

Amintæ Gaudia has a tenuous connection with *Amyntas:* the epistles show the development of Amintas's love and acceptance by Phyllis, and the eclogues celebrating the joys of their love end abruptly after Echo callously foretells the death of Phyllis. The fourth and longest eclogue, "The Dream of Amintas," demonstrates Watson's eclecticism and his irreverent delight in mocking the gods of pagan mythology, a practice begun in the *Hekatompathia.* The dream's purpose is to flatter the Sidney circle by showing Sir Philip's apotheosis; but Venus's vanity, energy, greed, and lust (meant no doubt to show how desirable Sidney was, even to a goddess) become the main event. The climax is humorous and occurs as Venus embraces Sidney; the Boyle translation captures the situational comedy:

> Forgetting Mars and the blacksmith, she threw her milk-white arms around Sidney's neck and poured out kisses upon his cheeks, eyes, and lips. The entire circle of Gods laugh at the clinging goddess, until Jupiter in order to suppress the passion of his daughter orders that the tables be taken away.

It is little wonder that Amintas tells Phyllis (at the end of Eclogue 5) not to be concerned about these stories of the gods, as he is more chaste than any god.

Although the *Amintæ Gaudia* is not as well structured as Spenser's masterpiece of high-mannered pastoral art, *Colin Clout,* it nonetheless demonstrates why Watson's contemporaries admired his learning, wit, and ingenuity. It is a pity that today Watson is remembered mainly as a Neo-Latinist, for his works show how poets of the 1580s saw themselves reviving the classics. It is also regrettable that Watson's original English compositions are neglected, since they illustrate the method by which gifted Renaissance writers transformed their sources in order to delight and instruct readers.

References:

Warren B. Austin, "Thomas Watson's Adaptation of an Epigram by Martial," *Renaissance News,* 13 (Summer 1960): 134–140;

Harry Herbert Boyle, "Thomas Watson, Neo-Latinist," Ph.D. dissertation, University of California, Berkeley, 1966 – includes a complete translation of *Amintæ Gaudia;*

Leicester Bradner, *Musae Anglicanae: A History of Anglo-Latin Poetry, 1500–1925* (New York: MLA, 1940);

C. Elliot Browne, "The Earliest Mention of Shakespeare," *Notes & Queries,* fourth series 11 (May 1873): 378–379;

Cesare Cecioni, *Primi Studi su Thomas Watson* (Catania: Università degli studi Seminario di lingua e letteratura inglese, 1964);

Cecioni, *Thomas Watson e la tradizione petrarchista* (Milan: Giuseppe Principato, 1969);

Louise George Clubb, "Gabriel Harvey and the Two Thomas Watsons," *Renaissance News,* 19 (Summer 1966): 113–117;

John T. Curry, "Edward de Vere, Earl of Oxford, and Thomas Watson," *Notes & Queries,* ninth series 11 (February 1902): 102–103;

Mark Eccles, *Christopher Marlowe in London* (Cambridge, Mass.: Harvard University Press, 1943);

Leonard Grant, *Neo-Latin Literature and the Pastoral* (Chapel Hill: University of North Carolina Press, 1965);

Hubert Hall, "An Elizabethan Poet and His Relations," *Athenæum,* no. 3278 (August 1890): 256;

Francis Meres, *Palladis Tamia,* edited by Don Cameron Allen (Urbana: University of Illinois, 1938);

G. C. Moore Smith, "Thomas Watson, Author of *Hekatompathia,*" *Notes & Queries,* twelfth series 7 (November 1920): 422;

William M. Murphy, "Thomas Watson's *Hekatompathia* (1582) and the Elizabethan Sonnet Sequence," *Journal of English and Germanic Philology,* 56 (1957): 418–428;

Wendy Phillips, "Thomas Watson's *Hekatompathia; or, Passionate Century of Love* (November 1582)," Ph.D. dissertation, University of California, Berkeley, 1990;

William Ringler, "Spenser and Thomas Watson," *Modern Language Notes,* 69 (November 1954): 484–486;

Walter F. Staton, Jr., "Thomas Watson's Authorship of 'Aurora Now,' " *Notes & Queries,* 207 (August 1963): 294–295;

Franklin B. Williams, Jr., "Biographical Notes: Thomas Watson and Henry VIII," *Library,* 2 (December 1980): 445–446.

William Webbe

(? – 1591)

Michael Pincombe
University of Newcastle upon Tyne

BOOK: *A Discourse of English Poetrie. Together, with the Authors iudgment, touching the reformation of our English Verse* (London: Printed by John Charlewood for Robert Walley, 1586).

Editions: *A Discourse of English Poetries,* edited by Edward Arber (London: Edward Arber, 1870); republished in *Elizabethan Critical Essays,* volume 1, edited by G. Gregory Smith (Oxford: Clarendon, 1904), pp. 226–302; Robert Wilmot, *The Tragedy of Tancred and Gismund,* edited by W. W. Greg (Oxford: Oxford University Press for the Malone Society, 1914).

OTHER: "To his frend R. W.," in *The Tragedie of Tancred and Gismund* (London: Printed by Thomas Scarlet for Richard Robinson, 1591).

William Webbe was the author of the first extensive printed treatise to deal specifically with English poetry: *A Discourse of English Poetry, Together with the Author's Judgment Touching the Reformation of Our English Verse,* written and published in 1586. Almost nothing is known of Webbe's life, but the lack of biographical details makes him all the more interesting as a representative figure of late-Tudor humanism. The *Discourse* is not without personal idiosyncrasy, but its virtual "authorlessness" renders it a particularly important index to the typical concerns and anxieties of classically educated readers and writers in the late sixteenth century.

It is not known when or where Webbe was born, but he signed himself "William Webbe, Graduate," and it appears that he had attended Cambridge University. A William Webbe took his B.A. at Saint John's College in 1573, and another man of the same name earned a B.A. at Catharine Hall in 1582. It would be useful to know which of these two was the author in question. If he was the first, then he might have been acquainted with Gabriel Harvey and Edmund Spenser, whom he praises as "two of the rarest wits and learned'st masters of poetry in England." But his uncertainty as to Spenser's authorship of *The Shepheardes Calender* (1579) would seem to count against this. If he was the other Cambridge Webbe, then he might have known Abraham Fraunce, to whom he seems to refer cryptically at one point in his *Discourse*. All three writers were connected in one way or another to Sir Philip Sidney, author of *An Apology for Poetry,* published in 1595 but written around 1579; Webbe would certainly have been interested in this book but does not appear to have been privileged to read it in manuscript before writing his own treatise. And all three shared Webbe's interest in reformed versifying; but again there is, unfortunately, very little to suggest that this shared interest came from or led to mutual acquaintance.

One of the few things known for certain about Webbe is that he wrote the *Discourse* while serving as tutor, almost certainly in the classics, to the sons of Edward Sulyard of Fleminges, near Runwell in Essex. In his dedication of the *Discourse* to that gentleman, Webbe explains that it was "compiled for recreation in the intermissions of [his] daily business, even these summer evenings." As one might expect from the casual and desultory nature of its composition, the *Discourse* is a magpie's nest of largely commonplace ideas "compiled" from other authors, but it contains one or two unusual thoughts as well. It lacks structure, as Webbe himself admits, sometimes "leaving out the chief colors and ornaments of poetry," and sometimes "stuffing in pieces little pertinent to true poetry." The result is a not-unpleasant hotchpotch that retains its informal, somewhat quirky character even after preparation for the press.

However, the treatise is given some coherence by Webbe's humanist interests. It begins, sensibly enough, with a definition of the word *poetry* as "the art of making" and goes on to make some general remarks about the estimation in which poetry was held by the ancients, particularly in its capacity to lead men "from a wild and savage kind of life to civility and gentleness and the right knowledge of hu-

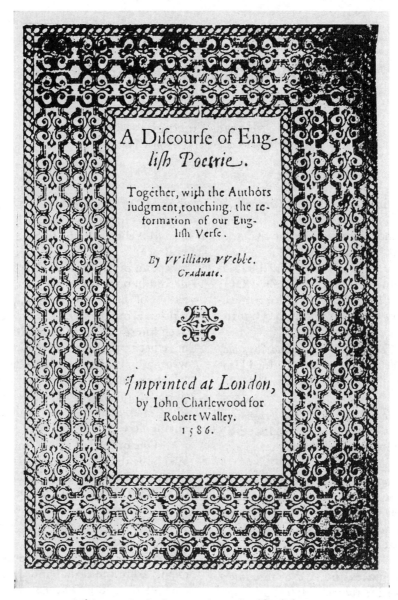

Title page for the first extensive study of English poetry

manity." Here is Tudor humanism in a nutshell: the arts of discourse, preeminently poetry and oratory, "humanized" those who practiced them (and their readers or listeners) by making them more civilized. Webbe's humanism belongs to the neoclassical school influenced by Roger Ascham's seminal treatise on teaching Latin, *The Schoolmaster* (1570). Ascham argues that the Greeks and Romans had perfected the art of versifying, but when they were overrun by their barbarian conquerors, their quantitative prosody based on the arrangement of long and short syllables was lost and replaced by the qualitative system of accent and rhyme, the traditional form of English verse. Webbe, who cites

Ascham's words almost verbatim, describes this kind of writing as "brutish poetry."

However, Webbe discerns a lack of interest in the project among his fellow writers. He had read Harvey's comments on meter in his *Letters* (written with Spenser and published in 1580) but regrets that they seem to have been made "between jest and earnest" and that he and Spenser now have more "serious businesses" to handle. And he is even driven to hope, somewhat wildly, that Harvey's brothers, neither of them noted or even known as poets, might turn their hands to metrical verses if their "great and weighty callings" might permit. It seems that only provincial tutors with time on their hands had leisure to study verse, and this is an indication of the demoralization of the humanist endeavor in the late sixteenth century.

Nonetheless, Webbe's own interest in the classical tradition is everywhere apparent in the *Discourse,* although he was not a scholar of the highest order. He states, for example, that Horace and Juvenal were contemporaries, although they belong to different centuries. Elsewhere one sees the pedant's hand, notably in the translation of George Fabricius's paraphrase into Latin prose of Horace's poem *Ars Poetica* – just the sort of crib that a young Elizabethan Latinist would find useful. The presence of this crib is also a sign of the decadent tendencies of late-Tudor humanism: instead of reading the original text in Horace, readers could turn to an easier prose version – in English, too, if their Latin was not good enough.

But if Webbe was only a modest scholar, he was an enthusiastic admirer of the classics, particularly Virgil. He spends several pages on Thomas Phaer's translation (1558–1562) of the *Aeneid* and shows some sensitivity in his appreciation of "how big and boisterous his words sound" in his Englishing of Virgil's battle scenes. On the other hand, Webbe's ear seems to have deserted him when he tried his own hand at a quantitative translation of the first and second of Virgil's *Eclogues.* The celebrated opening lines of eclogue 1 are rendered thus: "Tityrus, happily thou li'st tumbling under a beech-tree, / All in a fine oat pipe these sweet songs lustily chanting." The seven consecutive stressed syllables of the second line may meet the demands of neoclassical meter, but they sound very odd in English. Indeed, the real reason for the apparent neglect of meter was the fact that it often produced verses that sounded lumpish, as Webbe himself must have discovered in the lines quoted from his translation of Virgil, which he describes as a "troublesome and unpleasant piece of labor" – hardly an effective advertisement for the quantitative cause!

Webbe was undaunted, however, and applied his enthusiasm to the English poetry he most admired – Spenser's *Shepheardes Calender* – although he was not sure whether Spenser really did write this pseudonymously published collection of eclogues. Webbe decided to "translate" the "April" eclogue into sapphics, a popular quantitative form among English metricians. Spenser writes: "Ye dayntye nymphs that in this blessed brooke / doe bathe your brest, / Forsake your watry bowres, and hether looke, / at my request." Webbe translates: "O ye nymphs most fine, who resort to this brook, / For to bathe there your pretty breasts at all times, /

Leave the waterish bowers, hither and to me come / at my request now." Spenser is perhaps not heard at his best in these lines, but at least they flow prettily enough; Webbe's verse is choked and unidiomatic – indeed, it reads very much like a schoolboy's literal translation of a piece of Latin.

Despite his partisan affection for reformed versifying, Webbe is much sounder when he turns to traditional English poetry. Here he had before him the example of George Gascoigne's "Certain Notes of Instruction Concerning the Making of Verse of Rhyme in English," published in his *Posies* (1575). The "Notes" are no more than their title suggests: a collection of handy tips on how to write English verse, compiled for the use of a certain Edoardo Donati, an Italian. Webbe follows Gascoigne more or less closely. So, for example, he borrows Gascoigne's tip on finding the right rhyme by rehearsing rhyme words alphabetically; Webbe expands this hint into a brief discussion of extemporary versifying. And he keeps to the "principal observations" of prosody, word order, and rhyming, without including a catalogue of ornamental devices or "figures of speech."

This is where he chiefly differs from George Puttenham, whose *Art of English Poesy,* published in 1589 but written earlier, offers a useful comparison with Webbe's treatise (though, as in the case of Sidney's *Apology,* Webbe does not seem to have had access to a manuscript copy). Although Puttenham uses much the same sort of material as Webbe (their opening definitions of poetry are remarkably similar), his treatise is more detailed and more systematic, a genuine "art," in fact. By comparison, Webbe's piece seems a shambles. At one point, for example, he decides that all poetry may be divided into three kinds: "comical, tragical, and historical." At first one may be struck by the audacity with which he sorts delightful poems into the comical category and sorrowful ones into the tragical, only to be brought back to one's senses with his somewhat fatuous inclusion in the historical of "the rest of all such matters which is indifferent between the other two."

Webbe seems to have read quite widely in English poetry, from Geoffrey Chaucer, "the god of English poets," to contemporary poets such as Gascoigne and George Whetstone, and in translations by such writers as Barnabe Googe and Abraham Fleming. But he was, perhaps, most at home with the minor writers of collections such as *The Paradise of Dainty Devices* (1578), which – together with Ascham and Spenser – seems to have been influential in shaping his ideas and tastes. He mentions "Sand,

Hill, S. Y., M. D." among his favorite authors without even knowing their true identities. And he evidently had some problems in getting hold of manuscripts in rural Essex. He says that he knows that scholarly poets of the universities and Inns of Court have produced many poems, but he has not been able to see all he has heard of, "neither is my abiding in such place where I can with facility get knowledge of their works." This completes the picture of Webbe as an essentially minor yet basically open-minded writer, lacking the resources of those in the literary mainstream and resorting to his own not-always-adequate inventions to supply the want.

Webbe's allusion to the Inns of Court is significant. Sometime in the late 1580s he seems to have left Sulyard's service and removed to nearby Havering atte Bower, to Pyrgo, the house of Henry Grey, Sulyard's father-in-law. It was here, perhaps, that he became acquainted with Robert Wilmot, a clergyman who had attended the Inner Temple and was one of the authors of a play called *Gismond of Salerne,* performed before Elizabeth I at the Inner Temple in 1567. In 1591 Wilmot modernized the old manuscript version and had it printed as *Tancred and Gismund,* dedicating it to Grey's wife, Anne. Webbe supplied a complimentary letter "To his Friend R. W.," signed from his master's house at Pyrgo and dated 8 August 1591. Webbe must have been pleased with the way his friend had "revised and polished" the old play, for Wilmot had turned its quatrains into blank verse – a denial of rhyme that Webbe can only have applauded. But after this letter praising Wilmot's "true ornaments of poetical art" and "stateliest English terms," nothing more is heard of Webbe.

Webbe has never enjoyed a high reputation, either in his own time or the present. J. W. H. Atkins calls the *Discourse,* not without some justice, an "uninspired and uninspiring effort." And, compared to Sidney and Puttenham, Webbe is small-fry indeed. But the greatest minds are not always the best guides to the literature of an age, and, in Webbe's half-digested learning, pedantic enthusiasms, and humdrum commonplaces, one catches a glimpse of a more routine literary culture prevalent in late-sixteenth-century England.

References:

J. W. H. Atkins, *English Literary Criticism: The Renascence* (London: Methuen, 1947), pp. 151–156;

Derek Attridge, *Well-Weighed Syllables: Elizabethan Verse in Classical Metres* (London: Cambridge University Press, 1974), pp. 152–155, 198–199.

John Whitgift

(circa 1533 – 29 February 1604)

Mark Goldblatt
Fashion Institute of Technology, State University of New York

BOOKS: *An answere to a certen libel intituled, An admonition* (London: Printed by Henry Binneman for Humfrey Toye, 1572);
The defense of the aunswere to the Admonition, against the Replie (London: Printed by Henry Binneman for Humfrey Toye, 1574).
Collection: *Works,* 3 volumes, edited by John Ayre (Cambridge: Parker Society, 1851–1853).

The degree to which the life and work of John Whitgift, archbishop of Canterbury from 1583 to 1604, have been eclipsed by those of his protégé, Richard Hooker, is evinced in subtle ways. Whitgift's most recent biographer, P. M. Dawley, declares, somewhat defensively, that "he, not Hooker, is the typical Elizabethan churchman." Even here the word *typical* carries an unintentional double edge, suggesting Whitgift's centrality to the ecclesiastical controversies of the sixteenth century yet also perhaps conceding his mediocrity. Certainly his prose tends to be mediocre. He is not in Hooker's league as a stylist, in part the result of the ad hoc circumstances under which he composed. Nevertheless, if time has obscured his name, it should be noted that his stature among his contemporaries was as substantial as his office would indicate – far more substantial than Hooker's. Indeed, a case can be made that it was primarily Whitgift's energies that broke the ground for Hooker's eventual acceptance and that it was in the very act of breaking that ground that Whitgift undermined his own reputation.

John Whitgift was born sometime between 1530 and 1533 in the eastern port town of Great Grimsby, England. The first of several sons born to Anne and Henry Whitgift, a middle-class merchant and shipowner, the future archbishop was baptized under the auspices of a strife-ridden national church on the brink of formal separation from Roman authority. When the break came, with Henry VIII's Act of Supremacy in 1534, it is likely that the Whitgifts identified their own relative good fortune, and that of England, with their king. Since the separation entailed only minor changes in the day-to-day observance of their religion, it is also likely that the broader theological questions provoked by Henry's actions may have caused no great stir inside the Whitgift household. The fact that preachers might now dedicate prayers to Henry with the words "Our Sovereign Lord King Henry VIII, being immediately next under God the only and supreme Head of the Catholic Church of England" perhaps seemed cumbersome, but the reference to the "Catholic" character of the English church was also an explicit assurance of spiritual continuity. It was of course this very continuity, the unsettling sameness of the church under Henry as under the pope, that would eventually become a crucial point of contention between religious factions in Reformation England. But the impact of such controversies on a child growing up in Grimsby during the late 1530s was likely negligible.

In 1550 the Whitgifts sent their son off to Cambridge, where his undergraduate education was to straddle the turbulent reigns of Edward VI and Mary, as the English church moved first toward a more reformed position and then was yanked back violently in the direction of Rome. This time the effects of religious upheaval could not have been lost upon the young man. Within months after Mary's accession in 1553, many of his schoolmasters, themselves prominent Reformers, had disappeared from the scene at Cambridge – some into hiding, some into exile, and some into prison. Still, Whitgift rode out the turmoil and completed his bachelor's degree. He was graduated, ironically, in the company of the man who was to become his principal adversary for the remainder of the century, Thomas Cartwright.

"Bloody Mary's" demise in 1558 would prove the last gasp for reconciliation with Rome. Elizabeth's accession swung the church once more back

John Whitgift (portrait by an unknown artist; Cambridge University Library)

toward a reformed polity, and the new queen's influence would be decisive: the Church of England would remain Protestant. Elizabeth was determined, however, to find a settlement, an ecclesiastical structure to which both radical and conservative factions might consent. What she desired, in a word, was conformity. Achieving it, however, would be no easy task. The notion of an episcopacy (the hierarchy of priests and bishops upon which a central authority rests) was perceived by radical Puritans as a vestige of Catholicism; the monarch merely replaced the pope at the top. The Puritans sought the dissolution of Anglican episcopal order as the initial phase of a changeover to congregationalism, modeled after John Calvin's Geneva. Under this system individual congregations would have the freedom to follow their own consciences in matters of polity – a freedom that would challenge, albeit indirectly, the powers of the Crown itself.

The struggle against such reformation of the English church was to become the raison d'être of Whitgift's adult life. Ordained in 1560, first as deacon and then as priest, he ministered to a small congregation outside Cambridge. Besides his clerical duties, he also remained at the university as professor of divinity. For several years his career progressed uneventfully. But in late 1565 he was drawn into a dispute over church vestments. Three hundred undergraduates at Saint John's College, one of the more radical Cambridge schools, had turned up at the college chapel without their required surplices. Whitgift joined other professors in requesting moderation; in a letter to William Cecil, university chancellor, the professors argued that vestments might be left as a matter of conscience among students. Their request was denied. Two years later Whitgift was forced, in a letter to

Cecil, to defend his own loyalty for having pleaded the lenient position:

> As touching my non-conformity . . . I never encouraged any to withstand the Queen's Majesty's laws in that behalf; but I both have, and do by all means I can, seek to persuade men to conform themselves. . . . God hath moved you to love me. God hath hitherto by you provided for me: what it shall please God to put in your mind to do for me, I beseech you, let no reports . . . dissuade you. I trust hitherto I have not behaved myself that your honor doth repent you of any thing done for me. And I trust the day shall never come wherein your honor shall have cause to say, I would I had not done this for him.

This is the kind of letter that can be read as self-serving, if not obsequious, but to do so is an injustice to its author. (Certainly Puritans would make much of the fact that conformists were rewarded for their beliefs.) There was nothing in Whitgift's nature, as evidenced in his actions, to suggest that opportunism colored his beliefs. It is possible, after all, for a conscience to be genuinely conservative. Whatever his intentions, however, Whitgift's letter to Cecil apparently put the rumors of his nonconformity to rest, for two years later he was asked to preach before the queen. His subject, unsurprisingly, was the duty of conformity, and the impression he made upon Elizabeth was lasting. Within months he was appointed a royal chaplain, regius professor of divinity, and finally master of Trinity College at Cambridge.

At Trinity, Whitgift first exhibited those traits that would infuriate antagonists for the remainder of his life: he would tolerate neither disorder nor dispute. He ruled the college with an iron fist, demanding exact compliance among teachers and students to even the most minute statutes. The austerity was far from popular, but it was personal and heartfelt:

> I may not suffer those with whom I have to do to disquiet the university or college with false doctrine and schismatical opinions: I may not suffer them openly to break and condemn those laws and statutes which they are sworn to observe, and I to execute: I may not suffer any man, against the express words of his oath, against all honesty and conscience, to live under me, lest I be partaker of his perjury.

The tendency to personalize the dispute is characteristic; it is as if nonconformity represented a physical affront to his being. If, however, his insistence upon compliance with the statutes was absolute, he was not disinclined to reform the statutes themselves. The vestiarian skirmish had persuaded him that such reform was needed, and in 1569 he drew up new regulations that served, in effect, to consolidate his own administrative powers – and to drive out whatever overt nonconformist elements remained at Cambridge: "The college was never in better quietness," he would later declare.

At this point the adversarial figure of Cartwright reappeared. Having fled Cambridge during Mary's reign, Cartwright returned, after her death, to a fellowship; he began at once to undermine the "quietness" that Whitgift so prized. Cartwright was censured; when he refused to recant, Whitgift's new statutes were used to deprive him of his position – whereupon Cartwright departed in 1569 to Geneva.

Thus Whitgift's regulations brought a calm to Cambridge that had been absent for decades. The same could not be said, however, for England as a whole. Strife between Puritans and conformists in the early 1570s culminated in the anonymous *Admonition to the Parliament* in June 1572; it was a brief but bitter tract that detailed Puritan demands for a reformed English church. According to its author, the church was still tainted by vestiges of Rome. The traditions of episcopacy, clerical vestments, and the use of the Book of Common Prayer were condemned. The author demanded the return to a "primitive" church: a simplified Mass, a rejection of ceremonies whose origins were not obviously scriptural, and an equality of ministers within a congregational framework, on the Genevan model.

The *Admonition* cried out for a rebuttal, and Whitgift was summoned to the task by Archbishop Matthew Parker. The first draft of Whitgift's reply was completed barely three months after the initial printing of the *Admonition,* but whatever fanfare might have been built for its publication was drowned by the unanticipated appearance of another Puritan tract, *A Second Admonition to the Parliament.* Whitgift's reply thus seemed dated even before it appeared. Nevertheless, the book came out in February 1573 under the title *An Answer to a Certain Libel Entitled "An Admonition".* It was literally an "answer": the entire text of the first *Admonition* was reproduced paragraph by paragraph within Whitgift's book so that he could refute each point of the Puritan case. Two qualities evident throughout are Whitgift's strength as a logician – and his tactlessness as a politician:

> They earnestly cried out against pride, gluttony, etc. They spake much of mortification: they pretended great gravity, they sighed much: they seldom or never laughed: they were very austere in reprehending: they

spake gloriously ... thereby to win authority to their heresy among the simple and ignorant people.

Referring to one's opponents' followers as "simple and ignorant" is dubious strategy if one's goal is to unite the church. Yet Whitgift is personally appalled not only by the Puritan leaders' rhetorical approach but also by their sheer audacity:

They gave honor and reverence to none, and they used to speak to such as were in authority without any signification of honor, neither would they call men by their titles, and they answered churlishly.

Again, typically, the interpersonal aspects of the dispute seem to distract Whitgift from the deep-seatedness of the rift in the church. As a Christian, and more specifically as an English Christian, he cannot come to terms with the idea that he and the Puritans are not, in the final analysis, on the same side:

They went not to preach in such places where the gospel was not planted, but only they insinuated themselves into those places, wherein the gospel had been diligently preached, and, where there were godly and quiet men, there they made a stir, they raised up factions and bred discord.

Whitgift's response was quickly countered by Cartwright's *Reply to an Answer Made of Doctor Whitgift against the "Admonition"* (1573). To the consternation of both the queen and the religious hierarchy, Whitgift's tract had only one reprinting while both the original *Admonition* (which was banned) and Cartwright's *Reply* ran through "edition after edition," according to Dawley. This popularity was perhaps inevitable. The case for the status quo will never be as compelling or impassioned as the case for radical change. (As Hooker remarked years later in *Laws of Ecclesiastical Polity* [1593]: "He that goeth about to persuade a multitude, that they are not so well governed as they ought to be, shall never want attentive and favorable hearers.") This simple fact of human nature was to bedevil Whitgift and the conformist cause in general; the Puritans were, almost without exception, more dynamic polemicists. Their sermons drew larger crowds, their writings greater readership. If conformism brought the advantage of the queen's favor, it had also to bear the inertia of the familiar, the mundane. Drama will always accrue on the side of change.

Whitgift, though, remained undaunted. Turning his attention to Cartwright's *Reply,* he published in February 1574 his massive *Defense of the Answer to the "Admonition" against the Reply.* Within these eight hundred pages, he again reproduces, page by page, the earlier books of the controversy. The tome served not only as a rebuttal of the Puritan case but also as a compendium of arguments from both sides. The new material, addressed to Cartwright rather than the anonymous *Admonition* author, reflects some of the animosity of their feud. To Cartwright's charge that he had made selective omissions in his *Answer,* Whitgift's reply is terse: "I have omitted no matter of substance in either of the Admonitions. The words you here utter be contumelious: you only rail, you answer not." If, initially, Whitgift was shocked that the Puritans had willfully "made a stir ... / raised up factions and bred discord" by the writing of the *Defense,* he seems to recognize that discord is fundamental to Cartwright's agenda:

For if you would have written against the veriest papist in the world, the vilest person, the ignorantest dolt, you could not have used a more spiteful and malicious, more slanderous and reproachful, more contemptuous and disdainful kind of writing, then you use throughout your whole book.

The logical thrust of Whitgift's *Defense,* and indeed of the entire conformist case, is neatly summarized in his preface to the reader:

This Reply of Thomas Cartwright (which is of some counted so notable a piece of work) consisteth of two false principles and rotten pillars; whereof the one is, that we must of necessity have the same kind of government that was in the apostles' time, and is expressed in Scriptures, and no other; and the other is, that we may not in any wise, or in any consideration, retain anything that hath been abused under the Pope: if these two posts be weak, yea rotten (as I have proved them to be in this my Defense), then must the building of necessity fall.

In their rigid biblicism, as well as their determination to root out every trace of Roman Catholicism, the Puritans overlook that much of what forms the everyday religious experience of a man is comprised of indifferent things – "adiaphora" – matters that do not pertain to salvation. The crucial distinction for conformists is between polity and doctrine. Polity, including church government, does not directly affect the spiritual well-being of souls and may vary from time to time and place to place. Doctrine, on the other hand, is that by which souls are saved – and therefore it must be constant and in agreement always with Scripture. The Puritans would elevate all things, even the trivial, to the level

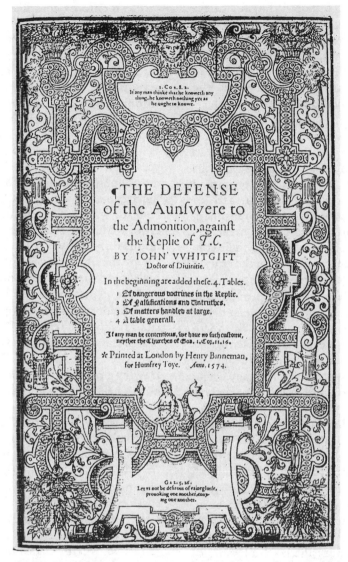

Title page for Whitgift's eight-hundred-page work attacking both the anonymous Puritan tract Admonition to the Parliament *(1572) and Thomas Cartwright's* Reply to an Answer Made of Doctor Whitgift against the "Admonition" *(1573)*

of doctrinal importance and turn to the Bible for justification. This literalism was, for Whitgift, both an overextension and debasement of the aim of Scripture. And he was confident that, doctrinally, the Church of England was well grounded:

> Here (thanks be to God) they allege not one article of faith, or point of doctrine, nor one piece of any substance, to be otherwise taught and allowed of in this church . . . than by the prescribed word of God may be justified; neither can they.

In other words, if the Church of England was doctrinally sound, there was no need for further reformation along the lines that the Puritans sought

simply for the sake of its polity. Rather, it was safer to keep things as they were – to preserve order. This is the central point of Whitgift's eight hundred pages.

Elizabeth, of course, was bound to notice such labors on behalf of the religious establishment. She had appointed the moderate Edmund Grindal to succeed Parker as archbishop – and soon came to regret her conciliatory gesture. When the see at Worcester became vacant in 1577, it seemed logical that she turn to the more zealous Whitgift. He was consecrated on 21 April of that year as bishop of Worcester. After a quarter century at Cambridge, he preached his final sermon at Trinity College that June: "Finally, brethren, fare you well," he urged. "Be perfect."

With his elevation to bishop, Whitgift's career was launched upon a new phase. His ecclesiastical responsibilities would now put a sudden end to his literary output. It is the great irony of his life: his tireless defense of the Elizabethan Settlement in effect ensured both his advancement within the church and the literary silence of his later years.

As bishop, Whitgift's modus operandi remained much the same as it was at Cambridge. He demanded conformity in all things and strove to root out dissent. He also drew up a more rigorous educational program for his clergy. He promoted the Book of Common Prayer as the standard for English worship; a literate clergy, he reasoned, would be less apt to improvise, as radical preachers often did, in the course of ministering to their congregations. At least if they varied from the prayer book, they could no longer plead ignorance.

For the next six years, Whitgift proved himself at each turn an able and unyielding defender of both the Crown and the church. Again, Elizabeth could not help noticing – especially by contrast to Grindal, her archbishop, with whom she often quarreled over his perceived leniency – and when Grindal died in 1583, Whitgift was named his successor. According to Dawley, upon Whitgift's confirmation in November of that year, a Puritan observer was moved to write: "The choice of that man at this time to be archbishop maketh me think that the Lord is determined to scourge his church."

Whitgift did much to fulfill the Puritans' worst fears. By the time he was enthroned at Canterbury, he had already drafted the Eleven Articles – a series of injunctions designed to tie up every loophole allowed to the Puritans under the lax leadership of Grindal. The sixth of these articles by itself ruled out the whole Puritan agenda. It forbade anyone to minister in any capacity within the church unless he subscribed to fundamentally conformist principles: the absolute sovereignty of the Crown in temporal and ecclesiastical affairs, the legitimacy of the prayer book and episcopal hierarchy, and the binding authority of all religious articles put forth under the Elizabethan Settlement. Within a month after consecration, Whitgift had effectively eliminated every ambiguity by which Puritans had been slipping through the cracks. His power had finally come to match his determination to stifle opposition. On the twenty-fifth anniversary of Elizabeth's accession (17 November 1583), he preached at Saint Paul's Cross, taking as his text "Railers shall not inherit the kingdom of God" (1 Cor. 6:10). No one in attendance could doubt which particular "railers" he had in mind.

To enforce compliance with his Eleven Articles, Whitgift set up the long-dormant "high commission" as an ecclesiastical court. The commission would summon a suspected minister and interrogate him under oath (the oath ex officio) about his activities, thus forcing him to incriminate himself without his being formally charged. He further empowered the commission to censor the press and impose fines and imprisonment for disobedience. With some justification the Puritans saw this as a version of the Inquisition. Even the House of Commons questioned the use of the ex officio oath, but the archbishop would not be moved. His response, instead, was to promulgate the Star Chamber decree, which in effect rendered public criticism impossible. Any press that published a manuscript that had not been approved by the archbishop or his commission would be destroyed, and the printer imprisoned for six months.

Against this backdrop the most notorious Puritan response surfaced. Printed in secret, the first Marprelate tract appeared in 1588, and pamphlets circulated regularly for the next two years. As Dawley remarks, "Seldom has a discomforted minority heaped such abuse upon its opponent as the Puritans poured upon John Whitgift." He is referred to as "John of Kankerbury, the Pope of Lambeth," "Beelzebub of Canterbury," "a monstrous Antichrist," and "a most bloody tyrant."

Whitgift's reaction to the Marprelate scandal was merciless. He sponsored not only the widespread manhunt for the authors but their subsequent imprisonment and (in the instance of John Penry) execution. This was Whitgift at his most unattractive, where his zeal had crossed the bounds of decency. As biographer Sidney Lee remarks: "In his examination of prisoners he showed a brutal insolence which is alien to all modern conceptions of justice or religion." The Marprelate episode may have indeed secured the only lasting victory the Puritans ever achieved over Whitgift, for many English historians have tended to view him in light of his overreaction. Dawley recounts that Samuel Gardiner judged Whitgift to be "narrow-minded to an almost incredible degree," while Thomas Macaulay summed him up as a "mean and tyrannical priest, who gained power by servility and adulation."

It is perhaps closer to the truth to view Whitgift as a man whose convictions were matched by a fierce, at times ruthless, determination to translate belief into action. If his words first brought him to the queen's attention, his deeds secured him her lasting favor. By under a year he outlived Elizabeth, who called him her "little black husband." When he died on the last day of February 1604, his final recorded words typified his life: "Pro ecclesia dei! Pro ecclesia dei!" (For the church of God! For the church of God!). He was interred at Croydon a month later.

From the standpoint of Whitgift's literary biography, it may be admitted that his greatest contribution to English letters was sponsoring Hooker. He supported him initially in Hooker's bitter clash with Walter Travers at the Temple in 1585, and he subsequently served as Hooker's principal benefactor through the composition of his *Laws of Ecclesiastical Polity*. As Whitgift's early biographer John Strype writes: "The same cause was here managed by Mr. Hooker in writing, which the Archbishop so painfully and vigorously in his place promoted by his actions." It would be an error, however, to disregard Whitgift's influence in the formulation of the conformist case. Stylistically, to be sure, Whitgift's prose has the feel of a sledgehammer; Hooker's, a sculptor's chisel. Yet it is no coincidence that throughout his masterpiece Hooker cites Cartwright, Whitgift's old antagonist, as representative of the Puritan position, rather than his own nemesis, Travers. Hooker in fact borrowed liberally from his mentor. Thus the relative dearth of Whitgift studies, as compared with the minor boom in Hooker criticism over the past decades, is something of an injustice.

Whitgift should best be viewed as a man whose devotion to his church and queen was constant, if at times perhaps excessive. His was an age in which religious questions were literally matters of life and death. Hence his concerns were for actions over words. And although he wrote a great many words, it is for his actions rather than his words that he is justifiably remembered.

Biographies:

John Strype, *The Life and Acts of John Whitgift, D.D.* (London, 1718; revised edition, 3 volumes, Oxford, 1822);

Sidney Lee, "John Whitgift," in *Dictionary of National Biography,* volume 61, edited by Lee and Leslie Stephen (London: Smith, Elder, 1899);

P. M. Dawley, *John Whitgift and the English Reformation* (New York: Scribners, 1954).

References:

Richard Hooker, *The Folger Library Edition of the Works of Richard Hooker,* edited by W. Speed Hill ([volumes 1–5] Cambridge, Mass. & London: Belknap Press of Harvard University Press, 1977–1990; [volume 6] Binghamton, N.Y.: Medieval & Early Renaissance Texts & Studies, 1993);

Peter Lake, *Anglicans and Puritans? Presbyterianism and English Conformist Thought from Whitgift to Hooker* (London: Unwin Hyman, 1988);

D. J. McGinn, *The Admonition Controversy* (New Brunswick, N.J.: Rutgers University Press, 1949).

Thomas Wilson

(1523 or 1524 – 20 May 1581)

Judith Rice Henderson
University of Saskatchewan

BOOKS: *The rule of Reason, conteinyng the Arte of Logique* (London: Printed by Richard Grafton, 1551; revised and enlarged editions, 1552, 1553);

The Arte of Rhetorique, for the vse of all soche as are studious of Eloquence (London: Printed by Richard Grafton, 1553; enlarged edition, London: Printed by John Kingston, 1560);

A discourse vppon vsurye, by waye of dialogue (London: Printed by Richard Tottel, 1572).

Editions: *Wilson's Arte of Rhetorique 1560,* edited by G. H. Mair (Oxford: Clarendon, 1909);

A Discourse upon Usury by Way of Dialogue and Orations, for the Better Variety and More Delight of All Those That Shall Read This Treatise [1572], edited by R. H. Tawney (London: G. Bell, 1925);

The Arte of Rhetorique (1553), edited by Robert Hood Bowers (Gainesville, Fla.: Scholars' Facsimiles & Reprints, 1962);

Demosthenes, *The Three Orations in Favour of the Olynthians (London 1570),* translated by Wilson (Amsterdam: Theatrum Orbis Terrarum / New York: Da Capo, 1968);

The Rule of Reason (London 1551), facsimile (Amsterdam: Theatrum Orbis Terrarum / New York: Da Capo, 1970);

The Rule of Reason Conteinyng The Arte of Logique, edited by Richard S. Sprague (Northridge, Cal.: San Fernando State Valley College, 1972);

Arte of Rhetorique, edited by Thomas J. Derrick (New York & London: Garland, 1982).

OTHER: *De obitu doctissimi et sanctissimi theologi doctoris M. Buceri, . . . epistolæ duæ. Item, epigrammata varia cum Græcæ tum Latinè conscripta in eundem ministrum,* edited by Sir John Cheke, with Latin epigram by Wilson (London: Printed by Reginald Wolf, 1551);

Vita et obitus duorum fratrum Suffolciensium, Henrici et Caroli Brandoni duabus epistolis explicata. Adduntur epitaphia. Affiguntur praeterea epigrammata, edited, with contributions, by Wilson (London:

Printed by Richard Grafton, 1551);

Walter Haddon, *Exhortatio ad literas,* with dedication and poem by Wilson (London: Printed by Richard Grafton, 1552);

Haddon, *Lucubrationes,* edited by Thomas Hatcher, with commendatory letter of Wilson to Hatcher and correspondence of Haddon with Wilson (London: Printed by William Seres, 1567).

TRANSLATION: Demosthenes, *The three Orations of Demosthenes . . . in fauour of the Olynthians . . . with those his fower Orations titled . . . against king Philip of Macedonie* (London: Printed by Henry Denham, 1570).

Thomas Wilson, B.A., M.A., D.C.L., was a Cambridge humanist and tutor under Edward VI; an exile, political activist, and victim of the Inquisition under Mary I; a civil lawyer, member of Parliament, diplomat, and statesman under Elizabeth I. His dialogue on usury and his tumultuous career merit more attention than they have received. He has been known primarily for *The Rule of Reason* (1551) and *The Art of Rhetoric* (1553) because these works, the first logic and the first comprehensive rhetoric in English, have offered this age an accessible survey of Tudor principles of composition and, as Hardin Craig shows, a mine of fool's gold for Shakespearean source study.

Wilson was the eldest of five sons of Thomas and Anne Wilson of Strubby, Lincolnshire. His father acquired lands by 1539, probably as a result of the dissolution of the monasteries. Wilson entered Eton College as a king's scholar in 1537. He matriculated at King's College, Cambridge, on 13 August 1542, telling the registrar he was eighteen and born at Lincoln. When his father died in 1551, he inherited property, so that in a deposition of 29 January 1553 on behalf of his former headmaster at Eton, Nicholas Udall, he could describe himself as "Thomas Wilson of Washingborough in the

*Thomas Wilson, 1575 (portrait by an unknown artist; National
Portrait Gallery, London)*

County of Lincoln. Gentleman of the age of XXIX years." Together with the inscription on his portrait in the National Portrait Gallery – "Aetatis LII 1575" – these records show that he was born in 1523 or 1524.

Cambridge University was the hotbed of the Reformation in England, especially after Henry VIII's break with Rome. Thomas Smith and Sir John Cheke trained a generation of Protestant scholars and statesmen. In 1544 this circle of Cambridge humanists took charge of the royal nursery. They hoped to ensure a Protestant future for the Church of England by educating Prince Edward, Princess Elizabeth, and other members of the royal family, such as Lady Jane Grey (the granddaughter of Charles Brandon, Duke of Suffolk, and the king's sister Mary, Dowager Queen of France). When Edward VI mounted the throne in 1547, the Cam-

bridge humanists helped to form his government and pushed church reform.

Wilson earned his B.A. about 1546 and began tutoring Suffolk's youngest son, Charles. Suffolk had sired Henry and Charles Brandon by his last wife, Catherine Willoughby, a Lincolnshire neighbor of the Wilsons. Henry, Duke of Suffolk after his father's death in 1545, shared Prince Edward's studies at court, while Charles studied at home. In 1549, the year Wilson became M.A., the Brandon brothers went up to Saint John's College, Cambridge. Wilson continued to tutor Charles and no doubt assisted in the studies of his brother. His deposition on behalf of Udall records that by 1553 he had also taught Charles Willoughby, son of the deputy of Calais.

Sorrow struck Cambridge in 1551. The Strasbourg Reformer Martin Bucer, regius professor of divinity since 1549, died 27/28 February, and Wilson contributed to a collection of tributes edited by Cheke. July brought a plague of sweating sickness. Henry and Charles Brandon, with friends and servants, fled to their mother's home at nearby Kingston. Their cousin Charles Stanley became mortally ill there, and the group moved on, leaving him in Wilson's care. The young Suffolk and his brother died after they reached Buckden Palace. Wilson edited *Vita et obitus duorum fratrum Suffolciensium* (1551), a collection of Latin and Greek eulogies of the Brandons and others by Cambridge and Oxford scholars. He contributed a prose biography and several poems in Latin, including one on Stanley. These deaths and Wilson's loss of his father took their toll on him. In a postscript to the first edition of *The Rule of Reason,* he complains, "I wrote this book in such a time, as when I had not so convenient leisure for the good placing and true examining thereof, as since I came to the printing of the same I wished that I had."

Wilson needed new patrons, and he sought them through these and other publications. While comforting their bereaved mother, he dedicated his tribute to the Brandons to the new duke of Suffolk, Henry Grey, the husband of their half sister Frances Brandon. His publisher, the royal printer Richard Grafton, suggested *The Rule of Reason,* which Wilson dedicated to Edward VI. He dedicated Walter Haddon's *Exhortatio ad literas* (1552) to Northumberland's eldest son, John Dudley, Earl of Warwick, and concluded the volume with a praise of the king in Latin verse. At Warwick's request he composed *The Art of Rhetoric* while spending the summer of 1552 in Lincolnshire as the guest of Sir Edward Dymock.

Except that he wrote his textbooks of dialectic and rhetoric in English rather than Latin, Wilson was following the customary career path of a master of arts. Humanist scholars often published textbooks in these core subjects of the arts curriculum soon after they had qualified as masters and begun to teach. Wilson's descriptions of the two arts are traditional. His dialectic is the scholastic elaboration of Aristotle's *Organon,* as modified by Rudolph Agricola and other humanists. His rhetoric is borrowed from the ancient Romans (Cicero, Quintilian, and the anonymous *Rhetorica ad Herennium*) and from Desiderius Erasmus. He may have drawn on Leonard Cox's *Art or Craft of Rhetoric* (1530?) and Richard Sherry's *Treatise of Schemes and Tropes* (1550), works in English on argument and style, respectively.

Wilson's decision to write in English reflects Protestant doctrine. Martin Luther and his followers wished to make the Scriptures accessible to their priesthood of all believers by extending education beyond the professional and governing classes. Wilson's textbooks teach his compatriots to think critically, especially about papal doctrine, to defend their beliefs, and to persuade others to a Christian life. Both rhetoric and dialectic offer techniques of finding and arranging arguments. Dialectic argues general principles; rhetoric applies them to specific situations. Dialectic is a tool for scholarly debate; rhetoric, for persuasion of a popular audience. Dialectic appeals to the reason; rhetoric, to the emotions as well. Therefore rhetoric also teaches orators how to remember a speech and how to delight and move their hearers through elegant language, voice, and gestures. Both textbooks found the popular audience Wilson sought. At least six editions of the logic and eight of the rhetoric appeared during the sixteenth century.

Wilson's examples of the rules of discourse promote the Protestant cause. In *The Rule of Reason* he enjoys exposing the false arguments of the papists, and he illustrates the places of invention by applying them to the question, "whether it be lawful for a priest to marry a wife or no." In *The Art of Rhetoric* he translates Erasmus's controversial *Encomium matrimonii* persuading a young man against celibacy. Wilson also suggests how the rules of rhetoric can be adapted to preaching, and his examples often urge godly living. Thus he praises the Brandons as models of virtue and persuades their mother to accept their deaths with Christian patience. Nevertheless, he writes at length on humor, "for except men find delight, they will not long abide. . . . And that is the reason that men commonly tarry the end of a merry play and cannot abide the half hearing of a sour checking sermon."

As he worked on these textbooks, Wilson developed his English style. The 1551 *Rule* is crabbed and sometimes confusing, but he revised and enlarged it for Grafton's two subsequent editions, in 1552 incorporating suggestions that Smith made in his own copy of the first edition and in 1553 citing by author that mispunctuated letter from *Ralph Roister Doister* (circa 1552) that proves the anonymous play is Udall's. As Thomas Sloane observes, Wilson found his voice in the *Art.* His prose speaks to the reader, and he often teaches by delighting, as when he parodies pretentious diction in his famous "inkhorn letter," purportedly written by a Lincolnshire man requesting a benefice:

There is a sacerdotal dignity in my native country, contiguate to me, where I now contemplate, which your worshipful benignity could soon impetrate for me, if it would like you to extend your schedules and collaud me in them to the right honorable Lord Chancellor, or rather Archigrammation of England. You know my literature, you know the pastoral promotion, I obtestate your clemency to invigilate thus much for me, according to my confidence, and as you know my condign merits, for such a compendious living. But now I relinquish to fatigate your intelligence with any more frivolous verbosity.

If Wilson intended to revise his rhetoric, he had no opportunity to do so before 1560. Edward VI died on 6 July 1553. Wilson's patrons, the Brandons, Greys, and Dudleys, his publisher, Grafton, and some of his Cambridge circle were involved in rebellions against the accession of Mary I, a Catholic, and her marriage to her Hapsburg cousin, Philip II of Spain. Wilson joined the Marian exiles, settling in Padua by 1555 to study law at its famous university and read Demosthenes with Cheke. When he returned to England in 1560, he added some jests to the section on humor and gave the "inkhorn letter" an introduction and conclusion; but in a new prologue he bitterly refused to revise more thoroughly a work for which he had been imprisoned and tortured during the Papal Inquisition.

The Protestant doctrine and diatribe in Wilson's textbooks were enough to indict him in the Rome of Pope Paul IV, but they were probably the excuse, rather than the reason, for his arrest. The English community in Padua, within the Venetian Republic, intrigued against Mary and Philip. Venice and Ferrara were two anti-Hapsburg states in an Italy largely controlled by that dynasty. Wilson gave the funeral oration in September 1556 for Edward Courtenay, Earl of Devon, a cousin of the Tudors who had conspired to usurp the English throne. By 17 November 1557 Wilson was in Rome as solicitor in a divorce case. The English ambassador, Sir Edward Carne, watched his movements suspiciously and finally delivered to him a royal summons of 17 March 1558 to appear before the Privy Council in England. When Wilson ignored the summons, Carne arranged his trial for heresy. Wilson escaped prison during riots against the Inquisition following the death of Paul IV in August 1559 and made his way to Ferrara. After receiving his degree there on 29 November 1559, he returned to England as doctor of civil law in 1560.

Wilson thrived during the reign of Elizabeth I. Although appointed master of the College of Stoke-by-Clare in 1560, he was soon practicing law in the Court of Arches and the Court of Requests. He was named master of Saint Katharine's Hospital near the Tower of London on 7 November 1561 and took up lodgings there. Wilson served in the Parliaments of 1563, 1571, and 1572 and on several foreign embassies, most notably to Portugal and the Netherlands. In 1571 he had the distasteful duty of interrogating Catholic rebels supporting the claim to the English throne of Mary, Queen of Scots. In 1577 he became a privy councillor and shared with Sir Francis Walsingham the office of principal secretary. Sometime after his return to England in 1560, he married a widow, Agnes Brook, sister of naval officer Sir William Winter. They had three children by 1565: a son, Nicholas, and two daughters, Mary and Lucrece. Agnes died in June 1574. Two years later Wilson married another widow, Jane Pinchon, daughter of Richard Empson of London. After her death in 1577 he settled with his children at Edmonton, Middlesex. In 1579, although a layman, he was awarded a benefice, dean of Durham Cathedral. He died on 20 May 1581, leaving a substantial estate. He had requested burial "without charge or pomp" at Saint Katherine's by the Tower.

Wilson's later works were a product of his political career. Threats to Elizabeth's rule occasioned his 1570 translation into English of seven orations of Demosthenes, the three *Olynthiacs* and the four *Philippics,* in which the Greek orator urges Athens to take action against the aggression of Philip of Macedonia. The title page bills them as "most needful to be read in these dangerous days, of all them that love their country's liberty and desire to take warning for their better avail by example of others." Wilson implies an analogy with Philip II of Spain, whose ambassador had encouraged a 1569 rebellion in England against Elizabeth. In 1570 the pope's excommunication of Elizabeth offered English Catholics a new incentive to rebel. Wilson dedicated his translation of Demosthenes to the cautious Sir William Cecil, Elizabeth's principal secretary. The work nevertheless serves humanist as well as political ends. The dedication pays tribute to Wilson's teacher, Cheke. Wilson supplies a biography of Demosthenes, arguments of the orations, and other editorial apparatus. His preface to the reader echoes the doctrine of classical imitation proclaimed in Roger Ascham's *Schoolmaster* (1570) but celebrates Demosthenes as an even better model than Cicero.

A Discourse upon Usury (1572) grew out of his experiences as a lawyer, parliamentarian, and diplomat in commercial negotiations. His stand against interest on loans is unattractive to the modern reader, but Tudor gentlemen such as Wilson, not understanding the nascent capitalism of their own time, looked with nostalgia to an age when land, not lucre, was the source of wealth and status. More-

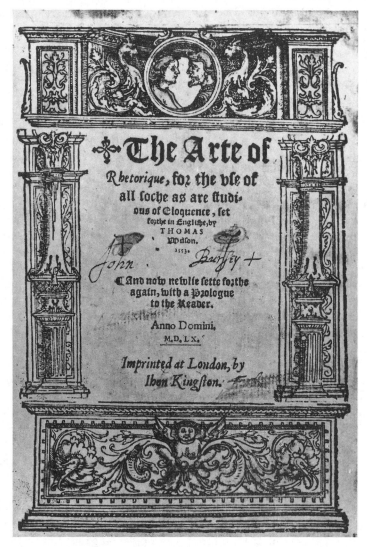

Title page for the enlarged edition (1560) of Wilson's textbook on rhetoric

over, usury was forbidden by Scripture and canon law, and Wilson believed firmly in a theocracy. He began a manuscript treatise of 2 April 1578 on the perils facing England with the principle that a government should "seek first and principally the glory of God and his righteousness to be faithfully settled everywhere." His dedication of *A Discourse upon Usury* to Robert Dudley, Earl of Leicester, dated 20 July 1569, calls for the execution of all usurers in England. Apparently he was not satisfied with the severity of the statute of 1552 under which taking any interest on loans might be punished by forfeiture of the principal and interest, imprisonment, and fine, even though that law had proved itself impossibly restrictive on English commerce. When in 1571 Parliament considered repealing the statute of 1552 and allowing interest of 10 percent, Wilson

spoke in opposition, drawing on his extensive research for the *Discourse,* but to no avail.

In spite of Wilson's stern conservatism, the *Discourse* is a lively dialogue debating all sides of the issue. The speakers are a merchant (Gromelgayner), his adolescent kinsman and apprentice, and his guests at a sumptuous dinner: a preacher (Ockerfoe), a temporal lawyer, and a civil lawyer. All but the apprentice defend their views in orations. While the characters are types, each has a style and personality reflecting his level of education and profession. Wilson's spokesmen are the learned and long-winded preacher and civil lawyer. Nevertheless, their opponents, the temporal lawyer and the merchant, are given such a fair hearing that their capitulation at the end is startling. Literary historians have only begun to study this dialogue, although C. S. Lewis considered it Wilson's best work and "the best preparation for seeing the *Merchant of Venice*."

The common threads running through Wilson's life and works are Protestant conviction and civic humanism. Like other members of the Cambridge circle, he devoted both his academic and political labors to the reform of church and state. Wilson did not write literature for its own sake; but, in his effort to reach a wide audience, he developed an English style both charming and flexible. He thus taught the arts of discourse in English not only by precept but by practice.

References:

E. J. Baskerville, "Thomas Wilson and Sir Thomas Smith at Cambridge," *Notes & Queries,* 27 (April 1980): 113–116;

Hardin Craig, "Shakespeare and Wilson's *Arte of Rhetorique:* An Inquiry into the Criteria for Determining Sources," *Studies in Philology,* 28 (October 1931): 618–630;

George J. Engelhardt, "The Relation of Sherry's *Treatise of Schemes and Tropes* to Wilson's *Arte of Rhetorique*," *PMLA,* 62 (March 1947): 76–82;

P. W. Hasler, ed., *The History of Parliament: The House of Commons, 1558–1603,* volumes 1 and 3 (London: Her Majesty's Stationery Office for The History of Parliament Trust, 1981), I: 102–110, III: 629–631;

Wilbur Samuel Howell, *Logic and Rhetoric in England, 1500–1700* (Princeton: Princeton University Press, 1956);

Catherine Jamison, *The History of the Royal Hospital of St. Katharine by the Tower of London* (London: Oxford University Press, 1952), pp. 69–79;

C. S. Lewis, *English Literature in the Sixteenth Century, Excluding Drama* (New York & Oxford: Oxford University Press, 1954), pp. 290–292;

A. W. Reed, "Nicholas Udall and Thomas Wilson," *Review of English Studies,* 1 (July 1925): 275–283;

Albert J. Schmidt, "A Household Inventory, 1581," *Proceedings of the American Philosophical Society,* 101 (1957): 459–480;

Schmidt, "A Humanist Prescribes and Describes: Thomas Wilson and Medicine," *Bulletin of the History of Medicine,* 34, no. 5 (1960): 414–418;

Schmidt, "Some Notes on Dr. Thomas Wilson and His Lincolnshire Connections," *Lincolnshire Historian,* 2, no. 4 (1957): 14–24;

Schmidt, "Thomas Wilson and the Tudor Commonwealth: An Essay in Civic Humanism," *Huntington Library Quarterly,* 23 (November 1959): 49–60;

Schmidt, "Thomas Wilson, Tudor Scholar-Statesman," *Huntington Library Quarterly,* 20 (1957): 205–218;

Schmidt, "A Treatise on England's Perils," *Archiv für Reformationsgeschichte,* 46 (1955): 243–249;

Thomas O. Sloane, *Donne, Milton, and the End of Humanist Rhetoric* (Berkeley: University of California Press, 1985), pp. 130–137;

Russell H. Wagner, "Thomas Wilson's Speech against Usury," *Quarterly Journal of Speech,* 38 (February 1952): 13–22;

Wagner, "Wilson and His Sources," *Quarterly Journal of Speech,* 15 (November 1929): 525–537;

Mark E. Wildermuth, "The Rhetoric of Wilson's *Arte:* Reclaiming the Classical Heritage for English Protestants," *Philosophy & Rhetoric,* 22, no. 1 (1989): 43–58.

Papers:

Wilson's unpublished letters and papers are in the Public Record Office and the British Library in London, and Cambridge University Library.

Sir Thomas Wyatt

(circa 1503 – 11 October 1542)

Ellen C. Caldwell
Clarkson University

BOOK: *The court of Venus. With the Pilgrim's Tale. In verse* (London: Printed by Thomas Gybson, 1538?) – first fragment of *The Court of Venus*; second fragment subtitled *A Boke of Balettes* (London: Printed by William Copland?, 1549?); third fragment titled *The courte of Venus. Newly and diligently corrected with many proper ballades newly amended, and also added therunto which haue not before bene imprinted* (London: Printed by Thomas Marshe, 1563?).

Editions and Collections: Henry Howard, Earl of Surrey, *Songes and sonettes,* edited by Richard Tottel (London: Printed by Richard Tottel, 1557);

Thomas Procter, *A gorgious gallery, of gallant inuentions,* compiled by Thomas Procter and Owen Roydon (London: Printed by William How for Richard Jones, 1578);

Nugae Antiquae: Being a Miscellaneous Collection of Original Papers in Prose and Verse . . . by Sir John Harington, 3 volumes (London: J. Dodsley & T. Shrimpton, 1769–1775, 1779, 1792); revised edition, 2 volumes, edited by Thomas Park (London: Printed by J. Wright for Vernor & Hood and Cuthell & Martin, 1804; New York: AMS, 1966);

The Poems of Sir Thomas Wyat and of Uncertain Authors, in *The Works of the English Poets,* volume 2, edited by Alexander Chalmers (London: J. Johnson, 1810; New York: Johnson Reprint, 1970–1971);

The Works of Henry Howard, Earl of Surrey, and of Sir Thomas Wyatt the Elder, volume 2, edited by George F. Nott (London: Longman, Hurst, Rees, Orme & Brown, 1816; New York: AMS, 1965);

The Poetical Works of Sir Thomas Wyatt, edited by Robert Bell (London: John W. Parker & Sons, 1854);

The Poems of Sir Thomas Wiat, 2 volumes, edited by Agnes K. Foxwell (London: University of

London Press, 1913; New York: Russell & Russell, 1964);

A Gorgeous Gallery of Gallant Inventions, edited by Hyder Edward Rollins (Cambridge, Mass.: Harvard University Press, 1926; New York: Russell & Russell, 1971);

Tottel's Miscellany (1557–1587), 2 volumes, edited by Rollins (Cambridge, Mass.: Harvard University Press, 1928–1929; revised edition, 1965);

The Poetry of Sir Thomas Wyatt: A Selection and a Study, edited by E. M. W. Tillyard (London: Scholartis, 1929; revised edition, London: Chatto & Windus, 1949);

" 'A Boke of Ballets' and 'The Courte of Venus,' " edited by Reginald H. Griffith and Robert A. Law, *University of Texas Studies in English,* 10 (1930): 1–12;

Plutarch's "Quyete of Mynde" Translated by Thomas Wyat, Reproduced in Facsimile from the Copy in the Henry E. Huntington Library, introduction by Charles Read Baskervill (Cambridge, Mass.: Harvard University Press, 1931);

Collected Poems of Sir Thomas Wyatt, edited by Kenneth Muir (London: Routledge & Kegan Paul, 1949; Cambridge, Mass.: Harvard University Press, 1950);

The Court of Venus, edited by Russell A. Fraser (Durham, N.C.: Duke University Press, 1955);

The Arundel Harington Manuscript of Tudor Poetry, 2 volumes, edited by Ruth Hughey (Columbus: Ohio State University Press, 1960);

Sir Thomas Wyatt and His Circle, Unpublished Poems Edited from the Blage Manuscript, edited by Muir (Liverpool: Liverpool University Press, 1961);

Songes and Sonettes, edited and compiled by Richard Tottel, facsimile edition (Leeds: Scolar Press, 1966);

Collected Poems of Sir Thomas Wyatt, edited by Muir and Patricia Thomson (Liverpool: Liverpool University Press, 1969);

A Gorgeous Gallery of Gallant Inventions, facsimile edition (Menston: Scolar Press, 1972);

Sir Thomas Wyatt (Collection of Her Majesty the Queen)

Sir Thomas Wyatt: Collected Poems, edited by Joost Daalder (London: Oxford University Press, 1975);

The Canon of Sir Thomas Wyatt's Poetry, by Richard Harrier (Cambridge, Mass.: Harvard University Press, 1975) — includes a transcript of the Egerton manuscript;

Sir Thomas Wyatt: The Complete Poems, edited by Ronald A. Rebholz (London: Penguin, 1978; New Haven: Yale University Press, 1981);

Sir Thomas Wyatt: A Literary Portrait. Selected Poems, with Full Notes, Commentaries, and a Critical Introduction, edited by H. A. Mason (Bristol: Bristol Classical Press, 1986).

TRANSLATIONS: Plutarch, *Tho. wyatis translatyon of Plutarckes boke, of the quyete of mynde* (London: Printed by Richard Pynson, 1528);

Certayne psalmes chosen out of the psalter of Dauid, called thee. vii. penytentiall psalmes, drawen into englyshe meter by sir T. Wyat (London: Printed by Thomas Raynald for John Harryngton, 1549).

No poet represents the complexities of the court of Henry VIII better than Sir Thomas Wyatt. Skilled in international diplomacy, imprisoned without charges, at ease jousting in tournaments, and adept at writing courtly poetry, Wyatt was admired and envied by his contemporaries. The distinction between his public and private life was not always clearly marked, for he spent his life at various courts, where he wrote for a predominantly aristocratic audience who shared common interests. Through and in this milieu he created a new English poetics by experimenting with meter and voice and by grafting Continental and classical forms and ideas to English traditions. Wyatt wrote the first English sonnets and true satires, projecting through them the most important political issues of the period: the Protestant Reformation and the centralization of state power under the reigns of the Tudors. For this combination of formalistic innovation and historical reflection, he is today considered the most important poet of the first half of the sixteenth century. Living and writing dangerously in an era of national and international, religious and secular transformations, Wyatt was the Henrician Renaissance man, and his poetry was the soul of his age.

Wyatt's position, attitudes, character, and fortunes were formed at the courts of the first two Tudor monarchs. One of the most important issues in scholarship on Wyatt remains the relationship between his poetry and his life as a Henrician courtier. With its extensive reproduction of primary sources, the best biography of Wyatt is still Kenneth Muir's *Life and Letters of Sir Thomas Wyatt* (1963). All letters and documents are quoted from this edition, while all poetry is cited from *Sir Thomas Wyatt: The Complete Poems* (1978).

Born around 1503 at Allington Castle in Kent, Thomas was the son of Sir Henry Wyatt of Yorkshire and Anne Skinner Wyatt of Surrey. Imprisoned more than once by Richard III, Sir Henry had become under Henry VII a powerful, wealthy privy councillor, and he remained so after Henry VIII's accession. In 1516 his son Thomas served as an honorary attendant at Princess Mary's christening. John Leland writes that Thomas attended Cambridge, and although there is no record to confirm the statement, it seems plausible that he did. It is often assumed that in 1516 he entered Saint John's College, Cambridge, but his name may have been confused with another Wyatt matriculating there. After marriage to Elizabeth Brooke, daughter of Thomas, Lord Cobham, in 1520 and the birth of a son in 1521, Wyatt progressed in his career at court, as esquire of the king's body and clerk of the king's jewels (1524). He probably acquired these posts through a combination of innate abilities and his father's influence. Stephen Miriam Foley suggests in *Sir Thomas Wyatt* (1990) that the positions were more significant than their titles might imply, for they helped to entrench him in the king's household. Members of that household sought power, struggling with the king's councillors to influence the king.

Sometime after the birth of his son, perhaps around 1525, Wyatt seems to have become estranged from his wife; all editors and biographers assume the reason to be her infidelity, for such were the rumors during his life. The *Spanish Calendar,* for instance, gives this detail: "Wyatt had cast [his wife] away on account of adultery." It is certain that in 1526, when Sir Thomas Cheney embarked for the French court on an official delegation, Wyatt accompanied him. There he may have met Clément Marot, whose poetry influenced his own work and whose epigram "Frere Thibault" is copied into the Egerton manuscript of Wyatt's poetry. In 1527 Wyatt asked for and was granted permission to attend Sir John Russell on his legation to Rome. On this journey he became acquainted with Continental political affairs and the methods of persuasive diplomacy, for when Russell was injured, Wyatt accomplished one part of the mission alone. He was briefly imprisoned by Spanish imperial forces, but he and Russell left Rome shortly before it was taken by the emperor's army.

Around 1527 Queen Catherine of Aragon, first wife of Henry VIII, asked Wyatt to translate Petrarch's *De remediis utriusque fortunae.* Wyatt translated in its place a piece he found less tedious, Guillaume Budé's Latin version of Plutarch's *De tranquillitate et securitate animi.* It was soon published by Richard Pynson as *The Quiet of Mind* (1528), and as several scholars have pointed out, the echoes of "quiet mind" in Wyatt's poetry indicate that the piece continued to hold philosophical importance for him. From around 1528 or 1529 to November 1530, Wyatt held the post of high marshal of Calais, and in 1532 he became commissioner of the peace in Essex. From this time forward he was under the patronage of Thomas Cromwell, Henry VIII's secretary and adviser on religious matters, one of the most powerful men in the kingdom. In 1533 Wyatt served for his father at the coronation of Anne Boleyn. Although in 1534 he was imprisoned in the Fleet for what was recorded as his involvement in a "great affray" in which a sergeant of London was slain, his rapid success as a courtier dates from this period. Also in 1534 he was given "command of all men able for war in the seven hundreds" and in various parishes of the county of Kent, and license "to have twenty men in his livery." He is thought to have been knighted in 1535. Around 1536 Wyatt formed an attachment to Elizabeth Darrell, who became his mistress for life. Some of his poems, such as "A face that should content me wondrous well" and "So feeble is the thread," almost surely allude to this relationship.

The woman with whom Wyatt has been notoriously associated, however, is Anne Boleyn, second queen of Henry VIII. Careful scholars acknowledge that although Wyatt's poetry is suggestive, the hard evidence for his role as Boleyn's lover, or scorned lover, is so bedeviled by legend and rumor as to affect even the most cautious statements. One poem long considered to allude to Boleyn is the riddle "What word is that that changeth not" (no. 54), for its solution (*anna*) is penned above the poem in the Egerton manuscript (though not in Wyatt's or the scribe's hand and, it seems, after the poem was copied there.) The third line of the poem puns on the solution: "It is mine answer" (*mine Anne, sir*). There is nothing, however, to indicate that the poem is about any specific Anne. Although anecdotes have circulated of the rivalry between Wyatt and Henry, it is very difficult and perhaps even impossible to gauge the extent of Wyatt's relationship with Boleyn, especially when Henry decided to divorce Catherine and marry her. Henry's doing so resulted in the Act of Supremacy (1534), whereby he broke from the hegemony of the pope and the Catholic church and proclaimed himself head of the church in England. This move had severe domestic and international consequences, in which Wyatt was implicated.

Although it has been widely debated, a poem historically thought to indicate Wyatt's loss of Boleyn to Henry is the sonnet "Whoso list to hunt, I know where is an hind" (no. 11). Wyatt altered the original poem, Petrarch's *Rime* 190, "Una candida cerva sopra l'erba," to center on the "chase," a courtly sport that provides an apt metaphor for the pursuit of love and power at Henry's court, as several scholars have acknowledged. In Wyatt's sonnet the speaker advises other suitors that they may pursue the hind/lady as vainly as he has and give her up with as much difficulty. The poem concludes that the chase should be given over, for the motto on the hind's collar suggests that although she has been claimed by someone more powerful than they, she will not be constrained by anyone:

> And graven with diamonds in letters plain
> There is written her fair neck round about:
> '*Noli me tangere* for Caesar's I am,
> And wild for to hold though I seem tame.'

Julius Caesar's deer are reported to have worn this motto on their collars. Wyatt's decision to retain the term *Caesar* from the Italian poem does suggest that the speaker or poet alludes to a royal master with powerful edicts, such as Henry VIII. Although the hind/lady might topically designate any one of several women, it could appropriately refer to Boleyn. To describe a lady of the court as an object of prey, bound by words or laws to a ruler absolute in name if not in reality, is to flatter neither the lady,

who is seen to be promiscuous or at least willful, nor "Caesar," who is seen to be unsuccessful in his attempt to "own" her with his inscription. In another sonnet also thought to refer to Boleyn in her role as court star, reformer, and the catalyst behind Henry's divorce, "If waker care, if sudden pale color" (no. 28), the speaker claims he has replaced his former love with another. The poem is found in the Egerton manuscript, where the line "Her that did set our country in a roar," so suggestive of Boleyn, has been revised, in Wyatt's hand, to "Brunet that set my wealth in such a roar."

The execution of Boleyn and her alleged lovers is one of the more sordid episodes of Henry's turbulent reign and has attracted a great deal of prurient interest. The episode does, however, indicate the violence attendant upon the very structure of dynastic succession and illustrates the instability of fortunes in a Renaissance court. Readers should consult the most reliable biographies and remember that theories about Wyatt's attachment to Boleyn involve the consideration not only of his life but also of the very densely recorded lives of Henry VIII and Boleyn. In 1536 Wyatt was arrested a few days after the arrests of Anne and five men alleged to have been her lovers. Most speculations about his relationship with Anne center on his arrest and imprisonment at this time. Muir gives three independent, sixteenth-century accounts, all of uncertain authority, which claim that before Henry married Boleyn, Wyatt told either Henry or his Council that she was not fit to become queen because she had been Wyatt's lover; but Muir adds that these anecdotes could have been devised to explain why Wyatt was not executed with the five men accused of adultery. Whatever the actions of Anne may have been, after she gave birth to Princess Elizabeth and then miscarried a second child, she lost Henry's favor; desperate for a male heir, he had already begun to look for her replacement. Cromwell is said to have instigated a plot to remove her by accusing her of adultery and therefore treason. A court musician, Mark Smeaton, was tortured and produced the names of four other men, some of them Wyatt's friends. Anne's brother, Thomas Boleyn, Viscount Rochford, was charged with incest, and Henry himself claimed that "more than a hundred had to do with her." There were no official charges against Wyatt, who in 1541 declared that his court enemy, Charles Brandon, Duke of Suffolk, was responsible: "My Lord of Suffolk himself can tell that I imputed it to him, and not only at the beginning but even the very night before my apprehension now last." A letter of petition from Wyatt's father to Cromwell does not reveal the nature of the charges beyond "the displeasure that [Wyatt] hath done to god otherwise."

One poem that seems to date from this period of imprisonment (no. 123) is headed *V. Innocentia / Veritas Viat Fides / Circumdederunt me inimici mei.* If one accepts that *Viat* indicates Wyatt, then the heading reads, "Innocence, Truth, Wyatt, Faith; my enemies have surrounded me." Editors have suggested that innocence, truth, and faith "surround" Wyatt's name in contradistinction to his enemies. The speaker asks that anyone "Who list his wealth and ease retain" should strive to live a private life, for there is danger, or "thunder," around seats of power. The refrain of the poem is *circa Regna tonat,* a phrase from Seneca's *Phaedra,* in which Jupiter "thunders about thrones." The opening line of the third stanza, "These bloody days have broken my heart," may refer to the fall of Anne and her courtiers. Even more powerful is the image Wyatt paints of the speaker in his cell, witnessing through its window grating what may have been Anne's execution:

> The bell tower showed me such sight
> That in my head sticks day and night.
> There did I learn out of a grate,
> For all favor, glory, or might,
> That yet *circa Regna tonat.*

In the last stanza the speaker learns that the wit to plead one's case or one's innocence is not always useful. This poem does not apologize for the speaker's conduct or his situation or the system in which he must live; rather, it vividly demonstrates the well-known fact that proximity to the king could be fatal. An elegy for Anne's putative lovers, "In mourning wise since daily I increase" (no. 197) is also dated to this period. The poem devotes a stanza to each man executed, naming him (Lord Rochford, Sir Henry Norris, Sir Francis Weston, Sir William Brereton, and Smeaton), acknowledging his guilt, yet mourning his death. This poem, which appears in one manuscript only, has not always been attributed to Wyatt.

After the executions of Anne and her alleged lovers, Wyatt was soon restored to favor, made sheriff of Kent, and asked to muster men and to attend on Henry VIII. In November 1536 his father died, and in 1537 he once again undertook a diplomatic mission, this time as ambassador to the court of Emperor Charles V. On his journey Wyatt wrote to his son, advising him to emulate the exemplary life of Sir Henry Wyatt rather than Wyatt's own: "And of myself I may be a near example unto you of my folly and unthriftness that hath as I well deserved brought me into a thousand dangers and hazards, enmities, hatreds, prisonments, despites, and indignations." He further admonished his son to "make God and goodness" his "foundations." An epigram in Wyatt's hand in the Egerton manuscript, "Of Carthage he, that worthy warrior," ends with a reference to Spain: "At Monzòn thus I restless rest in Spain" (no. 46). Henry VIII wished to prevent Charles V from forming what would amount to a Catholic alliance with Francis I and thus to prevent a concerted attack on England. Wyatt returned home in mid 1538; but when Charles and Francis, without Henry, reached a separate accord at Nice, the danger of an attack against England grew more grave. Wyatt's poem in ottava rima, "Tagus, farewell" (no. 60), probably dates from this period. With this poem, as with the letter to his son, scholars have tried to establish Wyatt's character. Despite his sufferings and despite his criticisms of the king and his court, he was a loyal servant to Henry VIII. In the last lines the speaker looks forward to returning to London: "My king, my country, alone for whom I live, / Of mighty love the wings for this me give."

Once more ambassador to the emperor in 1539, Wyatt was to watch his movements through France and to ascertain his intentions regarding England. But by mid 1540, after Henry VIII's marriage to Anne of Cleves threatened to create a Protestant league, and in the event of growing distrust between Charles and Francis, the danger of an attack against England was no longer imminent, so Wyatt returned home. On 28 July his patron, Cromwell, was executed. Historians attribute Cromwell's fall in part to factional resistance to his foreign and religious policies and in part to Henry's severe dislike of Anne of Cleves. He had married her sight unseen and claimed that descriptions of her beauty were untrue (historian John Guy notes that he called her "the Flanders mare"). An account found in the Spanish chronicle claims that at the execution Cromwell asked Wyatt to pray for him but that Wyatt was so overcome by tears he could not speak. It is thought that the sonnet Richard Tottel entitles "The lover laments the death of his love" refers instead to Wyatt's loss of his friend and patron, for it imitates Petrarch's *Rime* 269, "Rotta è l'alta colonna e 'l verde lauro," an elegy on the occasion of his patron's death, as well as the death of Laura. Wyatt's poem (no. 29) begins:

> The pillar perished is whereto I leant,
> The strongest stay of mine unquiet mind;
> The like of it no man again can find —
> From east to west still seeking though he went.

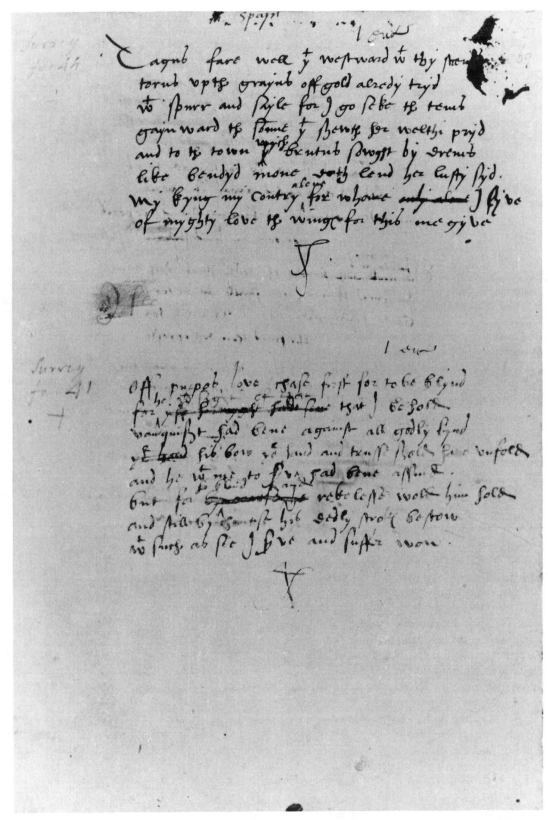

Drafts for two poems that Wyatt wrote shortly before his return to England in June 1539 from a two-year diplomatic mission in Spain (British Library, Egerton MS. 2711)

The "pillar" could easily designate Cromwell. The reference to an "unquiet mind" echoes Wyatt's translation of Plutarch and suggests an attempt to find some sort of relief from the uncertainties of life under Henry VIII. Cromwell's papers were investigated after his execution, and in 1541 Wyatt was arrested and imprisoned on the weight of old allegations that he had met with the traitor Reginald Pole and had otherwise misrepresented the king's interests. Wyatt had been cleared of those charges in 1538, but Cromwell's death left him open to further attack from his court enemies.

A poem addressed to Sir Francis Brian (no. 62) has traditionally been dated to this last period of incarceration:

Sighs are my food, drink are my tears;
Clinking of fetters such music would crave.
Stink and close air away my life wears.
Innocency is all the hope I have.

Besides its graphic depiction of the speaker's suffering and humiliation – "this wound shall heal again / But yet, alas, the scar shall still remain" – this poem echoes "Who list his wealth and ease retain" in its claim of the speaker's innocence. Wyatt had in 1536 suffered imprisonment in the Tower and, if scholarly dating is correct, had written of it. "Sighs are my food," though shorter, is more bitter in tone than the earlier poem. When commanded to answer in writing the accusations against him, Wyatt provided a declaration of his innocence. He insisted that "for my part I declare affirmingly, at all proofs whereby a Christian man may be tried, that in my life in crime toward the Majesty of the King my master or any his issue, in deed, word, writing or wish I never offended, I never committed malice or offense, or (as I have presently said before you) done thing wherein my thought could accuse my conscience." He then prepared a lengthy, sharply worded defense of his actions, turning the case against his accusers. At its end he declares: "Thus much I thought to say unto you afore both God and man to discharge me, that I seem not to perish in my own fault, for lack of declaring my truth; and afore God and all these men I charge you with my innocent truth that in case, as God defend, you be guilty of mine innocent blood, that you before his tribunal shall be inexcusable." No evidence of a trial survives; but the Privy Council later mentioned Wyatt's confession and pardon, both of which may have been wrought from this defense. At the time, the pardon was believed to have been urged by Queen Catherine Howard and to have rested on the removal of Elizabeth Darrell and the reinstatement

of Wyatt's wife. In 1541 Wyatt made his will, providing for Darrell and their son, Francis, and for his legitimate son, Thomas. There are indications that Wyatt was restored to favor, for later in 1541 he received some of the awards of Thomas Culpepper, who was charged with adultery with Queen Catherine Howard, and made an advantageous exchange of property with Henry VIII. Early in 1542 Wyatt was probably member of Parliament for Kent, and it is possible that he was to be made vice admiral of a fleet. On 11 October 1542, on his way to Falmouth to meet and escort to London the Spanish envoy, he died of a fever at the home of Sir John Horsey at Sherborne in Dorset.

It is clear, then, that although the records of Wyatt's life are not always reliable, they are numerous. Besides details in official records, in foreign chronicles, letters, and memoirs, there are letters in his hand, which help to establish his own concerns as a courtier and the demands placed on him by others. His letters to Cromwell and the king reveal a command of detail and dialogue as well as a sensitivity to delicate national and international issues. The two letters to his son have long been used to establish Wyatt's forthright character. His defense in 1541 demonstrates his acuity and his ability to outmaneuver his enemies. For Wyatt's poetry perhaps the most salient features of his life are his worldliness and his wavering fortunes as a courtier. Despite his imprisonments, which must surely have made him aware of the precariousness of his position, Wyatt remained a courtier and accepted diplomatic missions. Those years as ambassador must also have made him aware that diplomacy is a game of negotiation and refusal, that international alliances are quickly and of necessity broken with the changing expectations of new governments and the shifting needs of the state or the monarch. Wyatt's courtly poetry, then, transcribes, whether explicitly or obliquely, his life as a courtier.

Every aspect of Wyatt's poetry has been widely debated: the canon, the texts, the prosody, the occasion, the personae or voices, the significance of French and Italian influences, and the representation of court life. Wyatt's poems circulated widely among various members of Henry's court, and some may first have been published in a miscellany or verse anthology, *The Court of Venus,* of which three fragments survive. They were edited in 1955 by Russell A. Fraser, who dates the first fragment (Douce) to 1535–1539, the second (Stark) to 1547–1549, and the third (Folger) to 1561–1564, the subtitle of the Stark fragment running *A Book of Ballets.* Five of the poems in these fragments are Wyatt's, and others are thought to be his as well. The Douce fragment is, in fact, the earliest known printed miscellany in England. By far the most important of the miscellanies, however, is that compiled and edited in 1557 by Tottel: *Songs and Sonnets,* better known as *Tottel's Miscellany.* This collection of various verse forms and types, from the sonnet to satire, went through at least nine editions in thirty years. Intended to honor and represent "English eloquence," it is arranged by author, Wyatt being the best represented. Tottel or his editors exercised a great deal of license in altering Wyatt's poetry, omitting lines, rearranging the poems to resemble sonnets, regularizing the meter, smoothing out the irony, and giving them titles that prescribe their meanings. This collection includes about one-third of Wyatt's canon, concentrating on his lyrics and his adaptations from Italian sources, such as Petrarch and Serafino d'Aquilano. It is clear that Tottel thought this collection to represent the best of the courtly tradition and the best of Continental imitations, and although it is uneven in quality, it remains one of the most important publications of the sixteenth century.

Since Tottel's 1557 *Miscellany,* Wyatt's name has been coupled with that of a younger poet, another translator of Petrarch: Henry Howard, Earl of Surrey. The work of both poets is presented by Tottel, but Wyatt's metrical forms, rugged and experimental in the manuscripts, have been regularized into more-fluid and more-recognizably iambic-pentameter lines. Through George F. Nott's edition (1816) of the poems from manuscripts, it became apparent that Tottel had altered the poems, and Wyatt's prosody began to be studied independently of Surrey's. Wyatt both experiments with metrical forms and writes poems in various recognizable meters, but there is much disagreement over his facility in writing iambic pentameter. One view is that in his difficult lines the four-stress pull of the Anglo-Saxon line competes with pentameter. A common opinion in the twentieth century, however, is that although these lines are basically iambic pentameter, the language wrenches the meter to produce a more forceful and expressive line. For three centuries Surrey was generally considered the more aristocratic, harmonious, and therefore superior poet; but in recent times Wyatt has been judged the more individualistic, original, and complex of the two.

Despite the significance of *Tottel's Miscellany* as an influential text for later poets of the sixteenth century, any serious discussion of Wyatt's poetry must be grounded in his work as it is preserved in various manuscripts. The primary manuscript, British Library Egerton 2711, has been treated almost as if it were an "edition" of the poems, for it was certainly Wyatt's own book and contains poems in several hands, including his own, as can be ascertained from his autograph letters. It also contains poems with corrections and alterations (some in his hand) and some poems ascribed to him by the markers "Tho" or "Wyat." Several theories have been advanced to account for the chronology of the poems in this manuscript, but no firm conclusions have been reached. The poems need not have been copied in the order they were composed, and although a few can be dated, most editors do not think that poems following those datable were necessarily composed after them. One glance at the Egerton manuscript reveals some of the obstacles in deciding the texts of the poems: they are written in several hands and different inks, and the manuscript is scribbled over, having served its later owners as a commonplace book and calculation sheet. Peter Beal (1980) states that Egerton features copies of 107 poems by Wyatt, his paraphrase of the Penitential Psalms, two letters to his son (not in his hand), and three other poems that are not his. The first poem in the manuscript, "Behold, Love, thy power how she despiseth," imitates a poem by Petrarch. The poems in Wyatt's handwriting include "Of Carthage he, that worthy warrior," "Tagus, farewell," and "What rage is this?" Some of Wyatt's better-known poems in this manuscript, although not in his hand, are "The long love that in my thought doth harbor," "Whoso list to hunt, I know where is an hind," "Farewell, Love, and all thy laws forever," "I find no peace and all my war is done," "My galley charged with forgetfulness," "They flee from me that sometime did me seek," "My mother's maids," and "A spending hand."

While Egerton is acknowledged to be the primary manuscript of Wyatt's poetry, the significance of the Blage, Devonshire, and Arundel Harington manuscripts, to mention only the major ones, in determining Wyatt's canon is contested. The 1969 Muir-Thomson edition of the poems may have conflated the canon by including doubtful poems from these manuscripts. The Blage manuscript, compiled during the 1530s and 1540s and once owned by Wyatt's close friend Sir George Blage, is a collection of various types of poems, eighty-five of which have been attributed to Wyatt. It circulated among members of the court and, according to Ronald A. Rebholz, presents "versions" of poems earlier than those in Egerton. He claims the same dating for the Devonshire manuscript, also a verse collection, which circulated especially among members of the

Howard family and which contains the largest collection of Wyatt's love lyrics. The poems in Devonshire, 122 of which have been attributed to Wyatt, are written in the hands of Margaret Howard, Mary Fitzroy (Surrey's sister), and Mary Shelton. The Arundel Harington manuscript, yet another verse miscellany, was written by or for John Harington and is generally considered later than the Egerton. It contains the Penitential Psalms plus fifty-five other poems that have been attributed to Wyatt.

Although the canon is to this day disputed, it has in the past generally been decided with the following logic and hierarchy, according to Rebholz: certainly canonical are those Egerton poems in Wyatt's hand; those Egerton poems in the hand of a scribe but corrected in Wyatt's hand; those Egerton poems in various hands but designated "Tho." or "Tho"; those Egerton poems in various hands but designated "Wyat"; and those ninety-seven poems attributed to Wyatt by Tottel, fifteen without manuscript sources. Less certainly canonical are those poems found in Blage, Devonshire, or Arundel Harington, among poems known to be Wyatt's or ascribed to him. The extent of the controversy over canonical and textual problems is best illustrated by the fact that since 1969 four independent editions of the poems and one book-length critique of one of those editions have been published. While the Muir-Thomson *Collected Poems* (1969), with its lengthy notes and full texts of many original sources, is still considered to be the standard edition, Rebholz's *Complete Poems* (1978) is often cited as standard because of its accuracy in transcription, its modern spelling, and its comprehensive notes. The Oxford edition by Joost Daalder (1975) is also well regarded. H. A. Mason's *Editing Wyatt* (1972) prints tables of errors in transcriptions for the Muir-Thomson edition. Editors of Wyatt differ sharply over editorial principles and the hierarchy of the manuscripts, one of the most serious debates being whether, given various and varied copies, the poems should be transcribed or reconstructed, and on what grounds (for instance, metrical and stylistic) emendation should proceed.

Dating the poetry also raises serious problems. Editors can place a few poems with some degree of accuracy, according either to the dates of their sources or to genuine allusions to topical events. For example, the three epistolary satires were composed after 1532-1533, the publication date of the *Opere Toscane,* by Luigi Alamanni, whose tenth satire provides the source for Wyatt's "Mine own John Poyntz" and, it is thought, the terza-rima form for his three satires and his paraphrases of the Peniten-

tial Psalms. A few poems contain references to Spain, which date them during or after Wyatt's visit there from 1537 to 1539.

In most of his poetry Wyatt worked both with English models, notably Geoffrey Chaucer, and Continental sources. This combination gives his poems their peculiar characteristic of following the conventions of *amour courtois* yet implicitly rejecting those conventions at the same time. His canon falls into two subgenres: courtly poetry and religious poetry. The courtly poetry may be divided, with some difficulty, between the love poems and the satiric poems. The love poetry predominates and includes work in several forms, such as sonnets, epigrams, and what have traditionally been called songs. Many of Wyatt's Petrarchan sources had been set to music by the early sixteenth century, but recent scholars have doubted whether he wrote his poems for musical accompaniment.

Since the publication of Raymond Southall's *The Courtly Maker: An Essay on the Poetry of Wyatt and His Contemporaries* (1964), most scholars have recognized the importance of the "courtly" context for Wyatt's oeuvre. According to Southall, the love complaints, besides being personal expressions of love or pain, may also be stylized verses designed to win the favor of court ladies who could offer political advancement to a courtier. Southall notes that many of Wyatt's poems repeatedly stress the insecurity of a man's fortunes, an attitude consistent with the realities of court life. Others have suggested that love poetry masks the pursuit of power at court, and it now seems clear that Wyatt's metaphors serve a double purpose. This courtly context has been filled in by historicist scholars, who have more thoroughly explored the role-playing, submission to authority, and engaging in intrigue required for success at Henry VIII's court.

In the love lyrics, or "amorous" poetry, the lover complains of lost or unrequited love and begs the beloved for favor or mercy, as in the Egerton poem of four stanzas, corrected in Wyatt's hand (no. 106):

Though I cannot your cruelty constrain
For my goodwill to favor me again,
Though my true and faithful love
Have no power your heart to move,
    Yet rue upon my pain.

The same complaint, with variation and in several verse forms, may be found in many of Wyatt's poems. In the following doubled sonnet (no. 34), the lover's pain of rejection is expressed by his tears, sighs, moans, and, of course, his love poetry:

The flaming sighs that boil within my breast
Sometime break forth and they can well declare
The heart's unrest and how that it doth fare,
The pain thereof, the grief, and all the rest.

The eloquence of these sighs and complaints is counterbalanced by the pain they cause the lover. In much of Wyatt's love poetry, it is characteristic for the lover to protest his loyalty despite all odds against him and, further, despite the beloved's scorn and rejection of his suit, as here (no. 110):

I have sought long with steadfastness
To have had some ease of my great smart
But naught availeth faithfulness
To grave within your stony heart.

Although these courtly love poems lament personal loss or suffering, they take on added meaning read in the light of Southall's claim that such lyrics were often addressed to women of rank who could offer a courtier advancement. Southall notes that the vocabulary of Wyatt's love poetry often includes words that recall the patron/client relationship: *service, desert, suit, hope, reward, promise, fortune, grant* – a vocabulary suggesting that the dependency of the underling parallels the dependency of the lover. In a canzone that again boasts of the lover's steadfastness (no. 78), the refrain claims that the lover will "serve" the beloved, despite his "reward" of cruelty:

Though for goodwill I find but hate
And cruelty my life to waste
And though that still a wretched state
Should pine my days unto the last,
Yet I profess it willingly
To serve and suffer patiently.

This attitude of resignation, though traditional in courtly love poetry, has been seen by many scholars over the centuries as unseemly, and the poems themselves as slight. Read in the context of competition for preferment at court, for offices and awards, or for access to them, the poems reveal the courtier's relative lack of power. In the sonnet "My heart I gave thee, not to do it pain" (no. 14), the language of courtly love is barely distinguishable from the language of aristocratic patronage. The lover admits that he has entered a servant/mistress relationship, in which he expects to be remunerated for faithful service:

I served thee, not to be forsaken,
But that I should be rewarded again.
I was content thy servant to remain
But not to be paid under this fashion.

The speaker is so frustrated by his treatment that he rejects the lady as she has rejected him, acknowledging the hopelessness of receiving any gain for his service to her. In this and other love poems, Wyatt is distinguished by expressing anger over losing what he sees as his due by right and in questioning the codes of courtly love. This anger and contempt find their most sustained outlet in his satires of court life.

One of Wyatt's greatest poetic achievements is his adaptation of the sonnet form into English. Although he has been criticized by modern scholars for imitating the self-conscious conceits (extended comparisons) and oxymora (oppositions such as "ice / fire") of his sources, such language and sentiments would have found an appreciative audience at the time. A clear example of this type of sonnet is his translation of Petrarch's *Rime* 134, "Pace non trovo e non ho da far guerra." Wyatt's poem (no. 17) begins:

I find no peace and all my war is done.
I fear and hope, I burn and freeze like ice.
I fly above the wind yet can I not arise.
And naught I have and all the world I seize on.

Each succeeding line expresses a contradiction in the lover's situation: he feels both freedom and constraint; he wishes both life and death; he is both blind and seeing, mute and complaining, loving another and hating himself, sorrowful and joyful. The last line of this poem is typical of Wyatt in indicating that such internal divisions derive from the beloved: his "delight is causer of this strife."

Leonard Forster, in *The Icy Fire: Five Studies in European Petrarchism* (1969), reasons that because such devices are highly rhetorical and easily imitable, early English poets imitated them. Most of Wyatt's adaptations, however, express a highly dramatic situation and seem the overwrought outpourings of severe and personal pain, not the static result of artifice. Thus, even close translations often result in original beauty. Although it has not always been appreciated, an often-anthologized and haunting sonnet is "My galley charged with forgetfulness" (no. 19), a translation of Petrarch's *Rime* 189, "Passa la nave mia colma d'oblio." Here the comparison the speaker makes between a ship and love is not merely an exercise in sustained allegory but with its unexpected phrases and halting meter – "Thorough sharp seas in winter nights doth pass" – expresses the lover's inability to recover from his loss. The cause of his suffering is described with effective simplicity – "The stars be hid that led me to this pain" – and the couplet evokes a sense of true despair, for the lover knows he is beyond recovery precisely because love is not rational: "Drowned is reason that should me comfort / And I remain despairing of the port."

Perennially fascinated by Wyatt's use of French and Italian sources, scholars have continued to debate the significance of his Petrarchism. There is scholarly concern over what is meant by translation; Wyatt's tendency to imitate rather than transliterate has been widely discussed. Some take it as an indication that he adopted the principles for translation that Continental poets themselves used in turning classical poetry into the vernacular; therefore, Wyatt brought Renaissance humanism to England. Some scholars argue that he translated the Italian texts into an essentially English context or that he personalized that context, while others argue that many of the translations falter.

By far the most widely held view is that when Wyatt's poetry defies the beloved and denounces the game of love, or rejects the devotion to love found in his models, it approaches the anti-Petrarchism of the sort evident later in Elizabethan poetry. His sonnet beginning "Was I never yet of your love grieved / Nor never shall while that my life doth last" (no. 12), a translation of Petrarch's *Rime* 82, "Io non fu' d' amar voi lassato unqu' anco," declares that "of hating myself that date is past" and ends with the lines that project the speaker's disdain:

> If otherwise ye seek for to fulfill
> Your disdain, ye err and shall not as ye ween,
> And ye yourself the cause thereof hath been.

If this frustration of the beloved's satisfaction seems vengeful and petty, one must remember that it is bred by a system that seems arbitrary in its delegation of power and responsibility but is in fact closed and dependent on personal loyalties.

A sonnet often cited as an example of Wyatt's anti-Petrarchism is one for which no source has yet been found, "Farewell, Love, and all thy laws forever" (no. 31). As the first line indicates, the speaker has renounced love; he will replace it with the philosophy of Seneca and Plato and adopt a more Stoic attitude toward love. He decides to set no more store by such "trifles" and bids love "Go trouble younger hearts." The rejection of love as a waste of one's time and a sure means to suffer is complete in the couplet: "For hitherto though I have lost all my time, / Me lusteth no longer rotten boughs to climb." A similar theme is sounded in another poem whose source is likewise unknown,

"There was never file half so well filed" (no. 32). Here the speaker intends to abandon the passion or "folly" of youthful love for the "reason" of maturity. Expressing regret for wasted time and wasted trust, the poem ends by claiming that one who deceives should not complain of being deceived in return but should receive the "reward" of "little trust forever." Both these poems are more severely critical views of the artificiality and duplicity of courtly life than the one to be found in a translation such as "I find no peace and all my war is done"; and yet its juxtapositions of opposites may also indicate the underlying insecurity of that life.

Some of Wyatt's sourceless poems that are not sonnets, such as "My lute, awake" (no. 109), also convey a markedly anti-Petrarchan attitude. The several copies of this eight-stanza song, including those in the Stark and Folger fragments of *The Court of Venus,* suggest the extent of its popularity. It begins with the standard lover's complaint but then abandons the courtly love game and pronounces what amounts to a curse on the beloved:

> Vengeance shall fall on thy disdain
> That makest but game on earnest pain.
> Think not alone under the sun
> Unquit to cause thy lovers plain
> Although my lute and I have done.
>
> May chance thee lie withered and old
> The winter nights that are so cold,
> Plaining in vain unto the moon.
> Thy wishes then dare not be told
> Care then who list for I have done.

It is unclear whether the poem's bitter tone is a projection by Wyatt or by the speaker; and although its message may be traditional, it is a stark reminder of the importance of youth in Henry's court. These poems have an edge to them that jars with the very concept of courtly love poetry but that matches the tone of traditional court satire from other sources, including earlier English poets. This rejection or theme of lost beauty is carried to a misogynistic extreme in another of Wyatt's better-known poems, "Ye old mule" (no. 7). Here the faded beauty is compared to a worn-out beast of burden: she can no longer choose her lovers but must buy what is available.

In these and later anti-Petrarchan poems in English, the lover's pain is blamed on the beloved's artifice, guile, deceit, dissembling, fickleness, and hard-heartedness; in Wyatt's poems the lover's constancy is repeatedly compared to the beloved's lack of faith. In "Thou hast no faith of him that hath

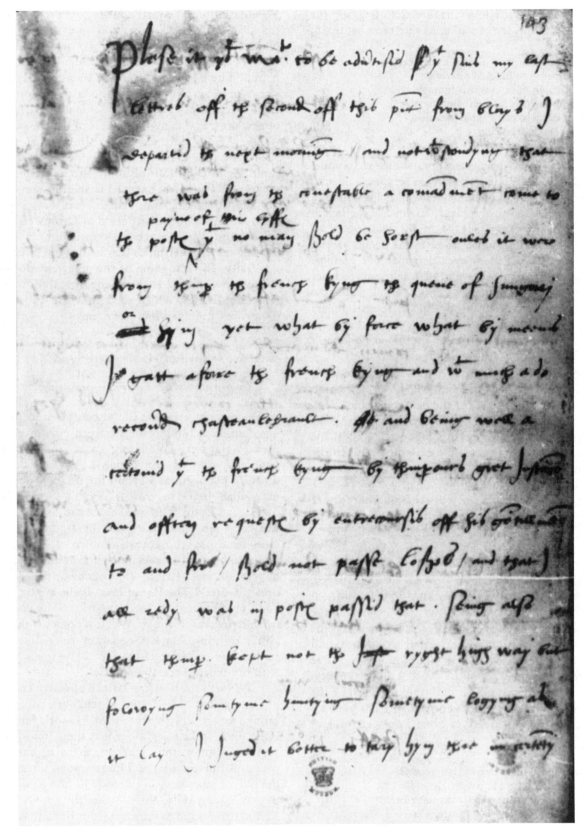

First page of a letter from Wyatt to Henry VIII, 12 December 1539 (British Library)

none" (no. 6), the lover, rather than begging for mercy or favor, is angered at having been betrayed:

> I thought thee true without exception.
> But I perceive I lacked discretion
> To fashion faith to words mutable:
> Thy thought is too light and variable.
> To change so oft without occasion,
>   Thou hast no faith.

Many of Wyatt's poems treat mutability as an undesirable characteristic for a lover, a servant, a patron, or a king; changefulness or betrayal is his common theme. It is not always clear, however, whether in these poems Wyatt speaks in his own voice or creates various personae. Some of the poems project a great deal of venom over personal and political events and seem to reveal an intelligent courtier struggling to define himself against a political structure he both criticizes and enjoys. Some scholars thus see Wyatt as a rebellious figure in a corrupt and corrupting system; others see him as hopelessly caught in that system and its dynastic concerns.

The poem that best illustrates these issues is "They flee from me" (no. 80), which combines eroticism with a contempt for the beloved's changefulness. This three-stanza poem, or ballade, moves between dreaming and waking, fantastic and realistic states of consciousness. It owes something to the amorous poetry of Ovid, perhaps something to Petrarch's sonnets, and much to Chaucer. The poem opens with the speaker remembering former love(s): "They flee from me that sometime did me seek / With naked foot stalking in my chamber." The poem's first few lines recall "Whoso list to hunt" in claiming that those who once sought the speaker were tamed but "now are wild"; further, "now they range / Busily seeking with a continual change" that the speaker finds problematic. In the second stanza the speaker recalls a time when the beloved caught him in her arms, kissed him, and asked, " 'Dear heart, how like you this?' " The poem shifts abruptly to the present and to reality: "It was no dream: I lay broad waking." Despite the lover's "gentleness" or "gentility," he has been rejected, and his loss leaves him, if not vengeful, at least sardonic:

> And I have leave to go of her goodness
> And she also to use newfangleness.
> But since that I so kindly am served
> I would fain know what she hath deserved.

"They flee from me," a poem of betrayal and remembrance, may be the definitive expression of Wyatt's attitude toward courtly love: it is a game that can cause real pain, and one in which the players are only half-aware of their own complicity.

Wyatt's Italian sources range beyond Petrarch. The epigrams, many of them based on the *strambotti* of Serafino d'Aquilano, also comment on the uncertainties of court life. Several are written in ottava rima, and many, like some of the classical epigrams of Martial, are biting. In a court where "none is worse than is a friendly foe" (no. 52), dissembling is common: "But well to say and so to mean — / That sweet accord is seldom seen" (no. 70). In "Lucks, my fair falcon" (no. 68), a poem most editors date to the period of Cromwell's execution and Wyatt's second imprisonment in the Tower, the speaker notes that he has few friends in adversity. In fact, some of the epigrams do mark Wyatt as a Stoic, such as the translation from Seneca's *Thyestes,* which describes the court as a dangerous and even foul place (no. 49):

> Stand whoso list upon the slipper top
> Of court's estates, and let me here rejoice
> And use me quiet without let or stop,
> Unknown in court that hath such brackish joys.

The poem suggests that life at court is uncertain if not dangerous, and again the word *quiet* marks the speaker's anxiety. While one must remember that anticourt satire is conventional, Wyatt's descriptions in this poem go beyond the original: Rebholz notes that "brackish joys" is Wyatt's own addition to Seneca's Latin. The speaker asks to be allowed to live away from the court and die among common men, for those who are well known often die ignominious deaths: "That is much known of other, and of himself, alas, / Doth die unknown, dazed, with dreadful face." The last phrase, again Wyatt's own addition, personalizes the translation. The common thread running through Wyatt's poetry – that the glitter of court life has a darker side, that court service has a "bitter taste" (no. 71) – is congruent with his experiences as a courtier.

Wyatt's most sustained and effective criticism of the court is to be found in what are commonly known as his "epistolary satires." Once again their immediate source is Italian, but their tone is definitely Horatian, thus marking them as humanist pieces. Although there is a known point after which the poems must have been written – the publication date of Alamanni's *Opere Toscane,* the source of the first satire – scholars disagree on the date of their composition in relation to the Penitential Psalms. In the first satire, "Mine own John Poyntz" (no. 149), addressed to a friend of Wyatt, the speaker explains that because he cannot meet the courtly requirements of duplicity, dissembling, and fraud, he has withdrawn to the country. The hundred-plus-line poem begins with a disclaimer: the speaker does not mock those whom Fortune has made rulers. Although the speaker at one time sought glory, he cannot now obtain it because he is unable to lie, to praise those who do not deserve it, to honor those who prey on others, to dissemble, to call deceit strategy, to gain profit from bending laws, to say that people have accomplishments that they have not, to cloak vice with virtue, to claim "tyranny / To be the right of a prince's reign," or to seem rather than to be. Rebholz notes that the polished Italian is often translated into homespun English proverbs, as if to underscore the speaker's inability to frame fair words to foul practices. Many scholars date this poem to the period of Wyatt's enforced exile in Kent in 1536; some argue that if he could, the speaker, whom they read as Wyatt, would be in the midst of that court, despite its demands and dangers, for he valued the active life.

The second satire, "My mother's maids" (no. 150), retells Aesop's fable of the country mouse and the city mouse, a story Wyatt could have taken from many sources, including Horace. Wyatt's version differs radically from most others in which the city mouse tempts the country mouse by describing the splendors of city life, criticizing country life, and inviting her to the city. The country mouse, after tasting the dangers of city life, returns home convinced of her error. Wyatt's country mouse, however, is described as living in desperate and destitute conditions, which she herself attempts to better by visiting her sister. This city mouse is frightened by the very noise the country mouse makes on her arrival. When a cat attacks the two mice, the city mouse escapes, but the country mouse is restrained by the cat and perhaps killed. The satire then offers a long moral on the best means to attain "quiet of mind," for "each kind of life hath with him his disease." The speaker counsels contentment with one's allotted life:

Then seek no more out of thyself to find
    The thing that thou hast sought so long before,
    For thou shalt feel it sitting in thy mind.

The poem's attitude of mental resignation to adversity is consistent with Wyatt's Stoicism. The poem ends with characteristic Wyattian disdain at those who stray from Virtue (here personified); the speaker hopes they will look behind them and "fret inward for losing such a loss."

Wyatt's third satire, "A spending hand" (no. 151), is a dialogue between the speaker and Sir Francis Brian, a courtier whom the speaker cynically advises to adopt the methods of flattery and fraud to obtain riches. Brian should learn to fawn, for then he "shall purchase friends where truth shall but offend." His best strategy is to seek out a rich old man to cozen; but if this does not work, he may marry the man's rich widow, no matter how old and unpleasant she might be, and still sleep with whom he pleases. To further his profit he may pander his own female relatives to his superiors. In the poem Brian ignores this advice, this "thrifty jest," because it would compromise his honor, and thus he seems to be the poem's ideal, although scholars have continued to debate Brian's historical appropriateness as an ideal. The poem, modeled roughly on Horace's *Satire* 2.5, takes on a life of its own, using proverbs, of which Brian was a collector, and examples appropriate to Henry's court. (Wyatt once lent money to Brian, but the extent or nature of their relationship is unknown.)

Although many have argued that Wyatt's Penitential Psalms were written before his satires (considered the better poems), the psalms deserve attention apart from the courtly poetry in part because they help to establish Wyatt as a poet of the Reformation. They are also written and corrected in his hand in Egerton, thus providing editors with an unparalleled instance of the poet at work. Published in 1549, the poems were composed sometime after the publication date of their most important sources: the paraphrase of the Penitential Psalms by Pietro Aretino (1534), another paraphrase by Joannis Campensis (1532), printed again in 1533 with a Latin translation by Ulrich Zwingli, and English translations of the latter two in 1534 and 1535. The Vulgate is evident in Wyatt's version, and paraphrases by other writers have also been cited as minor sources. The seven Penitential Psalms, used as a group in the medieval church, center on King David's repentance, after his denunciation by Nathan, for sending Uriah, husband of Bathsheba, to his death in battle. Wyatt, following Aretino's paraphrase, provides a prologue and narrative sequences between the psalms.

As with Wyatt's other poems, there is controversy over the date and meanings of these paraphrases. Some scholars link them to his 1536 or 1541 imprisonment. Others see the poems as unconnected to Wyatt's biography; instead, they are a psychological drama in which David does or does not progress. Several scholars think Wyatt's deviation from his sources may indicate his intention to present David as a "Reformed Christian," whose despair and suffering lead to permanent penitence. Or, the poems may constitute a transcription of Henry VIII into God the absolute ruler, who demands and obtains the complete submission of his "servant" (no. 152), or into David himself, whose adultery has brought hardships to the kingdom; David may also be read as a figure for Wyatt, whose poems acknowledge his own complicity, as psalmist, in the situation he describes. Wyatt seems to have been capable of projecting whatever persona he wished, but he was not blind to the political, national, and personal politics of the Reformation in England: neither should be the interpreters of his religious poetry. The prologue begins as an amorous poem in which David desires Bathsheba and sends Uriah to his death. After his crime is discovered, David removes himself to a cave, takes up his harp, and sings. The paraphrases explore themes common to all Wyatt's poetry: betrayal, loyalty, truth, submission, and particularly "the chastisings of sin . . . that never suffer rest unto the mind" (no. 152).

Those who wish to study Wyatt beyond his poems might begin by reading his letters, edited by Muir (1963). Wyatt's critical fortunes should also be explored through Patricia Thomson's *Wyatt: The Critical Heritage* (1974). This book begins with the preface to the first edition of *The Quiet of Mind* (1528) and ends with an excerpt from C. S. Lewis, who named Wyatt the father of Drab (as opposed to Golden) Age verse and who made the famous pronouncement that "poor Wyatt seems to be always in love with women he dislikes." In 1542 John Leland published a set of elegies extravagant in their praise of Wyatt's eloquence and forthright character. His paraphrases of the Penitential Psalms were highly regarded in the sixteenth century and, after the publication of *Tottel's Miscellany,* so were his courtly poems. In the seventeenth and much of the eighteenth century, Wyatt and other writers of Henry VIII's reign were eclipsed by the Elizabethans and later poets; when he again received critical attention, by Thomas Warton in 1781, it was as a satirist of "spirited and manly reflections," not a love poet, that he was admired. Nott first used Wyatt's manuscripts to edit the poetry and, although he is somewhat more generous, comes to much the same conclusions as Warton – that Surrey, the nobleman, is the better poet. Not until E. M. W. Tillyard published his edition in 1929 were the lyrics appreciated, and then because they represented what has come to be known as "the native English tradition." Wyatt's Petrarchan transla-

tions and imitations have not, since the sixteenth century, been generally admired, even by those who have studied the sources. H. A. Mason, in much of his work, has insisted that Wyatt is best in his "serious" poetry, especially the satires. Since Stephen Greenblatt's *Renaissance Self-Fashioning: From More to Shakespeare* (1980), most critical attention afforded Wyatt has been linked, once again, to his biography, to his struggle not merely to survive but to succeed as a courtier in a social order under stress. The latest study, Foley's excellent *Sir Thomas Wyatt* (1990), continues in this vein.

Until recently many critics have found it instructive to return to the first literary biographies of Wyatt, to learn from his contemporaries what they thought admirable about him. One of his earliest literary biographers was Surrey, whose reputation has fallen not only because he is now considered to be a more facile and less ambiguous poet than Wyatt, but also, perhaps, because he was an aristocrat whose family was involved in court intrigues throughout Henry's reign. Unlike Wyatt, Surrey *was* executed by his king; one might therefore expect to find in the work of the poet who managed not to be executed, despite his imprisonments and expected death, greater ambiguities than one finds in the work of the poet who was killed. In one of his poems on the occasion of Wyatt's death, "Wyatt resteth here, that quick could never rest," Surrey writes a *blason,* or stylized description of various parts of the body, in which he extols Wyatt's virtues and denounces his enemies; he also explains the conditions under which Wyatt wrote and the value of the work he produced. While the elegy is conventionally epideictic, praising its subject and blaming his detractors, it is clear that Wyatt saw his world in terms of this duality, both in his poems and in his defense (1541).

In the *blason* proper, Surrey describes "a head, where wisdom mysteries did frame," or an intelligent courtier who incessantly worked for his country's good, an ambassador whose "tongue . . . served in foreign realms his king." Unlike the courtiers he describes in his satires, Wyatt had "a visage, stern and mild," which condemned vice and praised virtue; his mind was "void of guile." In the midst of his discussion of Wyatt as a courtier, Surrey praises his craft as a poet: "A hand, that taught what might be said in rime; / That reft Chaucer the glory of his wit." It is no coincidence that Wyatt's success as a poet is associated with his work as an ambassador, for his contact with French and Italian cultures must have inspired him to imitate Continental poetry. The eighth stanza is the antecedent for all

Sir Thomas Wyatt (National Portrait Gallery, London)

those critical analyses aimed at describing Wyatt's attempt to define himself against the change, chance, and uncertainty of life at court. Surrey's premise is that the more Wyatt was envied, the better his life and works became; he was a singular man in a compromised world:

> A valiant corps, where force and beauty met,
> Happy, alas! too happy, but for foes,
> Lived, and ran the race that nature set;
> Of manhood's shape, where she the mold did lose.

The loss or the individuality lies in the power of Wyatt's poetry to evoke that precarious and ceremonialized life.

Bibliographies:

Michael C. O'Neel, "A Wyatt Bibliography," *Bulletin of Bibliography,* 27 (1970): 76–79, 93–94;

Burton Fishman, "Recent Studies in Wyatt and Surrey," *English Literary Renaissance,* 1 (Spring 1971): 178–191;

Peter Beal, *Index of English Literary Manuscripts, Volume I: 1450–1625, Part 2: Douglas-Wyatt* (London: Mansell / New York: R. R. Bowker, 1980), pp. 589–626, 636;

Clyde W. Jentoft, *Sir Thomas Wyatt and Henry Howard, Earl of Surrey: A Reference Guide* (Boston: G. K. Hall, 1980);

Ellen C. Caldwell, "Recent Studies in Sir Thomas Wyatt (1970–1987)," *English Literary Renaissance,* 19 (Spring 1989): 226–246.

Biographies:

Kenneth Muir, *Life and Letters of Sir Thomas Wyatt* (Liverpool: Liverpool University Press, 1963);

Patricia Thomson, *Sir Thomas Wyatt and His Background* (London: Routledge & Kegan Paul, 1964).

References:

Cecile Williamson Cary, "Sexual Identity in 'They Flee From Me' and Other Poems by Sir Thomas Wyatt," *Assays,* 4 (1987): 85–96;

Helen Cooper, "Wyatt and Chaucer: A Re-Appraisal," *Leeds Studies in English,* new series 13 (1982): 104–123;

Joost Daalder, "Are Wyatt's Poems in Egerton MS 2711 in Chronological Order?" *English Studies,* 69 (1988): 205–223;

Daalder, "Editing Wyatt," *Essays in Criticism,* 23 (October 1973): 399–413;

Daalder, "Seneca and Wyatt's Second Satire," *Etudes Anglaises*, 38, no. 4 (1985): 422–426;

Reed Way Dasenbrock, "Wyatt's Transformation of Petrarch," *Comparative Literature*, 40 (Spring 1988): 122–133;

Stephen Miriam Foley, *Sir Thomas Wyatt* (Boston: Twayne, 1990);

Leonard Forster, *The Icy Fire: Five Studies in European Petrarchism* (Cambridge: Cambridge University Press, 1969);

Agnes K. Foxwell, *A Study of Sir Thomas Wyatt's Poetry* (London: University of London Press, 1911; New York: Russell & Russell, 1964);

Joe Glaser, "Wyatt, Petrarch, and the Uses of Mistranslation," *College Literature*, 11 (Fall 1984): 214–222;

Stephen Greenblatt, *Renaissance Self-Fashioning: From More to Shakespeare* (Chicago: University of Chicago Press, 1980);

Thomas M. Greene, *The Light in Troy: Imitation and Discovery in Renaissance Poetry* (New Haven: Yale University Press, 1982);

John Guy, *Tudor England* (Oxford: Oxford University Press, 1988);

Alexandra Halasz, "Wyatt's David," *Texas Studies in Literature & Language*, 30 (Fall 1988): 320–344;

Robin Hamilton, review of *Sir Thomas Wyatt: A Literary Portrait*, edited by H. A. Mason, *Renaissance Studies*, 2 (March 1988): 102–105;

Richard Harrier, *The Canon of Sir Thomas Wyatt's Poetry* (Cambridge, Mass.: Harvard University Press, 1975);

Harrier, review of *Collected Poems of Sir Thomas Wyatt*, edited by Kenneth Muir and Patricia Thomson, *Renaissance Quarterly*, 23 (Winter 1970): 471–474;

Harrier, review of *Sir Thomas Wyatt: Collected Poems*, edited by Daalder, *Modern Language Review*, 73 (January 1978): 154–155;

Harrier, Ronald A. Rebholz, and Mason, "Replies to Joost Daalder," *American Notes & Queries*, 1 (October 1988): 146–152;

Ingeborg Heine-Harabasz, "Courtly Love as Camouflage in the Poems of Sir Thomas Wyatt," *Studia Anglica Posnaniensia*, 14 (1982): 305–313;

Charles A. Huttar, "Frail Grass and Firm Tree: David as a Model of Repentance in the Middle Ages and Early Renaissance," in *The David Myth in Western Literature*, edited by Raymond-Jean Frontain and Jan Wojcik (West Lafayette, Ind.: Purdue University Press, 1980), pp. 38–54, 186–191;

E. W. Ives, *Anne Boleyn* (Oxford: Blackwell, 1986);

Jonathan Z. Kamholtz, "Thomas Wyatt's Poetry: The Politics of Love," *Criticism*, 20 (Fall 1978): 349–365;

Dennis Kay, "Wyatt and Chaucer: 'They Fle From Me' Revisited," *Huntington Library Quarterly*, 47 (Summer 1984): 211–225;

Anthony LaBranche, "Imitation: Getting in Touch," *Modern Language Quarterly*, 31 (September 1970): 308–329;

C. S. Lewis, *English Literature in the Sixteenth Century, Excluding Drama* (Oxford: Clarendon, 1954);

H. A. Mason, "*Ecce iterum Crispinus* – Progress in Wyatt Studies?," review of *Sir Thomas Wyatt: The Complete Poems*, edited by Ronald A. Rebholz, *Cambridge Quarterly*, 10 (1981–1982);

Mason, "Editing Wyatt," *Sewanee Review*, 84 (Fall 1976): 675–683;

Mason, *Editing Wyatt: An Examination of "Collected Poems of Sir Thomas Wyatt" Together with Suggestions for an Improved Edition* (Cambridge: Cambridge Quarterly Publications, 1972);

Mason, "Editing Wyatt: Further Reflections on the Possibility of Literary Study," *Cambridge Quarterly*, 5 (1971): 355–371;

Mason, *Humanism and Poetry in the Early Tudor Period: An Essay* (London: Routledge & Kegan Paul, 1959);

Mason, "Wyatt's Greatest Adventure?," *Cambridge Quarterly*, 7 (1977): 151–171;

Michael McCanles, "Love and Power in the Poetry of Sir Thomas Wyatt," *Modern Language Quarterly*, 29 (June 1968): 145–160;

Jerry Mermel, "Sir Thomas Wyatt's Satires and the Humanist Debate over Court Service," *Studies in the Literary Imagination*, 11 (Spring 1978): 69–79;

Anthony Mortimer, ed., *Petrarch's Canzoniere in the English Renaissance* (Bergamo: Minerva Italica, 1975);

Ivy L. Mumford, "Petrarchism and Italian Music at the Court of Henry VIII," *Italian Studies*, 26 (1971): 49–67;

Shormistha Panja, "Ranging and Returning: The Mood-Voice Dichotomy in Wyatt," *English Literary Renaissance*, 18 (Autumn 1988): 347–368;

Joseph Pivato, "Wyatt, Tudor Translator of Petrarca: Italian Plain Style," *Canadian Review of Comparative Literature*, 8 (Spring 1981): 239–255;

Elizabeth W. Pomeroy, *The Elizabethan Miscellanies: Their Development and Conventions* (Berkeley: University of California Press, 1973);

J. J. Scarisbrick, *Henry VIII* (Berkeley: University of California Press, 1968);

Raymond Southall, *The Courtly Maker: An Essay on the Poetry of Wyatt and His Contemporaries* (Oxford: Blackwell / New York: Barnes & Noble, 1964);

Southall, " 'Love, Fortune and My Mind': The Stoicism of Wyatt," *Essays in Criticism,* 39 (January 1989): 18–28;

David Starkey, "The Court: Castiglione's Ideal and Tudor Reality; Being a Discussion of Sir Thomas Wyatt's *Satire Addressed to Sir Francis Bryan,*" *Journal of the Warburg & Courtauld Institutes,* 45 (1982): 232–239;

Starkey, *The Reign of Henry VIII: Personalities and Politics* (New York: Franklyn Watts, 1986);

Henry Howard, Earl of Surrey, *The Poems of Henry Howard, Earl of Surrey,* edited by Frederick Morgan Padelford (Seattle: University of Washington Press, 1920; revised, 1928);

Patricia Thomson, *Sir Thomas Wyatt and His Background* (London: Routledge & Kegan Paul, 1964);

Thomson, ed., *Wyatt: The Critical Heritage* (London: Routledge & Kegan Paul, 1974);

Robert G. Twombly, "Thomas Wyatt's Paraphrase of the Penitential Psalms of David," *Texas Studies in Literature & Language,* 12 (Fall 1970): 345–380;

George Watson, "Petrarch and the English," *Yale Review,* 68 (Spring 1979): 383–393;

George T. Wright, "Wyatt's Decasyllabic Line," *Studies in Philology,* 82 (Spring 1985): 129–156.

Papers:

The most important Wyatt manuscripts are the Egerton (British Library Egerton MS. 2711), which contains poems in Wyatt's hand; Blage (Trinity College, Dublin MS. 160); Devonshire (British Library Add. MS. 17492); and Arundel Harington (Arundel Castle). Some poems are found separately or in groups in other poetry collections in manuscript. Wyatt's letters are in the British Library (Harleian MS. 282).

Checklist of Further Readings

Bibliographies and other reference materials:

Arber, Edward, ed. *A Transcript of the Registers of the Company of Stationers of London, 1554–1640 [Stationers' Register]*, 5 volumes. London, 1875–1894.

"English Literature/1500–1599," *MLA Bibliography of Books and Articles on the Modern Languages and Literatures.* New York: Modern Language Association, annually.

Fédération international des sociétés et instituts pour l'étude de la Renaissance. *Bibliographie internationale de l'humanisme et de la Renaissance.* Geneva: Droz, annually.

Hamilton, A. C., gen. ed. *The Spenser Encyclopedia.* Toronto: University of Toronto Press, 1990.

Harner, James L. *English Renaissance Prose Fiction, 1500–1660: An Annotated Bibliography of Criticism.* Boston: G. K. Hall, 1978, and supplements.

Ijsewijn, Jozef. *Companion to Neo-Latin Studies.* Amsterdam: North-Holland, 1977.

Lanham, Richard A. *A Handlist of Rhetorical Terms,* second edition. Berkeley: University of California Press, 1991.

Lievsay, John L., ed. *The Sixteenth Century: Skelton Through Hooker.* Goldentree Bibliographies. New York: Appleton-Century-Crofts, 1968.

Marcuse, Michael J. "Literature of the Renaissance and Earlier Seventeenth Century," section O in *A Reference Guide for English Studies.* Berkeley: University of California Press, 1990, pp. 323–338.

O'Dell, Sterg, ed. *A Chronological List of Prose Fiction in English Printed in England and Other Countries, 1475–1640.* Cambridge, Mass.: MIT Press, 1954.

Ousby, Ian, ed. *The Cambridge Guide to English Literature.* Cambridge: Cambridge University Press, 1988.

Pollard, A. W., and G. R. Redgrave, eds. *A Short-Title Catalogue of Books Printed in England, Scotland, and Ireland, and of English Books Printed Abroad, 1475–1640 [STC],* 3 volumes. London: Bibliographical Society, 1926; revised and enlarged by W. A. Jackson, F. S. Ferguson, and Katharine F. Pantzer. London: Bibliographical Society, 1976–1991.

Preminger, Alex, and T. V. F. Brogan, eds. *The New Princeton Encyclopedia of Poetry and Poetics.* Princeton: Princeton University Press, 1993.

"Recent Studies in the English Renaissance," *Studies in English Literature, 1500–1900.* Annually, Winter.

Ruoff, James E. *Crowell's Handbook of Elizabethan and Stuart Literature.* New York: Crowell, 1975.

Schweitzer, Frederick M., and Harry E. Wedeck, eds. *Dictionary of the Renaissance.* New York: Philosophical Library, 1967.

Stephens, Leslie, and Sidney Lee, eds. *The Dictionary of National Biography from the Earliest Times to 1900 [DNB].* London: Oxford University Press, 1885–1900; reprinted with supplements, 1967–1968.

Watson, George, ed. *The New Cambridge Bibliography of English Literature [NCBEL] volume 1: 600–1600*. Cambridge: Cambridge University Press, 1974.

Anthologies, collections:

Alexander, Nigel, ed. *Elizabethan Narrative Verse*. Cambridge, Mass.: Harvard University Press, 1968.

Byrne, Muriel St. Clare, ed. *The Lisle Letters,* 6 volumes. Chicago: University of Chicago Press, 1981.

Dodd, A. H., ed. *Life in Elizabethan England*. New York: Putnam, 1961.

Donno, Elizabeth Story, ed. *Elizabethan Minor Epics*. New York: Columbia University Press, 1963.

Henderson, Katherine Usher, and Barbara F. McManus, eds. *Half Humankind: Contexts and Texts of the Controversy about Women in England, 1540–1640*. Urbana: University of Illinois Press, 1985.

Hurstfield, Joel, and Alan G. R. Smith, eds. *Elizabethan People: State and Society*. New York: St. Martin's Press, 1972.

Manley, Lawrence, ed. *London in the Age of Shakespeare: An Anthology*. London: Croom Helms, 1986.

May, Steven W., ed. *The Elizabethan Courtier Poets: The Poems and Their Contexts*. Columbia: University of Missouri Press, 1991.

Millward, J. W., ed. *Portraits and Documents: Sixteenth Century* [1485–1603]. London: Hutchinson, 1961.

Myers, James P., Jr., ed. *Elizabethan Ireland: A Selection of Writings by Elizabethan Writers on Ireland*. Hamden, Conn.: Archon, 1983.

Rollins, Hyder E., and Herschell Baker, eds. *The Renaissance in England: Non-dramatic Prose and Verse of the Sixteenth Century* [1954]. Prospect Heights, Ill.: Waveland Press, 1992.

Smith, G. Gregory, ed. *Elizabethan Critical Essays,* 2 volumes. Oxford: Oxford University Press, 1904.

Travitsky, Betty, ed. *The Paradise of Women: Writings by Englishwomen of the Renaissance*. Westport, Conn.: Greenwood, 1981.

Williams, Penry, ed. *Life in Tudor England*. New York: Putnam, 1964.

Wilson, Katharina M., ed. *Women Writers of the Renaissance and Reformation*. Athens: University of Georgia Press, 1987.

Recommended works:

Allen, Don Cameron. *Mysteriously Meant: The Rediscovery of Pagan Symbolism and Allegorical Interpretation in the Renaissance*. Baltimore: Johns Hopkins University Press, 1970.

Alpers, Paul J., ed. *Elizabethan Poetry: Modern Essays in Criticism*. New York: Oxford University Press, 1967.

Bainton, Roland H. *The Reformation of the Sixteenth Century*. Boston: Beacon, 1952.

Bakhtin, Mikhail M. *Rabelais and His World* [1968], translated by Hélène Iswolsky. Cambridge, Mass.: MIT Press, 1984.

Beilin, Elaine V. *Redeeming Eve: Women Writers of the English Renaissance*. Princeton: Princeton University Press, 1987.

Black, J. B. *The Reign of Elizabeth, 1558–1603*, second edition, volume 8 of *The Oxford History of England*, edited by George Clark. Oxford: Clarendon, 1959.

Booty, John E., and others, eds. *The Godly Kingdom of Tudor England: Great Books of the English Reformation*. Wilton, Conn.: Morehouse-Barlow, 1981.

Bradner, Leicester. *Musae Anglicanae: A History of Anglo-Latin Poetry, 1500–1925*. New York: Modern Language Association, 1940, with supplement in *Library*, fifth series, 22 (1967): 93–103;

Briggs, Julia. *This Stage-Play World: English Literature and Its Background, 1580–1625*. Oxford: Oxford University Press, 1983.

Brooke, Tucker, and Matthias A. Shaaber. *The Renaissance (1500–1600)*, book 2 of *A Literary History of England*, second edition, edited by Albert C. Baugh. New York: Appleton-Century-Crofts, 1967.

Burckhardt, Jacob. *The Civilization of the Renaissance in Italy* [1860], translated by S. G. C. Middlemore. Oxford: Oxford University Press, 1944.

Bush, Douglas. *The Renaissance and English Humanism*. Toronto: University of Toronto Press, 1939.

Dubrow, Heather, and Richard Strier, eds. *Historical Renaissance: New Essays on Tudor and Stuart Culture*. Chicago: University of Chicago Press, 1988.

Ferguson, Margaret, and others, eds. *Rewriting the Renaissance: The Discourse of Sexual Difference in Early Modern Europe*. Chicago: University of Chicago Press, 1986.

Foucault, Michel. "What Is an Author?" [1979], translated by Josué V. Harari, in *The Foucault Reader*, edited by Paul Rabinow. New York: Pantheon, 1984, pp. 101–120.

Grant, Leonard. *Neo-Latin Literature and the Pastoral*. Chapel Hill: University of North Carolina Press, 1965.

Greenblatt, Stephen Jay. *Renaissance Self-Fashioning from More to Shakespeare*. Chicago: University of Chicago Press, 1980.

Greene, Thomas M. *Light in Troy: Imitation and Discovery in Renaissance Poetry*. New Haven: Yale University Press, 1982.

Guy, John. *Tudor England*. New York: Oxford University Press, 1988.

Hannay, Margaret P., ed. *Silent but for the Word: Tudor Women as Patrons, Translators, and Writers of Religious Works*. Kent, Ohio: Kent State University Press, 1985.

Helgerson, Richard. *Self-Crowned Laureates: Spenser, Jonson, Milton, and the Literary System*. Berkeley: University of California Press, 1983.

Howell, Wilbur Samuel. *Logic and Rhetoric in England, 1500–1700*. Princeton: Princeton University Press, 1956.

Hull, Suzanne W. *Chaste, Silent, and Obedient: English Books for Women, 1475–1640*. San Marino, Cal.: Huntington Library, 1982.

Javitch, Daniel. *Poetry and Courtliness in Renaissance England*. Princeton: Princeton University Press, 1978.

Keach, William. *Elizabethan Erotic Narrative: Irony and Pathos in the Ovidian Poetry of Shakespeare, Marlowe, and Their Contemporaries*. New Brunswick, N.J.: Rutgers University Press, 1977.

King, John N. *English Reformation Literature: The Tudor Origins of the Protestant Tradition*. Princeton: Princeton University Press, 1982.

Levin, Harry T. *The Myth of the Golden Age in the Renaissance*. Bloomington: Indiana University Press, 1969.

Lewis, C. S. *The Discarded Image: An Introduction to Medieval and Renaissance Literature*. Cambridge: Cambridge University Press, 1964.

Lewis. *English Literature in the Sixteenth Century, Excluding Drama,* volume 3 of *The Oxford History of English Literature,* edited by F. P. Wilson and Bonamy Dobrée. Oxford: Clarendon, 1954.

Lovejoy, Arthur O. *The Great Chain of Being: A Study of the History of an Idea*. Cambridge, Mass.: Harvard University Press, 1936.

Mackie, J. D. *The Earlier Tudors, 1485–1558,* reprinted, with corrections, as volume 7 of *The Oxford History of England,* edited by George Clark. Oxford: Clarendon, 1978.

Marcus, Leah S. "Renaissance / Early Modern Studies," in *Redrawing the Boundaries: The Transformation of English and American Literary Studies,* edited by Greenblatt and Giles Gunn. New York: Modern Language Association of America, 1992, pp. 41–63.

Mason, H. A. *Humanism and Poetry in the Early Tudor Period: An Essay*. London: Routledge & Kegan Paul, 1959.

Matthiessen, F. O. *Translation: An Elizabethan Art*. Cambridge, Mass.: Harvard University Press, 1931.

May, Steven W. *The Elizabethan Courtier Poets: The Poems and Their Contexts*. Columbia: University of Missouri Press, 1991.

Norbrook, David. "Introduction," in *The Penguin Book of Renaissance Verse, 1509–1659,* edited by Norbrook and H. R. Woudhuysen. London: Penguin, 1992, pp. 1–67.

Norbrook. *Poetry and Politics of the English Renaissance*. London: Routledge & Kegan Paul, 1984.

Parker, Patricia A. *Literary Fat Ladies: Rhetoric, Gender, Property*. Berkeley: University of California Press, 1987.

Parker, and David Quint, eds. *Literary Theory / Renaissance Texts*. Baltimore: Johns Hopkins University Press, 1986.

Patterson, Annabel. *Censorship and Interpretation: The Conditions of Writing and Reading in Early Modern England*. Madison: University of Wisconsin Press, 1984.

Peterson, Douglas L. *The English Lyric from Wyatt to Donne: A History of the Plain and Eloquent Styles,* second edition. Princeton: Princeton University Press, 1990.

Pitcher, John. "Tudor Literature (1485–1603)," in *The Oxford Illustrated History of English Literature,* edited by Pat Rogers. Oxford: Oxford University Press, 1987, pp. 59–111.

Ricks, Christopher, ed. *English Poetry and Prose, 1540–1674,* revised edition, volume 2 of [*Sphere*] *History of Literature in the English Language*. London: Barrie & Jenkins, 1986.

Rivers, Isabel. *Classical and Christian Ideas in English Renaissance Poetry: A Students' Guide*. London: Allen, 1979.

Rubel, Veré L. *Poetic Diction in the English Renaissance from Skelton through Spenser.* New York: Modern Language Association, 1941.

Salzman, Paul. *English Prose Fiction, 1558–1700: A Critical History.* Oxford: Clarendon, 1985.

Schmitt, Charles B., and others, eds. *The Cambridge History of Renaissance Philosophy.* Cambridge: Cambridge University Press, 1988.

Sloan, Thomas O., and Raymond B. Waddington, eds. *Rhetoric of Renaissance Poetry from Wyatt to Milton.* Berkeley: University of California Press, 1974.

Smith, Hallett. *Elizabethan Poetry: A Study in Conventions, Meaning, and Expression.* Cambridge, Mass.: Harvard University Press, 1952.

Southall, Raymond. *The Courtly Maker: An Essay on the Poetry of Wyatt and His Contemporaries.* Oxford: Basil Blackwell, 1964.

Stauffer, Donald A. *English Biography before 1700.* Cambridge, Mass.: Harvard University Press, 1930.

Stevens, John. *Music and Poetry in the Early Tudor Court.* London: Methuen, 1961.

Stone, Lawrence. *The Crisis of the Aristocracy, 1558–1641.* Oxford: Clarendon, 1965.

Stone. *The Family, Sex and Marriage in England, 1500–1800.* New York: Harper & Row, 1977.

Tillyard, E. M. W. *The Elizabethan World Picture.* New York: Macmillan, 1944.

Tuve, Rosemund. *Allegorical Imagery: Some Medieval Books and Their Posterity.* Princeton: Princeton University Press, 1966.

Tuve. *Elizabethan and Metaphysical Imagery: Renaissance Poetics and Twentieth-Century Critics.* Chicago: University of Chicago Press, 1947.

Vickers, Brian. *In Defence of Rhetoric.* Oxford: Clarendon, 1988.

Waller, Gary. *English Poetry of the Sixteenth Century.* London: Longman, 1986.

Whigham, Frank. *Ambition and Privilege: The Social Tropes of Elizabethan Courtesy Literature.* Berkeley: University of California Press, 1984.

Winters, Yvor. "The 16th Century Lyric in England: A Critical and Historical Reinterpretation," *Poetry,* 53 (1939): 258–272, 320–335 and *Poetry,* 54 (1939): 35–51; reprinted in Winters, *Forms of Discovery: Critical and Historical Essays on the Forms of the Short Poem in English.* Chicago: Alan Swallow, 1967, pp. 1–120; reprinted in Alpers, ed., *Elizabethan Poetry: Modern Essays in Criticism,* pp. 93–125.

Woodbridge, Linda. *Women and the English Renaissance: Literature and the Nature of Womankind, 1540–1640.* Urbana: University of Illinois Press, 1984.

Wright, Louis B. *Middle-Class Culture in Elizabethan England.* Chapel Hill: University of North Carolina Press, 1935.

Zocca, Louis R. *Elizabethan Narrative Poetry.* New Brunswick, N.J.: Rutgers University Press, 1950.

Contributors

Elizabeth Archibald...*University of Victoria*
Peter Auksi ....*University of Western Ontario*
Kenneth R. Bartlett..*Victoria College, University of Toronto*
Priscilla Bawcutt ....*Liverpool University*
Steven Berkowitz...*Fu Jen University, Taipei*
Joseph Black ....*University of Toronto*
Ellen C. Caldwell ....*Clarkson University*
David R. Carlson ....*University of Ottawa*
John T. Day...*St. Olaf College*
Bradford R. DeVos ....*Marshall University*
Maria Dowling..*University of London*
A. S. G. Edwards ....*University of Victoria*
Carmel Gaffney ....*Northern Territory University, Australia*
Louis V. Galdieri...*Massachusetts Institute of Technology*
Albert J. Geritz...*Fort Hays State University*
Lee W. Gibbs ....*Cleveland State University*
Mark Goldblatt ....*Fashion Institute of Technology, State University of New York*
Nancy A. Gutierrez...*Arizona State University*
William Keith Hall..*University of North Carolina at Chapel Hill*
Judith Rice Henderson ....*University of Saskatchewan*
Wyman H. Herendeen ....*University of Windsor*
Peter C. Herman ....*Georgia State University*
Christopher Hodgkins...*University of North Carolina at Greensboro*
Judith M. Kennedy...*St. Thomas University*
John N. King ....*Ohio State University*
George Klawitter ....*Viterbo College*
Robert Lane...*North Carolina State University*
Carole Levin....................................*State University of New York College at New Paltz*
Daniel T. Lochman...*Southwest Texas State University*
Thomas F. Mayer ....*Augustana College*
Michael O'Connell...*University of California, Santa Barbara*
David Parkinson...*University of Saskatchewan*
Michael Pincombe...*University of Newcastle upon Tyne*
James A. Riddell ....*California State University, Dominguez Hills*
Michael Rudick...*University of Utah*
W. R. Streitberger ....*University of Washington*
John N. Wall ....*North Carolina State University at Raleigh*
D. R. Woolf...*Dalhousie University*

Cumulative Index

Dictionary of Literary Biography, Volumes 1-132
Dictionary of Literary Biography Yearbook, 1980-1992
Dictionary of Literary Biography Documentary Series, Volumes 1-10

Cumulative Index

DLB before number: *Dictionary of Literary Biography*, Volumes 1-132
Y before number: *Dictionary of Literary Biography Yearbook*, 1980-1992
DS before number: *Dictionary of Literary Biography Documentary Series*, Volumes 1-10

A

C

E

G

K

L

M

Munroe and Francis DLB-49

Munsell, Joel [publishing house] DLB-49

Munsey, Frank A. 1854-1925 ....DLB-25, 91

Munsey, Frank A., and Company DLB-49

Murdoch, Iris 1919- DLB-14

Murdoch, Rupert 1931- DLB-127

Murfree, Mary N. 1850-1922 ....DLB-12, 74

Murger, Henry 1822-1861 ....DLB-119

Murger, Louis-Henri (see Murger, Henry)

Muro, Amado 1915-1971 ....DLB-82

Murphy, Arthur 1727-1805 ....DLB-89

Murphy, Beatrice M. 1908- DLB-76

Murphy, Emily 1868-1933 ....DLB-99

Murphy, John H., III 1916- DLB-127

Murphy, John, and Company DLB-49

Murphy, Richard 1927- DLB-40

Murray, Albert L. 1916- DLB-38

Murray, Gilbert 1866-1957 ....DLB-10

Murray, Judith Sargent 1751-1820 ....DLB-37

Murray, Pauli 1910-1985 ....DLB-41

Musäus, Johann Karl August 1735-1787 ....DLB-97

Muschg, Adolf 1934- DLB-75

Musil, Robert 1880-1942 ....DLB-81, 124

Mussey, Benjamin B., and Company DLB-49

Mwangi, Meja 1948- DLB-125

Myers, Gustavus 1872-1942 ....DLB-47

Myers, L. H. 1881-1944 ....DLB-15

Myers, Walter Dean 1937- DLB-33

N

Nabbes, Thomas circa 1605-1641 ....DLB-58

Nabl, Franz 1883-1974 ....DLB-81

Nabokov, Vladimir 1899-1977 ...... DLB-2; Y-80, Y-91; DS-3

Nabokov Festival at Cornell Y-83

The Vladimir Nabokov Archive
   in the Berg Collection Y-91

Nafis and Cornish DLB-49

Naipaul, Shiva 1945-1985 ....Y-85

Naipaul, V. S. 1932- DLB-125; Y-85

Nancrede, Joseph [publishing house] DLB-49

Narrache, Jean 1893-1970 ....DLB-92

Nasby, Petroleum Vesuvius (see Locke, David Ross)

Nash, Ogden 1902-1971 ....DLB-11

Nash, Eveleigh [publishing house] DLB-112

Nast, Conde 1873-1942 ....DLB-91

Nathan, Robert 1894-1985 ....DLB-9

The National Jewish Book Awards Y-85

The National Theatre and the Royal Shakespeare
   Company: The National Companies DLB-13

Naughton, Bill 1910- DLB-13

Neagoe, Peter 1881-1960 ....DLB-4

Neal, John 1793-1876 ....DLB-1, 59

Neal, Joseph C. 1807-1847 ....DLB-11

Neal, Larry 1937-1981 ....DLB-38

The Neale Publishing Company DLB-49

Neely, F. Tennyson [publishing house] DLB-49

Negri, Ada 1870-1945 ....DLB-114

"The Negro as a Writer," by
   G. M. McClellan DLB-50

"Negro Poets and Their Poetry," by
   Wallace Thurman DLB-50

Neihardt, John G. 1881-1973 ....DLB-9, 54

Nelligan, Emile 1879-1941 ....DLB-92

Nelson, Alice Moore Dunbar 1875-1935 ....DLB-50

Nelson, Thomas, and Sons [U.S.] DLB-49

Nelson, Thomas, and Sons [U.K.] DLB-106

Nelson, William 1908-1978 ....DLB-103

Nelson, William Rockhill 1841-1915 ....DLB-23

Nemerov, Howard 1920-1991 ....DLB-5, 6; Y-83

Ness, Evaline 1911-1986 ....DLB-61

Neugeboren, Jay 1938- DLB-28

Neumann, Alfred 1895-1952 ....DLB-56

Nevins, Allan 1890-1971 ....DLB-17

O

S

Y

Z

ISBN 0-8103-5391-1

90000

(Continued from front endsheets)

Documentary Series

Yearbooks